LINDLEY J. STILES
Dean of the School of Education, University of Wisconsin
ADVISORY EDITOR TO DODD, MEAD & COMPANY

THE ROLE OF THE SCHOOL
IN AMERICAN SOCIETY

Second Edition

THE ROLE OF
THE SCHOOL IN
AMERICAN SOCIETY

by V. T. THAYER
and MARTIN LEVIT

DODD, MEAD & COMPANY
NEW YORK   TORONTO   1966

EDITOR'S INTRODUCTION

When Dr. V. T. Thayer published the first edition of this book, it was called by critics a classic. Agnes Meyer in a lead review for *The Washington Post* observed: "Of all the books on education pouring from the presses, *The Role of the School in American Society* is one of the most useful and illuminating. For Thayer treats education not as something that takes place in isolation but, as his title indicates, as a reflection of society and an influence on it." The quality of the author's scholarship, the clarity of his writing, the vigor with which he related theory to the vital issues and conflicts in education soon established the book as the standard text in educational foundations courses for prospective teachers.

To make certain that the revision of *The Role of the School in American Society* would be more than an extension and updating of the original book, Dr. Thayer invited the collaboration of a younger scholar, Dr. Martin Levit. The two authors have reexamined historical assumptions and evidence, related freshly the past to the developing realities of the present and predictable future, and added new content and documentation. As a consequence, they have produced an entirely new book—one that retains the strength of the original treatment and adds the force of theoretical assumptions retested by recent research as well as educational issues and programs illuminated by contemporary applications.

The Role of the School in American Society places the spotlight of analysis on American education just as the rest of the world is seeking to understand how our system of education undergirds the fabric of democratic life in a free society. Gains as well as failures of educational efforts are illuminated. Problems as well as programs are analyzed. Conflicts as well as convictions are aired. This is, in short, a college textbook based on sound scholarship, lucidly written, and designed for reflective learning.

Dr. V. T. Thayer is one of the world's leading educational scholars. No armchair philosopher, he has tested theory with reality in various types of educational positions ranging from classroom teacher, principal, and superintendent of schools to college professor. His books, including his recently published *Formative Ideas in American Education* (Dodd, Mead & Co., 1965), have been widely read and studied by laymen as well as professional educators.

Dr. Martin Levit of the University of Missouri at Kansas City is a well-known scholar in his own right. An educational philosopher of repute, he is distinguished as a teacher of teachers who prizes intellectual freedom and reflective inquiry. He brought to this partnership an independence of mind and variations in background that made the teamwork of writing a constant cross-examination of ideas, facts, and concepts as well as conclusions.

As advisory editor for education textbooks for Dodd, Mead and Company, I take pride in presenting to students and teacher educators, as well as to all interested in the work of schools, this revised edition of *The Role of the School in American Society*. I believe that readers will find it as refreshing as the air of freedom that our schools seek to preserve.

LINDLEY J. STILES

PREFACE

A major revision of the original edition of this book has been necessitated by the swift pace of events. Moreover, on the principle that two educators who are in essential agreement in their philosophic outlook but differ in background and experience can contribute better than one to an understanding of the problems of education today, the author of the first edition has welcomed a collaborator in the writing of the second.

A common point of view has enabled the authors, in the main, to write as one. Major exceptions are Chapters 12 and 13, for which Martin Levit is chiefly responsible, and the chapters of Part IV, which are primarily the work of V. T. Thayer. Revisions have been most extensive in those chapters (10 through 23) which deal most directly with contemporary trends and issues in society and education. However, the need to indicate the relevance of selected historical material for current educational practice and theory has generated some revisions in Chapters 1 through 9.

Public education in the United States confronts a situation both unique and contradictory. On the one hand, the traditional importance of education in the mind of the average citizen has been enhanced by a number of contemporary social developments. A technological society requires more and more highly educated experts. A complex society, if it is to be democratically controlled, requires of its people deepened wisdom and widened breadth of concern. Under these conditions, and as "knowledge explodes" and a mounting number of young people and adults spend a larger proportion of their time in schooling, the school becomes an ever more central institution of society. Moreover, since the launching of Sputnik I by the Russians, it has become increasingly clear that education plays an indispensable role in the world-wide struggle for the loyalties of men. Means must be found to channel young people talented in science, mathematics, and engineering into these fields. To the discerning, it is no less obvious that an education designed to perpetuate and develop the institutions of a free society cannot safely be limited to the training of specialists and technicians. Consequently, there is an urgent need for expanded programs in the social sciences, the humanities, and the arts, programs which will bring to the fore minds informed and disciplined in methods of thinking and ways of living that will not only safeguard but develop and enrich an open society.

In short, the times emphasize a one-to-one relationship between a high level of education, both general and technical, and the welfare, indeed the survival, of free nations.

Nevertheless, a strange lethargy seems to pervade many American communities. Despite some encouraging signs and activities in recent years, the educational effort falls far short of the educational need. Bond issues designed to offset building shortages and inadequate teaching facilities are defeated with alarming frequency. Overcrowded classrooms persist and farsighted planning to accommodate the expanding school enrollments of tomorrow fails to enlist wide or enthusiastic public attention. Teachers' salaries, although improved over several years back, are conspicuously below wage and salary schedules in occupations less demanding in preparation and training, a situation which makes it difficult to man the schools with a quality of personnel competent to meet contemporary challenges to American education.

One explanation for this unique situation is a want of confidence in public education caused, in no small measure, by attacks upon the schools which have been characteristic of the past two decades. During this period, the electorate have been told repeatedly that their schools fail to measure up to normal requirements. The able and the gifted children are crippled rather than encouraged in the full realization of their powers, and the handicapped and mediocre are taught neither to read nor to write with any degree of proficiency nor to perform the simplest operations in mathematics. To these indictments are commonly added the serious charge that neglect of character education and instruction in moral and spiritual values explains a rising tide of juvenile delinquency.

Indictments of the curriculum are equally severe. Efforts to meet the needs of a diversified student body, it is asserted, have resulted in a general lowering of standards, thus fostering a flabbiness of mind at precisely the time when our international competitors are cultivating to the full the talents and abilities of their young. When, in recent years, liberal arts professors turned their attention to the curriculum, many of them declared large portions of the curriculum to be obsolete or otherwise inadequate.

Nor is this situation bettered by a confusion of tongues characteristic of educational discussions. One group of educators envisages the speedy disintegration of American society unless the schools return to a type of education characteristic of yesterday. Still others, impressed by the influence of work upon character, ascribe many of our difficulties to an excess of zeal for universal and compulsory education. This, they believe, has been carried too far. Accordingly, they suggest that steps be taken to separate the sheep from the goats. Raise the standards for the academically competent, they urge, and shorten the period of compulsory schooling for the incompetent. Others, again, believe that school and home and community face today genuinely novel conditions—that we are living in one of those dramatic periods of human history in which men engage in the creation of new institutions and the formulation of new ideas and ideals of living relationships. Under these circumstances, the failure of old institutions to function vitally or of people to devise adequately substitutes for long-confirmed ways of thinking, feeling, and acting exact a heavy toll. But this in no way implies ultimate disaster. It constitutes, rather, a challenge for home and school and community agency to adopt an experimental attitude and to travel hopefully with a faith grounded in the conviction, as L. P. Jacks once emphasized, that "It is precisely when his circumstances are easiest that he [man] gives the poorest account of himself, and the best when he is fighting against odds. Never is he more at home in this universe than when he finds himself 'upon an engagement very difficult.'"

Different as these suggestions are (and we might have added to the list others equally at odds with each other), one common note may be detected in them. Schooling is important and decisive if the school will but define its boundaries, recognize and concentrate upon its legitimate functions, and slough off the irrelevant!

This shared faith in the importance of schooling would seem to justify an attempt to survey the task of public education in the light of changes that have taken place in American culture from the colonial period to the present and to consider the impact of these changes upon the school, changes in the economic and social status of young people, in the psychology of learning, and in the bearing of these many factors upon the theory and practice of education today.

The Role of the School in American Society consists of four parts. Part I draws attention to certain basic assumptions or formative ideas in American life and education of the past which still serve to guide all concerned with education on local, state, and national levels. Part II provides further background, historical and psychological, with which to understand the development and current status of the curriculum, methods of teaching, and the administrative structure of the school. Stages of development in American culture are described, together with the influence of each stage upon conceptions of the nature of the individual and how he best learns, as well as the influence which these varying conceptions have exercised upon educational ideals and practices. Part III is devoted to an analysis of fundamental transformations in the status of children and adolescents in American society, together with their implications for the curriculum of the school. The concern here is to identify significant changes in the status and life patterns of young people which should give character to aims, subject matter, and method; to the guidance function of the school; and to relations between school and home and community. Finally, in Part IV, consideration is given to a number of critical issues in public education today. The effort in this section has been to describe briefly the origin and background of a critical issue and the circumstances that make it a crucial problem in education today, and to review suggested solutions. As in other sections of the book, the authors attempt to do justice to all relevant points of view without necessarily disguising their own conclusions. To know where a writer stands, we believe, is the privilege of the mature reader.

The authors gratefully acknowledge indebtedness to the many publishers who have granted permission to quote from publications cited in the text.

V. T. Thayer
Martin Levit

CONTENTS

PART IV.   CRITICAL ISSUES IN CONTEMPORARY
         EDUCATION

PART I

BASIC ASSUMPTIONS
IN AMERICAN EDUCATION

Chapter 1

Faith in Education

A Common Faith

From their earliest establishment, settlements upon the American continent have been characterized by diversity. Varying in national origin and ethnic background, in religion, language, and customs, Americans have always faced problems of forging unity from difference and stability from change.

The schools of America have played a major role in the process of evolving a common culture. Even in the relatively homogeneous communities of seventeenth-century New England, schools were established to realize objectives more comprehensive than those of similar institutions in England and on the Continent. High on the list was the resolve to offset the disintegrating effects of new living conditions upon family life and long-established values. While less ambitious, legislation for education in the Middle and Southern colonies during the colonial period had much the same purpose.

The school's share in the development of American civilization has been continually growing. The transition from a predominantly rural and agricultural society to one industrial and urban has called for ever higher levels of education for ever more people; this extension of educational opportunities, in turn, has resulted in a level of productivity that has permitted—indeed, required—larger numbers to prolong their education. The developing American economy has given rise to a new class structure, to new professional and managerial positions, and to a socioeconomic mobility closely identified with democracy and access to the "good life" by an ever-increasing proportion of the population.

In international relations the American dream of individual liberty and progress has been translated into revolution, expansionism, and a general belief in the Manifest Destiny of the United States to carry its way of life to other lands. In the course of these changes, the schools have been called upon to help develop a spirit of national unity, to instruct students in the changing definitions of allies and enemies, and, in recent decades, to provide the trained manpower essential for the specialized needs of a modern great power.

At different periods and under differing conditions the individual equipment required for effective participation in American life has varied from the barest literacy to the acquisition of complex technical and professional skills; from a high level of personal ambition and a disciplined zest for work (that is, from the ability to play a lone hand successfully) to ability to get along well with people; from a modicum of knowledge and a maximal acceptance of the status quo to competent inquiry into the problems of impending change. Again, the schools have been asked to contribute by providing the means for the individual's acquisition of skills for today's needs.

Often the shifting and contradictory demands upon the schools, as well as their admitted failures and defects, have resulted in waves of criticism against the schools. Generally speaking, however, criticism has reflected less a lack of faith in public education itself than conflict and division with respect to the *ends* the schools should serve and the *methods* they should employ to realize these ends. These social conflicts and divisions find their correlates today in the confused and contradictory beliefs of many individuals as to the function of education in American society.

Historians tell us that in appending their names to the Declaration of Independence, with its revolutionary assertion that "all men are created equal" and are "endowed . . . with certain unalienable Rights," the members of the Continental Congress had in mind no more than the principle that all men are equal in the sight of the law and should be so treated by government. Very quickly, however, under the unique conditions of American life, there developed a mutually sustaining relationship between popular psychology and the material conditions of living. Life in the United States seemed to confirm the theory that all men are born essentially equal in their potentialities. As a result, within seventy years of the signing of the Declaration of Independence, that vigorous advocate of public schools, Horace Mann, could assert, with little fear of contradiction that "there is by nature little or perhaps no distinction among men with respect to their original power of intellect. The seeds of knowledge, of refinement, and of literary excellence are implanted with a liberality, nearly or completely equal, in the mind of the ignorant peasant, and in the mind of the most profound philosopher."

The School as an Open Frontier

Life on the ever-expanding frontier, with its democratic faith in the potentialities of each individual, seemingly reinforced this assumption of original equality among men. The frontier invited the oppressed and the underprivileged of the earth to seek their fortunes in America. So alluring, indeed, was this invitation that in the colonial period many an ambitious soul became a bonded servant, subject to purchase and sale, in order to pay for his passage from Europe to America. Others cheerfully accepted the hardships involved in clearing the forests and breaking virgin soil in order to insure for themselves and their children a fresh start in life. For a period these opportunities derived principally and directly from the open country, but in the course of time the opportunities of an industrial economy proved equally attractive. With the exploitation of these later opportunities, however, both general and technical education assumed ever more importance.

The agricultural and industrial attractions of the frontier thus led Americans to ascribe to education, and, in particular, to a system of tax-supported education on all levels—elementary, secondary, and higher —a status unique in history.

This is not to say that determination of an "adequate" education has been the same at all times or in all places. The level for functional literacy, for example, and for other skills essential for individual competence in practical affairs has risen with developments in the American economy. It once involved little more than the ability to write one's name and to read the simplest sentences. Later, the mastery of the three R's to a degree somewhat less than that now provided in the curriculum of the elementary school became a minimum requirement, with the result that throughout the nineteenth century the term "common school" was used to designate the elementary school. In the early 1900s the junior high school came into existence with a view to providing a "terminal education" for a rapidly expanding school population. But after a relatively short period, the need for further schooling was recognized. Soon the upper years of the secondary school were confronted with a similar obligation, and it is today widely recognized that graduation from the secondary school constitutes an inadequate preparation for successful and responsible participation in contemporary life. Indeed, with the emergence of the junior college, terminal education has invaded the college years.

Paralleling, or should we say supporting, these increasing demands for additional formal schooling has been confidence in the magical powers of an education. Often this has been of a materialistic and narrowly practical character. The school was conceived of as a great democratic opportunity, an agency designed to enable those who wanted to better their lot in life to do so. Poor and rich alike might attend it and thus acquire the information and training indispensable for individual advancement.

Some see in this faith in education little more than an expression of the materialism that dominates American life. That there has been and still is a materialistic core to it is no doubt true. Horace Mann, for example, despite his idealism, was shrewd enough to know that his fellow citizens required hard-headed arguments if they were to agree to tax themselves on behalf of public schools. Consequently, he sought to demonstrate that ". . . education has a market value; that it is so far an article of merchandise, that it may be turned to pecuniary account; it may be minted, and will yield a larger amount of statuable coin than common bullion. . . . The aim of industry is served, and the wealth of the country is augmented, in proportion to the diffusion of knowledge."

Witness, too, the numerous publications throughout the years that, presenting evidence of the financial rewards that come with schooling, are designed to persuade youth to resist the inducements of immediate earnings out of school. One typical set of figures compares the annual mean incomes for males twenty-five years of age and over by years of school completed. These statistics indicate that college graduates earn well over three times more than those who have had less than eight years of schooling, well over twice as much as those with just eight

years of schooling, and about 40 per cent more than high school graduates. Moreover, since 1939 the differences between these incomes have
been increasing.[1]

Or, take the results of a national poll conducted in 1963 by the
Survey Research Center of the University of Michigan. The survey
found that 96 per cent of the public believes a college education is
more important now than it was about thirty years ago. Of those
polled, 72 per cent believe that the most important benefit from a
college education is "training for a good job." The reasons given next
most frequently for going to college were "social acceptance" and
"getting to know the right people."

We agree that these expressions of faith in education are materialistic. It is easy, however, to oversimplify one's judgments. Frequently, an
educated man is able to enjoy the refinements of living commonly
denied to those who "work with their hands." Moreover, this way of
life might well include nonmaterialistic as well as materialistic values.
And often his work is more stimulating and, therefore, enjoyable in itself. It is not uncommon for the "cultured," or the fortunate possessor
of conditions that make for ease and comfort, to condemn as evidence
of the "materialistic spirit of the times" the strivings of a submerged
group for similar refinements of living!

Broad relations among certain educational, economic, political, and
intellectual factors suggest that a rigid division between so-called
"materialistic" and "higher" values may be misleading. It is clearly
false, for example, that among nations a high degree of social mobility
and the widespread availability of education are invariably associated
with a high level of political democracy.[2] On the other hand, it is quite
generally true that a low level of political democracy is associated with
a low level of social mobility and with limited educational opportunities.[3] An extensive and careful comparison of preindustrial and industrial societies reveals the key role played by industrialization in increas-

1. U.S. Office of Education, *Digest of Educational Statistics* (Washington, D.C.:
Government Printing Office, 1964), p. 126.
2. See, for example, Seymour M. Lipset, "The Value Patterns of Democracy:
A Case Study in Comparative Analysis," *American Sociological Review*, August
1963, pp. 515–31.
3. See John Vaizey, "Comparative Notes on Economic Growth and Social
Change in Education," *Comparative Education Review*, June 1961, pp. 7–12. See
also Theodore L. Reller and Edgar L. Morphet, eds., *Comparative Educational
Administration* (Englewood Cliffs, N.J.: Prentice-Hall, Inc., 1962), pp. 375, 377.

ing social mobility and the proportions of middle- and upper-class occupations.[4] In the United States there has been a close association between movements directed at expanding educational opportunities and movements toward political, social, and economic reforms.[5]

Although the economic motive for education is a dominant drive, education often has expanded more than economic horizons. Many studies have revealed that people of lower-class status who have had a limited education strongly tend to favor intolerant, authoritarian forms of political and religious behavior.[6] Even when individuals are grouped according to social class status, persons within each class who have higher levels of education tend to be characterized by more liberal and humanitarian attitudes, greater cultural awareness, and a higher level of interest in civic and international affairs.[7] Level of education seems to be associated with these characteristics and values even when such variables as age, occupation, and income are controlled or taken into account.

These findings do not justify the claim that more formal education produces unadulterated virtues. Nor can one assume that the person who defends, say, the political rights of other persons necessarily has a profound understanding of why he does or should defend those rights. Moreover, like other American institutions, education is heavily endowed with various brands of anti-intellectualism.[8] Indeed, in a number of chapters to follow we will argue that the schools have often repressed rather than released critical intelligence and creative, contemplative tendencies.

At all events, it is well to recognize that the schooling an individual prizes initially for its promise to better his status economically may also

4. Robert M. Marsh, "Values, Demand and Social Mobility," *American Sociological Review*, August 1963, pp. 565–75.

5. For an excellent analysis of these movements, see Rush Welter, *Popular Education and Democratic Thought in America* (New York: Columbia University Press, 1962).

6. For a review of some relevant studies, see Melvin L. Kohn, "Social Class and Parent-Child Relationships: An Interpretation," *American Journal of Sociology*, January 1963, pp. 475–79.

7. Burton R. Clark discusses some of these studies in his book *Educating the Expert Society* (San Francisco: Chandler Publishing Company, 1962), pp. 30–37. See also Robert M. Frumkin, "Dogmatism, Social Class, Values, and Academic Achievement in Sociology," *Journal of Educational Sociology*, May 1961, pp. 398–403.

8. See Richard Hofstadter, *Anti-intellectualism in American Life* (New York: Alfred A. Knopf, 1963), chaps. XII–XIV.

open his eyes to values to which he had previously been blind. We can thus draw the moral that one possible way to transform the material aspirations of an individual or a people into values of a higher order is to provide more education. In the case of an individual as well as a group, economic well-being constitutes a soil more favorable than poverty and undernourishment for the cultivation of the values of a liberal education.

Free Schools and the Conservation of Values

Thus far we have emphasized the individualistic expression of the American's faith in education. This is but half the story. Equally significant has been a vision of the social mission of the school.

The social conception of the functions of education in America dates from the origin of the first schools. In New England and the Middle Colonies a primary purpose in establishing schools was to insure the perpetuation of the religious faith of the community. To be sure, what constituted religious truth varied as one moved from one colony to another. In New England, to which the Puritan had journeyed, impelled by the conviction that "the God of Heaven had carried a nation into the wilderness upon the designs of a glorious transformation," schools were a major means for insuring allegiance to what Cotton Mather also described as "the pure and full dispensations of the Gospel." [9]

Similar motives prompted the good people of the Middle Colonies to establish schools, but heterogeneity of religious faith rather than homogeneity prevailed. Each community in this checkered pattern was convinced of the validity of its own faith, and schools were recognized as essential in order to perpetuate "truth" in competition with "error." Thus schooling, both in subject matter and method, served the com-

9. In a number of the following chapters, we shall return to the influence of early religious motives upon education. However, it may be well to state here that religious ardor waned after the middle of the seventeenth century, and that in both early and later expressions, religious motives were often used to justify concerns other than religious. Nevertheless, the early colonial mind generally identified social health with religious orthodoxy and, as Oscar Handlin states, "seventeenth century schools [were] mainly religious in orientation . . . the Bible was the primary text." (See his *The Americans: A New History of the People of the United States* [Boston: Little, Brown and Company, 1963], p. 121.) It is possible that some current skepticism concerning the potency of the religious motive in the colonial period is, in part, a reflection of certain contemporary attitudes that find their expression in historical interpretation.

monly accepted purpose of education for conformity. So axiomatic was this conception of education, even with respect to higher education, that the authors of Statutes of the College of William and Mary were constrained to enjoin instructors to "take special care that if the author is never so well approved on other accounts, he [the Master] teach no such part of him to his scholars as insinuates against religion and morals." [10]

With the advent of manhood suffrage and the increasing participation of the common man in government, the attempt to use education as a means of forming the mind of the young assumed political importance. Members of the upper classes now envisaged the possibility of government by "the mob." As Catherine Beecher put it, the common people had become masters, and consequently "the education of the common people . . . is the point around which the wisest heads, the warmest hearts, the most powerful energies should gather for conservation, for planning, for unity of action, and for persevering enterprise."

As Richard D. Mosier amply illustrates in his careful study of the influence of the McGuffey readers, the compilers of these books turned to the Beechers, along with many others, for material with which to influence the minds of the young, and thus "safeguard[ed] established institutions from the inroads of Jacksonian hordes" by instilling the proper political as well as social and moral concepts.[11]

There is a temptation to see (as some critics have done) in this deliberate and earnest effort to form the minds of the young the selfish attempts of once dominant groups to perpetuate their ideals and ways of living in a shifting and changing situation. Although partially true, this explanation fails to do justice to the generous aspirations of many a pioneer in early American education. Some of these people were ardently committed to change, and saw in public education an instrument with which to insure for all the blessings commonly enjoyed only by the few. Certainly we should hesitate to describe the motivations of Horace Mann and Henry Barnard exclusively in terms of class consciousness, even though their concepts of the good life may have been

10. See Elmer Ellsworth Brown, *The Making of Our Middle Schools* (New York: Longmans, Green & Company, 1914), chap. VII, for an excellent account of education in colonial schools. See also Adolphe Meyer, *An Educational History of the American People* (New York: McGraw-Hill, Inc., 1957), chap. VI.

11. *Making the American Mind* (New York: Kings Crown Press, 1947), chaps. I, IV.

identical with the virtues and values of one class of society rather than another.[12] It is more accurate to credit them with insight, rare in their day, into the relationship between free schools and a free society.

At the same time, profiting from the record, we can identify an excess of optimism in some of the arguments put forth in support of a system of tax-supported schools. Thus, we find Horace Mann looking to popular education as an automatic cure for the dangers that follow from an excess of wealth in one class and poverty in another. "Education," he asserted in his famous report of 1848 to the Massachusetts State Board of Education, "is the great equalizer of men, the balance wheel of the social machinery."

Not all individuals, however, are equally moved by broad, general social objectives. They require more direct and immediate evidence of ways in which new proposals will better their lot. The advocates of free schools early in the nineteenth century were keenly aware of this fact. Accordingly, not only educators, such as Horace Mann and Henry Barnard in the North, Caleb Cushing in the South, and Calvin Stowe in the West, but liberal-minded laymen, labor leaders, and statesmen emphasized the practical importance of a free education in a free society. To stubborn objectors, such as the irate Rhode Island farmer who threatened to do bodily harm to Henry Barnard for "preaching such a horrible heresy as the partial confiscation of one man's property to educate another man's children," [13] the advocates of tax-supported schools put this question: "Which do you prefer: to tax yourselves for jails or for schools?"

Thaddeus Stevens employed this argument most effectively in the Pennsylvania legislature in 1834, when engaged in one of the most dramatic and influential battles over the issue of free education. In an address later printed and distributed widely throughout the country, Stevens answered virtually all the common objections to publicly supported education and also demonstrated the benefits that would flow from it.

To the argument that it is unjust, if not immoral, to tax people to provide educational facilities from which they can observe no direct or

12. For an excellent presentation of these views, see Merle Curti, *The Social Ideas of American Educators* (New York: Charles Scribner's Sons, 1935), chaps. III, IV.
13. Edgar W. Knight, *Education in the United States* (Boston: Ginn & Company, 1934), p. 250.

indirect return, Stevens replied that it is nevertheless for their own benefit since it sustains government and the laws that protect their lives and property. Furthermore, inquired Stevens, why not urge the same objections to other taxes? "The industrious, thrifty, rich farmer" pays taxes to support courts, jails, sheriffs, and other officials whom he will probably never use, "but loudly complains of that which goes to prevent his fellow-being from becoming a criminal and to obviate the necessity of these humiliating institutions." [14]

The virtues of an education for citizenship, as Thaddeus Stevens and his associates envisaged it, were essentially political. It is understandable, therefore, that a predominantly rural population, accustomed to relatively simple institutions and face-to-face relations with their public servants, should have remained skeptical of the indispensable character of formal education. For many decades, in fact, the friends of tax-supported schools were confronted with arguments similar to those of a rural correspondent for a Raleigh (N.C.) newspaper who inquired whether it might not be of as much advantage to young people, as well as to the state, "if they should pass their days in the cotton patch, or at the plow, or in the cornfield, instead of being mewed up in a school-house where they are earning nothing." [15]

In the rapidly growing cities of America the importance of schooling was more obvious. Here the children of immigrants, together with the children of families accustomed only to rural living, were growing up under slum conditions. This fact profoundly disturbed many who were accustomed to thinking of America as a land of open opportunities and who were resolved to keep it so. To these individuals—representatives of labor, humanitarians, statesmen, educators—we are indebted for the concept of the school as an agency designed to serve the children of all classes in much the same way as the open country with its free land had long served adults by providing an opportunity to better their status in life. Out of their efforts came, eventually, the decision of all states in the Union to provide schooling free to all able and willing to profit therefrom.

Nor did schools fail in this objective. They were so conspicuously successful that with steady progress in industrialization and the grad-

14. Thomas Frederick Woodley, *Thaddeus Stevens* (Harrisburg, Pa.: Telegraph Press, 1934), pp. 153–67.
15. Knight, *op. cit.,* p. 244.

ual transformation of a predominantly rural and agricultural economy into an urban and industrial economy a schooling that was once optional for the young became compulsory. Massachusetts was the first state to set this example with the passage of a compulsory school attendance law in 1852. Other states followed with varying degrees of rapidity. In 1918 the circle was complete when Mississippi, the last of the states to do so, finally adopted its compulsory school attendance law.[16]

Many of the conditions that seemed to dictate free education and, later, compulsory school attendance likewise suggested an ever enlarging area of responsibility for the school. For children of the foreign-born and children of underprivileged rural families the school has functioned as a melting pot in the sense that it has striven to instill in the young ideas and ideals, specific habits and dispositions of ways of life unlike their original backgrounds. Indeed, the process of assimilation has not infrequently been carried so far that the school has been charged with creating unfortunate gaps between the generations, with the further result that potential contributions of peoples from widely different cultures have been lost to American life.

Be this as it may, economic, social, and political life since the day of Thaddeus Stevens has complicated and extended the services of the school far beyond what Stevens and his fellow pioneers envisaged. Today even many traditionalists who would restrict the schools largely to the teaching of "basic subjects" and "fundamental disciplines" think of these subjects in ways that go far beyond most nineteenth-century and early twentieth-century conceptions of subject matter. Arithmetic, for example, may be seen not as merely a collection of numbers, tables, and simple mathematical operations, but as an example of inductive and deductive modes of thought and of other logical concepts and operations.[17] Or American history may be seen as loaded and spiced with problems of causation, interpretation, and verification.[18]

Moreover, many traditionalists assume or assert that the schools

16. It is one thing to pass a law and altogether another to provide adequately for its enforcement. In a number of instances states made no provision for the enforcement of these acts. Even today considerable variation exists as to the years covered by compulsory acts and the means of enforcement.

17. Stewart S. Cairns, "Mathematics," in James D. Koerner, ed., *The Case for Basic Education: A Program of Aims for Public Schools* (Boston: Little, Brown and Company, 1959), pp. 155–69.

18. Ray A. Billington, "American History," in Koerner, *op. cit.*, pp. 27–48.

should perform functions that would have seemed preposterous in, say, 1875 to many reformers urging an expansion of educational functions. For example, Mortimer Smith, an executive of the Council for Basic Education—which is probably the most active private organization advocating that the schools confine themselves essentially to teaching the "basic subjects"—writes as follows:

> The advocate of basic education maintains that education . . . must deal primarily with intellectual training, with making young people literate in the essential fields of human knowledge, with transmitting the heritage and culture of the race. He acknowledges that formal education also plays a role in the social adjustment of the individual child, that it contributes to his physical welfare, the development of his personality, and his vocational competence; he is even ready to agree that the school on occasion must be a combined social-service and baby-sitting agency, even sometimes an amateur psychiatric clinic. He acknowledges that the teacher and the administrator have many important things to do besides cultivate the youthful intellect. At the same time, however, he would insist that schools must have some priorities, must decide what is primary and what is secondary.[19]

The world today is one of science and technology, of accelerating change, of complex and closely knit parts. These descriptions help explain the rapid decline of "common sense" and traditional practices as sufficient responses and the increasingly central role of education in our times. Whether we desire wealth and security or an understanding of ourselves and society, we turn to education to find ways and means.

The American's faith in education, then, has both persisted and expanded throughout the years. However, as a result of the uses to which this faith has been put, problems have arisen. Principles and procedures that in a simple and relatively homogeneous community seemed self-evident have become less so—have even become questionable—in today's complex and heterogeneous society. Take for illustration the colonial concept of teaching as synonymous with the instilling of approved ideas in the minds of the young. This was once widely accepted as the legitimate function of the school. This concept of education,

19. "Fundamental Differences Do Exist," in Paul Woodring and John Scanlon, eds., *American Education Today* (New York: McGraw-Hill, Inc., 1963), p. 28.

however, is difficult to apply once communities become genuinely heterogeneous in politics, in religion, and in social and cultural background.

Out of the practical necessity of maintaining peace and furthering understanding within diversity in American life has emerged the concept of freedom of thought and expression and the discipline of free inquiry as an essential value in American society. This second tradition is the younger, although older by far than the public school, and is grounded in principles sanctioned by the federal Constitution.

Thus it is that two traditions in education are in conflict, each contending for a central position in the school: one a tradition of conformity and orthodoxy, the other a tradition of free inquiry, each with its appropriate discipline of thought. One of the problems in present-day education is to determine the relations that should obtain between these two traditions and the educational procedures that derive from each.

Consistent with the first tradition is the tendency of earnest individuals and groups to use education as an instrument for implanting in the minds of the young the information and convictions that these elders believe to be all-important.

The second tradition has the problem of rendering more explicit than it has done thus far the relation of the discipline of free inquiry to the entire program of the school and to areas of knowledge not visibly subject to change as well as to areas still uncertain and controversial.

The adherents of both traditions are, however, as one in their faith in education. To this faith, in large measure, we may ascribe the phenomenal growth and development of the public school system of the United States.

Suggested Reading

Bailyn, Bernard, *Education in the Forming of American Society* (New York: Random House, Inc., 1960), pp. 3–49.

Curti, Merle, *The Social Ideas of American Educators* (New York: Charles Scribner's Sons, 1935), chaps. II–IV.

Gross, Carl H., Stanley P. Wronski, and John H. Hanson, eds., *School and Society* (Boston: D. C. Heath and Company, 1962), pp. 220–34, 409–37, 472–507.

Lottich, Kenneth V., "What Is Indigenous in American Education?" *Heri-*

tage of American Education, Richard E. Gross, ed. (Boston: Allyn and Bacon, Inc., 1962), chap. XI.

Spindler, George D., "Education in a Transforming Society," *Education and Culture,* George D. Spindler, ed. (New York: Holt, Rinehart and Winston, Inc., 1963), pp. 132–47.

Welter, Rush, *Popular Education and Democratic Thought in America* (New York: Columbia University Press, 1962), chaps. XI–XV.

Wiggin, Gladys A., *Education and Nationalism* (New York: McGraw-Hill, Inc., 1962), chap. II.

Wright, Louis B., *The Cultural Life of the American Colonies: 1607–1763* (New York: Harper & Brothers, 1957), chaps. 4–5.

Chapter 2

Acceptance of Change

Constancy and Change in Western Thought

The good teacher, it is said, does not expect children to learn a mass of messy details. She helps them understand the basic concepts or, in current nomenclature, the "structure" of a subject. The assumption often is that there are principles which express the regularities that in fact rule the many specific details studied in a discipline. In another version of this same mode of thought the good teacher is said to be one who understands the motives or needs of a child. The common assumption in this view is that there are predispositions that lie behind and control the varied specific behaviors exhibited by a child. The "basic structure" of a discipline or the "fundamental needs" of a child are commonly regarded as self-contained entities or forces that exist independently of the other factors in a situation.

We will consider some possible limitations of this approach in later chapters. The point to be emphasized here is that it represents a widely accepted and very ancient way of thinking in Western culture. So pervasive and deeply embedded in our thinking, so apparently natural and self-evident is this approach that we use it even today, when there are good reasons to believe that it is not self-evident, but dubitable. We use it even though some of its assumptions are in conflict with some of our other beliefs—beliefs that have emerged more from a conscious and controlled study of events than from a sub- or semiconscious assimilation of customary ways of thinking.

This bit of traditional ideology in Western culture makes a fairly radical distinction between things that are constant and things that change.[1] Whether in theology, philosophy, traditional science, or mundane thought, that which is constant usually has been exalted over that which changes. Like the perfect God who created imperfect man, the Commandments that guide the behavior of men, the laws of evolution that act to transform the species, the law of supply and demand that governs economic decisions, constancies have been seen as the directors and creators of changing particulars. Compared to what changes, they have been accorded a higher level of reality, of causal efficacy, and of explanatory power.

There is a social and moral side to this view of life. The belief in fixities has been closely associated with various divisions and fixities in society that have marked off the respective rights and roles of freemen and slaves or serfs, of rich and poor, of men and women, of adults and children. Superior or inferior roles have been assigned, and the actors have been pressed or trained to play their proper parts. Dictionaries remind us that we use the term "constancy" to refer not only to the "unchanging quality" of things but also to "steadfastness or faithfulness in purpose, action, or affection." The belief in exalted constancies and the exaltation of abiding beliefs have gone hand in hand. After all, do we not want children to think correctly? And what can "thinking correctly" mean other than thinking in accord with natural and moral principles as these are represented in, for example, our "solid" subjects?

During the past six or seven centuries, increasingly rapid social and intellectual transformations have altered some conceptions of the relations between constancy and change. But the alterations are by no means complete or clear. A brief glance at some aspects of the American experience in school and society may bring into focus certain aspects of the alterations, including the ambivalences and confusions.

1. We have stressed the fact that we are speaking of *Western* cultural traditions because anthropologists find that some other cultures interpret natural and social events in quite different ways. Moreover, in our own culture, particularly in the more advanced sciences, there have been some modifications—even transformations—of this approach. In these connections, see Dorothy Lee, *Freedom and Culture* (Englewood Cliffs, N.J.: Prentice-Hall, Inc., 1959), pp. 89–140. For references to other relevant studies, see Anthony F. C. Wallace, *Culture and Personality* (New York: Random House, Inc., 1961), pp. 94–104. See also Norwood R. Hanson, *Patterns of Discovery* (New York: Cambridge University Press, 1958), chap. III.

Change Optimistically Viewed

"No other people," writes Henry Steele Commager, "ever demanded so much of education as have the American people. None other was served so well by its schools and education."

The American school, Commager continues, has discharged three important tasks. It has provided "an enlightened citizenry in order that self-government might work," it has created "unity out of diversity, nationalism out of particularism," and it has Americanized millions of newcomers. "Economic and social distinctions and privileges, severe enough to corrode democracy itself, had to be fought. To our schools went the momentous responsibility of inspiring a people to pledge and hold allegiance to the principles of democracy, nationalism, Americanism, egalitarianism." [2]

These achievements are the more remarkable when we consider that they run counter to the original intentions of the fathers of American education. Had John Cotton and his New England associates foreseen that the schools they were so eager to establish would evolve into the instruments of "democracy" and "egalitarianism" they would indeed have concluded that the ultimate victory was Satan's. Schools, as they envisaged them, were to confirm known truths in the minds of the young and to perpetuate the status quo.

Two hundred years later a new and different spirit had come to permeate the land. In the process of pushing back the frontier and developing what seemed to be the inexhaustible resources of a new continent, a concept of man and his possibilities as extravagantly optimistic as John Cotton's was pessimistic pervaded the consciousness of people. As a French observer, André Maurois, remarked, the American is an optimist "because he lives in a country that has never betrayed him and he knows that a strong daring man may always succeed a little farther on."

Two basic assumptions in American education thus have reinforced each other: faith in education, with which we have dealt in Chapter 1, and faith in tomorrow. These two assumptions are closely related.

A frontier thinker in more than one sense, Thomas Jefferson had

2. "Our Schools Have Kept Us Free," *N.E.A. Journal,* January 1951, pp. 18–19.

hoped that the school would enable the state to avail itself "of those talents which nature has sown as liberally among the poor as the rich, but which perish without use, if not sought for and cultivated." Expansion of material opportunities for the lower classes, he believed, would become translated into a more common faith in the common man and into the ideal of equality of educational opportunity. Though this ideal has certainly not been realized,[3] we must recognize the extent to which the open-door policy in education has been successfully pursued and the extent to which current concerns about deficiencies in the realization of this policy are reflections of raised expectations.

From 1890 to 1963, the percentage of the population fourteen to seventeen years of age enrolled in the schools rose from less than 7 per cent to 93 per cent.[4] Within a century, the nation has raised its sights from universal elementary education to universal high school education to a policy proposal that at least two years of free college education be made available to all high school graduates.[5] In part, this policy is the child rather than the parent of the present situation. Margaret Mead is only one of many persons who now urge that a democratic and technological society would do well to rid itself of the "outworn idea" that higher education is for those who can afford it.[6]

The economic and educational ascent of large segments of the population has brought a certain widening of social, political, and cultural horizons; those who bewail the uniform, apolitical, and sensual state of mass culture are to be complimented on their aspirations, but they are probably wrong in their evaluation of the mass culture of today as compared with that of yesteryear. Moreover, the variety and variability of occupational and leadership roles have generated at least two prerequisites of democratic change: (1) increasing recognition of differences in ability and talent within student bodies—differences that require recognition whether our aim is to create uniformity or to release creativity; (2) growing awareness of problems in adjusting or reconciling personal choices and social requirements or priorities.

3. See Chapter 5.
4. U.S. Office of Education, *Digest of Educational Statistics* (Washington, D.C.: Government Printing Office, 1964), p. 14.
5. Educational Policies Commission (National Education Association), "Universal Opportunity for Education Beyond the High School," *N.E.A. Journal*, January 1964, pp. 58–60.
6. "Questions That Need Asking," *Teachers College Record*, November 1961, pp. 89–93.

Conflicting Concepts of Law and Morality

Another item of contrast between education in a changing and heterogeneous society and in a relatively stable and homogeneous society
merits attention. When people live together over long periods of time
and under conditions essentially similar, their accepted ways of earning
a living, their political forms of government, and the relations among
the classes that compose their society tend to assume a fixed and eternal
character. Moreover, the origins of these institutions often date from
beyond the memory of man, and thus seem to be grounded in the
structure of the universe rather than in the obvious needs of people.
Indeed, insofar as time succeeds in exercising an influence upon them it
often seems to confirm their benefits for the few rather than to bring
them into line with the needs of the many. Their theoretical justification is often found, therefore, not in the nature of man and his relationships but in the laws of nature.[7] Thus the office of king came to be
grounded in a divine right to rule and the nature of the peasant and
the tradesman to be considered qualitatively lower than that of the
nobleman. The revolutionary who ventured to challenge or to destroy
these arrangements was thought to offend against God as well as man.

In a society of this character, the task of the school is clear and circumscribed. It is to instill in the young a loyalty to convictions not subject to question and to principles that serve as the major premises from
which the student can infer the specific answers to his daily problems.

The American continent was settled by people who accepted this external conception of government and law and the existence of rigid distinctions among social classes. But the American climate was unfavorable to its perpetuation. For generations, Americans enjoyed first-hand
evidence of their ability to transform their physical environment and to
create organized communities in localities where none had previously
existed. They pushed back the forest, literally made the desert to blossom as the rose, and developed marts of trade and commerce and cultural centers where no civilized man had trod before. All this was done
within the memory of living men. Under those circumstances, class distinctions were forced to give way before a new ideal of social mobility

7. See, in this connection, John Dewey, *Freedom and Culture* (New York: G.
P. Putnam's Sons, 1939), chap. V.

and the potential equality of man—an ideal that seemed to find repeated verification as individuals, through the exercise of their own initiative, raised themselves from the position of humblest to highest in the land. Moreover, in the process of transforming a continent, Americans were forced to create new institutions and to modify those institutions as occasion necessitated, to write their own laws, and to insure their enforcement. From this experience, it was easy for them to conclude that institutions—political, social, economic—are born of men and designed to meet the needs of men.

This revolution in thought was, of course, no straight-line development. Nor has there been a clear-eyed and conscious replacement of one concept of man and nature by another. Rather, we find operating in the thought and the practice of the average person two contradictory concepts of government, of law, and of institutions in general.

No one has pointed this out more clearly than Boyd H. Bode.[8] He shows, for example, that the founding fathers, in adopting the Constitution, had in mind both restricting the powers of the new government—on Jefferson's theory, born of hard experience with arbitrary rulers, that the best government is one which governs least—and creating an instrument that would, as the Preamble to the Constitution states, "establish justice, insure domestic tranquility, provide for the common defense, promote the general welfare, and secure the blessings of liberty to ourselves and our posterity." The second purpose, states Bode, "was clearly staking out considerable new ground and not just paring down the operations of government." Continuing, Bode remarks:

> According to the Declaration of Independence the new government was to be founded on the *self-evident truths* that all men are created equal and that they are endowed by the Creator with certain inalienable rights, such as the right to life, liberty, and the pursuit of happiness. In other words, the purpose of government was to seek conformity to the will of God. The Declaration also states, however, that governments derive their just powers from the consent of the governed, which seems to say that government

8. See chapter on "Reconstruction in Education" in *Modern Education and Human Values*, Pitcairn-Crabbe Foundation Lecture Series, vol. I (Pittsburgh: University of Pittsburgh Press, 1947).

is only an instrumentality for securing what the people want, and that the test of its worth is conformity to the will of the people.[9]

The criteria of social well-being and of obedience to principles that derive their authority from improved relations among people have transformed the concept of law and rendered more flexible the judgments of the courts. No longer are decisions based solely on precedents and legal principles that have little reference in their application to unique situations or to the peculiarities of the context in which they operate. As the late Chief Justice Vinson of the United States Supreme Court remarked in the case of Eugene Dennis and his fellow Communists, "Nothing is more certain in modern society than the principle that there are no absolutes, that a name, a phrase, a standard has meaning only when associated with the considerations which gave birth to the nomenclature."

When Abraham Lincoln spoke at Gettysburg of "a government of the people, by the people, and for the people," he was not so much stating an ideal as he was summarizing the results of two hundred years of political experience on this continent. Law is no longer an injunction or a principle originating in a manner foreign or external to the interests of those who must obey. It is rather analogous to the rules of a game which the players have agreed to observe in order that they may get the most out of the game. It is "an instrument of social policy" dependent for its origin as well as for its validity upon the consent of the governed. Legal justice, in ideal at least, becomes one with social justice, and, as Justice Brandeis once remarked, "the dry bones of legislation" can no longer serve to screen the courts from the political, economic, and social realities of the real world.[10]

The step from a redefinition of law in civil society to a revision of the concept of law in the moral field is a short and inevitable one. Here, too, the principle of "by their fruits ye shall know them" has gained increasing recognition in a society marked by religious diversity. The general pattern of American communities was in the beginning religious, and the assumption that both individual and social morality were grounded in religious orthodoxy was well-nigh universal. But life on the changing frontier, where men and women of many

9. *Ibid.*, p. 5.
10. Alpheus Thomas Mason, *Brandeis, A Free Man's Life* (New York: The Viking Press, Inc., 1946), p. 250.

religious backgrounds and affiliations came to share a common lot, tended to undermine an extreme interpretation of this formula. In communities where no one religious sect was in a position to enforce its dicta there grew up a secular morality, a morality of consensus, that concerned itself with channeling and harmonizing the interests of the inhabitants because of the obvious necessity of regulating intercourse in all of the essential relationships of living.

Similarly, in education the evolution of the nonsectarian school led to the stressing of moral principles that various religious groups of the community held in common. This soon rendered it difficult to convince the young that the virtues of everyday living emanated solely from items of creed that marked a man off from his neighbor's faith rather than from those that were accepted in common. Ultimately, this concept gave birth to the secular state and the secular school.

Needless to say, these developments have complicated the task of education in school. The dualism which Bode tells us characterized the thinking of the founding fathers continues to exist in the minds of many today. In certain areas of living, people are experimental and pragmatic; in others, they remain loyal to authoritarianism. Nor are the experimentalists free of difficulty. When "right" human relations—in politics, economics, or person-to-person relations—are determined with an eye to consequences in the future, as well as to the past, the subject matter as well as the procedures in education must undergo reexamination. Emphasis shifts from the acquisition of knowledge and truths firmly rooted to a training in methods of thinking and ways of living that foster the ability to cope with, if not to control, events that may come as well as those at hand. Principles, in the form of funded experiences, and expressions of wisdom gleaned from the past remain of value and cannot safely be ignored, but novel data and the import of new situations likewise intrude upon the scene and demand consideration—perhaps even the replacing of old truths with generalizations more in harmony with the times.

The Technical and the Moral

An analysis of the distinction our culture makes between technical and moral matters may throw some light on the trends and conflicts we have noted.

That there is an essential and enduring distinction between these matters is rarely doubted. Means—techniques, machines, and other devices—are one thing; ends—values, standards, and goals—are quite another thing. Roughly, the sciences and the humanities correspond to the different ways in which we consider and come to know these different matters. Generally, even those who believe that social norms should be matters for continual decision-making tend to accept change in the technical realm much more readily than in the ethical.

Yet the conception of a radical and natural distinction between these two realms may be questionable. Anthropologists find that societies differ greatly as to the areas of their culture in which they accept or seek change, and that it is by no means always the material part of a culture that is the most variable.[11] Some societies even treat their entire culture rather experimentally.[12] They deliberately take it apart and put it back together again. In our own society, many questions that were once settled by dogmatic "oughts" and "musts" have become subject to more or less rational—or, in a sense, technical—procedures. This has happened to questions in such diverse fields as astronomy and political science, biology and economics, criminology and race relations. When a change has been accepted for a long time, we may use scientific or rational criteria of evaluation and call the older view a superstition, dogma, or prejudice. Note, however, that when we speak of improvement in the ethical domain we refer usually to closer adherence, by ourselves or others, to established norms, rather than to changes in the norms themselves.

In any event, it seems that at least some characteristics we associate with our technical culture—such as flexibility, or a scientific attitude—are not delimited by nature or necessity to certain areas of life. Perhaps, as Harold L. Hodgkinson suggests, part of our difficulty in dealing with problems of constancy and change is our failure to recognize the intimate association between different levels or kinds of technology and different patterns of values.[13]

For example, in both preindustrial and industrial societies, a rise in

11. See Felix M. Keesing, *Cultural Anthropology: The Science of Custom* (New York: Rinehart and Company, Inc., 1958), pp. 384–411.
12. See Edward T. Hall, *The Silent Language* (Greenwich, Conn.: Fawcett World Library, 1961), p. 84.
13. *Education in Social and Cultural Perspective* (Englewood Cliffs, N.J.: Prentice-Hall, Inc., 1962), pp. 110–21.

the level of technology tends to be associated with decreased emphasis on hereditary social-class status and with increased stress (up to a point) on individualism, secularism, and rationalism.[14] In the United States, as productivity has increased and as responsibility for capital accumulation has shifted from the individual to industrial, financial, and governmental organizations, the religion of hard work, thrift, and rising from rags to riches has been replaced in part by the religion of consumption, security, and work as a necessary evil. Also, the occupational, social, and geographical mobility of an industrial population has made social ties ephemeral and thin. Family and community influences and pressures are diluted, and a more attentive eye is turned toward the corporate and national trends that outline ways of getting along in our society.

On the one hand, shifting contacts and situations seem to require a kind of education that will help young people adjust to this pattern of life. So generally useful are the skills of adaptability that, for many people, questions about the values and purposes of adjustment become almost irrelevant. Like other highly useful techniques of the past, adaptability becomes an end, a value in and of itself. To many people, a good grade on an isolated scale labeled "social adjustment" is a highly meaningful and valuable sign.

On the other hand, a technological society requires experts in various areas and at various levels. Increasing pressure directs the schools' attention to the values and skills represented in the subjects of instruction. The demands for specialization are heavy and professional schools are steadily gaining in prestige and influence. As a group, they have begun to award more first degrees than are awarded by the liberal arts colleges.[15] By and large, students and parents, high schools and colleges, exhibit more concern for specialized education than for a broad general or liberal education which, in a past era, was thought to be the education needed by citizens of a free society. Specialization, in the form of departmentalization, now appears even in elementary schools.[16]

14. Alvin W. Gouldner and Richard A. Peterson, *Technology and the Moral Order* (Indianapolis: The Bobbs-Merrill Company, Inc., 1962), pp. 29–36.
15. Earl J. McGrath, *The Graduate School and the Decline of Liberal Education* (New York: Bureau of Publications, Teachers College, Columbia University, 1959).
16. National Education Association, *The Principals Look at the Schools* (Washington, D.C.: National Education Association, 1962), pp. 14–15.

Moreover, since expertness now is required at various occupational or technical levels, there is a growing feeling, especially in our larger schools, that it is efficient to vary the standards, or expected levels of performance, for different student groups. For example, there has been a sharp rise recently in the number of elementary and secondary schools which group students by ability and achievement levels.[17] This kind of organization of students for instruction is also felt to be "good." For, honoring an older value while changing some of its meanings and emphases, many people say that this procedure permits schools to serve the needs and abilities of different individuals.

Resistance to Change

Now, if it is true that values and techniques are interdependent, what are the uses of a dualistic view of them? Perhaps, on the one hand, such a view permits the innovator or modernist to operate on a "purely" technical level. New techniques or devices can be introduced and used freely without inquiry into the wide range of consequences that may emerge from their use. In a complex society devoted to specialization this is a welcomed privilege readily bestowed. But, insofar as this happens, society loses not only the opportunity for a comparative evaluation of the old and new value-technique systems, but also the comprehensive vision that might generate even better systems.

If there is no frame of reference other than technical efficiency, factors that lead to consideration of alternative values and frameworks become irrelevant. The highly trained specialist can then keep his eye on his "own" subject matter; thus anthropology, social philosophy, history, and other areas become irrelevant to the problems examined by some teachers of educational psychology.

On the other hand, the "dispossessed" [18]—those who are threatened by some emerging change or those who stand more or less outside the long-run or current streams of change—can call for a return to the constancies, the traditional values of the American way of life. The life patterns of the dispossessed embrace an older but, often, still somewhat venerable moral-and-technical culture. The dispossessed may

17. *Ibid.*, pp. 15–17.
18. Daniel Bell, ed., *The Radical Right*, rev. ed. (Garden City, N.Y.: Doubleday & Company, Inc., 1963), pp. 1–38. It will be evident that the term "dispossessed" does not refer simply to an economically underprivileged group.

even comprise a fading majority of the population. In any event, their values may still have a strong appeal, and when a society of increasing complexity and diversity feels threatened as a whole, these traditional values may become its unifying and rallying symbols.

In a world whose name is Change, each of us, to some degree, is among the dispossessed. We continually are "on edge," on the dividing line between the old and new in fashions, occupational skills, and —as the fantasies of yesterday become the realities of today—in beliefs. This may produce apathy or a submissive readiness to adjust to changes brought by such phantom agents as "technology" or "modern times." But it may also produce irritability and insecurity. As international tensions persist at a fluctuating but generally high level in an age of overkill, many domestic modernists are inclined to join the domestic dispossessed in their search for security.

In their bearing on the schools, these conditions have tended to stifle the spirit and limit the scope of free inquiry. For example, the free-enterprise system that the fading independent or small businessman has in mind is clearly not the free-enterprise system of the modern executive whose corporation may be engulfing some of these businessmen. Yet both the small businessman and the executive may agree that schools now must teach more vigorously the values of the American way of life and the evils of communism. These values probably will include *the* free-enterprise system, and may embrace freedom of religion, including the freedom to inculcate beliefs on which both the fundamentalist and the generally lukewarm religionist can agree. As another illustration, both the tradition-directed superpatriot and the modern man who feels he is merely being realistic in an age of hot and cold wars may believe that the overriding obligation of education today is to contribute to national power. One educator who accepts this obligation believes that the schools are fulfilling it by stressing the "power" subjects (like the natural sciences) and neglecting the "contemplative" subjects. This, he believes, is necessary and justifiable.[19]

In such an atmosphere, many people are only too ready to identify the schools' efforts to foster the spirit of inquiry with the fostering of subversion. Teachers who fail to inculcate in their students an uncritical acceptance of the status quo have been identified with the enemies

19. Harold W. Stoke, "National Necessity and Educational Policy," *Phi Delta Kappan,* April 1959, pp. 266–69.

of democracy. When traditions and tensions generate a radical division between means and ends, it is easier to "fight communism" by abandoning democratic procedures. Confined to the realm of the technical, reason becomes a tool of unexamined purposes and "necessities."

The level of tension in the public mind moves up and down with the fluctuating temperature of the cold war. Within the schools, however, there is still little disposition to develop the kind of personality which, in Tennyson's words, is prone to follow "knowledge as a sinking star beyond the utmost bounds of human thought." Nor has there been any conspicuous evidence of the repeal of restrictive acts passed by boards of education and state legislatures which bear upon teachers and the selection of textbooks—acts which, so long as they remain unrescinded or unmodified, will continue to hamper the legitimate functions of the teacher. Nor is the continuing shortage of competent teachers likely to encourage the average school administrator to strike out boldly from conventional shores.

Despite these evidences of "loss of nerve," it would be unwise to conclude that Americans as a whole have lost confidence in the future or that they have abandoned the hope that their schools will equip the young "to grasp the winds of change in their fists." By and large, they remain friendly to equality of opportunity and to social mobility.

Effects of Transition from a Stable to a Changing Society

Acceptance of change in its educational applications is not an unmixed blessing. Social mobility, the opportunity for individuals to move freely up and down the ladder of social recognition, can create pains of adjustment. Under these conditions children often find it difficult to maintain free and easy relations with their parents and friends who fail to keep pace with them, whereas those who are left behind tend frequently to nurse feelings of hurt and inferiority. Moreover, since change so often involves the discovery of new knowledge and the attendant necessity to revise accepted facts—even to revise the codes of yesterday—a transformation in age-long attitudes in education becomes imperative. The traditional confidence in the past as the custodian of the truth gives way to dependence upon, sometimes even an uncritical faith in, the future.

Let us consider some of the consequences that follow upon an education keyed to a changing society in contrast with one that is static or relatively stable. In the latter what is important to transmit from generation to generation is easily determined by analogy. Children and youth are raised without question in the image of the past, and parents and teachers may draw with confidence upon their own experiences or the recipes of earlier generations in selecting materials, goals, and procedures for home and school.

But when change calls the tune, the selection of materials, goals, and procedures becomes a difficult, bewildering problem. In their professional education teachers are urged to draw upon a variety of sources in the construction of a curriculum. This involves consultations with experts who may differ as to what is most significant or valid. For example, specialists in child development and educational psychology often differ in their emphasis on aims in education, advocate different approaches to teaching, and stress different specific techniques. Similarly, experts on social trends, whose advice may be sought in order to establish the relevance of various principles, skills, and attitudes in the modern world, disagree frequently in their interpretations and values.

How may the teacher best put together suggestions and cues? How shall he reconcile the recommendations of a psychologist who insists that, above all, the child should grow in self-understanding with those of a subject-matter specialist who places the mastery of a subject first? Can these objectives—not to mention many other possible objectives— be realized by the same general procedures? Moreover, what influence is or will be exerted on the curriculum by the textbooks and standardized tests, the community, the administrator, and the other teachers? There are no easy answers to these and similar questions. In this situation, a teacher may be tempted to rely on just one or two areas of consideration or to accept the practices of a school system as necessary and good. Then, too, since the values and techniques advocated by teacher-training institutions often differ from the practices accepted by a school system, it is easy to conclude, in a mood of surrender to the practical, that professional education is loaded not only with vagueness but also with impracticality.

Although they may be neglected, moral problems remain even for the person who is practical and thoroughly adjusted to current trends. Indeed, if it is desirable to promote careful, critical inquiry into any set of assumptions or practices, moral problems continually confront each of us. As an illustration, we can take the following general situation: Despite important qualifications that we have already noted, the accelerating pace of change has produced a tendency to promote "education for a changing society" and to demote "education for the transmission of the cultural heritage." Often, however, it is not clear whether bondage to the past is to be exchanged for thralldom to a mad rush somewhere—anywhere—or whether questions about democratic values and control of change are to become essential elements in the emerging educational scene. The words of John W. Gardner, Secretary of the United States Department of Health, Education, and Welfare, express both this tendency and this ambiguity:

> If we indoctrinate the young person in an elaborate set of fixed beliefs, we are insuring his early obsolescence. The alternative is to develop skills, attitudes, habits of mind, and the kinds of knowledge and understanding, that will be the instruments of continuous change. . . .
>
> This suggests a standard for judging the effectiveness of all education—and so judged, much education today is monumentally ineffective. All too often we are giving young people cut flowers when we should be teaching them to grow their own plants. We are stuffing their heads with the products of earlier innovation rather than teaching them how to innovate.[20]

Certainly, there are valid ideas in this statement. But all too often questions about the purposes of change or the criteria for accepting change are neglected or passed over with vague words. We are not suggesting that there are constant moral principles which, though isolated from the field of change, must yet provide the goals for change. We are suggesting that changes become part of networks of activities that have directions and purposes. The same techniques, devices, and arrangements may indeed be used within different institutions or cultures and for different purposes. This is precisely why the value of a technique or innovation is not revealed by considerations restricted to the technique or innovation. In part, the moral element in education lies in a comprehensive view of the networks of relations and consequences of our activities; in part, it lies in the ability to consider, crea-

20. Carnegie Corporation of New York, *Annual Report* (New York: Carnegie Corporation of New York, 1962), p. 11.

tively and critically, alternative relations or frameworks. Yet, as
Bertrand Russell and others have suggested, too few people are disturbed by the fact that an innovation that promotes "efficiency" within
an established social or educational framework may be widely ac-
claimed, whereas a proposal for the reformation of the framework itself may be wildly, almost automatically, attacked.

For example, over a long period of time, the curriculum of the
schools has been changing from a fairly uniform program of studies to
a highly diversified set of programs. Often, however, what has passed
for "an adjustment to and respect for individual differences" has been
an attempt to adjust individuals with different abilities to different
levels and functions within a complex society. Adjustment to society
and creative criticism of society are not necessarily or completely in-
compatible objectives. But on the whole, children with diverse talents
have been guided or pressed into different curricula and prepared to
assume "appropriate" future roles much more systematically than they
have been encouraged to examine critically the existing core values
and the attendant roles and rules of the society in which they live. It
may fairly be questioned whether becoming an adequate functionary
within a changing society is understood to include a fair share of the
attitudes and abilities needed by critics and controllers of the social
framework.

Fickle Theories in Education

Consequences of the confusions and contradictions in a changing society can be both amusing and tragic.

Some disciplines that usually serve as the "foundations" of educational theory seem to be either impervious to changing experience, as
in the case of some philosophies of education, or to be influenced more
by shifts in social climates than by a critical evaluation of comprehensive and controlled experiences, as in the case of some psychological
theories. "Scientific" psychology profoundly influenced classroom teaching and school organization during the first third of this century. Job
analysis and scientific management as applied to industry served as
models for schools to follow in determining the curriculum and methods of teaching. All learning is habit formation, it was concluded, a

mere matter of cementing connections between situations and responses (S → R bonds). This became a psychological dogma which earnest teachers sought to translate into the particulars of subject matter and the details of method in the instruction of their pupils.

With the onset of disillusionment in the 1920s and the Depression in the 1930s, a more broadly sympathetic understanding of childhood and youth found its way into the schools. Clinical studies and research into personality development, influenced in large measure by the Europeans Freud, Jung, and Adler and their American disciples, began to transform traditional conceptions of discipline and methods of teaching as well as the purposes and functions of subject matter. "Child-centered" schools sprang up in great numbers to shock conventional educators out of their complacency, and often, unfortunately, to encourage a skewed emphasis upon the individuality of the child so extreme that it left many incapable of living sympathetically and responsibly with their fellows.

These limitations were quickly sensed, however, since they were basically out of key with a closely knit and sensitively interrelated society. Respect for the integrity and the uniqueness of child nature remained, but attention came to center more upon "developmental tasks" (social as well as individual and personal) than upon interests in the raw. Thereupon, education on both the elementary and secondary levels set about the task of reorganizing the curriculum of the school with an eye to the factors of *interplay* between the child and *his* community.

These new trends were scarcely at the point of yielding educational fruit when "the lights of the world went out," and mankind plunged itself into World War II, a war that concluded with little evidence of a lasting peace. War and its aftermath, as we have seen, generated a spirit quite different from that which seemed on the point of emerging from the Great Depression of the 1930s. Whether a tender and understanding concern for the inner sensibilities of childhood and youth can survive the corroding influences of an atmosphere permeated by often unexamined fears, is a grave question. Heavy demands for technical excellence coupled with the uncertainties of the world, including the ever-present possibility of global war, tend to create an atmosphere unfriendly to the development of a warm and generous, open and inquiring nature. Not surprisingly, the demands in recent years for firmer knowledge and loyalties have been accompanied by demands for and justifications of a firmer discipline.[21]

"Permissiveness" may mean many different things; it may be conjoined with a variety of aims, criteria, and techniques. Like automobiles and morphine, like knowledge and charity, permissiveness may be put to beneficial or harmful uses, depending on purposes, persons, and situations. But in the minds of many today, permissiveness has become such a bad thing that we should begin to suspect that we are dealing with a caricature and a social mood rather than with a careful analysis of the complex process of education.

Growing Pains in Parent-Child Relationships

A final contrast between education in a fairly stable society and that in a relatively changeful society relates to the respective roles of young and old. In a stable society, the old tend to be wise and the fruits of their experience tend to dominate the education of the young. In a changing society, these roles are often ill-defined or reversed.

In the United States today, the variety of social contacts, the "knowledge explosion," the more or less anonymous "experts," and the mass media provide the background for our changing parent-child relationships. Parents may not be able to help even elementary-school children with the "new mathematics." Comparisons of family standards and customs with those suggested by a variety of reference groups with which the child might identify himself, such as school or peer groups, may work to the disadvantage of the home to which the child belongs.

In later chapters we shall return to a consideration of some of the factors that seem bent upon changing the traditional patterns of family living and the long-accepted roles of its members. The point of these preliminary observations is to draw attention to the fact that parents today are finding it increasingly difficult to raise children with the confidence formerly felt by parents. The young, in turn, are often confused by factors of change encountered at a time when each is prone to picture for himself the kind of person he wishes to become. Consequently, both young and old need the assistance that a good school can provide, and this dual need today constitutes a major challenge to education.

21. See Keith F. James, *Corporal Punishment in the Public Schools* (Los Angeles: University of Southern California Press, 1963), pp. 88–89.

We should observe, however, that in assuming the task of professional guide in an era of contradiction and confusion, the school helps to shape the future. No longer is it restricted to the teaching of salted-down truths or to the inculcation of habits specified in advance. It now ventures to break new soil and to assume the role of an agency of the community charged with the responsibility of preparing young people to live significantly with their fellows in a changing society.

But when should one hold fast to the old and when should one welcome the new? In what areas should the school encourage the experimental method and in which, if at all, should it follow tradition? How should it deal with factors of change when the community is fearful of change or is not of one mind? These are questions with which we must deal in chapters to come.

Suggested Reading

Bereday, George Z., and Bonnie B. Stretch, "Political Education in the U.S.A. and the U.S.S.R.," *Comparative Education Review,* June 1963, pp. 9–16.

Corwin, Ronald G., *A Sociology of Education* (New York: Appleton-Century-Crofts, 1965), chaps. 4–5.

Edman, Irwin, *John Dewey, His Contribution to the American Tradition* (Indianapolis: The Bobbs-Merrill Co., Inc., 1955), chap. VI.

Gardner, John W., *Excellence: Can We Be Equal and Excellent Too?* (New York: Harper & Brothers, 1961), chaps. IV, XI, XIII.

Hodgkinson, Harold L., *Education in Social and Cultural Perspective* (Englewood Cliffs, N.J.: Prentice-Hall, Inc., 1962), pp. 110–21.

National Society for the Study of Education, *Social Forces Influencing American Education,* Sixtieth Yearbook (Chicago: University of Chicago Press, 1961), pt. II, chaps. V, VI, X.

Torrance, E. Paul, *Education and the Creative Potential* (Minneapolis: University of Minnesota Press, 1963), pp. 4–32, 137–44.

Chapter 3

The School as a Supplementary Institution

Education and the "Permanent Studies"

Two attitudes toward change, as set forth in Chapter 2, are influencing education today: the one hopeful and optimistic, the other timid and fearful. We should not conclude, however, that all who oppose the keying of instruction in the schools to the concept of change do so in response to the threatening aspects of modern life. A third group of laymen and educators consider the contemporary emphasis upon change to be a serious error. What appears as change, this group insists, is no more than the variations of a constant. They consider the novel in human society somewhat like the surface currents on a lake caused by a passing breeze. Upon inspection and reflection, the novel idea reveals itself as little more than the individual expression of an unchanging principle or law. Accordingly, to tamper with the true and tried content of the curriculum or to change its emphasis in response to what seem to be fundamental transformations in contemporary society is to do violence to a valid education.

Vigorous justification of this point of view, together with an attack upon what he considers to be the fallacies of "progressive education," are found in the writings of Robert M. Hutchins and his fellow advocates of a curriculum grounded in the "permanent studies." Thus, Hutchins insists that any schooling which aims at adjusting youth to the currents, the sights and sounds, vocations and manners, of any particular society is a kind of animal training rather than an education. It is instruction in mores rather than in morals, in what divides rather than unites men, in the superficial and changing opinions of science rather than in basic issues and perennial truths. According to Hutchins, the major purpose of education is the same for all times and societies. It is to develop man's distinctive quality, his capacity to reason. This is to be accomplished through an education in the liberal arts, especially in the classical exemplars of the tools and truths of reason.[1]

Hutchins draws deep lines of division between what is permanent and what changes, between schooling and social or practical experience, between intellectual and emotional aspects of behavior, between rational ways of knowing and empirical (which he identifies with scientific) ways of knowing. Assuming that intellectual aspects of behavior are the direct expression of a rational "faculty" whose capacities can be developed without significant attention to empirical, social, and emotional qualities of behavior, he asserts that the sole concern of education should be the development of the intellect.

Hutchins' basic thesis has received support in recent years from an influential group of writers, including Walter Lippmann, Bernard Iddings Bell, Mortimer J. Adler, and Louis Bromfield.[2] For example, Dorothy Thompson, in a series of articles written for the *Ladies' Home Journal*, questioned the wisdom of equipping young people to cope with change by means of instruction in contemporary materials and the use of contemporary problems. It would seem to be far better to insulate the young from the tensions of the present and to introduce them instead to the tried and true materials of the traditional curriculum. Miss Thompson illustrated the superiority of the training provided by the high school of her day over that of the present by calling attention to the "avoidance" in the former "of the transient and the currently controversial."

A further virtue in the old education, as Miss Thompson viewed it, was its refusal to adapt instruction to individual differences. These

1. Robert M. Hutchins, *Freedom, Education, and the Fund* (New York: Meridian Books, 1956), pp. 106–44.
2. See, for example, Walter Lippmann, *The Public Philosophy* (Boston: Little, Brown and Co., 1955), chap. VII; Mortimer J. Adler, "In Defense of the Philosophy of Education," *Forty-First Yearbook*, National Society for the Study of Education (Chicago: University of Chicago Press, 1942), pt. I, pp. 197–249.

were safely ignored, since the training afforded the student enabled him to "turn his training to his particular bent" by virtue of the fact that "the same training would serve anyone of any bent." [3]

The members of the Council for Basic Education—an organization of educators and laymen advocating rigorous teaching of the basic subjects as the heart of education—represent a spectrum of educational philosophy broader than the "new humanism" of Hutchins. But the new humanism is well represented on the Council,[4] though usually in a somewhat diluted or unsystematic form. For many members of the Council, the basic subjects are above all the humanistic subjects—languages, literature, philosophy, history, the fine arts, and so on. For many, the only alternative to an education in the liberal arts, which presumably develops a highly generalized ability to reason, is a freedom-constricting education in the trivia of daily living, in vocational skills, and in the changing and essentially insignificant data of the sciences.[5]

Moreover, many members of the Council, though they might insist less on the permanence of certain truths or insist more on the values of a certain kind of science, still would agree with Hutchins in many respects.[6] One general point of agreement—even among those whose premises, purposes, and definitions may differ somewhat—is that education should aim at the development of theoretical knowledge and rational capacities, and that this objective is thwarted if major attention is paid to the development of technical skills or qualities of personality.

Whatever we may conclude with respect to the concepts of human nature and society underlying Hutchins' philosophy of education, the history of curricula, as these have operated in schools in this country and abroad, would indicate that education has not been everywhere the same. There has been considerable variation in the actual content

---

3. Dorothy Thompson, "Do Our Schools Need an S.O.S.?" *Ladies' Home Journal*, February 1953, p. 60.

4. Robert H. Beck, "The New Conservatism and the New Humanism," *Teachers College Record*, March 1962, pp. 440–41.

5. See Clifton Fadiman, "The Case for Basic Education," *The Case for Basic Education: A Program of Aims for Public Schools*, James D. Koerner, ed. (Boston: Little, Brown and Co., 1959), pp. 3–14; Thomas Molnar, *The Future of Education* (New York: Fleet Publishing Co., 1961), pp. 49–97.

6. See, for example, Arthur Bestor, "The Education We Really Need for a Changing World," *Harvard Educational Review*, Winter 1957, pp. 1–8.

of the seven liberal arts—the trivium and the quadrivium—which, we are told, constitute today as yesterday the valid instruments of a liberal education. A careful inspection of these arts as taught throughout the years reveals clearly that factors other than unchanging criteria have given them whatever validity they possess. An inspection of the curricula of schools and colleges indicates not only constant change in subjects taught but transformations in the content of the "permanent studies," changes in response to what the times have brought forth, in terms of human values and aspirations as well as changing circumstances. There is little resemblance, for example, between the concept of human nature and its destiny which the colonial school sought to convey and that promoted by the school of today. In purposes and goals as well as in subject matter taught, methods of instruction, and administration of the school, profound transformations have taken place.

In one respect, however, education in this country is the same today as yesterday. Throughout their history, as we indicated in Chapter 1, Americans have attributed almost magical qualities to the influence of the school. It was this influence which Governor Berkeley of Virginia feared when he thanked God that there were no free schools or printing presses in his colony, just as this magical influence was welcomed by the Puritans of New England, who envisaged the establishment of schools, primary through college, as the indispensable means for realizing what Cotton Mather termed "the designs of a glorious transformation," the establishment and perpetuation of the Holy Commonwealth on this continent.

Faith in education and conscious recognition of change have led to a third formative principle or concept: that of the school as a supplementary institution. The school has been viewed as an educational agency established by society in order to afford to its young, through collective effort, what its adults value for them but are unable to provide individually. The vagueness of this formulation is necessitated by the variety and changes in the kinds of tasks assigned to the school and by the vagueness of the criteria for selecting these tasks. Clarification of alternative criteria is a problem so basic and of such magnitude that it could not be worked through by this entire book, let alone by this chapter. Here we can do no more than emphasize some of the intricacies of this concept of the school's function.

The Curriculum Responds to the Times

The colonial school began with an exclusive emphasis upon academic education. In this respect it bore witness to its European origin and the persistence of European influences upon the intellectual life of the colonies; but it was by no means a passive imitator. In New England, which is frequently spoken of as the cradle of public education, its founders saw in the school one means of rendering children immune to the wiles of that "old deluder Satan." This required instruction in the written word, and so determined was the New Englander on this point that within a few short years of his landing on the shores of the New World he had established a complete system of education, extending from the primary school through college.

The curriculum, however, was narrow, centering primarily upon literary materials (if we may apply the term literary to the catechetical contents of the *New England Primer* and the *Hornbook,* as well as to the classical materials used in secondary schools and colleges), and only incidentally upon mathematics. Science was nonexistent. Life in home and community was comparatively rich in practical experiences essential for the preparation of the young for adult life, so that schools were deemed necessary as a means of access to books and the values which books alone might develop.

These values loomed large in the Puritan mind. In large measure both the Puritan and his neighbor, the Pilgrim (or Separatist), had left their homes because of religious conviction. The truth, of which they believed they were in possession, derived from the Bible and from learned commentaries upon its meaning. The substance of this truth they wished the school to convey to the young: the elementary school to the mass, the secondary school and college to the future leaders of church and state.

As schools followed the pioneers into the virgin territory of the West, they continued to afford virtually the only opportunity young people had of acquiring the rudiments of an academic education. Consequently, the three Rs loomed large. Public libraries were, of course, nonexistent, and the scarcity, if not total absence, of books in the home was a common phenomenon. With the appearance of the academy as a successful competitor of the colonial grammar school, the curriculum was enlarged to include practical subjects relevant to the needs of young people in a rapidly expanding commercial and industrial economy.

Nor was there a significant change of emphasis as the academy gave way to the public high school. What the schools continued to provide, by and large, was an ever richer and fuller curriculum in the elementary school and an expanding curriculum on the secondary and college levels to which was added for special groups the specific skills and techniques of a vocation.

What of today?

Books and academic education are still indispensable and properly occupy a central place in the school. Indeed, we might say that books and the abstract education they symbolize are more important today than yesterday. We have become a verbal civilization and are heavily dependent upon the ability to communicate with people beyond the range of our immediate senses. This dependence carries with it the necessity of familiarity with and ease in the use of abstract symbols. But, at the same time, the out-of-school conditions which once gave import and meaning to abstractions, such as number concepts and economic and social principles, are not so prevalent today. Consequently, alert teachers seek to bring into the classrooms of both the elementary and secondary schools experiences that will infuse abstract symbols and principles with the breath of contemporary life. Children from urban homes are thus encouraged to manipulate objects in order to develop concepts of numbers that come naturally to the rural child who gathers the eggs daily and reports the number to his elders. So, too, with other concepts conveyed by the printed word. By means of excursions and out-of-school projects, the use of the arts and crafts, and an early introduction to the science laboratory, the modern school strives to infuse good red blood into classroom experiences which without this enrichment would take on a pale and hollow look.

Many critics of modern procedures in the schools do not appreciate this need to provide fertile soil in which abstractions can germinate and grow. They fail to sense the full implications of the fact that children of today, in contrast with the children of yesterday, begin their schooling at a younger age than formerly and are thus introduced earlier to verbal materials and abstract concepts while, at the same time, modern children are increasingly denied the experiences outside of school which once gave substance and meaning to these concepts.

Nor is the attempt to fuel the imagination and intelligence appropriate only on the elementary level. Secondary school and college are likewise finding it essential to give reality to the concepts and principles basic to subjects such as economics, political science, and sociology. We live today in a world of chain reactions. Increasingly, the well-being—perhaps even the existence—of people is intimately affected by events occurring far away. What we decide to do or not to do in one locality may spell life or death for individuals in another with whom we have no first-hand acquaintance. Young people have to learn, as many of their elders have not yet learned, that principles—economic, political, social—are descriptions of living relationships among people, not mere abstract formulations. A strike or a lockout, for example, is more than a local economic phenomenon or an instrument of limited effect used by one party in a labor dispute in order to fix wages or to acquire profits. It is also an act of far-reaching import for the lives of many people who are not the immediate contestants in the dispute. The terms of settlement of a steel strike, for example, may have profound ramifications for the whole economy—which means inconvenience for everyone in the country, no matter how far their interests seem to lie from that industry.

Until young people have learned to translate concepts and principles into living relationships and to sense them as descriptions of transactions among men caught up in the complicated web of modern life, the school will not have discharged its educational responsibility. But to achieve this objective, more than the written word is required. First-hand observation, excursions, radio and television, the visual and dramatic arts, and, on occasion, work projects must supplement the written words so that each may reinforce the other.

Emphasis upon nonverbal experiences need not distract from or be a weak substitute for an academic education. Rather, these experiences, at their best, give vitality to it. Much the same may be said of many (though not all) additions to the curriculum which have been subject to criticism and ridicule. These indictments are valid only when the subject or the course in question is proved to be a substitute for an academic subject of importance.

From Specific to General Vocational Education

The contrast between education for vocation today and that of yesterday illustrates further the supplementary function of the school. Under the relatively simple conditions of the colonial period and the frontier, the vocational responsibilities of the school were easily discharged. Once mastered, the three Rs constituted a sufficient equipment for economic life. The specific skills and processes employed in carrying on a trade after the academic foundations were laid were commonly acquired through an apprenticeship with a master craftsman, and essential preparation for a profession, such as law or medicine, was obtained from direct association with a practicing attorney or physician.

This is not the method of acquiring skills in the intricate, complex, and rapidly changing economic society of today. Without guidance there is no way in which young people can know about—let alone perform—the operations required in a modern industrial plant. Some preliminary introduction and training therefore become essential. On the other hand, specialization and the rapid spelling out of new functions and processes require a sensitive adaptation and readaptation to the vocation, including, on occasion, the ability to scrap one skill and to acquire a new one rapidly. This calls for a vocational education that cuts through numerous specialized performances and introduces the student to "families" of occupations and to the basic principles of science which are easily translated into practical skills. Moreover, as we shall stress later, the comparatively simple operations called for in many occupations suggest that character traits may be as important as specific skills in the initial preparation of a good worker. If so, a general education which centers upon desirable qualities of personality becomes of immediate concern in vocational education. What this suggests for the school is strikingly different from the original functions of the "common branches" of the school or the early limited attempts to equip young people in school with the specific skills employed on the job. To these are now added concern for the social functions of a profession or a vocation, as well as its exclusively technical requirements.

Vocational education is still often viewed as the acquisition of some narrow technical skills and as a lure to keep potential dropouts in school. Also, there are educators other than the new humanists who believe that vocational education has little or no place in the program of the school.[7] Both of these groups see work experience and techniques as quite distinct from an intellectual or general education. It seems probable, however, that under both conceptions it will be difficult for students to develop a vital appreciation of the ways in which certain technical routines are tied to social, moral, and intellectual problems of the most profound import.[8] Not surprisingly, many adults approach many economic, social, and political problems in terms of narrow occupational or social-class interests. What better way is there to preserve this unfortunate situation than to divorce vocational and general education, intellectual and technical affairs, rational and emotional aspects of behavior?

A Broadened Responsibility for Citizenship Education

Education for citizenship has a history similar to education for vocations. For a period the former was identical with religious instruction. Since no line divided church and state, it was natural for church authorities to translate religious teachings into their implications for public and private conduct. In New England, for example, the clergy more or less proclaimed the law, moral and religious, and the magistrates saw to its enforcement, whereas the schoolmaster instructed his pupils in the virtues of obedience. The Blue Laws of Connecticut, and similar legislation in other colonies, testify to the dominance of religious ideas in regulating the transactions of men in all areas of living. Gradually, as people became more tolerant in religion and the citizen acquired the right to worship according to the dictates of his own conscience, moral conduct and religious behavior ceased to be identical, and citizenship, as one phase of a secular morality, undertook to stand on its own feet.

With suffrage for adult men citizenship education became increasingly secular. Its emphasis centered chiefly upon political office and the information and knowledge adults might require as voters to win political preferment for themselves. The emphasis upon the political in civic

7. For one argument in this direction, see Harry S. Broudy, B. O. Smith, and Joe R. Burnett, *Democracy and Excellence in American Secondary Education* (Chicago: Rand McNally and Co., 1964), especially pp. 11–23, 31–42.
8. See Chapter 12.

education continued well into the period following the Civil War—
indeed, until industrial development and the growth of cities, with
their magnetic attraction for people unaccustomed to urban living, of
necessity promoted broader preparation of young people for civic responsibility. Contrast, in this connection, Reverend James E. Lap-
ham's description of Townsend's *Analysis of Civil Government,* a secondary school textbook published in 1868, with the table of contents in
a modern text.

> He has drawn the materials for his work from original sources
> and from commentaries and from classic excellence. We see
> traces of interminable rumblings of *The Madison Papers, The
> Federalist, Elliott's Debates,* Story and Rawle on the Constitu-
> tion, Kent and Blackstone's *Commentaries,* as well as the most
> patient gleanings from official statistical and chronological ta-
> bles.[9]

The steady drift to the city of a people once predominantly rural, the
growth of cities, and the multiplication of services communities now
render their inhabitants; the struggle for greater integrity and efficiency in civil government; the entrance of women and children into
industry, with the resulting necessity of correcting attendant abuses
and rendering protection to them; the rise of labor organizations and
the growth of corporations—to mention but a few developments
within the last century—made obvious the need for a many-sided
orientation of the young to economic, social, and civic institutions.
Obviously, this orientation requires more than a course in "civics," or,
to adopt a more recent term, the "social studies," important as "knowledge about" political government and politics assuredly is. Certainly
the intelligent citizen requires professional assistance in order to
acquaint himself with the institutions and resources of the local community which serve his daily needs and stand ready to assist him in an
emergency. Similarly, on the state, national, and international levels,
information is indispensable. But today it is essential to have more than
"knowledge about" these matters, in the sense of an exclusively intellectual preparation for citizenship. Young people require assistance in

9. Quoted in J. E. Stout, *The Development of the High School in the North
Central States from 1860 to 1918,* Supplementary Educational Monographs, no. 3,
University of Chicago, p. 182.

learning how to understand and to get along with people, how to respond sensitively to and live creatively with their fellows. They need to acquire through practice in relatively simple situations the qualities and insights they must later apply in the solution of complex problems. Moreover, democracy has become a way of life in which the rules and regulations that govern conduct emerge from the thinking of the governed and derive their validity from the consent of the governed. Such a democracy presupposes an association of healthy personalities. Consequently, education for citizenship both begins and ends with attention to sound emotional and social attitudes. Accordingly, we find the school slowly reorganizing its work in the classroom, its administrative structure, and its relations with institutions and agencies outside the school in the light of a fuller and richer concept of what constitutes education for healthy citizenship.

An "understanding of democracy" achieved by learning the words and routines representing the existing social norms is indeed a kind of animal conditioning that Hutchins and others condemn. So, also, is the development of a sociable and healthy personality, whether by benevolent manipulation or by coercion, which renders a person unable to inquire seriously and capably into what he and his society consider sociable and healthy. But surely the only alternative to these sad procedures is not recourse to some permanent truths—a procedure which is as authoritarian as the others we have mentioned.

Nor is the only alternative a procedure which, though it rejects the notion of transmitting permanent truths, still insists that education must be concerned "essentially" with the development of abstract, theoretical knowledge, and that technical skills, emotional dispositions, and personality traits should be learned outside the school, outside a context of inquiry. Such a procedure is based on ancient but very dubious assumptions that such abstractions as reason and emotion and reason and sensation (or interpretation and observation) are essentially separate processes which can be developed independently.

It seems clear, for example, that knowledge is acquired within and in the light of a larger culture, an interrelated system of behaviors, attitudes, and beliefs. For both the expert and the pupil, this larger personal and social system exerts a directive and limiting effect on interpretation, evaluation, and observation. A pupil may learn something in order to compete successfully and "get ahead," or because the context of personal and social concerns facilitates recognition and appreciation of the broad moral and intellectual implications of that knowledge. In any case, the fuller meanings, at least for the student, of what is taught are not known or explored by teachers who omit from their concerns the personal and social system into which a bit of knowledge enters.[10]

To take another illustration, both conservatives and liberals may intellectually, for some limited academic purposes, know the same facts and theories. But so long as the teacher's attention is riveted to certain intellectual abstractions, the dissimilar dispositions which lead conservatives and liberals to assign different interpretations and uses to these elements of knowledge remain largely unexplored. Then, since they are not intellectualized, we call these dispositions "personal" attitudes and values. Moreover, the task of exploring and intellectualizing these dispositions involves careful and systematic attention to them as means and ends in education.

In these and in many other ways, reason and emotion, interpretation and observation, individual and social experiences interpenetrate. Aspects of human behavior that can be separately classified and discussed do not necessarily function as disengaged, insulated parts of behavior. Thus, an enlightening education in democracy, or in anything else, becomes a much more complex matter than instruction in a set of symbols or mere acceptance or manipulation of personal feelings and attitudes.

Moral and Spiritual Values in a Changing Culture

Contemporary emphasis upon the school's responsibility for education in moral and spiritual values will serve as a final illustration of the school as a supplementary institution.

This task assigned to education had its origin in an exclusively religious orientation. The religious motive loomed large in the early settlements of this country. Many people had migrated from Europe in order to develop in the New World a way of life in harmony with what they conceived to be religious truth. Once here, they established

10. In this connection, it is interesting to contrast the interpretations of formal education provided by an anthropologist and an educator. See Jules Henry, *Culture Against Man* (New York: Random House, 1963), chaps. II, VII, VIII; Carl F. Hanson, *The Amidon Elementary School: A Successful Demonstration in Basic Education* (Englewood Cliffs, N.J.: Prentice-Hall, Inc., 1962).

schools both to safeguard the young from ignorance of the Scriptures and to train the future leaders in church and state, that is, the ministers who would interpret the law and the magistrates who would see to its administration.

The desire for freedom of religion, so dominant in the early colonial period, differed nevertheless from our present conception of religious liberty. The religious freedom, so essential for the conscience of one, often was denied to others. Accordingly, Massachusetts drove the dissenters Anne Hutchinson and Roger Williams into the wilderness and warned all religious "heretics" on pain of death not to pollute her soil. Virginia was equally intolerant of Congregationalists. In each instance, intolerance was grounded upon the assumption that religious orthodoxy is essential to individual morality and civic well-being.

The inhabitants of the Middle Colonies were the first to weaken, if not to undermine, this assumption. Here people of diverse religious affiliation dwelt side by side. Quakers and Mennonites, Lutherans and Baptists, Methodists and Presbyterians, together with a scattering of Catholics and Jews, gradually evolved a community of interests. They raised their crops, exchanged their wares, practiced their professions, determined the laws to govern them, and united for defense. In short, they evolved a common way of life that was more firmly rooted in interlocking interests than in their separate theologies.

For a time, each religious sect assumed the responsibility for educating its own children, but in a mixed population where numbers were small this was no easy undertaking. Ultimately, there developed the nonsectarian school, a device first employed by the Quakers but soon adopted by others. This was a school in which religious instruction centered upon items common to several denominations rather than upon creedal differences. It proved to be admirably adapted to the needs of a growing country and a population heterogeneous in religion.

Nonsectarian instruction continued to rest, nevertheless, on the assumption of a one-to-one relationship between morality and religious orthodoxy. It merely broadened the religious base from which morality seemed to flow. To a Protestant child attending a school with children of varying sects who was thus instructed in religious tenets common to all, it soon became obvious that the virtues of honesty, truthfulness, dependability, and the like bore no exclusive relation to the doctrines which divided Protestants even though he continued to believe, as he was taught, that he must be on his guard when dealing with Catholics or Jews or atheists. Not until Catholics and Jews gained admission to the schools in considerable numbers was it possible to broaden still further the basis of a common morality. Finally, with the passage of laws forbidding all instruction of a sectarian character in public schools the secular school was born.

The exclusion of sectarian instruction from public education was an act in no way unfriendly to religion. On the contrary, as the Superintendent of Schools in New York State wrote in 1853, it seemed the only way to avoid either an official religion or a multiple establishment in religion.

> To form for the schools a course of instruction . . . which could bear the name of a religious one, and which would meet the views of all, was manifestly impossible. To give to every sect a pro rata share of the school monies to enable it to support its own schools and teach its own system of religious faith in them, would be . . . to divide the children . . . into a dozen or more schools. . . . In view of the above facts, the position was early, distinctly, and almost universally taken by our statesmen, legislators, and prominent friends of education—men of the warmest religious zeal and belonging to every sect—that religious education must be banished from the common schools and consigned to the family and church. . . . Accordingly, the instruction in our schools has been limited to that ordinarily included under the head of intellectual culture, and the propagation of those principles of morality in which all sects, and good men belonging to no sect, can equally agree. . . .[11]

Moral education which centers upon "the propagation of those principles of morality in which all sects, and good men belonging to no sect, can equally agree" is vital, as verbal instruction, only so long as the principles taught reflect or summarize the obvious facts of common experience. The moral maxims in *Poor Richard's Almanac*, for example, embodied in apt phrase the wisdom of this common experience, and from this fact came their influence. Thus, "The sleeping fox catches no poultry. Up. Up," "Early to bed and early to rise makes a man healthy,

11. Quoted in R. Freeman Butts, *The American Tradition in Religion and Education* (Boston: Beacon Press, Inc., 1950), p. 136.

wealthy, and wise," "Keep thy shop and thy shop will keep thee," reflect the experience of generations of a frugal and industrious people under simple and relatively stable conditions of living. When taught in school, they enabled children to verbalize in a happy phrase the pressures and influences of home and community consistently playing upon them. Precept and example worked hand in hand. But, like the Biblical warning that "Whatsoever a man soweth that shall he also reap," these wise sayings were keyed essentially to and their effectiveness was dependent upon a consistent relationship between verbal statement and daily event.

Change the cultural setting, and these words lose their convincing quality. Two families, for example, live side by side on the same street in a suburban community. The one wishes its children to retire at night at what it considers to be a reasonable hour. The other is lax in its regulations. Should the mother of the first seek to bolster her position by quoting from Poor Richard, "Early to bed and early to rise, makes a man healthy, wealthy, and wise," she is likely to receive the reply: "But Mother! the children next door don't have to go to bed as early as we do, they are healthy; and they have more money than we do!"

Once life outside the school began to deprive children and adolescents of first-hand experiences in coping with the serious problems of living and life in the city transformed family relationships that were peculiar to the country, moral maxims and verbal instruction appropriate to a simpler order weakened in influence and education in moral and spiritual values was forced to enlist new allies.

Increasingly these allies have been found in new forms of educational experience in the classroom and in projects that grip young people and relate them intimately to institutions and agencies in their community. Such experiences, in William H. Kilpatrick's happy phrase, enable them to learn what they live and to live what they learn.

The times have also changed in other respects since the colonial period. Moral instruction within the school, by means of sectarian religious material no longer insures the spirit of brotherly love. Nor are religious tenets recognized as the exclusive source of the moral values common to all members of the community. Equally inadequate is an education that depends chiefly upon verbal materials, the roots of which do not permeate deep into the soil of daily experience. New wine thus flows into old bottles, but the old bottles remain, in the sense that the school still functions as an institution dedicated to the task of bringing to flower in the lives of the young the values cherished by the community.

Some Problems of a Supplementary Institution

The adaptation of the school to social changes has not been a straight-line development. Despite the rapidly growing influence of the federal and state governments, education in the United States still remains largely a local enterprise. This is both an asset and a liability, since a progressive and experimentally minded community may profit from relative autonomy, whereas the same freedom enables a backward community to impose atavistic concepts and ways of living upon its children. Nor are all the educational needs of rural, slum, and suburban communities identical.

Then, too, practices at variance with each other may appear even when the material conditions of communities are similar, for differences in educational practice also reflect differences in educational theory, conflicting notions of child nature and of the ways in which children learn best. Thus, philosophies and psychologies of education are as relevant to our study as are the more obvious consequences of change. Theories of education, like the general instructional practices with which they are associated, are expressions of the culture and can be dated. Not infrequently they are intellectually obsolete and are used by counterrevolutionists to "reform" education and restore it to the "fundamentals." In other cases they represent efforts to utilize the most recent findings of the science of education and of other disciplines in a manner most appropriate to the hour.

In short, a competent student of education can find no fixed or commonly agreed upon set of criteria for selecting appropriate tasks for a school. Indeed, the lack of commonly recognized criteria is a major source or reflection of educational conflict and confusion. The confusion and conflict are compounded when, as now, the school is overtaxed with instructional tasks relating to such diverse matters as sports, character and personality development, safe driving, juvenile delinquency, dancing, a wide variety of vocational skills, and dozens of subjects whose content seems bent on changing or expanding.

We have suggested that attempts to allocate educational tasks to different institutions in terms of radical divisions between intellectual, technical, and moral or emotional aspects of behavior rest on infirm grounds. Still, it is impossible for any single social institution to undertake the "total" education of youth. Perhaps one of the major tasks of the school is to encourage and help other social institutions and agencies—the family; various civic, social welfare, and youth-serving agencies; libraries; industrial organizations; the mass media; and so on—to become better educational agencies. These and other institutions do develop attitudes, understandings, skills, tastes. If, as it sometimes does now, the school can help these institutions substitute educational procedures for emotional, punitive, indoctrinative, or "purely" recreational or technical aims or methods, it may be possible to strengthen not only the work of the school but our entire social structure. At times, in many communities, more of these agencies may be able to take over some functions of the school.

Although it will be difficult or impossible for the school to develop significant intellectual abilities without serious attention to technical and emotional matters, it is true that some schools are so immersed in these latter matters that they fail to lead children into an exploration of wide social and intellectual structures. And it is in this critical, intellectually responsible, and personally meaningful exploration that the essential work of the school lies. Just as the school selects and concentrates on certain intellectual matters, so it must select and concentrate on certain technical and attitudinal matters.

Yet it is difficult to know which might be the "lesser evil" for the future citizen, as for the future doctor or anthropologist—an education in manners, applicative routines, and unquestioned facts or an education in theoretical structures and formal logic which makes little or no meaningful contact with a world of brutal facts, blinding emotions, and apathy.

Suggested Reading

Broudy, Harry S., B. O. Smith, and Joe R. Burnett, *Democracy and Excellence in American Secondary Education* (Chicago: Rand McNally and Co., 1964), chaps. I–IV.

Brubacher, John S., *Modern Philosophies of Education* (New York: McGraw-Hill Book Co., Inc., 1962), chaps. IV, V.

Ginzberg, Eli, ed., *The Nation's Children,* Vol. II: *Development and Education* (New York: Columbia University Press, 1960), pp. 70–92.

Hutchins, Robert M., *The Conflict in Education* (New York: Harper and Brothers, 1953), chaps. I–III.

Kneller, George F., ed., *Foundations of Education* (New York: John Wiley and Sons, Inc., 1963), chap. 18.

Project on the Instructional Program of the Public School, *Deciding What to Teach* (Washington, D.C.: National Education Association, 1963), chaps. 4–5.

Sayers, E. V., and Ward Madden, *Education and the Democratic Faith* (New York: Appleton-Century-Crofts, Inc., 1959), pp. 104–57, 395–405.

Chapter 4

Local Autonomy in Education

The Citizen and His School

One morning at breakfast Johnny Miller became involved in an argument with his father over the question of municipal ownership of the local transportation system. To the father, the head of the largest plumbing supply firm in town, this was clear evidence that his son had become infected by "creeping socialism." Imagine his alarm, therefore, in learning that the boy's teacher was considering in class the issue of public vs. private ownership of public utilities and had organized the class into two sections, one to gather all possible data and arguments favorable to public ownership and the other in opposition; and his son was chairman of the group giving support to the affirmative! As the father saw it, there was but one thing to do: to snuff out heresy as quickly as possible.

Accordingly, Mr. Miller decided to stop at the school and speak to either the principal or the boy's teacher on his way downtown to his office. Upon arriving at the school, he observed the teacher in earnest conversation with a group of students. Rather than arouse the curiosity of the young people, or create a scene in their presence, he resolved to speak immediately to the principal. This he did, only to be informed calmly, but firmly, that the topic under consideration by the class was an inherent part of the course of study in the field of the social studies, and as long as the teacher handled the topic objectively and with an eye to furthering an understanding of all points of view, the father should welcome the inclusion of the topic rather than its exclusion.

However, if Mr. Miller were still unsatisfied, he was free to appeal to the superintendent and/or the board of education.

"So this is the way I must cope with subversion in the schools," muttered Mr. Miller to himself. "Well, where duty points, I shall go." The result was that he shortly found himself at the head of a body of like-minded citizens who were determined to discipline the teacher and the principal through the board of education. In addition, to avoid similar difficulties in the future, they wished to survey courses of study, textbooks, and supplementary teaching materials in the schools with a view to weeding out anything conducive to the introduction of un-American ideas in the minds of their youth. Moreover, in the event the board of education should refuse to grant these demands, they were resolved to take their case to the people and thus insure the election of proper members to the incoming board of education.

Mr. Miller, in the above illustration, is a fictional character, but the incident described has been duplicated on numerous occasions in communities of the United States, for one of the unique features of education in this country is the high degree of community autonomy. In the vast majority of instances the school board is elected directly by the people of the school district. This board selects the administrative and instructional staff; prepares the budget; writes the rules and regulations governing the functions and the behavior of the administrative staff, the teachers, and students; approves the curriculum; and, in many other respects, acts as the governing body of the schools.

So conspicuously, indeed, is the average board of education in charge of the public schools that Mr. Miller and his associates have little cause to consider, as we shall do in a moment, that these functions are delegated functions and are subject to the will of the state. They conceive of their schools, as does the average American, as directly expressive of the will of the people of each locality.

How do we explain the fact that school systems which are both created by the state and subject to its control and regulation are, nevertheless, thought of as essentially local in authority and responsibility?

The Child Is Father of the Man

The answer is found, in part, in the American tradition of local self-government, a tradition which derives from the peculiarities of settlement in the colonial period and which was reaffirmed by each generation thereafter as individuals and groups, in the course of the conquest of the continent, constantly penetrated into new areas and established new communities in advance of a central government. In part, also, the explanation lies in the manner in which the state related itself to education in the early stages of development. Were we to consider the relation of local schools to the state as analogous to that of child and parent, we should have to say that the child is father of the parent!

In early New England, for example, a number of communities in their town meetings established schools in advance of legislation by the General Court requiring all towns to do so.[1] Moreover, with the advent of general legislation in 1642 and 1647, the responsibility for enforcement was lodged directly in the hands of the "chosen men appointed to manage the prudential affairs" of the town, rather than in state officials. In the course of time, as towns came to grant to outlying districts the privilege of establishing and maintaining their own schools, local self-determination in the conduct of education became firmly grounded in practice and theory. A century and a half after the mandatory act of 1647 a state agency of education was established in Massachusetts.

In the Middle Colonies, as in New England, a motivating factor in the establishment of schools was the religious concern that young people grow up possessed of the faith of their fathers. But, here, diversity rather than uniformity of religious conviction prevailed. As Edwards and Richey point out, in no other section were Protestants more divided in their concepts of the relation of God to man, nor in any other section was the population more heterogeneous in social origins and social outlooks. To these colonies came representatives from all northern Europe, and "the only non-English people to found settlements within the limits of the original thirteen colonies established them in this middle region."[2]

Under these circumstances, the state soon found it inexpedient to enforce religious orthodoxy through education and willingly left the responsibility for schooling in the hands of family, church, and other religious and philanthropic organizations. The sole exception, but one

1. For example, Boston in 1635 and Ipswich and Salem in 1641.
2. Newton Edwards and Herman G. Richey, *The School in the American Social Order*, 2d ed. (Boston: Houghton Mifflin Co., 1963), p. 148.

pregnant with later possibilities, was state provision for the education of the poor as charity pupils.

Much the same condition prevailed in the South. There no school system as such existed prior to the Revolution or, indeed, for some time later. Despite the influence of Thomas Jefferson and others of broad vision, there was little public sentiment for the concept of general education either as a public obligation or as a public asset, least of all for "taxation of one man's property for the education of another man's child." Nevertheless, in the South as in the North, there were scattered seeds of a future public school system in the form of public provision for the education of the "children of barbarians" and of the poor.[3] There, too, were to be found transient and isolated schools sustained by private initiative and serving private interests.

On the whole, then, as we have said, individual and local efforts tended to antedate state efforts in the establishment of schools, although, in the course of time, it became necessary for the state to intervene in order to require lagging communities to follow in the footsteps of more progressive communities. The states either enacted mandatory legislation, similar to that enacted in Massachusetts in 1647, requiring the towns to make provisions for the education of all children in the rudiments of knowledge or else they established, as did Pennsylvania in its constitution of 1790, the less ambitious but nevertheless pioneering requirement that "the legislature shall, as soon as conveniently may be, provide for the establishment of schools throughout the state in such a manner that the poor may be taught gratis." But legislation that was mandatory in form was in fact only hortatory and was dependent for its enforcement upon the enlightened will and determination of the people of each community. Moreover, details of administration, such as the selection of teachers, the determination of subjects to be taught, and other items affecting the operation and administration of the schools, were locally determined and lacked both

3. Ten years after the settlement at Jamestown (1617) King James I wrote a letter to the bishops of the English churches ordering them to instruct the bishops in Virginia "to give orders to ministers and other zealous men of their Dioceses" to encourage contributions in support of churches and schools for the education of the children of "barbarians." Two years later, some 1500 pounds had been raised for this purpose, as well as for "a seminary for the breeding of good ministers." These efforts marked the beginnings of the College of William and Mary, the actual opening of which as a college was delayed until 1710 because of wars and hardships and official apathy.

central determination and central supervision. The result, of course, was that wide differences in the amount and quality of education provided by communities characterized schools well into the nineteenth century. For example, when Massachusetts, in 1837, established its State Board of Education and selected Horace Mann as its secretary, the "gnarls of a century's growth" had to be smoothed out. Private schools viewed the development of public education with jealous eyes and placed obstacles in the way of its progress. Churches, fearing the encroachments of nonsectarian education, were likewise commonly opposed. Teachers were ill-prepared and both professional education and professional standards waited upon future efforts.

During Mann's dozen years in office, the annual state appropriation for public education doubled, local taxation for education increased even more rapidly, the average school term was considerably lengthened, and instructional methods and materials were notably bettered. These and other improvements marked the establishment of a secular public school system on a fairly firm basis. Yet, the glaring defects in the system which Mann worked so hard to improve are only barely indicated by the fact that during his early years as secretary up to half the children of Massachusetts were not attending school regularly.[4]

Conditions elsewhere in New England in the early nineteenth century were no better. In Connecticut, for example, according to the report of Henry Barnard in 1839 to the State Board of Commissioners, expenditures upon the education of 12,000 pupils in private schools were as large as those upon the education of 40,000 in public schools. Children in primary grades were neglected in both. There was virtually no gradation of schools. Public funds for education were often misappropriated, and although in the cities and populous districts of the state provision for education was as good as elsewhere in New England, there were wide differences in the quality of education provided.[5]

Developments in the Middle Colonies and the South

Outside "enlightened" New England, conditions were even worse. But, as in Massachusetts and Connecticut, ardent advocates of reform

4. Harry G. Good, *A History of American Education*, 2d ed. (New York: Macmillan Co., 1962), pp. 158–67.
5. Richard G. Boone, *Education in the United States* (New York: D. Appleton and Co., 1909), p. 105.

were also succeeding in arousing the public mind and convincing state legislatures of the necessity of state provision for education and the exercise of state authority and control over education.

Active efforts at state provision for education date roughly from the period following the Revolution. Most frequently mentioned in this connection is Jefferson's plan for the universal establishment of common schools in Virginia. An act embodying his ideas was introduced in the Virginia legislature in 1779 but failed of passage.[6] Not until 1796 was legislative provision made in Virginia for a comprehensive system of elementary schools, and not until 1810, with the establishment of a literary fund, was assistance from the state extended to counties in support of public education. The influence of Jefferson's ideas, however, was not limited to Virginia. Nor was his voice as one in the wilderness. In 1786 Benjamin Rush in Philadelphia produced a plan for the education on a national scale of all American youth, including both sexes, a plan specifically designed to emphasize the principles of democracy and to insure an understanding of the machinery of government with which to maintain the institutions of democracy.[7] Others, similarly inspired, produced equally interesting plans with a view to the promotion of national progress and national unity. Active in this connection were the members of the American Philosophical Society, an organization founded by Benjamin Franklin and others and to which many of the leading minds of America belonged.

Following the adoption of the federal Constitution in 1789 and the approval of the Tenth Amendment to the Constitution in 1791 with its provision that "The powers not delegated to the United States by the Constitution, nor prohibited by it to the States, are reserved to the States respectively, or to the people," comprehensive schemes for the education of the young were of necessity confined within state boundaries. Within the states, however, a number of practical as well as theoretical considerations favored the gradual development of state systems of education.

6. This plan was designed, in Jefferson's words, "to avail the state of those talents which nature has sown as liberally among the poor as the rich, but which perish without use, if not sought for and cultivated." It was, therefore, selective in character. Schools for the teaching without cost of reading, writing, and arithmetic were to be established in districts of convenient size, from which competent children might go on to middle schools, also without cost, and, again, from these, all who demonstrated their ability to do so, might go on to college.

7. For an excellent discussion of these plans, see Allan Oscar Hansen, *Liberalism and American Education in the Eighteenth Century* (New York: The Macmillan Co., 1926), pp. 48–63.

Factors Stimulating State Responsibility for Education

First was the obvious need for wise administration of funds which the states set aside to assist communities in the discharge of their educational responsibilities.

In a number of states a "literary fund" was established with which to encourage education in the subdivisions of the state—counties in the South, towns or districts in the North. These funds were intended, in the first instance, to assist communities in the education of the poor; they provided, nevertheless, a nucleus for wider employment later.

The sources of these funds were varied: income from lotteries, liquor licenses, marriage licenses, and, as in Virginia, in accordance with an act of 1810, the income from all escheats, confiscations, penalties, and forfeitures, together with all rights in personal property found derelict. Substantial additions to state funds were made in 1837 by a grant of $28,000,000 from the federal government under the Surplus Revenue Act and in 1841 and 1850, respectively, by the Federal Internal Improvement Act and the Swamp Land Grant Act. In the West, public lands constituted a boon for the cause of education. As early as 1785 the Continental Congress, in adopting the Northwest Ordinance, provided for the setting aside of the sixteenth section of each township for the maintenance of schools. This served as a suggestive precedent for later action by both state and federal governments. Thus, when Connecticut, in 1786, agreed to cede to the United States her claims to lands in what is now northeastern Ohio, it was stipulated that a portion of this area, called the "Western Reserve," be used in support of education. Eventually this yielded the sum of $1,000,000 which was turned into a school fund. Similar restrictions were placed upon the sale of land granted to the states by the United States government, with stimulating effects upon the development of public education, despite the unfortunate circumstances of theft and waste and unwise practices which often accompanied the disposal of public land and its resources.

In both the West and the East the emergence of state funds in support of education led to the creation of committees and boards of control charged with the responsibility, in the first instance, of distributing the income of these funds equitably and, later, of stimulating local initiative on a matching basis not unlike the various forms of state aid employed at present.

By the middle of the nineteenth century every state in the Union had established a school fund and every state, with the exception of Arkansas, had, as a further step, enacted legislation authorizing localities to impose taxes in support of education. This legislation stemmed from the realization that resources more substantial than the income from state school funds were essential to meet new demands of the people for education.

These demands were for nothing less than schools to be maintained at public expense and open and free to all children, without the taint of charity.

As we have seen, the origins of this demand were plural. In New England it derived in large measure from the religious concern of the early New Englander that each child be provided with the means of determining his own salvation. In other colonies these seeds were found rather in their faltering provisions for the education of the "poor." By the first quarter of the nineteenth century, however, the commercial and industrial development of the country gave birth to forces other than religious and humanitarian in favor of a free education. These forces derived from an alliance of groups strikingly different in complexion and motivation but, nevertheless, united in support of schools.

One was the growing importance of labor. Although weak according to present standards, labor, by the second quarter of the nineteenth century, had become outspoken in its demands for an education which would enable young people to better themselves economically and to share more abundantly in the advantages of a general education. Labor was also becoming aware of its growing political power through united action. "Let us unite at the polls and give our vote to no candidate," declared the constitution of the Association of Working Men of New Castle, Delaware, in 1830, "who is not pledged to support a national system of education to be paid for out of public funds." And as early as 1820, the workingmen of Philadelphia requested of each candidate for the state legislature that he state his attitude toward an equal and general system of education for the state.[8]

8. William E. Drake, *The American School in Transition* (Englewood Cliffs, N.J.: Prentice-Hall, Inc., 1955), pp. 205–18, gives an excellent summary of these developments.

The early effects of industrialization and urbanization upon children as well as adults were not altogether friendly to the American ideal of an open road to opportunity. One authority states that two fifths of all laborers in factories in 1832 were children, few of whom had an opportunity to learn to read and to write.[9] The historian Carl Russell Fish informs us that "As late as 1840 only one-half of the children of New England were given a free education, one-seventh of those of the Middle States, and one-sixth of the West." [10] As Edwards and Richey point out, the mills and factories were attracting children as well as adults from the farm. These factories and the cities which grew up about them were increasing more rapidly than the social insight required to solve the problems generated by their development. "Illiterate and unruly children roamed the city streets uncared for and considered only as potential workers in factories which took them at a tender age." The mother as well as the father of the family was employed, but the wages of the entire family provided only a bare subsistence.[11]

Fortunately, to many Americans these conditions came as a shock. Nor was the emerging "common man" disposed to accept them as necessary and inevitable. Labor, as we have said, proceeded to organize in order to better its condition and to demand schools free from the taint of charity or dependence upon philanthropy. Individuals from all classes (members of the rapidly increasing middle class, who saw in education an indispensable means for the advancement of their children, humanitarians, political leaders, educators in all sections of the country, and forward-looking businessmen, from whose resources the increased revenues for public education would have to be drawn) united with labor in demanding the establishment of a tax-supported public school system.

As we have also seen in Chapter 1, Horace Mann and others sought to convince the business community of the market value of education. Merle Curti has shown that motives of fear as well prompted many to support a broadening of the base of education. "Anxious to wring support for public schools from propertied interests, then opposed to taxation for such a purpose," writes Curti, "educational spokesmen warned

9. *Ibid.,* p. 209.
10. Quoted in Charles and Mary Beard, *The American Spirit* (New York: The Macmillan Co., 1942), pp. 251–52.
11. Edwards and Richey, *op. cit.,* p. 296.

them of the dangers to property rights from universal suffrage, Jacksonian democracy, and even, possibly, revolution—any of which might result if the masses were left undisciplined by education." [12]

Equally urgent words of warning and admonition came from intellectuals and statesmen of the caliber of Edward Everett, who saw dangers to the status quo from the use of the ballot by frontier folk as well as by labor. Thus, in addressing a group of Boston capitalists in 1833, Everett used the following argument in support of contributions to education in the far-off state of Ohio: "We can, from our surplus, contribute toward the establishment and endowment of the seminaries where the mind of the West shall be trained and enlightened," . . . in order "to give security to our property, by diffusing the means of light and truth throughout the region where so much of the power to preserve or to shake it resides." [13]

Eventually, united effort brought about the establishment of free schools in a manner characteristically American, that is, by means of state authorization for individual communities to levy taxes upon the local population in support of public schools. Typical of these acts was the passage of a law in Missouri in 1824 which permitted school districts to levy taxes in support of schools, provided two thirds of the voters approved so doing. Only after experimentation with local autonomy in taxation did it become common practice for the states to enact laws which made it mandatory for communities to levy taxes on behalf of their schools. So acceptable, however, had the principle become by the third quarter of the nineteenth century that every state admitted to the Union since 1876 has been required by Congressional resolution to provide in its constitution "for the establishment and maintenance of a system of public schools which shall be open to all children of the State and free from sectarian control. . . ." [14]

The final step in the assumption of state responsibility for the education of all children came with the passage of compulsory school attendance laws. In this, as in earlier developments in education, Massachusetts led the way in 1852. New York followed in 1853. By 1895,

12. Merle Curti, *The Social Ideas of American Educators* (New York: Charles Scribner's Sons, 1935), p. 81.

13. Edward Everett, *Importance of Practical Education and Useful Knowledge* (New York: Harper & Brothers, 1856), pp. 169–70.

14. See in this connection, footnote 9 in Justice Frankfurter's concurring opinion in *McCollum* v. *Board of Education*, 333 U.S. 203 (1948).

according to the report of the United States Commissioner of Education, W. T. Harris, 28 states and the District of Columbia had passed compulsory school attendance laws.[15] Not until 1918, however, had all the states fallen into line.

Provision for free and universal education within a state requires more in the way of financial assistance than irregular appropriations from school funds derived from miscellaneous sources. It requires legislation designed to yield revenues upon which local school boards can depend both in the process of constructing their annual budgets and in laying plans for the future. It also requires, as we have seen, the creation of boards of control to insure the proper distribution and use of these funds. It was not long, however, before even this setup proved insufficient. As school attendance grew in volume and, eventually, became mandatory for all children within a given age bracket, leadership and encouragement on the part of the state became ever more imperative. It is not surprising, therefore, to find each of the states eventually rounding out its provision for education by the establishment of some form of supervision and control over the operations of educational programs within the various school communities of the state.

Local Autonomy with the Consent of the State

From this brief survey of the evolution of public education in the United States it should be clear that a unique relationship between locality and state has existed from the beginning. Generally speaking, one or more localities have pioneered in meeting the needs of the community—needs, however, in no way peculiar to one place or to one people. These efforts have stimulated other communities to follow the example of the pioneers, and, eventually, the state has entered the picture to render general or binding upon all what were for a time the innovations of the few.

Observe, however, that ultimate authority to stimulate or to retard experimentation resides in the state, and in the exercise of their educational functions local school officials act as agents of the state. Although

15. See J. L. Blair Buck, *The Development of Public Schools in Virginia* (Richmond: State Board of Virginia, 1952), p. 117. It is well to bear in mind, however, that for a time, in a number of states, no machinery was provided for the enforcement of compulsory school attendance laws. Even today enforcement is far from uniform.

significant variations exist among the states with respect to the structural or organizational pattern of education, the general outlines are strikingly similar. In each instance, the constitution, as an expression of the will of the people, instructs the legislature to provide for the establishment of free schools. In most states, the legislatures have set up state boards of education, charged with specific functions, and, at the same time, have assigned other functions to local boards (city, county, town, or district, as the case may be). Within these respective areas, each acts as a direct representative of the state. As Mort and Ross emphasize in their *Principles of School Administration,* the state legislature may be viewed as a state board of education and the state department of education as its executive agent, with power to act in strictly defined areas. In other areas, local districts are authorized to act. "Neither is justified under this theory in encroaching upon the powers of the other. Both are state agents. With respect to these powers they are coordinate." [16]

Considerable variation exists within the states with respect both to the powers and responsibilities of state boards and to the relations of local communities to the state. These range from extreme home rule, as in New Jersey and Rhode Island, to a high degree of centrally controlled education in others.

The degree of responsibility lodged in state boards of education also varies from state to state. In a majority of states, state boards exercise considerable control over elementary and secondary education, whereas in others this authority is more restricted. [17] Methods for the selection of state boards and their officers also vary. For example, in a few states the members of state boards are elected directly by the people. In others they are appointed by the governor or the legislature. Likewise with the chief executive officer of the state board (commonly called the commissioner or superintendent of public instruction). In some states this officer is elected directly by the people. A second method is appointment by the governor; a third method, which is considered preferable, is appointment by the state board of education.

But to return to the major theme of this chapter, however varied may be the structural and organizational pattern among the states or

16. New York: McGraw-Hill Book Co., 1957, p. 269.
17. See Arthur W. Foshay, ed., *The Rand McNally Handbook of Education* (Chicago: Rand McNally and Co., 1963), chap. 2, for a summary of state school systems.

the assignment of powers and responsibilities to local school authorities, on the one hand, and to state officers, on the other, education in each instance is a state function and is thus subject to the control and direction of the state, as expressed through the legislature.[18] For example, it is the legislature which decides whether or not school boards are to be elected or appointed or whether the locality may decide this question by referendum. Unless there are other provisions in the constitution, the legislature also determines the functions which the state board of education and local school boards, respectively, shall exercise with respect to items such as the selection and retention of teachers, salary schedules, content of the curriculum, choice of textbooks, construction of buildings, and the like.

Interesting confirmation of the potential domination of the state over the locality in educational matters has been afforded recently by the attempts of southern states to resist the decisions of the United States Supreme Court on segregation in education. Many of these attempts remove virtually all authority from local school boards to determine policies for the admission of pupils. When Arlington County, Virginia, for example, announced its plans for complying with the decision of the United States Supreme Court, an indignant state legislature deprived it of the privilege of electing its school board and lodged this authority in the county board. Moreover, to discourage any school system in the state from admitting a Negro student into a white school, the legislature adopted an act which transferred final authority for the placement of pupils from the locality to a state commission. A Virginia act provided further that any public school in the state which "mixed the races," even on court decree, should be deprived of its share of state funds. Acts of similar intent have been passed by other southern states. On the other hand, in the North, acts of quite a different character have found their way into the statute books. Illinois, for example, prohibits the distribution of state funds to any school district which maintains segregated schools and requires school officials to certify that their schools are nonsegregated as a condition for receiving their share of state appropriations.

Fear of "subversion" in education has also induced state legislatures in recent years to intervene directly in the educational concerns of local communities through the enactment of laws respecting the selection of

18. In some instances state constitutions place limitations upon the powers of the legislature in certain areas.

textbooks and library materials, the imposition of loyalty oaths for teachers as a condition of employment, and the creation of investigating committees charged with the responsibility of identifying un-American activities on the part of teachers and un-American ideas in textbooks and other instructional materials. Mandatory legislation with reference to what schools should or should not teach in the way of specific ideas—ranging from the effects of alcohol and tobacco upon the human system to concepts such as the validity or lack of validity of the concept of evolution—are familiar illustrations, not only of the authority which resides in state legislatures but of a willingness to exercise that authority. Apparently, the only limits upon actions of this character are those imposed by constitutions, state or federal, as determined by the courts.

To those who prize local initiative in education, the increasing cost of education and the apparent inability of local school units to bear the full cost of conducting their schools constitute a threat to local autonomy. The proportion of the cost of education borne by local school systems, in comparison with that assumed by the state, varies widely, both within a state and among the states. For a number of decades, however, funds from local taxation have constituted a shrinking proportion of total school revenue. In 1930, local funds provided about 82 per cent and state funds provided about 17 per cent of total public school revenue. By 1960, the respective figures were 56 per cent and 40 per cent.[19]

Of course, these over-all figures do not disclose the great variations within and among states. For example, in the school year 1963–64, local funds provided about 89 per cent of the school revenue in Nebraska but only about 11 per cent in New Mexico.[20] Often these discrepancies testify to paralysis of will or an unfortunate disposition on the part of local school districts to draw upon the funds available from the state rather than to impose local taxes. In many instances, however, they testify to the differences between a wealthy area and a poor one and to the existence of obsolescent methods of financing education in a period of sharply rising demands for and costs of education. In any case, the trend toward increased financial support of the schools by the state can have serious effects upon local initiative.

19. U.S. Office of Education, *Trends in Financing Public Education: 1929–30 to 1959–60* (Washington, D.C.: U.S. Government Printing Office, 1961), p. 39.
20. U.S. Office of Education, *Digest of Educational Statistics* (Washington, D.C.: U.S. Government Printing Office, 1964), p. 57.

The common assumption that he who pays the piper will eventually call the tune also explains the opposition of many to the extension of federal aid to education.

As we have seen, the federal Constitution contains no specific provision for the support of education. Under the Tenth Amendment this remains one of the powers reserved to the states. However, various clauses of the Constitution have been interpreted as clearly conferring implied powers over education to the federal government.[21] These constitutional provisions include several guarantees of civil rights and they include the "general welfare" clause, which confers on Congress the power to provide for the common defense and general welfare of the United States. Since 1936 the Supreme Court has held to the so-called broad interpretation of the general-welfare clause: the implication is that the federal government may support "any" activity that promotes the general welfare. Moreover, since such terms as "liberty" and "general welfare" are extremely broad or vague, the limits of federal power in education have not been defined.[22]

Still, with the exception of educational activities which clearly serve the national interest (such as military training and a generous list of activities subsumed under the title "emergency training," together with a wide variety of departmental programs of education, all financed and administered directly by the federal government), the national government has been content to assist education in the states rather than to give body to the dream of Benjamin Rush of a national system of education. This assistance has been both substantial and varied in character, as, for example, grants of public lands to the states upon their admission to the Union, outright appropriations in support of general education, the distribution of surplus revenue, grants-in-aid to special types of education, and so on.[23]

---

21. Charles A. Quattlebaum states that a total of fourteen constitutional warrants for federal activities in education have been found or used. See "Federal Policies and Practices in Higher Education," *The Federal Government and Higher Education*, Douglas M. Knight, ed. (Englewood Cliffs, N.J.: Prentice-Hall, Inc., 1960), p. 36.

22. Lee O. Gerber and Newton Edwards, *The Public School in Our Governmental Structure* (Danville, Ill.: Interstate Printers and Publishers, 1962), pp. 3–7.

23. For a comprehensive survey of federal assistance to education, as well as educational programs conducted by the federal government, see Committee on Education and Labor, House of Representatives (Eighty-Eighth Congress, First Session), *The Federal Government and Education* (Washington, D.C.: U.S. Government Printing Office, 1963).

With the exception of certain grants for special educational purposes, the federal government has refrained to a remarkable degree from exercising control over the educational activities it has fostered and assisted. Many educators would agree with the following statement recently issued in the name of the National Education Association:

> Federal participation in the financial support of education has strengthened and will strengthen the public schools enormously, providing that it follows appropriate principles. Federal financial support for the schools should take the form of general funds allocated to and administered by the states rather than special aid measures. The latter are likely to result in unbalanced, even haphazard, instructional programs. Determination of what to teach and when to teach it according to federal appropriation of money is neither a rational nor a desirable method of procedure.[24]

Federal leadership and financial aid, but *without control,* express the prevailing judgment of educators and legislators today as to the desirable relation of the federal government to public education. It is this policy, for example, which has defined the activities of the United States Office of Education within the Department of Health, Education, and Welfare.

Nevertheless, the development of a technologically based national community within a precarious international situation seemingly dictates more direct and extensive forms of federal intervention in education within the states. For instance, so important is education today in providing adequate personnel for economic and military affairs that the national government cannot afford to remain indifferent to the nature of the education provided at all levels within the state. Recognition of this intimate relationship between education and the welfare of the nation prompted the national government in the 1930s to assist education directly through such instruments as the National Youth Administration, and more recently to provide scholarships for individuals within the fields of science, mathematics, and language and grants to

24. Project on the Instructional Program of the Public School, *Deciding What to Teach* (Washington, D.C.: National Education Association, 1963), p. 212.

institutions within the states for purposes of guidance, instruction, and research.

Decisions of the United States Supreme Court in recent years have also drawn attention to a number of areas in which national principles take precedence over both state and local self-determination in education. These principles have to do with civil rights, as defined in the Constitution of the United States. For example, the First Amendment to the Constitution, as interpreted by the Supreme Court, prohibits public schools from engaging in religious instruction of a sectarian character. Similarly, according to the decisions of the Supreme Court in May 1954 and May 1955 on segregation in education, no school can lawfully exclude a child from attendance in that school on grounds of race. Moreover, to enforce this decree, the lower courts are specifically instructed, when cases of violation are brought to their attention, "to take such proceedings and enter such orders and decrees consistent with this opinion as are necessary and proper to admit to public schools on a racially non-discriminatory basis with all deliberate speed the parties to these cases."

Neither as a matter of practice nor as a matter of law can education in the United States be described in terms of local autonomy. We can say, however, that both in practice and law, school communities in the United States are encouraged to exercise a high degree of local self-determination and, in large measure, to adapt their educational programs to the needs of their own communities. In at least 85 per cent of our school districts, the people elect the members of their boards of education by direct vote.[25] Although these boards are commonly required to meet standards set by state authorities, such as minimum qualifications of teachers, minimum salaries, and the teaching of specific subjects, they are, nevertheless, permitted and usually encouraged to better the minimum requirements. As a result, the quality and character of education provided by the wisest or wealthiest communities continue to serve as beacons for others. Moreover, state departments of education generally have exercised their powers of supervision and direction with an eye to stimulating self-direction rather than passive compliance by localities. As we have indicated, this self-direction does permit many localities to perpetuate intellectual and material poverty.

25. U.S. Office of Education, *Local School Boards: Organization and Practices* (Washington, D.C.: U.S. Government Printing Office, 1962), pp. 1, 8–12.

On the other hand, no community is condemned, as a result of control by a central bureaucracy, to mediocrity or conformity.[26]

The dynamics of an expert and corporate society draw large-scale units into increasingly influential roles in the control of education. Not only the state and national governments, but also professional, philanthropic, industrial, and other organizations have a growing influence on the direction of education. In this situation, the problem of finding a vital and viable role for the local community becomes complex. Merely clinging to traditional sentiments and arrangements is probably no more promising than turning the direction of education over to the federal government or to professional educational organizations.

We will return to this problem in several of the following chapters, particularly in the final chapter.

Suggested Reading

Chandler, B. J., Lindley J. Stiles, and John I. Kitsuse, eds., *Education in Urban Society* (New York: Dodd, Mead & Co., 1962), pp. 107–16.

Cramer, John F., and George S. Browne, *Contemporary Education: A Comparative Study of National Systems*, 2d ed. (New York: Harcourt, Brace and World, Inc., 1965), chaps. 2–6.

Edwards, Newton, and Herman G. Richey, *The School in the American Social Order*, 2d ed. (Boston: Houghton Mifflin Co., 1963), chap. 9.

Gerber, Lee O., and Newton Edwards, *The Public School in Our Governmental Structure* (Danville, Ill.: Interstate Printers and Publishers, 1962).

Knezevich, Stephen J., *Administration of Public Education* (New York: Harper & Row, 1962), chaps. 4–6.

Lieberman, Myron, *The Future of Public Education* (Chicago: The University of Chicago Press, 1960), chaps. 3–4, 9.

U.S. Office of Education, *Ministries of Education: Their Functions and Organization* (Washington, D.C.: U.S. Government Printing Office, 1962), chaps. 3–5.

26. For a different and pessimistic view of the values of a high degree of local autonomy in education, see Myron Lieberman, *The Future of Public Education* (Chicago: The University of Chicago Press, 1960), chap. 3.

Chapter 5

Equality of Educational Opportunity

The Concept of Equality

Perhaps the most familiar affirmation of the ideal of equality for Americans occurs in the Declaration of Independence: "We hold these truths to be self-evident: that all men are created equal; that they are endowed by their Creator with certain inalienable rights; that among these, are life, liberty, and the pursuit of happiness; that to secure these rights governments are instituted among men, deriving their just powers from the governed. . . ."

Two basic assumptions have been associated with this statement: (1) the psychological assumption that all men are born essentially equal in their potentialities and (2) the political assumption that a primary function of government is to insure to individuals an opportunity to realize the rights of life, liberty, and the pursuit of happiness with which they are endowed.

The psychological principle derives in large measure from the philosophy of John Locke, an intellectual godfather of the leaders of the American revolution. According to Locke, men bring little into this world by way of inheritance. Contrary to the assumptions of the rationalists and hereditarians of his time, he denied the existence of innate ideas (a native tendency to accept and apply specific logical and moral principles). Rather, according to Locke, men are born with minds analogous to a sheet of paper upon which experience writes all of the originals of knowledge. Thus, what an individual is at a given moment represents the outcome of the experiences he has had and the use he has made of them.

"As it is in the body," writes Locke in *The Conduct of the Understanding*, "so it is in the mind: practice makes it what it is; and most even of those excellencies which are looked on as natural endowments, will be found, when examined into more narrowly, to be the product of exercise and to be raised to that pitch only by repeated action." [1]

Locke did not deny altogether that natural disposition may "give the first rise" to rare ability, but he insisted "that [it] never carries a man far without use and exercise, and it is practice alone that brings the powers of the mind, as well as those of the body, to perfection."

As so frequently happens, the disciples of the master very shortly outdid Locke in their assertions of innate equality. In France, for example, Helvetius in the eighteenth century expounded the doctrine that all intellects in their original state are equal and the differences which do in fact distinguish men result from their education.

Moreover, many educated men in the eighteenth century saw an intimate connection between this psychological principle and some political principles. For example, if inequalities among men are due to differences in opportunities and experiences, then, by properly organizing social and educational conditions, government can be a key factor in the perfection of man and the creation of social equality. It is not surprising that the eighteenth century was characterized by optimism with respect to the future and that throughout our history reformers have appealed to government to provide the conditions that make for equality.

In America, the concept of innate equality fell upon fertile soil and soon brought forth revolutionary fruits. The constantly expanding frontier seemed to confirm the principle that men are to be judged by what they demonstrate themselves to be, rather than by accidents of birth and inheritance. As Oscar Handlin remarks:

> Man was not a creature endowed at birth with all his attributes and located by Providence in a situation in which he would remain fixed and helpless in the face of forces he could not control.

1. See Bohn's Standard Library, *The Philosophical Works of John Locke* (London: George Bell and Sons, 1902), vol. I, sec. 14, p. 35.

Certainly that had not been his fate in America. Man at birth was all potentials, his mind a clean slate; he acquired habits, skills and ideas by training and by contact with the environment.[2]

Plural Sources of the Doctrine of Equality

It would be a mistake, however, to assume that the principle of equality, as Americans have conceived and applied it, is grounded exclusively in John Locke's theory of the mind as analogous at birth to a sheet of paper upon which experience is to write. Precisely the opposite assumption, namely, that men are originally endowed by their Creator with an infinite worthiness, has been equally potent. Emerson gives expression to this view in his well-known definition of reform in his essay on *Man the Reformer*. "The power, which is at once spring and regulator in all efforts at reform," he writes, "is the conviction that there is an infinite worthiness in man which will appear at the call of worth, and that all particular reforms are the removing of some impediment." [3]

But how should we conceive of this infinite worthiness? As essentially alike in all to be developed through essentially similar means or as a uniqueness or distinctiveness calling for infinitely varied instrumentalities of development?

The answer Emerson gave was clear. "To thyself be true"; and being true meant having the courage to develop one's individuality and to follow one's own reason, regardless of whether or not the world was in agreement. Freedom, he wrote in his journal in 1834, is rooted in the sacred truth that "every man hath in him the divine reason," and, although few have lived according to its dictates, all "are created capable of so doing. That is the equality and the only equality of all men." With respect to the state, its only interest "is persons; . . . the highest end of government is the culture of men." [4]

What this might imply in the way of the education of a young person is suggested in Emerson's poem, *Culture*.

2. *The Americans* (Boston: Little, Brown and Co., 1963), p. 118.
3. *The Prose Works of Ralph Waldo Emerson* (Boston: Fields, Osgood and Company, 1870), vol. I, p. 135.
4. Irwin Edman, *Fountainheads of Freedom* (New York: Reynal and Hitchcock, 1941), p. 147. Now published by Harcourt, Brace and World, Inc.

Can rulers or tutors educate
The semigod whom we await?
He must be musical,
Tremulous, impressional
Alive to gentle influence
Of landscape and of sky,
And tender to the spirit-touch
Of man's or maiden's eye:
But, to his native centre fast,
Shall into Future fuse the Past,
And the world's flowing fates in his own mould recast.[5]

This, however, was too strong a medicine for the educators of the period, even for those who, in their own minds, were dedicated to the task of eliciting the worth they posited within the soul of each child.

For example, Froebel, the founder of the kindergarten, and his American followers likewise saw in each child a replica of the Infinite Spirit, a divine spark which defined his original nature. This elicited their reverence and respect and dictated to them the methods they should employ in order to transform the spark into a steady flame. Or, to change the analogy, just as the successful gardener adapts soil and moisture and light to the nature of the plant, so the educator and the parent were to take as their cue the nature of the child and the laws of his development. Materials and methods thus became instrumental to the major purposes of education, the spiritual growth of the child.

Following the lead of the child, however, was in no way identical with a hands-off policy. On the contrary, it imposed a heavy obligation upon child and adult alike, since both were required to regulate their activities so as to bring to fruition the full promise of child nature. Discipline, materials of instruction, methods of teaching, all the instrumentalities of education, were thus subordinated to the supreme end of education, the spiritual development of the individual.

Inspiring as this program was in its beginnings, it suffered eventually from its assumption that the spiritual potentialities within the child are reflections of a spiritual unity. The curriculum it developed soon became rigid and formal, leaving little room for individual differences.

5. *The Complete Poetical Works of Ralph Waldo Emerson* (Boston: Houghton Mifflin Co., 1910), p. 273.

Thus, although the movement drew attention to childhood as a distinctive stage of development with its own criteria for education, in contrast to the earlier tendency to consider children merely as adults in miniature, it did little to transform the conventional notion that schooling should be identical for all.

Not until the end of the nineteenth century did educators give serious consideration to the significance of uniqueness of personality, or, to use the jargon of the educator, individual differences. One of the first of these was Felix Adler, a pioneer in the establishment of the kindergarten in the United States and the founder of a school in New York, in 1878, dedicated to what he termed the "creative principle" in education.

Adler, too, grounded his educational philosophy in the metaphysical assumption of an original uniqueness in people. Just as in the empirical world each individual is demonstrably different in essential respects from his fellows, so he is also unique as a member of a spiritual universe, of which the empirical is merely a reflection. Moreover, to Adler, healthy development, individual and social, consists in each person's fostering this uniqueness through mutually stimulating and creative relations with others. He enjoined his fellows to act in such a manner as to further the distinctive expression of others and thereby further their own distinctive expression.

This conception obligates the educator to search for the unique potentiality within each individual, to observe the inner life of the child as well as his outer behavior. Moreover, all acts of discipline and all educational materials and methods are evaluated in terms of their effects upon personality. This conception dictates a subordination of the professional activity of the teacher and the functions of parenthood to an overarching ideal at once individual and social, an ideal of equality predicated upon widening opportunities for the expression and development of differences as well as similarities.

Needless to say, this conception of equality, which is grounded in an assumption of primary differences among people, is fraught with significance in a society that is essentially characterized by heterogeneity rather than homogeneity.

It appears that the principle of equality in education, as in other relationships of life, has served as a guiding light for reformers who have nevertheless grounded their convictions in quite different metaphysical, even theological, premises. Nor would our description be complete without calling attention to the fact that still others, who accept and live by the principle of equality, see no impelling reason for grounding it in either philosophy or religion. For example, Sidney Hook, writing as a pragmatist, contends that democracy, together with its concept of equality, can be demonstrated as superior to other forms of government by pointing to its results, to the qualities of relationships it yields in contrast to the qualities fostered by a nondemocratic society. In the long run, Hook would hold, there is no more convincing criterion than, "By their fruits ye shall know them."

Hook is not concerned with establishing that all men are at birth equal in their potentialities. He is quite willing to accept the idea that there are individual differences. But he is vitally concerned with grounding the principle of equal opportunity in terms of its "consequences for weal and woe." What are these consequences? Of them, and of the justification for turning to them, Hook writes:

> If we ask, then, why we should treat individuals of unequal talents and endowments as persons who are equally entitled to relevant consideration and care—the central idea underlying democratic institutions—we can point to consequences of the following type: it makes for greater tranquillity, justice, freedom, security, creative diversity, reasonableness, and less cruelty, insensitiveness, and intellectual intolerance than any other social system that has so far been devised or proposed. There are more widespread commitments among men to these values, and a greater agreement on the methods by which evidence is reached concerning whether or not they are present in any situation, than to any metaphysical or theological system which allegedly underlies them. Any one of these values has been or can be challenged in the course of experience. Its rejection or vindication depends on whether or not it furthers other values. There is no last resting point, nor is there a circle. We rest at each problem, until a new one arises.[6]

Without attempting to mediate among these different methods of justifying the principle of equality (whether in terms of the conse-

6. Sidney Hook, *Education for Modern Man* (New York: Alfred A. Knopf, 1963), p. 63.

quences of its application in a democratic society or of metaphysical and theological presuppositions respecting the original nature of man), it is evident that the concept of equality is both flexible and plural in its applications. In one set of circumstances, it implies identical treatment for all. In another, it implies not only the right to be different, but conscious provision for the exercise of this right so long as it does not interfere with the development of other free personalities. Hook, for example, believes that "equality of concern is not the same thing as equal treatment. It is compatible with unequal [that is, dissimilar] treatment, provided this treatment is required by the necessities of intellectual and emotional growth in each case." [7] Hook goes on to add that "mediocrity is the consequence of imposing one uniform pattern on individual differences, of the attempt to make everyone talk and sing and think alike about the same things at the same time." [8] Clearly, this is a description not only of mediocrity but also of conformity.

So much for the assumption that "all men are created equal" as applied to education. What this has led to in actual practice, we shall observe in a moment. But first, let us recall the second basic affirmation in the Declaration of Independence: the assertion that "governments are instituted among men" to insure the realization of rights which derive from equality.

Since conceptions of these rights, of the purposes for which the rights are to be exercised, and of the means by which the rights are to be realized have varied greatly, this statement has meant different things to different people. Some, especially those who possess property, have claimed that the proper sphere of government is limited largely to protecting the right of property and freedom in the use of property. Generally, economic individualism has been the shibboleth of such men. Others, even when speaking of economic rights, have emphasized that equality of opportunity is not adequately assured merely by having the same laws apply to all men. As Morris R. Cohen has stated, "the legal freedom to earn a million dollars is not worth a cent to one who has no real opprtunity." [9]

More broadly, greater emphasis has gradually been given to the belief that in the absence of the essential social and educational means, a

7. *Ibid.*, p. 37.
8. *Ibid.*, p. 38.
9. *Reason and Law* (New York: Collier Books, 1961), p. 102.

guarantee of political and social rights is often a hollow mockery. In the words of Alan Gewirth, "the political rights whose equal distribution constitute justice include considerations which are closely related to, if they are not identical with, welfare or beneficence." [10]

The slow drift in thinking about equality has been away from a stress on original and fixed rights or potentialities toward a stress on powers that emerge from social and educational experience. Many social and intellectual developments have supported this trend. Logically, one of the strongest forces has been a growing awareness that almost any of the many "original" human distinctions—of sex, color of skin, wealth, place of birth, number of fingers or toes, and so on—have been used as sanctions for traditional inequalities of status and opportunity in different cultures.[11] To many people this particular kind of appeal to tradition seems to be highly irrational.

Especially in a changing society, the assumption that government should take an active role in promoting conditions favorable to the growth of personal integrity and to the realization of the rights that derive from equality, seems to assign to government a never-ending task. From a review of American education, we may conclude that there has been fairly steady progress in the direction of equalizing the opportunities of education, although much remains to be done.

The Road to Equality Has No Ending

Efforts at equalizing educational opportunity have consistently encountered prior assumptions of inequality as natural and normal, assumptions that time and circumstance have firmly established in the warp and woof of daily practice. Distinctions of class, for example, received conspicuous attention in our early schools, from infant school through college. Thus, when John Adams was a student at Harvard, classes were graded according to the social standing of the student's family rather than according to academic ability. Consequently, if one were the son of a governor or a judge or a prominent minister, he was ranked first and assigned the best room in the hall, the upper seat at the table, the first place in academic processions, and the privilege of

10. "Political Justice," in *Social Justice*, Richard B. Brandt, ed. (Englewood Cliffs, N.J.: Prentice-Hall, Inc., 1962), p. 154.
11. See Melvin Tumin, "On Inequality," *American Sociological Review*, February 1963, pp. 19–26.

helping himself first at the commons.[12] Need we add, as well, that he stood first in amount of attention he received from the professor?

Tuition charges for education necessarily constituted a barrier which children of the poor could not surmount. With the institution of scholarship grants and the establishment of charity schools for young people willing to be labeled objects of charity, the doors of opportunity were opened slightly. Not until the advent of free schools, which all might attend as a matter of right, did the principle of equality bring about significant change. Nor was it a matter of accident that the movement on behalf of free schools gained little momentum until the period of Jacksonian democracy with its "leveling tendencies." Finally, with the passage of compulsory school attendance laws, the benefits of an education were extended to all children—even in opposition, if necessary, to parental will.

Outside the South, the principle and, in general, the fact of public support for the elementary school were established by the time of the Civil War. During and after the 1820s high schools began to appear on the American scene. In the 1870s, a series of court decisions (the most famous was the Kalamazoo decision of the Michigan Supreme Court in 1874) upheld the right of communities to tax themselves for the support of public high schools. Shortly after the Civil War the high school replaced the more or less privately controlled and supported academy as the dominant secondary school. Moreover, by 1860 twenty states had free (or relatively free) public universities. Thus, the high school, serving both terminal and college-preparatory students, became the central rung in a common-school ladder system of education, a system which reflected a less rigidly stratified society than the traditional dual, or two-track, system of education in Europe.

The adoption of each measure designed to enlarge educational opportunity has revealed the necessity of still further change in order to insure its fuller realization. Thus to free instructions we find added, in the course of time, free textbooks, free materials of instruction, free lunches, free transportation, and so on, all designed to offset limitations beyond the control of the recipient. Similarly, as we move up the educational ladder into college and graduate school, we encounter plans and programs designed to keep open the road to advancement for all

12. Catherine Drinker Bowen, *John Adams and the American Revolution* (Boston: Little, Brown & Co., 1950), p. 78.

who demonstrate not only the ability and willingness to progress, but for all those whose talents are recognized as potential contributions to society. Indeed, growing recognition today of a shortage of personnel and an increasing inability to man the strategic positions in our society —the classrooms of our schools, our scientific research laboratories, positions in business and the professions which call for a high degree of technical proficiency—have introduced a note of urgency in plans for widening opportunities in education still further.

These steps, however, may be classified as primarily administrative in character. The gradual enrichment and diversification of the curriculum in school and college with an eye to serving a student body ever more diversified in composition are, of course, efforts in the same direction. Until recent years, major emphasis in curriculum development, as in other provisions for differences in ability and interest, has been largely that of ministering to the underprivileged—the underprivileged economically and the underprivileged in terms of academic neglect. This has been true to such an extent that critics of American education often charge that our schools have become keyed to the mediocre and thus deny to the able their educational birthright.

The Call for Excellence in Education

Much of the concern about bettering the quality of American education is rooted in our high level of technology and the complexity of our social organization. Our society has an enormous appetite for experts in almost all areas of daily life and work. The need is not for people who are barely literate but for citizens and workers who can make fairly complex judgments in the light of extensive information, broad sensitivities, and a discriminating intelligence. Consideration of a local problem of taxation, for example, may lead into broad questions of social policy, questions which involve complicated political, economic, ethical, and other concerns.

The implications of this general situation for education are clear. Both the average educational level and the typical occupational skills of young adults are now rising from secondary to college levels. Within twenty-five years, by the early 1960s, the average educational level of the adult population as a whole had risen from the completion of elementary school toward the completion of high school—and the end is not in sight.[13]

Documentation of the demands of an expert society emphasizes the need for trained manpower in the national economy. In 1910, for example, unskilled workers comprised well over one third of the total labor force; by the early 1960s, this proportion had dropped to just over one fifth.[14] The United States Department of Labor has estimated that during the 1960s the number of people employed in professional and technical occupations will increase by 44 per cent, the number of semiskilled workers will increase by 13 per cent, and there will be no increase in the number of unskilled workers.[15] In recent years, much of the concern about the high school dropout reflects the need for trained personnel. Judging from the intensity and frequency of the expressed concerns, one would hardly guess that in recent decades there has been an increase in both the number and the proportion of those who complete twelve years of schooling.[16] According to Paul Woodring, the percentage of the age group that graduated from high school was 16.8 in 1920, 50.8 in 1940, and 65 in 1962.[17]

The shortage of trained personnel is felt to be particularly grave at the higher levels of skill, especially in mathematics and many fields of science.[18] Competition with Russia, for example, is becoming ever more keen in spheres of activity where scientific training is one of the crucial factors determining success or failure. Yet, although such subjects as physics, chemistry, and geometry are taught to all Soviet children, many American children receive no instruction in these subjects.[19] Again, although the categories, numbers, and needs are not strictly comparable, the Soviet stock of professionals in engineering is

13. "51 Million and More," *School Life*, October 1963, p. 17.

14. U.S. Department of Labor, *Labor in America: 1913–1963* (Washington, D.C.: U.S. Government Printing Office, 1963). The pages of this pamphlet are not numbered.

15. *Mobility and Worker Adaptation to Economic Change in the United States* (Washington, D.C.: U.S. Government Printing Office, 1963), p. 34.

16. Leonard M. Miller, "The Dropout: Schools Search for Clues to His Problem," *School Life*, May 1963, pp. 31–33.

17. "Dropouts," *Saturday Review*, February 16, 1963, p. 59.

18. See, for example, Committee on Education and Labor, House of Representatives (Eighty-Eighth Congress, First Session), *The Federal Government and Education* (Washington, D.C.: U.S. Government Printing Office, 1963), pp. 134, 137.

19. Edmund J. King, *Other Schools and Ours*, rev. ed. (New York: Holt, Rinehart and Winston, Inc., 1963), p. 177.

larger than that of the United States, and the planned (and probable) annual additions are about three times greater.[20]

Then, too, the rapid growth of knowledge in many disciplines has stimulated the development of many projects which aim at reforming the curriculum. Often these plans bring new and rather abstract concepts into education. At the same time, subjects or concepts once studied at higher levels of education have been pushed down into the elementary school.[21] These developments have strengthened the traditional concern for the "disciplines" as the focus of educational attention.

Of course, this concern has been strengthened also by the increasing number of high school graduates who go on to college. In 1930, 1.1 million youth, 12.4 per cent of the college-age group, were enrolled in college; in 1961, 3.8 million, 37.7 per cent, were enrolled.[22] In 1900, only 6.4 per cent of the seventeen-year-old age group graduated from high school; in 1963, 65 per cent of that age group graduated from high school and 58 per cent of these graduates entered college.[23] Moreover, "the generally accepted assumption that college enrollments will double in the 1960s includes an expectation that the percentage of the age group entering college must continue to increase." [24]

However, the appetite for talent remains unsatisfied, and a number of "talent hunts" are being conducted in an effort to ascertain the extent and causes of the "waste of talent." Indicative of the nature of this concern and of the way talent is usually conceived is a rather typical finding that among high school graduates in the early 1960s, 20 per cent of the top 25 per cent in "academic aptitude" did not enter college, whereas 18 per cent of the lowest 25 per cent did enter college.[25]

In light of such developments, it is not surprising that the "pursuit of excellence" has become a catchword in discussions about education.

20. See Nicholas DeWitt, "Soviet Science Education and the School Reform," *School and Society,* Summer 1960, p. 298; U.S. Office of Education, *Higher Education in the U.S.S.R.* (Washington, D.C.: U.S. Government Printing Office, 1963), pp. 105, 108.
21. Helen Heffernan and William M. Alexander, "Using Current Curriculum Developments," *Using Current Curriculum Developments* (Washington, D.C.: Association for Supervision and Curriculum Development, N.E.A., 1963), pp. 2–3.
22. *N.E.A. Research Bulletin,* February 1963, p. 7.
23. *Phi Delta Kappan,* February 1964, p. 264.
24. George H. Hanford, "1963–65: Peak Years for Admissions Offices." Reprinted from the *College Board Review,* Fall 1962.
25. John C. Flanagan, "Project Talent," *N.E.A. Journal,* January 1964, p. 10.

Excellence has many meanings, but there is a strong tendency to assume that it refers to the ability to learn organized bodies of knowledge, the basic disciplines—although learning and the basic disciplines may themselves be variously conceived. In this conception of excellence such devices and arrangements as ability grouping, teaching machines, and ungraded schools, are often regarded as providing equal opportunity for all children to advance as rapidly as their talents (for learning subject matter) permit. Moreover, it is vigorously denied that all subjects are of equal value, provided only that students like them equally well. The expert society, many people say, requires more attention to academic subjects and less attention to the narrowly practical subjects of "life adjustment" education. Consequently, there is a tendency to tone down, if not to derogate, any emphasis on developing "sociability" or other qualities of personality.

As we have indicated, the call for excellence often includes the charge that equalitarianism in education has deprived the gifted child of his right to equal concern and opportunity. Jerome S. Bruner has written that "the top quarter of public school students, from which we must draw intellectual leadership in the next generation, is perhaps the group most neglected by our schools in the recent past." [26] Like many other educators, James B. Conant, an influential critic of education, equates the gifted child with the "academically talented" child, as measured by I.Q. scores and superior achievement in subject matter.[27] At times, Conant defines academically talented children more specifically as the minority (the top 15 to 20 per cent) who are "able to study effectively and rewardingly a wide program of advanced mathematics, science, and foreign language." [28] In schools today, acceleration, enrichment, or independent study programs, advanced placement programs, honors programs, and other arrangements are increasingly used to provide opportunity for academically talented children to learn bodies of organized subject matter as rapidly as they can.

In the light of our concern in this chapter, it becomes important to inquire whether these conceptions of excellence and opportunity are

26. *The Process of Education* (Cambridge: Harvard University Press, 1960), p. 10.

27. *Slums and Suburbs* (New York: McGraw-Hill Book Co., Inc., 1961), pp. 88–91.

28. *The American High School Today* (New York: McGraw-Hill Book Co., Inc., 1959), p. 20.

adequate to the principle of equality, to other values, and to the needs of the day.

Equality, Talent, and Individual Differences

There is very little reason to think that the hierarchies of academic ability and intelligence, especially as these are now measured, are the same as the hierarchy of all human values. For example, many studies reveal that the correlations between abilities in problem solving and critical thinking, on the one hand, and knowledge of subject matter and intelligence, on the other hand, are usually low to quite moderate.[29] Other components of personality or cognitive style may contribute more than knowledge or intelligence to problem-solving and critical-thinking skills.[30]

Such evidence—and similar evidence bearing on other educational and social values could be cited—leads many educators to sense a grave danger in the tendency to identify the gifted student with one type of mind, the "academically talented" as currently defined. Even if we assume that the gifted students of today are to be the leaders in the increasingly complex society of tomorrow, it is highly important for us to recognize that leadership will demand plural abilities and that it is highly diversified, not singular or uniform in character. Consequently, it calls for an education of many types of minds in many different fields, in the humanities and social sciences as well as in the natural sciences. It should be noted that a similar argument would be relevant if we substituted the criterion of citizenship for that of leadership.

Human abilities do not develop from innate capacities that express themselves regardless of social conditions and educational opportunities. Nor do specified social and educational conditions generate only

29. Some relevant studies are summarized in William H. Burton, Roland B. Kimball, and Richard L. Wing, *Education for Effective Thinking* (New York: Appleton-Century-Crofts, Inc., 1960), pp. 241–45. See also Edward J. Furst, "Relationship Between Tests of Intelligence and Tests of Critical Thinking and of Knowledge," *Journal of Educational Research*, April 1950, pp. 614–25; E. E. Socher, "Literal and Critical Reading in Social Studies," *Journal of Experimental Education*, September 1958, pp. 49–56. Owing, perhaps, to the renewed emphasis on learning of subject matter, studies such as those mentioned above have been far less numerous in recent years.

30. Richard Christie and Florence Lindauer, "Personality Structure," *Annual Review of Psychology*, Paul R. Farnsworth, ed. (Palo Alto, Calif.: Annual Reviews, Inc., 1963), pp. 208, 223.

certain abilities regardless of differences among individuals. Human abilities are products of transactions between individuals and their environments. Thus, it is unlikely that a relatively uniform set of educational experiences will be equally beneficial for all individuals or will be equally useful in the development of all desirable abilities. If we desire to detect (much less to develop) the unrealized potentialities of individuals, we need a reasonably varied set of educational experiences.

This is not an argument for an education in trivia or in watered-down courses. It is an argument for a meaningful recognition of the amazing differences among individuals—though it is neither possible nor desirable to develop all unique characteristics. The argument does support a broader and more differentiated conception of educational aims and values than is now generally held. Society certainly should not permit any individual to become, say, a teacher or doctor regardless of the level of his relevant abilities. But, in many cases, it is wiser, more liberating and equitable, for an individual to compete with his own stimulated and growing potentialities than to run a race with other individuals. Thus, the "average" student may well be encouraged to enter college if the college helps to broaden his intellectual horizons.

This orientation is quite compatible with the belief that a certain common body of skills, knowledge, and sensitivities must be developed among all students. There are some things everyone should know, but it is a mistake in logic and an educational blunder to infer from this statement that all children must be exposed to the same courses and experiences. Just as an adequate diet may be found in a wide variety of foods, some of which are enjoyed for reasons other than health, so common abilities may be developed through a wide variety of experiences. In general, the more uniform the educational outcomes we seek, the more varied must be the procedures and materials we use. The identification of the student with the subject studied, or his lack of identification with it, for example, may be a crucial factor in determining whether or not learning takes place.

Creativity and the Problem of Equality

Some of these general ideas may be more concretely examined as they apply to recent findings concerning the development of creativity.

Creativity is now generally regarded by psychologists not as a special gift possessed only by a few individuals but as a capacity that all normal people have to some degree.[31] It is not conceived as a mystical, internal power but as a capacity that develops in and through experience and that may be expressed in any area of life—in play and in the routines of daily life, in politics and in business, in art and science.[32]

The ability to approach things in novel and constructive ways is a very complex ability, involving many cognitive operations, skills, and attitudes, and varying with many factors (such as age, sex, and kinds of problems or materials).[33] Only rarely is a person equally creative in different fields or areas of education and life. Creativity seems to involve some common traits that cut across various areas and some traits that differ greatly among different areas.[34]

A number of studies, conducted at elementary, high school, and college levels, have found that, generally, there is a low positive correlation between scores on intelligence and creativity tests. A typical finding is that if, in a school population, the highest 20 per cent on an I.Q. test are selected as the gifted students, this selection omits about 70 per cent of those who ranked in the highest 20 per cent on tests of creativity.[35] Clearly, intelligence tests do not measure some of the primary abilities of creativity.

Although some highly creative children have high I.Q.s, the cognitive styles and motivational structures of the highly creative child and the child with a high I.Q. tend to differ significantly.[36] For example, the child with a high I.Q. tends to work hard for good grades. His task, as he sees it, is to assimilate and reproduce bodies of knowledge. This preservative or conservative orientation is exhibited also in his social

31. Elliot W. Eisner, "Research in Creativity: Some Findings and Conceptions," *Childhood Education*, April 1963, p. 371.
32. Gardner Murphy, *Human Potentialities* (New York: Basic Books, Inc., 1958), pp. 143–45, 158–74.
33. See, for example, J. P. Guilford, "Factors that Aid and Hinder Creativity," *Teachers College Record*, February 1962, pp. 380–81.
34. *Ibid.*, p. 387.
35. E. Paul Torrance, *Guiding Creative Talent* (Englewood Cliffs, N.J.: Prentice-Hall, Inc., 1962), pp. 54–59.
36. Summaries of these differences can be found in Calvin W. Taylor and John L. Holland, "Development and Application of Tests of Creativity," *Review of Educational Research*, February 1962, pp. 91–103; Paul Nash, "Characteristics of the Creative Scientist," *Journal of Education*, February 1963, pp. 26–53; Jacob W. Getzels and Philip W. Jackson, *Creativity and Intelligence* (New York: John Wiley and Sons, Inc., 1962), pp. 11–14, 35–42, 65–83, 118–26.

aspirations and behavior. He is inclined to follow the accepted patterns of behavior and to strive for success as defined by relatively unquestioned adult standards. On the other hand, the highly creative child tends to have a much more questioning and exploratory attitude. He searches for new meanings, new definitions of problems, and alternative solutions to problems, often seeking to relate things that, to many people, seem to be unrelated. He has what Frank Barron has called a "moral attitude." [37] He is less inclined than is the child with a high I.Q. to sacrifice intellectual and ethical principles in the interests of personal success and acceptance.

When the scholastic achievement of highly creative children is compared with that of children with top I.Q. scores, it is usually found that these creative children do equally superior work despite sizable differences in average I.Q.s of the two groups. In one study, the difference was 23 I.Q. points; [38] in another study, the difference was 25 I.Q. points.[39] As Getzels and Jackson note, since the creative children are not at the top of their class in I.Q., their superiority in scholastic achievement places them in the somewhat pejorative category of "overachievers." On the assumption that the I.Q. is a full and true measure of intellectual capacity, "overachievement" is usually regarded as a function of emotional or motivational factors. But, if the I.Q. is the full and true measure of intellectual capacity or potential, a logical dilemma arises. How can achievement exceed capacity? How can a person do more than he is able to do? [40]

Even if it is said that achievement is due to capacity plus motivation, the dilemma remains. However, the problem is resolved if, for one thing, the intelligence test is *not* a full measure of intellectual resources; and the fact that it is not this full measure is becoming increasingly clear. Some researchers report that about fifty different factors or variables are involved in intellectual operations. Other researchers report well over 100 factors. In general, the number of reported factors is growing. It is clear that there are various kinds of

37. "Creative Vision and Expression," *New Insights and the Curriculum*, A. Frazier, ed. (Washington, D.C.: Association for Supervision and Curriculum Development, 1963), p. 297.

38. Jacob W. Getzels and Philip W. Jackson, *op. cit.*, pp. 23–25.

39. E. Paul Torrance, *op. cit.*, pp. 4–5.

40. *Op. cit.*, pp. 25–26.

intellective abilities and styles, and that intelligence tests measure only a very limited set of them.[41]

Many activities, such as communication, cooperation, decision-making, and planning, are probably at least as complex as creative activities. Even without exploration of the numerous factors involved in such activities, the findings concerning creativity should give serious pause to those who make a radical distinction between emotional and intellectual elements and whose primary criteria are I.Q. scores and scholastic achievement as they contemplate the problems of quality and equality in education. Teachers generally give much more consideration and stimulation to children with high I.Q.s than to creative children. The general lack of concern about the development of creativity is reflected in statements of educational aims, in the tests used by teachers, in the kinds of learning activities found in schools, and in the means used to identify talent.[42]

Often irritation is the reaction of teachers to creative children. Teachers have a decided tendency to prefer the child with high I.Q. over the highly creative child even when their academic achievement is the same.[43] Indeed, two of the most consistent findings in studies of creativity are that children with high I.Q. are better known by teachers and are considered more desirable as pupils than are highly creative children.[44] The evidence of unequal opportunity is strengthened by the fact that I.Q. scores and recommendations from teachers are two of the most important criteria for admission to college.

Yet, if ever the world has needed creativity, we need it today. We need it not only in artistic and scientific endeavors but also in our attempts to solve the basic social and ethical problems of our time. We ought to be deeply disturbed by the fact that many teachers are offered courses in creative arts but not in creative economics, creative politics,

41. See Calvin W. Taylor, "Many-Sided Intelligence," *Childhood Education*, April 1963, pp. 364–66; J. P. Guilford, "Traits of Creativity," *Creativity and Its Cultivation*, Harold H. Anderson, ed. (New York: Harper & Brothers, 1959), pp. 142–61.

42. E. Paul Torrance, *Education and the Creative Potential* (Minneapolis: University of Minnesota Press, 1963), pp. 4–5, 16.

43. See, for example, John L. Holland, "Creative and Academic Performances Among Talented Adolescents," *Journal of Educational Psychology*, June 1961, p. 145.

44. Jacob W. Getzels and Philip W. Jackson, *op. cit.*, pp. 30–31.

and so on. Would not individual and social growth be promoted more by the wonderful ability to wonder, to be puzzled, than by complacency and apathy; more by the ability to redefine problems and seek alternative solutions than by clashes of stubborn viewpoints in domestic and international arenas; more by individuality and the "moral attitude" than by a cog-in-a-machine style of life?

Moreover, there is every reason to think that the school could contribute greatly to the development of creative tendencies, although this would require major changes in emphases and procedures.[45] It is unlikely that creative abilities will emerge automatically after an education in closed systems of thought and behavior. It is more likely that an education which uses systems of thought and behavior as material for developing creative abilities will contribute to this objective.

The purpose here is not to propose a choice between intelligence and creativity. Intelligence and creativity are not completely different characteristics, nor do they encompass all educational and social values. The example of creativity has been used mainly to illustrate the need for broader, more complex conceptions of equality and talent than those now underlying so much educational practice.

Many gifted children have been educationally neglected. Social exigencies may require emphasis on only certain types of educational excellence. But these claims do not erase the fact of individual differences even among pupils with the same kind of talent. They do not erase the existence and value of many kinds of talents and of many different ways of fostering these talents. They do not erase the probability that, in principle, the pursuit of excellence is compatible with the pursuit of equality.

Obstacles to Realizing Equality

Schools in a democracy need not be passive in determining what values will be honored in education. Nevertheless, broad cultural forces raise many obstacles to the realization of equality of educational opportunity, and schools are generally none too successful in overcoming these hindrances. Although we shall return to some of these obstacles in later

45. Jacob W. Getzels, "Creative Thinking, Problem-solving, and Instruction," *Sixty-Third Yearbook*, National Society for the Study of Education (Chicago: University of Chicago Press, 1964), part I, pp. 257–67.

chapters,[46] they merit at least brief mention here.

It is obvious, for example, that children born and raised in a "poor" section of the country do not receive educational advantages equal to those afforded children more favorably placed. Many factors other than wealth influence the quality of an educational program. But the significance of disparities in financial resources is increased by the fact that, in general, where economic circumstances are at their worst, children and youth are most plentiful. As is shown in Table 1, the top eight states according to personal income per child of school age tend to rank at the bottom in terms of the number of school age children per 100 adults, and the bottom eight states in personal income tend to rank at the top in the ratio of children to adults.

Perhaps there was a time when the consequences of local and state differences in educational opportunity were chiefly of local and state

TABLE 1

Rank by *Personal Income per Child* *of School Age (5–17), 1961*		*Rank by* *Number of School Age* *Children (5–17) per 100* *Adults (22–64), 1960*
1	New York	50
2	Nevada	48
3	Connecticut	45
4	Delaware	38
5	New Jersey	49
6	California	40
7	Illinois	43
8	Massachusetts	46
43	Georgia	14
44	North Carolina	10
45	Louisiana	8
46	North Dakota	6
47	Arkansas	9
48	Alabama	7
49	South Carolina	3
50	Mississippi	1

SOURCE: *Ranking of the States,* Research Report 1963-R1 (Washington, D.C.: Research Division, National Education Association, 1963), pp. 14, 41.

46. See especially chaps. 13, 22, and 23.

import. This is not so today. Mobility has become more and more characteristic of our people, and what one section of the country sows in the education of its young another commonly reaps. One fourth of the American people now live in a state other than the one in which they were born, and this percentage is increasing.[47] The facts of political and economic interdependence, and the high rate of rejection from military service on grounds of educational deficiencies cause many people to believe that the nation as a whole should attempt to equalize educational opportunity for youth just as most states have attempted to equalize these opportunities within their borders.

Race, Too, Is a Handicap

Perhaps the most stubborn factor contributing to inequality in education is race. Children born of one race are from birth denied opportunities which invite the young of more fortunate background. Moreover, since these differences are more analogous to differences of caste than of class, their effects are the most difficult to overcome. A conspicuous illustration of this fact is, of course, the resistance not only in the South but in other sections of the country to the injunctions of the United States Supreme Court with respect to segregation in education.

It should not be forgotten, however, that the Negro is not the sole victim of segregation. Similar obstacles confront the Indian and the Mexican in the Southwest. In milder form, other racial and national groups are subject to discrimination in various sections of the country —groups such as Jews, Italians, Chinese, and Japanese. When discrimination results in blocking opportunities to enter college or professional school, as it often does, or closing certain vocations to members of minority groups, its effects upon the personalities of young people early in their careers can be serious.

Social Class As an Obstacle to Equality

Socioeconomic status is perhaps the most obvious general factor in determining whether or not young people are to enjoy equal educational opportunities. Using various sources, Robert J. Havighurst has esti-

47. *Education for a Changing World of Work*, Report of the Panel of Consultants on Vocational Education (Washington, D.C.: U.S. Government Printing Office, 1963), pp. 9–10.

mated that while four fifths of the high school graduates from the upper and upper-middle classes enter college, only one fifth from the upper-lower class and less than one tenth from the lower-lower class enter college.[48] The differentiated curriculum of the secondary school often serves as an index of the socioeconomic status of students within a community, students of upper socioeconomic status tending to gravitate toward the college preparatory courses and students of lower status toward curricula of a more immediate vocational application.[49] The large number of academically able children from the lower classes who do not go on to college represents by far the major part of the widely publicized "waste of talent." [50] As Havighurst and Neugarten state:

> It is clear that the educational system selects and carries along most of the ablest youth of upper and upper-middle status, but that able youth of working-class status (upper-lower and lower-lower classes) tend to stop their formal education at the end of high school. The reasons for this lie partly in the inability of most lower-class youth to pay for a college education, and partly in the lack of motivation of most lower-class youth for higher education.[51]

It would not be fair to charge the schools with the sole or, perhaps, even the major responsibility for lack of motivation. As education and financial resources become more widely distributed, the educational aspirations of the lower social classes continue to rise. However, educational aspiration is closely associated with parental stress on prolonged education,[52] and this stress is much stronger among upper-status families than among lower-status families.[53] Among middle- and upper-

48. "Social-Class Influences on American Education," *Sixtieth Yearbook,* National Society for the Study of Education (Chicago: University of Chicago Press, 1961), part II, p. 123.

49. See, for example, Patricia C. Sexton, *Education and Income* (New York: Viking Press, 1961), p. 177.

50. Burton R. Clark, *Educating the Expert Society* (San Francisco: Chandler Publishing Co., 1962), pp. 60–62.

51. Robert J. Havighurst and Bernice L. Neugarten, *Society and Education,* 2d ed. (Boston: Allyn and Bacon, Inc., 1962), p. 233.

52. See, for example, David J. Bordua, "Educational Aspirations and Parental Stress on College," *Social Forces,* March 1960, pp. 262–69.

53. In this connection, see Harry J. Crockett, Jr., "The Achievement Motive and Differential Occupational Mobility in the United States," *American Sociological Review,* April 1962, pp. 191–204.

class families, prolonged education is likely to be a tradition, financial resources are often available, and individuals are accustomed to postponing marriage and the earning of money in favor of a long and costly period of education. In a national poll, Elmo Roper found that 97 per cent of parents in the "high economic level" expected their children to go to college, but only 44 per cent of parents in the "below-average economic level" had this expectation.[54]

The School May Not Serve All Equally

Teachers, too, have their limitations. It is clear that teachers often find it easier to work with children of the middle and upper classes than with those from the lower class. Methods of discipline, ways of dealing with children in school, the faith and the confidence in the individual which teachers express in their person-to-person relationships, "actions that speak louder than words," are not altogether free from cultural backgrounds and the class distinctions to which these testify.

This is but another way of saying that teachers are predominantly of middle-class origin and are emotionally identified with the values and customs and the morals and manners of the upper- and middle-class segments of society. As a result, they find it difficult to deal objectively and unemotionally with child or adolescent behavior that runs counter to their accustomed and cherished ways. It is not always easy, in short, to temper the wind to the shorn lamb.

Obviously, the difficulties teachers encounter in their training continue to operate later in the practice of their profession. The manners and customs of members of an "out-group" are often as emotionally disturbing as the more serious violations of moral standards by a likable member of an "in-group." Consequently, where experience and training have not conditioned a middle-class teacher to the normal behavior of the lower-class child, in a community where class lines are fairly rigidly defined, the latter is usually at a disadvantage, even

54. "College Ambitions and Parental Planning." *Public Opinion Quarterly*, Summer 1961, p. 161. These two levels, the highest and lowest on a four-level scale, are not further defined. Income level is one major index of social class but, in most definitions, is not necessarily the same as social-class level.

though the teacher may be unconscious of either prejudice or willful discrimination.[55]

Teachers often expect lower-class children to be "difficult." These anticipations are communicated to children in many ways and, thus, a self-fulfilling prophecy may be initiated.[56] Children who perceive teachers as having favorable attitudes toward them tend to be children from middle- and upper-class backgrounds.[57] These limitations of teachers are particularly unfortunate since, with the exception of the immediate family, teachers may be the principal stimulaters of interest in education among lower-class children.[58]

Many aspects of the school militate against lower-class children.[59] Lacking the social drives and skills of many middle-class children and made to feel "out of place" by the status system within the school, lower-class children join student organizations much less frequently than do middle-class children. At times, too, membership in a social class seems to be at least as potent as aptitude in determining the awarding of grades and the assignment to groups of different ability levels. In lower-class districts, as compared with middle-class districts, school buildings and their facilities are generally less adequate, the class size is often larger, and both pupil turnover and teacher turnover are greater. On the whole, there are more substandard teachers in lower-class districts; higher salaries and more favorable working conditions elsewhere tend to siphon off the more competent teachers.

Moreover, the subject matter used in schools is much more familiar to middle-class children than to lower-class children. Many of the words, skills, and patterns of thought used in schools are unlikely to be used in low-status homes. Intelligence tests well illustrate this dispar-

55. See Samuel Tenenbaum, "The Teacher, the Middle Class, the Lower Class," *Phi Delta Kappan*, November 1963, pp. 82–86.
56. Harold L. Hodgkinson, *Education in Social and Cultural Perspective* (Englewood Cliffs, N.J.: Prentice-Hall, Inc., 1962), pp. 97–98.
57. See, for example, Helen H. Davidson and Gerhard Lang, "Children's Perceptions of Their Teachers' Feelings Toward Them Related to Self-Perception," *Journal of Experimental Education*, December 1960, pp. 107–18.
58. Robert A. Ellis and W. C. Lane, "Structural Supports for Upward Mobility," *American Sociological Review*, October 1963, pp. 755–66.
59. For more detailed accounts of these inequalities, see Frank Riessman, *The Culturally Deprived Child* (New York: Harper & Row, 1962), chaps. 1, 3; Patricia C. Sexton, *op. cit.*, pp. 58–68, 78–97, 108–35, 194–215.

ity. It has been shown that the ordinary intelligence tests favor high-status children.[60] Take, for example, the following test item:

A symphony is to a composer as a book is to what?

( ) paper ( ) sculptor ( ) author ( ) musician ( ) man

Compared with lower-class children, middle-class children are more likely to have heard symphonies or discussions about symphonies. Since the ordinary intelligence tests include many items of this type, they tend to penalize lower-class children. Attempts to construct "culture-fair" tests have met with only limited success.[61] For one thing, high-status children are wiser in the ways of test-taking. Their achievement drive is stronger. Speed and efficiency come more "naturally" to them from their home training.

Such findings are of great significance when we recall the reliance widely given to the prognostic value of intelligence tests and the not uncommon assumption that a close correlation exists between "real" intelligence and socioeconomic status. These reservations concerning the value and the use of intelligence tests in education throw light upon the lack of appeal in the conventional curriculum for many young people in the lower economic and social levels of society. We are becoming increasingly sensitive to the fact that much of the subject matter and content of the curriculum is foreign to the experience of lower-class children and that they require a reinterpretation, if not a reorganization, in order to yield the richest educational fruit.

It seems fair to conclude that both in concept and in application much remains to be done if Americans are to assure all their youth a full realization of the blessings of "life, liberty and the pursuit of happiness" insofar as these are attainable through education. As we shall note in several later chapters, a growing variety of efforts are currently being made to improve educational opportunities for underprivileged children. Most significant and portentous is the Elementary and Secondary Education Act of 1965. This act marks the assumption by the federal government of a major role in attacking inequalities of educational opportunity by providing federal funds to local educational

60. Robert J. Havighurst and Bernice L. Neugarten, *op. cit.*, p. 236.
61. See Frank Riessman, *op. cit.*, pp. 52–53; J. E. Stablin, D. S. Willey, and C. W. Thomson, "An Evaluation of the Davis-Eells (Culture-Fair) Test Using Spanish and Anglo-American Children," *Journal of Educational Sociology*, October 1961, pp. 73–78.

agencies on the basis of the financial needs of the families from which public school children come.

Suggested Reading

Brookover, W. B., and D. Gottlieb, "Social Class and Education," *Readings in the Social Psychology of Education*, W. W. Charters, Jr. and N. L. Gage, eds. (Boston: Allyn and Bacon, Inc., 1963), pp. 3–11.

Brubacher, John S., *Modern Philosophies of Education* (New York: McGraw-Hill Book Co., 1962), chap. VI.

Conant, James B., *Slums and Suburbs* (New York: McGraw-Hill Book Co., 1961), chaps. III–IV.

Douvan, E., and C. Kaye, "Motivational Factors in College Entrance," in *The American College*. Nevitt Sanford, ed. (New York: John Wiley and Sons, Inc., 1962), pp. 119–224.

Gardner, John W., *Excellence: Can We Be Equal and Excellent Too?* (New York: Harper & Row, 1961), chaps. I, IV–VII.

Getzels, Jacob W., and Philip W. Jackson, *Creativity and Intelligence* (New York: John Wiley and Sons, Inc., 1962), chaps. 1–2.

Gewirth, Alan, "Political Justice," in *Social Justice*. Richard B. Brandt, ed. (Englewood Cliffs, N.J.: Prentice-Hall, Inc., 1962), pp. 119–69.

Havighurst, Robert J., and Bernice L. Neugarten, *Society and Education*, 2d ed. (Boston: Allyn and Bacon, Inc., 1962), chaps. 1, 4, 6, 9.

Hook, Sidney, *Education for Modern Man* (New York: Alfred A. Knopf, 1963), pp. 34–45, 54–67.

Hughes, Emmet J., ed., *Education in World Perspective* (New York: Harper & Row, 1962), chaps. 5, 10.

Kaplan, Bernard A., "Issues in Educating the Culturally Disadvantaged," *Phi Delta Kappan*, November 1963, pp. 70–76.

Miner, Jerry, *Social and Economic Factors in Spending for Education* (Syracuse: Syracuse University Press, 1963), chap. 2.

Rudy, Willis, *Schools in an Age of Mass Culture* (Englewood Cliffs, N.J.: Prentice-Hall, Inc., 1965), chaps. 5, 10.

Torrance, E. Paul, "Cultural Discontinuities and the Development of Originality in Thinking," *Exceptional Children*, September 1962, pp. 2–13.

PART II

CONCEPTIONS OF LEARNING IN THEIR AMERICAN SETTING

Chapter 6

Our Colonial Inheritance

Early Motives for Establishing Schools

Frequent mention has been made of the influence of religion upon American education. This was particularly true of the colonial period in all of the colonies, but its manifestations in New England were perhaps most conspicuous and most dramatic, for there it was that the vision of the Holy Commonwealth long dominated both civil and ecclesiastical establishments. For a period, indeed, church and state were united, with the church the dominant partner. "We came hither," wrote Cotton Mather, in his *Magnalia*, "because we would have our posterity settled under the pure and full dispensations of the gospel; defended by rulers that should be ourselves."

Historians have cautioned us not to read too generous or enlightened a conception of the nature and purpose of education into early legislation on compulsory education in Massachusetts or, for that matter, in other New England colonies which followed the example of Massachusetts. The Beards, for example, emphasize that the acts of 1642 and 1647 [1] did not represent the intention of the state to assume responsibility for the education of all children as much as it represented a theological determination to impose upon all the sectarian creed of the

1. The act of 1642 required parents and masters to teach children and apprentices to "understand the principles of religion and the capital laws of the country." The act of 1647 ordered towns of fifty householders to appoint a master "to teach all children as shall resort to him to write and read" and towns of one hundred householders to set up a grammar school to prepare youth for the university.

Puritans.[2] The fact that this education was ordered by the state, they insist, was of little significance since the state and the church were one.

Again, we should bear in mind that although the religious motive loomed large in legislation, other interests were also operative. The New Englander was determined that children acquire the means of self-support. Consequently, all compulsory educational legislation provided that parents or guardians who failed to teach their children the elements of some lawful calling, labor, or employment should be deprived of their guardianship and the children apprenticed to someone more responsible.[3]

Observe also that although the state enacted legislation, enforcement was left to localities. Moreover, as was indicated in Chapter 4, state legislation respecting the establishment of schools followed upon rather than antedated prior action by localities.

Nor is it without significance that the Puritan adopted universal education as a means of perpetuating orthodoxy in preference to the device of Governor Berkeley of Virginia for achieving the same end, namely, keeping the masses in ignorance. Two important phrases occur in the preamble to the law of 1647: (1) "It being one chief object of that old deluder Satan, to keep men from the knowledge of the Scriptures, as in former times by keeping them in an unknown tongue . . ." and (2) "that learning may not be buried in the graves of our fathers in Church and Commonwealth. . . . It is therefore ordered. . . ."

The interests of scholarship were highly valued by the Puritans, and despite the later failure of towns to obey the education laws, an abiding respect for books and the fruits of learning long characterized the people of New England.

Granted significant differences between the motives of the Puritans and those which animated the advocates of publicly supported schools in the nineteenth century, the lines of connection between the two are nevertheless evident. The early religious determination to use the schools as a means of insuring religious orthodoxy and civic conformity is not unrelated to the later objective of using them for moral and civic

2. Charles and Mary Beard, *The Rise of American Civilization* (New York: The Macmillan Co., 1930), vol. I, pp. 179–80.

3. Max Weber believed that Protestantism, by sanctifying the virtues of work, was instrumental in the rise of capitalism and a new middle class. See his study, *The Protestant Ethic and the Spirit of Capitalism* (New York: Charles Scribner's Sons, 1930).

purposes. In each instance schools were viewed as instruments for realizing in the lives of the younger generation the vision of the good life as envisaged by the older.

Time has done much to transform the objectives of both school and college since the colonial period. Nevertheless, Americans still conceive of the school as the custodian of the morals of the young, and one of its purposes—indeed, a primary purpose—is to raise the young in the paths of virtue. Consequently, when the rate of juvenile delinquency increases, there is a natural tendency to hold the school as well as the home responsible.

To the moral purpose of education we may also ascribe the fact that the school, in contrast with other institutions of government, has been kept relatively free from political manipulation. Not that politics and favoritism have been totally excluded from the public school! That is too much to expect of an American community. But this is more nearly true of the school than perhaps of any other public agency, with the result that when evidence of political influence becomes clear the public is easily persuaded to "turn the rascals out." [4]

As we have seen, the ideal state for the Puritan was one in which the church and state were merged, but with the religious influence dominant. In the early church the elders were the elect and the elect ruled.

Not until the revision of the charter in 1691 was the right to vote in Massachusetts extended to nonchurch members. With a widening of the suffrage, however, and the rise of a wealthy merchant class, the foundations of the Holy Commonwealth began to yield to the acids of secular influence. Nevertheless, something of the earlier spirit has persisted in the American's conception of the missionary function of his way of life, so that a genealogist might trace without too much difficulty a relationship between faith in the "manifest destiny" of the American Republic and the earlier conviction that "the God of Heaven had carried a nation into a wilderness upon the designs of a glorious transformation."

This intense conviction also gave vital importance to education, since upon each generation rested the responsibility of fostering, but not altering, the basic structure of the state. Consequently, we have the rare

4. To be sure, the schools of any society may be agents of indoctrination rather than education, even though they teach only the "core" or commonly agreed upon values of a society, while carefully refraining from teaching the "alternative" values—those, say, of particular sects or classes.

phenomenon of a devoted people establishing within a few short years of their sailing into Boston harbor a complete system of schools—an elementary school to educate all young people sufficiently to enable them to read and understand the Bible and the religious and civil laws; a secondary school to equip the future leaders of church and state for college; and a college that would insure an educated ministry as well as an adequately prepared professional class.

Education, even dogmatic education, often has a way of stimulating people to think for themselves. Education in early New England was no exception to this rule, with the result that serious differences in theology soon manifested themselves, a fact which did much to populate new communities with heretics and dissidents. Challenging official doctrine was not only a personal sin; it undermined the health of the community as well. Consequently, when Roger Williams, Anne Hutchinson, and less well-known folk began to propagate offensive ideas they were driven into the wilderness to fend for themselves.

On the other hand, the New Englander was a Protestant. As such, he was committed to the proposition that salvation is an individual matter, dependent not upon official intermediaries between God and man, but upon direct relations between each person and his Maker. This imposed upon one the obligation to read and interpret the Bible for himself, with its possibilities of deviation from the straight and narrow path of truth. Successive generations proceeded to exploit this opportunity to the full. But this possibility also demonstrated the importance of censorship and meticulous attention to methods of teaching which might insure the acquisition of truth and avoidance of error.

Colonial Influences in Contemporary Education

Were it possible for a colonial schoolmaster to visit a modern classroom, it is doubtful that he would recognize it as a school. Imagine, for example, the horror with which an Ezekiel Cheever might view the activities of teacher and pupil today, or the qualities or relationship between the two which a competent teacher strives to develop. Would he not conclude that the "old deluder Satan" had at last succeeded in his designs upon education?

Nevertheless, a number of educational assumptions which influence both educator and layman still survive from the colonial period.

Man's Dual Nature

Take, for example, the assumption that man's nature is dual, in that a distinction of kind exists between body and soul. This continues to operate as a basic assumption for many and has yielded abundant fruit in education. Originally it was grounded more in theology than in philosophy and psychology. In the hands of Jonathan Edwards, theology and philosophy united to prepare the mind for the later more distinctly psychological distinctions between mind and body which, as formulated by John Locke, dominated educational thought and practice in America well down to the end of the nineteenth century.

According to the colonial conception of man, the traditional conflict between good and evil is reflected in the constitution of each individual, with the body and its impulses oriented toward evil and the soul alone aspiring to higher things. Moreover, in this contest, the devil seems to have an initial advantage, since children are born in sin and are thus natively disposed toward evil. Consequently, Cotton Mather could describe the child as a "little viper" and John Wesley was prompted to enjoin parents to "break your child's will in order that it may not perish. . . . Break its will, in order that its soul may live." [5]

As we page through the literature of the seventeenth and eighteenth centuries to which children were customarily introduced, we can detect little that was designed to develop in them what psychologists today emphasize as all-important, namely, a sense of inner confidence and security. Imagine, for example, the inspiration they must have derived from Cotton Mather's "A Token for the Children of New England, or some examples of children in whom the feare of God was remarkably budding when they died in several parts of New England." Or consider the manner in which their eyes would turn eagerly toward their own future after reading Janeway's "Tokens for the Children: An exact account of the Conversions, holy and exemplary Lives and Deaths of several young Children." What picture was a child expected to form of himself as he encountered these words in a manual widely used in an infant school of something more than a century ago?

> Yes, I was ever born in sin,
> And all my heart is bad within.

5. Quoted in William Heard Kilpatrick, *Source Book in the Philosophy of Education* (New York: The Macmillan Co., 1923), p. 334.

A textbook entitled *Youth's Instructor,* published as late as 1757, carried this introduction for the eager youth to read: "Lord, what is man: Originally, dust, engendered in sin, brought forth in sorrow, helpless in his infancy, extravagantly wild in his youth, mad in his manhood, decrepid in his age; his first voice moves to pity; his last commands grief." [6]

It follows from this conception of man's original nature that discipline from without is a first essential. Discipline and hard work are necessities from the earliest years if the young are to succeed in following the straight and narrow path of virtue.

We can appreciate how general and persistent this concept of childhood has been when we consider the manner in which Charles Dickens was moved to use his pen in order to arouse the public to a more humane conception of child nature and a reform in methods of schooling. Observe the satire in this passage from *Old Curiosity Shop:*

> "Don't you feel how naughty it is of you," resumed Miss Monflathers, "to be a wax-work child, when you might have the proud consciousness of assisting to the extent of your infant powers, the manufacturers of your country; of improving your mind by the constant contemplation of the steam engine; and of earning a comfortable and independent subsistence of from two and nine pence to three shillings per week? Don't you know that the harder you are at work the happier you are?" (Chapter XXXI).

And Mrs. Pipkin in *Dombey and Son:*

> There is a great deal of nonsense—and worse—talked about young people not being pressed too hard at first and being taught and all the rest of it, sir . . .
>
> It was never thought of in my time, and it has no business to be thought of now. My opinion is; keep 'em at it (Chapter XI).

Nor is this view of human nature, to say nothing of child nature, inactive today. It is often implied by the common expression, "You can't change human nature" and by the suggestion so commonly heard in these days of public concern over juvenile delinquency that more frequent visits to the woodshed would bring desirable results.

6. Quoted in Newton Edwards and Herman G. Richey, *The School in the American Social Order,* 2d ed. (Boston: Houghton Mifflin Co., 1963), p. 108.

The past decade has witnessed a rise in the demand for stricter discipline of children and youth. Although there may have been a leveling off during the most recent years, this demand generally rises and falls with the level of domestic and international tensions.[7] Permissive or "child-centered" approaches have been strongly condemned, and it is not unfashionable to urge again that the child's will must be broken [8] and that he must "learn to respect authority," even if it is the authority of force.[9]

Probably at least as significant as this development is the revival in certain theological circles of the doctrine of innate depravity, although a substitute for this ancient term may be used. Take, for example, the concept of morality expounded by the eminent theologian, Reinhold Niebuhr, in his *Moral Man and Immoral Society*.[10] According to Niebuhr, individual people may succeed in climbing to moral heights but groups, as groups, find it virtually impossible to do so. This follows from the fact that an individual can tame and discipline his naturally selfish impulses through the exercise of reason. With groups, however, reason is not sufficiently potent to achieve this end. The result, as Niebuhr sees it, is that in relations between groups might alone can establish the right. Although Niebuhr has softened his pessimism in recent years—as have some other theologians [11]—in 1960 he wrote that he was "still committed" to this "central thesis" of *Moral Man and Immoral Society*.[12]

Two contradictory theories of child development thus confront the modern parent and teacher: one which continues to emphasize the native tendency of children to kick against the pricks and to become "soft" unless acclimated to hard work and effort with or without (perhaps better without) interest; and the other which stresses the impor-

7. See Alfred Auerback, "The Anti-Mental Health Movement," *American Journal of Psychiatry*, August 1963, pp. 105–11.

8. Sherwood B. Chorost, "Parental Child-Rearing Attitudes and Their Correlates in Adolescent Hostility," *Genetic Psychology Monographs*, August 1962, p. 65.

9. Paul Nash, "Corporal Punishment in an Age of Violence," *Educational Theory*, October 1963, pp. 295–98, 307.

10. (New York: Charles Scribner's Sons, 1960). The date of original publication is 1932.

11. See, for example, Karl Barth, *The Humanity of God* (Richmond, Virginia: John Knox Press, 1960), pp. 5–6, 37–65.

12. See also Niebuhr's *Pious and Secular America* (New York: Charles Scribner's Sons, 1958), pp. 1–23, 113–22.

tance of fostering in the young an inner confidence and an inwardly directed discipline, both of which are furthered when a child, in a friendly and nourishing atmosphere, is encouraged to identify himself with the manners and the morals of the society in which he is to live, move, and have his being.

Without Orthodoxy the Health of the Community Is Endangered

That orthodoxy in religion is an essential for individual morality and the well-being of the community is a second assumption which originated in the colonial period, an assumption which continues to function as an operative principle in contemporary education.

As a policy of governments, the conviction that the health and welfare of the community require uniformity in religion was in no way original with the American colonies. Consequently, when Nathaniel Ward announced that "All Familists, Antinomians, Anabaptists, and other Enthusiasts shall have free liberty to keep away from us," he was but applying to Massachusetts a policy of which the Puritans themselves had been victims. As they had been dealt with, so they proposed to do unto others!

Nor was this principle confined in application to Massachusetts. Although the religious faith it safeguarded varied from colony to colony, the principle of orthodoxy was applied generally. In time, however, it gave way to one of live and let live, and, eventually, to the concept of noninterference by the state in matters of religious conviction, or, as we now term it, the principle of separation of church and state.

The assumption that morality derives from and is dependent upon religious conviction continues, however, to influence the minds of many educators and laymen, with one essential difference between today and yesterday. The assumed *necessary* relationship between creed and moral behavior has become less specific. Few Protestants will insist today that their own version of Protestantism (Baptist, Methodist, and so on) is alone in its underwriting of morality, and, obviously, members of the Jewish faith can hardly agree with the dictum that the Christian faith carried by the Catholic Church must guide intellectual and moral life.[13] The common view today is that although men may

13. George Brantl, ed., *Catholicism* (New York: George Braziller, 1962), pp. 197–209.

legitimately disagree as to the validity of one faith as compared to another, nevertheless, religious faith in some form is essential for morality.

The assumption that religion and morality are inseparably related explains the determination of many earnest people "to bring God into the school," although they profess neutrality as to the concept of God thus introduced and deny that they attempt to foster the acceptance of one religious faith over another. As Professor William O. Stanley has pointed out, although there exists a general "agreement on prohibition of teaching a particular sectarian doctrine," there is, nevertheless, "a considerable, and perhaps growing, body of opinion in Catholic, Protestant, and even Jewish circles that the public schools must recognize the importance of religion in the American way of life." [14] Various domestic and international developments probably will be influential in determining the future history of this trend and of Supreme Court decisions bearing on the place of religion in the public schools.[15]

Eliminate the Controversial from the Classroom

To teach with an eye to orthodoxy implies the exclusion from the classroom of views which run counter to prevailing opinion. Only as doctrines to be refuted may the latter receive attention in the classroom. It is not surprising, therefore, that the principle we are considering finds application in areas other than religion. It is to this principle of orthodoxy that we must ascribe responsibility for the widely held assumption that since education is a public function and teachers are the hired agents of the public, they should instill in the minds of children only ideas approved by the public. In practice this means that the school board, or groups in the community to whom the school board owes its selection, should determine what doctrines might legitimately be fostered in the school. It is this conviction, evidently, that prompts a southern community dominated by the white population to insist that schools teach nothing which runs counter to the "southern way of life"; prompts members of patriotic organizations to insist that schools promote their version of Americanism; prompts leaders in business to urge

14. "Educational and Social Policy," *Review of Educational Research,* February 1961, p. 93.

15. See Donald E. Boles, *The Bible, Religion, and the Public Schools,* 2d ed. (Ames, Iowa: Iowa State University Press, 1963), pp. 281–85.

that both textbook and teacher deal with the history of American economic development and the issues of contemporary economic society in ways designed to insure adherence to the principle of "free enterprise"; prompts lay groups of every shade—reformist, conservative, radical—to look to the schools for the spread of their doctrines.

Nor are liberals in education in agreement as to where the line should be drawn in dealing with problems of this character, even when teaching for "understanding" as against "conviction." Some hold that on all issues upon which men disagree the proper educational objective is to develop the method or the discipline which emerges best from wrestling with problems that cannot be answered by looking in the back of the book; that is, to teach *how* to think but not *what* to think. Others contend that an institution established and maintained by the public is under obligation to develop an allegiance to the basic principles of the society which sustains it. This second group would argue that although the individual problems which thus confront a democracy should receive only objective consideration (and that students should be permitted—even encouraged—to arrive at their own conclusions), there should emerge, nevertheless, from study and discussion a common loyalty to the principles of democracy and the methods of free inquiry without which a free society cannot long exist.

To the problems which inevitably emerge from these rival conceptions of the function of the school, we shall return in the chapters dealing with freedom to learn and freedom to teach.

To Read Is To Believe

Closely allied to teaching for conformity is the tendency to identify reading with believing. This, too, as indicated in Chapter 1, is an inheritance from the colonial period but it has received sufficient nourishment in later periods of our history to insure its continued health and vigor.

Doubtless the early prominence of the Bible in men's thinking and the central position of religious materials in the curriculum were responsible for the assumption that what one reads he is both inclined and expected to believe. On this view, a major purpose in schooling is to stock the mind with the facts and principles from which one might later deduce the appropriate solutions to life's problems. Accordingly, when difficulties present themselves or disagreements among men arise, the first step toward ultimate resolution of points at issue is to identify the relevant precept, principle, or major premise which might serve as a starting point toward a happy solution. In the relatively simple Protestant communities of the past, the Bible served as this fountainhead of basic principles. Nor has it lost this position altogether, as evidenced by the common tendency for people today, when confronted by a burning issue, such as racial segregation, to quote the Scriptures in support of their position. In a similar manner, when Roger Williams wrote his treatise on *The Bloody Tenent of Persecution etc.* and John Cotton replied with *The Bloody Tenent Washed and Made White in the Blood of the Lamb etc.*, only to be answered by Roger Williams in *The Bloody Tenent Yet More Bloody: By Mr. Cotton's Endeavor to Wash It White in the Blood of the Lamb etc.*, both grounded their positions in the words of the Scripture.

Not so long ago, the study of the law followed this "read and believe" method. Aspiring lawyers read the law for the purpose of familiarizing themselves with the principles of the law in its various categories, together with their applications in the past, which later as judges and advocates they would be called upon to apply to individual cases.

Advocates of a return to "the old books" in education, or to a curriculum similar to that which prevailed in school and college during the nineteenth century, take a position similar to that under discussion. Thus Walter Lippmann has charged that American education, by catering to mass demands and teaching primarily the "know-how of success" in business life, has failed to "transmit the moral system, indeed the psychic structure of a civilized society." [16] According to Lippmann, it is the cultural heritage "which contains the whole structure and fabric of the good life," and this heritage must be "transmitted from one generation to the next." [17]

The view that education is a process of transmitting truths and that reading is believing is by no means the exclusive possession of some intellectual aristocrats, a few stubborn "traditionalists," or some other minority group. For example, that the great majority of elementary school teachers today pay very little attention to the development of

16. *The Public Philosophy* (Boston: Little, Brown and Co., 1955), pp. 73–78.
17. *Ibid.*, p. 95.

critical thinking as they teach reading (even when "reading for comprehension" is stressed) is the conclusion of a recent and comprehensive survey of reading practices in over a thousand of the nation's public school systems. The authors of the report write as follows about this point:

> Many boys and girls understand and recall the literal meanings of printed material but are unable to evaluate their accuracy or to determine their relevancy to a specific problem. Studies have shown that some pupils lack the ability to read discriminatingly, even when they have achieved satisfactory comprehension scores on standardized reading tests. . . . It was rare indeed that members of the study staff heard teachers trying to help children draw conclusions from what they had read, make inferences or comparisons, evaluate the facts, or participate in other activities that would help develop critical thinking skills.[18]

Thus far, our attention has centered upon certain aspects of colonial thought and practice which continue to influence men's minds and to give character to education today. Some readers will doubtless cherish these as a valuable inheritance. Others will consider them atavistic, appropriate and relevant in their time, perhaps, but handicaps to progress today.

To what we have stressed should be added items discussed in earlier chapters. Thus friends of public education recognize their indebtedness to the early New Englander for his conviction that the education of all young people is a public as well as a private obligation. Significant also is the fact that from the beginning, local communities, along with (and sometimes even before) the state, assumed this responsibility, thus assuring a high degree of local initiative in education and the disposition to adapt education to needs peculiar to the local community.

Finally, we should not forget that many aspects of the colonial mind were more European than American in origin. Under the impact of conditions in the New World, together with a gradual loosening of ties with Europe, quite different conceptions of man and his destiny came into being.

These changes were reflected, eventually, in education. Material suc-

18. Mary C. Austin and Coleman Morrison, *The First R: The Harvard Report on Reading in Elementary Schools* (New York: Macmillan Co., 1963), pp. 39–40.

cess and material well-being led to new demands upon the school, both elementary and secondary, and, eventually, on the college. Gradually the elementary school began to enrich its offerings and the grammar school, with its exclusive emphasis upon classical and literary materials, gave way to the academy and, later, in the nineteenth century, to the high school. Both these latter institutions endeavored to serve interests and needs of a wider range than those recognized by the grammar school.

To these developments we now turn.

Suggested Reading

Childs, John L., *Education and Morals* (New York: Appleton-Century-Crofts, Inc., 1950), chap. VIII.

Edwards, Newton, and Herman G. Richey, *The School in the American Social Order*, 2d ed. (Boston: Houghton Mifflin Co., 1963), chaps. 1–5.

Handlin, Oscar, *The Americans: A New History of the People of the United States* (Boston: Little, Brown and Co., 1963), chaps. 4–5, 8–9.

Meyer, Adolphe E., *An Educational History of the Western World* (New York: McGraw-Hill Book Co., 1965), chap. 13.

Miller, John C., ed., *The Colonial Image* (New York: George Braziller, 1962), pp. 115–31, 169–78, 207–14, 479–98.

Roucek, Joseph S., "The Protestant Heritage in American Education," *Heritage of American Education*. Richard E. Gross, ed. (Boston: Allyn and Bacon, Inc., 1962), pp. 163–231.

Wright, Louis B., *The Cultural Life of the American Colonies* (New York: Harper & Brothers, 1957), chaps. 1–2, 4–5.

Chapter 7

Education and the Conquest
of the Continent

An Expanding Economy Transforms the Colonial Mind

The religious motive loomed large in colonial America, but it was by no means the only one to influence education. Even the *Mayflower,* on its memorable voyage in 1620, included among its passengers a considerable number of adventurers whom William Bradford characterized as an "undesirable lot." Indeed the Mayflower Compact was, in part, designed to prevent this group of "undesirables" from realizing their boast that once on shore they would "use their liberties" as they wished. In the South, the desire to improve one's fortunes in a material way clearly overshadowed spiritual aspirations. Likewise in the Middle Colonies, which set an example in religious toleration novel for the period, the lure of economic success commonly competed with the religious motive. In all of the colonies the inducements of material success became ever more attractive with each succeeding generation.

Only in New England did the vision of the Holy Commonwealth succeed for a considerable period in dominating the policies of state as well as church. But even here, eventually, preoccupation with the conditions of salvation gave ground before the attractions of the world of the flesh and the devil. Nor were these attractions lessened by the happy discovery that the Puritan virtues were evidently designed to insure worldly success as well as the salvation of the soul. From the prac-

114

tice of these virtues the spiritually elect soon found themselves possessed of the power and influence of the materially elect.

As a background for understanding developments in education in the latter part of the eighteenth century and throughout the nineteenth century, we should bear in mind the influence of the frontier or, better, perhaps, the effects of the conquest of the continent upon successive generations of individuals who faced a continuing invitation to better their stations in life through the development of natural resources that gave no hint of exhaustion. Hard as life was on the frontier, it afforded the underprivileged, the oppressed, and the submerged an opportunity to share in the goods of this world. Under these conditions class lines became less rigid. In the South, the young surveyor of limited means could gain entrance into the planter class and, eventually, become an outstanding representative of Virginian aristocracy. In New England, the son of a poor candlemaker, by judicious use of the Puritan virtues of temperance, order, resolution, frugality, industry, honesty, and so forth, rose to a position not only of wealth and influence in the business and professional communities but of leadership in the affairs of state. The expression "While there is life, there is hope" became more than a happy phrase with which to assuage disappointment; it described a confirmed attitude toward discouragement, even defeat, in an atmosphere in which failure was never final.

To be sure, there were regressions and depressions in the development of the economy of the colonies as well as of the later Republic; but, despite the "ups" and the occasional severe "downs" throughout the years, Americans have lived consistently in a steadily expanding economy. This condition has contributed to a gradual change in man's conception of himself and the human drama. The virtues of religious individualism, as we have said, were transformed into the conditions of worldly success. What Benjamin Franklin records in his autobiography as his own observations and conclusions were shared by many:

> Revelation had no weight with me, as such; but I entertained an opinion, that though certain actions might not be bad, *because* they were forbidden by it, or good, *because* it commanded them; yet probably these actions might be forbidden *because* they were bad for us, or commanded *because* they were beneficial to us, in their own natures, all the circumstances of things considered.

For many, the nature of the Deity likewise underwent significant change. Less emphasis was placed upon the stern and forbidding qualities of a jealous God and more upon his characteristics as a beneficent planner, the designer of the universe, who operates in accordance with laws and principles that make of this the best of all possible worlds. Thus Alexander Pope could pen for the American as well as for the Englishman with little fear of contradiction:

> All are but parts of one stupendous whole,
> Whose body Nature is, and God the soul; . . .
> All Nature is but art, unknown to thee;
> All chance, direction, which thou canst not see;
> All discord, harmony not understood;
> All partial evil, universal good:
> And, spite of pride, in erring reason's spite,
> One truth is clear, whatever is, is right.[1]

Nowhere was the swing of the pendulum, from the concept of man's innate depravity to one of optimistic faith in his possibilities for continuous progress toward perfection, more evident than in the intellectuals of New England. "For two hundred years," writes Parrington, "the dogmas of Calvin had lain as a heavy weight on the mind of New England." [2] By 1850, however, Calvinism had found a formidable rival in French liberalism and its New England expression in Unitarianism, a religion which Parrington describes as "essentially a humanistic religion, rational, ethical, individual, yet with deep and warm social sympathies." [3]

Unitarians and others, too, experienced an upsurge of confidence in God's love and man's potentialities for perfection, which, when married to the spirit of social reform, led to passionate and far-reaching attempts to transform the institutions of this world into forms more appropriate to man's new status. All the passionate determination which once seemed bent upon establishing the Holy Commonwealth in New England now centered upon removing impediments to prog-

1. *Essay on Man.*
2. Vernon Parrington, *Main Currents in American Thought* (New York: Harcourt, Brace & Co., 1927), p. 321.
3. *Ibid.*, p. 327.

ress—economic, political, social—or conditions which hampered expressions of that infinite worth of which each individual soul is possessed.

Nor was this liberal and reformist spirit confined to New England. The influence of a William Ellery Channing or a Theodore Parker, a Ralph Waldo Emerson, a Henry Thoreau, or a William Lloyd Garrison was welcomed by kindred souls in all sections of the country. There, too, soil and climate, material and spiritual, were favorable to visions of a potential heaven on earth.

Typical of this new faith in man and his universe were the writings of Ralph Waldo Emerson. Contrast, for example, the following selections from his essays on *Fate* and *Culture* with the quotation on page 106 from the introduction to the *Youth's Instructor:*

> The book of nature is the book of fate. She turns the gigantic pages leaf after leaf, never re-turning one. One leaf she lays down, a floor of granite; a thousand ages, and a measure of coal; a thousand ages, and a layer of marl and mud; vegetable forms appear; her first misshapen animals, zoophyte, trilobium, fish; then saurians, rude forms, in which she has only blocked her future statue, concealing under these unwieldly monsters the fine type of her coming king. The face of the planet cools and dries, the races meliorate, and man is born. . . .
>
> We call these millions men; but they are not yet men. Half engaged in the soil, pawing to get free, man needs all the music that can be brought to disengage him. If love, red love, with tears and joy, if want with his scourge; if war its cannonade, if Christianity with its charity, if trade with its money, if art with its portfolios, if science with her telegraphs through the deeps of space and time, can set his dull nerves throbbing and by loud taps of the tough chrysalis can break its walls and let the new creature emerge erect and free, make way and sing paean. The age of the quadruped is to go out, the age of the brain and of the heart is to come in. . . . And if one shall read the future of the race hinted in the organic effort of nature to mount and meliorate, and the corresponding impulse to the better in the human being, we shall dare to affirm that there is nothing he will not overcome and con-

vert, until at last culture shall absorb the chaos and gehenna. He will convert the furies into muses, and the hells into benefit.[4]

Evidences of the New Spirit

These changes did not come overnight; nor was the rate of change identical in all colonies. The normal expectation of the early immigrants to this country was, of course, to perpetuate the ways of life they brought with them. Only gradually did differences in soil and climate become manifest in developments as divergent as the plantation aristocracy of the South with its tobacco-cotton-slave economy and the more fluid society of the North which rested by contrast upon trade and commerce, manufacturing, farming, and free labor. In less than a century following the first settlements, differences between American and European society as well as significant contrasts among the colonies themselves had become evident. Important as the latter were to become in subsequent relations among the sections, one trait was common to all: an optimism which expressed itself in developments both novel and revolutionary.

One was the extension of the suffrage and the gradual participation of ever larger numbers in the affairs of government. The first step in this direction was the elimination of the religious test for both voting and the holding of public office. A second was a modification in the property qualification for voting and officeholding. In 1789, only four states permitted nonproperty holders to vote, with the result that less than one fifth of the male population of the original thirteen states was privileged to vote. Then came the admission to the Union of new states, each with liberal provisions for manhood suffrage: Vermont in 1790, Kentucky in 1792, Tennessee in 1796. Ohio, in 1803, required that voters be taxpayers, but abolished this requirement in 1804. By 1840 the battle for manhood suffrage had been won.

Other evidences of the new spirit were prison reform, the gradual humanizing of the criminal code, and agitation on behalf of the freeing of the slaves.

Political and social reform was, of course, an outgrowth of economic developments. Again, with the possible exception of the South (in

4. *The Prose Works of Ralph Waldo Emerson* (Boston: Fields, Osgood and Co., 1870), vol. II, pp. 323, 402.

which the plantation system created new divisions of class as well as caste) birth and family origin tended to lose importance, and individuals were judged more in terms of what they demonstrated themselves to be than in terms of background. This was particularly true of the frontier, where it was not always wise to inquire of the stranger what brought him to his present location! On the frontier, too, work ceased to be a mark of class distinction, something to be avoided, and became more a badge of honor. The employer commonly worked side by side with his employee and took pride in his ability to do more or better than what he asked his helpers to do. The "hired man" or the "hired girl" was not considered a hireling or a member of a subordinate class; rather, he or she was temporarily dependent upon earning the means with which to achieve independence. Accordingly, it was more common than not for the "help" to eat at the same table and to share in the activities of the family in which they occupied more the status of assistants than of servants.

Since the East, with its unquenchable thirst for manpower, was faced constantly with loss of population to the West, these characteristics of an open society soon operated to undermine old ways and to bring about "low visibility" of class lines there as well.

To these characteristics of a dynamic and changing society we should add the influence of science and conditions favorable to empirical methods of thinking, in contrast with those which lean heavily upon authority. Yankee ingenuity and inventiveness were in no way confined to New England, although they flourished there in abundance. As Americans moved west they encountered ever new conditions of soil and climate and people of novel backgrounds and life assumptions. Consequently, they were called upon repeatedly to modify old precepts and principles and customs in order to sow and to reap to advantage and to evolve fruitful ways of living with their fellows. Major premises once accepted as fixed and final became subject to modification in the light of new situations or contexts different from those which once gave them validity. As indicated earlier, these factors of change not only encouraged methods of solving problems other than by an appeal to authority, but tended to generate as well a confidence in the creative power of men's minds and an unwillingness to accept what is as necessarily what must be.

In certain important areas of life there thus occurred a change in both the nature and the location of truth, as men envisaged the truth. No longer was it a proposition or a principle external to men's interests which came to them from tradition and the past. Rather, was it conceived to be a product of man's inventiveness and was oriented in large measure to the future.

This is not to say that tradition and precedent and external truths were wholly discarded and a new logic substituted for the old. More accurately, we should say that this shift was characteristic of only certain areas of experience. For the bulk of individuals, two contradictory schemes of values and methods of thinking came to dwell together in the same person (as for many today), with now one dominant, now the other.

In no place, however, were the potential conflicts between the old and new less well recognized than in school and college. Indeed, by and large, the methods of thinking fostered by the schools tended to lag behind those employed outside the school in business, in politics, and in social relations. Even in the teaching of science emphasis was placed more upon the acquisition of facts than upon scientific methods of inference and discovery.

John Locke: Representative of a Formative Influence

One way in which to appreciate developments in the curriculum and the evolution of educational method in the late eighteenth and the nineteenth centuries is to observe the influence of John Locke's philosophy and psychology upon men's minds. Not only was Locke a founder of modern psychology, but his theory of how the mind operates was designed specifically to provide a theoretical foundation for fundamental changes in society: the substitution of representative government for government based upon the concept of the divine right of kings to rule; toleration in religious thought and the separation of church and state; an education for the young which stressed the importance of direct observation of the world about them and the encouragement of many-sided interests, in contrast with the narrow and exclusively bookish practices of the pedagogues of his day.[5]

5. Locke's *Two Treatises on Government* were written with a view to justifying the revolution which brought William and Mary to the throne of England. Other writings to which the liberal minds of the period turned repeatedly for inspiration and guidance were his *Letters on Toleration, The Conduct of the Understanding, Essay on the Human Understanding,* and, of course, *Thoughts on Education.*

In *Jefferson and His Time,* Dumas Malone tells us of requests which Jefferson, when serving as minister to France, made of his friend Trumbull for the procurement of busts and pictures. High on this list were life-sized busts of Bacon, Newton, and Locke, which he wished copied for him as a picture. His reason was that he regarded these men as "the three greatest men that have ever lived, without any exception, and as having laid the foundations of those superstructures which have been raised in the physical and moral sciences." [6]

Observe that these three men were distinctive, in turn, for the development of an inductive logic, a mathematical and scientific explanation of the operations of the universe, and an empirical explanation of the operations of the mind. They developed ways of thinking, in other words, that were hospitable to an open universe and none too friendly to tradition and custom.

Jefferson and his associates in the American Philosophical Society (which included in its membership the leading minds of the period) doubtless first encountered Locke's ideas as students in the academy. Central in the curriculum of the academy was Isaac Watt's *Improvement of the Mind,* a popular rendition of John Locke's *The Conduct of the Understanding.* For generations this document served as a practical logic for all who passed through the academy. When we reflect that this included the future teachers of America as well as the future statesmen and leaders in the professions and business, it is difficult to overemphasize its influence on the American mind.

What were some of these formative ideas?

The Mind at Birth As a White Sheet of Paper

First was Locke's denial of innate ideas, "some primary notions . . . characters, as it were, stamped upon the mind of men, which the soul receives in its first being, and brings into the world with it." [7]

Locke's purpose was to refute the rationalists in philosophy who assumed that the mind is so constituted that it accepts, without proof or prior experience, the truth of certain logical principles or axioms as well as those practical and moral principles which constitute the foundation of universally accepted moral values. As evidence of his posi-

6. Boston: Little, Brown & Co., 1951, vol. II, p. 211.
7. John Locke, *An Essay Concerning the Human Understanding,* Book I, chap. II, sec. 1.

tion, Locke argued that the recognition and acceptance of "innate ideas" come not at birth but with maturity and experience. He also contended that, far from being universally accepted, moral principles, in particular, vary with time and place, or, as we would say, with cultures.

What Locke denied is the existence of inborn tendencies to think, feel, and act on the basis of beliefs or ideas predetermined and unrelated to the experience of the individual, a concept of human nature of revolutionary significance for a people long accustomed to rigid distinctions of class and now ready to exploit the resources of a new continent.

From whence, then, come the obvious differences in talent and interest which clearly mark off one individual from another? Locke answers,

> From experience. . . . Let us suppose the mind to be, as we say, white paper, void of all characters, without any ideas; how comes it to be furnished? Whence comes it by that vast store which the busy and boundless fancy of man has painted on it with an almost endless variety? Whence has it all the materials of reason and knowledge? To this I answer in one word, from experience; in that all our knowledge is founded, and from that it ultimately derives itself.[8]

Once furnished with simple or unorganized ideas and impressions, the mind has the power to organize them in such a way that they come to picture or represent the external world of objects and events, through the "powers" or "faculties" of perception, memory, imagination, reason, and so on.[9] In other words, to experience in its raw or original form Locke adds the contribution of "ideas of reflection" or the operations of the mind upon simple ideas. Thus, while rejecting the doctrine of innate ideas, Locke carries forward the ancient dichotomy between "reason" and "perception." Raw experience furnishes the materials upon which reason operates; reason has its own faculties or modes of operation. In "bare, naked perception," he wrote, the mind is largely "passive, and what it perceives it cannot avoid perceiving." On the other hand, at a *later* stage, in thinking or reflection, the "mind is active." [10] This doctrine is similar to the present popular belief that the

8. *Ibid.*, Book II, chap. I, sec. 2.
9. *Ibid.*, Book II, chap. I, sec. 5.
10. *Ibid.*, Book II, chap. IX.

young child must first "learn the facts" before he or she can think. Moreover, Locke assumes the existence of a faculty of "volition" or willing, separate and distinct from the general faculty of reason.[11] In this assumption, and in some other statements, Locke seems to have accepted the dichotomy between reason and emotions or attitudes.

All Men Are Essentially Equal

Locke's theories, combined with cultural influences in America, in various ways gave character to American education down to the end of the nineteenth century. Most conspicuous, perhaps, is the encouragement Locke gave to the individual's own experience, in contrast with inheritance, in determining his worth. This view gave to and received support from the concepts of equality native to the frontier where daily experience seemed to confirm the principle that a man should be judged in terms of what he reveals himself to be rather than by what he inherits either in worldly goods or social status from his forebears.

It was this basic assumption, as we have seen, which induced Horace Mann and others to labor on behalf of a system of tax-supported public schools open and free to all. As these educational pioneers saw it, a democratic society can do no less for its children than it does for its adults. What free land and open economic opportunities were for adults, free schools might become for children. Naive as Mann's assertion may seem to the effect that "there is by nature little or perhaps no distinction among men with respect to their original power of intellect," we may question seriously whether the American people would have developed public school systems as we have them today but for an assumption of this character in preference to the notion prevalent in the early part of the twentieth century that each individual is endowed at birth with a fixed quantum of intelligence.

On the other hand, the concept of an essential equality among individuals may also imply that the failure has only himself to blame, and that although the school's doors should be open to all on equal terms, this does not imply that it should attempt to make a silk purse out of a sow's ear. In other words, in this analogy between the school and free land, it also follows that the child should fit himself to the curriculum, not the curriculum to the child! Consequently, just as it has taken time

11. *Ibid.*, Book II, chap. VI, sec. 2.

for the public to hold society as well as the individual responsible for poverty and other social disadvantages which beset men in the complicated world of today, so the school, thanks to an individualistic psychology, has been slow to adapt its program to the varying needs of those who are to benefit from it.

There Is a Typical Mind

Second, Locke's psychology assumed that all minds are essentially alike,[12] an assumption which gave support to the notion that education, both in content and method, can properly be the same for all. Do we need to know how the mind works or how one best learns? Then examine one's own learning experiences. As our parents and teachers dealt with us, and as we responded, so may we conclude the children entrusted to us will respond to our treatment of them. Thus educators derive their ideas of method and the kinds of knowledge most worth while largely from analogy. Since, moreover, teachers have tended to be verbal-minded, it was natural that they should favor the verbally inclined over other types of mind and find them easier to instruct. Likewise, with the advent of intelligence tests—instruments which have consistently been skewed in favor of the verbally intelligent— educators as well as laymen have been prone to infer that the verbally intelligent are over all the more intelligent.

The assumption that minds are essentially alike influenced educational theory and practice until relatively recently. William James once remarked that the significance of individual differences received little recognition in psychology until Fechner's work in 1863. Not until the last decade of the nineteenth century do we find Edward L. Thorndike and other psychologists calling attention to their significance for education.

Mind, as Locke envisaged it, is twofold in its operations. In its original state, as we have seen, it is analogous to a white sheet of paper waiting to be written upon. Once impressions are received from the various senses, however, it proceeds to give order and pattern to them. In this way it comes to reflect, or to know, albeit partially, the outside world.

Here are two characteristics of mind which developed eventually

12. Locke recognized differences in degrees of ability, but the abilities or "powers" which he recognized were few and essentially uniform in kind.

into two contradictory theories of its nature. One group—including Rousseau, Pestalozzi, G. Stanley Hall—transformed Locke's notion of the original powers of the mind into "original tendencies" and inner drives which those responsible for the education of the young are to observe and follow. A second group concentrated upon the essentially passive and receptive nature of the mind and thus envisaged the responsibility of the adult as that of furnishing the growing individual with appropriate information and ideas which are to form his character.

Learning Becomes a Receptive Process

It was this second interpretation of the nature of mind and of learning which largely characterized schooling throughout the nineteenth century, and which is not without influence today. The child's mind was likened to a wax sheet upon which the educator and the textbook are to write what he should know. Again, the child's mind was likened to a cabinet full of pigeonholes in which one files bits of information which reside there until needed. Consequently, schooling was neither expected nor required to concern itself with what immediately appeals. Its values were oriented toward later life. The significance of schooling and what one learns in school were to be taken largely on faith.

There was much in the cultural setting in the early days of the Republic to give support to this conception of education. The advent of manhood suffrage had drawn attention to the importance of acquainting young people with the nature and operations of our political institutions and, as the guardians of the status quo saw it, with the principles of both private and public morality without which a stable society cannot endure.[13]

Moreover, the purposes which prompted parents to send their children to school, as, indeed, the motives of young people themselves in subjecting themselves to education, gave weight to a conception of learning as basically a receptive process. The school was envisaged as a means for bettering one's station in life. This gave to learning the appearance of an instrument for purposes practical and ornamental and to culture an external aspect. It was something one might acquire more or less as he buys a new suit of clothes with which to improve his ap-

13. See Richard D. Mosier, *The Making of the American Mind* (New York: King's Crown Press, Columbia University, 1947), chaps. II, III, IV.

pearance and to gain status, rather than the cultivation of interests and talents genuinely one's own. For a time, indeed, it was considered a sign of weakness or inefficiency in a teacher were he to gear instruction to the interests of his students. Effort for the sake of effort was considered valuable since it developed persistence, a valuable asset in life.

This schoolmaster's attitude is well expressed in Dr. Alexander Hill's defense of the classics, recorded in John Adams' *Modern Developments in Educational Practice.* The worthy doctor valued the classics, as he evidently taught them, for the discipline they provide "of working at a subject which offers in itself no temptation to work." From the schoolboy's point of view, the "only motive for learning his lesson is that his master tells him to do so." And this, concludes Dr. Hill, "should always be sufficient." [14]

Basic to Locke's psychology was the distinction between mind and body. The sense organs are physical and are stimulated by physical events, but the ideas conveyed by them to the mind are nonmaterial impressions or pictures of the real world outside.

This gives crucial importance to the sense organs since, in the first instance, it is they and they alone which enable us to know the outside world. Decrease their number or impair any one of them, and the nature of reality as we know it undergoes change.

Keep the Channels of Inquiry Open

This carries with it profound implications. For example, in his *Conduct of the Understanding,* Locke, in concerning himself with ways in which men fail to reason correctly, mentions among other things "the want of having that which we may call large, roundabout sense" or "a full view of all that relates to the question, and may be of moment to decide it." In this, he continues, the angels have a permanent advantage over man, being endowed "in their several degrees of elevation above us" with "more comprehensive faculties; and some of them perhaps, having perfect and exact views of all finite beings that come under their consideration can as it were in a twinkling of an eye, collect all their scattered and almost boundless relations; a mind so furnished, what reason has it to acquiesce in the certainty of its conclusions!"

14. John Adams, *Modern Developments in Educational Practice* (London: University of London Press, 1922), p. 209. (Published in the United States by Harcourt, Brace & World, Inc.)

But man is mortal and his senses necessarily limited, a fact that carries a moral quite different from the dogmatic and authoritarian spirit Locke undertook to undermine. In religion, it favored the point of view that each individual and each sect sees through the glass but darkly, and although each may have found rays of valuable insight, other individuals and other sects may also have contributions to make toward a larger and more comprehensive vision of the truth. From this it follows that he who genuinely seeks the kingdom of heaven will encourage freedom of religious belief and the right—nay, the obligation—to subject all views to critical inspection. This is similarly true in areas other than religion. No longer was it wise to identify the well-being of the state with orthodoxy, be it political, economic, social, or what not.

We are not saying that it was Locke's philosophy alone which brought about this change in intellectual orientation. Nor are we suggesting that the climate of opinion veered immediately or conclusively from one direction to its opposite. One has only to look about him today to realize that the old habits still persist. What we are saying is that in Locke liberals found a philosophical and psychological justification for freedom of thought and expression, which, in conjunction with other trends of the period, enabled them, eventually, to incorporate the principle of freedom of thought and expression in the constitutions of both state and national governments. Here also were sound reasons to justify the intellectual's pursuit of a "round-about-knowledge" in contrast with narrow specialization—as evidenced in Benjamin Franklin, Thomas Jefferson, and other members of the American Philosophical Society—and the support of studies in physics, mechanics, astronomy, mathematics, and so on, together with the implications of these studies for the development of the natural resources of the country.

New Life Values and the Curriculum

Not even the schoolmaster could withstand completely the intellectual trends of the time or the determination of the people to use education for practical as well as theoretical ends. As a result, by the end of the eighteenth century the primary and elementary school, as well as secondary school and college, had taken steps to liberalize the curriculum. In the former, arithmetic shortly edged out religion as the third R (although readers with heavy emphasis upon morality and the virtuous life continued to provide a generous substitute for the earlier emphasis upon items of creed). In quick succession came the addition of history, civics, and geography, together with the subdivision of reading into grammar, word analysis, spelling, oratory, and so on. By the end of the nineteenth century, the typical elementary school pupil found himself occupied with some ten or more subjects: reading, writing, spelling, arithmetic, geography, history, nature study, physiology or hygiene, music, and drawing.[15]

Benjamin Franklin's announcement of his plan for the Philadelphia Academy, published as early as 1749, expresses very well the new conception of education that was to characterize both the academy and its eventual successor, the public high school, for decades to come. Concerning the studies he would offer, Franklin said, "it would be well if they could be taught everything that is useful, and everything that is ornamental," but since "art is long and their time short . . . it is therefore proposed that they learn those things that are likely to be most useful and most ornamental; regard being had for the several professions for which they are intended."

How varied were the offerings that eventually found their way into the academies of the country may be inferred from the fact that, in 1837, the academies of the state of New York reported some seventy-five or more subjects as included in their curricula.[16]

Nor did this picture change materially as the public high school, roughly from 1830 on, came to replace the academy. Indeed, the difference between the academy and the high school, until well after 1900, was essentially that of control and sources of support rather than curriculum. What an individual school decided to teach was a matter of local self-determination. College admission requirements, at this stage, were of little concern to the secondary school educator.[17]

15. Ralph W. Tyler, "The Curriculum—Then and Now," *The Elementary School Journal*, April 1957, pp. 364–74.

16. See Alexander Inglis, *Principles of Secondary Education* (Boston: Houghton Mifflin Co., 1918), p. 180.

17. Up to the year 1800, Latin, Greek, and arithmetic were the only subjects required for admission to the leading American colleges. Between 1800 and the outbreak of the Civil War, five new subjects were commonly added: geography, English grammar, algebra, geometry, ancient history. As Elmer Ellsworth Brown tells us in his pioneer work on *The Making of Our Middle Schools*, the disposition of the secondary schools for a considerable period was to add subjects to their programs "at their own sweet will." (New York: Longmans, Green & Co., Inc., 1914), pp. 232–33.

This setup worked well enough, until the college preparatory function of the academy and the high school began to assume importance.
By 1890, however, the lack of uniformity in school programs had become a serious problem for administrators of school and college alike.
Some agreement seemed essential in order to determine which subjects
or phases of subjects were appropriate for treatment on the college
level and which for secondary school; and, with respect to the latter,
some principle or principles of organization had to be established if
order were to be brought out of chaos.

No one was more insistent upon drawing the attention of the profession and the lay public to this problem than Charles W. Eliot, President of Harvard University. In an address before the Massachusetts
Teachers Association in November 1890, President Eliot asserted that
it was literally impossible to determine what work was being done
in the secondary schools of the United States.[18] Indeed, he went on to
say, it was equally impossible to answer the same question with respect
to the state of Massachusetts, or even a municipality, such as Boston, so
great were the differences among schools. In rural areas also "an ex-
traordinary variety of conditions and results" might be found.

This condition resulted, according to Eliot, from a number of causes:
(1) the absence of an "elaborate system of national or State superin-
tendence, and no permanent bodies of experienced inspectors";
(2) local control and administration of education, each municipality
or town conducting its affairs, with little cooperation or coordination
among communities; (3) the nonexistence of any accepted standards
for schools to follow.

This situation prompted the educators of the country to organize a
number of national committees charged with the responsibility of
bringing order out of confusion: the Committee of Ten on Secondary
School Studies, 1891; the Committee of Fifteen on Elementary Schools,
1893; the Committee on College Entrance Requirements, 1895. From
the work of these committees a remarkable degree of agreement resulted on such matters as the appropriate subjects to be taught, the
order of their appearance in the curriculum, and the length of time
each should be pursued. Out of the three committees concerned with

18. *Educational Reform, Essays and Addresses* (New York: The Century Company, 1898), pp. 179–94.

secondary school and college there also eventually evolved standardizing agencies whose influence still continues.

In most modern texts, the reports of these committees are usually labeled as conservative in their orientation. To a large extent, they were. With some reservations in the case of the committee on elementary schools, the committees generally assumed that the major task of curriculum planning was to organize subject matter into logical sequences, that time spent in class was one adequate measure of learning, and that the contribution of a subject to "mental discipline" should be one criterion for judging the value of the subject. Yet, as Wiggin writes, referring to the committees on the secondary school and on college entrance requirements, "he who would be misled by the Latin, Greek, mathematics, and history with which both committees dealt would be missing the direction of secondary education which was being reinforced by both committees." [19]

The development being reinforced, whether for good or ill, was the twentieth-century American pattern of secondary education. Even in laying the groundwork for the "standard unit" for purposes of college admission—a time-based measure of learning which helped create undue stress on separate subjects and a specious equivalency of courses —these two committees promoted the "constants plus electives" system in the differentiated curriculum of the comprehensive high school. They promoted the concept and the realization of a broad general education for all secondary students, and they encouraged the delayed choice of career which has been built into the common ladder system and which sharply distinguishes American practice from European practice.[20]

Classroom Method Takes On New Form

Thus far we have centered upon curriculum developments which had their origin in the liberalizing influences of the nineteenth century. The educational picture would not be complete were we to omit developments in classroom method in this same period.

19. Gladys A. Wiggin, *Education and Nationalism* (New York: McGraw-Hill Book Co., Inc., 1962), p. 178.
20. See, for example, "Report of the Committee on College-Entrance Requirements," *Journal of Proceedings and Addresses, Thirty-eighth Annual Meeting of the National Education Association*, 1899, pp. 632–68.

At no time in their history have American schools been blessed with an adequate supply of professionally trained teachers. In the early days (a situation to which we seem to have returned in recent years!), teachers were largely transients in the profession. They were young people who were using teaching as a means of accumulating resources with which to pursue a more desirable career, individuals who were on the verge of retirement, or those who were none too successful in other lines of work who had turned to teaching as one way of recouping their fortunes. Few, in consequence, would claim to know more than the textbook or presume to teach without its assistance.

In addition, teachers who are transients in the profession do not contribute to a stable teaching staff. Consequently, American schools have been faced from the beginning with a heavy turnover in teaching personnel. To this we must add the fact of rapid growth in both rural and city population, with cities springing up overnight and rural schools expanding rapidly into city school systems. Under these conditions it was natural for textbook writers to prepare their books with an eye to offsetting or supplementing the deficiencies in the knowledge of both the teacher and the pupil and for supervisors and administrators (once these officials came into existence) to see in the text an instrument for insuring some degree of continuity in the pupil's education.

Developments in educational theory and their reflection in practice contributed to the same end. The advocates of the Pestalozzian method, for example, felt constrained to prepare manuals and texts which would indicate how specific subject matter was to be taught under the new method. As object teaching developed, books were written which indicated in detail procedures for teacher and pupil to follow. The Herbartian theory, which came into prominence near the end of the last century, likewise called for revolutionary changes in content and method. Readers, geographies, arithmetics, and other texts were carefully written so that a teacher, without too clear an understanding of the five steps of Herbartian procedure, might nevertheless teach in a fairly acceptable manner.

To make the contents of the textbook the be-all and the end-all of instruction is, of course, to substitute uncritical acceptance of what is read for what might otherwise become food for thought. And who will say that this has not characterized much of the teaching and learning in the schools? Taken together with the wax-tablet concept of the mind and the cultural influences to which we have drawn attention above—all favorable to the notion that teaching exists for the purpose of instilling in the minds of the young the information, the principles, and the ideals deemed important by adults—we can understand how Locke's psychology was transformed into one encouraging education for conformity.[21]

From Individual to Class Instruction

Prior to 1800, instruction in both elementary and secondary schools was mostly individual. The master's chief occupation seems to have been whittling goose quills, and although school legislation usually required pupils at twelve or thirteen years of age to whittle their own pens, we are told that, like many laws of today, these regulations were seldom enforced. The results were wasteful of time for both master and pupil. Not only was the former unable to give attention to the latter's study habits, but the practice of calling pupils to the master's desk to recite individually severely limited the amount and the character of attention available for each individual.

This system persisted much longer than is generally supposed. As late as 1855, Grimshaw, writing in *Barnard's Journal*, deplored the waste of time resulting from "the old-fashioned and false" method of individual instruction.[22]

The invention of steel pens and blackboards enabled resourceful teachers to take the first steps toward group instruction, the former by freeing the teacher from his traditional task of whittling pens and the latter by making it possible for the master to gather together pupils who were at the same point in their progress in order to clear up common difficulties or to present new material. Henry Barnard has recorded his surprise upon viewing a blackboard for the first time. It was the winter of 1813–1814. While still a student at Harvard, Barnard visited a Boston school and there saw a group of pupils gathered about a blackboard undergoing what he described as "analytical and inductive teaching."

Considerable credit must be given to Joseph Lancaster and his fel-

---

21. In this connection, see Mark M. Krug, " 'Safe' Textbooks and Citizenship Education," *School Review*, Winter 1960, pp. 463–80.
22. S. C. Parker, *History of Elementary Education* (Boston: Ginn & Company, 1912), p. 88.

low monitorians for developing in minute detail the methods of group instruction. Under his direction, pupils were organized into small groups, usually of ten, with an older pupil in charge of each group. Thus supervised, the children were marched to and from class in military fashion. They recited in unison in answer to questions posed and responded as one to instructions such as "hats off!" "show slates!" and so on.

David Solomon, in his *Joseph Lancaster,* describes Lancaster's method of saving time in the taking of attendance.[23] Each pupil was assigned a fixed number. Corresponding numbers were written in a row on the wall. To determine absences it was necessary only for the class to take positions, each pupil under his own number.

Steps in learning were organized in similar detail. For example, the monitor's manual in arithmetic consisted of examples and a key which revealed not merely the complete solution of the problem but the steps by means of which the answer was to be obtained. If the question were one of simple addition, the monitor would find instructions of this character: "First column 7 and 9 are 16, and 3 are 19, and 5 are 24. Set down 4 under 7 and carry 2 to the next column"; after reading this instruction the monitor would so instruct the class.[24] Evidently by repetition rather than from explanation proficiency was expected to result.

Crude and mechanical as was this method of instruction, with its tendency to confuse overt performance and memorization with genuine learning, its results were startling when compared with individual instruction. David Solomon records an incident of a worried father who was impelled to call upon his pastor to stop the practices of the monitorial school attended by his son for the reason that the master must be engaged in magic. How else might one account for his son's making such rapid progress in mastering arithmetic!

Not only are we indebted to the monitorial system for many of the practices still employed in group instruction, but it must also be credited with rendering feasible the idea of free public schools manned by professionally trained teachers, since the cost of group instruction by any other method would have seemed impossible, if not fantastic, in its drain upon the taxpayer. For example, in Philadelphia, in 1819,

23. David Solomon, *Joseph Lancaster* (New York: Longmans, Green & Co., Inc., 1904), p. 9.
24. *Ibid.,* p. 12.

there were ten monitorial schools, each with one teacher in charge and an average of 284 pupils per teacher. As late as 1834, in the same city, the average number of pupils per teacher was 218.

To be sure, the followers of Pestalozzian methods likewise contributed to the art of group instruction, but an analysis of these contributions as well as those of Herbart and Froebel would reveal numerous items of indebtedness to the monitorians.

Take, for example, Pestalozzian methods which, in theory, start from quite different premises, the theory that learning should begin with the actual experiences of children and proceed by carefully graded oral instruction to systematic and organized knowledge. Children's experiences were thus to replace exclusive dependence upon books and the teacher's direction of learning activity was to replace the passive method of hearing lessons.

These ideas brought profound changes in elementary courses of study. Arithmetic was reorganized on the basis of object teaching so that pupils passed gradually from the observation of sensible objects to an understanding and manipulation of abstract numbers. "Mental arithmetic" assumed a prominent place in schoolwork. Object teaching likewise led to oral instruction with heavy emphasis upon oral language training. Geographies of a "dictionary-encyclopedia" type were replaced by home geography; and natural science as an outgrowth both of object teaching and oral language received recognition.

When we turn, however, to the methods of teaching into which Pestalozzian procedures quickly crystallized, we encounter a dismal formalism. It is said that a French-Swiss officer once remarked to Pestalozzi, when the latter was explaining his methods, "I see, you want to mechanize instruction." Whether or not Pestalozzi believed his psychological procedure was identical with mechanical routine there is no doubt that his followers, at least, succeeded in mechanizing instruction. And they mechanized it in the direction of formal group work, which, in the hands of the average teacher, became deadly routine. Parker states of oral instruction that a proper method of questioning became the sole requisite and a teacher's knowledge unimportant. Frequently, a teacher "simply questioned the children about their experience and told them nothing." [25]

In their bright promises and their ambiguous results these early

25. Parker, *op. cit.*, p. 329.

efforts to cope with an increased influx of pupils into the schools were not unlike some current efforts to reorganize instructional procedures and raise the level of technology in education.[26] In Chapter 12, we shall examine the new technology and the "new designs for learning" —educational television, teaching machines and programed instruction, flexible organization of pupils and teachers for instructional purposes, and others.

The Herbartians Professionalize Instruction

Important as Pestalozzi's influence was upon classroom teaching, it is probably to the Herbartians that chief credit should be given for professionalizing teaching procedure. By 1890, as we have seen, a number of factors had combined making it imperative to create order out of the chaos which characterized both the curriculum and the administrative structure of the schools. Conspicuous among the leaders in education who devoted themselves to this task was G. Stanley Hall. Others who were to exercise a determining influence for some decades to come were Charles DeGarmo, Frank and Charles McMurry, William C. Bagley, and John Dewey. A number of these men had studied in Germany and had become ardent disciples of Johann Herbart. All were profoundly impressed with the latter's theories even when, as with John Dewey, they constituted a foil for their own thinking. In 1892 they joined with others in forming the National Herbart Society, which, under the name of the National Society for the Study of Education, still functions as one of the leading educational organizations in the United States devoted to the scientific study of education.

Herbart was in agreement with Locke's emphasis on the importance of experience in the formation of the mind. He went even farther in that he denied the existence of the mind as a substance or as an entity which receives impressions (except as a logical entity used to explain the fact that the first impressions are responded to either by attraction, repulsion, or indifference). Sensations thus received respond in one of these three ways to subsequent impressions and thus, purely through

26. William Clark Trow, *Teacher and Technology: New Designs for Learning* (New York: Appleton-Century-Crofts, 1963), chaps. 4–5.

association, a self is created. What men speak of as the mind is nothing other than the ordering and the organization of the experiences one has encountered since birth. In this view, Dewey commented, "the 'furniture' of the mind is the mind." [27]

Obviously, this conception of the mind carries to an extreme Locke's assumption of the nature of experience and contradicts the notion of an inner nature or an original contribution on the part of the individual in giving character and quality to his experience. What one becomes or makes of himself is manifestly the result of the ideas or experiences presented to him and the method (the laws of association) employed in their presentation.

The effects of the Herbartian movement upon education were twofold: (1) to direct attention to the appropriate content of study and (2) to standardize methods of instruction. Had the pedagogues of the period applied the doctrines of Herbart to children in the *concrete* rather than to children in *general,* they would doubtless have been impressed with the significance of individual differences in backgrounds and interests and the consequent necessity of organized instruction in harmony with these facts. This possibility, however, was not grasped for some time. Rather the importance of the teacher's activity was accentuated and the "method of the recitation" used to mold the performances of children in groups, in accordance with the laws of thought.

Out of these efforts came the Herbartian "steps" in teaching and learning. These "steps" or stages influenced the ordering and the presentation of materials in textbooks and the details of procedure within the classroom. The "Inductive Lesson" as developed by Professor Bagley will serve as one example.[28] This included five steps: (1) preparation, which called for questions and answers and was to consume no more than one fifth of the period; (2) presentation, in which the pupil was to acquire the facts from textbooks, lecture, or other means; (3) comparison and abstraction, which called for the question-and-answer method again, the time varying depending upon whether one or more generalizations were sought; (4) generalization, which consisted in the summing up in a class definition the results of previous labor and which was to consume no more than three or four minutes;

27. John Dewey, *Democracy and Education* (New York: The Macmillan Co., 1916), pp. 81–84.

28. William C. Bagley, *The Educative Process* (New York: The Macmillan Co., 1907), chap. XIX.

and, finally, (5) application, either direct or indirect, which might be elastic in method as well as in the time involved.

Beginning in about 1890, the Herbartian influence tended to dominate theory and practice in the normal schools and teacher training institutions of the United States. Despite the fact that it led in many ways to an enrichment of the curriculum, through its emphasis upon history, literature, and the arts, and brought into prominence the concept of interests as central in education, its basic assumption of education as an activity to be controlled and directed from outside the learner resulted inevitably in what came to be called "lockstep methods" of teaching.

It would seem, then, that education in the period under review moved out of one type of formalism, through an intervening period of liberalism and expansion, only to end in another period of formalism. Under the influence of an expanding economy and the evolution of new political and social institutions, together with a philosophy of rugged individualism, schools on all levels came to serve a multitude of interests and purposes. These developments were reflected in an increase in the number of subjects taught in both elementary and secondary schools as well as in a broadening of the curriculum and the purposes of the college. Moreover, just as the classical grammar school gave way to the academy, so the academy, as a private institution, in the nineteenth century began to give ground to the public high school, a reflection of public recognition of the increasing importance of education. Following the Civil War compulsory school attendance gradually replaced voluntary attendance on the elementary school level; and the number of graduates from secondary schools, particularly in the latter part of the century, increased substantially. Indeed, in the 1890s the number was sufficient to create demands for uniformity and standardization of the curriculum of the secondary schools and to promote common agreements between colleges and secondary schools on conditions of admission to college.

These new demands for a reorganization of education, together with efforts to bring about standardization, resulted from the marriage of new psychologies of learning with emerging factors in American society. These factors of change will be discussed in the chapter to follow.

Suggested Reading

Brauner, Charles J., *American Educational Theory* (Englewood Cliffs, N.J.: Prentice-Hall, Inc., 1964), chaps. 2, 4.

Commager, Henry Steele, *The American Mind* (New Haven: Yale University Press, 1952), chaps. I–IV.

Meyer, Adolphe E., *An Educational History of the Western World* (New York: McGraw-Hill Book Co., 1965), chap. 26.

Nash, Paul, Andreas M. Kazamias, and Henry J. Perkinson, eds., *The Educated Man: Studies in the History of Educational Thought* (New York: John Wiley and Sons, Inc., 1965), chap. 8.

Price, Kingsley, *Education and Philosophical Thought* (Boston: Allyn and Bacon, Inc., 1962), chap. VI.

Thut, I. N., *The Story of Education* (New York: McGraw-Hill Book Co., 1957), chaps. 14–15.

Wiggin, Gladys A., *Education and Nationalism* (New York: McGraw-Hill Book Co., Inc., 1962), pp. 153–81.

Chapter 8

Inner Development as a Criterion for Education

Rousseau and the Doctrine of the Original Goodness of Man

As we have seen, the Lockian conception of the mind dominated educational thinking during the period of the conquest of the continent. According to Locke, all knowledge begins with sense impressions and all of the content of mental life is traceable, ultimately, to those objects of sense outside the organism which instigate mental activity. If one ignores what Locke termed ideas of reflection—the power of the mind to work over the original impressions of sense, to combine them in diverse ways, and thus to create objects of imagination as well as to draw inferences from them respecting matters that have no counterpart in the real world—it is easy to credit the nature of an individual's personality primarily to environmental influences. This some successors of Locke proceeded to do, notably Helvetius and his colleagues in France and, somewhat later, the extreme Herbartians in this country and abroad. By the end of the nineteenth century, in the hands of the latter, the concept of education as essentially a formative process had not only assumed prominence as a theory but had found expression in the details of the curriculum, in methods of teaching, and in the administrative structure of the school.

Beginning roughly with Rousseau, however, a different conception of original nature found expression which was to provide new criteria for educative materials and methods. This conception placed the beginnings of education squarely within the nature of the child, making of his nature and his needs the basic considerations in the educative process. Here, once again, we have a matching or mutal reinforcement of psychological theory and cultural factors.

Attention was drawn in the preceding chapter to the new confidence in man and his inner nature which developed in this country during the first half of the nineteenth century. It was also suggested that the supreme confidence in the individual, the affirmation of the integrity and worth of personality, which prompted Emerson to make the following assertion, found little concrete application within the actual practices of the schools: "No law can be sacred to me but that of my nature. Good and bad are but names very readily transferable to that or this; the only right is what is after my constitution, the only wrong is what is against it." [1] Much the same can be said of England and the continent. Contrast, for example, the schoolmaster's concept of child nature as pictured by Charles Dickens with that of William Wordsworth in his ode, *Intimations of Immortality*.

> Not in entire forgetfulness,
> And not in utter nakedness,
> But trailing clouds of glory do we come
> From God, who is our home.
> Heaven lies about us in our infancy!
> Shades of the prison house begin to close
> Upon the growing Boy.
> But he beholds the light, and whence it flows;
> The Youth who daily farther from the east
> Must travel, still is Nature's
> Priest;
> And by the vision splendid
> Is on his way attended;
> At length the Man perceives it die away,
> And fade into the light of common day.

Nevertheless, as early as 1762, in his *Emile*, Rousseau had outlined a program of education keyed to the developing nature of the child,

1. *The Prose Works of Ralph Waldo Emerson, Essay on Self-Reliance* (Boston: Fields, Osgood and Company, 1870), p. 244.

which, once the situation was ripe, was to influence profoundly both the practice and the science of education.

We will glance briefly at some of his germinal ideas.

In contrast with the notion that children are born in sin and thus are originally corrupt in nature, Rousseau boldly proclaims the original goodness of man. Thus the opening words of the *Emile:* "God makes all things good; man meddles with them and they become evil."

It follows that the native impulses and desires of the child, rather than the demands of society, should constitute the criteria to observe in planning his education. The child, like the man, is an end in himself. That is to say, man is too noble a being to serve as a mere instrument of others. Consequently, in planning the future of the young person it should be borne in mind that "men are not made for their stations but their stations for men." [2]

This approach implies both a respect and a reverence for child nature and, in consequence, a revolutionary approach to education. Educators became concerned not with preconceived subject matter or preordained ground to be covered, but with the selection and adaptation of learning experiences in harmony with the evolving characteristics of children. "Thus are we taught by three masters. If their teaching conflicts, the scholar is ill-educated and will never be at peace with himself; if their teaching agrees, he goes straight to his goal, he lives at peace with himself, he is well educated. . . . What is this goal? As we have shown, it is the goal of nature. Since all three modes of education must work together, the two that we can control must follow the lead of that which is beyond our control." [3]

This principle of adapting educational materials and methods to child nature accounts for the program which Rousseau outlined for the education of his Emile. Since the child's first impulses and desires are sensuous and relate to his physical well-being, his early training should concentrate upon the physical. To substitute books for sense experience "does not teach us to reason, it teaches us to use the reason of others rather than our own; it teaches us to believe much and to know little." [4]

2. For an excellent summary of Rousseau's thought, see Kingsley Price, *Education and Philosophical Thought* (Boston: Allyn and Bacon, 1962), chap. VII.
3. Jean Jacques Rousseau, *Emile* (New York: Everyman's Library, E. P. Dutton & Co., Inc., 1925), p. 6.
4. *Ibid.*, Book II, p. 90.

Until the age of twelve, then, Rousseau would have Emile's education confined primarily to physical activity and the manifold active relations with his sensible environment. Similarly with other stages in his development. His intellectual education (in the sense of coping with abstract ideas and principles) should not begin until he is from twelve to fifteen, and from fifteen to twenty he should receive his moral and social training. By this time, it is assumed, the senses and the brain have developed to the point where it is appropriate and necessary to temper the heart. "Man's proper study is that of his relation to his environment. So long as he knows that environment through his physical nature, he should study himself in relation to things; this is the business of his childhood; when he begins to be aware of his moral nature, he should study himself in relation to his fellowmen; this is the business of his whole life, and we have now reached the time when that study should begin." [5]

It is interesting to observe that although Rousseau would organize education in accordance with stages of development common to children *in general*, he nevertheless repudiated Locke's concept of a typical mind, thus anticipating the modern educator's concern for individual differences by more than a century. Each mind, he insisted, has a form of its own which carries a moral for the teacher's efforts, if he would be successful.

Perhaps, however, his idea of an education appropriate for members of the female sex was less progressive! Since women, in his view, are not like men in character or temperament their education should be different, and, since men are the stronger the education of the girl should prepare her for a role subordinate to man. [6]

To Rousseau must be given credit (some would insist blame!) for formulating in suggestive terms a concept of education in striking contrast with that prevalent in his day. Children, according to his theory, were no longer to be viewed as adults in miniature. Their minds are unique and peculiar to them, and their development proceeds in stages which manifest themselves in a serial and predetermined order.

From today's vantage point, Rousseau's insight into child nature may seem naive. In appraising its importance, however, we should distin-

5. *Ibid.*, Book IV, p. 175.
6. See *Emile, ibid.*, Book V, pp. 321 ff. for a detailed outline of the education of Sophie, Emile's future wife.

guish between the specific applications of his doctrines, as he made them, and their later influence upon the history of education.

His basic principle was that nature is right, and, in consequence, the wise parent and teacher will follow its lead. Two conclusions from this premise have exercised a determining influence upon education: (1) that the child's spontaneous and natural interests and impulses are essential ingredients in his education; (2) that the child and the adolescent, in the course of their progress toward maturity, pass through identifiable stages, each with characteristics of its own, which must be given opportunities for expression if development is to be healthy.

This concept of child development and its translation into educational procedures may be divided into two phases, one which antedated developments in biology and the doctrine of evolution, the other biological and evolutionary.

Preevolutionary Conceptions of Inner Nature and Education

Both Pestalozzi and Froebel are representative of the first phase.

Pestalozzi, for example, pictured the child's nature after the analogy of the seed of a tree, on the assumption that within the seed the mature tree exists in miniature.

> Sound education stands before me symbolized by a tree planted near fertilizing waters. A little seed, which contains the design of the tree, its form, and its properties, is placed in the soil. The whole tree is an uninterrupted chain of organic parts, the plan of which existed in its seed and root. Man is similar to the tree. In the new-born child are hidden those faculties which are to unfold during life. The individual and separate organs of his being form themselves gradually into unison, and build up humanity in the image of God. The education of men is a purely moral result. It is not the educator who puts new powers and faculties into man, and imparts to him breath and life. He only takes care that no untoward influence shall disturb nature's march of development. The moral, intellectual, and practical powers of man must be nurtured within himself and not from artificial substitutes. Thus, faith must be cultivated by our own act of be-

lieving, not by reasoning about faith; love, by our own act of loving, not by fine words about love; thought, by our own act of
thinking, not by merely appropriating the thoughts of other men;
and knowledge, by our own investigation, not by endless talk
about the results of art and science.[7]

In practice, Pestalozzi's theory of education found expression in object teaching, an effort to educate the child in the first instance through
the senses, since these develop and require discipline prior to other faculties, such as memory, imagination, reason. In practice, contradictory
results followed from Pestalozzi's efforts. On the one hand, the emphasis upon the child's first-hand observations led not only to fundamental
changes in the organization of subject matter and the content of learning experiences, but to carefully graded lessons as well. As a result, the
curriculum of the elementary school was enriched by the addition of
materials in science, geography, arithmetic, oral language, and other
areas. On the other hand, Pestalozzi's concept of general faculties of
the mind which evolve in a serial order, but are assisted in so doing by
the stimulation of outside material, lent itself to a concept of formal
discipline (the notion that once the faculties of memory, reason, and so
on, are trained and disciplined by one sort of material they will function efficiently in any situation calling for their exercise). This was, of
course, grist for the mill of the traditionalist who might then justify the
teaching of his subject by virtue of its disciplinary value, when hard
pressed to demonstrate its relevance on any other basis.

Similarly, in the realm of method Pestalozzian emphasis upon object
teaching and the art of questioning associated with it was twofold in its
educational effects. It opened the door of the classroom to the outside
world of objects and events, but, in the course of time, it also degen-
erated into a barren verbalism, a trend fostered rather than retarded by
the publication and distribution of "Pestalozzian methods" with detailed instructions for teachers to follow. Take, for example, the following language lesson conducted by Pestalozzi himself and reported by
one of his students. The lesson was intended to develop ideas by means
of gradually enlarged sentences.

7. Quoted from Paul Monroe, *A Text Book in the History of Education* (New
York: The Macmillan Co., 1905), pp. 611–12. By permission of The Macmillan
Company.

Thus he would ask: "Boys, what do you see?"
(He never addressed the girls.)
Answer: "A hole in the paper."
Pestalozzi: "Very well, say after me:
"I see a hole in the paper.
"I see a long hole in the paper.
"Through the hole I see the wall.
"Through the long, narrow hole I see the wall.
"I see figures on the paper.
"I see black figures on the paper.
"I see round black figures on the paper.
"I see a square yellow figure on the paper.
"By the side of the square yellow figure I see a round black one.
"The square figure is joined to the round figure by a large black stripe, etc." [8]

Pestalozzi's major influence upon American education probably dates from the publication of Warren Colburn's *First Lessons in Arithmetic on the Plan of Pestalozzi,* published in Boston in 1821. This was followed by descriptions in American periodicals of European practices. Henry Barnard, for example, used his *American Journal* and the Connecticut *Common School Journal* (1838–1842) toward this end. Most potent, however, was the influence of Oswego, New York, during the superintendency of Edward A. Sheldon. Under the latter's direction, Pestalozzian methods were not only introduced into the Oswego schools, but, through his efforts, they were widely publicized. In 1866, the Oswego training school was established, to be followed by others throughout the country, all devoted to the spread of the new gospel.[9]

Froebel and the Kindergarten Influence

A second conspicuous illustration of the doctrine of inner development is that of Froebel and the kindergarten movement. Although a few kindergartens were established in this country between 1850 and 1875,

8. Quoted in Samuel Chester Parker, *A Textbook in the History of Modern Elementary Education* (Boston: Ginn & Company, 1912), p. 326.
9. For a comprehensive description of Pestalozzian theory and practice in this country and Europe, one can do no better than to read Samuel Chester Parker's account in *A Textbook in the History of Modern Elementary Education* (Boston: Ginn & Company, 1912), chaps. XIII–XVI.

the movement did not assume significant proportions until about 1875.[10]

Froebel, like Pestalozzi, believed that each child contains within himself the germs of his future possibilities and, therefore, that a major purpose of education is to adapt instruction to the laws of development. Froebel, moreover, conceived of child nature as the offshoot of the divine nature which unfolds according to the laws of self-activity but which, at the same time, is dependent upon the quickening influence of outer conditions for adequate expression. Hence the mission of the school as a kindergarten. Education, when truly conceived, consists in no more than the proper relating of the inner and the outer, with the latter subordinate to the former. When given adequate outlet for its divine energy and appropriate materials with which to concern itself, the child's inner nature will develop in a healthy manner. When it is thwarted, stunted growth and perversion will follow.

It thus follows that for Froebel educative materials and activities serve a divine purpose. As described in his *The Education of Man*, "Education consists in leading man, as a thinking, intelligent being, growing into self-consciousness, to a pure and unsullied, conscious and free representation of the inner law of Divine Unity and in teaching him ways and means thereto." [11]

This involved for Froebel differing emphases and different activities at different stages in the child's development, but with one common purpose throughout: to relate the individual to the whole. In practical terms, this consisted in engaging cooperatively in the activities of the social environment. In childhood, this was accomplished quite largely through play in which phases of domestic life were imitated; in boyhood, by participating in the work of the home, as well as sharing vicariously in racial experiences through story and song. It was assumed that through this process of sharing, actually and vicariously, the spiritual truths which objects and activities and stories symbolize would emerge in the consciousness of the child.

Although Froebel outlined an educational program which should extend beyond the first years of childhood, it is with the kindergarten

10. For an interesting description of Elizabeth Peabody's pioneer efforts in the establishment of kindergarten education in this country, see Louise Hall Tharp, *The Peabody Sisters of Salem* (Boston: Little, Brown & Co., 1950), chap. 25.

11. Friedrich Froebel, *The Education of Man*, Hailmann translation (New York: D. Appleton and Company, 1897), p. 2.

that his name is most commonly associated. His germinal ideas, however, were of far-reaching importance.

In the first place, he envisaged each child as a sacred personality, a replica of the Infinite Spirit. This inspires reverence for child nature as such. Childhood and youth, as unique stages in development toward maturity, are thus possessed of laws and characteristics uniquely their own, which must be known and followed by those responsible for child rearing in a manner analogous to that of a skillful gardener who tends his plants with an ever watchful eye upon the inner conditions of healthy growth. In the best sense of the term, education is thus to be child centered.

Second, the conditions requisite for healthy development constitute a regimen or a discipline binding equally upon guardian and child. Discipline is thus taken out of the category of mere external pressure, the arbitrary imposition of the will of a superior upon the will of a weaker individual, and assumes instead the character of an overarching ideal to which teacher and pupil alike must subordinate themselves.

Finally, Froebel introduces a concept of growth that is social rather than individualistic in nature. It is through *shared* activities and *participation* in the concerns of the family and the community that one becomes a *personality*, a concept which contrasts with the idea of maturity as a goal of self-containment.

These ideas have profoundly influenced education, not merely on the kindergarten and primary levels, but at later stages as well. On the other hand, a number of difficulties soon emerged from the Froebelian concept of education. These derived from the fact that two sets of criteria were employed in selecting and organizing educational experiences for the child: one, his needs as empirically observed; the other, these needs as metaphysically interpreted. Theoretically, what best serves the interests of the child, as determined by the direct observations of the "skilled gardener," also functions best to liberate the infinite nature within the young person, as determined by metaphysical insight, and vice versa. In practice, however, the observations and the conclusion drawn from them by empirical observers have often been in disagreement, whereas in the realm of pure thought and mystical experience no such stubborn obstacle confronts the individual engaged in its operations. It was not strange, therefore, to find the Froebelians following the easier path and selecting the activities of the kindergarten more by reference to their symbolic or metaphysical value than their appropriateness to child nature as determined by observation and experiment.

Although in the mind of one and the same individual there may be no inconsistency between educative materials selected from actual observation and experiment and those logically approved by means of mystical insight into the purposes of the infinite, this seldom holds true of different interpreters. Mysticism as a method of curriculum building and as a means of constructing helpful teaching procedures suffers from the same difficulty as mysticism in other areas of life; it is satisfactory and reassuring only to the individual translator of the deliverances of the ultimate reality. Consequently, it is not strange that efforts were made to discover criteria for education by resort to science.

G. Stanley Hall and the Child Study Movement

Few individuals in the course of their lifetime have exercised greater influence upon American education than G. Stanley Hall, President of Clark University from 1888 to 1920. Under his leadership, able scholars representing all fields of higher education were attracted to Clark University, giving to this institution an enviable status for many years. Hall's advice was sought on educational questions from all parts of the country, with the result that directly, as well as indirectly through his students, his ideas found wide application. To the theory and the practice of education he brought contributions from his knowledge of many fields—biology, history, geology, comparative psychology, among others—as well as conclusions from first-hand observation and study of children. Quite appropriately he earned the title of father of the child study movement in this country.

Hall and his students devised many of their own methods and procedures, as well as utilizing theories and inferences drawn from other fields. Thus, from biology they derived the recapitulation theory and from psychology the theory of instincts, two theories which served as lenses through which they read and interpreted many of the data derived from their own investigations.

According to the biological theory of recapitulation, each individual, prior to birth, passes through well-defined physical stages reminiscent of that line of evolution to which he belongs. Thus, at one stage in its development, the human embryo possesses a fishlike tail and gill slits which shortly disappear to be replaced by still other nonhuman characteristics in the progress toward eventual human structure.

Now, if we assume, as did Hall and his followers, that the cultural and historical development of Western civilization reappears as stages of development—intellectual, emotional, social—in the lives of young people as they move from infancy to adulthood, we have what became known as the culture epochs theory. In shorthand terms this theory affirms that "ontogenesis recapitulates phylogenesis."

Observe, also, that for this school of thought, the stages of individual development which parallel racial history manifest themselves more or less suddenly (a saltatory conception of development) and in an order or series (serial development) similar to their appearance in history. These stages, as described by one follower of Hall, are (1) prehistoric; (2) patriarchal; (3) tribal; (4) feudal, with absolute monarchy; (5) revolutionary, with constitutional monarchy; (6) republican, or self-governing. According to the same author, the corresponding stages in the development of the individual are: (1) infancy; (2) child-hood; (3) preadolescence; (4) early adolescence; (5) middle ado-lescence; (6) late adolescence.[12]

One more item requires mention, the doctrine of catharsis, according to which the suppression or repression of tendencies characteristic of one stage may affect unfavorably development in a subsequent stage. More positively stated, the undesirable original tendencies must be given expression either because they are necessary preliminaries to, or correlates of, other quite different impulses or because free expression in early life safeguards the individual from their appearance in later life.

The cultural epochs theory, together with the doctrine of catharsis, carried revolutionary implications for education with respect to the content of the curriculum, methods of discipline and guidance, and the administrative structure of the school. Its greatest impact upon educa-tion in the United States was in the last decades of the nineteenth century and the first quarter of the present century, although, in modi-fied form, a number of its tenets are still evident in the theories of Freud and Jung as applied to individual guidance and therapy.

12. R. W. Pringle, *Adolescence and High School Problems* (Boston: D. C. Heath & Company, 1922), pp. 16–17.

The Curriculum Takes Its Cue from Nature

In 1901 Hall delivered an address before the National Council of Education on the topic "The Ideal School As Based on Child Study," [13] which stated in short compass the applications of his conception of the nature of the child to the curriculum and the organization of the school. Thus he observed that during the years from eight or nine to puberty "there is a decreased rate of growth, so that the body relatively rests; but there is a striking increase of vitality, activity, and power to resist disease." This stage, he believed, corresponds to the period of human development well above the simian and before the historic period, "when our early forebears were well adjusted to their environment." It does not suggest, therefore, an emphasis upon reasoning, creative thinking, appeals to judgment or originality, but it is admirably adapted to "drill, habituation, and mechanism." Accordingly, the teacher will seek to establish the fundamentals of an education in reading, writing, arithmetic, and so on. "Accuracy, which, when out of season, is fraught with so many dangers for mind and body, is now in order." Arithmetic should be mechanized, "with plenty of mental exercises, and later with rules and processes for written work, with only little attempt at explanation."

Similarly, the other subjects presented between the ages of eight or nine and the onset of puberty are to be selected and organized in terms of cues and criteria supplied by the nature of the child. Thus this period is most favorable for beginning the study of foreign languages, although these will be taught by ear and mouth. "The child has a natural desire to express himself in many vocal forms other than the vernacular, for it is the age when all kinds of gibberish, dog Latin, and inventive words culminate. It represents the stage when human speech evolved fastest." Geography, to take another example, should be organized on the basis of the fact that the child's interest in primitive life and animals culminates in the ages of nine and ten, and interest in trade and government does not appear until the ages from sixteen to twenty.

Methods of discipline and teaching advocated by Hall and others

13. *Proceedings and Addresses,* National Education Association, 1901, pp. 474–88.

during the elementary school period likewise take their cue from nature. This leads to quite different procedures at different stages; at one time the most rigorous disciplinary measures are applied and at another time a *laissez faire* policy is followed. Thus, when speaking of the methods employed during the period from eight or nine to puberty, Hall contended that to explain instructions yields only self-consciousness and conceit. "Obedience should be a law, if not a passion." Even with respect to morals and conduct the chief duty of the child at this age is to obey.

In a similar vein, Pringle advises against an appeal to the higher reasoning powers during the period of preadolescence. To get the best results, he insists, instruction in this period should be dogmatic and authoritative, even mechanical. "So far as the fundamentals are concerned, it is a case of drill and inculcation rather than true teaching." [14]

On the other hand, with the dawn of adolescence, not only do rich and varied experiences become imperative, but the manner of their presentation is of strategic consideration. To drill at this stage is to retard development. Now is the time for encouraging the reasoning powers, thoughtfulness, and reflection.

To the layman the applications of the catharsis theory were shocking. Take, for example, the property instinct and its implications for parent and teacher as discussed by Kline and France, and quoted by Hall:

> Selfishness is the corner-stone of the struggle for existence, deception is its very foundation, while the acquiring of property has been the dominant factor in the history of men and nations. These passions of the child are but the pent up forces of the greed of thousands of years. They must find expression and exercise, if not in childhood, later. . . . It does no good to make the child perform moral acts when it does not appreciate what right and wrong mean, and to punish a child for not performing acts which his very nature compels him to do, is doing that child positive injury.
>
> During the period of adolescence, generosity and altruism spring up naturally. Then why try to force a budding plant into

14. Pringle, *op. cit.*, p. 19.

blossom? Instruct them by all means, teach them the right; but if this fails, do not punish, but let the child be selfish, let him lie and cheat, until these forces spend themselves. Do not these experiences of the child give to man in later life a moral virility? [15]

The Secondary School Becomes the Common School

As we have said, the culture epochs theory exercised its greatest influence in the last decades of the last century and the early years of the present century. This was a period of extreme growing pains in education on both the elementary and secondary levels. Prior to this time the elementary school had been the "common school" in the sense that only a fraction of its graduates anticipated further education. Consequently, it was under no impelling obligation to organize its curriculum with an eye to work in the secondary school. Nor would this have been an easy task, considering the chaotic condition of curricula in the latter. From 1890 on, however, it became more evident to observers that the high school was in process of becoming the common school, insofar as that term implies the enrollment of the bulk of the school population within a given age range and the point at which most young people terminate their formal education.

On the other hand, the number of pupils who were dropping out of school between the first and last years of the secondary school was creating general concern. According to data provided by Alexander Inglis, the first year of public secondary schools in 1914–1915 included 40.86 per cent of all pupils enrolled in these schools, whereas the fourth year included only 13.99 per cent, a fact which suggested not only that something was wrong with the holding power of the secondary school but also that the elementary school was failing to equip pupils adequately for work on the secondary level.[16]

Several demands upon educators emerged from this situation: a demand for reorganization of the curriculum in the upper years of the elementary school which would provide learning materials more relevant to the interests and future intentions of this age group and a demand for reorganization of the secondary school keyed to the fact

15. G. Stanley Hall, *Aspects of Child Life and Education* (Boston: Ginn & Company, 1907), pp. 266–67.
16. Alexander Inglis, *Principles of Secondary Education* (Boston: Houghton Mifflin Co., 1918), p. 121.

that it was no longer concerned exclusively with a selected school population but, in its first years at least, should minister to the needs of all graduates of the elementary school.

Thus was the stage set for the apostles of G. Stanley Hall to insist that a new school unit was required, one adapted to the age commonly embraced by the upper years of the elementary school and the first two years of high school. Many objectives contributed to the reorganization of the elementary and secondary schools in this period, objectives such as the need for economy of time in education and provision for some form of vocational education for boys and girls who were to terminate their education at this point, but the psychological need to adapt education to the characteristics of early adolescence was of general appeal. Thus a new school unit, the junior high school, came into being. The junior high school would, it was hoped, by virtue of its administrative structure and its curricular and extracurricular offerings, meet the unique needs of young people—intellectual, emotional, social, moral, and vocational—in the early years of adolescence.

Administrators were not slow in meeting their responsibilities. Within a few short years fundamental changes were inaugurated in the curriculum, the methods of teaching, and the types of activities in which young people might engage. For example:

1. It was observed that in this stage irregularities in physical growth are common, together with rapid changes in aptitudes and interests. This suggested a broad sweep of subject matter in contrast with narrow and specialized concentration upon one area or one field, with the result that general science, general history, general mathematics, general literature, and "try-out" courses in the arts and crafts were substituted for special subjects such as physiology and ancient history.

2. It was observed that this period was one of budding social interests, marked by new relationships between the sexes, keen sensitiveness with respect to group approval or disapproval, especially of one's peers. These interests suggested the wisdom of socializing the work of the school at this point through the introduction of extracurricular activities, special-interest clubs, assemblies, dramatic work, and so on, and utilizing the social motive in the teaching of the regular subjects through the project method and the "socialized recitation."

3. In this period intellectual interests were seen to center upon the concrete and the immediate rather than upon the abstract and the re-

mote, with the implication that instruction should foster the development of the practical, rather than the theoretical, reason.

4. Since individual differences in interests and life goals become prominent in this period, it was concluded that a differentiated curriculum was called for. In practice, however, this eventuated all too often in provision for individual differences in interests and life goals as viewed by the administrative office: a commercial curriculum, an industrial arts curriculum, or a general and a college preparatory curriculum, each with a specialized purpose but from which it was often difficult for a pupil to transfer to another curriculum.

5. Finally, the junior high school period was seen to be one in which young people are concerned with the immediate environment, which, as the educator saw it, suggested vocational education for those who would terminate their education at this point. Thus came into being *terminal courses* to serve a function not unlike that assigned today to the junior college.

A large measure of credit must be given to psychologists for the emergence of the junior high school and the stimulus for a reorganization of education on all levels. In all fairness, however, we should add other factors such as (1) the concern of social reformers over the large numbers of dropouts in the early years of the secondary school and (2) the insistence of business and industry that the vocational needs of youth receive attention. To this latter insistence we shall return in our next chapter.

An Appraisal of the Culture Epochs Theory

How shall we appraise the contributions of the culture epochs theory?

Most obvious were its positive contributions to the enrichment of the curriculum, particularly in the elementary and the junior high schools. Not only was new subject matter introduced which served a wider range of interests, but methods of teaching were vitalized and what were once considered "fads and frills"—art, music, dramatic work, clublike activities—now attained the status of essentials.

On the other hand, the presentation of appropriate materials and the use of methods keyed to a given stage of development were assumed to exercise a magical influence. That is to say, the child's response was supposed to spring forth like a jack-in-the-box, by virtue of a pre-established connection between inner nature and outer stimulus. For example, Indian life was studied in the early years of the elementary school, not so much because primitive life, in its simplicity, serves as a happy introduction to an understanding of the operations of a modern community, such as the providing of food, clothing, and shelter, but rather because it affords channels of expression for atavistic tendencies in the life of the young child.

Moreover, the fact that stages of development were conceived of as inborn tendencies to think, feel, and act in ways characteristic of racial experiences gave an aspect of inevitability and imperativeness to child behavior. Since John or Mary's behavior was thus known in advance, teachers easily forgot John and Mary as individuals in order to lay their plans for children in general. Thus the explanation for misbehavior on the part of an individual child was sought for in the past history of the race, which was thus reasserting itself rather than in the circumstances peculiar to that child's environment. (See the quotation from Kline and France on p. 151.) This theory was not at all helpful in advancing the diagnosis of growing pains in children, although it doubtless had the advantage of easing the conscience of a negligent parent whose child might give indications of waywardness!

The uses to which subject matter might be put were also limited by this theory. Movements and events in history easily yielded to the interpretation that what is, or, at least, what has been, is right inasmuch as these were manifestations or expressions of a cosmic process in which human beings function more or less as pawns, not as responsible agents.

It was this interpretation of history, indeed, which prompted an outstanding educator of the time, Charles McMurry, to introduce "project teaching" in the study of history and literature. The project differed from the daily recitation in that it concerned itself with the solution of a problem, the understanding of a movement in history, a masterpiece in literature, or the operations of a social, industrial, or economic institution as a unified experience in contrast with the daily nibbling process of assign, study, recite characteristic of the daily recitation. From the standpoint of the pupil, it was purposive, designed to capture his interest and to enlist his continued efforts until either a solution of the problem or a unified understanding emerged. Second, the project departed from conventional teaching in that it employed "plural routes to learning," research in textbook and library, yes, but other media as well, such as the arts and crafts, music, kitchen, and shop—whatever might contribute a real-life character to the study.

The obvious advantages of the project method led to its widespread adoption and later development into "units of work" of both an academic and real-life character. It also contributed to the spread of free, informal, and diversified procedures within the classroom, thus rescuing teaching from lockstep methods. As its originators conceived it, however, the project had other purposes to serve as well. It was designed to enable young people "to gather up and organize" the world's experience and wisdom by reliving, so to speak, "the actual evolution of the main life processes in a practical world" and thus to bring to a focus in the mind of the pupil a progressive revelation of the world, past and present.[17]

The kinship of the project, so conceived, to the theory of recapitulation is clear, as is the danger it entailed that school experiences might be used for the purpose of having children relive the experiences of others with a view to identifying themselves with their purposes and ideals. What better way might one devise for forming the minds of the young in harmony with the status quo?

A second contribution of the culture epochs theory consisted in fostering an objective attitude toward children. Once children ceased to be adults in miniature and were thought to pass through stages unique and peculiar to them, it was natural to conclude that both the causes and the significance of their behavior were to be appraised and dealt with in a manner different from that warranted by similar behavior in adults. Theft and lying in a child, for example, were no longer conclusive evidence of a criminal nature. This encouraged the development of a professional attitude toward children. Absurd as we now believe the explanation by Kline and France of lying and stealing to be, it nevertheless suggested methods of diagnosis and treatment relevant to children. As confidence in the theory of recapitulation weakened, psychologists were encouraged to seek the explanations of delinquent behavior in the circumstances which play upon children, in the situation rather than in heredity.

As we have seen, the culture epochs theory, together with the notion that stages of development are saltatory in character, rather than grad-

17. For example, Charles McMurry, *Teaching by Projects* (New York: The Macmillan Co., 1920), p. 4.

ual in transition, seemed to justify, psychologically, school units, each organized with special reference to stages of development.

Both experience and careful observation of children eventually undermined the validity of this conclusion. It was found, for example, that children of the same chronological age are not necessarily at identical points in their development, intellectual, social, or emotional. Consequently, even though we may grant the validity of stages of development (which educators do, although not as recapitulations of the past), individual children of the same age may differ significantly in maturity.

Likewise, the assumption that administrative units must correspond to age range should be taken with liberal grains of salt. Other factors peculiar to the community, such as its size, the geographical distribution of the school population, and the like, are as relevant as an assumed stage of development. Relevant as the junior high school was to conditions of some years ago, factors which were nonexistent at that time are today suggesting new groupings of administrative units. Thus the increasing tendency of young people to continue both their general and their vocational training beyond the period served by the conventional senior high school is leading to the emergence of new units, such as a six-year elementary school, a four-year junior high school, and a four-year senior high school, the latter embracing what were formerly the last two years of high school and the first two years of college.

This 6–4–4 pattern has been favorably discussed among educators for several decades. However, other plans—such as the 6–3–3–2 pattern—which provide for a separate two-year junior or community college are much more frequently adopted. Usually providing both vocational and academic programs, "the community two-year college today is the most rapidly growing phenomenon in American education," [18] a phenomenon which has had relatively little concern with the psychological traits of age groups considered in isolation from socioeconomic factors. Similarly, the recent development of 4–4–4 plans has more to do with pressures for continuing education in college than with ideas about stages of child development.

What, by way of conclusion, shall we say of the concept of inner development and the culture epochs theory?

18. Fred E. Crossland, "Fantasy, Facts, and the Future of College Admissions," *Journal of Educational Sociology*, March 1962, p. 334.

Internal Criteria in the Light of Modern Theories

For one thing, the biological foundations of the recapitulation theory no longer sustain it in the form accepted and applied by its child study advocates. It is now established that although an individual embryo roughly repeats, in the course of its development, the phylogenetic series, there are large omissions and gaps in this series. Moreover, studies in heredity have thrown doubt upon the theory of acquired characteristics which underlies the notion that the individual inherits and thus relives the cultural experiences of his ancestors. Furthermore, a detailed comparison of cultural periods with stages in the development of the individual reveals only superficial resemblances between the two. It would appear, then, that the validity of the cultural epochs theory varies inversely with a detailed knowledge of history and a careful and meticulous observation of child development.

A somewhat similar fate has befallen the theory of instincts as inherited habits, or as specifically organized ways of thinking, feeling, and acting which derive from inheritance rather than from experiences in the lifetime of the individual. As a result of Edward L. Thorndike's insistence, for example, that instincts as natively organized responses be described in terms of the *specific* elements within a situation to which *specific* responses in the individual are related, Hall's instincts began to shrink in number. Later observations of infant behavior have reduced the number of instincts still further. Moreover, those instincts which seem to have survived have lost their specific characteristics, with the result that the "instincts" of love, fear, and anger are described as variable ways of responding to varying circumstances.

"In higher animals and most of all in man," writes the biologist, Theodosius Dobzhansky, "instinctual behavior is intertwined with, overlaid by, and serves merely as a backdrop to learned behavior." Instincts are "subject to environmental modification, including modification by learning." [19] More broadly, research in biology and anthropology has cast grave doubt upon the idea that specific cultural patterns of behavior—whether these be economic institutions or methods of child rearing—are necessitated by or can be deduced from biological

19. *Mankind Evolving* (New Haven: Yale University Press, 1962), p. 204.

propensities or drives.[20] Major cultural changes seem to occur independently of prior genetic changes; and, on an individual basis, whether the "brain" thinks of money or of poetry is not biologically determined.

Similarly, the older view of a necessary unilinear development—of progress through fixed stages and in a single direction—in both biological and cultural evolution has been generally abandoned in favor of a theory of multilinear evolution.[21] This theory postulates the probability of divergent evolutionary development in species and cultures and finds the source of these developments neither in an "unfolding from within" nor an "imposition from without" but in the interplay of organic and environmental factors.

Finally, in the psychology of John Dewey, instinctive behavior as "impulse" becomes a source of novelty and change in behavior! Although recognized as first in time in the life of an individual, impulses lack specificity and meaning prior to their interaction with the surrounding medium. Thus Dewey writes as follows in his *Human Nature and Conduct:* "In conduct the acquired is the primitive. Impulses although first in time are never primary; they are secondary." Since impulses in their original expression are without form and acquire form only through interaction with an individual's surroundings, "the *meaning* of native activities is not native; it is acquired, . . ." and so "we need to know about the social conditions which have educated original activities into definite and significant dispositions before we can discuss the psychological element in society." [22]

Does this mean that educators have abandoned the concept of stages of development? Not at all. It is still recognized that childhood is a unique period of growth and development and that children, as they move from infancy into childhood and adolescence and on toward the mature status of adulthood, pass through relatively distinct stages of emotional and social development, a knowledge of which is helpful for parent and teacher alike. Each of these stages is marked by emo-

20. See, for example, C. H. Waddington, *The Nature of Life* (New York: Atheneum, 1962), p. 101; Anthony F. C. Wallace, *Culture and Personality* (New York: Random House, 1961), p. 83.

21. See Dobzhansky, *op. cit.,* pp. 8–17; Julian H. Steward, *Theory of Culture Change* (Urbana, Ill.: University of Illinois Press, 1955), pp. 11–29.

22. See John Dewey, *Human Nature and Conduct* (New York: Henry Holt & Co., Inc., 1922), part II. Also John Watson, *Behaviorism* (New York: The Peoples' Institute, 1924), chaps. V, VI.

tional and social characteristics sufficiently definite to carry a moral for the guidance and education of the individual. But observe that they are no longer conceived of as "instincts" but rather as the resultants of an *interplay* between the impulses and urges of the individual and cultural and environmental factors. They are thus idiomatic as well as cultural in their expressions and cultural as well as native.[23]

A Modern Version of Inner Development

All this recent reevaluation by educators does not mean that willingness to search for the essential cues and criteria for education within a relatively self-sufficient human nature has been entirely abandoned. This tendency persists in several schools of thought and in several different ways. The client-centered therapy and student-centered teaching of Carl R. Rogers and of certain phenomenological or perceptual psychologists [24] are illustrations of this fact.

In Carl Rogers' view, for example, ideal development occurs when "the person comes to *be* what he *is*," [25] when an individual's "own" unique potentialities are being realized. All individuals have a "self-actualizing" tendency, the only motive postulated by Rogers. It is "the inherent tendency of the organism to develop all its capacities in ways which serve to maintain or enhance the organism." [26] Thus moved, the "self" both discovers and actualizes itself. Rogers relies on what Coleridge called the "fountain within." Any direction from without, whether based on authority and custom or on instruction, logic, and evaluation of the consequences of behavior, is rejected as an "imposition" and a subversion of the drive toward autonomy and away from control by external forces.

23. For a helpful discussion of the growth process in these terms, see Morris L. Bigge and Maurice P. Hunt, *Psychological Foundations of Education* (New York: Harper & Row, 1962), chap. 9.

24. See, for example, A. W. Combs and D. Snygg, *Individual Behavior: A Perceptual Approach to Behavior* (New York: Harper & Brothers, 1959); Robert H. Bills, "Education in Human Relations," *New Insights and the Curriculum*, A. Frazier, ed. (Washington, D.C.: Association for Supervision and Curriculum Development, 1963), pp. 165–87.

25. Carl R. Rogers, *On Becoming a Person* (Boston: Houghton Mifflin Co., 1961), p. 104. Emphases in original.

26. Carl R. Rogers, "A Theory of Therapy, Personality, and Interpersonal Relationships as Developed in the Client-Centered Framework," study I, vol. III of *Psychology: A Study of a Science*, Sigmund Koch, ed. (New York: McGraw-Hill Book Co., Inc., 1959), p. 196.

In Rogers' view, the ideal counselor or teacher does not modify the nature of the self.[27] He is a catalyst. By providing "unconditional"[28] acceptance of the pupil or client as he is, the teacher or counselor frees the "helped" person from any feeling of threat and, thus, frees him so that he can accept and be himself.

Rogers believes that "anything that can be taught to another is relatively inconsequential, and has little or no signficant influence on behavior."[29] The only real learning is that which is "self-discovered," and this learning "cannot be directly communicated to another."[30] The ideal teacher does not set lesson tasks. "He does not assign readings. He does not lecture or expound (unless requested to). He does not evaluate and criticize unless the student wishes his judgment on a product. He does not give examinations. He does not set grades."[31] Assignments, examinations, and so on would indicate mistrust of the internal directions and norms supplied by the freely developing young person; in Rogers' bipolar system, they would substitute "external controls" for "self-direction."

Many elements of Rogers' thought are valid and attractive. However, viewed as a logical system and a social instrument, his theory has a number of significant weaknesses.[32] For example, he posits a single, inherent, and vague motive, the actualizing tendency. Since, in Rogers' view, this motive accounts for all kinds of behavior under any circumstances, its existence and nature are unverifiable. There is no indication of what evidence would constitute a refutation of this postulated tendency.

Rogers' system is internally inconsistent, and some of his basic ideas

27. Carl R. Rogers, "Some Observations on the Organization of Personality," *The Phenomenological Problem,* Alfred E. Kuenzli, ed. (New York: Harper & Brothers, 1959), pp. 51–57, 72–73.

28. *On Becoming a Person,* p. 283.

29. *Ibid.,* p. 276.

30. *Ibid.*

31. Carl R. Rogers, "Learning To Be Free," in *Conflict and Creativity,* part II of *Control of the Mind,* Seymour M. Farber and Roger H. L. Wilson, eds. (New York: McGraw-Hill Book Co., Inc., 1963), p. 282.

32. For critical evaluations of Rogers' thought, see Paul F. Secord and Carl W. Backman, "Personality Theory and the Problem of Stability and Change in Individual Behavior: An Interpersonal Approach," *Psychological Review,* January 1961, pp. 21–32; Melvin H. Marx and William A. Hillix, *Systems and Theories in Psychology* (New York: McGraw-Hill Book Co., Inc., 1963), pp. 338–41; Richard W. Dettering, "Philosophic Idealism in Rogerian Psychology," *Educational Theory,* October 1955, pp. 206–14.

are inconsistent with the evidence from a number of sciences. For example, he often indicates that all judgments are merely matters of "personal opinion," in a subjective sense.[33] Yet, he is wont to offer "objective" research evidence to support his own theory.[34] Also, while at times Rogers acknowledges that the self is fundamentally constituted and changed in and through social interactions, at other times he insists that only the self can produce fundamental changes in itself. Moreover, when Rogers assumes that internal agents are the sufficient causes of stability or change in personality, he is inconsistent with a large body of evidence in the biological and behavioral sciences that direct attention to the interplay between organism and environment.

Finally, Rogers' theory in fact subordinates all other values to the value of developing a person who recognizes and accepts his own characteristics—whatever these characteristics may be. For recall that any attempt by, say, a teacher to change any of these characteristics would be an "imposition from without." Moreover, some of the relations that Rogers does at times posit between self-acceptance and other values seem to be doubtful or erroneous. For example, contrary to his blanket assumption that self-acceptance is positively associated with open-mindedness, studies of creativity, along with other studies,[35] strongly suggest that at least some aspects or kinds of self-acceptance tend to be associated with dogmatism or insensitivity.

New Motives and Criteria for Education

Before the older doctrines of inner development were transformed into the modern theories of Rogers and others, new social forces and a quite different theory of education gained prominence in America during the late nineteenth century and the early twentieth century. As the concept of instincts as racial urges which reappear in the lives of growing individuals weakened in the minds of educators, new influences were quick to assert themselves. The junior high school, as we have seen, owed its inception in large measure to the doctrine of culture epochs and the assumption that administrative school units should parallel stages of

33. See, for example, "Learning To Be Free," p. 281.
34. See, for example, *On Becoming a Person*, pp. 41 ff.
35. See, for example, E. D. Pannes, "The Relationship Between Self-Acceptance and Dogmatism in Junior-Senior High School Students," *Journal of Educational Sociology*, May 1963, pp. 419–26.

development. But we have also pointed out that a second motive was to provide a terminal education for that large proportion of young people who were to conclude their schooling at a point between graduation from the elementary school and entrance into the senior high school. Educational planning of this character had its source not so much in the psychology of adolescence as in the response of educators to economic trends. American society was rapidly becoming industrialized. Industry called for workers, and the education of future workmen, as the hardheaded businessman or industrialist conceived it, called for habit training and the development of skills. This, in turn, had use for a psychology of "adjustment," a psychology, in short, less sentimental and romantic than that of inner development.

And, once again, the times brought forth the man!

Suggested Reading

Bigge, Morris L. and Maurice P. Hunt, *Psychological Foundations of Education* (New York: Harper & Row, 1962), chaps. 2–5, 7, 9.

Dewey, John, *Human Nature and Conduct* (New York: Henry Holt and Co., Inc., 1922), parts I, II.

Dobzhansky, Theodosius, *Mankind Evolving* (New Haven: Yale University Press, 1962), chap. I.

National Society for the Study of Education, *Child Psychology*, Sixty-second Yearbook (Chicago: University of Chicago Press, 1963), part I, chaps. II, XII.

Rogers, Carl R., *On Becoming a Person* (Boston: Houghton Mifflin Co., 1961), pp. 163–82, 275–310.

Thut, I. N., *The Story of Education* (New York: McGraw-Hill Book Co., Inc., 1957), chaps. 9–10.

Ulich, Robert, *History of Educational Thought* (New York: American Book Co., 1950), pp. 211–24, 258–70, 284–314.

Chapter 9

Education as Adjustment

Industrial Development Creates New Problems

On October 3, 1876, Thomas Huxley delivered an address in Baltimore, Maryland, on the occasion of the opening of Johns Hopkins University. He spoke of the impression he received as an Englishman in landing upon the American shore for the first time and "traveling for hundreds of miles through strings of great well-ordered cities, seeing your enormous actual and almost infinite potential wealth in all commodities, and in the energy and ability which turn wealth to account."

It was not so much the evidences of bigness and matchless natural resources, however, which impressed Huxley most, since he realized that "size is not grandeur, and territory does not make a nation." Rather was he moved to inquire of this country's future:

> The great issue, about which hangs a true sublimity, and the terror of overhanging fate, is what are you going to do with all these things? What is to be the end to which these things are to be the means? You are making a novel experiment in politics on the greatest scale which the world has yet seen. Forty millions at your first centenary, it is reasonably to be expected that at the second, these states will be occupied by two hundred millions of English-speaking people, spread over an area as large as that of Europe, and with climate and interests as diverse as those of Spain and Scandinavia, England and Russia. You and your descendants have to ascertain whether this great mass will hold together under the form of a republic, and the despotic reality of

universal suffrage; whether state rights will hold out against centralization, without separation; whether centralization will get the better, without actual or disguised monarchy; whether shifting corruption is better than a permanent bureaucracy; and as population thickens in your great cities, and the pressure of want is felt, the gaunt spectre of pauperism will stalk among you, and communism and socialism will claim to be heard. Truly America has a great future before her; great in toil, in care, and in responsibility; great in true glory if she be guided in wisdom and righteousness, great in shame if she fail. I cannot understand why other nations should envy you, or be blind to the fact that it is for the highest interest of mankind that you should succeed; but the one condition of success, your sole safeguard, is the moral worth and intellectual clearness of the individual citizen.

By the turn of the century, some of the questions so forcefully posed by Thomas Huxley had become even more imperative than they were in 1876. The trend toward industrialization had reached a point where it was clear that a predominantly rural and agricultural economy was to be superseded by an urban and industrial economy. As Arthur Schlesinger put it, "rural America, like a stag at bay, was making its last stand." [1] By 1890, three fifths of the population of the North Atlantic states had become city dwellers, and in sections of New England and the Middle Atlantic states many rural areas were falling into decay. Moreover, this shift from rural to urban living was proceeding at an ever accelerating pace.

These changes were of significance to education in that they testified to fundamental transformations in the lives of people and thus had an impact upon children. Parents who had been accustomed only to rural life were now moving to cities in large numbers, there to confront not only the necessity of engaging in new vocations but of rearing children under circumstances novel and disturbing to adults and children alike.

Large numbers of the foreign-born were also coming to the cities. Between 1865 and 1900, about fourteen million immigrants came to America. By 1900, they were coming at the rate of one million a year. Prior to 1880, the bulk of immigrants had come from Great Britain and the north of Europe. The 1880s marked a change in this tide and the

1. Quoted in Newton Edwards and Herman G. Richey, *The School in the American Social Order*, 2d ed. (Boston: Houghton Mifflin Co., 1963), p. 407.

beginnings of immigration from southern and eastern Europe, where customs and institutions were sufficiently different from those encountered in this country to create severe growing pains. Between 1881 and 1890, for example, 75.6 per cent of all immigrants into the United States came from Great Britain, Germany, Ireland, Norway, Sweden, Denmark, and Canada. By 1901, this proportion had shrunk to 21.3 per cent. In the same period, however, the percentage of immigrants from Austria-Hungary, Italy, Russia, and Poland increased from 17.6 per cent of the total to 68.5 per cent.[2]

How different were the ways of living thrust upon these immigrants may be seen from the fact that in Europe they had lived primarily in rural areas and small villages and had earned their living, in the main, as farm laborers, an occupation from which they hoped to free themselves upon coming to America. Once here, they flocked to the cities or to mining towns, there to share slum conditions of living with relatives and friends and there, too, to create complicated patterns of diversity out of what had once been relatively homogeneous communities.

Finally, a sizable proportion of the immigrants were illiterate (12.9 per cent, according to the twelfth census, as compared with 5.7 per cent of native whites and 1.6 per cent of native whites of foreign parentage),[3] competent only to enter unskilled occupations.

One more factor of concern to educators early in the century requires mention. Not only were new technological developments absorbing large proportions of a population once accustomed to rural life in this country and abroad, but change was invading the home and undermining the family through the employment of women and children. Thus, in 1900, 18.2 per cent of all children between the ages of ten and fifteen years of age were engaged in gainful occupations, of whom about one sixth, or 17.2 per cent, were under twelve years of age. Moreover, according to the census of 1910, 70 per cent of all girls between the ages of ten and fifteen who were engaged in gainful occupations were so engaged outside the home.[4]

To the credit of Americans it should be said that these conditions weighed heavily upon their conscience, and eventually, laws were passed with a view to improving both working and living conditions

2. Thomas Sewall Adams and Helen L. Sumner, *Labor Problems* (New York: The Macmillan Co., 1905), p. 73.
3. *Ibid.*, p. 89.
4. *Ibid.*, p. 27.

and, in the case of children, limiting hours of labor and encouraging attendance at school.

The passage of compulsory school attendance laws had the effect of rendering more complex the task of education. Into the schools now flocked large numbers of young people of a type who had previously received little or no education. For them an exclusively academic curriculum on either the elementary or secondary level no longer seemed adequate. New subjects and new criteria for the selection of materials within the traditional subjects seemed essential. "Civics" no longer concerned itself with matters exclusively political, but undertook as well to acquaint young people with the agencies and institutions and the problems of the community. Thus "community civics" came into being. Similarly, in the elementary school, particularly, the need for health education was obvious, education that would safeguard the health of children even when this involved correcting the erroneous practices and ideas of parents. Still again, as a result of the alarming exodus of women from the home and an increase in child labor, particularly of girls, home economics (chiefly cooking and sewing) gained entrance into the curriculum, as did shop of a practical character for boys.

The changes in American society to which we have drawn attention affected education on all levels. But the contrast between programs of education keyed, on the one hand, to the inner nature of the young person and, on the other, to the demands of society were most obvious on the junior high school level. Here genetic psychology was emphasizing the dynamic and instinctive potentialities of the young person, with the clear implication that nature was to be followed; whereas life outside the school, in home and community, in business and industry, stressed the importance of education for adjustment, one that would give specific and detailed attention to the formation of desirable habits and skills and techniques.

Confronted with this necessity of choice, educators turned to a psychology that would further education for adjustment.

The Rise of Behaviorism in Psychology

In the discussion of Herbart and the Herbartians it was pointed out that the fundamental postulates of this movement lent themselves to a concept of learning in which the schoolmaster conceives of his task as that of forming the character of youth. Since the mind and the personality of the individual are nothing other than the organized experiences that have come to him (the ideas presented to him and the method of their organization), it is easy to conclude that all learning is habit formation. Although Herbart and his followers explained the details of the mental life in terms of psychic phenomena (mental states), there is little difference in spirit between their conception of learning and that implied in the assertions of John Watson, except that the latter conceives of all learning in physiological terms. Thus, according to Watson, there is nothing within to develop. Let an individual begin life with the right number of fingers and toes, plus the few elementary movements which are present at birth, and we need nothing more "in the way of raw material to make a man, be that man a genius, cultured gentleman, a rowdy, or a thug." [5]

What Watson is saying, in the above reference, is that human behavior is best explained in purely physical and physiological terms. At the time of his writing, this seemed a logical conclusion to draw from developments in psychology. With the rise of a physiological psychology, there seemed less and less occasion to explain human nature and behavior by reference to mental states or to the mind as a nonmaterial entity. Briefly summarized, the stages in this process (shall we say the manner in which psychologists came to lose their minds?) were as follows:

1. Mind as an all-embracing substance, an immaterial agency in contrast with body as a physical substance, shrinks to the status of a collective noun. In Herbart, for example, it designates an association and organization of ideas with no more objective reality than the woods over and above the trees which comprise its existence. This was also the position at which William James had arrived when he demonstrated in his *Principles of Psychology* that each "passing thought" includes within itself all that is essential in order to explain the operations of the mental life. [6]

2. Further observation and analysis of mental activity seemed to establish the fact that what were once described as mental states, or

5. *Psychological Care of Infant and Child* (New York: W. W. Norton and Company, Inc., 1928), p. 41.
6. New York: Henry Holt & Co., Inc., 1890, vol. I, pp. 360–73.

ideas, are dependent upon an underlying physical or neural activity. Given interference with the latter, such as a blow upon the head, consciousness seemingly disappears for a time, but the physical processes and neural activity continue to function without dependence upon mental activity. This tended to place mental phenomena in a position subordinate to the physical, but at least they were tolerated for a time as "epi-phenomena" or psychic correlates of the physical with a capacity to register, if not to initiate and control, behavior.

3. As so often happens, however, when the lion and the lamb lie down together, the lamb shortly disappears. So it was in this instance. Before long, a dominant school of psychology arose, of which Watson was one member, which repudiated mental states and attempted to explain all behavior in purely physical terms (physiology, physics, chemistry).

In this transition from a psychology of mental states to a psychology of behaviorism or physiological processes, few played a role more decisive than Edward L. Thorndike.

Thorndike Investigates the Doctrine of Formal Discipline

Early in his career, Thorndike, as we have seen, subjected the concept of instincts, as conceived by G. Stanley Hall and his followers, to critical examination. If instincts actually exist as inherited tendencies to think, feel, and act under given circumstances, he insisted, then an observer should be able to identify the specific situations in the environment which cause or accompany their manifestations and also the specific responses of the individual to these stimulating conditions. Confronted by this necessity to be definite and precise, the cohorts of the instinct psychology and the culture epochs theory began slowly to fold their tents and to disappear over the educational horizon.

The guns which Thorndike leveled at the formal disciplinarians in education were equally devastating. It will be recalled that in Chapter 7 we spoke of the conservative influences in education which, near the end of the nineteenth century, sought to bring order out of chaos in the curriculum of the secondary school and in relations between school and college. One purpose of the Committee of Ten, in its report issued in 1893, was to identify the subjects most appropriate for study by young people "who are going to college, for those going to a scientific school, and for those who, presumably, are going to neither," and to determine how these subjects might best be taught.[7]

In answer to the first question, the Committee took the position that there should be no essential difference in the content of subjects taught for those who intend to continue their education upon graduation and those who do not so plan. The principle enunciated was that an education best designed for the noncollege bound is also best for the college bound, although a careful reading of the recommendations of the various subcommittees suggests that what the Committee really meant was precisely the opposite. Thus, out of the list of subjects endorsed by the Committee (English, the classics, foreign language, mathematics, science, and history), only minor provision was made for the fact that some students would not be going on to college.[8] The reason for this was that despite differences in their educational plans, the two groups were essentially alike in that they constituted "a small proportion of all the children of the country." [9]

This conception of the secondary school as an institution designed to serve mainly a selected group was shortly to undergo significant change.

In defense of its policy of limiting the curriculum to a few, well-selected subjects, the Committee stated: "Every youth who entered college would have spent four years in studying a few subjects thoroughly; and, on the theory that all the subjects are to be considered equivalent in educational rank for the purposes of admission to college, it would make no difference which subjects he had chosen from the programme—he would have had four years of strong and effective mental training." [10]

The assumption that the educational values of one subject can be equated with the values of another was challenged by one member of the Committee, James H. Baker, President of the University of Colorado. Baker pointed out that the recommendations of the majority

7. *Report of the Committee of Ten on Secondary School Studies* (New York: Published for the National Education Association by the American Book Company, 1894), p. 17.

8. The Committee did recognize the possibility of electives in bookkeeping and commercial arithmetic. It also suggested that "if it were desired to provide more amply for subjects thought to have practical importance in trade or the useful arts, it would be easy to provide options in such subjects for some of the science in the third and fourth years of the English program."

9. *Op. cit.*, p. 51.

10. *Ibid.*, p. 53.

assumed as valid the doctrine of "formal discipline," which held that the mind is possessed of general powers—memory, imagination, reason, and so on—which, when trained by appropriate materials, will function better thereafter in all situations calling for their exercise.

Were this doctrine valid, the task of education would be relatively simple. The only preparation a schoolman would need to insure the effectiveness of schooling would be to identify the mental powers most important for training and the subject matter best adapted toward this end, knowing the future would take care of itself.

But suppose that the assumption of general powers or faculties is without valid foundation, that we have only specific memories, not a faculty of memory, that we engage in individual acts of reasoning but have no faculty of reason which we can employ in general. Then should we not, as educators, seek to identify the specific items of information, the most important habits, skills, and techniques employed in adult life, and help young people to become possessed of them?

Herculean as this task might seem, some educators, under the influence of a behavioristic psychology, concluded that it was of necessity the only practical alternative to the "false doctrine" of formal discipline.[11]

Here are two conflicting theories of learning with quite different implications for the curriculum and methods of teaching, two theories which Thorndike and other investigators were quick to subject to investigation and experimentation. From his studies, Thorndike concluded that there are no general powers, such as those of reasoning and memory, which when trained by one sort of material and in one situation will thereby function better with other materials and in other, quite different situations. He concluded that there is no reason to believe, for example, that the discipline which comes from memorizing Latin verbs will improve the functioning of memory in other areas. On the other hand, Thorndike succeeded, as did others, in identifying certain situations in which "transfer of training" clearly takes place. From careful analysis of these occasions, he concluded that instances of improvement followed from the presence of "identical elements" present in the two situations, or from identical procedures, or from both.

11. See, for example, Franklin Bobbitt, *How to Make a Curriculum* (Boston: Houghton Mifflin Co., 1924), chap. II. Bobbitt identified the objectives of the curriculum with the specific activities which make up or ought to make up the lives of men and women in the major fields of human action.

Thus an actor who has memorized his part in one play may discover that he learns his part in a second play more easily or in a shorter period of time by virtue of similarities in content or of certain tricks and devices with which he has become familiar.

All Learning Becomes Habit Formation

Observe that this explanation of improvement in learning by means of identities of content and identities of procedure assumes that learning situations are reducible to specifics of stimulus and response!

It is this assumption which constitutes Thorndike's contribution to educational psychology, an assumption eagerly received and employed by educators concerned with both curriculum construction and methods of teaching, since it seemed to insure for education advantages similar to those being derived at the time from the employment of scientific management in business and industry.

The crucial factors in learning thus became for a period what Thorndike termed S → R bonds; that is, original and innate tendencies within the individual to respond favorably to certain specific situations and to be indifferent or hostile to others. Out of these original *connections* between situations to which one is innately sensitive and the responses one makes to the situation in a manner *native* to the individual, each person, it was believed, develops his personality and character. As Thorndike wrote in his *Educational Psychology:*

> Any man possesses at the very start of his life, that is, at the moment when the ovum and the spermatozoon which are to produce him have united—numerous well-defined tendencies to future behavior. Between the situations which he will meet and the responses he will make to them, pre-formed bonds exist. It is already determined by the constitution of these two germs, that under certain circumstances he will see and hear and feel and act in certain ways. His intellect and morals, as well as his bodily organs and movements, are in part the nature of the embryo in the first moment of its life. What a man is and does throughout life is a result of whatever constitution he has at the start and of all the forces that act upon it before and after birth.[12]

12. Edward L. Thorndike, *Educational Psychology, Briefer Course* (New York: Teachers College, Columbia University, 1917), p. 2.

Observe the three components in each learning situation: the S, or situation to which one is natively disposed to respond; the R, or response, also, in its elements, of an inherited character; and the connection, or bond between the two, which also derives from inheritance. These S → R bonds vary in degrees of complexity and specificity of response, and in accordance with the degree of response they are termed reflexes, instincts, and capacities.

The reader will observe a similarity between Thorndike and Herbart in that for both the education of the young consists in control and direction of a meticulous and detailed character. From this point of view the difference is one of vocabulary rather than of spirit. Thorndike, however, avoids the terminology of earlier psychologists. Mental states, impressions, ideas conceived of as something distinct from physical reactions are no longer mentioned. Attention centers rather upon response units, or S → R bonds, which may be viewed either as mental or physical or, perhaps, better as the two in one.

There is, however, one significant difference between the two. For Herbart, there are no inherited ideas. All derive from experience. For Thorndike, on the other hand, the manner in which one responds to the experiences of life finds its explanation, ultimately, in his stock of inherited tendencies to respond to specific situations. These tendencies Thorndike terms original satisfiers and annoyers. As he puts it, "The original basis of the wants which so truly do and should rule the world is the original satisfyingness of some states of affairs and annoyingness of others. Out of such original satisfiers and annoyers grow all desires and aversions; and in such are found the first guides of learning." [13]

Thorndike's Influence on Education

It was not long before Thorndike's influence in education rivaled that of G. Stanley Hall. Indeed, few men have succeeded in extending their influence more widely than he did. As with Hall, from Thorndike's classroom and laboratory future teachers and supervisors and administrators and research workers went forth to translate his ideas into practice.

On the surface, at least, the S → R bond concept of learning simplifies the task of instruction. All learning, we are told, reduces itself to a

13. *Ibid.,* p. 50.

matter of relating situation elements to response units already given. It follows that what one learns is less a novel experience than a matter of making explicit associations with which one is already endowed, of encouraging one group of associations and discouraging others. Two basic laws of learning thus emerge for parents and teachers to apply: the *Law of Exercise or Use* and the *Law of Effect*. That is, repetition tends to perpetuate and give prominence to an $S \rightarrow R$ bond; failure to exercise tends to push these connections into the background. Second, learning experiences which are accompanied by or followed by feelings of satisfaction tend to become confirmed, whereas the opposite is true of those not so favored.

From these two basic laws, Thorndike derived certain subsidiary laws of learning which he sought to validate in the laboratory. An analysis of these laws and their application reveals that they are formulated from the standpoint of the observer, or the manipulator of learning situations, rather than from that of the learner.[14]

Take, for example, the manner in which a child is taught the meaning of the abstract idea of "fiveness." This consists first "in having the learner respond to the total situation containing the element in question with the attitude of piecemeal examination, and with attentiveness to one element after another." [15] By naming five boys, five girls, five pencils, etc., and having the learner respond in such a way as to favor "the partial and predominant activity of 'how-many-ness' as far as may be," it is thought that a bond is ultimately established between the element "fiveness" and the response to "fiveness" on the part of the learner. A second way in which a connection between the desired element in the situation and the response may be effected is by means of dissociation of varying concomitants. By associating a response of five to a variety of situations such as five pencils, five boys, five girls, and so on, which differ in all respects except in the element five, this element of "fiveness" finally becomes distinctly associated with the response. Third, "fiveness" may be learned by having a child respond to situa-

14. For an analysis of Thorndike's theory, including the revisions of his earlier laws of learning, see Melvin H. Marx and William A. Hillix, *Systems and Theories in Psychology* (New York: McGraw-Hill Book Co., Inc., 1963), pp. 116–26. We are not concerned here with some informal suggestions in which Thorndike did recognize a more active role for the learner. Nor are we concerned with the later modifications of his views which brought him out of his "pure" behaviorist or $S \rightarrow R$ position—see Edward L. Thorndike, *The Psychology of Wants, Interests, and Attitudes* (New York: Appleton-Century, 1935). We concentrate here on the major theoretical and practical thrusts of his influential views.

15. Thorndike, *op. cit.*, p. 159.

tions which "pair by pair, present the element in a certain context and present that same context with *the opposite of the element in question,* or with something at least very unlike the element in question." [16] Thus a child being taught to respond to one fifth of a pie, a cake, or the like will have the bond between situation and response brought out and strengthened by contrasting five pies, five cakes, and so on.

But, again, observe that nothing new has been learned! According to Thorndike the response of "fiveness" is in the nervous system as an inherited potential response, and the association of the correct response with the proper element in the situation needs only to be made explicit by exercise and effect. Unless the response were already there, the teacher's efforts would be futile.

Thorndike's psychology encouraged the use and development of intelligence tests with which to discover the native equipment of children and thus to determine in advance of their education the possibilities and the limits of this education. For a time, it looked as though these tests might be used in a manner fatal for the futures of many. There were, for example, school systems in which alert supervisors undertook to administer intelligence tests to children in the primary grades with an eye to their assignment in groups graded according to "native intelligence," a procedure which it was hoped would render teaching more efficient. In the course of time, however, confidence in the tests as indicators of inherited as against acquired ability weakened somewhat, and they came to be used instead as instruments with which to gauge a child's present working capital, without dogmatic inference as to its original source.

The Curriculum Centers Upon the Acquisition of Specific Habits

Thorndike's psychology of learning came as manna from heaven to harassed superintendents and supervisors who, during the first quarter of the century, were unexpectedly confronted with the problems of mass education. Into their schools were flocking large numbers of young people of varied backgrounds, interests, and abilities. For these young people the times seemed to suggest an education in habits and skills relevant to a society to which neither they nor their parents were as yet adjusted. School systems were increasing in size more rapidly than adequately trained teachers could be found to man them. At the

16. *Ibid.,* p. 160.

same time, business and industry were capturing the imagination of people with manifestations of efficiency that seemed to follow from the applications of scientific management to the details of the manufacture and distribution of goods, results which clearly followed from the detailed analysis of processes and the applications of a psychology of habit formation to the acquisition of skills and techniques. Why not apply these same methods, it was asked, to the task of education, thus simplifying the work of both teacher and taught? The steps required for so doing were relatively simple. Identify the relevant facts and skills children need to acquire, together with the abilities requisite for their acquisition, provide teachers with suggestions for inculcating these facts and skills, test from time to time the effectiveness with which both teacher and children have followed the plans thus formulated. Do this faithfully and an effective education will be assured.

This new emphasis in the selection and organization of subject matter received support in 1918 from the Report of the National Commission on the Reorganization of Secondary Education. This commission stated the functions of the secondary school in the form of life objectives. Its preliminary statement read as follows: "In order to determine the main objectives that should guide education in a democracy, it is necessary to analyze the activities of the individual. Normally he is a member of a family, of a vocational group, and of various civic groups, and by virtue of these relationships he is called upon to engage in activities that enrich family life, to render important vocational services to his fellows, and to promote the general welfare." [17]

There followed a more detailed breakdown of these three areas and a formulation of the fundamental principles which should guide educators in the reorganization of subjects and of curricula. These "cardinal principles" were health, command of fundamental processes, worthy home membership, vocation, citizenship, worthy use of leisure, and ethical character.

Curriculum Construction Becomes "Scientific"

With the areas of education thus defined, research workers, wedded to a psychology of adjustment, began the task of organizing subjects of study in terms of "scientifically determined specific objectives."

17. Bureau of Education, *Bulletin*, 1918, no. 35.

The methods resorted to in order to realize this "simple" program were not impressive when viewed from the perspective of today. The professed aim was to be "scientific," precise, and definite. But what does "scientific" mean when it is a matter of determining the important facts and principles within a given field for a child to master, as well as the appropriate habits and skills for him to acquire? The methods of business and industry were, of course, to serve as a model. For example, job analysis was the method followed in business and adopted with evidences of success in vocational education. It seemed natural, therefore, to apply the techniques of job analysis and activity analysis to other aspects of education as well.

There was one significant difference, however, between vocational education and general education. In the former, the specifics of the job were known. In the latter, the components of the job, as well as its purposes, had to be defined, unless tradition were to be followed. What, for example, were the habits and skills most appropriate for attainment in first-year English? or the most relevant processes to teach in arithmetic? or the most significant facts and principles in a course in science or the social studies?

Search for an answer to questions of this character led to some interesting solutions. One method followed was to cull from contemporary magazines and newspapers references to the subject being organized, such as history or general science, in order to determine from frequency of mention the relative importance of facts pupils were to digest. Another was to question members of a faculty, or a parent body, regarding the abilities or traits of character which adults deemed most important for a child to acquire. In one instance, the appropriate materials for a course in physics were validated by asking parents of children what applications of the principles of physics they had made in their daily lives. Whatever the method, the general tendency was to emphasize subject matter which pertained to adult life rather than to child life or adolescence and to accept the existing state of adult culture as the criterion for determining what adults of tomorrow should know.

Nor were the applications of education as adjustment in any way confined to trade and vocational school, on the one hand, or to the curriculum of elementary and secondary schools, on the other. Just as early in the century it was assumed that large numbers of pupils who were then pouring into secondary schools would conclude their education upon graduation from the junior high school, so in the 1920s and the 1930s, the junior college developed as a terminal institution designed to serve that mass of students which was now engulfing the senior high school and beginning to encroach upon the lower levels of college and professional school.

To meet these new demands upon education, terminal courses were devised for the junior college much as they had been originated earlier for the junior high school. These courses operated in large measure on the assumption that the vocational preparation afforded should be of a specific character, leading to the acquisition of specific skills and operations.

In support of this assumption educators called attention to several trends in industry, business, and the professions. One was a trend toward the upgrading of certain types of work in such a way that entrance to occupations that once called for little if any preliminary training now required considerable preparation. Thus a contractor frequently evolved into an engineer or a domestic servant into a trained nurse. Second, many professions were being subdivided into parts, each part requiring a period of intensive preparation, and, thereafter, tending to exist in its own right. Dentistry, for example, had come to include not only the profession of the dentist, but that of the orthodontist, the research dentist, the dental nurse, the dental hygienist, the dental mechanic. Third, there was evidence that individuals moved from one occupational level to another with less frequency than formerly. A dental mechanic, for example, might improve his status in salary and position, but he tended to remain a mechanic and not to become a dentist.[18]

A similar point of view influenced the organization of courses in general education in the first two years of college and lower division of universities. An example of the general education course is the survey course which evolved out of the laudable desire to give unity and consistency to the student's education by means of an overview of representative fields of knowledge or an equally complete introduction to the facts and principles and activities within a functional area of living. Probably the most ambitious effort along this line was made by Col-

18. Robert J. Leonard, "Professional Education in Junior Colleges," *Teachers College Record*, May 1925, p. 729.

gate University, where students in the freshman year were required to devote two thirds of their time to five survey courses: a survey of the physical sciences, the biological sciences, the social sciences, the fine arts, and philosophy and religion. It was the ambition of Colgate, in this way, to enable the student at the beginning of his college education to survey "the whole domain of human knowledge." [19]

Still other institutions adopted the method of introducing students to "functional areas of living." Stephens College, a girls' college in Missouri, attracted wide attention to its curriculum which was organized on this plan. Under the direction of W. W. Charters, surveys were made of the activities in which women engage and the problems and needs they encounter in the course of their lives. These were classified under seven different categories of activities and problems, following which courses were devised with an eye to enabling the students to acquire the facts and principles and skills essential for effective functioning as women.

Observe that the assumptions underlying these approaches to the organization of the curriculum were similar to those followed in the applications of job analysis to vocational education. In each instance, the student was viewed as primarily a recipient of ideas, skills, and habits defined for him. To insure their acquisition, the educator leaned heavily upon behavioristic psychology and the statistical and scientific tools its devotees had developed for identifying and selecting those adult activities which, when viewed objectively and quantitatively, seemed of most importance.

It was not long before the limitations in these methods of determining what knowledge is of most worth became evident. Nevertheless, the determination to apply scientific method to the organization of the curriculum had the advantage of bringing to the forefront of educational discussion a search for the criteria that should operate in defining the task of the school. The result was that the curriculum of both elementary and secondary schools, and, eventually, that of the college, became for educators a central problem of study and experimentation.[20]

19. See statement of President Cutten in the *Thirty-first Yearbook,* National Society for the Study of Education, Part II, pp. 46–47.

20. See, for example, the *Twenty-sixth Yearbook,* National Society for the Study of Education, Parts I, II. Also Harold B. Alberty and Elsie J. Alberty, *Reorganizing the High School Curriculum,* 3d ed. (New York: Macmillan Co., 1962), chaps. 5–8.

Teaching Methods Take Character from Scientific Management

The psychology of adjustment and attempts to introduce the spirit and methods of scientific management into the school not only led to new methods of curriculum organization, but also revolutionized teaching procedures and classroom methods.

Both Pestalozzi and Herbart, as we have seen, did much to professionalize the task of the teacher. Their efforts, however, centered pretty much upon the acts of the instructor. Under the $S \rightarrow R$ bond, or stimulus-response concept of learning, attention centered more specifically upon a meticulous direction of the activities of the child.

One of the first attempts in this direction was the supervised study movement. This resulted from both psychological and sociological considerations. On the psychological side attention was directed toward the acquisition of study habits in contrast with exclusive emphasis upon the recitation.

On the sociological side, educators had become impressed by the large number of pupils who lacked facilities for study at home. Investigations of home conditions seemed to establish a one-to-one relation between home conditions for study and quality of schoolwork. These facts, together with accumulated evidence that home assignments were often poorly given and inadequately understood by children, gave support to the suggestion that schools should develop methods of instruction which would bring the entire learning activity of the student under the direction and control of the teacher.

Supervised study (the "directed period," as it was sometimes called) involved three steps: review, study, recite. Not infrequently, the conscientious administrative officer insisted upon specific time limits for each phase!

One advantage in supervised study quickly became evident. As the classroom was transformed into a place for supervised study as well as for reciting, attention began to center upon difficulties students encounter in learning and the work habits appropriate to each field of study. Studying, in other words, became professionalized, and manuals and texts, as well as directions for study within the conventional textbook, began to make their appearance.

Supervised study soon drew attention to the need for lengthening the conventional class period, and, somewhat later, instruction was organized in terms of units of work, and the daily recitation period was abolished altogether. Thus the time consumed in completing each phase of a unit was variable, depending upon the nature of the unit or topic under study. In these cases, as in the Morrison Plan and in what became widely known as the "contract plan," emphasis still centered upon what William Heard Kilpatrick has called "pre-digested subject matter" (information, ideas, principles, habits and skills, all carefully planned in advance) but there was, nevertheless, more generous provision for individual differences in rate of learning and even for differences in interests and abilities than existed under the traditional system of recitation.

Investigations of the results of supervised study, in contrast with the conventional recitation, clearly established its value, but they also indicated that further improvements in method were still needed, for, although the poor student obviously did better, good students either did no better or actually did worse! Analysis of these unexpected results led to the conclusion that methods of work differ from one individual to another and that what is best for one is not necessarily best for another. These conclusions led to a second development in methods of teaching—individual instruction.

Experiments with individual instruction took on different forms but two types, in particular, received wide attention, not only in this country but abroad. These two were known as the Dalton and the Winnetka plans. They are representative of the period in their efforts to model instruction on characteristics of business life and a psychology of adjustment.

Common to both plans was provision for each pupil to progress at his own rate. For certain purposes, primarily social education, the class group in each instance retained its organization. In the Dalton Plan, as conducted by its originator, Helen Parkhurst, administrative provision was made for group conferences once a week. In other schools adopting the plan, more numerous conferences were held. On occasion, in Miss Parkhurst's school, certain assignments in certain subjects were deliberately planned so that pupils might work together, as in conducting experiments in science, or the writing and production of a play in which teachers and pupils in English, history, and the arts might cooperate. Since, however, the original purpose of the Dalton Plan was to provide for individual progress, these cooperative and group ventures were not easily devised. In the Winnetka Plan, pupils were both expected and encouraged to go it alone. Assignments were completely individualized. Subjects were organized in the form of tasks, or "goals," in such a way that pupils, by following directions, might proceed alone. When a goal, or a logical portion of a goal, was completed, the pupil took a self-administered test in order to determine whether or not he was ready to submit to the teacher's examination, which was the final criterion for determining his mastery of one step and his fitness to advance to the next.

In the Winnetka Plan there was no effort to relate the achievements of a pupil in one subject, such as arithmetic, to his achievements in another, such as history or geography. Thus it frequently happened that a child might be working on fourth-grade arithmetic at the same time that he had advanced to the fifth or sixth grade in another subject.[21] Under the Dalton Plan, the conventional time schedule of subjects was also abolished, thus giving a pupil the opportunity to work on a subject in which he might be less able or slower for a longer period of time than would be necessary for a subject he could master more easily or quickly. For example, he might report to the science laboratory on a given morning and work there continuously for the entire day, thus completing a number of "contracts" in advance and saving time for subjects upon which he might work more slowly. However, he was not permitted to undertake a second month's contract in any one subject until the month's contracts for all subjects were completed.

Characteristic of both the Dalton and the Winnetka plans was the careful preparation of assignments, directions for individual progress, self-testing devices, and the final tests administered by the teacher to determine a pupil's competence to move from one "goal" or "contract" to another. In short, as their advocates envisaged their plans, partial learning and the conventional marking systems which sanctioned partial learning were replaced by an emphasis upon mastery. What was required in the way of assimilative material might vary among individuals, but no one advanced from one task to another until he had assured himself and his instructor that he was ready to do so.

Both plans, as we have said, drew their inspiration from the business

21. In describing the Winnetka Plan in the *Twenty-third Yearbook* of the National Society for the Study of Education, part II, p. 257, Superintendent Washburne cited one case of a gifted boy who was one year and six months ahead of his grade in arithmetic and two years and two months ahead in language.

world. The Dalton Plan emphasized the importance of budgeting time and entering into a "contract" to perform a task agreed upon. The Winnetka Plan divided the day into two parts, a period of hard work in which the child, like his father, worked individually at a job and a period of recreation and group activities in which he functioned as a social being. Under both plans, group and social activities, as well as art, music, and leisure-time activities, were assigned primarily to the afternoon portion of the day. However, the Dalton Plan was somewhat more flexible (or, shall we say, less consistent) than the Winnetka Plan in that work in the "common essentials" was frequently motivated by having pupils engage in group projects.

Schools adopting either of these plans found it necessary to abolish the conventional time schedule for recitations and to abandon the assumption that all pupils should begin and end a semester's assignment in a subject at the same time. Not all schools considered it wise to carry the plan of individual instruction to such an extreme. Accordingly, a number adopted the concept of mastery and individual progress while retaining the conventional class organization. The "unit method" of instruction followed at the University of Chicago Laboratory School, under the direction of H. C. Morrison, represents one such attempt.[22] Morrison's influence, like that of Carleton Washburne and Helen Parkhurst, was far-reaching. His was essentially the Herbartian psychology and method applied to instruction on the secondary level. Although he developed techniques for the teaching of understandings different from those for appreciations and skills, his influence was probably greatest in the teaching of what he called the science technique (the teaching of "understandings" in science, history, mathematics, and so on). This consisted of five steps, or stages: exploration, presentation, assimilation, organization, and recitation.[23] It was in the assimilative period that provision was made for individual rates of learning and for individual interests and abilities.

Teaching Machines and B. F. Skinner

In a recent book on the Winnetka plan, Carleton Washburne describes a "step-by-step procedure" used to teach arithmetic. "The process un-

22. The Morrison Plan was described in H. C. Morrison, *The Practice of Teaching in the Secondary School* (Chicago: The University of Chicago Press, 1926).
23. For an excellent analysis of Morrison's plan, see Alberty and Alberty, *op. cit.*, pp. 312–16.

der study," he writes, "was itself broken into small steps, each containing just one element of difficulty. We did an intensive job of what is now called 'programming' instruction." [24] Describing sets of little cards devised to teach the basic number facts of addition, subtraction, and such, Washburne indicates that he regards them as an early form of a modern teaching machine.[25]

These comparisons are quite accurate. Educational practices which are apparently based on S → R psychologies are extremely widespread, but programed instruction presented in teaching machines (and in some texts) represents the most obvious extension and refinement of practice based on Thorndike's psychology of learning. Subjects—from mathematics to psychology to the study of the Old Testament [26]—are broken down into very small units and these items are ordered in a carefully planned sequence. The student, proceeding at his own pace, operates the machine to reveal each item. Normally, each item poses a question or task and the student usually writes his response on a strip of paper revealed through a window in the machine. He then operates the machine to make his response inaccessible, though visible, and to reveal the correct response for comparison and, hopefully, for "reinforcement" or reward. Beginning with simple situations and tasks and with whatever knowledge the student brings to the situation, the program proceeds to "shape" behaviors toward desired terminal performances through a small step-by-small-step linkage of items, reinforcement, and repetition or review. As the Harvard psychologist, B. F. Skinner, writes, "Even with lower organisms, quite complex behavior can be 'shaped' in this way with surprising speed; the human organism is presumably far more sensitive." [27]

Teaching machines have had more publicity than use. Their use is feared by some educators and enthusiastically encouraged by others.[28] Although teaching machines do not constitute a "revolution" in education, their use will undoubtedly continue to increase during the

24. Carleton W. Washburne and Sidney P. Marland, Jr., *Winnetka* (Englewood Cliffs, N.J.: Prentice-Hall, Inc., 1963), p. 26.
25. *Ibid.*, pp. 30–31.
26. James G. Holland and B. F. Skinner, *The Analysis of Behavior* (New York: McGraw-Hill Book Co., Inc., 1961), p. v.
27. "Reflections on a Decade of Teaching Machines," *Teachers College Record*, November 1963, p. 169.
28. Frank L. Steeves, *Fundamentals of Teaching in Secondary Schools* (New York: Odyssey Press, Inc., 1962), pp. 135–36, 227.

coming years.[29] Many theoretical and practical differences are represented by various teaching machines and their programs. Most programs, however, are based on B. F. Skinner's theory of operant conditioning,[30] a modern version of the stimulus-response psychologies of Thorndike and Watson.[31]

Skinner is fond of comparing man with a machine.[32] Like many other neobehaviorists he is far more concerned with controlling or "shaping" behavior than he is with the "ultimate" origins or causes of behavior.[33] He urges educators "to employ available engineering technique which would efficiently build the interests and instill the knowledge which are the goals of education." [34] In this process, human behavior is the dependent variable, and the independent variable consists of those external conditions of which behavior is a function.[35] It is erroneous to ascribe the causes of behavior "to events taking place inside the organism." [36] Skinner rejects the use of terms like "idea," "purpose," and "sensation," which refer to some covert "mental" activities, in favor of terms referring only to observable behavior. He even objects to Thorndike's phrase, "trial and error," as reading "mental" attributes into the organism.[37]

According to Skinner's "law of operant conditioning," the important stimulus is the one immediately *following* the response, not the one preceding it. Any kind of "emitted response" (operant) which leads to reinforcement is thereby strengthened; that is, the probability of recurrence of that response is increased.[38] ("Reinforcement" is Skinner's

29. See, for example, Research Division, The Center for Programed Instruction, *The Use of Programed Instruction in U.S. Schools* (Washington, D.C.: U.S. Government Printing Office, 1963), pp. 2, 10, 21.

30. See Wilbur Schramm, *Programed Instruction: Today and Tomorrow* (New York: Fund for the Advancement of Education, 1962), pp. 8, 12–13, 25; Edward B. Fry, *Teaching Machines and Programmed Instruction* (New York: McGraw-Hill Book Co., Inc., 1963), p. 17.

31. For a summary of Skinner's theory, see Ernest R. Hilgard, *Theories of Learning*, 2d ed. (New York: Appleton-Century-Crofts, Inc., 1956), chap. 4.

32. B. F. Skinner, *Science and Human Behavior* (New York: Macmillan Co., 1953), pp. 45–47.

33. B. F. Skinner, *Cumulative Record* (New York: Appleton-Century-Crofts, Inc., 1959), pp. 275–77.

34. *Ibid.*, p. 228.

35. *Ibid.*, pp. 100–31.

36. B. F. Skinner, *Verbal Behavior* (New York: Appleton-Century-Crofts, Inc., 1957), p. 5.

37. *Science and Human Behavior*, p. 64.

38. Holland and Skinner, *op. cit.*, pp. 42–51.

technical term for reward.) Thus a reinforcement does not elicit a response but makes it more probable that the response will occur in the same way again. Skinner believes that most teachers have no carefully organized program for shaping and reinforcing behaviors. Moreover, with large classes, it is impossible for a teacher to provide an adequate number of reinforcements for each child at each small and necessary step.[39] It is clear to Skinner that the educational situation demands the widespread use of programed instruction and teaching machines.

What is most significant is that Skinner, like many others today, regards the teaching machine as an instrument for helping teachers accomplish their major task, the task of building firm, even rigid sets of behavior patterns which serve as "mind." This is often what is meant today by vaguer phrases such as "developing knowledge and skills" or "teaching subject matter."

Administrative Reform Reflects Corporate Organization

We thus see that both the psychology of learning and conditions within American society during the first third of the twentieth century, broadly speaking, cooperated in developing types of curriculum organization and methods of teaching which emphasized the acquisition of information, habits and techniques for adjustment, and even the development of those attitudes which empirical studies of society seemed to validate. Moreover, our discussion of Skinner and teaching machines reveals that the concept of education as adjustment is not merely a matter of historical interest.

These were developments within subject matter and method. The spirit of science and business efficiency were equally potent in bringing about administrative reforms. Originally, the people in public assembly administered their schools as they conducted other affairs of the community. Here they voted to establish a school, to employ a teacher, and to provide the essentials of maintenance. In time, it seemed advisable to delegate the details of administration to a committee or to an individual. Before long, however, this method, too, proved inadequate for the proper conduct of the school, and a specially designated officer came into being charged with the responsibilities of executive secretary

39. *Cumulative Record*, pp. 150–54.

or school superintendent. In Connecticut, for example, "school visitors" or a "school committee" undertook the task of preparing courses of study, supervising methods of instruction, and enforcing discipline, but eventually these functions were delegated to one individual. However, the inferior service rendered by laymen resulted, in time, in the selection of a trained educator with the title of superintendent.[40]

The school committee has also set the pattern for the administration of city school systems. Since our cities have commonly enlarged through the absorption of communities that were once independent, school systems have grown by a similar process. Often these new additions insisted upon maintaining a direct interest in their schools, with the result that the central board of education became an aggregate of semi-independent committees, each tending to put the interests of its own district first. In other instances, a central board was established with control over the schools as a whole. In either case, it was the general practice to perpetuate district or ward representation, with the result that city boards of education increased in size with the growth of the city. As late as 1902, for example, the Philadelphia board of education was composed of some five hundred members.

It soon became obvious that large boards with district representation and the inevitable log-rolling methods of arriving at decisions on critical matters could result only in the demoralization of the schools. Committeee administration of matters such as the purchase of school supplies, employment of teachers, selection of textbooks, and so on, not only fostered inefficiency but encouraged graft and favoritism.[41] Maladministration of public education became one aspect of what Lincoln Steffens, writing early in the century, characterized as the "shame of the cities," and the rescue of the schools from the clutches of special interests was one of the leading objectives of all who labored for reform.

In their search for ways and means of bettering school administration,

40. Frank P. Graves, *The Administration of American Education* (New York: The Macmillan Co., 1932), pp. 407–08.
41. Samuel T. Dutton and David Snedden point out that in the city of Rochester, New York, lay members of the board of education once served on the following committees: finance, qualification and employment of teachers, organization of schools and grievances, textbooks, library and apparatus, repairs, buildings, supplies, fuel and fire fixtures, printing, free academy salaries, janitors, and law apportionment. [*Administration of Public Education in the United States* (New York: The Macmillan Co., 1915), p. 141.]

reformers turned to business organization as a model. Nor is it strange that they did so. Both the conduct and the structure of large business corporations seemed at the time to possess characteristics the schools were sadly lacking, which lack had brought school systems to their low estate. In contrast with the large board of education, whose operations involved waste of time, log-rolling, and, all too often, the subordination of the public interest to special interests, the governing boards of corporations were small, evidenced a singleness of purpose, and concerned themselves with the formulations of policy as distinct from the details of administration. Superintendents of schools, as the executive officers of boards of education, were commonly checked in their administration of details by the self-seeking and petty interference of laymen. Boards of directors of corporations defined general policies, assigned the task of their execution to a manager, and encouraged him from that point on to exercise initiative and independence.

A similar comparison can be made of the internal structure of the business corporation. The general manager appointed the heads of departments on the basis of merit, and department heads were held immediately responsible to the manager for results. Centralized responsibility and control, clearly defined functions, and single-hearted concentration of each functionary upon his own sphere of duties seemed ideal, a method worthy of incorporation in the conduct of public affairs.

Out of these contrasts came the general pattern of school organization and administration as we see it today in the United States. The large board has been replaced by the small board, which, in ideal at least, concerns itself with the formulation of policy rather than the details of administration. Ward or district representation has given way largely to citywide or nongeographical representation, either by appointment or election. Within the school system, there are clear-cut divisions of labor and authority which run from the board of education to the superintendent and from him to associate or assistant superintendents, to principals, to heads of departments, to teachers. There are some variations, to be sure, in the internal structure of administration and supervision. For example, in one city or county, assistants to the superintendent, as supervisors, may be assigned responsibilities on a geographical basis, and in another, assignments may be along functional lines, as, for example, elementary schools, junior high schools, senior high schools, or some division of the curriculum such as elementary education, home economics, physical education, and the like.

Especially from 1910 to 1930, as Professor Raymond E. Callahan shows in his scholarly study, *Education and the Cult of Efficiency*,[42] great pressure was brought to bear upon school administrators to adopt a businesslike, cost-conscious attitude. The education of school administrators became heavily loaded with finance, accounting, public relations, buildings and equipment, and the like. A statement by Ellwood P. Cubberly, perhaps the leading teacher of educational administrators during most of that period, conveys the spirit of the times:

> Our schools are, in a sense, factories in which the raw products (children) are to be shaped and fashioned into products to meet the various demands of life. The specifications for manufacturing come from the demands of the twentieth-century civilization, and it is the business of the school to build its pupils to the specifications laid down. This demands good tools, specialized machinery, continuous measurement of production to see if it is according to specifications, the elimination of waste in manufacture, and a large variety in the output.[43]

Horizons were narrowed as the administrator became more an efficiency expert than an educational leader. But, in a technical sense, these developments resulted in more "efficient" administration. Then, too, assisted by legislation designed to protect the schools from interference, either from members of the board when acting as individuals or from outside pressure groups, school systems and school officials are today relatively free to concentrate upon their educational functions in a manner often denied them in the past. Not until approximately the second quarter of the century did the question of the appropriateness of an organization of education in harmony with the structure and purposes of business disturb educators or the general public. With the advent of totalitarianism abroad, however—especially the rise of Mussolini in Italy and Hitler in Germany and the challenge these dictators hurled at the "effete" democracies of the West—misgivings developed. Educators, like others, began to question themselves seriously as to the meaning of democracy and democratic education. From this it was but

42. Chicago: University of Chicago Press, 1962.
43. Quoted in Raymond E. Callahan, *op. cit.*, p. 152.

a step to inquire: How relevant is the administrative organization of the school to the purposes of a democratic education? Is the organization of an education on an essentially authoritarian and autocratic pattern best designed to prepare young people for responsible participation in democratic life? What changes would follow in the administration of the school, as well as the conduct of the classroom, if public schools undertook literally to raise young people for responsible participation in a government of the people, by the people, and for the people?

To many, the answer to this question involved the application of a psychology of learning and a response to factors in American life different from education for adjustment.

Suggested Reading

Alberty, Harold B., and Elsie J. Alberty, *Reorganizing the High School Curriculum*, 3d ed. (New York: Macmillan Co., 1962), chaps. 5–8.

Callahan, Raymond E., *Education and the Cult of Efficiency* (Chicago: University of Chicago Press, 1962), chaps. 1–2, 6, 8–10.

Cremin, Lawrence A., *The Transformation of the School* (New York: Alfred A. Knopf, 1961), chaps. 1–4.

Holland, James G. and B. F. Skinner, *The Analysis of Behavior* (New York: McGraw-Hill Book Co., Inc., 1961). (This is a programed textbook on Skinnerian psychology.)

Kolesnik, Walter B., *Mental Discipline in Modern Education* (Madison, Wisconsin: University of Wisconsin Press, 1958).

Nash, Paul, Andreas M. Kazamias, and Henry J. Perkinson, eds., *The Educated Man: Studies in the History of Educational Thought* (New York: John Wiley and Sons, Inc., 1965), chap. 15.

Thorndike, Edward L., *Educational Psychology, Briefer Course* (New York: Teachers College, Columbia University, 1917), chaps. I, X.

Wolman, Benjamin, *Contemporary Systems and Theories in Psychology* (New York: Harper & Row, 1960), pp. 32–41, 76–85, 125–40.

Chapter 10

Education in an Interdependent World: Theories of Learning

Theories of Learning As Expressions of the Culture

Thus far we have considered four psychologies of learning in their American setting, together with their influence upon classroom and school. The first was called the *mind-substance* theory, since it conceived of the mind as an all-embracing substance, analogous in one of its aspects to a container or a receptor of experience and in another aspect to an active agent endowed with faculties or powers which work over original impressions, giving order and character to them. In each instance man is viewed as dual in nature, consisting of body and soul. Body is a physical substance and operates in accordance with the laws of the material world; the mind, or the soul, in contrast, is an immaterial substance (defined in terms precisely the opposite of material substance) which, by virtue of its power to receive and organize sensations and ideas, can mirror and even anticipate objects and events in the external world. It thus serves as the directive agent in the partnership.

A second theory emphasizes the importance of *inborn tendencies,* instinctive ways of thinking, feeling, and acting which make their appearance at well-defined stages of development in the life of the individual as he progresses from infancy to adulthood. We characterize adherents of this conception of learning as the *follow-nature* group, since the nature and the sequence of instinctive expressions dictate what is appropriate in the way of learning experiences and the methods of instruction employed by those responsible for dealing with the young.

A third conception of learning, the theory of *mental states* (clearly represented by the Herbartians), rejects the concept of the mind as an entity separate and distinct from its content. Rather it considers this relationship as similar to that of a woods to its trees. That is to say, the mind lacks objective reality. It is nothing more or less than a collective noun. On this view, the operations of the mental life are explained entirely by means of the laws of association. Mental states (sensations, perceptions, images, ideas, and so on) are, however, intimately associated with the nervous system—so intimately, indeed, that psychologists soon observed that no psychic state can make its appearance without neural activity, although physical processes obviously can perform their functions with or without consciousness. This observation shortly led many to pose the question: "Is consciousness anything other than a spectator of events, an epi-phenomenon, and thus an impotent by-product of physical activity?"

Finally, in *behaviorism,* or what we have termed education for adjustment, we have a psychology which endeavors to explain all learning in terms of the acquisition of habits. In Thorndike (whose views serve more as a transition from a psychology of mental states to behaviorism than as an outright expression of the latter) there is no open disavowal of dualism or of mental states, although the new units of learning ($S \rightarrow R$ bonds) are clearly designed to avoid the issue of mental versus physical and to center attention in learning solely upon the conditioning of the nervous system. There is, however, one significant difference between Thorndike and behaviorists such as John Watson with respect to the originals of learning. According to Thorndike, these are inherited. Consequently, it is to heredity that we must look to determine the limits and the possibilities of education in the individual. Watson, on the other hand, stresses the influence of environmental factors. For both, however, all learning, from the simplest physical act to the most original and seemingly creative intellectual activity, is habit formation. Education, accordingly, is conceived of as an operation in which one generation gives character to its successor through carefully controlled and directed exercises. To improve himself, man must learn to lift himself by his own bootstraps!

Each of these theories of learning has influenced American education at one time or another, depending upon cultural factors that are at one time dominant and at another time recessive, and each is represented in the educational forum of today. For example, John Locke's individualism seemed admirably adapted to frontier conditions and a period when nature was lavish with its resources. Similarly, a psychology of inner development flourished during a period when cultural factors seemed to confirm man's confidence in the innate goodness of original nature in contrast with the corrupting influences of society. Finally, with the rapid transition of a rural and agricultural economy into an urban and industrial one, learning became identified with "conditioning," which is essentially a one-way process. Having before him direct evidence of his ability to change his society fundamentally by means of machines of his own invention, man studies himself and concludes, "Lo! I, too, am a machine!"

We come now to still another concept of learning, one that has profoundly influenced methods of teaching, the selection and organization of learning experiences, and the administrative and supervisory practices of the schools in the past half-century. No one term is used consistently to identify it, because its assumptions are drawn from a number of different disciplines. Although many individuals less well known than Charles Peirce, William James, John Dewey, and William Heard Kilpatrick are entitled to credit for its formulation and its applications, these four, within the disciplines of logic, philosophy, psychology, and education, are most conspicuously associated with it under various designations such as, "pragmatism," "instrumentalism," "functionalism," "experimentalism." Kilpatrick frequently employed the term "organismic learning." Within the field of education, the term "progressive education" was used for many years to identify methods and procedures which looked to "organismic learning" for their justification, although the term "progressive" has also been used to describe practices which can be justified only by distorted interpretations of this theory of learning. To avoid confusion we shall employ the terms "organic learning" and "experimentalism."

In line with our previous procedure, let us glance briefly at factors in American society which seem relevant to a psychology of learning that emphasizes interrelations and interdependence.

International Trends Emphasize Interdependence

First were the obvious changes of an economic and political character which, since the turn of the century, have undermined policies of isolation of the United States in relations with other nations and concepts of *laissez faire* and rugged individualism in economic and political relationships at home. World War I probably marked the first general realization on the part of the American people that the modern world no longer permits either nations or individuals to live unto themselves alone. Few question today that we live in what Wendell Willkie termed One World, even though this world is like a house divided against itself. World War II and international events since have taught young people in the most remote backwoods settlements that a decision of a foreign office in some small nation, the name of which they do not know, or the manner in which a colonial power deals with its subject people may decide whether they are to lay down their lives in battle.

Nor are international issues related solely to those of war. What was known early in the century as "dollar diplomacy" has evolved into relationships among people of a thousand and one varieties. Since the creation of the United Nations with its Economic and Social Council (to mention but one of the organs of the United Nations), all manner of previously existing international agencies concerned with the economic and social welfare of peoples have come into one organization, an agency which knows no rigid national boundaries. A plague in India, for example, quickly brings relief in the form of vaccine gathered from all parts of the world through the instrumentality of the World Health Organization. Similarly, through the efforts of other organizations of international membership (such as UNESCO in education), individuals and associations of individuals from all parts of the globe are learning to merge their interests and to work together in the realization of common purposes. Thus are men in the process of laying the foundations of an international morality through the welding of interests which bind the people of one nation to the people of another.

Increasingly, the "national interest" must be defined so as to include the interests not only of allies but of a larger community of nations.[1]

1. See Andrew W. Cordier, "Diplomacy Today," *Journal of International Affairs,* Number 1, 1963, pp. 3–4.

Indicative of this trend is the fact that during the period from 1901 to 1925 the yearly average number of international conferences in which the United States participated was 7.2, whereas in the period from 1956 to 1958 the average was 342.3.[2] Indicative, also, is a recent statement issued by the U.S. Department of Defense that "in a major attack upon our country, millions would be killed. There appears to be no practical program that would avoid large-scale loss of life."[3] This historic admission suggests that a reasonably adequate "provision for the common defense" is a problem that now transcends national boundaries; it indicates some reason for the predictions of a probable decline in the system of independent states and the evolution of some kind of world order.[4]

Economic Developments Undermine Rugged Individualism

In 1893, in an epoch-making article, "The Significance of the Frontier in American History," Frederick J. Turner drew attention to the closing of the American frontier. Americans, he pointed out, now faced a future in which free lands and easy access to seemingly inexhaustible natural resources would no longer play the roles that had been so significant in the past. Within two or three decades of Turner's article, the consequences of the uncontrolled exploitation of the nation's natural resources gave rise to the conservation movement on both state and national levels. It has been increasingly acknowledged that conservation is unavoidably a problem of social control and planning, and that a key to the problem is a recognition of the "interdependence of processes."[5] Water conservation, for example, cannot be divorced from soil conservation, land-use practices, electric power generation, research, and many other factors; these processes affect and, in turn, are affected by urban development, transportation, the location of industries, waste disposal, and so on.

Rugged individualism and *laissez faire* in other areas have also been

2. Amry Vandenbosch and Willard N. Hogan, *Toward World Order* (New York: McGraw-Hill Book Co., Inc., 1963), p. 26.
3. Quoted in Gerard Piel, *Science in the Cause of Man,* 2d ed. (New York: Alfred A. Knopf, 1962), p. vii.
4. See Norman J. Padelford and George A. Lincoln, *The Dynamics of International Politics* (New York: Macmillan Co., 1962), chap. 8.
5. Robert A. Brady, *Organization, Automation, and Society* (Berkeley and Los Angeles: University of California Press, 1961), pp. 402–04.

on trial. For example, the evils of unrestricted conditions of employment for women and children particularly, but of men as well (freedom of contract!), suggested to liberals, who had hitherto objected to governmental interference in economic matters, the necessity of legislation designed to control conditions of work and, in the case of children, to raise the age at which they might be employed and to compel their attendance at school prior to this point.

Moreover, large-scale economic operations with their requirements of large capital were rapidly changing the status of the "independent producer" and the small businessman. During the past two or three decades, the 500 or 600 largest industrial corporations have produced from two thirds to three fourths of America's total industrial production.[6] Oligopoly, the concentration of a major share of production in a very few firms, is the general characteristic of American industry.[7] Furthermore, a giant corporation is itself often merely a subsidiary unit in a larger corporate structure, such as the trust or holding company,[8] and, in turn, many smaller firms depend not upon competition with the giants but upon establishing "symbiotic relations" with them (supplying parts and materials, for example).[9]

As for workers, it seems that by the beginning of the 1960s only 15 per cent were self-employed.[10] About 85 per cent were "employees," and about half of these employees worked in organizations big enough to be called corporate organizations. In manufacturing, 361 corporate organizations (out of a total of 263,000 firms) employed 40 per cent of the employees in this field. Roughly similar proportions prevailed in finance, trade, transportation, and other fields.[11]

Within the corporate organizations, the general separation of management from ownership has created a novel situation in American economic life. Ownership in corporations has become relatively widely

6. A. A. Berle, Jr., "The Corporation in a Democratic Society," *Management and Corporation, 1985,* Melvin Ansken and George L. Bach, eds. (New York: McGraw-Hill Book Co., Inc., 1960), pp. 69–70.

7. See Donald Dewey, "Mergers and Cartels: Some Reservations About Policy," *American Economic Review,* May 1961, pp. 256–59.

8. Lawrence L. Bethel, *et al., Industrial Organization and Management,* 4th ed. (New York: McGraw-Hill Book Co., Inc., 1962), pp. 3–4.

9. Peter M. Blau and W. R. Scott, *Formal Organizations: A Comparative Approach* (San Francisco: Chandler Publishing Co., 1962), pp. 218–19.

10. Robert Presthus, *The Organizational Society* (New York: Alfred A. Knopf, 1962), pp. 78–79, 206.

11. W. Lloyd Warner, *The Corporation in the Emergent American Society* (New York: Harper & Row, 1962), p. 26.

diffused, but control is narrowly limited, with the result that the vast majority of shareholders have very little, if anything, to say with respect to the management and direction of what they "own." In 1962 there were seventeen million stockholders in America, although only 2.1 per cent of them held 58 per cent of the total shares.[12] There are over two million stockholders of American Telephone and Telegraph; none of them owns over ½ of 1 per cent of the stock; and the corporation is directed by a small managerial group.[13]

It would seem that the individual worker or operator of a business in the "free enterprise system" has lost his status as a self-determining individual. Even the captains of finance and industry are not captains of their own souls, since they too are parts of larger wholes over which they have little control. To be sure, within a fairly large range of discretion, many prices today are "administered prices," set by managerial policy rather than by free market conditions. But costs today are increasingly determined by public policy rather than being merely "objective" data from which policy is derived. As Robert A. Brady puts it, "cost is a function of policy as much as the reverse." [14] That is to say, public policy decisions concerning the allocation of the costs of education (what part of these costs should be regarded as a component of the "labor price"?), or the costs of road construction, concerning taxation of mass-consumption goods, concerning dozens of other matters, all are major influences in the determination of costs in many areas.

Success or failure of a product or an enterprise has become more and more dependent upon complex and sometimes unforeseeable factors. Witness the distress of the producers of silk in Japan following the invention of rayon and nylon in the United States. Economic operations now go on in a highly sensitive and delicately balanced economic society, with the result that a disturbance in one basic industry, or abnormal conditions in one section of the globe, bring maladjustment and distress in another. Rugged individualism and self-determination have given way before a closely knit and interdependent economic society.

Large organizations of capital were followed by large organizations of labor and the emergence of a variety of organized interests, all of which recognized that the individual alone is relatively helpless, but,

12. Michael D. Reagan, *The Managed Economy* (New York: Oxford University Press, 1963), pp. 35, 38.

13. *Ibid.*, p. 15.

14. Robert A. Brady, *op. cit.*, p. 22.

through association, his integrity might be insured and many of his interests and needs realized. Only through union and collective bargaining did it seem possible for the workingman to reap the advantages of "freedom of contract" and to insure for himself and his family the benefits of wages and conditions of work in harmony with the American ideal of a constantly rising standard of living.

The facts of interdependence have led liberals also to abandon the earlier notion that the best government is one that governs least and to substitute for it the ideal of government as a mutual insurance association, an agency by means of which individuals may through associated action serve needs which cannot be served when individuals operate on their own. Thus state legislatures and the national Congress have been prevailed upon to pass all manner of legislation (health laws, social security acts, provisions for unemployment insurance, laws defining standards for the manufacture and distribution of goods, minimum wage legislation, and similar laws) including measures which bring relief to business and industry in times of distress, such as the establishment of the Reconstruction Finance Corporation or acts authorizing the President to declare certain sections of the country disaster areas in times of misfortune and to bring them the assistance which only the resources of the national government can provide. After World War II, governmental responsibility for maintaining economic prosperity, developing atomic technology, promoting scientific research, and assuring an adequate supply of scientists was taken almost for granted.[15]

As we review these many developments, it becomes apparent that realization of interdependence is often accompanied by a sense of futility and weakness on the part of the individual. Confused and bewildered by the complexities of events, he has been described as apathetic and insecure, normless and rootless, an "other-directed" organization man seeking cues for behavior and belief from a shifting social pattern which he neither understands nor controls.[16] The trend of events seems to have deprived him of his one-time imperial status and assurance of significance as the architect of his own fortune and often of the fortunes of others.

15. William H. McNeill, *The Rise of the West* (Chicago: University of Chicago Press, 1963), pp. 797–98.

16. In Chapter 13, we attempt to interpret some of the analyses of the changing "American character" or style of life. An interesting introduction to this vast topic is provided by Jules Golden, *et al.*, "A Summary Description of Fifty 'Normal' White Males," *American Journal of Psychiatry*, July 1962, pp. 48–56.

A Social Concept of the Individual Emerges

On the positive side, recent social changes and concepts have developed a respect for the individual quite different from that which characterized the era of *laissez faire* and rugged individualism.

The rise of traditional democratic ideals in Europe was associated with efforts (1) to free individuals from restraints imposed by absolute governments or by groups foreign to the interests of the governed; (2) to gain freedom of operation in trade and commerce; and (3) to rise in the world without limitations of class distinctions. In America, these characteristics of the democratic ideal were encouraged by the loneliness of frontier existence and the remoteness of government and organized social institutions. Similarly, economic conditions were for a long time favorable to the concepts of *laissez faire*, with the result that for a considerable period in our history all branches of government cooperated in perpetuating the ideal of the individual as self-sufficient and of society as little more than a collection of such individuals.

In furtherance of this ideal and its associated purposes, traditional democratic theory insisted that certain individual or "natural" elements were superior to and directive of political and economic institutions. Thus the "inalienable natural rights" of individuals were not established by society; society was established to protect these rights. Thus the "natural profit motive" was not born and nurtured in social experience; rather, the economy must be such (*laissez faire*) as to insure the natural operation of this motive.

Later, this conception of the individual and society began to yield sour fruit, with the result that the meaning of democracy was brought under critical review. In both philosophy and psychology the social nature of growth and development began to receive attention hitherto denied it, and the nature of society was redefined. In contrast to the concept of society as a mere collection of individuals or as an entity separate from the individual, society was now conceived of, in one of its essential aspects, as habitual and confirmed ways in which people think, feel, and act in association. Just as the concept of democratic government was redefined, so, also, the concept of government in general underwent redefinition. No longer was government envisaged as a necessary evil or an organization external to the interests of the individual, or merely as a referee between rival and competing interests. Rather, it was recognized as an indispensable instrument for realizing interests and values and meeting needs through associated actions which individuals alone could not realize.

In this revision of democratic ideals, equality was no longer identified with sameness of individual natures or of external conditions but, rather, with an equal and effective right of participation in the social process from which both common purposes and individual differences develop. Thus, in relations between personalities and groups, new conceptions of what constitute "right relations" have come into being. For example, the cultural background of an individual or group becomes an important factor in the determination of "the right," even to the extent of modifying at times the abstract principle which once dictated an answer.

Democracy was seen as placing emphasis on the recognition of the worth and integrity of the individual. This assumption continues as a be-all and an end-all; but the new definition is unique in its insistence that only through relationships, that is, through qualities of relationship between individuals and groups, can the democratic ideal be realized. Democracy is thus no longer a political or an economic ideal, merely; it has evolved into a social and a moral ideal, "signifying the possession and continued use of certain attitudes, forming personal character and determining desire and purpose in all the relationships of life." [17]

Finally, a democratic society is viewed as one which abides by the principle stated by Charles Sanders Peirce: "Do not block the way of inquiry." [18] Though formed and informed by past experience a democratic society reserves the right to generate its own norms and institutions through a rational, social, and continuing decision-making process. Like any other open and rational process of inquiry, social decision-making may alter its assumptions and conclusions, unencumbered by alleged absolutes which are presumed to emanate from "nature" or from any source external to the social process.

17. For this description of democracy as a moral ideal, see the address prepared for delivery by John Dewey at the celebration of his eightieth birthday and reprinted in Irwin Edman, *John Dewey, His Contributions to the American Tradition* (New York: The Bobbs-Merrill Company, Inc., 1955), chap. VIII.

18. See Thomas L. Thorson, *The Logic of Democracy* (New York: Holt, Rinehart and Winston, 1962), pp. 120–24.

Science Emphasizes Interrelationships

Not only changes in political, economic, and social relations have given rise to a social conception of the individual; science, too, has contributed toward that end. In biology, for example, the concept of traits once basic to Thorndike's explanation of behavior in terms of S → R bonds is no longer viewed as analogous to the unit characters in the Mendelian theory. Traits are now believed to be the resultants of relationships between inner and outer factors, an interpretation which renders untenable the once rigid division between heredity and environment.

In the first place, "the development of an organism cannot be adequately understood as the outcome of a gradual accretion of 'characters' [traits], each produced by a separate gene. The genes function as members of an ensemble, like players in a symphony orchestra rather than like soloists." [19] Thus, a gene A may be harmful in combination with B, beneficial with C, neutral with D, and contributory toward quite different results with E and F.[20]

Moreover, genetic materials do not by themselves produce "blue eyes" or any other traits. With the same genetic materials, alterations in a wide variety of "internal" and "external" conditions may trigger differential developmental patterns and help produce different results. "No final resulting character is 'purely hereditary,' " writes Hampton J. Carson. "Genes must react with and operate through the environment to produce the characters. . . . The character is always the outcome of two forces. . . ." [21]

The central role of interrelationships in determining part-characteristics is illustrated in the development of animal embryos. Under normal conditions, certain cell sections of an embryo will produce, say, the eye, others the skin, the spinal cord, and so on. But whether or not these sections will actually do so depends not only upon materials within the

19. Theodosius Dobzhansky, "Evolution and Environment," in *The Evolution of Life*, vol. I of *Evolution After Darwin*, Sol Tax, ed. (Chicago: University of Chicago Press, 1960), p. 415.
20. See, for example, George W. Beadle, *Genetics and Modern Biology* (Philadelphia: American Philosophical Society, 1963), p. 54; Morton Beckner, *The Biological Way of Thought* (New York: Columbia University Press, 1959), p. 5.
21. *Heredity and Human Life* (New York: Columbia University Press, 1963), p. 98.

cells but also upon conditions outside the cells and relations among cells. In numerous experiments, cell sections have been transplanted, grafted into another embryo. A small piece of prospective skin, if transplanted to the center of an eye-producing region, will be transformed into an eye; if transplanted to a muscle-producing region, it will form part of the muscle. These transplanted sections "can differentiate into muscle, or into nervous tissue, into notochord, or kidney, gut, or liver. In other words, practically all the tissues of the body can be formed by this material." [22] As the eminent biologist Norman J. Berrill writes: "In developing systems of unspecialized cells, the cells acquire special differentiation according to their position in the system." [23]

Of course, there comes a time when plasticity ends, when the cell sections become specialized. But the dominant role of patterned relations over the functions and characteristics of parts is maintained in many other ways—for example, in the mutually sustaining relations among the circulatory, respiratory, and nervous systems; in the relations between organism and environment, relations so intimate that "we have to remember that events inside the individual and outside form connected systems and that our separation is purely a matter of convenience." [24]

This general emphasis on interrelationships may be found today in many scientific disciplines and in various specific forms. Einstein's theory of relativity assumes that the fundamental concepts of physics (e.g., space, time, mass) are "relational" terms, having no determinable meaning outside a given field or frame of reference which includes the observer—just as being "on the right" or "on the left" are relational concepts. [25]

Modern theory in social anthropology stresses that the "same" cultural trait or institution may have quite different meanings or functions in different cultures, depending on the relations of that institution to

22. C. P. Raven, *An Outline of Developmental Physiology* (New York: Pergamon Press, 1959), p. 114.

23. *Growth, Development, and Pattern* (San Francisco: W. H. Freeman and Co., 1961), p. 137.

24. Marston Bates, "Ecology and Evolution," in *The Evolution of Life,* vol. I of *Evolution After Darwin,* Sol Tax, ed. (Chicago: University of Chicago Press, 1960), p. 549.

25. See Percy W. Bridgman, *A Sophisticate's Primer of Relativity* (Middletown, Conn.: Wesleyan University Press, 1962), pp. 28–31, 91–95.

other elements of a culture. Two cultures might have almost identical lists of traits and still be quite different. As Harry Hoijer writes: "Cultural anthropologists, during the last twenty-five years, have gradually moved from an atomistic definition of culture, describing it as a more or less haphazard collection of traits, to one which emphasizes pattern and configuration." [26] Again, anthropologists do not regard the "mind" as some kind of "antecedent and ready-made thing" with its own built-in response tendencies, motives, and so on. Mind is viewed as a complex of concrete behaviors, the working of beliefs and dispositions which vary with and are functions of social experience. [27]

Several versions of Gestalt psychology, developed during the past half century, have emphasized that "wholes"—a melody, a shape, a quality of (say) roughness, a theory—cannot be understood merely in terms of the properties of parts. Certain "Gestalt qualities," which are not derivable from the traits of the "ultimate" components, emerge from the relationships of parts. Thus we may recognize the same melody even though the specific notes are different. Originating in studies of perception, principles of Gestalt psychology have been fruitfully applied in studies of learning, memory, thinking, and motivation. [28] Borrowing heavily from Gestalt psychology, certain "open system" personality theories [29] and several "field theories" in the social sciences [30] focus attention on a kind of "organism-environmental gestalt." While recognizing that not everything can be studied at the same time, these theories take the organism-in-an-environment as the basic unit of study rather than this or that fragment (trait, motive, perception, and so on) of the individual or some self-sufficient bit of the environment.

Now, in all these varied theories, qualities or traits are seen as

26. "The Relation of Language to Culture," in *Anthropology Today*, A. L. Kroeber, ed. (Chicago: University of Chicago Press, 1953), p. 554.

27. A. Irving Hallowell, "Self, Society, and Culture in Phylogenetic Perspective," in *The Evolution of Man*, vol. II of *Evolution After Darwin*, Sol Tax, ed. (Chicago: University of Chicago Press, 1960), pp. 315–16. See also Edward T. Hall, *The Silent Language* (Greenwich, Conn.: Fawcett Publications, Inc., 1961), pp. 45–58, 133–42.

28. See Mary Henle, ed., *Documents of Gestalt Psychology* (Berkeley and Los Angeles: University of California Press, 1961).

29. See Gordon W. Allport, "The Open System in Personality Theory," in *Current Perspectives in Social Psychology*, E. P. Hollander and R. G. Hunt, eds. (New York: Oxford University Press, 1963), pp. 151–62.

30. See J. Milton Yinger, "Research Implications of a Field View of Personality," *American Journal of Sociology*, March 1963, pp. 580–92; Kurt Lewin, *Field Theory in Social Science* (New York: Harper & Row, 1951), chaps. 3–4.

emerging from relations, including the relations of the organism and the environment. The search for adequate descriptions and explanations becomes a multidimensional search, following converging lines of energies and events and not resting content with some single, simple factor—gene, stimulus, motive, or whatever. Simple cause-effect relations are recognized as being elliptical and possibly misleading, as when we say "the discarded match caused the forest fire," even though we know that the presence of oxygen, the low kindling temperature of dry leaves, the absence of moisture, carelessness (due to . . . ?) were all involved in this matter. In the same way, when a teacher believes that her class became noisy *because* she stepped out of the room for a moment, she is probably turning away from a consideration of many relevant factors.

In relations between the organism and the environment, causal efficacy does not seem to be located in either internal or external factors taken separately. Pain is neither in a needle and then transferred to a person, nor in a person regardless of the needle, but is something that emerges from a certain kind of relationship. In general, internal factors seem to draw out and limit environmental influences and, at the same time, environmental factors condition the nature and influence of internal factors. This conception of interrelationship as a mutually conditioning, two-way process contributed to the development of a psychology strikingly different from those which assume that the environment impresses its own meaning upon mind, or that mind's dispositions and actions are the ultimate source of significance or behavior.

A Psychology of Organic Behavior Competes with a Psychology of Adjustment

The psychology which emerged rejects the concept of a mind as analogous to a blank sheet of paper upon which experience writes, a container to be filled, or a substance endowed with faculties that grow and develop under the stimulus of external application. Insofar as the term *mind* serves a purpose, according to this view, it is best thought of as a verb rather than a noun. It is a name for a distinctive type of behavior, behavior of an *organic* character, which occurs when objects and events take on meaning and significance (implications for the future) which the individual thus anticipates and seeks to control or direct in ways friendly to ends and purposes envisaged. It is, in short, a process of minding.

Mind, for this school, moreover, is but one form of organic behavior, if organic behavior is conceived as other than adjustment or mere habit formation of a one-way type of reaction. It contrasts with behaviorism as implicit in Thorndike and explicit in Watson. The origins of behavior, as we saw in Thorndike, are S → R bonds (observe the direction of the arrow!) or original and innate tendencies to respond in specific ways to stimuli of a specific character. In Watson, emphasis is placed upon the original plasticity of the organism, but plasticity in the sense of readiness to take on form and character from external pressure and direction, more or less as putty responds to the pressure of the hand. The concept of an organism here presented, in contrast, emphasizes the two-way character of behavior. The baby, in responding to its parents, transforms them as well as itself! What distinguishes an organism is the fact that a unique type of interplay or transaction between itself and its surroundings is a condition and means of its survival and prospering, an interplay in which both factors in the situation undergo change.

This conception of an organism and of organic behavior flatly repudiates the analogy between a machine and an organism. A machine functions properly only so long as its parts remain unchanged. An organism, on the other hand, continues to function only by virtue of a continuous alteration and re-creation of its parts (organs, tissues, cells, fluids) in response to changes it is at the same time effecting in its surroundings.

John Dewey introduced the idea of interaction (or, as he later expressed it, *transaction* between inner and outer) with the publication in 1896 of a paper on the reflex-arc concept in psychology. In this paper he attempted to refute the conventional idea of stimulus-response as essentially a one-way process in which an external stimulus impinges upon a sense organ, passes through a central system, and emerges as a response, which, when repeated frequently, creates a channel, so to speak, in the nervous system of a reflex or habitual character. As against this conception, Dewey held that activity (stimulus and response) constitutes a cycle (a "reflex current") in which the response may seek out or "constitute" the stimulus. That is, one gives character to the other.

Thus, an object may have different meanings in different situations and in relation to individuals with different problems, purposes, and experiences. A book may be perceived (responded to) as "overdue at the library," "too expensive," "something I must read," or, by a child, as a strange object diverting the mother's attention from the child.[31] These varying responses help constitute the book as a stimulus to further and varying responses. Moreover, not all organisms can perceive a book as something to be read. Nor have people developed books or knowledge about anything (about, say, trees and the connection of wood pulp with the paper in books) by the mere reception of impressions which mirror qualities "out there" or by the expression of innate drives. The familiar objects of our environment gradually take on the characteristics by which they are known as a result of give-and-take between ourselves and them.

Thinking Conceived of As an Interrelationship

It is this fact of a mutually creative relationship between the individual and his environment that the earlier psychology of habit formation neglects. Take an act of reflective thought, for example. According to Thorndike and the behaviorists, an original and creative act is neither original nor creative in any genuine sense. Inspect it carefully, break it down into its constituent parts, and one finds that it is composed of "preformed bonds." For Thorndike an act of thought is little different except in its complexity from reflex action. As Thorndike put it, "We trust to the laws of cerebral nature to present us spontaneously with the appropriate idea and also to prefer that idea to others." [32] Watson describes thinking as "talking to oneself"; that is, as a purely physiological process of a habitual character. To the experimentalist, these explanations are inadequate in that they attempt to explain a total process in terms of merely one of its aspects. One distinctive characteristic of thinking, for example, is the use of meanings. Items of present

31. For some indication of the many factors entering into the complex process of perception, see Eleanor J. Gibson, "Perceptual Learning," in *Annual Review of Psychology*, Paul R. Farnsworth, ed. (Palo Alto, Calif.: Annual Reviews, Inc., 1963), pp. 29–56; John A. Swets, Wilson P. Tanner, Jr., and Theodore G. Birdsall, "Decision Processes in Perception," *Psychological Review*, September 1961, pp. 301–40.

32. Edward L. Thorndike, *Educational Psychology, Briefer Course* (New York: Teachers College, Columbia University, 1917), p. 172.

experience point to, imply, and suggest things not present. Let us suppose that I am driving along an unfamiliar highway and come to a fork in the road. Which route shall I take? To decide this question, I look for "signs," highway markings and others. I trace in imagination, with what data I can muster, the consequences of one choice or the other, and, finally, test in action the decision arrived at. In other instances, the past may function in such a way as to give certain characteristics to present data (such as an established principle or a cherished ideal or a precept which has often demonstrated its applicability to similar situations) and to charge these data with future implications.

For the experimentalist, then, thinking is a unique type of interrelationship, roughly analogous to other forms of give-and-take behavior between an organism and its environment. It is a relationship, however, on a much higher level than one of physical contact. In thinking and the higher forms of learning, the environment includes things absent as well as things present, the remote as well as the immediate. Thinking originates in a disturbed situation. The customary flow of events is halted. In a complete act of thought, there follows an attempt to locate the difficulty, to define the problem. Then follows a process not unlike trial-and-error behavior. Suggested ways of resolving the difficulty present themselves and are examined in terms of what they promise. Those which seem to meet the conditions of the problem are tried out and tested. If inadequate, they are rejected, and new candidates in the form of inferences and hypotheses are examined. This procedure continues until a final solution is found.

According to the experimentalist, thinking, as we have described it, "is the method of an educative experience," [33] and, conversely, the most effective methods of learning are identical with the method of reflective thinking. Consequently, he would have the subject matter of instruction planned with this in mind.

The scientist goes farther. He believes that when learning follows the method of reflective thinking, which is also the method employed in science, it not only develops an intellectual discipline most relevant to the nature of modern life, but lends itself as well to the development of democratic values. And, to achieve this result, he insists, is a primary responsibility of the school. John L. Childs writes:

33. John Dewey, *Democracy and Education* (New York: The Macmillan Co., 1916), p. 192. See also H. G. Hullfish and Philip G. Smith, *Reflective Thinking: The Method of Education* (New York: Dodd, Mead and Co., 1961), part IV.

In their attempt to care for democratic values, in the sphere of education . . . the experimentalists hold that children should be accepted as persons and treated accordingly. They affirm that to treat an immature human being as a moral end requires that he be educated in such a way that he will progressively develop into a self-directing person, equipped to make an intelligent manifestation of preference, and qualified to share in the determination of the social arrangements under which he lives, including the ends for which he spends his energies. In the development of democratic attitudes and skills, as in the development of scientific attitudes and skills, the experimentalist holds that it is essential for the young to practice that which we would have them learn and become. It is at this point in education that the scientific and democratic procedures meet as one, for both call for a person who can think, who has respect for evidence and consequences, and who is willing to bring his ideas of truth and value to the test of group examination, criticism, and validation. In fact, the self-correcting procedures of scientific inquiry and the self-governing procedures of democratic living, both internalize authority within the shared experiences of ordinary men and women, and they call for the nurture of the young in that pattern of morality and character which is the correlative of these co-operative human procedures.[34]

The experimentalist's concept of learning, as we have seen, rejects a dualism in which a mind as an immaterial substance receives impressions in some mysterious way from the sense organs and then proceeds to give form and character to them. It also rejects the concept of mental states, together with its description of learning as no more than an association of ideas. This, it holds, differs from the psychology of behaviorism only superficially. Change the vocabulary by substituting "the laws of cerebral nature" for the "laws of association" and the difference between the two fades away.

A New Theory of Instincts

On the other hand, the experimentalist likewise refuses to accept the concept of instincts as inner drives or organized systems of responses

34. *The Experimentalist Educational Theory*, Bode Memorial Lectures, 1957 (Columbus, Ohio: College of Education, The Ohio State University), pp. 14–15.

which come to us from inheritance. He conceives of original impulses as unorganized and unformed, but which, in interaction with the culture (as the anthropologist conceives of culture) or the "ordered relations" of the environment, take on a form and character that is both new and old. It is this conception that led Dewey to assert that "the meaning of native activities is not native, it is acquired," and, again, "we need to know about the social conditions which have educated original activities into definite and significant dispositions before we can discuss the psychological element in society." [35]

Dewey's position is thus a mean between two extremes. In contrast with the idea of education as adjustment, Dewey's emphasis is on the importance of seeing in native impulses the possibilities of novel response to environmental factors. Instead of following nature, he would encourage an accommodation between native impulse and cultural factors. Take language, for example. The unformed utterances of the child are soon channeled in such a way as to conform to the verbal expressions of his family and community. He speaks the words with the accent and the meaning others give to them. But not without variation! He adds his own enunciation, and he may also give to his words shades of meaning slightly different from common usage, deviations which, in some instances, are adopted by others. In this way the language we use is both idiomatic and common to the group to which we belong.

So it is with other responses of the young person to his culture. No generation follows exactly in the footsteps of its elders. In these variations of response which individuals make to the customary and the traditional as well as to the novel in their environment reside the possibilities of change and progress. Consequently, the wise parent and teacher are sensitive to the potentialities within novel responses of the young as well as to the nourishing and sustaining effects of identification with group pattern, whether these be in the interpretation and use of objects and events or in the realm of manners and morals.

The above is a sketchy presentation of the experimental or organic concept of learning. Basic to understanding of the concept is the idea of a "transaction" between an organism and the environment as a condition of survival and development. On all levels, from the responses of a simple one-celled organism to those of the most complex

35. John Dewey, *Human Nature and Conduct* (New York: Henry Holt & Co., Inc., 1922), pp. 90–91.

organisms, "transaction" involves an *adaptation,* of a give-and-take character, to the environment—adaptation in the sense that the organism and its medium are engaged in a mutually transforming relationship. In the evolutionary process this mutually responsive relationship goes hand in hand with structural developments or changes in the organism. On all levels, organisms have interests or goals which they seek to realize consciously or unconsciously. With the acquisition of distance receptors (eyes, ears, nose) these interests come to involve the future as well as the immediately present and the distant as well as the tangibly near. With these acquisitions also, the environment takes on new qualities. Eventually, too, the past contributes to the nature of present experience. In man, gestures and symbols and language enable the remote in time as well as space, the future as well as the past, to function in the present, and the interests of others as well as of oneself become an inherent part of each individual.

As the experimentalist sees it, this conception of organism renders inadequate previous explanations of learning, either in terms of a mind (as distinct from body) which receives and organizes experiences, or the concept of stimulus and response (body without mind) as a conditioning process. As viewed by the experimentalist, the organism, as body, has more mind in it than the behaviorist will grant, and, as mind, the organism has more body in it than the traditional conception of mind permits. This is true, whether we view the responses of the organism from within or in response to external stimuli.

Consider, for example, the relationship between the blood stream and the organs of the body. This can be described only as a form of communication, a highly sensitive relationship in which the blood is kept in a relatively uniform condition by various organs which, responding to the composition of the blood, help regulate that composition; the blood, in turn, conveys to the same organs (the lungs, kidneys, liver, and so on) what they require for their healthy functioning.[36]

In much the same way, the organism communicates with its environment. Breathing, wrote Dewey many years ago, is an affair of the atmsophere as well as of the lungs.

36. For a more comprehensive summary of complex physiological transactions, see Maurice Sussman, *Animal Growth and Development* (Englewood Cliffs, N.J.: Prentice-Hall, Inc., 1960), pp. 85–91.

Learning Viewed As a Unique Form of Communication

Learning, too, is a form of communication. It is purposive in that meanings and goals operate as selective factors in relationships between "inner" and "outer," the individual and his environment. Were we to employ the term *mind* in this connection, we should say it signifies the *process of "minding,"* a process in which objects and events suggest future consequences in such a way as to influence present behavior. Again, learning is a process in which experiences in the past operate along with factors in the present with an eye to their future implications. To continue in paradoxes, learning may be described as a process in which an individual maintains his integrity, continues to be himself, by consistently reconstructing and remaking himself and his environment into something different. When an organism ceases to learn, it dies.

Students of the biological and behavioral sciences agree that rigidities—in biological structures, beliefs, or anything else—often become maladaptive as situations change. Proponents of organic learning have stressed that, particularly in a world rocking with change, the *ability to go on learning* is a suitable description of the over-all aim of education. This ability to grow embraces the various sub-aims of education within a unified, directive whole. It includes wide and deep knowledge—but the kind that stimulates inquiry and the integration of relevant data in a multidimensional approach, rather than a series of conclusions that close inquiry (for example, that protect psychological theory from relevant concepts in logic, anthropology, sociology, and biology). It includes a wide range of interests and sensitivities, for without depth and liberality of concern thought is likely to be absent, superficial, or narrowly focused. It includes an intimate communication between theoretical and practical matters so that words and deeds, ends and means, may confront and illuminate each other.

Finally, learning is organic in the sense that cognitive, emotive, and other abstracted aspects of behavior are not ultimate and self-sufficient parts of behavior. As Gordon W. Allport writes, "all motives are an inextricable blend of feeling and cognition." [37] Indeed, it is misleading

37. *Pattern and Growth in Personality* (New York: Holt, Rinehart and Winston, Inc., 1961), p. 274. See also, William H. Starbuck, "Level of Aspiration," *Psychological Review*, January 1963, pp. 51–60.

to abstract intellectual and emotive aspects of unified behavior and then to convert one "separate" part into the leader and the other into the follower.[38] For example, there are many complex relations between rigid "attitudes" and rigid "beliefs," but there is no indication that one—an "attitude" or a "belief"—is the servant of the other.[39] It is not surprising to learn that children whose behavior indicates a relatively deep "understanding" of the complex forces affecting human behavior and who seek alternative explanations of these forces also manifest an "attitude" of flexibility in such matters.[40] Learning, wrote Kurt Lewin a number of years ago, "is a process in which changes of knowledge and beliefs, changes of values and standards, changes of emotional attachments and needs, and changes of everyday conduct occur not piecemeal and independently of each other, but within the framework of the individual's total life in the group."[41] Even our many inconsistencies between verbal knowledge and actual conduct are learned as related aspects of a unified, though logically defective, behavior.

So much for the theory of learning as an interrelationship. We now turn to its practical applications.

Suggested Reading

Bennis, Warren G., Kenneth D. Benne, and Robert Chin, eds., *The Planning of Change* (New York: Holt, Rinehart and Winston, 1961), chap. 3.

Childs, John L., *American Pragmatism and Education* (New York: Henry Holt and Co., Inc., 1956), chaps. 3–5.

Corwin, Ronald G., *A Sociology of Education* (New York: Appleton-Century-Crofts, 1965), chap. 5.

Dewey, John, *Democracy and Education* (New York: Macmillan Co., 1916), chaps. XIII–XIV.

38. Gordon W. Allport, *op. cit.*, pp. 258 ff.

39. See, for example, Serge Moscovici, "Attitudes and Opinions," *Annual Review of Psychology*, Paul R. Farnsworth, ed. (Palo Alto, Calif.: Annual Reviews, Inc., 1963), pp. 231–60; Sheila M. Chown, "Rigidity—A Flexible Concept," *Psychological Bulletin*, May 1959, pp. 195–223.

40. R. E. Muuss, "The Relationship Between Causal Orientation, Anxiety, and Insecurity in Elementary School Children," *Journal of Educational Psychology*, June 1960, pp. 122–29. For other relevant examples, see Stanley Schacter and Jerome E. Singer, "Cognitive, Social and Physiological Determinants of Emotional State," *Psychological Review*, September 1962, pp. 379–99.

41. *Resolving Social Conflicts: Selected Papers in Group Dynamics* (New York: Harper & Brothers, 1948), p. 58.

Hullfish, H. Gordon, and Philip G. Smith, *Reflective Thinking: The Method of Education* (New York: Dodd, Mead & Co., 1961), chaps. 2–4, 9, 11.

National Society for the Study of Education, *Theories of Learning and Instruction* (Chicago: University of Chicago Press, 1964), chaps. I, III, XVII.

Price, Kingsley, *Education and Philosophical Thought* (Boston: Allyn and Bacon, Inc., 1962), chap. X.

Roe, Anne, and George G. Simpson, eds., *Behavior and Evolution* (New Haven: Yale University Press, 1958), chaps. 5, 16, 20, 22, 23.

Thorson, Thomas L., *The Logic of Democracy* (New York: Holt, Rinehart and Winston, 1962), chaps. 7–9.

Voget, Fred W., "Man and Culture: An Essay in Changing Anthropological Interpretation," *American Anthropologist*, December 1960, pp. 943–65.

Chapter 11

Education in an Interdependent World: Educational Practices

The Child Becomes a Participant in Educational Planning

A wise teacher once remarked that the verb "teach," in the sentence, "I teach John Latin," governs two objects. Consequently, to teach well, one must know the object "John" as well as the object "Latin" in order to make the most of the potential relationships between the two. At its best, the experimentalist's conception of learning has contributed fruitfully to the potentialities of a creative interrelationship between student and subject matter. Of primary importance, it emphasizes the importance of encouraging the pupil's active participation in his own learning; of bringing about his identification with the task in hand by virtue of its known bearing, directly or indirectly, upon his interests, needs, and future hopes as these relate to wider social and intellectual concerns.

Writing early in the century, John Dewey stated that the subject matter of instruction has two aspects,[1] one for the scientist as scientist, the other for the teacher as teacher, each involving a somewhat different organization. For the scientist, that organization of a subject is best which enables its user to solve problems, to locate new problems, and to "carry them through to a verified outcome." For the teacher, on

1. John Dewey, *The Child and the Curriculum* (Chicago: University of Chicago Press, 1902), p. 30.

214

the other hand, the relevant organization of his subject is that which best relates to the child's experiences at a given stage of development. In other words, the teacher's major concern is with "the subject-matter as a related factor in a total and growing experience."

It proved to be but a step from a sense of direction and identification on the part of the pupil to first-hand participation in the planning of his program. The improved attitude of young people toward school, once their interests were enlisted, led many teachers early in the century to engage in radical departures from tradition. On the assumption that facts, skills, habits, attitudes, and ideals are best acquired in the context of a practical endeavor, or in the solution of a "real-life" problem, a number of schools resolved to abolish traditional subjects and to substitute "projects." For example, in place of separate periods for arithmetic, reading, spelling, geography, and other subjects, one class group in an elementary school might concern itself with a study of family life, another might conduct a school store, still another might center upon city living. Not uncommonly, these "areas of interest" became as conventionalized as "subjects," with the result that children of a given age would be expected this year to be interested in the same type of project, or "center of interest," as were children of the same age last year. Nevertheless, these centers of interest, in the eyes of their practitioners, had the advantage of providing vital occasions for development in reading, writing, arithmetic, art, music, industrial work, and so on, as concomitant learning which compared more than favorably with the old subject-matter curriculum.[2]

In the hands of a skillful teacher, one keenly aware of the bones to be covered by the flesh and blood of active learning, the project method of teaching, particularly on the elementary school level, yielded superior results. However, with an unskillful teacher, the active participation of pupils in the planning of a project often led to the selection of trivial activities and to the partial mastery of the facts and the skills which incidental learning was to achieve. In these instances only skewed development could result. In one well-known school, for instance, it was the practice of teachers and pupils at the opening of each school year to decide "cooperatively" upon the units of work or

2. For two excellent accounts of project teaching in its early stages, see Ellsworth Collins, *An Experiment with a Project Curriculum* (New York: The Macmillan Co., 1923), and Margaret E. Wells, *The Project Curriculum* (New York: J. B. Lippincott Co., 1921).

the major themes of the year. In one class group the unit might be primarily scientific; in another, historical or literary. The result was that, although the learning of the pupils within each area of interest was impressive, pupils in the science units experienced little history and the historically minded group learned little science.

"Progressive" Practices Criticized

Extremes of this kind were certain, of course, to bring a reaction. Indeed, experimentalists have been as severe as conservatives in their criticisms of the project method thus employed and its successor, the "activity curriculum." Professor Boyd H. Bode, for example, was a consistent critic of incidental learning, pointing out that although it has its values, it is likely to be "too discontinuous, too random and haphazard, too immediate in its functions, unless we supplement it with something else," [3] and John L. Childs, while emphasizing the values in the activity curriculum which come from the fact that it enables children to learn by employing the methods of scientific thinking, also warned that "In our zeal for pupil initiative, pupil planning, and pupil problem-solving, we must never forget that education is a deliberate effort to provide the young with a course of experiencing which makes the maximum use of these meaningful and charged stimuli of the culture." [4] Childs wrote that there is "an irreducible difference between a form of inquiry in which the aim is to introduce the young to that which is already known and functioning in the life of a people, and the pattern of research in inquiry in which the aim is to discover knowledge which no one has as yet achieved." [5] To the method of the project and the activity curriculum, then, Childs would add "more effectual procedures by which the young can master well-organized bodies of knowledge. In some fields the logical order of the materials to be learned may have to be given priority." [6]

Other critics have directed their attacks upon what they consider to be a superficial interpretation of the nature of scientific method as

3. *Modern Educational Theories* (New York: The Macmillan Co., 1927), pp. 150–51.
4. *The Experimentalist Educational Theory*, Bode Memorial Lectures (Columbus, Ohio: College of Education, Ohio State University, 1957), p. 25.
5. *Ibid.*
6. *Ibid.*, p. 26.

embodied in the activity curriculum. No scientific problem is solved, they insist, without heavy indebtedness to the past. Granted that thinking begins with a problem, it follows, nevertheless, that full understanding of a serious problem and inferences and hypotheses for its solution involve the use of funded experience. A thinker may have to draw heavily upon the accumulated results of generations who have gone before and have provided the present generation with the assumptions and systems of belief which constitute an indispensable framework for inquiry and valid reasoning today. This in no way lessens the importance of a pupil's identification with the task in hand or his participation in planning. However, it renders questionable the assumption that he is an equal partner in determining what knowledge is worth while. The relation of an apprentice to a master craftsman is not an unwise analogy in this connection.

Some of Dewey's Views on Education

These criticisms of experimentalism as practiced by its overly enthusiastic disciples are of value in calling attention to the twofold nature of experience as originally described by Dewey. It is not Dewey but his so-called followers who have neglected the part that the experience of mankind plays in learning. Consider, for example, these words with which Dewey concludes his discussion of *The Child and the Curriculum:*

> The case is of the child. It is his present powers which are to assert themselves; his present capacities which are to be exercised; his present attitudes which are to be realized. But save as the teacher knows, knows wisely and thoroughly, the race-experience which is embodied in that thing we call the Curriculum, the teacher knows neither what the present power, capacity, or attitude is, nor yet how it is to be asserted, exercised, and realized.[7]

Dewey certainly did not imply that it is sufficient for education to serve the immediate or "felt" needs of children. Rather, he insisted that it make contact with, engage, these inclinations so that "impulse" might

7. Dewey, *op. cit.*, p. 40.

be gradually transformed into "intelligence." [8] Nor did he suggest that education should merely teach subject matter, but that it should develop well-informed and reflective minds that are open, not empty—that are creative, not rigidly "programed." [9]

Dewey generally advocated an educational procedure which would start with significant life experiences that run into perplexities, that are provocative of thought and interest. For, as Brubacher writes, "inquiry starts in doubt, and doubt is personal." [10] Emotions and tensions are active even though the situation and posture are intellectual. In defining and solving problems, in evaluating ends and means, a child learns not only data and skills, but also the discipline of reflective thought.[11]

In this process there would be no exaltation of the student's own unreflective thought. As Dewey often stated, "independent thinking" that was unchecked by logical criteria and unfertilized by the social heritage was quite likely to be flabby and fruitless.[12] In this process the "psychological" systems of meanings would be progressively organized into richer and fuller systems that approximate the "logical" systems of subject matter used by mature students or experts.[13] But these more rigorous systems, learned in their interrelationships and their applications to vital problems, could be effectively used, Dewey believed, in experiences later in life.

Dewey was opposed not to subjects, but to the isolation of subjects from each other and from personal–social concerns. Furthermore, while advocating experimentation with different curriculum designs, he had a definite place in his over-all design for the intensive study of subjects at appropriate times. And speaking of the "problem" or "project"

8. John Dewey, *Experience and Education* (New York: Macmillan Co., 1938), pp. 77–81. See also, John Dewey, *The Quest for Certainty* (New York: Minton, Balch and Co., 1929), chap. 10.

9. John Dewey, *Democracy and Education* (New York: Macmillan Co., 1916), pp. 204–10.

10. John S. Brubacher, *Modern Philosophies of Education*, 3d ed. (New York: McGraw-Hill Book Co., Inc., 1962), p. 276.

11. John Dewey, *How We Think* (Boston: D. C. Heath and Co., 1933), pp. 106–07.

12. See, for example, John Dewey, "Progressive Education and the Science of Education," *Progressive Education*, August 1928, pp. 197–202.

13. John Dewey, *Experience and Education*, pp. 86–89. See also, Sing-nan Fen, "The Logical, Psychological, and Educational Approach to Subject Matters," in *Proceedings of the Nineteenth Annual Meeting of the Philosophy of Education Society* (Lawrence, Kansas: University of Kansas, 1963), pp. 105–11.

method of instruction, he wrote: "I do not urge it as the sole way out of educational confusion, not even in the elementary school, though I think experimentation with it is desirable in college and secondary school." [14]

Moreover, Dewey had a deep appreciation of the fact that as children acquire information, they are developing, usually unconsciously, many basic dispositions, expectations, and beliefs. For example, they may be learning that some things are "active" (causes) and some are "passive" (effects)—note the active and passive voices in our grammar, note the self-action indicated by such statements as "the roots search for water" and "the moon is rising." Children may learn to accept an unquestioned social or intellectual structure or they may learn to seek and evaluate social and intellectual alternatives. [15] They may be learning, in Professor Arnstine's words, "submission to—or intolerance of—authority, and any number of other things as well." [16] Thus, as anthropologists tell us, children usually are developing a largely unexamined philosophy about the nature of the world and of society as they consciously learn the specific details of their culture.

What Dewey urged was recognition of the fact that education has more or less concomitant moral, esthetic, practical, and intellectual aspects. He argued continually against the rigid conceptual separations of content from method, one subject from another subject, theory from practice, attitudes from intellect—dualisms which, he believed, impoverished education. On the intellectual side, he insisted that the vital concern of education is with "cultivating the attitude of reflective thinking." "Otherwise," he wrote, "practical activity is mechanical and routine, morals are blind and arbitrary, and esthetic appreciation is sentimental gush." [17]

However, Dewey's basic "transactional" approach usually has been disregarded by both his subject-centered critics, who have complained that he neglected subject matter, and by his child-centered "followers," who have concentrated their attention mainly on the child's interests and feelings.

14. John Dewey, *The Way Out of Educational Confusion* (Cambridge: Harvard University Press, 1931), p. 36.
15. John Dewey, "Education and Social Change," *Social Frontier*, May 1937, pp. 236–37.
16. Donald G. Arnstine, "The Language and Values of Programmed Instruction: Part Two," *Educational Forum*, March 1964, p. 344.
17. *How We Think*, p. 78.

One-Sided Emphases

It is not surprising that in the period between the two World Wars the time-honored position of the "subjects" as organizing centers of the curriculum would be challenged by the "child's needs," "social problems," and so on. Many forces were pushing toward a revitalization of the curriculum and the provision of a more adequate general education for youth.

The "fragmentation of life caused by the extreme specialization of a complex, interdependent society" [18] had generated what many people regarded as a fragmented educational curriculum. It was a curriculum dominated by "watertight compartments" (the subjects) and excessively devoted to the production of specialists at various levels of life. This specialism, it was felt, often operated to confine the student's intellectual horizons to a narrow field of concern. At the same time, shocking events, especially the war and the Depression, were shaking the common social structure. The conjunction of these developments gave added impetus to the general-education movement. Aimed at developing the common values, skills, and understandings necessary for effective control of and participation in the common social structure, the general-education movement was a central part of many reform and experimental trends in education.[19] It was also an expression of what Cremin has described as "the inextricable relationships between social reform, reform *through* education, and the reform *of* education." [20]

The Depression of the 1930s, with its disastrous effects upon American youth, stimulated studies of American youth on a nationwide scale. The studies conducted by the American Youth Commission were particularly influential. A preliminary report of the work of this commission, entitled *How Fare American Youth?* [21] revealed clearly that the schools were failing to meet the increasingly diverse needs and abilities of a large proportion of youth. It seemed, for example, that more

18. Philip H. Phenix, *Realms of Meaning: Philosophy of the Curriculum for General Education* (New York: McGraw-Hill Book Co., 1964), p. 5.

19. See Russell Thomas, *The Search for a Common Learning: General Education, 1900–1960* (New York: McGraw-Hill Book Co., 1962), chaps. 4–5.

20. Lawrence A. Cremin, *The Transformation of the School* (New York: Alfred A. Knopf, 1961), p. 85.

21. By Homer P. Rainey, Director of the American Youth Commission (New York: D. Appleton–Century Co., 1937).

young people were dropping out of school because of lack of interest than because of lack of family funds. Other studies reported that many young people who did graduate from secondary schools did not later use effectively what they presumably had learned.[22]

As we have already indicated in this chapter and in the preceding chapter, new conceptions of experience, knowledge, and democracy were emerging. Many educational reformers saw the "authoritarian transmission of subject matter" as inconsistent with a philosophy of continuing personal–social reconstruction. Organic or integrative conceptions of personality, knowledge, and the educational process provided theoretical bases for condemnations of conventional educational practices. For example, the usual time schedules did not seem to provide sufficient time in which to engage in learning experiences of a "real-life" character. Again, a largely subject-centered curriculum seemed to offer little opportunity for the integration and use of subjects in significant personal–social problems. Thus, "block-time classes," "unified studies," "units," and "projects" were proposed as remedies.

Out of these and other currents emerged numerous suggestions for improving education from the elementary school through college. As might be expected, in this period of social and educational controversy, conflicting and one-sided emphases often substituted for a balanced and unified program. For example, although many proponents of "life-adjustment" education paid their verbal respects to "creativity," "the needs of each child," and so on, their operational emphasis was on the *adjustment* of youth to existing conditions. Nor did they show much hesitation in enlisting, erroneously, the views of John Dewey as theoretical support for their programs.[23]

Again, some educators, noting the rapidity of change, emphasized the skills and procedures (the "process values") needed for solving problems rather than the funded content of the cultural heritage. Others, departing from the same point, laid stress on the "intellectual disciplines," or updated content, or on "truths which, in the midst of change, do not change" as the means of preparing youth to grapple

22. William M. French, *America's Educational Tradition: An Interpretive History* (Boston: D. C. Heath and Co., 1964), p. 164.

23. Representations of "life-adjustment" views and practices can be found in Charles Prosser, *Secondary Education and Life* (Cambridge: Harvard University Press, 1939); U.S. Office of Education, *A Look Ahead in Secondary Education: Report of the Second Commission on Life Adjustment Education for Youth* (Washington, D.C.: U.S. Government Printing Office, 1954).

with change. Still others, reacting against "external imposition" of any kind, gave authority to the child's "own" interests and needs in providing curriculum guidelines. Nor did *this* group hesitate to appeal, erroneously, to the authority of Dewey as a support for their views.

Thus many educators found it difficult to avoid what Taba has described as the "unnecessary *versus* thinking with its unfortunate juxtaposition of considerations that should be combined into one comprehensive curriculum theory: interest *vs.* subject matter; life-centeredness *vs.* subject-centeredness; method *vs.* content; emotional development *vs.* intellectual growth; basic skills *vs.* the growth of the whole child, and so on." [24]

Developmental Tasks and the Curriculum

However, some notable progress was made in developing an integrated and comprehensive curriculum theory, a theory which avoided the limited child-centered, society-centered, or subject-centered approaches. For example, in the 1930s a group of educators undertook to survey the task of the school with an eye to defining the "needs" of pupils, or what were later termed "developmental tasks." This represented an effort to avoid a one-sided emphasis upon the individual, his nature and his interests, and an equally one-sided emphasis upon the "demands of society." As a result of its study, this group concluded that curricular experiences should meet the following criteria:

> *First,* they must relate meaningfully to the prevailing desires, inclinations, and quests of the particular students for whom they are designed, since needs are personal in reference. Curricular experiences, in other words, must have identifiable connection with the individual student's desires for a sense of security, of belonging, of achievement, and the like, must contribute to their fulfillment in socially desirable ways.
>
> *Second,* they must be relevant to significant current social, economic, political, and cultural trends as they bear upon the adolescent, since needs are also always social in reference. In

24. Hilda Taba, *Curriculum Development: Theory and Practice* (New York: Harcourt, Brace and World, Inc., 1962), p. 3.

other words, they must further the individual's adjustment within the basic relationships of living.

Third, they must further the realization of democratic values, since education cannot meet needs without giving direction to their expression. Curricular experiences must be conducive to the growth of that kind of personality which is capable of democratic living under modern conditions.[25]

In line with this concept of needs, various subject matter committees within the field of secondary education associated with the Commission on the Secondary School Curriculum undertook to examine the resources of their fields—science, social studies, mathematics, language, literature, art—with a view to suggesting materials and methods appropriate for meeting the needs of young people in the areas of immediate personal-social relationships, social-civic relationships, economic relationships, and in personal living.[26]

The attempt to provide educational experiences for young people with an eye to both individual and social criteria soon influenced the organization of courses of study and the curriculum in both the elementary and secondary schools. Nor was it without influence upon college curricula.

This was a particularly fruitful period of experimentation in college education. Colleges such as Sarah Lawrence, Bennington, Bard, and Black Mountain, although not large, nevertheless attracted wide attention for their departures from conventional curricula and methods. Others, such as Reed College, Stephens College, Goucher College, together with curricular experimentation in the lower divisions of state universities (Wisconsin, Minnesota, and others), elicited equal attention, although the emphasis in these latter schools was less than with the first group upon what might be called the adolescent study approach. Somewhat later, curricular revisions at Harvard, Yale, Princeton, and other institutions invited critical study in higher education circles.

25. The Commission on the Secondary School Curriculum, in V. T. Thayer, Caroline Zachry, and Ruth Kotinsky, *Reorganizing Secondary Education* (New York: D. Appleton–Century Company, 1939), p. 415.

26. *Ibid.,* chaps. IV–IX. See also *Science in General Education, Art in General Education, Mathematics in General Education, Language in General Education, The Social Studies in General Education, Prose Fiction in General Education: A Bibliography of 1500 Novels* by Elbert Lenrow. All of these volumes were published by D. Appleton–Century Co., New York.

Curriculum Designs for General Education

Despite the ferment and innovation, the subject-centered curriculum has clearly retained its dominant position during the past four decades. However, especially in junior high schools and in some junior-senior high schools, there has been a significant development of "core curriculum" courses. This term has extremely varied meanings; indeed, it may refer merely to that portion of the curriculum, however organized, which is required of all students. Here we shall use the term to refer to diverse organizational patterns—sometimes called correlated studies, unified studies, broad fields curriculum, common learnings, or block-time courses—which seem to display some concern with one or more types of integration. The integrations or interrelationships may be that of one subject with another subject; of subjects, social problems, and adolescent needs; of knowledge and critical-thinking skills; of emotional, behavioral, and intellectual dispositions, or of still other groupings.[27]

One type of core curriculum provides for the "correlation" of courses. The courses are taught separately, but more or less systematic plans are made to show the relationships of the materials to each other or to some overarching theme or topic. Thus, while a social studies teacher is dealing with a certain period in American history, her students may be studying the literature of that period in their English classes. Or teachers may relate their special subjects to some common concept or theme, such as "Living in the Community." The degree of correlation of these separately taught subjects is often quite small.

A somewhat less conservative approach is the "fusion" of certain related courses into a single, more comprehensive structure. History, geography, and civics may be combined in a social studies course. History (or social studies) may be taught in combination with English (or the "language arts"). Divisional courses on the college level are often similar to these broad field courses in the secondary schools. Frequently these courses display very little unification of materials. A gen-

27. With some modifications, our description of curriculum patterns follows the accounts provided by Harold B. Alberty and Elsie J. Alberty, *Reorganizing the High School Curriculum*, 3d ed. (New York: Macmillan Co., 1962), chap. 6; and Hilda Taba, *op. cit.*, chap. 21.

eral science course, for example, may provide brief and rather separate surveys of materials from chemistry, physics, geology, astronomy, and zoology. If there is no balanced provision for depth as well as breadth, there is danger that a broad course may replace trivial details with unintelligible generalizations, with no more opportunity for active inquiry than is found in many separately taught subjects.

If the materials of broad field courses are organized around culture epochs or overarching concepts and generalizations (Man's Control of Nature, Interdependence in a Changing World, and so on), these courses represent or merge into a third approach to the core curriculum. For example, some years ago the Horace Mann School for Girls in New York City adopted as a general theme for its three upper years Modern Civilization and Culture. Under this heading, the tenth grade concentrated upon American Civilization and Culture; the eleventh grade upon Other Modern Civilizations and Culture (Russia, Germany, China, and others); the twelfth grade upon Modern Problems and Issues in America. An effort was made to use each subject— English, social studies, science, mathematics, the fine, industrial, and household arts, and music—so as to give students a comprehensive picture of society in each of these periods. Work was planned cooperatively by teachers drawn from several fields, and each course was conducted by a coordinating teacher.

In the "activity" or "experience" curriculum, projects usually are based upon the interests of students and the suggestions of the teacher in a given class. Learning activities are developed cooperatively by the teacher and the students. This type of curriculum is rarely found in the secondary schools.

Much more frequent than the activity curriculum but less frequent than the broad-fields curriculum are the "social problems," "life functions," or "areas of living" approach and the approach organized around the predicated, common problems, needs, and interests of youth. Actually, when the needs of youth are defined as personal-social needs (as in the preceding section), there may be little difference between these two approaches. Such titles as Family Living, Protecting Life and Health, Making Ideas Clear, Participating in Government, or Intergroup Relations can be found in both the "social functions" and the "adolescent needs" approaches. Problem-centered and function-centered curricula often provide many opportunities for students to learn planning and problem-solving skills and to work on individual and small-group problems within a unifying framework.

In the elementary school, the "unit" or "unit teaching" is roughly the equivalent of the secondary school core curriculum. "Units of work form the heart or core of the modern elementary school program." [28] There is general agreement that "the unit of study occupies the central position in the curriculum patterns of a large number of elementary schools." [29] The practices and techniques of integrative teaching are more widely developed in elementary schools than in secondary schools.

Usually one or two hours are scheduled for unit study. However, if the unit is large enough in scope, many of the day's activities will center around it. For example, the activities carried on by children in a unit on railroads may involve many learnings in social studies and the language arts. Science may be included as related to steam and diesel locomotives. Construction and art skills may be learned as children build different kinds of railroad cars for dramatic activities and as they paint a railroad mural for their room. [30]

Many kinds of units can be found in elementary schools. There are "contemporary event" units (the Presidential Election, for example) and "culture area" or "culture period" units (Life in Japan, Pioneer Life, and such). There are "problems or areas of living" units—Living Together in the School, Living Together in Our Community, How We Live with Other Countries, How the Natural Environment and the People Affect Each Other. Many units concentrate largely on learnings in a separate subject. However, many cut across the subject fields, though the emphasis may be in some one field. Possibly the most widely taught units are those which are centered in the social studies.

Experimental Practices Evaluated

Under the impetus of the Eight-Year Study in the 1930s the core curriculum and other tendencies toward integrative education seemed

28. Lavone A. Hanna, Gladys L. Potter, and Neva Hagaman, *Unit Teaching in the Elementary School* (New York: Holt, Rinehart and Winston, Inc., 1963), p. 1.
29. U.S. Office of Education, *Unit Planning and Teaching in Elementary Social Studies* (Washington, D.C.: U.S. Government Printing Office, 1963), p. 14.
30. *Ibid.*, p. 11.

destined to receive wide adoption. Through a cooperative arrangement between some three hundred colleges and thirty secondary schools, operating under the general direction of The Commission on the Relation of School and College of the Progressive Education Association, these thirty schools were to be freed for a period of eight years from the usual requirements for admission to college in order that they might experiment with the curriculum of the secondary school.[31]

The thirty schools differed greatly in the degrees and ways in which they departed from traditional educational practices. However, the general tendencies were to emphasize (1) some form of integration of subjects with each other, with social problems and adolescent needs; (2) individual guidance and evaluation, teacher-pupil planning, and the use of a variety of learning experiences adapted to variations in individual interests and abilities; and (3) the development of social concerns, critical-thinking skills, creativity, and other often neglected objectives.

The records of 1475 graduates were followed carefully in thirty-nine colleges, and comparisons were made with the records of a like number of graduates from traditional schools. The graduates from the traditional and experimental schools were matched, pair by pair, on "all" basic variables—scholastic aptitude, interests, socioeconomic background, and other relevant factors—so that, presumably, the only major general difference was the difference in high school programs. It was found that the graduates of the thirty experimental schools earned a slightly higher total grade average and earned higher grade averages in all subjects except foreign languages; they received slightly more academic honors each year; they were more often judged by college faculties to possess clarity, precision, and objectivity in thought, higher intellectual curiosity and drive, and greater resourcefulness in meeting new situations and personal problems; and they demonstrated a more active concern for what was happening in the world.[32]

Now, worthwhile research in the social sciences is difficult to conduct and assess. It is impossible to control "all" relevant variables; operational meanings of "integrated studies," "critical thinking," and other such concepts vary considerably, and there are other problems which

31. See Wilford M. Aikin, *The Story of the Eight-Year Study* (New York: Harper & Brothers, 1942).
32. *Ibid.*, pp. 110–12. See also Dean Chamberlin *et al.*, *Did They Succeed in College?* (New York: Harper & Brothers, 1943).

call for tentativeness and a historical sampling process. But several significant factors seem to add weight to the general indications provided by the Eight-Year Study.

For one thing, even though the enthusiasm of both teachers and students who engage in experimental procedures may be high, this possible advantage is likely to be counterbalanced by the confusion and mistakes resulting from a lack of historically and personally accumulated experience with the new procedures. Then, too, it was found that, in general, the graduates of those experimental schools which made the most fundamental revisions in curriculum design and teaching procedure had better college records than the graduates of the less experimental schools and "achieved in college distinctly higher standing than that of students of equal ability with whom they were compared." [33] Finally, and most important, many other studies (probably several hundred) at all levels—elementary, secondary, and college—tend to show essentially the same results as the Eight-Year Study. The most consistent general findings are that in the learning of subject matter, students in experimental programs do as well as or better than students in conventional programs, and that students in experimental programs usually are significantly better on measures of critical-thinking skills, personal adjustment, and interest in social problems.[34]

In the light of evidence available now, the data bearing on the adoption of integrative teaching–learning practices are disappointing. Experimentalists have left an enduring impression on the schools. Some of their practices have been incorporated into the schools at large. But the impression has probably been much less than the opponents have feared and the proponents have hoped.

In higher education and in the last three or four years of secondary education, by far the greatest portion of generally required courses are taught in the form of separate subjects and are organized around the

33. Aikin, *op. cit.*, p. 117.
34. For reviews or summaries of some of these studies, see Norman E. Wallen and Robert M. W. Travers, "Analysis and Investigation of Teaching Methods," in *Handbook of Research on Teaching*, N. L. Gage, ed. (Chicago: Rand McNally and Co., 1963), pp. 470–74; Grace S. Wright, *The Core Program: Unpublished Research, 1956–1962* (Washington, D.C.: U.S. Government Printing Office, 1963); "Progressive Education," *NEA Research Bulletin*, December 1957, pp. 137–41; John M. Mickelson, "What Does Research Say About the Effectiveness of the Core Curriculum?" *School Review*, Summer 1957, pp. 144–60; Winslow R. Hatch and Ann Bennett, *Effectiveness in Teaching* (Washington, D.C.: U.S. Government Printing Office, 1962), pp. 15–26.

internal logic of the respective subjects.[35] Although unit teaching is a dominant characteristic in the elementary school, there are good reasons to believe that many, perhaps most, units are more integrative in print than in practice, that critical-thinking skills are often neglected, and that some subjects (for example, mathematics and spelling) are often taught in isolation from other materials and activities.

The core curriculum has been used most extensively in junior high schools. The results of a nationwide survey made in 1960 indicated that about 40 per cent of junior high schools and 16.4 per cent of junior-senior high schools had some form of "block-time" classes.[36] However, core classes are used in descending frequency from grade seven to grade nine, and the fields drawn upon in organizing the core are limited. For example, 80.8 per cent of the junior high schools with block-time classes had a language arts–social studies combination in the seventh grade, but only 16.3 per cent had a science–mathematics combination in that grade. For the ninth grade the percentages were 16.4 (language arts–social studies) and 2.3 (science–mathematics).[37] Moreover, changes of titles and scheduled combinations of subjects often do not signify the actual presence of integrative education.

Experimentalism and Tradition: Departures and Returns

There are many reasons for this rather timid departure from tradition.[38] In departing from tradition, experimentalists were hampered by the weight of tradition. In substituting "the child's needs" for "the subjects," some progressives unconsciously brought into the movement the traditional practice of oversimplifying complex processes. Reacting overvigorously against certain traditions and searching for new routes

35. See, for example, U.S. Office of Education, *What High School Pupils Study* (Washington, D.C.: U.S. Government Printing Office, 1962), pp. 20–24, 114; U.S. Office of Education, *The Junior High School* (Washington, D.C.: U.S. Government Printing Office, 1963), pp. 18–24; Joseph Katz and Nevitt Sanford, "The Curriculum in the Perspective of the Theory of Personality Development," in *The American College*, Nevitt Sanford, ed. (New York: John Wiley and Sons, Inc., 1962), pp. 418–24.

36. U.S. Office of Education, *The Junior High School*, p. 20. These figures are roughly in agreement with other indices of the extent to which some form of core curriculum is employed.

37. *Ibid.*, p. 21.

38. For two conflicting interpretations of this matter, see Lawrence A. Cremin, *op. cit.*, pp. 324–53; Paul Nash, "The Strange Death of Progressive Education," *Educational Theory*, April 1964, pp. 65–75, 82.

in a relatively uncharted area, some progressives were more clearly *against* something than *for* something. The traditional mind found it difficult enough to understand (and many never did understand) Dewey's views. The traditional mind found it easier to understand and, understanding, to reject the accusations and *unconventional* oversimplifications of some others in the experimental movement. For many conventional-minded teachers and parents, the whole experimental movement became identified with certain immoderate "progressive" practices. At the same time, experimentalists differed among themselves as to principles, and internal dissension weakened the movement.

Then, too, one of the most obvious obstacles has been the lack of qualified teachers. Integrative education called for teachers who not only knew *a* subject but who were broadly educated, who understood children and could work with them, who had a working knowledge of logic and scientific method, and so on. Few conventionally educated teachers could measure up to the tasks posed by the new education.

The reports of the Eight-Year Study were published during World War II when attention and energies were focused on the struggle against totalitarianism. Thus the reports did not receive the consideration they deserved. After the war, conservative influences became prominent in American society and education, influences we shall want to consider in several other chapters.

In any event, although some experimentalist tendencies have been partially absorbed into the schools, there are today strong countercurrents. Consider one small indication of these countercurrents: the number of articles on "core" in the *Education Index* decreased rather steadily from fifty-seven in the 1953–1955 volume to fifteen in the 1961–1963 volume. "There has been little recent effort," writes Professor Goodlad in an analysis of recent curriculum trends, "to combine related fields; in fact, the current movement is predicated upon the discreteness of subjects and the importance of organizing and teaching them as separate disciplines." [39]

Guidance Programs Enlarge Their Responsibilities

As the variety and number of students, courses, and career opportunities increased and as more comprehensive conceptions of the learning

39. John I. Goodlad, *School Curriculum Reform in the United States* (New York: Fund for the Advancement of Education, 1964), p. 78.

process evolved, many schools established guidance positions to help the school meet educational responsibilities. Originally, guidance was chiefly vocational and narrowly academic in its function. These services remain of importance, as contemporary emphasis upon identifying and stimulating the gifted renders clear. It is now recognized, however, that these functions can be performed more effectively in the context of emotional and social development. For this reason, guidance and counseling have enlarged their responsibilities in recent years to include an understanding of the emotional and social development of children and adolescents, profiting from the insight which has come out of the mental hygiene movement and the contributions of child guidance clinics and research into child and adolescent development. What are commonly spoken of as "traits" of character and personality are no longer viewed as relatively independent entities (cooperation, reliability, honesty, or the reverse) which an individual either acquires or inherits and carries around with him in fixed quantities. Rather are they conceived of as qualities of relationships, the outcomes of interplay between oneself and others, and thus flexible and subject to change as conditions change. The conditions of health of personality are thus seen to be the conditions of mutually creative communication between a child and others—parents, siblings, playmates, teachers. High on the list of essentials for mental health are first-hand assurance to a child that he is accepted and loved, that he is needed and that others are thus dependent upon him in certain essential respects, that he is recognized for his achievements in some area of importance in the eyes of others, and that he is free, in the sense that he feels he is progressively acquiring the "know-how" with which to walk on his own feet and to make his own decisions.

This concern for the emotional and social aspects of growth and development, of health of personality, explains the emphasis educators have placed upon the "whole child" in recent years. As so often happens, this phrase is easily misinterpreted in its applications. It does not mean that the school should now undertake to provide all of the young person's education, thus replacing or invading the territories of home, church, and the like, although it may mean that the school should, on occasion, seek to offset serious deficiencies in these areas. It does mean that what the school undertakes to do should contribute positively to health of personality. It means, too, that in their professional preparation teachers should acquire knowledge of personality development in addition to knowledge of subject matter so that the verb "teach" may, in fact, govern two objects.

As C. Gilbert Wrenn indicates,[40] what is called the "guidance point of view" is characterized by (1) an expectation and acceptance of individual differences among students, and a concern and respect for these differences; (2) an effort to see the student "totally," as a person with motivations "which originate in his family, in his age peers, in his community life—a total world, of which classroom and school are often only a minor part"; (3) an effort to see the student as he sees himself while helping him to take stock of himself, cope with his life situation, and plan for the future. It is a point of view which must "permeate the school staff and program if the personnel service is to be effective."

The Concept of Democracy Examined

Mention has been made of the fact that, prior to World War II, both theories of learning and the dangers to American democracy posed by the rise of totalitarian governments abroad led to soul searching on the part of educators in this country. To what extent, they began to ask themselves, do classroom procedures and the administrative structure of the schools contribute toward the conscious realization by young people of the principles of democracy and their applications in daily living? The answer was not always flattering to the school.

Obviously, if we are to educate for democracy, clarification of its meaning as applied to relationships among people becomes essential.

Three of its aspects are relevant here. First and foremost, it implies the attribution of worth to the individual—respect for the integrity of his personality in "the conviction that personality is the center of value and that all social organizations get their significance from their promise to enhance the individual: to guarantee the sacredness of his person, to safeguard his rights, to extend his opportunities." [41] In a heterogeneous society, this means respect for differences in origin and background, in interests, abilities, and skills. It implies the right of a child to grow up with a sense of security and an inner self-respect by virtue of what he himself is, rather than to be judged and classified in

40. "School Counseling," in Van Cleve Morris and others, *Becoming an Educator* (Boston: Houghton Mifflin Co., 1963), pp. 334–35.
41. John Dewey, "Education and Social Change," *The Social Frontier*, May 1937, p. 238.

terms of a stereotype or factors of origin over which he has no control. It means freedom of thought and inquiry and the right of individual conscience.

Second, democracy contrasts with both totalitarianism and rugged individualism. Totalitarianism requires that an individual merge his interests with the interests of the whole and subordinate his convictions and his talents to the requirements of a central authority. Rugged individualism places the individual above society and its institutions.

Democracy, on the other hand, implies a mutually creative relationship between society and the individual, the whole and the part. Society and its institutions find their justification in promoting the distinctive nature and the well-being of the individual, and the individual, in turn, validates his right to be unique, his self-expression, through his contributions to the whole or through the creative impact of his gifts upon the self-expression of others. A democratic personality by its very nature is thus a social personality and the democratic ideal a moral ideal.

Finally, the democratic ideal, when applied to the resolution of conflicts and disputes between individuals and groups, relies upon the use of intelligence rather than upon force and attempts to solve problems and to resolve differences through the process of creative compromise discussed earlier.[42]

Using the Classroom to Educate for Democracy

To employ a conventional term, a "lesson" commonly involves at least three phases: assignment, study and work period, recitation and evaluation. Although subjects differ, the study of each utilizes these steps. Within each step, moreover, there are ample occasions for the promotion of democratic ways of thinking and acting.

For example, the assignment period has as a major purpose introduction of the task at hand in such a way that the student will understand its importance and be encouraged to identify himself with the work ahead. A skillful teacher is skillful by virtue of his ability not only to relate new experiences to old, but to sense the varied reactions of

42. For a fuller discussion of the democratic ideal and its bearing upon "desirable directions of growth," together with its implications for classroom and school, see Thayer, Zachry, and Kotinsky, *op. cit.*, chaps. III, IX.

members of his class to the new undertaking; to hold in reserve more than one route for individuals to follow; and to invite the participation of members of the group in the selection of routes in accordance with their interests, needs, and abilities. This does not mean that the uninformed are to pass upon what the informed must know or that the apprentice is to substitute for the master. It does mean, however, that there are areas in which the pupils can participate with profit in defining the part they will play in their own education. One aspect of this education, indeed, consists in learning to distinguish between those occasions on which one may legitimately cooperate with the master in outlining the course he is to follow and when he must accept and follow instructions more or less on faith. For the teacher, it also means an attempt to apply the results of contemporary research into the nature of group behavior and the comparative effects upon motivation of democratic, autocratic, and laissez-faire methods of leadership.[43]

The working period likewise affords opportunities for democratic practices. It is in this period that both individual and group interests may be served. There is, of course, in every subject a common body of information, principles, and skills to be mastered, but each subject offers in addition abundant opportunities for interesting side excursions which can be made in such a way as to enrich the group as well as the individuals engaged in them. Often the problem or topic under study lends itself to committee work. This is of increasing importance today in the light of the tendency of Americans to solve their problems—political, social, civic, scientific—through cooperative research. This should suggest to educators the importance of helping young people to acquire the discipline and the techniques of cooperative research and committee activity which alone will render those activities effective rather than wasteful.

Within the committee as well as in the class recitation period there are ample opportunities to employ the techniques of democratic group discussion. Each student will have some occasion to function as discussion leader, as participant, as observer and critic, and as research worker who gathers data for the group in an objective spirit, without regard for his own conclusions and prejudices.

Finally, in the evaluation period, members of the group should be

43. See *The Dynamics of Instructional Groups, Fifty-Ninth Yearbook,* National Society for the Study of Education (Chicago: University of Chicago Press, 1960), part II, chaps. V, VI, VIII.

encouraged to review their work with a critical eye to their failures as well as their successes. In this phase, as in others, students may be led to understand the nature of a problem, the manner in which it has grown out of the past, how it implies a disturbed or unsatisfied present, and, in the process of its solution (whether finally solved or not), the way in which it may give character to the future. Thus, too, will students come to appreciate the vital importance of experimental thinking and freedom of inquiry in a democracy and, indeed, the dependence of free institutions upon disciplined freedom of thought.

In this hasty summary of ways in which a lesson period may be used to further the understanding and appreciation of democratic values, there is no intention to discount the importance of thorough intellectual accomplishment. On the contrary, it is assumed that the conscious use of democratic procedures will not only lend vitality to learning, but will foster and encourage intellectual discipline.

Applying Democracy to Administrative and Supervisory Relationships

Attempts to use the school in the interests of democratic thought and action (over and above the direct study of the origins, development, and nature of democracy and its methods) have not been confined to the classroom. They have led to new relationships between faculty and students and new departures in the administrative and supervisory functions of school officials.

Basic to these changes is a conception of democratic leadership which contrasts with leadership in both an autocratic society and one characterized by heavy accent upon individualism. Traditionally, the leader is thought of as one gifted with a dominant personality, one who by virtue of a strong will and an aggressive personality can impose his will upon others or through the exercise of magnetic qualities can induce others to identify their wills with his. In either case, the leader is thought of as one who determines for others what they should think and the course they are to follow.

The democratic leader is of a different breed. He conceives of his relationships with the members of his staff less as one between superior and inferiors than as one between functionaries in which each is charged with a distinctive task and each complements the other in the realization of an overarching ideal. As against the notion, then, that he has a will or a program to impose upon others, he seeks for mutually stimulating and creative relations between his colleagues and himself. In the formulation of policies, as in their execution, he realizes that he, as supervisor or administrator, by virtue of his central position has one function to serve and the members of his faculty have other functions; but when each contributes in the light of these different points of view, decisions are likely to be more relevant than when each operates without reference to the other. In his relations with individual teachers, heads of departments, or other functionaries, the democratic administrator encourages initiative and originality. At the same time he acts, when need be, as a constructive critic who, by virtue of his more varied experience or his central position, is likely to be sensitive to factors of which the specialist is unaware. As chairman of a meeting or as conference leader, he is "permissive," if this term means one who fosters a free play of ideas and suggestions while retaining the privilege of using his central position to call attention to and to round out the limited, partial, and often slanted proposals of those who speak from one vantage point only. In the school situation again, it is the leader's responsibility to foster harmonious relations among the members of his staff through mutual understanding and appreciation, to keep alive the overarching purposes and philosophy of the school, and to stimulate his colleagues to identify themselves with this philosophy in such a way as to promote all possible unity within difference. Finally, an administrator should conscientiously provide his colleagues with the essential tools of their craft and earnestly strive to safeguard them from unnecessary interference and distraction in the performance of their distinctive functions.

This conception of a democratic leader differs in a number of respects from that common in the management of industrial and business corporations. The specific pattern of organization, however, will vary with different school situations. In a small school, little in the way of formal structure may be required; the spirit is all important. In a large and complex situation, on the other hand, faculty participation in the formulation of policies may call for a formal organization of the faculty, together with the establishment of joint faculty-administrative committees.[44]

44. See *Behavioral Science and Educational Administration, Sixty-Third Yearbook,* National Society for the Study of Education (Chicago: University of Chicago Press, 1964), part II, chaps. VI, VII, IX–XI.

Logic would seem to suggest an extension of the principle of functional representation to the composition of boards of education. It must be admitted, however, that neither the small board which came into existence early in the century nor experiments in group representation on boards of education for public schools have entirely realized the ideals of their advocates. The small board often lends itself to the influence of pressure groups and even to capture by special interests (taxpayers' associations, religious and patriotic groups, and so on).[45] School board surveys have consistently shown that the composition of school boards tends to be heavily weighted in favor of certain social groups, usually business and professional groups,[46] and that school board members tend to identify their own motives with those of special-interest groups.[47] Attempts have been made to insure the representation of "all" legitimate interests. But in this respect also results have not been altogether happy. Not infrequently one group has combined with other groups to realize its limited and selfish purposes in accordance with the principle, "If you scratch my back, I'll scratch yours!"

This, of course, defeats the primary purposes of group representation. These purposes can only be realized when representatives of groups recognize that their primary obligation is to the institution as a whole and that as members of the central governing body they are selected *from* a group because of the special contributions they can make to the whole. They can discharge this obligation only when they contribute from their special backgrounds what is relevant to the formulation of general policies and then serve as successful interpreters of these policies to their groups. If this ideal be out of the reach of frail human beings, a substitute procedure might insure selection of members of boards of education from the community at large, with conscious provision for group representation upon advisory bodies—representation from parents, the professional staff, the whole community, and civic organizations within the community. The form and structure matter less (although they are not without importance) than general

45. See Neal Gross, *Who Runs Our Schools?* (New York: John Wiley and Sons, Inc., 1958), pp. 49–56.
46. See Edward L. Dejonska, "School Board Members: Their Opinions, Status, and Financial Willingness," *Journal of Educational Sociology*, January 1963, pp. 193–99; Alpheus L. White, "An Analysis of School Board Organization," *American School Board Journal*, April 1963, pp. 7–8.
47. See, for example, Donald J. McCarthy, "School Board Membership: Why Do Citizens Serve?" *Administrator's Notebook*, Number 1, September 1959.

understanding on the part of the public at large of the primary function an educational system is to serve in a democracy. In this respect, it must be recognized that the public school system, widely regarded as the main intellectual bulwark of democracy, has often failed to stimulate the interest and informed participation of citizens in school affairs.[48]

As one of the writers stated a number of years ago:

> We thus conclude that it is not solely in its relation to the learner that the school should observe the precepts of education. In all of its dealings it should bear witness to its major function. This implies the fostering and creation of living arrangements which permit of an intelligent sharing of experiences. It means an organization of such a character that each one participating performs his own special work with a full realization of its implications and effects upon his associates and the larger aims of which he is a means. In short, a school system should typify and exemplify in its operations as a whole and in the functioning of its parts the process which is the be-all and the end-all of its existence. It should stand forth clearly as an educational institution. And to make these purposes manifest is the distinctive function of school administration.[49]

Suggested Reading

Alberty, Harold B., and Elsie J. Alberty, *Reorganizing the High School Curriculum*, 3d ed. (New York: Macmillan Co., 1962), chaps. 5–6, 8, 13.

Cremin, Lawrence A., *The Transformation of the School* (New York: Alfred A. Knopf, 1961), chaps. 1, 3–4, 9.

Dewey, John, *Democracy and Education* (New York: Macmillan Co., 1918), chaps. IV, VII, IX.

Handlin, Oscar, *John Dewey's Challenge to Education* (New York: Harper & Brothers, 1959).

Hanna, Lavone A., Gladys L. Potter, and Neva Hagaman, *Unit Teaching in the Elementary School* (New York: Holt, Rinehart and Winston, Inc., 1963), chaps. 4–6.

48. See, for example, Roscoe C. Martin, *Government and the Suburban School* (Syracuse: Syracuse University Press, 1962), p. 57; Luvern L. Cunningham, "Executive Sessions and 'Informal' Meetings," *American School Board Journal*, May 1963, pp. 7–9.

49. V. T. Thayer in William Heard Kilpatrick and others, *The Educational Frontier* (New York: The Century Company, 1933), p. 256.

Phenix, Philip H., *Realms of Meaning: A Philosophy of the Curriculum for General Education* (New York: McGraw-Hill Book Co., 1964), pp. 267–321.

Taba, Hilda, *Curriculum Development: Theory and Practice* (New York: Harcourt, Brace and World, Inc., 1962), chaps. 1–2, 21–22.

U.S. Office of Education, *Local School Boards: Organization and Practices* (Washington, D.C.: U.S. Government Printing Office, 1962), chaps. 2–5, 8.

Wrenn, C. Gilbert, *The Counselor in a Changing World* (Washington, D.C.: American Personnel and Guidance Association, 1962), chaps. 1, 5–7.

PART III

YOUTH AND EDUCATION
IN TODAY'S WORLD

Chapter 12

Education in Corporate Society

Toward Organized Complexity

A little more than a century ago in America there were few business corporations, few and small labor unions, and practically no farm organizations or employers' and trade associations. In the federal government there was no Department of Agriculture, no Department of Labor, and, until 1867, no Department (now Office) of Education. Today, however, the significant units of business, the mass media, religion, government, philanthropy—once predominantly small and local in orientation—have become increasingly complex, large-in-scale, hierarchical, and often national or international in character.[1]

Essential to this organizational revolution have been the advances made by science and technology in certain areas of life. These have been areas where, to achieve control and power, it was decided to treat things as complex, problematic, and improvable rather than simple, known, or unknowable. The systematic study of certain phenomena by scientific procedures triggered the explosions of knowledge, productivity, population, and atoms, generated a highly diversified occupational structure of specialists, and provided rapid communication networks throughout the social systems.

With increasing heterogeneity came the need to coordinate specialized functions. This need, along with the apparent need to assign

1. For descriptions of the development and structure of "organizational society," see Philip Olson, ed., *America as a Mass Society* (New York: Free Press of Glencoe, 1963), part II; Robert Presthus, *The Organizational Society* (New York: Alfred A. Knopf, 1962), pp. 59–92. It should be noted that sociologists often attach more specific meanings to such terms as "organization" than we do here.

decision-making authority to coordinators, has resulted in a "proliferation of bureaucracies" [2] and a differential distribution of power according to principles of hierarchy.[3] To achieve predictable and efficient behavior, most complex organizations rely on bureaucratic principles, that is, on formal, impersonal, and "rational" procedures. Informal procedures and groups do facilitate or impede the working of the formal organization. However, the modern organization is primarily bureaucratic,[4] and when roles are highly specialized, specified, and interlocked, the individuality of the role-filler tends to be minimized and even "personal" relations become objects of study and standardization.

Organized complexity has been the way to success, that is, to efficiency and power, in many areas of life. In domestic and international arenas, affluence and organized complexity have generally marched hand in hand. Not only do the 500 largest industrial corporations in the United States account for the major share of the sales of all manufacturing and mining companies,[5] but their average rate of profit is higher than that of smaller firms. In 1963 their profits were 6.05 per cent of sales as compared with 4.79 per cent for all industrial firms.[6] During the past three or four decades in the United States (the societal acme of organized complexity), the gross national product, in constant dollars, has increased about three times as fast as the population.[7] In recent years the United States has been producing close to 50 per cent of the noncommunist world's values in manufacturing industries whereas Latin American countries, for example, have been producing a combined total of 4 per cent of these values.[8]

2. V. Williams, "Bureaucratic Proliferation: A Theoretical Approach," *American Journal of Economics and Sociology,* July 1963, pp. 337–45.

3. See Herbert A. Simon, "New Developments in the Theory of the Firm," *American Economic Review,* May 1962, p. 6.

4. Bernard Berelson and Gary A. Steiner, *Human Behavior: An Inventory of Scientific Findings* (New York: Harcourt, Brace and World, 1964), p. 364. On the page cited the authors state that "in much of the sociological literature, the terms 'bureaucracy' and 'organization' are synonymous, or virtually so (and 'bureaucracy' is by no means limited to governmental organizations)."

5. "The Fortune Directory: The 500 Largest U.S. Industrial Corporations," *Fortune,* July 1963, p. 177.

6. "Directory of the 500 Largest Industrial Corporations," *Fortune,* July 1964, p. 179.

7. John K. Norton, *Changing Demands on Education and their Fiscal Implications* (Washington, D.C.: National Committee for Support of the Public Schools, 1963), p. 10.

8. United Nations, *Statistical Yearbook, 1962* (New York: United Nations Publishing Service, 1963), p. 70.

Within the United States, whether we turn to labor unions or professional associations, to military or political units, to the mass media or the churches, we find roughly similar organizational developments. For example, while our population doubled between 1910 and 1960, the number of independent daily newspapers dropped by a third, and in 1962 competition between dailies survived in only 60 of the country's 5911 cities.[9] In religion the ecumenical movement has influenced American Protestantism so that "since 1905 no less than sixteen mergers and reunions have combined many of the major Protestant groups and reduced their number from thirty-six to fifteen." [10]

A National Community Is Emerging

Power, prestige, and people flow into great urban centers, the agglomerates that symbolize technology, transiency, and organized complexity. In 1890 two thirds of the population was rural, but by the early 1960s over 70 per cent was urban.[11] A typical prediction is that by 1980, 80 per cent or more will be urban. Moreover, we are in the "age of the supermetropolis. It is characterized by the merging of towns with towns, and cities with cities, overlapping state boundary lines to form continuing giant urban complexes—a phenomenon called 'megalopolis.'" [12]

The headquarters of the big organizations are concentrated in the metropolises. Although decisions take local situations and views into account, they must be made in terms of the "big picture." [13] Particularly at the top levels of the hierarchies, the complex organizations interact in making policies that spill over local, organizational, state, and national boundaries. The organizations even blend—as in the passage

9. James M. Burns and Jack W. Peltason, *Government by the People* (Englewood Cliffs, N.J.: Prentice-Hall, Inc., 1963), p. 236. See also, V. O. Key, Jr., *Public Opinion and American Democracy* (New York: Alfred A. Knopf, 1963), pp. 370–405.

10. Robert Lee, "The Organizational Dilemma in American Protestantism," *The Dilemma of Organizational Society*, H. M. Ruitenbeek, ed. (New York: E. P. Dutton and Co., Inc., 1963), p. 155.

11. Leo. F. Schnore, "Some Correlates of Urban Size: A Replication," *American Journal of Sociology*, September 1963, pp. 186–87.

12. B. J. Chandler, Lindley J. Stiles, and John I. Kitsuse, eds., *Education in Urban Society* (New York: Dodd, Mead and Co., 1962), p. v.

13. M. K. Jennings, "Public Administration and Community Decision Making," *Administrative Science Quarterly*, June 1963, pp. 18–43.

of industrial, military, governmental, and professional leaders from one kind of organization to another, or in the formation of various associations and national commissions.

To regulate powerful and interlocking organizations, to protect public interests and provide public goods and services (water, education, and so on), to redirect and synchronize the national effort in a changing world—above all, to provide for the national defense—the power of government has grown enormously in recent decades. Especially is this true of the federal government. The fear that disturbed Alexander Hamilton—"a nation without a national government"—need concern us no longer. In 1883 there was one federal government worker for every 400 Americans; by 1963 there was one for every 76 Americans.[14] For the past several years, total federal expenditures have amounted to at least 20 per cent of the annual gross national product.[15]

Thus "The Great Society" is emerging.[16] It is a national community in which complex, hierarchical organizations penetrate deeply and pervasively into individual life and provide much of the direction, structure, and content of daily activities. They provide individual opportunities, definitions of domestic and international situations, and a partially new national morality in which organizational and national interests weigh heavily. In this fluid society with its demands for unity and trained manpower, individuals must be poised for geographical, social, and ideological mobility.[17] They must be more or less unfettered and interchangeable, available for changing uses and ways in a changing society.

The big organizations are not deeply embedded in or controlled by local communities. Local and traditional determinants of status and behavior—family origins and wealth, race, religion, and sex—have lost much of their former significance. Organizational achievements and associations, only partially correlated with these traditional criteria,

14. Frank C. Porter, "So You Want to Work for the Government," *Saturday Review,* April 11, 1964, p. 21.
15. *The Budget of the United States Government for the Fiscal Year Ending June 30, 1964* (Washington, D.C.: U.S. Government Printing Office, 1963), p. 6.
16. W. Lloyd Warner, *The Corporation in the Emergent American Society* (New York: Harper & Row, 1962), pp. 1–23.
17. For a discussion of the influence of organizational society on values and personality (a problem we shall consider in the next chapter), see Solon T. Kimball and James E. McClellan, *Education and the New America* (New York: Random House, 1962), chaps. 6–7, 9.

have assumed increasing significance.[18] A Catholic President, deseg-regation problems, the weakening of local control over education, and the growing involvement of women in socioeconomic life are only some of the signs of our corporate age. The 1964 presidential election was in part a triumph of representatives of modern society (many executives of federally connected corporations, the majority of newspapers, many scientists, engineers, and union members, for example) over represen-tatives of traditional society.

Centrality of Education in Corporate Society

As hereditary and ancestral factors become less significant deter-minants of status and roles, educational achievement becomes an in-creasingly significant determinant. Of course, social-class origin, for example, is an important determinant of later status. However, a rather typical finding today is that "education is a more important deter-minant of occupational achievement than is father's occupation." [19] In an expert society, success in climbing up the educational ladder has be-come a general prerequisite for entry into career opportunities and for movement up many other organizational ladders.[20] The centrality of education is reflected in the schools' burgeoning relations with large-scale and national organizations—state and federal agencies, profes-sional organizations, philanthropic foundations, and so forth. Whether purposes are defined in terms of training scientists and other special-ists, contributing to national economic and military strength, achieving a unity of outlook and effort in a precariously divided world, or devel-oping individual freedom and responsibility, a growing number of leaders in all walks of life recognize the centrality of education in shap-ing and implementing national policy.[21]

18. S. N. Eisenstadt, "Bureaucracy, Bureaucratization, and Debureaucratization," *Complex Organizations,* Amitai Etzioni, ed. (New York: Holt, Rinehart and Winston, Inc., 1961), p. 268.

19. Otis D. Duncan and Robert W. Hodge, "Education and Occupational Mobility: A Regression Analysis," *American Journal of Sociology,* May 1963, p. 637.

20. See Suzanne Keller, *Beyond the Ruling Class: Strategic Elites in Modern Society* (New York: Random House, 1963), pp. 58–59, 96–98, 115–20, 175, 178, 181–82.

21. See, for example, Paul R. Hanna, ed., *Education: An Instrument of National Goals* (New York: McGraw-Hill Book Co., 1962), pp. 11–49, 72–117, 192–210.

At the same time, limited concerns, vision, authority, and funds have made most local board members, teachers, and administrators insensitive to or unable to cope with many educational problems of modern society. Many recent emphases and innovations in education—development of new curricula; stress on science, mathematics, and foreign language; reform of teacher education; search for talent; and others—have been promoted, at least initially, by individuals and organizations not identified primarily with education at the local level.

Strategic control over education has been moving up from local districts to state and federal agencies; it has been moving out from the so-called "educational establishment" (public school teachers and administrators, professors of education, and officials in state departments of education) to a broader array of influences. In a recent national survey, elementary and secondary principals rated the influence of local school officials and faculties lower in stimulating educational changes than the influence of national studies in the subject areas, state and national professional associations, philanthropic foundations (such as the Ford and Carnegie foundations), and educational programs sponsored by the federal government.[22] The greater financial resources of large-scale organizations, existing constitutional authority and a climate favorable to the active use of government to achieve public goals, the prestige of experts and national figures, the professional educators' general lack of expertness in the disciplines which are under continual revision—these and other influences are reducing, though by no means erasing, the traditionally heavy degree of local and professional control in education.

In diverse ways the operations of an organizational-technological society work toward shifting the areas and kinds of control over education. Take, for example, the specialization of educational functions according to grade level and specific duties. This specialization has promoted multiplicity and specificity in state certification requirements, and staff assignments tend, thus, to become a state function rather than a local administrative function.[23] Again, the rapidly increasing use of nationally standardized tests, such as those adminis-

22. Project on the Instructional Program of the Public Schools, *The Principals Look at the Schools* (Washington, D.C.: National Education Association, 1962), p. 29.

23. Lucien B. Kinney, *Certification in Education* (Englewood Cliffs, N.J.: Prentice-Hall, Inc., 1964), p. 29.

tered by the National Merit Scholarship Program and the College Entrance Examination Board, tends to exert a heavy influence on instructional emphases.[24]

Some Proposals for Shaping Educational Policy

As James B. Conant has remarked, "the national concern for education and the revolution in techniques have together made obsolete our past methods of determining educational policy in the United States," [25] and we are groping toward new arrangements for controlling education. Extending some current tendencies, Conant proposes greatly increased reliance on state educational agencies and on an "Interstate Commission" which, with federal participation, would act as a fact-finding and policy-recommending body "for Planning a Nationwide Educational Policy." [26] Leaders in education and in other fields have proposed the establishment of national educational standards,[27] the formation of a national board of education [28] and of various national curriculum commissions,[29] the elevation of the U.S. Office of Education into a department with representation in the President's cabinet,[30] and other plans designed to strengthen the schools' financial base and coordinate the educational leadership found in various professional organizations and levels of government.[31]

Numerous efforts and proposals are being made to reform teacher education, including efforts to strengthen the role of liberal arts professors in teacher education and in the National Council for Accreditation of Teacher Education (NCATE), the body which accredits teacher

24. *Sixty-Second Yearbook,* National Society for the Study of Education (Chicago: University of Chicago Press, 1963), part II, pp. 82–102, 193–210.

25. *Shaping Educational Policy* (New York: McGraw-Hill Book Co., 1964), p. 4.

26. *Ibid.,* pp. 31–43, 121–28.

27. Franklin Parker, "Recent Events in World Education," *Comparative Education Review,* October 1963, p. 197.

28. George W. Angell, "Do We Need a National Board of Education?" *School and Society,* Summer 1963, pp. 238–39.

29. See, for example, Paul R. Hanna, "Revising the Social Studies: What is Needed," *Social Education,* April 1963, pp. 190–96.

30. Donald W. Robinson, "Commissioner of Education: Our Least / Most Important Government Post," *Phi Delta Kappan,* December 1962, pp. 106–15.

31. See, for example, Committee on Educational Finance, *Long-Range Planning in School Finance* (Washington, D.C.: National Education Association, 1963), pp. 22–27, 36–41, 62–68, 122–28.

training institutions.[32] It is interesting to note that probably the single most influential proposal about teacher education has been made by James B. Conant in *The Education of American Teachers*.[33] Conant is a scientist, a past president of Harvard University, a former ambassador to West Germany. His several studies and reports on education have been supported by funds from philanthropic foundations. Few individuals so well represent the organizational–technological currents which impinge on education today.

Many members of the teaching profession are urging that professional educators must themselves seek wider powers in licensing procedures, negotiations for salaries and suitable conditions of work, and the shaping of educational policy. However, there is no single organization of professional educators, and what is often meant is that the National Education Association (NEA) should receive the increments of power.[34] The NEA, the single largest organization of public school teachers and administrators, is far from being representative of all professional groups directly concerned with some phase of the complex educational process. It has, in fact, often been identified with a rather narrow and unscholarly approach to raising the quality of instruction.

Some Principles for Shaping Educational Policy

As we search for new modes of controlling education, it is useful to remind ourselves that we often oversimplify problems, sometimes by clinging to outworn customs and sometimes by exaggerating one or two new elements of a complicated situation. Today, those who are fairly directly concerned with the operations of our educational institutions represent a multiplicity of "interacting groups which are increas-

32. See Lindley J. Stiles, "Role of Liberal Arts Colleges in Teacher Education," *Educational Forum*, January 1964, pp. 171–77, Joe Park, "Toward Reconstructing Schools and Departments of Education," *Educational Theory*, April 1963, pp. 108–18. For two quite different views on NCATE, see *Phi Delta Kappan*, October 1963, pp. 31–42.

33. (New York: McGraw-Hill Book Co., 1963). For some reactions to Conant's many recommendations, see "A Symposium on James Bryant Conant's *The Education of American Teachers*," *Journal of Teacher Education*, March 1964, pp. 5–49; *New York Times*, November 8, 1964, pp. 1, 43.

34. See, for example, T. M. Stinnett and A. J. Huggett, *Professional Problems of Teachers*, 2d ed. (New York: Macmillan Co., 1963), pp. 68, 147, 295–315. See also, Lawrence R. Klein, "The NEA Convention and the Organizing of Teachers," *Monthly Labor Review*, August 1964, pp. 882–85.

ingly separated from each other in their specializations and, for that reason, increasingly dependent upon each other for their operation." [35] This situation places a premium upon communication among the groups and calls for an expanded role of comprehensive organizations —"umbrella" or unifying associations and commissions, state and federal agencies, and so on—in coordinating diverse but interdependent elements.

Nevertheless, no complete set of decisions can be made "at the top" of even a single complex organization. Moreover, effective top-level decision-making requires much participation and information "from below," and much of this information—through selection, interpretation, and emphasis—already contains decision-orienting influence. As in the case of other technical activities of modern society, there is and should be an increasing role for experts in the related aspects of education.[36]

Thus, for example, broader authority for professional educational organizations is necessary. However, authority is misplaced when, for instance, those who are not experts in the training of teachers have a dominant voice in accrediting teacher-training institutions. And exaggeration of the role of professional educational organizations, as a group, can lead to defensiveness and conflict with other groups. Among the many realities which make professional provincialism unrealistic is the fact, emphasized by James B. Conant, that curriculum revisions *"can not now be discussed or planned without participation of subject matter professors."* [37]

On another point: great fear of federal control over education is not warranted by the history of federal activities in education, by constitutional and customary restrictions on federal activity in this area, and by the general ability of the electorate to control and use governmental agencies. Again, a national curriculum committee in a subject area may be quite useful, particularly if it bears in mind that "national" need not mean "uniform" and, thus, aids in developing a number of different

35. John Useem, "American Society as a High Civilization: Implications for Education," *Changes in Teacher Education: An Appraisal,* National Commission on Teacher Education and Professional Standards (Washington, D.C.: National Education Association, 1964), p. 15.

36. For an excellent survey of communication and decision-making processes in complex societies, see Alfred Kuhn, *The Study of Society: A Unified Approach* (Homewood, Ill.: Dorsey Press, Inc., 1963), chaps. 14–16, 24–25, 36, 40.

37. *Shaping Educational Policy,* p. 27.

approaches to an area. On the other hand, excessive concentration on national agencies can deflect attention from the key problem of selecting and developing teachers who are more than presenters of texts and tests prepared by others, teachers who can evaluate and use materials wisely and for varied purposes, who are competent and concerned enough to select able representatives in professional organizations and textbook selection committees. Yet to obtain career-oriented teachers of high quality will require vastly increased state and federal funds for education, the assistance of liberal arts professors, and aid from other sources.

What is most essential for achieving democratic control over education is not that particular powers be located in particular agencies, but that the public develop a deep and informed concern about education. Directly or indirectly, and whether by default or positive action, the public can determine the deployment of powers exercised over education. It can suffer or erase federal, state, or local abuses of power. It can use professionals wisely or place unreasonable restrictions on their judgments. There is much evidence that very few citizens are actively concerned with the complex procedures and problems involved in determining educational policy.[38] Contributions to the general education of citizens, including an understanding of the role of education in society, may be the most effective contributions the schools can make to the unending problem of shaping educational policy, a policy increasingly one with shaping the kind of society we desire in our technological age.

Where "Knowledge Explodes," There Inquiry Is Honored

Basic to our organizational-technological age is an only slightly appreciated "knowledge explosion." In some disciplines, knowledge is being accumulated or revised at an almost incredibly accelerated rate.

According to one authority, "there has been more technological knowledge gained in the last fifty years than in all previous history, and the growth is accelerating." [39] The biologist Bentley Glass estimates that, in comparison with the year 1900, the fund of biological

38. See, for example, Nicholas A. Masters, Robert H. Salisbury, and Thomas H. Eliot, *State Politics and the Public Schools* (New York: Alfred A. Knopf, 1964), p. 265.
39. Walter Buckingham, "Gains and Costs of Technological Change," *Adjusting to Technological Change*, Gerald G. Somers, *et al.*, eds. (New York: Harper & Row, 1963), p. 1.

knowledge had increased 4 times by 1930 and 16 times by 1960, and will increase about 100 times by 2000.[40] A manuscript prepared in 1964 by Joseph C. Shipman [41] reveals the following examples of the knowledge explosion: (1) Fifty years ago the known properties of crystals were summarized in five volumes; today these volumes represent less than 1 per cent of what is known about crystals. (2) Two estimates roughly agree that if an organic chemist devoted eight hours a day, six days a week, to reading the important literature now coming out in his field, in ten years he would be nine years behind in his reading.[42]

The impact of modern science upon society and education cannot adequately be conveyed by scattered data. Here, however, we wish to emphasize a point that often is overlooked: the new knowledge is socially produced; it is the product of a complex and costly process in which there is a rather deliberate and massive allocation of money and effort to selected problems.[43] Outstanding scientists like Einstein may command public attention. However, it is no disparagement of these individuals to say that they stand on the shoulders of a crowd of past and present colleagues, themselves encouraged by social stimulations promoting scientific progress in certain areas.

More important than the bits of knowledge already available is the growing awareness that continually improved theory and technique can be produced in a multiplying set of areas.[44] It is often said that no industry has ever grown as fast as the research and development (R and D) industry. In 1920 the total funds spent in the United States on R and D amounted to 0.09 per cent of the gross national product; in 1963 these funds represented 3 per cent of the gross national product,[45] well over half the total expenditures for public education. From

40. "Information Crisis in Biology," *Bulletin of the Atomic Scientist*, October 1962, p. 6.
41. Mr. Shipman is Director of Linda Hall Library of Science and Technology (Kansas City, Missouri).
42. For varying, though always startling, estimates of the extent of the knowledge explosion, see National Bureau of Economic Research, *The Rate and Direction of Inventive Activity: Economic and Social Factors* (Princeton, N.J.: Princeton University Press, 1962), pp. 19–51, 53–90; Fritz Machlup, *The Production and Distribution of Knowledge in the United States* (Princeton, N.J.: Princeton University Press, 1962), pp. 122, 170–75.
43. See Jacob Schmookler and O. Brownlee, "Determinants of Inventive Activity," *American Economic Review*, May 1962, pp. 165–76.
44. See Hugh J. Miser, "Operations Research in Perspective," *Operations Research*, September–October 1963, pp. 669–77.
45. William W. Ellis, "The Federal Government in Behavioral Science: Fields, Methods, and Funds," *American Behavioral Scientist*, May 1964, p. 23.

1920 to the early 1960s, the personnel in industrial laboratories increased by 400 per cent, while the number of production workers increased by only 6 per cent.[46] The prediction is that this trend will accelerate, despite critical manpower shortages in scientific and technical fields.[47]

Expenditures for R and D are concentrated in the most powerful of our interlocking organizations and are used primarily for military and economic purposes. In recent years the federal government has been providing well over two thirds of the total R and D funds.[48] Although private industry has been providing just one fifth of these funds, about three fourths of all R and D is performed by industry, mainly under contracts with the federal government.[49] A relatively few large industrial firms spend the major share of federally provided research funds. Over 95 per cent of federal dollars for research in universities goes to less than 100 of the over 2000 institutions of higher education; some 71 per cent of this money goes for research in the physical sciences and 26 per cent for research in biology.[50]

R and D efforts tend to be concentrated where, for certain purposes, creativity and careful inquiry are most honored, advances have been most spectacular, and the fact is widely recognized that "funds invested in research yielded a higher return than funds invested in other ways." [51] R and D funds in the aircraft and missile fields, for example, have been running at about a quarter of the total R and D outlay in this country.[52]

For an increasing variety of wonderful and terrible purposes—to control cancer and develop bloodless surgery by sound waves, to stimu-

46. J. W. H. Clare, "Current Trends in the Organization of Industrial Research," *Research Management,* March 1963, p. 137.

47. U.S. Department of Labor, *Mobility and Worker Adaptation to Economic Change in the United States,* rev. ed. (Washington, D.C.: U.S. Government Printing Office, 1963), pp. 14–15, 29, 34.

48. William B. Farrington, "Squeezing Research Dollars," *International Science and Technology,* September 1963, pp. 80, 82.

49. James R. Killian, Jr., "The Crisis in Research," *Atlantic Monthly,* March 1963, p. 69.

50. Charles G. Dobbins, ed., *Higher Education and the Federal Government* (Washington, D.C.: American Council on Education, 1963), pp. 18, 61.

51. W. A. Wallis, "Some Economic Considerations," *Automation and Technological Change,* John T. Dunlop, ed. (Englewood Cliffs, N.J.: Prentice-Hall, Inc., 1962), p. 107.

52. *New York Times,* September 22, 1963, sec. 3, pp. 1 ff. The Department of Defense, the National Aeronautics and Space Administration, and the Atomic Energy Commission administered well over 13 billion dollars of the nearly 15 billion dollars laid out by the federal government for R and D in 1964. See *The Budget of the United States Government . . . 1964,* pp. 390–91.

late the production and consumption of goods, to make possible the destruction of civilization or the creation of life by man—there is a growing awareness that systematic research is the great invention of our time and that scientific theory is our greatest incorporeal capital and product.

Education Is an Under-researched Area

In education, as in the social sciences generally, the situation has been quite different from that just described. Total R and D funds in the United States are distributed about the same as the federal R and D funds—97 per cent goes to the natural sciences, less than 3 per cent to the social sciences.[53] The U.S. Department of Health, Education, and Welfare administered about 778 million dollars of the nearly 15 billion dollars of federal R and D funds in 1964. However, within the Department, the Public Health Service expended 721.8 million dollars of the total amount allocated. The U.S. Office of Education, showing a sharp increase over 1963, spent 24.3 million dollars, about 3.5 per cent of the research money spent by the Public Health Service.[54]

At least until very recent years, federal money for educational research has been less than that provided for research in such agencies as the Forest Service and Commercial Fisheries.[55] Although funds for educational research have been growing rapidly in the past few years, it is estimated that "considerably less than one per cent," [56] perhaps $\frac{1}{10}$ of 1 per cent,[57] of the annual education budget is spent on research.

Some Deficiencies in Educational Research

Tradition and dogma, liberal or conservative sentiments, undergird more educational policies and practices than does research.[58] After

53. William W. Ellis, *op. cit.,* p. 23.

54. *The Budget of the United States Government . . . 1964,* pp. 390–91, 395–96.

55. David L. Clark, "Educational Research: A National Perspective," in *Educational Research: New Perspectives,* Jack A. Culbertson and Stephen P. Hencley, eds. (Danville, Ill.: Interstate Printers and Publishers, Inc., 1963), p. 12.

56. David R. Krathwohl, "Comment on the Briggs Proposal," *Phi Delta Kappan,* November 1964, pp. 103–04.

57. David L. Clark, *op. cit.,* pp. 8, 12.

58. For detailed analyses of deficiencies in educational research see Paul F. Lazarsfeld and Sam D. Sieber, *Organizing Educational Research* (Englewood Cliffs, N.J.: Prentice-Hall, Inc., 1964), chaps. 3–4; Matthew B. Miles, ed., *Innovation in Education* (New York: Bureau of Publications, Teachers College, Columbia University, 1964), chaps. 1, 13, 16, 22, 25.

surveying the status of educational theory and research, two social scientists concluded that "to a marked extent, education is thus characterized by the development of very general philosophic theories on the one hand, and relatively simple empirical inquiries on the other. . . . Sometimes very little appears between these extremes." [59] Historical explanations of this enfeebling disjunction between theoretical and empirical materials can be given; however, few logical justifications can be given.

Much educational research consists of surveys of trends in practices and policies. Often the trends that are found seem to serve as cues for climbing on a bandwagon—apparently on the assumption that if something is becoming popular it must be good. Or a trend may be criticized in terms of scientifically unchecked beliefs. Also, much research, particularly in large urban school systems is merely service-oriented; it is geared to "improving" rather than understanding education, to doing more efficiently what the system believes it should be doing rather than to developing better ideas about what to do. In general, research based on the assumption that we already know what we need to know does not inspire imaginative development and testing of alternative approaches to education.

Basic research, designed to develop and test fundamental and potentially broadly applicable theory, is largely neglected in education. Yet most scientists believe that basic research is *the* key to dramatic advances in knowledge, and in the stronger sciences there is much concern about increasing the proportion of R and D funds spent on basic research. Most educational research lacks both systematic theoretical work and extensive testing in a variety of school situations.

The common practice is to neglect "system analysis"—in education, inquiry into how a limited set of procedures and aims (in counseling, the teaching of reading, and so on) might fit into, modify, and be modified by the system of means and ends which constitute a comprehensive, long-range educational program. This fragmented approach, with its neglect of systems, field testing, dissemination of findings, and development and feedback, further impedes construction of theory.

Fragmented research often seems to proceed on the assumption that a strong theory is only a set of generalizations drawn from a body of

59. Rollo Handy and Paul Kurtz, *A Current Appraisal of the Behavioral Sciences* (Great Barrington, Mass.: Behavioral Research Council, 1964), p. 92.

accumulated data and that, therefore, inquiry must go forward by the initial gathering of "facts" followed by formulation of a theory. However, as Karl R. Popper has written, "the belief that we can start with pure observations alone, without anything in the nature of a theory, is absurd. . . ." [60] We do not begin an inquiry by going around and "observing carefully." We observe selected phenomena. We have in mind just certain purposes, criteria by which we accept data as relevant and weighty, assumptions about causal relations, and so on. If we do not carefully and explicitly formulate these ideas, we slip away from scientific procedure into the unquestioned and therefore untestable certainties of common sense, or we confuse a simple regularity or hypothesis ("a rewarded child will learn more than a punished child," for example) with a developed theory.

Even when the evidence at hand is quite limited, many of the natural sciences and a few of the social sciences increasingly use carefully constructed theories to "explain" and interconnect presumed regularities, suggest new and testable ideas, and so on.[61] As used in education, however, the term "theory" usually refers to a few simple regularities or to vague, untestable doctrines about "ultimate" causes or goals.

With its emphasis on the study of just a few factors evaluated in terms of one or two criteria, fragmented research assumes that the full meaning of a very limited set of variables can be known independently of a larger context of relations and criteria.[62] This is highly doubtful. For example, the long-range effects of a particular practice may be quite different from the short-range effects; or a procedure in teaching history may be effective in teaching facts but make a negative contribution to the ability to select, evaluate, and use historical data in a problem situation; or, when conjoined with other emphases in different educational programs, a procedure useful in developing "sensitivity to others" may contribute to open-mindedness, herd-mindedness, the subtle manipulation of others, or a tolerance that borders on amorality.

60. *Conjectures and Refutations* (London: Routledge and Kegan Paul, 1963), p. 46.
61. See Rollo Handy and Paul Kurtz, *op. cit.*, pp. 5–14, 77–87; M. Bunge, "The Weight of Simplicity in the Construction and Assaying of Theories," *Philosophy of Science*, April 1961, pp. 120–49.
62. For a more detailed criticism of what is here called fragmented research, see Lee J. Cronbach, "Course Improvement Through Evaluation," *Teachers College Record*, May 1963, pp. 672–86.

Improving Our Knowledge of Education

In recent decades, interdisciplinary work and deliberate theory construction have been carefully cultivated in the more rapidly advancing sciences.[63] An increasing number of scientists work cooperatively with colleagues in other disciplines; some scientists specialize in applying concepts and methods of one field to problems in other fields; some specialize in constructing overarching theories that bring together concepts and data from a number of different fields. Such measures promote powerful linkages of resources in dealing with complex problems. They permit evidence in one field to serve as a partial check on the usefulness and limitations of theories in another field. They contribute to what is paradoxical to common sense—the development of well-grounded theories which, ideally, are tentatively held and are continually being revised.

However, system analysis, (theoretical) model building, and operations research, terms which refer to the practical and theoretical activities involved in modern research, are rarely found in the literature of educational research. Yet, it seems clear that the intellectual and organizational patterns of fragmented research must be replaced by those of modernized and massive research.

Support for individual investigations should be strengthened, but our ability to synthesize research efforts conceptually and operationally should also be strengthened. The agenda might include these items: (1) establishment of national and regional institutes of research for work on projects which exceed the powers of a single researcher or university; (2) provisions for the continuing collection of data in long-range studies of "systems" that embrace significant variables in the social backgrounds and general education of teachers, professional education programs, administrative and curricular practices of school systems, social characteristics of communities, and personal characteristics of pupils and educators; (3) sharing of teaching and research personnel whose abilities and interests cut across the administrative lines that now separate professional education from potential resources in the liberal arts and other faculties; (4) development of theories which

63. See Richard H. Brenneman, "Interdisciplinary Approach to Research in Solving Modern Problems," *California Journal of Educational Research,* May 1963, pp. 97–107.

provide a rationale for meshing separately conducted studies; and (5) extensive studies of the conduct and organization of educational research in order to improve this agenda.

No science studies "all" aspects or relations of anything. Finding interrelationships among a selected set of variables that are significant for certain purposes is an essential feature of scientific procedure. Eye color and a million other variables may be irrelevant for certain purposes. Nevertheless, massive research on a "systems" scale could involve expenditures that rival those in military research programs. Nothing in physical research makes it intrinsically more costly than social science research. Although money is not everything, fragmented research is in part the rather passive adjustment education has made to the limited funds available for research.

The potential benefits of improved research are so great that educators might well make the modernization of educational research a major aim. To understate the case, the achievement of more adequate educational theories seems to be a reasonable and socially useful goal. Few other achievements could contribute so much to the professionalization of education. No profession can or should go its own way, totally immune to larger social forces. With more adequate theory, educators would be in a better position to follow the suggestions of theory and to resist some of the unwarranted interference or pressures from "external" agencies, such as philanthropic foundations, local pressure groups, or governmental bodies.

Science, Values, and the Spirit of Inquiry

Many people argue that science can play only a minor or "merely instrumental" role in education, for education is a thoroughly value-laden activity. Science may tell us how to get somewhere but it does not tell us where to go.[64] At least our ultimate values, it is said, are not provided by science.

One can agree wholeheartedly that education is permeated by value choices without subtracting an iota from the potential role of scientific procedures in decision-making. Experience in democratic societies war-

64. For one version of this general argument, see George S. Maccia, "Science and Science in Education," *Foundations of Education*, George F. Kneller, ed. (New York: John Wiley and Sons, 1963), chap. II.

rants the claim that people do not have to believe in the same gods or "ultimate" values in order to live, work, and inquire together. Moreover, the nature of our rules for making social decisions indicates that we do not regard our social values as being so subjective that no rational justification of them can be given. We do observe common procedural rules, but they need not be justified by a common and "ultimate" philosophy. Indeed, we would label undemocratic any attempt to impose such a philosophy. There seems to be no reason why we cannot adopt in education the working principle we adopt in social life—a posture of continuing inquiry into our basic practices and purposes.

No scientific law or ethical principle causes people to be reasonable. People can be reasonable and open-minded or emotional and dogmatic about both factual and ethical questions. In science, at least ideally, we have chosen to honor those kinds of ideas, attitudes, and skills which promote critical and competent inquiry, which permit us to go on learning. We can do the same in education.

Improving educational research is not merely a technical enterprise. Nor is it aimed at converting teachers into researchers. It is a value-laden activity, for, among other things, it could invigorate the spirit of inquiry in teacher education and in the public school classrooms. Teachers are more likely to understand education as an opportunity for inquiry if they have experienced an educational program conducted by professors who, in their various capacities, view education as a field of inquiry rather than as an opportunity for transmitting largely theory-less "facts," unquestioned values, or ungrounded "theories." Teachers who experience education as a field of inquiry could learn not only the knowledge and skills required for teaching but also something about the theoretical-empirical foundations of the principles they use. They would probably be better prepared to develop in their own pupils the kind of knowledge, attitudes, and skills required for competent inquiry.

Of course, there would be many significant differences between the preparatory programs of teachers and of researchers. However, there would be some common elements, although the depth of study would vary. In any event, research cannot be adequately conducted or interpreted merely on the basis of some knowledge of statistics, research design, and research technique. Among other items, the nature of theory, the relations among the concepts and data of cognate fields, the nature of scientific method and validation, and the relation between the general purposes of science and the purposes of a particular study would be examined more extensively by researchers and teachers. If something like this occurs, major changes in teacher education will occur.

In recent years, there have been encouraging indications of reform in educational research. More adequate construction of theory has been a subject of growing interest.[65] Largely with federal funds, some progress is being made in expanding the cooperative and comprehensive aspects of R and D.[66] The tempo of innovation in education has increased in recent decades.[67] However most of the reform work is still to be done, and many of the new efforts provide cause for concern.

A Bewildering Array of Innovations in Education

Today unprecedentedly massive waves of children move through the public schools. Faced with shortages of funds and teachers, public schools also have been confronted with widespread criticism of their effectiveness in providing for individual differences among children, educating gifted and culturally disadvantaged children, training scientists and technicians, and so forth. Stimulated by this situation and by successful uses of technology in raising levels of expertness and productivity in military and industrial tasks, educators are considering and using many plans for employing new instructional devices, grouping students and staff, and changing curricula.[68] "The past decade, probably more than any other in history, has witnessed an almost bewildering array of innovations and its share of educators on bandwagons." [69]

Traditional ways of organizing students and staff for instructional purposes are being modified. The formerly rather limited practice of

65. David L. Elliott and Arthur W. Foshay, "Chart or Charter: Recent Developments in Educational Discourse," *Review of Educational Research*, June 1963, pp. 233–44.

66. See Gerald R. Smith, "Progress Through the Cooperative Research Program," *Phi Delta Kappan*, March 1964, pp. 303–06; Panel on Educational Research and Development, *Innovation and Experiment in Education* (Washington, D.C.: U.S. Government Printing Office, 1964).

67. Matthew B. Miles, *op. cit.*, p. 320.

68. Certain aspects of the new curricula will be considered in Chapter 15.

69. Project on the Instructional Program of the Public Schools, *Planning and Organizing for Teaching* (Washington, D.C.: National Education Association, 1963), p. 120.

grouping students by ability and achievement has been widely extended at both elementary and secondary levels.[70] An increasing number of honors and advanced placement programs, work-study programs, and plans for promoting independent study embody attempts to provide for differences in abilities and interests among students and to meet the needs for trained manpower at various levels. The impact of the knowledge explosion and of the intensified specialization of functions are reflected in the introduction of more separate subjects at the secondary level and in the trend toward departmentalization at the elementary level.[71]

Challenging the usual practice of promotion or retardation at the end of fixed periods is the nongraded (mainly elementary) school which permits individual advancement when required competencies are achieved. Among other plans which facilitate flexible scheduling and grouping of pupils and, also, greater specialization among teachers, are various forms of team teaching. Working cooperatively, two or more teachers take over the responsibility for all or much of the instruction of a group of pupils. During a day, instruction may be carried on in groups or sub-groups comprising 3 to 150 pupils; independent study and ability grouping may be included in this plan. Some typical features of complex organizations (specialization, hierarchy, and so on) are visible in the large instructional teams which may have a team leader, several "master teachers," various specialists and aides, and apprentices. A small but growing minority of schools use team teaching or ungraded sequences.

Rapidly increasing use is being made of a growing variety of mechanical devices for individual and group instruction—videotapes, overhead projectors, record players, teaching machines, for example. Although the great majority of schools still do not use teaching machines, the number of programs available (for teaching machines or in textbook form) grew from a handful in 1960 to well over 500 in 1964.[72] It seems likely that within a decade or so the majority of school systems will be making some use of programed instruction.[73]

70. *The Principals Look at the Schools,* pp. 15–17.
71. *Ibid.,* pp. 11–14.
72. Fund for the Advancement of Education, *Four Case Studies of Programed Instruction* (New York: The Fund, 1964), p. 9.
73. Research Division, The Center for Programed Instruction, *The Use of Programed Instruction in U.S. Schools* (Washington, D.C.: U.S. Government Printing Office, 1963), p. 10.

Concerning educational television, a rather typical estimate is that by 1970, 90 per cent of public school students will receive part of their instruction through television.[74]

Evaluation of Educational Innovations

An organizational–technological revolution in education has not yet occurred, but it is in the making. In general the rate of innovation is most rapid in some large urban districts and in some well-supported suburban schools. Proponents cheer and opponents fear the introduction of a new device or procedure. However, the evidence available provides little reason for either wild enthusiasm or gnawing fear, though it does suggest that we have often accepted a proposal without adequate research.

The findings concerning ability grouping, for example, "seem to follow no definite pattern. Available evidence indicates that factors other than the particular grouping methods used account for any differences that may show up in achievement tests between children grouped according to ability and those grouped heterogeneously." [75] Very little evidence is available on the merits of nongraded sequences, and what evidence there is suggests that this structural change does not necessarily affect teaching procedures and results, and that individual differences can be met just as well in graded schools.[76] Several hundred studies of educational television indicate that the most common finding is "no significant difference" in the learning of subject matter when educational television is compared with conventional classroom procedures.[77]

In evaluations of programed instruction, "the 'no difference' studies comparing programmed instruction with live teachers have been the rule rather than the exception," and "the most consistent finding is that students learn at least equally well compared with other methods of

74. *Planning and Organizing for Teaching*, p. 127.
75. Jane Franseth, "Research in Grouping: A Review," *School Life*, June 1963, p. 6. See also Stuart E. Dean, "The Nongraded School: Is There Magic in It?" *School Life*, December 1964, pp. 19–23.
76. See Walter W. Cook and T. Clymer, "The Impact of Testing on School Organization," *Sixty-Second Yearbook*, National Society for the Study of Education (Chicago: University of Chicago Press, 1963), pp. 75, 79; Robert F. Carbone, "A Comparison of Graded and Non-graded Elementary Schools," *Elementary School Journal*, 1961, pp. 82–88.
77. *Phi Delta Kappan*, February 1964, p. 266.

instruction." [78] Some studies indicate that students may learn material more rapidly through programed instruction, but usually "the experimental groups [those using teaching machines or programed texts] only worked on test-relevant material, while control groups covered a wider range of topics." [79] In all, the fragmentary nature of the research, the limited effects evaluated (mainly assimilation of information), and the probability that the Hawthorne or novelty effect temporarily favors the experimental groups, suggest to Professor Lee J. Cronbach that "we are not able to greet teaching machines, self-teaching texts, and the other products of this new movement as a great breakthrough. . . ." [80]

Numerous studies of attempts to improve learning of subject matter by changing one or two variables in the complex process of education show that "differences in achievement of pupils exposed to different teaching methods are small and are not generally consistent from study to study." [81] As Philip W. Jackson has suggested, it is not that teaching is some kind of "mysterious art," but that the educational process is too complex to be adequately studied by fragmented approaches. [82]

The lack of a system-analysis approach in evaluation of recent innovations is particularly obvious in the limited criteria used to evaluate success. Achievement in subject matter has been the major, often the sole, criterion. Thus, research reports on team teaching "give no evidence on whether or not team teaching produces gains with respect to learning critical thinking, creativity, competencies in inquiry, or self-

---

78. Lawrence M. Stolurow, "Implications of Current Research and Future Trends," in *The Teacher and the Machine*, Philip Lambert, ed. (Madison, Wisc.: Dembar Educational Research Service, Inc., 1962), p. 520. Analyzing 36 comparisons of programed instruction with conventional classroom instruction, Wilbur Schramm found that 18 showed no significant difference, 17 favored programed instruction, and only 1 favored conventional instruction. However, many of Schramm's conclusions and words of caution are similar to our own. See U.S. Department of Health, Education, and Welfare, *The Research on Programed Instruction: An Annotated Bibliography* (Washington, D.C.: U.S. Government Printing Office, 1964), pp. 2–5.

79. Harry F. Silberman, "Self-Teaching Devices and Programmed Materials," *Review of Educational Research*, April 1962, p. 185.

80. *Educational Psychology*, 2d ed. (New York: Harcourt, Brace and World, Inc., 1963), p. 416.

81. Robert M. W. Travers, *Essentials of Learning* (New York: Macmillan Co., 1963), p. 4.

82. "The Teacher and Individual Differences," *Sixty-First Yearbook*, National Society for the Study of Education (Chicago: University of Chicago Press, 1962), part 1, pp. 77–83.

instruction." [83] In studies of ability grouping, "little research has been conducted to determine the possible effects of different ways of grouping on children's growth in such areas as ability to think, on the development of creativity, or on the development of human values— respect for the worth of all individuals, human dignity, and the like." [84]

In programed instruction, it may well be that programs can be constructed and used to contribute to a variety of educational aims. At present, however, they are constructed and used to transmit rigid structures of knowledge, with little attention to critical thinking, comparisons of different conceptual approaches, applications to nonverbal situations, and so on.[85] It may well be that extensive use of teaching machines will free teachers so they can devote more time to developing critical thinking and other abilities. Perhaps, however, they will devote more time to reinforcing the programs presented by the machines. We do not know. If we are to be better informed about what we are doing in education, programed instruction, team teaching, and other variables need to be analyzed in terms of a system of means and ends.[86]

Mass Processing in the Schools

The over-all pattern of educational experiences in the United States increasingly resembles the patterns of life in the larger society and in complex, bureaucratic organizations. Specialization of functions, diversification of curricula, and some kinds of grouping and scheduling plans lead to student interaction with a larger number of adults, but for briefer periods of time and, in general, for increasingly specialized purposes. The teacher's familiarity with varied aspects of a student's experience and personality decreases. Using an often unhappy combination of formal, impersonal procedures and unchecked subjective judgments, counselors, administrators, and staff specialists are taking

83. Glen Heathers, "Research on Team Teaching," in *Team Teaching,* Judson T. Shaplin and Henry F. Olds, Jr., eds. (New York: Harper & Row, 1964), p. 329.
84. Jane Franseth, *op. cit.,* p. 6.
85. Lee J. Cronbach, *Educational Psychology,* p. 417; Wilbur Schramm, *Programed Instruction: Today and Tomorrow* (New York: Fund for the Advancement of Education, 1962), pp. 8, 12–13, 25.
86. See William C. Trow, *Teacher and Technology: New Designs for Learning* (New York: Appleton-Century-Crofts, 1963), chap. 5.

over guidance functions, control of conduct, and special services and treatments.[87]

Some of the consequences of this mass processing [88] are beneficial. Nevertheless, there is some reason to think that emotional depth and richness and active concern for others emerge from more rounded and intimate relations than the schools generally provide. To explore and integrate subject matter in ways charged with both scholarly and personal potentials, to promote an intellectually respectable and personally meaningful appreciation of subtle human affairs, to develop civilized people rather than skilled functionaries of a technological society may require that students and teachers experience each other in ways significantly different from those of yesterday or today.

What is tragic is not that the above "allegations" are true. What is tragic is that we do not know reasonably well whether they are true or false. With our narrow conceptions of scientific method and excellence in education, we are left without firm grounds for acceptance or rejection of educational proposals, without bold and rigorous plans for adequate evaluation of comparative educational programs.

Suggested Reading

Berelson, Bernard, ed., *The Behavioral Sciences Today* (New York: Basic Books, Inc., 1963), chaps. 1, 3–5, 11, 20.

Clark, Burton R., *Educating the Expert Society* (San Francisco: Chandler Publishing Co., 1962), chaps. 1, 8.

Conant, James B., *Shaping Educational Policy* (New York: McGraw-Hill Book Co., 1964), chaps. 1–2, 5.

De Cecco, John P., *Educational Technology: Readings in Programmed Instruction* (New York: Holt, Rinehart and Winston, 1964), pp. 27–50, 393–423.

Ehlers, Henry, and Gordon C. Lee, *Crucial Issues in Education* (New York: Holt, Rinehart and Winston, 1964), part 6.

Kaplan, Abraham, *The Conduct of Inquiry: Methodology for Behavioral Science* (San Francisco: Chandler Publishing Co., 1964), sections 3–4, 7–8, 33, 37, 43–46.

87. See Aaron V. Cicourel and John I. Kitsuse, *The Educational Decision-Makers* (Indianapolis: Bobbs-Merrill Co., Inc., 1963), pp. 83–84, 100–22, 141–47.
88. The concept of "mass processing" in this application is from Burton R. Clark, *Educating the Expert Society* (San Francisco: Chandler Publishing Co., 1962), pp. 281–85, 288–91.

Lazersfeld, Paul F., and Sam D. Sieber, *Organizing Educational Research* (Englewood Cliffs, N.J.: Prentice-Hall, Inc., 1964), chaps. I, III–IV.

Miles, Matthew B., ed., *Innovation in Education* (New York: Bureau of Publications, Teachers College, Columbia University, 1964), chaps. 1, 9, 13, 17, 20–21, 23, 25.

National Commission on Teacher Education and Professional Standards, *Changes in Teacher Education: An Appraisal* (Washington, D.C.: National Education Association, 1964), pp. 1–5, 9–19, 89–120, 320–31.

Olson, Peter, ed., *America as a Mass Society* (New York: Free Press of Glencoe, 1963), part II.

Project on the Instructional Program of the Public Schools, *Education in a Changing Society* (Washington, D.C.: National Education Association, 1963), chaps. 2–4, 7–10.

Chapter 13

Youth, Education, and
the Way of Life

The Acquisitive Society

In this chapter we consider just a few modal features of the American style of life, characteristics which carry their moral for education.

One basic fact of our life is our intense devotion to the production and consumption of goods and services. We are the world's greatest producer of material things, and "Americans consume three times as much in the way of goods and services per capita as their fellow inhabitants of industrial civilizations."[1] Nevertheless, to whip up our desires, we have been spending on advertising about 50 per cent of the total funds we spend for all levels of public education.[2]

We invest in this business not only capital but also much of ourselves. Not wisdom or spiritual values but the pleasures of goods and services are what we usually plan to attain tomorrow. Though the correlations are far from perfect, we distribute rewards and status broadly in accord with ability to produce, sell, and consume or to manage these activities.[3]

Many of our theories—religious, social, biological—of the relation-

1. Gerard Piel, "The Advent of Abundance," *Bulletin of the Atomic Scientists*, June 1963, p. 3.
2. Cf. Michael D. Reagan, *The Managed Economy* (New York: Oxford University Press, 1963), p. 105; and U.S. Office of Education, *Digest of Educational Statistics* (Washington, D.C.: U.S. Government Printing Office, 1964), p. 129.
3. See Wendell Bell, Richard J. Hill, and Charles R. Wright, *Public Leadership* (San Francisco: Chandler Publishing Co., 1961), pp. 34–41, 97–120.

ships of men with each other and with the powers and principles of the universe have been bent to support of the acquisitive society. Far more than in many other cultures, our traditional and popular economic theory views man as "economic man," driven by his very nature to maximize sensual pleasures or "profits" in a postulated world of scarcity and insatiable wants.[4] Erich Fromm has depicted the typical American as one who has a "marketing orientation" even toward himself. This person sees himself as a commodity to be sold; his self-esteem depends upon his success. Historically and generally, American conceptions of equality and equal opportunity did not deny the need for status differences. Indeed, these conceptions probably intensified competitive drives by calling upon each person to make something of himself by climbing up the socioeconomic ladder.[5]

People are made of finer and much more complex materials than acquisitive and competitive motives. Nevertheless, this aspect of the American style of life bears heavily upon the education of our youth.

Youth Learn the Ethics of Competition

Although specific means of competition and definitions of success vary greatly with individuals and social groups, acquisitive drives are learned early and thoroughly by most of our youth. An extensive series of studies of adolescents led to the following conclusion: "The values and ambitions common to youth in all areas [social classes] spell the image of *individual success*. . . . The ingredients of the image are comfortable living, cars, attractive clothing, money to spend, leisure, and entertainment." [6] Characteristically, a study found that college students rated occupations they associated with "honorable and morally good work" and "service to humanity" generally lower in prestige and desirability than occupations they associated with security, good income, and high socioeconomic status.[7]

4. George Dalton, "Economic Theory and Primitive Society," *American Anthropologist*, February 1961, pp. 2–5, 9.
5. See Seymour M. Lipset, "Social Stratification and the Analysis of American Society," in *The Behavioral Sciences Today*, Bernard Berelson, ed. (New York: Basic Books, Inc., 1963), pp. 199–202.
6. Muzafer Sherif and Carolyn W. Sherif, *Reference Groups: Exploration into Conformity and Deviation of Adolescents* (New York: Harper & Row, 1964), p. 257.
7. Albeno P. Garbin and Frederick L. Bates, "Occupational Prestige: An Empirical Study of the Correlates," *Social Forces*, December 1961, pp. 131–36.

Socialization for competition involves learning questionable ethical criteria and a sloppy "morality with elbowroom." Children learn that to succeed, to be accepted, is good, and to lose, to be rejected, is bad. For example, many children give the possibility of punishment as a reason for judging an act morally wrong.[8] Adolescents generally view responsibility and other values as being equivalent to following the socially accepted rules of conduct.[9] And yet the accepted rules include a large gap between ideal and real morality. Children learn, by unconscious assimilation or by observation of concrete situations, that being truthful often conflicts with being "practical," that there are many ways to cut corners and still be legitimate, that the most important thing about cheating is not the ethical fact but keeping the fact secret.[10] Several hundred interviews with seniors in twenty colleges left the clear impression that, as a group, they were cynical, expected to receive and give large doses of hypocrisy in socioeconomic life, and felt that, in some large measure, all occupations were "rackets."[11]

Education for Competition

Numerous educational practices encourage self-seeking motives. For example, many educators believe that current evaluation and grading practices all too frequently neglect desirable educational purposes—such as the detailed diagnosis of individual weaknesses or the evaluation of skills and attitudes associated with democratic living—and overemphasize competition and invidious comparisons among pupils. These practices, it is felt, often generate cheating and disorganizing tensions.[12]

However, education for competition does not originate within the schools. Numerous studies have revealed that the great majority of par-

8. Lawrence Kohlberg, "Moral Development and Identification," *Sixty-Second Yearbook*, National Society for the Study of Education (Chicago: University of Chicago Press, 1963), part I, pp. 321–22.

9. Paul H. Mussen, John L. Conger, and Jerome Kagan, *Child Development and Personality*, 2d ed. (New York: Harper & Row, 1963), p. 577.

10. See Ernest A. Smith, *American Youth Culture* (New York: Free Press of Glencoe, 1962), pp. 37–38, 127–29; Jules Henry, *Culture Against Man* (New York: Random House, 1963), pp. 205–06, 280.

11. David Riesman, "The College Student in an Age of Organization," in *The Dilemma of Organizational Society*, H. M. Ruitenbeek, ed. (New York: E. P. Dutton Co., Inc., 1963), pp. 105–07.

12. See, for example, J. S. Ahmann and M. D. Glock, *Evaluating Pupil Growth*, 2d ed. (Boston: Allyn and Bacon, 1963), pp. 579–80.

ents and high school and college youth value education primarily for its contribution to individual success in attaining a good job and social acceptance.[13] Only a small minority desire schools to develop wisdom. A recent national survey found that 72 per cent of a representative sample of adults believed that the most important reason for going to college was to obtain "training for a good job." The next most often given reasons were "social acceptance" and "getting to know the right people." [14] Reporting on an interview study of boys from working-class homes, Joseph A. Kahl wrote:

> None was interested in learning for the subtle pleasures it can offer; none craved intellectual understanding for its own sake. The most common phrase in the entire body of interviews was "nowadays you need a high school diploma (or a college degree) to get a good job." Often a distinction was made between the diploma and the education it symbolized; the boys wanted the parchment, not the learning.[15]

Particularly in middle-class families, girls are socialized for a far greater degree of independence than they were a generation or two ago.[16] In old and new ways, girls learn competitive behavior. However, girls are still reared toward more passive and dependent behavior than are boys. Boys are expected to be more independent, aggressive, "manly." [17] As Jules Henry has remarked, our society does not seem

13. For a review of some of these studies see W. H. Ferry, "College Responsibilities and Social Expectations," *Teachers College Record,* November 1963, pp. 99–111.

14. *Kansas City Star,* November 13, 1963.

15. "'Common' Man' Boys," *Education, Economy, and Society,* eds. A. H. Halsey, Jean Flood, and C. Arnold Anderson (New York: Free Press of Glencoe, Inc., 1961), p. 357. Here, as elsewhere in this chapter, the reader should bear in mind that (1) there may be great differences between motives as revealed in questionnaires or interviews and those revealed in more complete living situations; (2) such "traits" as egoism and altruism are not necessarily independent or separable in reality—they may partake of each other, as when a person finds satisfactions in being cooperative and generous; and (3) taken as a whole, psychological and social reality is far richer and probably brighter than this chapter indicates. No single chapter can present anything like a "complete" picture of modern life and its motivations, and unqualified emphasis on certain matters that may need improvement can lead to overemphasis and distortion.

16. See Carl N. Dengler, "Revolution Without Ideology: The Changing Place of Women in America," *Daedalus,* Spring 1964, pp. 655–59.

17. See, for example, Urie Bronfenbrenner, "Towards a Theoretical Model for the Analysis of Parent-Child Relationships in a Social Context" in *Current Perspectives in Social Psychology,* E. P. Hollander and Raymond G. Hunt, eds. (New York: Oxford University Press, 1963), p. 139.

able to tolerate tenderness between men, possibly because it might frustrate our competitive economic system.[18] Despite anthropological evidence to the contrary, do we not regard tenderness as being "naturally" a feminine characteristic?

In schools, teachers (with some differences between male and female teachers) also evaluate boys and girls in terms of different criteria of social adjustment. Moreover, men are still the major breadwinners; girls still look forward principally to a housewife's role; and a mother's learning is not yet popularly regarded as a significant legacy for her children. Thus, despite historical advances, the amount of education received by girls is less than that received by boys. In 1962, although girls comprised 53 per cent of high school graduates, only 43 per cent of college entrants were girls, and women received only one third of the bachelor's and master's degrees and one tenth of the doctoral degrees.[19]

Changing socioeconomic conditions and the increasing amount of education obtained by lower-class families are raising the educational aspirations of these families. Robert J. Havighurst writes: "Whereas in 1920 it was extremely rare for a student of working-class background to enter college, by 1960 the gross numbers of college students from working-class homes exceeded the numbers from upper- and upper-middle-class homes." [20] Moreover, earlier studies have sometimes overlooked the fact that correlations between lower-class background and lack of interest or ability in education are usually low-moderate or moderate.[21]

Nevertheless, higher social status is generally associated with a higher regard for education as an essential step toward success. Although upwardly mobile children from lower-class backgrounds also display a generalized anxiety about achieving in school and an ability to defer gratification of impulses in the interest of long-range plans, this "achievement syndrome" is more often found among middle-class

18. Jules Henry, *op. cit.,* p. 141.
19. Esther Peterson, "Working Women," *Daedalus,* Spring 1964, pp. 676–77. These percentages of university degrees received by women represent a significant decline since the 1930s.
20. "Social Class Influences on American Education," *Sixtieth Yearbook,* National Society for the Study of Education (Chicago: University of Chicago Press, 1961), part II, p. 122.
21. Wilbur B. Brookover and David Gottlieb, *A Sociology of Education,* 2d ed. (New York: American Book Co., 1964), pp. 170–73.

children.[22] It has been estimated that at the beginning of this decade the percentages of youth from the various social classes who entered college were as follows: from the combined upper and upper-middle classes, 85 per cent of males and 75 per cent of females; from the lower-middle class, 60 per cent of males and 38 per cent of females; from the upper-lower class, 30 per cent of males and 18 per cent of females. Very few youth from the lower-lower class were college entrants.[23]

In short, teachers are faced with a formidable problem if they believe that general education should make a vital contribution to breadth of vision and interests in later life and if they believe that the kind of motivation students have for education affects what is learned and the uses of learning. However, there are deep sources of hope and strength in the American character. For example, the ideal of a "fair chance" is a widespread working ideal, and whatever its origins may be, it has a bearing on more than merely economic matters. Moreover, there is evidence that, under certain conditions, sheer amount of education has a low to moderate influence in opening hearts and minds, and that some kinds of educational programs have a "peculiar potency" in this direction.[24] In later pages of this chapter we will return to a consideration of this problem.

Social Consciousness Is Inadequate to the Level of Social Complexity

Particularly in an affluent society, the self-indulgent pursuit of happiness is a general possibility. Moreover, a number of other characteristics of our society make it difficult for thought and concern to reach far beyond narrowly construed boundaries of personal life.

The complex and protean nature of social structure makes it easier to accept or complain about it than to attempt to understand and control it. The rate of social change seems to reduce the possibility that many significant events can be ingested (much less digested) and inures us to

22. Murray A. Straus, "Deferred Gratification, Social Class, and the Achievement Syndrome," *American Sociological Review*, June 1962, pp. 321–35.

23. Robert J. Havighurst and Bernice L. Neugarten, *Society and Education*, 2d ed. (Boston: Allyn and Bacon, 1962), p. 252.

24. See James C. Davis, "Intellectual Climates in 135 American Colleges and Universities: A Study in Social Psychophysics," *Sociology of Education*, Winter 1963, pp. 110–28.

living rather complacently in the midst of things and events we do not understand. Perhaps the frequency of anxiety-arousing and belief-upsetting communications engenders intellectual and moral indifference and the tendency to accept simple and certain answers in an uncertain world. In any event, feelings of "powerlessness" (or abject acceptance of structure) and "normlessness" (or cynical moral relativism) are widespread,[25] and many contemporary forces work toward keeping the level of social consciousness inadequate to the level of social complexity and the ideals of democracy.[26]

If we glance only at the political arena, we find that "American democracy proceeds without even the minimum involvement of voting for about 40 per cent of the electorate in presidential elections and many more than that in local elections." [27] Even those who do vote are often uninformed or vaguely informed about the issues at stake. "Scholarly studies of American voting are but twenty years old," writes David Wallace, "yet already they have largely demolished the myth of Rational Man in the democratic process: the alert voter who sees issues, seeks knowledge about them, weighs alternatives, and comes to an intellectual decision on the merits of the case." [28] Comparatively few adults have a considered, comprehensive social ideology (as distinguished from, say, economic interests) which unites diverse issues, and even the great majority of "public leaders" become immersed in local civic affairs without consistently connecting these affairs with larger structural matters.[29]

The following indications of the lack of public knowledge about public affairs are quite representative findings: (1) in 1962, only 13 per cent of a national sample of adults had a reasonably correct idea of

25. See, for example, Arthur G. Neal and S. Rettig, "Dimensions of Alienation Among Manual and Non-Manual Workers," *American Sociological Review*, August 1963, pp. 599–608.

26. For relevant and suggestive studies, see Philip Olson, ed., *America as a Mass Society* (New York: Free Press of Glencoe, 1963), pp. 13–47, 187–204, 262–312; David Riesman, *Abundance for What?* (Garden City, New York: Doubleday and Co., Inc., 1964), pp. 196–225, 258–69, 300–23.

27. John C. Livingstone and Robert G. Thompson, *The Consent of the Governed* (New York: Macmillan Co., 1963), p. 419.

28. "Some Functional Aspects of Stability and Change in Voting," *American Journal of Sociology*, September 1963, p. 161.

29. See Thomas R. Dye, "The Local-Cosmopolitan Dimension and the Study of Urban Politics," *Social Forces*, March 1963, pp. 239–46; Joseph R. Gusfield, "Mass Society and Extremist Politics," *American Sociological Review*, February 1962, pp. 19–30.

what the European Common Market was; [30] (2) national polls have revealed widespread public ignorance of the population explosion, the effects of technology on our lives, and the importance of the Bill of Rights.[31]

Although political information and participation in public affairs tend to increase with amount of education, high school and college youth share many of the characteristics we have just noted. Nationwide studies indicate that the majority of both high school and college youth seem to rest content with the beliefs that politics is a dirty business and that the average citizen should have little to do with politics, the science and art of government.[32] A study of college seniors revealed, characteristically, that these students had significantly more information about entertainment, sports, and brands of merchandise than about public affairs. For example, only 13 per cent could identify UNESCO and only 5 per cent could name the U.S. Secretary of Health, Education, and Welfare, but 97 per cent identified Liberace.[33] A survey of a national sample of high school students disclosed that "abridgment of the freedom of the press is by no means abhorrent to many if not most of our young citizens," and that the typical teen-ager believes that "police and other groups" should have the power to impose censorship on books and movies.[34]

The Dominance of "Privatism"

With the public world relatively meaningless and obscure, many Americans turn to the private world. As revealed by a number of studies, the typical American adult is much more concerned with attaining his own happiness—at home, on the job, and among personal friends—than he

30. Hazel G. Erskine, "The Polls: The Informed Public," *Public Opinion Quarterly*, Winter 1962, p. 677. See also Hazel G. Erskine, "The Polls: Exposure to Domestic Information," *Public Opinion Quarterly*, Fall 1963, pp. 491–500.

31. Stuart Chase, "What Americans Believe: Report on a Young Science," *Saturday Review*, June 16, 1962, p. 11.

32. Alex S. Edelstein, "Since Bennington: Evidence of Change in Student Political Behavior," *Public Opinion Quarterly*, Winter 1962, pp. 564–65, 569; Stanley E. Dimond, "Citizenship Education," *Encyclopedia of Educational Research*, Chester W. Harris, ed. (New York: Macmillan Co., 1960), p. 209.

33. Joseph E. Garai, "Information of College Students on Current Affairs," *Journal of Educational Sociology*, October 1962, pp. 58–60.

34. H. H. Remmers and R. D. Franklin, "Sweet Land of Liberty," *Phi Delta Kappan*, October 1962, p. 23.

is with exploring his accepted definition of happiness and the structural forces which limit and channel desire and activity.[35] One national study of adults found that "international tensions, fears of atomic extinction, and the anxious atmosphere of a troubled world do not figure importantly among the things the American people say trouble them. Fewer than one in ten expressed an outstanding concern for community, national, or world problems." [36]

Compared with adolescents from some other societies, American adolescents display much more concern about a "happy family life," "economic security," and "ample vacations and leisure," and much less concern about "a life of service to people and the nation" and making "a contribution of some outstanding value" in a chosen field.[37] Reporting a comparative study of the values of college youth in ten nations, Gordon W. Allport wrote:

> . . . the most important finding was that within these 10 nations, American students were the most self-centered, the most "privatistic" in values. They desired above all a rich, full life for themselves, and showed little concern for national welfare or for the fate of mankind at large. The context of their outlook was private rather than public, passive rather than pioneer.[38]

As we shall see, the data do *not* imply that teachers should concern themselves above all with teaching the facts about our public affairs or with exhorting students to exercise, when they are of age, the right to vote. Indeed, the data suggest that learning the facts is not enough. These facts change rapidly. Nor is good citizenship restricted to voting, even when there is reasonably full awareness of the issues. The data do imply that the informal and formal education of youth have not developed a high and general interest in public affairs, an activating appreciation of democratic principles, a drive to comprehend and co-

35. See, for example, Serge Moscovici, "Attitudes and Opinions," *Annual Review of Psychology,* Paul R. Farnsworth, ed. (Palo Alto, Calif.: Annual Reviews, Inc., 1963), pp. 231–60; Jules Golden and others, "A Summary Description of Fifty 'Normal' White Males," *American Journal of Psychiatry,* July 1962, pp. 48–56.

36. Gerald Gurin and others, *Americans View Their Mental Health* (New York: Basic Books, Inc., 1960), p. xiii.

37. Lyle M. Spencer, "The Changing Face of Children's Heroes," *PTA Magazine,* November 1962, pp. 7–10.

38. "Values and Our Youth," *Studies in Adolescence,* Robert E. Grinder, ed. (New York: Macmillan Co., 1963), pp. 19–20.

operatively control the social structure which is so powerful in shaping individual character and thought.

Patterns of Life and Thought in Organizational Society

Place of residence, personal friends, international allies, knowledge and occupational skills change today at an unprecedented rate. We adjust, and we expect that others will adjust, to swiftly changing roles and groups. Increasingly, whether as buyer or seller, teacher and parent or pupil, policeman or civilian, we see each other mainly in terms of specialized roles and limited purposes. We experience each other as more or less replaceable units.

There is a general awareness that personality in its depth, breadth, and uniqueness has much to do with the fulfillment of specific roles, and we attempt to develop patterns of interpersonal behavior which will substitute for those that emerged from stable communal living and intimate familiarity with "whole" personalities. A ready smile and a "cooperatve attitude" are generally useful. Newsletters and psychologists flourish in large organizations, including the schools. Special subject teachers are carefully instructed in the techniques of knowing each child "as an individual" and of holding "informal" discussions with parents. In all, the demand for skills and behavior that facilitate adjustability and hasty familiarity is a heavy and continuing one, even while the demand for expert knowledge gains strength.[39]

Patterns of social behavior are intimately related to patterns of individual feeling and thought. When contacts are fleeting, fragmented, and directed toward narrow purposes, thought and emotion tend to be superficial, fleeting, and restricted.[40] Narrow specialization of tasks often leads to narrowness of viewpoint, a loss of sense of the "whole." [41] Studies suggest that continual exposure to rapidly changing situa-

39. For some interesting indications of the ways in which these two demands (for sociability and for expertness) blend, conflict, or support each other, see George D. Spindler, ed., *Education and Culture: Anthropological Approaches* (New York: Holt, Rinehart and Winston, 1963), chaps. 7–11, 14.

40. For quite different, but suggestive, studies of this general topic, see S. Messick and J. Ross, eds., *Measurement in Personality and Cognition* (New York: John Wiley and Sons, Inc., 1962), pp. 183–215; Vernon L. Allen and Richard S. Crutchfield, "Generalization of Experimentally Reinforced Conformity," *Journal of Abnormal and Social Psychology*, October 1963, pp. 326–33.

41. See Peter M. Blau, "Patterns of Choice in Interpersonal Relations," *American Sociological Review*, February 1962, pp. 41–55.

tions and values tends to produce cognitive and emotional disorganization, conformist behavior, or irrational and highly variable behavior.[42]

Variations in Education for Organizational Life

Among the many factors influencing participation in organizational life are social class, differences between manual and nonmanual work, and differences between "bureaucratic" and "entrepreneurial" settings of life. The head of a "bureaucratic family" is employed in a large organization where specialization of tasks is prominent and harmonious relations among specialists is essential. The head of an "entrepreneurial family" is much more on his own; he is self-employed or employed in a small organization. These categories are not necessarily exhaustive or exclusive. A manual worker, for example, may belong to the lower-middle class or the upper-lower class and may work in either a bureaucratic or entrepreneurial setting. Of course, the differences presented below are statistical trends; they are not definitive for any particular family or child.

In their child-rearing practices, middle-class families in both bureaucratic and entrepreneurial settings exhibit greater concern than do working-class or lower-class families for "internal states of mind"—motives, feelings, and self-control. Working-class values cluster around overt obedience, conformity to external prescriptions.[43] Entrepreneurial middle-class families tend to train children for a more active and independent approach to the world than do their bureaucratic counterparts, whereas bureaucratic middle-class families encourage a more accommodating, adjustive way of life.[44] There is evidence that the bureaucratic setting is more conducive to conformist behavior than is the entrepreneurial setting.[45]

42. See, for example, Mary A. Sarvis, "Reactions of Children from Crowded Areas," *Childhood Education*, May 1963, pp. 413–15.
43. Melvin L. Kohn, "Social Class and Parent-Child Relationships," *American Journal of Sociology*, January 1963, pp. 474–79; Yehudi A. Cohen, ed., *Social Structure and Personality: A Casebook* (New York: Holt, Rinehart and Winston, 1961), pp. 52–53, 96, 149–53.
44. See, for example, Phillip Fellin and Eugene Litwak, "Neighborhood Cohesion Under Conditions of Mobility," *American Sociological Review*, June 1963, pp. 364–76.
45. See Albert D. Biderman and Herbert Zimmer, eds., *The Manipulation of Human Behavior* (New York: John Wiley and Sons, 1961), pp. 234, 237–40, 257.

In recent years, and particularly in bureaucratic settings, lower- and middle-class families have moved closer together in their attitudes toward permissive-restrictive training practices. However, control of impulses and of overtly aggressive behavior and the ability to defer gratification of desires in the light of long-range plans are still established earlier and more firmly in middle-class families. Middle-class parents use mainly "psychological" techniques of discipline—reasoning, appeals to guilt, giving and witholding of affection. Lower-class parents often use more direct methods—scolding, threats, physical punishment.[46] Middle-class parents, especially those in bureaucratic settings, generally exhibit great interest in techniques of "personality management." It is significant to note that neither manipulative, love-withdrawal, nor severe and authoritarian techniques of discipline seem to promote independence and spontaneity in children.[47]

The differences we have noted seem to be related to differences in the styles of life of the various groups. The middle-class person tends to work with people, symbols, and ideas. Although he is a conformist in many ways, the conditions of his life require a greater degree of independence and self-direction than is the case for the working-class person, who deals with things and whose work is generally subject to more detailed supervision and standardization. Moreover, in interpersonal relations (especially for middle- and upper-class people), the bureaucratic setting requires less overt competitiveness and risk-taking and more adjustive, accommodating behavior.

Compared to entrepreneurial families, the increasingly numerous bureaucratic families lead mobile and fragmented lives. They move frequently; their work and home neighborhoods are often far apart; they have few contacts with relatives; and they form and dissolve friendships with comparative ease. They learn to integrate themselves into new and diverse settings, but they also learn not to become deeply and emotionally committed to friends, communities, or, perhaps, ideas.[48]

46. Urie Bronfenbrenner, *op. cit.*, p. 141; Seymour M. Lipset, *op. cit.*, pp. 197–98.

47. Willard W. Hartup, "Dependence and Independence," *Sixty-second Yearbook*, National Society for the Study of Education (Chicago: University of Chicago Press, 1963), part I, pp. 334–39, 349–57.

48. See Robert P. Stuckert, "Occupational Mobility and Family Relationships," *Social Forces*, March 1963, pp. 301–07; Ernest R. Mowrer, "Sequential and Class Variables of the Family in the Suburban Area," *Social Forces*, December 1961, pp. 107–12.

Although they are estranged in many ways from adult life, youth also learn to float and flit along the surface of life. If changing social pressures require greater attention to learning subject matter, youth —especially those from the higher classes—learn to give parents and teachers what they want,[49] but strong indeed is their tendency to live for the present moment without deep or notably developing concern for social questons.[50] "Good-natured," "popular," "leadership abilities" —such are the terms adolescents use to identify and evaluate their peers; and the adolescents give almost no thought to questions about criteria of popularity or aims of leadership.[51] While generally learning to conform to the basic values of society and of their social class, adolescents also learn to "fear and shun the holding of positions deviant to those of their peer groups." [52]

For both adults and youth, participation in social, organizational life declines with descent along the socioeconomic ladder. It is estimated that about two thirds of upper-class adults, one third of middle-class adults, and less than one fifth of lower-class adults belong to at least one formal social organization.[53] Correspondingly, and characteristically, a study of high school youth found that about 36 per cent of students from high-income families, but only 4 per cent of students from low-income families, participated in five or more school activities, whereas 20 per cent of students from low-income families, but only 2 per cent from high-income families, participated in no school activities.[54] Compared with middle-class youth, lower-class youth lead relatively unprogramed lives; they have more time for "bumming around." [55] Moreover, not only are middle-class students more readily accepted by teachers than are lower-class students, but they also re-

49. Morris E. Eson, *Psychological Foundations of Education* (New York: Holt, Rinehart and Winston, Inc., 1964), pp. 36–37.
50. See Jessee Bernhard, "Teen-Age Culture: An Overview," *Annals of the American Academy of Political and Social Science,* November 1961, pp. 1–12.
51. Alice Van Krevelen, "Characteristics Which 'Identify' the Adolescent to His Peers," *Journal of Social Psychology,* 1962, pp. 285–89.
52. Ernest A. Smith, *op. cit.,* p. 10.
53. Paul F. Lazersfeld, "Political Behavior and Public Opinion," in *The Behavioral Sciences Today,* Bernard Berelson, ed. (New York: Basic Books, Inc., 1963), p. 183.
54. John K. Coster, "Some Characteristics of High School Pupils from Three Income Groups," in *Studies in Adolescence,* Robert E. Grinder, ed. (New York: Macmillan Co., 1963), p. 215.
55. Muzafer Sherif and Carolyn W. Sherif, *op. cit.,* p. 219.

ceive a somewhat more realistic education about social issues and the struggle for political power.[56]

Youth Are Excluded From Adult Responsibilities

A few years ago, Professor James S. Coleman reported that the majority of adolescents in a number of high schools located in different social settings believed that sports, dating, and personal appearance were more important than academic achievement.[57] Coleman concluded that the adolescent "fun subculture" was a major deterrent to academic achievement. Since Coleman's useful but perhaps one-sided study, international rivalries and the rising educational requirements of an expert society have brought increased pressure for academic excellence, and the fun subculture is being squeezed from many sides. However, the fun subculture, "bumming around," and the heavy incidence of juvenile antisocial behavior are not merely expressions of youthful tendencies which must be curbed. They reflect many characteristics of our society, including a pervasive, almost systematic, exclusion of youth from adult concerns.

In recent years, the belief that adolescence is naturally a period of stress and strain has been refuted by anthropologists who have described societies in which the transition from a child's role to an adult's role is made with relative ease. In our society, however, bridges between the generations are inadequate. Typically, the American adolescent is economically and socially dependent for a number of years after he reaches biological maturity. "Denied by law the right to work except under controlled conditions, required to attend school where he is often treated as a child, generally excluded from adult social, political, and civic activities and intellectual life, the adolescent bands together with his age-mates in self-defense." [58] Both the influence of the peer culture on adolescents and the conflict between the generations are

56. Eugene Litt, "Civic Education, Community Norms, and Political Indoctrination," *American Sociological Review*, February 1963, pp. 69–75.

57. *The Adolescent Society* (New York: Free Press of Glencoe, 1961), pp. 240–46, 308–10.

58. Grace Graham, *The Public School in the American Community* (New York: Harper & Row, 1963), p. 467.

probably stronger today than they were a generation or two ago.[59]

In the next chapter we shall consider the world of work in some detail, but the social and moral significance of the changing nature of work should be noted here. More and more, the world's work is being monopolized by age groups above twenty. With the continuing reduction in the number of "unskilled jobs," many lower-class youth and high school dropouts encounter increasing difficulty in finding employment. Moreover, the great majority of young people no longer receive their preparation for life work in direct association with their parents, relatives, and friends. The exclusion of youth from significant work under conditions wherein work is much more than a "job" has an obvious bearing on the formulation of youthful ideas and standards.

Consider, for example, the influence upon a young person's ideal of good workmanship when he worked with his father on the farm or in the shop or the local mill and acquired directly from his parent not only the skill of the specific operation but the style which gave quality to the skill and won the approbation of the neighbors. Or consider the stimulus to improve that came with his gradual promotion, on the basis of performance, from a boy's to a man's work. Once we recognize that the specifics of morality and character grow best out of membership in face-to-face relationships, out of shared experiences with others, that they are as much caught as they are taught, we can appreciate the potency of the intimate associations in the small community of yesterday in contrast with the more superficial and impersonal contacts afforded children and youth today.

This denial of opportunities to participate with one's intimates in the serious concerns of life bears directly upon the attitudes toward work and toward people which many young people are encouraged to develop today. It is one thing, for example, to absorb ideals and standards from one's elders and quite a different matter to work under circumstances in which personal identity is lost. What a contrast between the picture a young person tends to develop of himself as a worker under the more simple conditions in which men prided themselves upon the quality and the quantity of work each might do and the picture drawn from association with strangers on a job for an employer known

59. See, for example, Robert J. Smith, and others, "Parental Authority and Job Choices: Sex Differences in Three Cultures," *American Journal of Sociology,* September 1963, p. 143.

only through a foreman, and in the performance of work in which each one's stint is but a fraction of the complicated whole! [60]

Youth's Changing Role in Home and Community

Parallel with the exclusion of young people from responsible participation in economic activities has been a corresponding elimination from responsibilities in home and community which once fostered social maturity. Obviously, the one-time participation of children and adolescents in the concerns of adults in store and shop and on the farm contributed to their social development as well as to their economic education. Indeed, it is difficult to overemphasize the importance in the life of a young person of adult recognition of his present contribution to the group and of the tasks of even greater significance which he may undertake tomorrow. In the rural home there was often a gradation of jobs, beginning with the simple chores for the young child and continuing through a series of promotions, on the basis of merit, to the full-fledged work of man or woman. With what pride, for example, did the small boy on the farm move from assignments in and about the house to the man's work in the barn! Or from the minor jobs in the garden and the fields to the skilled work of a grown man, such as guiding the plow or building a haystack that would withstand wind and rain and snow! Work, in other words, was suffused with social significance, and as such it was an indispensable means of furthering the social and moral development of the young.

Opportunities for children and youth to play a corresponding role in home and community are today decreasing, since many of the services and functions which were once personal and individual have become institutionalized and are clothed with a public or semipublic garb.

For example, contrast the role of a young person today with what it was yesterday when sickness afflicts the family next door. This once confronted the neighboring boy or girl with an opportunity to assume the functions of an adult. The adolescent girl was sent into the afflicted home to do the housework or to tend the children, perhaps to help in nursing the sick. The boy assumed temporarily the responsibility for

60. For discussions of the social and moral significance of work, see Sigmund Nosow and William H. Form, eds., *Man, Work, and Society* (New York: Basic Books, Inc., 1962), chap. II.

the chores or the work out-of-doors. Today, the seriously ill more or less automatically are sent to a hospital and group insurance or a social agency is relied upon to help the family meet the incidents of illness. And, of course, the obvious need of avoiding contagion necessitates keeping the young uncontaminated by contact with the unfortunate family!

The commercializing and institutionalizing of assistance to the unfortunate has invaded a similar sphere of social and emotional development. We no longer consider it appropriate to house the homeless or to feed the stranger who knocks upon the gate. Indeed, it is safe to assume that the stranger, in obvious distress, who accosts us on a city street and solicits a coin with which to purchase "a cup of coffee" or a hot meal is not at all times in the dire straits he appears to be in. In some instances he is employed at a fixed wage to ply his craft. Consequently, we harden our hearts and instruct our children to pass him by. But, what are the effects of this seeming indifference upon the child? And what can we substitute for the child to encourage his generous impulses and to avoid the corrosive influences of an impersonal society?

Obviously, the complex society of today cannot operate on the old system of voluntary services. When a fire breaks out in the middle of the night, we rejoice over the fact that we are no longer dependent upon the bucket brigade of men of good will but little skill to fight the fire or upon the hastily improvised tactics of the volunteer fire department. Nevertheless, old as well as young pay a price in spiritual coin for the comfort of returning to their slumbers with an easy conscience once they are assured it is not their house that is on fire. Again, hospitalization and professional medical attention are far superior to that which the home can provide, no matter how generous or devoted the neighbors may be, and few would exchange the benefits that derive from associated effort for the earlier types of individual and personal service.

Not only are opportunities for children and adolescents to participate responsibly in the life of the home and community fewer and less significant than was once the case, but there are positive influences today which encourage irresponsibility and the evasion of social and moral standards. Prior to the development of modern facilities of transportation, life in the city, as well as in the small town and rural community, involved much more of a community feeling than exists today. Cities were collections of neighborhoods in which families came to know each other in a manner no longer true. Today they move frequently or their members live in one section of the city and earn their living in another. This condition contributes to a sense of anonymity and frees the individual from the discipline of the observing eye as well as the tender concern of his neighbor.

The moment a child steps out of the school building in New York City he is amongst strangers and what he does or refrains from doing is seemingly unobserved. As a member of the gang, he and his comrades can "snitch" from the corner grocery and quickly lose themselves in the crowd, with little sense of having injured someone whose feelings are as theirs. In the New England village, by contrast, the boy was known to everyone and the standards his parents sought to have him adopt were obviously and consistently the standards of the community. Consequently, the temptation to deviate from the common code was quickly associated with public disapproval.

We are suggesting that there has emerged in American life a relatively new and distinctive stage of development for adolescents as well as for children. Young people have drunk deep from the fountain of youth, with results not altogether to their advantage or their inner satisfaction. Fundamental changes of this nature bring confusion and frustration, as many a parent will testify. But they need not result in pessimism. The lengthening of the period of adolescence holds genuine promise for this age group and for society as a whole, provided we deal with it creatively.

The Family as a Socializing Agency

As the influence of nonfamily institutions on the socialization of young people increases, it might seem that the significance of the family in this regard is declining. However, the family remains by far the single most important agency in the socialization of the young.

A word of caution is in order. We must be careful in thinking about "the" American family, for there is no single pattern to which all families conform. Indeed, interfamily differences in ways of life are major sources of intrafamily conflicts as youth (and adults, too!) gaze with sometimes envious eyes upon the family next door. The exemplar of contemporary trends in family life is the middle-class family in a bureaucratic setting, although there are great variations even within this group. Lower-class and rural families, upper-class "old families," and the families of various ethnic and religious groups move more slowly toward modal family patterns.

Authorities generally agree that while the effects of early family socialization may be modified by later experience, early family experiences are crucial in the formation of personality.[61] Through the family, the young child receives his first and most comprehensive introduction to the ways and values of the culture and of the subcultures of class, religion, ethnic group. In this womb of personality, the child is initiated into the basic mode of human existence—the social organization of interacting persons. Before reason comes, he learns sets of behaviors and expectations which bear on how to be a child or an adult, boy or girl, sister or brother, mother or father, friend or foe; what to value and how to achieve aspirations; what can be openly discussed and what must be felt in silence; what is the significance of religion, education, government, and other social institutions.

The powerful nature of early family experience is related to the child's dependence upon adults for the satisfaction of basic biological and psychological needs. Not only the physical immaturity but also the social and intellectual immaturity of the child makes him dependent and impressionable. Moreover, his learnings are continually reinforced in a network of intimate relations characterized by emotional ties that are stronger and more complex than those in most other groups.

Then, too, the learnings occur at an age which makes them relatively inaccessible to later conscious memory. Thus, they tend to become not sets of responses which, among other possible sets, a person voluntarily (and perhaps hesitantly) chose to acquire, but deeply embedded criteria which guide aspiration and evaluation in later life. Little wonder, then, that students of child development agree that "the learning situation within the family is a particularly sensitive one, with a quality very different from other learning situations. . . . The lessons the child learns at the hands of his family tend to go deep and last long. . . ."[62]

61. Benjamin S. Bloom, *Stability and Change in Human Characteristics* (New York: John Wiley and Sons, Inc., 1964), pp. 214–16.
62. Robert J. Havighurst and Bernice L. Neugarten, *op. cit.*, p. 103.

Contemporary Trends in Family Relationships

The modern family tends to be a small and mobile unit with a narrowing circle of intimate and continuous interpersonal relationships. There has been a long-term decline, with a recent mild rise, in the size of the average household (a category which may include single persons living alone). Representative figures are 7 members in 1700, 5 in 1870, 4.7 in 1910, 2.5 in 1950, and 3.4 in 1962.[63] Although the fertility rate has declined slightly in recent years, we probably will have a sudden spurt in population growth. In part, this is due to the fact that large numbers of young women, products of the prolonged baby boom which began in 1946, are now reaching child-bearing age.[64] However, there is not likely to be any major change in the average size of families.

Between 1870 and 1962 the median age of marriage dropped from 22.0 to 20.3 for women and from 26.1 to 22.7 for men.[65] Not only does marriage occur earlier, but parents tend to have their children earlier and more rapidly and to terminate their major child-rearing activities before the age of forty.[66] When children marry, they usually leave home and live by themselves; three-generation families are rare. Moreover, one of five families moves annually, and one third of the families that change their place of residence move across county lines.[67] The network of deep, long-lasting, and common ties which supports internal family relations is further weakened with the scattering of relatives and former friends.

Basic social changes have brought decline in the functions of the family. At one time the family cooperated in *making* a living. Today, the fact that the burden of *earning* a living falls upon one or two members of the family means that parents and children are usually not drawn together by the formerly shared activities. Vocational skills, many intellectual competences, and employment are acquired outside the home. In some large measure, "family fun" has been supplanted by

63. Reuben Hill, "The American Family Today," *The Nation's Children: The Family and Social Change*, Eli Ginzberg, ed. (New York: Columbia University Press, 1960), vol. I, p. 88; and Donald J. Bogue, "Population Growth in the United States," *The Population Dilemma*, Philip M. Hauser, ed. (Englewood Cliffs, N.J.: Prentice-Hall, Inc., 1963), p 81.
64. Donald J. Bogue, *op. cit.*, p. 76.
65. Esther Peterson, *op. cit.*, p. 675.
66. Carl N. Dengler, *op. cit.*, p. 667.
67. Reuben Hill, *op. cit.*, p. 84.

commercialized activities. Indeed, the family as a whole functions more as a consuming than as a producing unit. Moreover, certain responsibilities relating to character- and health-building, sex education, and welfare have been taken over by the school, youth-serving organizations, and governmental and other agencies.

This profound change in family functions has been accompanied by a shifting and blurring of roles within the family.[68] Smaller families, labor-saving devices in the home, better education, and increased opportunities for participation in economic, social, and political life have altered the traditional role and status of women. For example, the female component of the labor force rose from 22 to 34 per cent between 1930 and 1962, and in the early 1960s, one third of all married women were in the labor force.[69] While the typical lower-class family remains more patriarchal and authoritarian, middle-class families have generally moved toward the "companionship" and "equalitarian" models. Joint decision-making practices frequently include the voices of children.

Although the equalitarian family may well provide a more nourishing environment for the development of free spirits than did the authoritarian family of the past, many tensions are associated—often within an individual—with the changing and ill-defined roles of family members. Thus, training children for independence often conflicts with training them for dependence.[70] The role of women in modern society is especially ambiguous. Many husband-wife and parent-child tensions are generated by the conflict between modern and traditional role expectations.[71]

In a competitive and impersonal world, the home can be "an island of security in a sea of insecurity," a haven where the healing qualities of a degree of autonomy, altruism, and recognition of individuality may be found. While other functions of the family decline, its affectional function becomes increasingly significant. To be sure, exposed to immature cultural notions about "love at first sight" and to cultural vacillations between sensuality and prudishness, youth have difficulty

68. See Norman W. Bell and Ezra F. Vogel, eds., *A Modern Introduction to the Family* (Glencoe: Ill.: Free Press, 1960), chaps. 10–11, 26–27, 29.
69. Esther Peterson, *op. cit.*, pp. 672, 674.
70. See Richard Centers and Louise Centers, "Social Character Types and Beliefs About Childrearing," *Child Development*, March 1963, pp. 69–78.
71. Roland G. Thorp, "Psychological Patterning in Marriage," *Psychological Bulletin*, March 1963, pp. 97–117.

learning that strong and lasting love emerges from a complex set of relations in a process requiring continual readjustment.[72] Nevertheless, love has become the basic reason for marriage and procreation, a major disciplinary force in child-rearing, and lack of love is the principal reason for divorce.

There has been a long-term rise in the divorce rate, although since the high mark of 1 divorce for every 2.5 marriages in 1946, the rate has declined to 1 for every 4 or 5 marriages in recent years (and 3 out of 4 divorced persons remarry within 5 years).[73] These data undoubtedly are significant of many things, including the growing independence of women, a changing climate of opinion about divorce, and the loss of common concerns and community bonds which formerly supported the affectional function.

Family, Society, and the Aims and Means of Education

What can schools do to increase the amount of altruism in society and decrease the amount of "privatism"; to lead love and concern beyond the borders of the family so that love within the family may be enriched; to prepare children to make a life and not merely a living; to help people control social structure and not merely forage or fume within it?

Apparently, it will not do simply to maintain a heavy disciplinary hand and exert pressure on pupils to buckle down and learn subject matter in the hope that they then will become rational, self-disciplined, and altruistic. This kind of treatment is more likely to beget dependent and conformist or, perhaps, rebellious and aggressive behavior.[74] In general, altruistic and independent children have received loving, trustful, and relatively democratic treatment which, while stressing social responsibility, also respects individuality and a questioning spirit.[75]

72. Herman R. Lantz and Eloise C. Snyder, *Marriage* (New York: John Wiley and Sons, Inc., 1962), pp. 81–100, 127–28, 212–13.
73. Reuben Hill, *op. cit.*, p. 86.
74. Martin Hoffman and Lois W. Hoffman, eds., *Review of Child Development Research* (New York: Russell Sage Foundation, 1964), pp. 192–97, 267, 302–03, 369, 426–27.
75. See, for example, Robert F. Peck and Herbert G. Richek, "Personality and Social Development: Family Influences," *Review of Educational Research,* December 1964, pp. 582–84; Jacob W. Getzels and Philip W. Jackson, *Creativity and Intelligence* (New York: John Wiley and Sons, Inc., 1962) pp. 52–54, 63–64, 69–72.

Moreover, the correlations between actual behavior and verbal knowledge of intellectual and moral principles are much too low for educators to rest content with the belief that putting information and precepts into minds is the most effective method of influencing behavior.[76] Referring to this procedure, Lawrence Kohlberg states that "recent research provides little reason to revise the conclusions . . . that formal or conventional character education classes or programs in the school or church have little or no effect upon children's moral conduct."[77]

The usual or "formal" educational procedures are relatively ineffective in these matters because they fail to recognize that the individual develops as a "behavioral unit" in a process wherein cognitive, emotional, and motor elements are learned together. Even inconsistencies among these "elements" are learned together. If, for example, principles are indeed treated as academic, if they are largely confined to verbal situations, then many people will learn to refute in social practice what they acknowledge in theory.[78]

In order to develop "independent judgment" and also the "ability to cooperate" in matters of public interest, teachers must as a first necessity formulate these aims seriously and clearly. They must provide situations which permit and elicit the appropriate behaviors, situations in which, for example, pupils can both personally experience and intellectualize the often thin line between conformity and sensitivity to others. If teachers want to develop an interest in social problems, a concern for social structure, they must provide meaningful, satisfying, and direct experience with selected aspects of social structure. This experience must facilitate identification with both communal concerns and with intellectual and moral principles. The situations often will involve interactions with parents and other community groups in settings infused with both social reality and educational objectivity.

76. Vernon Jones, "Character Education," *Encyclopedia of Educational Research*, Chester W. Harris, ed. (New York: Macmillan Co., 1960), pp. 187–88.

77. "Development of Moral Character and Moral Ideology," in Martin L. Hoffman and Lois W. Hoffman, eds., *op. cit.*, p. 426.

78. For evidence and discussion relevant to this general topic, see Norman E. Wallen and Robert M. W. Travers, "Analysis and Investigation of Teaching Methods," in *Handbook of Research on Teaching*, N. L. Gage, ed. (Chicago: Rand McNally and Co., 1963), pp. 470–74; Warren G. Bennis, Kenneth D. Benne, and Robert Chin, eds., *The Planning of Change* (New York: Holt, Rinehart and Winston, 1961), pp. 493–527.

We are not suggesting that standards externally imposed are the most vital, or that standards are essentially moral so long as they can be put on or taken off according to circumstances. On the contrary, genuine morality is an inner possession, a self-directive principle, a way of thinking, feeling, and acting toward people and with people which are as one's own. Its origin and development are social in the sense that morality grows out of membership and deep-rooted interests one shares with his fellows. The home and the community must supply these necessary conditions, or, if circumstances render it difficult for these institutions to function with their one-time vitality, the school, as a supplementary institution, must obviously find ways of offsetting serious undernourishments of personality.

More concretely now, what positive efforts are being made or could be made to adapt education to the needs of youth?

Minimum Essentials in a Context of Meaning

The most obvious effort is the attempt to give body to the three Rs, the "tools" or minimum essentials of education. These attempts take cognizance of the fact that children enter school at an earlier age and remain in school for a longer period than was common some generations back. They are thereby introduced to verbal symbols and abstractions before life outside the school has provided a ground in first-hand, active experiences sufficient to give meaning and substance to these abstractions.

What can be the meaning of a "job" for most urban children in the primary grades? Can the school begin to extend the narrow meanings provided by life outside the school into a personal sense of the social significance of work? Again, while it is true that the "new mathematics" can be taught successfully in the early grades, this seems to require a wealth of guided and intellectualized experience, for the symbols and operations are viewed not in the light of a few concrete things—5×5 does not mean that 5 nickel apples cost a quarter—but, rather, in the light of pervasive ideas of the "set" (any class of like or unlike elements), relatedness, and so on.[79]

Now, what holds true of the elementary school is equally pertinent

79. See Benjamin DeMott, "The Math Wars," in *New Curricula*, Robert W. Heath, ed. (New York: Harper & Row, 1964), pp. 54–67.

on the secondary and college levels. Unless the bony structure of a verbal education is covered with healthy flesh and blood, it will fail of its purpose. Accordingly, liberal-minded educators on all levels are searching for ways to relate students to the community, not merely to help them to grasp better the full implications of theory, but also to foster intellectual and social maturity.

Enriched experiences thus serve the purpose of vitalizing an otherwise abstract and verbal education. They function, too, as plural routes to learning, thus opening the doors of insight and understanding to the nonverbal as well as to the verbally minded pupil. A visit to the health department, a conference with a public official, or a moving picture of services rendered the people by the agencies of government may enable the "slow reader" or the concrete-minded boy or girl to grasp the functions and purposes of community agencies and the operations of government as intelligently as does the pupil with the academic mind from the printed word. So, too, the child who, following an introduction to his community in the manner described, records his impressions in an art form may testify to the value of that experience for him and may heighten its value for others as effectively as one who resorts to the pen.

The use of plural media of instruction may help a child converse in many tongues and enjoy nuances of experiences often denied those who lack plural channels of communication. An alert teacher can help children appreciate the possible bearing of common tasks on almost all areas of social interaction, including family relationships. The parent, for example, cannot segregate children into homogeneous sections and minister to the idea-minded to the neglect of the thing-minded child. Indeed, the wise parent soon learns that these and other qualities are intimately related to each other. Education for parenthood involves an introduction to many-sided interests and abilities out of which to provide a varied and fertile environment in which children can grow.

Relating the School to the Community

Field experiences and the increasing use of social service and work projects on the secondary school level likewise testify to the school's assumption of the obligation to guide youth in the direction of social maturity.

Social service projects may develop naturally out of classroom work or as an independent but nevertheless inherent part of the school program. An example of the first type is provided by a class in an urban junior high school. While discussing a story which dealt with the problem of working out conflicts among values, a class member remarked that a traffic signal represented a compromise between various needs. The question arose as to who decided (and upon what bases) that a signal should be established, since there seemed to be no logical explanation for the presence or absence of traffic signals at certain crossings close to the school. Encouraged by the teacher, the students themselves obtained various kinds of traffic data, drew up tables and charts, and formulated something like a "statement of principles." Threading their own way, more or less, through a maze of suggestions, civic organizations, and public offices—a process which brought parents, a traffic engineer and a lawyer (who contributed their services), and city officials into the picture—the students eventually presented their data and suggestions to the city manager. In their own school neighborhood and in other areas of the city, the (modified) results of their work soon became visible to the children.

In this project, the youth learned many things. Above all, they probably learned to translate principles into action, to work cooperatively on a problem they could feel and intellectualize as being at once personal and public, to regard at least a bit of social structure as manmade and malleable. It is important to note the essential role of a teacher who had definite plans to make school and community meet in the hearts, minds, and muscles of her students.

A large city school affords a second illustration. The science department of this school has established close relationships with the officials of the city's botanical garden. Students with interests in science are permitted to serve as apprentices in the gardens, thus rendering valuable assistance to the experts, on the one hand, and receiving the stimulus of first-hand association with experts in the field, on the other.

Similar possibilities of a two-way relationship between school and community can be identified in most localities. Opportunities for service in public health departments, public libraries, museums, and social and civic agencies will be seen to exist in abundance once both public officials and educators envisage their potential contributions to education. Nor need this extension of function interfere with or handicap the present activities of these agencies. On the contrary, once the department of government add to their service functions that of education, it may well follow that the one will give quality to the other.

The program of the school as a whole can often be geared to the need of involving students in socially useful work with an eye to furthering their responsible participation in the wider community.[80] For example, one school in New York City requires "community service" of all students registered in the senior high school. This varies in character and is related as nearly as possible to the needs and interests of the students. It may consist of actual work, under professional supervision, in a settlement house, a day nursery, or a hospital or service as a volunteer in an agency devoted to a social-civic purpose. This school likewise searches out opportunities for its students to engage in work projects with a social agency on weekends and vacations. The projects include jobs such as painting and repairing buildings for a fresh-air camp for children or serving as junior counsellors in a summer playschool or a camp for underprivileged children.

Many states and local communities have inaugurated the practice of including representatives of young people on councils and boards dedicated to community improvement. In organizing drives, making surveys, writing letters and petitions, and attending conferences and meetings relating to community problems—intergroup relations, juvenile delinquency, social welfare, employment of youth, and so on—youth learn more than verbal statements about the relations between public and personal problems, family and social problems, knowledge and its uses in life. There is room for considerable expansion of these kinds of activities, expansion which should include not only increased representation of youth on councils but also the formation of affiliates or branches composed of young people and associated with adult organizations.

The Role of the School in the Community

Many educators do not believe that by expanding the connections between school and community experiences the school can significantly offset the undernourishment in youth's social development. Some point

80. For an elaboration of this point, see Franklin Patterson, *High Schools for a Free Society* (Glencoe, Ill.: Free Press, 1960), pp. 47–64.

to the larger social structure, which cannot be sensed in immediate experience, and to the academic disciplines which do lead out to these molar problems. Thus, while giving some consideration to social interactions within the school and to limited school-community relations, some educators emphasize a more "intellectual" approach in education, centered on developing understanding of the disciplines and various intellectual skills.[81]

We have urged, however, that guided enrichment of primary experience provides essential channels for integrating what is social and intellectual with the growing experience system of the child. Indeed, this enrichment is particularly necessary today when "remote" social forces impinge upon local events and complex intellectual structures are available for analyzing concrete events. However "remote" the social forces may be and however abstract the intellectual structures, they have meanings and influences which extend into specific events. Certainly, as we will emphasize later, the world of immediate sights and sounds does not exhaust the world of possible meanings. It never has. The "law of gravity" may seem obvious to us now that we are (or think we are) familiar with it. The impression that a person is "abnormal" may be immediate and clear. But our perceptions are packed with historical, cultural, and intellectual influences that extend far beyond our clear and immediate judgments. If we do not see, feel, and question the remote and theoretical in the sensory and personal, then social forces are indeed remote and intellectual structures are indeed abstract —or, as we say, academic.

To be sure, the school is not our only socializing agency. It is not the only institution that enables old and young to participate jointly in meaningful experiences. Indeed, in recent years many national and local agencies, using public and private funds and often cooperating with schools, have initiated programs to meet some of the needs of youth, particularly of culturally disadvantaged youth. However, while many of these programs are valuable, many of them could benefit by the integration of sometimes narrow and isolated purposes—such as the provision of work experiences or of recreational opportunities— with a program of general education.

81. For one excellent elaboration of this general viewpoint, see Harry S. Broudy, B. Othanel Smith, and Joe R. Burnett, *Democracy and Excellence in American Secondary Education* (Chicago: Rand McNally and Co., 1964), pp. 24–31, 43–60, 214–43.

As an institution devoted to the general education of youth, as an *educational* institution rather than a pressure group or an organization with narrow purposes, and as an institution which is broadly representative of the people and the interests of a community, the school often can be our most effective instrument for bringing together a community's material and human resources for the education of youth. Through the aid of the school, parents and children can be led together, in practice and in intellectual appreciation, into larger public concerns.[82]

The growing functions of parents' associations illustrate this conception of the potential contributions of the school.[83] Not only do these organizations serve as interpreters between the school and the parent body—explaining the school's curriculum to the parents and relaying the concerns of parents to the school—but, in many instances, they have become the means whereby parents solve their problems as parents through cooperative effort.

Parents' organizations have likewise come to realize that in union there is strength with which to face the problem of unhealthy environmental forces playing upon young people. When parents are united, their status increases. Amusement centers respond more sensitively to their suggestions. Movie theaters solicit their endorsement of pictures. With the advice of a wise school administration, organized parents can establish good relations between the school and other agencies concerned with the health and welfare of young people. On occasion, a broad-gauged health and guidance program, including health examinations, a counseling system in mental health, and vocational guidance, has had its origin in the informal relationships of the school with the local medical association, mental hygiene society, labor unions, and employer associations. When parents are organized they can develop a constructive interest in underprivileged sections of the community and demonstrate to the less discerning members of the community that conditions which make for diseased personalities are as disadvantageous to the well-being of the community as a whole as are breeding spots of physical infection.

82. See Fred A. Sloan, Jr., "Helping Parents to Help Their Children," *NEA Journal*, March 1960, pp. 49–50.

83. During the period between 1943 and 1964, the National Congress of Parents and Teachers (PTA) enjoyed an increase from 2.6 million to well over 12 million members.

Possibilities of cooperation between the school and the parents are not limited to the extracurricular life of the school. Virtually every subject taught in the school represents the interests, often vocational, of competent and resourceful members of the community. One effective means of vitalizing instruction and of breathing unity and significance into topics that might otherwise remain foreign and remote is to draw upon these adults for the purposes of enriching the curriculum and giving to students first-hand evidence of ways in which activities within the school are representative of worthy adult interests out of school.

These are but a few of many ways in which the school and the parents, united, can both meet problems of "undernourishment" in the lives of boys and girls and contribute positively to the enrichment of their lives. To achieve these goals the school must envisage its responsibility as a community responsibility and conceive of its work with young people in terms broader than conventional notions of the development of the "mind." It takes seriously the established fact that healthy intellectual growth involves healthy emotional and social relationships as well. It implies a disposition on the part of the school to bridge the traditional gap separating the two. Finally, it assumes that the school, through its administrative machinery, will exercise initiative in bringing about this change.

Criteria Are Important

In all attempts to relate the school to the community, it is essential to keep in mind that the primary purpose of this relationship is educational. Its function is to provide young people with specific occasions for participating responsibly in life about them and, through this participation, to acquire qualities of personality which further identification with others and with the concerns of an ever enlarging community. Not infrequently, schools have leaped suddenly from a state of virtual nonparticipation into one in which activities are so numerous and varied that their educational value has been lost. To extract their full educational value, community projects should, to every extent possible, (1) grow naturally out of class work and bear an obvious and direct relationship to the objectives of the course of study; (2) serve the needs of children rather than those of pressure groups or propaganda agencies outside the school (worthy as these may be); (3)

afford opportunities for pupils to identify themselves emotionally as well as intellectually with institutions and agencies that are furthering the interests of the community as a whole; and (4) be keyed to the social maturity of the students who are asked to engage in them.

The School Is a Community

A classroom and a school as a whole are small social systems in which, as in any socialization process, young people learn much more than what is explicitly taught. Often these "concomitant" or "silent" learnings have much more influence on a child's working values and beliefs than do the explicit teachings.[84] The influences upon character of the atmosphere and the norms, roles, and social interactions that comprise the culture of a school are constant and powerful. Thus, no new dimension, alien to education, is introduced if the attention of the teacher is directed toward these matters. What is introduced is an opportunity to become aware of these factors and to make them yield intended, rather than unintended, results.

Take the case of third-graders who hear a teacher explain and uphold the belief that "all individuals, regardless of race, status, or religion, are equally worthy of respect," and, at about the same time, see the teacher exhibit deferential, submissive behavior toward the principal who has entered the room. The children are being provided with material for learning, possibly subconsciously, an accepted inconsistency between principle and practice.

Again, an alert citizen defines problems, seeks and evaluates relevant data, reaches a conclusion, and revises his views when reason so dictates. Yet how often are children faced with the difficult and significant problem of selecting a problem worthy of their attention? And do not most learning experiences in school push children toward learning an answer which terminates inquiry rather than a formulation which opens up new questions? Note that we are not suggesting that teachers should permit children to do whatever they want to do, nor that students must always be engaged in defining problems and evaluating

84. For further discussion of these points and of related topics, see *Fifty-ninth Yearbook*, National Society for the Study of Education (Chicago: University of Chicago Press, 1960), part II, chaps. 4–8; W. Warren Kallenbach and Harold M. Hodges, Jr., *Education and Society* (Columbus, Ohio: Charles E. Merrill Books, 1963), pp. 197–257.

evidence. We are suggesting that problem-solving activities are significant and are often neglected in education.

Consider the numerous educational provisions made to encourage "individual achievement." Compared with these provisions, the measures taken to promote a child's feeling of responsibility for the personal and intellectual development of other children are generally meager. Rarely do the phrases "gifted child" or "excellent student" evoke images of a young person rich with love for others, excelling in the ability to enrich the lives of others. And, concerning the gifted student, do we not interest ourselves most of all in ways of accelerating his own acquisition of knowledge and skills?

The school has many opportunities for creating meaningful interactions between children of different interests and abilities, socioeconomic and ethnic backgrounds, ages and sexes—interactions which can contribute significantly to the development of sensitive and cooperative relations in many areas of life. For example, attempting to realize certain objectives relating to social responsibility and family relationships, some institutions have found occasions to bring high school students, both boys and girls, into contact with young children in day nurseries or kindergartens. Here they not only learn how to care for babies and young children physically, but how to observe their behavior and gain some understanding of how to cope with problems of child-rearing.

Many schools and classrooms are characterized by routines and expectations which are so fixed and unquestioned that individual and group activities must constantly yield to the "system" and cooperation becomes equated with role fulfillment within the system. Attention is often so exclusively focused on attaining the correct answer that the significance of the answer for individual children is overlooked. These and other conditions are hardly conducive to the development of an atmosphere in which young people feel free to express their doubts, fears, and cynicism, feelings which may involve the relation of intellectual and moral principles to their expression in the family, school, or other social situations. The ability of a teacher tactfully and sensitively to encourage the expression of unpopular ideas, personal problems, and doubts is not merely a pleasant "personality" characteristic; it is an essential element in uniting what seem personal and private matters with what is public and intellectual.[85]

85. For a general introduction to some aspects of this large topic, see Josephine Klein, *Working With Groups* (London: Hutchinson and Co., Ltd., 1963), chaps. 5–10.

The reader may wish to consider the possible implications of the fact that the school is a social system for such topics as homogeneous grouping, teacher-pupil ratios, the place of independent study and of group work, student government, the relations between the teacher's aims and those of students, and so on. The area of possible concern is as wide as the total life of the school.

Relating Youth to the Wider Social Structure

An education which restricts itself to exhortation and to teaching facts or the structure of a discipline often cannot contribute much toward linking social structure, the structure of the discipline, and the structure of individual thought and character, a linkage which is essential for self-fulfillment, social consciousness, and social intelligence. And an education which immerses youth in the community without developing the art of reflection and growing awareness of the moral and intellectual principles implicit in the working of the social structure is hardly an education; it is an effective instrument of "adjustment." Moreover, such an education may dangerously confine thought and concern. Today, for example, "citizenship and perhaps even survival call for more than face-to-face charity and kindliness. We can no longer plead ignorance of the plight of starving Armenians, Indians, and African tribesmen." [86]

A high degree of detachment and objectivity are needed in the midst of participation. Concern and inquiry must move out from personal and community relations to larger social and intellectual structures and to the evaluation of alternative patterns of life found among men. To do less is to leave a person so much the less free to know himself, the forces that work upon him, the alternative specific goals available, and the possible means of working toward these goals. It is the distinctive function of the school to intellectualize primary experience—a function which manifestly calls for the use of primary experience. Thus, there is a major place in general education for the study of social institutions.

It is desirable to use widely varied resources and modes of relating observation, study, and interpretation.[87] Literature, art, and science are, in a significant sense, parts of the social sciences. For some chil-

86. Harry S. Broudy, and others, *op. cit.,* p. 29.
87. For a number of suggestions, see the valuable booklet by Franklin Patterson, *Public Affairs and the High School* (Medford, Mass.: Lincoln and Filene Center for Citizenship and Public Affairs, 1962).

dren in an elementary school, acclimatization to the music of India—hearing it change from "strange" to "rather pretty"—was an excellent introduction to the realities and ideas which they might someday call ethnocentrism. One high school combines (1) the performance of needed work-services in school and community, (2) the study of community life, and (3) an intensive study of national and international problems which parallel or bear on community problems.

Many schools and colleges provide units of study or courses in family life. These deal with such items as responsibilities of family members; relations between the older and younger generations; relations of the family to community institutions and to larger social forces; the social, mental, and physical growth of children; factors essential in the selection of a mate; the physiology of reproduction; and the history and purposes of the family and its multiple forms in modern society.

Provisions are made and should increasingly be made for the study of other social institutions and problems. We must go beyond the usual social studies–history–civics–geography approach of most schools and deal more directly with the social and moral significance of literature, art, and the natural sciences, and with the principles and findings of anthropology, comparative religion, economics, psychology, and the other behavioral sciences. One of the most urgent needs today is for studies which provide an objective and comparative analysis of the American experience with the experiences of other societies. Like other societies, we have been ethnocentric in our education, concentrating on a much too unquestioning transmission of our way of life. Critical and comparative studies are needed below the college level since, for one thing, the majority of youth between the ages of eighteen and twenty-one still do not attend college.[88] In high schools today a very small minority of students studies such subjects as economics, psychology, and sociology—and anthropology is not even listed in a "comprehensive report" of subject offerings in public high schools.[89]

In short, we are not urging that "activity" and "participation" be confused with education. We are urging an effort to intellectualize the habits and feelings of daily life, an attempt to make principles one with concrete relationships among people.

88. U.S. Office of Education, *Digest of Educational Statistics* (Washington, D.C.: U.S. Government Printing Office, 1964), p. 75.
89. U.S. Office of Education, *Summary of Offerings and Enrollments in High School Subjects* (Washington, D.C.: U.S. Government Printing Office, 1964), p. 13.

The Functions and Morality of Rich
and Varied Primary Experience

It should be noted that the kinds of experiences we propose as appropriate for education constitute the elements of a broad general education. In terms of subject matter, such experiences would cumulatively involve the content found in the humanities, social sciences, and natural sciences. But the subject matter would not be treated in isolation from activities which can pour personal and social significance into them, and which demonstrate that schools envisage their task as helping young people meet their needs in all the relationships of life. Focusing on common situations, while encouraging a variety of mutually enriching individual responses; teaching intellectual and moral principles, while developing a concern for their application and improvement—such experiences could develop the community of concerns and the variety and variability of individual responses and interests which are needed by a democratic society in flux.[90]

As an illustration, take the case of the modern family. We have noted that its functions are declining and that its members have fewer shared, continuous, and intimate relations with people outside the immediate family. These conditions imply that to fulfill its mission the family must learn to build personality through shared experiences that are less economic and more social, cultural, and recreational in character, experiences which lead the family out into a public world where concerns and principles, if not friends and relatives, are shared and stable. This accents the importance of finding numerous and varied activities and interests congenial to different talents and ages, activities which bring friends into the home and cement the ties between parents and between parents and children.

The rush of experience in daily life may foster apathy, conformity, and other ailments. Nevertheless, there are seeds of objectivity and cosmopolitanism in the modern human condition, since binding and blinding attachments may be discouraged.[91] These are seeds which the school must carefully cultivate. In terms of the question of "teaching values," we have suggested, in effect, that the school cannot in fact be

90. See Donald W. Fiske and Salvatore R. Maddi, *Functions of Varied Experiences* (Homewood, Ill.: Dorsey Press, Inc., 1961), pp. 355–79.

91. Kenneth D. Benne, *Education in the Quest for Identity and Community* (Columbus, Ohio: College of Education, Ohio State University, 1962), p. 18.

neutral and merely teach facts, and that it should not attempt to impose or confirm unquestioned values but, rather, should attempt to make the choice of values a matter of reflective and socially responsible concern. Perhaps, in a mobile and changing society, identification with social concerns and with reason is a viable alternative to careless drift or careful self-centeredness.

Finally, it should be noted that a salient characteristic of the suggested experiences is the inclusion of a wide range of interlocking activities from the daily round of life. This feature is essential in promoting the translation of principles into practice and the engagement of personal and youthful interests with public and mature concerns. As we have seen, children from culturally disadvantaged backgrounds are usually those most excluded from responsible concerns, both in school and society. Therefore, special care must be devoted to the education of these children. This problem, among others, is one we will consider in the next chapter.

Suggested Reading

Benne, Kenneth D., *Education in the Quest for Identity and Community* (Columbus, Ohio: College of Education, Ohio State University, 1962).

Broudy, Harry S., B. Othanel Smith, and Joe R. Burnett, *Democracy and Excellence in American Secondary Education* (Chicago: Rand McNally and Co., 1964), chaps. 1–3, 13–14.

Graham, Grace, *The Public School in the American Community* (New York: Harper & Row, 1963), chaps. 4, 8, 12–15.

Havighurst, Robert J., and Bernice L. Neugarten, *Society and Education*, 2d ed. (Boston: Allyn and Bacon, 1962), chaps. 4–6, 12–13, 18, 20.

Kimball, Solon T., and James E. McClellan, Jr., *Education and the New America* (New York: Random House, 1962), chaps. 6–7, 9, 13.

Klein, Josephine, *Working With Groups* (London: Hutchinson and Co., Ltd., 1963), chaps. 3–9.

Olson, Philip, ed., *America as a Mass Society* (New York: Free Press of Glencoe, 1963), pp. 13–47, 262–312, 415–40.

Patterson, Franklin K., *Public Affairs and the High School* (Medford, Mass.: Lincoln and Filene Center for Citizenship and Public Affairs, 1962).

Riesman, David, *Abundance for What?* (Garden City, New York: Doubleday and Co., 1964), pp. 162–83, 196–225, 300–48.

Westby-Gibson, Dorothy, *Social Perspectives on Education: The Society, The Student, The School* (New York: John Wiley and Sons, Inc., 1965), chaps. 6–8, 14, 15.

"The Woman in America," *Daedalus,* Spring 1964.

Chapter 14

Youth and the World of Work

The Need for Orientation to Economic Life

As we noted in Chapter 13, the preparation of youth for economic life in the society of yesterday was linked closely with the gradual involvement of youth in a network of relationships, services, and gratifications that extended far beyond purely economic aspects of life. Under the old order the child might learn from first-hand experience at home and in the community not only the nature of economic processes, but also their significance for the community. The crops he helped to plant and tend and, eventually, to harvest and market were charged with meaning that transcended the profit motives. Economic operations transcended their expression in abstract economic formulas, and economic principles, within the compass of the child's experience, were identical with concrete and many-sided human relationships. In the words of Robert J. Havighurst, "work has been the usual way by which people have made a principal personal commitment to a stable society." [1]

Under the new order, profound socioeconomic changes have disrupted the channels through which youth have traditionally assumed adult roles, including economic roles. The fact that, in general, young people are no longer an economic asset is a major factor in the organized exclusion of youth from the adult community. Nevertheless, work is still the road to the symbols and realities which mark adult status, and preparation for economic life has been increasingly turned over to

1. "Youth in Exploration and Man Emergent," *Man in a World at Work*, Henry Borow, ed. (Boston: Houghton Mifflin Co., 1964), p. 233.

the school. In a rapidly changing world of work the school's responsibilities have been many and varied; its funds of money and of reliable guiding principles have been limited; and, particularly for the 80 per cent of youth who do not complete a college education, the school has too often failed to provide adequate orientation to economic life.

One weakness, described by Grant Venn as "first-job preoccupation," is characterized by the narrow, highly specialized vocational and technical curricula of many high schools and junior colleges. These programs are not equal to the demands of a society wherein "swiftly changing job patterns mean that the subprofessional person must look forward to five or six occupational shifts over the next forty years. . . ." [2] A second and perhaps even more significant weakness is that preparation for economic life, as carried on within the school, has tended to replace the concept of work, with its broad psychological, social, and moral connotations, by the narrower (and mainly economic) concept of the job. In a large measure, this has been the result of the isolation of academic occupational preparation from community experiences, an ungenerous conception of vocational education which has separated it from enriching connections with general education and the view that vocational education consists primarily of the acquisition of specialized skills and compartmentalized information. Finally, the school has failed to provide even simple, marketable occupational skills for more than a small fraction of the majority of high school youth for whom high school experience is still the basis of entry into the world of work.[3]

Recent decades have witnessed a rather steady decline in the school dropout rate. The percentage of former fifth-graders who went on to graduate from high school rose from 30.2 in 1932 to 50.5 in 1950 and to 66.7 in 1964.[4] However, the dropout rate has become a matter of increasing public concern because many more young people are going to school than in former years, because of manpower shortages in fields requiring prolonged education and training, and because the school is now the major avenue to adult occupational competence and status.

2. Grant Venn, *Man, Education, and Work* (Washington, D.C.: American Council on Education, 1964), p. 32.
3. *Education for a Changing World of Work: Report of the Panel of Consultants on Vocational Education* (Washington, D.C.: U.S. Government Printing Office, 1963), pp. 108–10.
4. U.S. Office of Education, *Digest of Educational Statistics* (Washington, D.C.: U.S. Government Printing Office, 1964), p. 120.

If schooling is the major alternative to unemployment or a blind-alley job for an increasing number of youth, what should be the nature of this experience? What can the school do to help youth gain not only occupational skills but also a sense of worth, identification, and involvement in the world of work? Before offering suggestions, it will be useful to glance at certain basic characteristics of the world of work.

The Changing Age Structure of the Population

One important factor is the changing age distribution of the population. In the early nineteenth century persons under twenty years of age comprised the majority of the total population. Since about the middle of the nineteenth century, and until very recent years, this age group has constituted a declining proportion of the population. "Roughly speaking, 52 per cent of the population were under twenty in 1850, 44 per cent in 1900, and 38 per cent in 1960. There were 2.5 per cent over sixty-five in 1850; 4 per cent in 1900; and 9.2 per cent in 1960." [5] The tendency, until very recent years, for older people to become an increasing proportion of the population is reflected in the rise of the median age: 18.8 years in 1850, 22.9 in 1900, 29.0 in 1940, 30.0 in 1950, and 29.44 in 1960.[6]

Of particular significance in this connection are the relative gains made by different age groups within the adult population. The size of the group sixty-five years of age and above has been increasing greatly in proportion to other age groups. This group showed a more than ten-fold increase between 1850 and 1930, compared with a fivefold increase in the population as a whole. In 1940 there were 9 million persons sixty-five years of age and over; in 1963 this age group comprised 17.6 million persons,[7] a near doubling of the group during a period when the total population increased from 151 million to 189 million persons. Moreover, as a percentage of the population, the "65 years and over" group rose from 8.1 to 9.3 per cent between 1950 and 1964, at the same time as the "18 to 24 years" group declined from 10.5 to 9.6 per cent, the "25 to 34 years" group declined from 15.8 to 11.6 per cent,

5. Robert J. Havighurst and Bernice L. Neugarten, *Society and Education,* 2d ed. (Boston: Allyn and Bacon, 1962), p. 413.

6. See "Projections of the Population of the United States, By Age and Sex, 1964 to 1985," *Current Population Reports* (Population Estimates), July 1964, p. 8.

7. *Ibid.,* p. 7.

and the "35 to 44 years" group declined from 14.2 to 12.8 per cent.[8]

The rise in the birth rate since the 1940s and the continuing (although recently slightly declining) high fertility rate have modified the long-term trends we have noted. Between 1950 and 1964 the "under 5 years" group increased from 16.2 million to 20.6 million (and from 10.7 per cent to 10.8 per cent of the population), the "5 to 13 years" group increased from 22.2 to 35.1 million (14.7 to 18.4 per cent of the population), and the "14 to 17 years" group increased from 8.4 to 14.2 million (5.6 to 7.4 per cent of the population).[9] The median age of the population, which had been 30.0 in 1950, declined to 29.4 in 1960 and to 28.5 in 1964.[10]

Old Age Competes with Youth

Thus, within a rapidly expanding population, two age groups—the young and those sixty-five years and over—have recently shown the largest increases.[11] In 1964 the "5 to 17 years" group comprised 49.3 million persons and the "65 years and over" group included 17.8 million persons. The recent variations in the growth rates of different age groups have resulted in an increase of the "dependency ratio," that is, the ratio of *persons under 18 plus those 65 and over* per *100 persons 18 to 64 years of age*. Since the "18 to 64" group constitutes the bulk of the labor force, this ratio provides a rough measure of the relative proportions of "dependents" and "workers." The table on page 308 shows the dependency ratio in recent years, including the relative contributions of the two groups, "under 18 years" and "65 years and over."

The long-term trend toward a middle-aged and old population has been a major factor in freeing children from the necessity of working and in permitting children to remain in school for a longer period of time, since relatively more adults were available to do the work of society. This changing age distribution of the population was particularly significant during the period when productivity (output per man hour) was not as high as it has been in recent years. In recent decades, how-

8. "Estimate of the Population of the United States By Age, Color, and Sex: July 1, 1964," *Current Population Reports* (Population Estimates), October 21, 1964, p. 1.
9. *Ibid.*
10. "Projections of the Population . . . ," *op. cit.*, p. 8.
11. "The U.S. Labor Force: 1950–1960," *Population Bulletin*, May 1964, p. 62.

ever, these changes have intensified some points of conflict between the
young and the old.

Take, for example, the influence of the changing age structure upon
the intellectual and moral climate in which education is to carry on.
Traditionally, Americans have welcomed change. Their attitude toward the future has been youthful—as might be expected in a predominantly young population. A middle-aged and old population is
less disposed to venture far from the shore unless the wind is promising

TABLE 2

DEPENDENCY RATIO OF THE POPULATION: 1930 TO 1964

Year	Under 18 Years	65 Years and Over	Total	Percentage Change Since Previous Date
1964	67.7	17.3	85.0	+ 3.8
1960	65.1	16.8	81.9	+27.2
1950	51.0	13.4	64.4	+ 7.5
1940	48.9	11.0	59.9	−11.9
1930	58.9	9.1	68.0	—

Source: "Estimate of the Population of the United States, by Age, Color, and
Sex: July 1, 1964," *Current Population Reports* (Population Estimates), October
21, 1964, p. 2.

and the waters are calm.[12] In recent years, the international atmosphere has been, when not ominous, at least something less than peaceful. From these two facts alone—international tensions and an aging
population—we can understand the concern with which many have
been scrutinizing the ideas educators may be "planting" in the minds of
the young.

Then, too, the data we have mentioned bear directly on the extent to
which our people are ready and willing, as well as able, to finance public education. Along with other factors, the recent wave of births has
enormously increased the burden of financing public education. At current prices, the GNP (gross national product) increased by less than 70
per cent from 1954 to 1964; at the same time public school expenditures increased about 135 per cent, almost double the rate of increase

12. See, for example, John Crittendon, "Aging and Party Affiliation," *Public
Opinion Quarterly*, Winter 1962, pp. 648–57.

in the GNP.[13] As a percentage of the GNP, expenditures for public education increased from 3.1 in 1929 to 4.8 in 1957 and to 5.8 in 1963.[14]

Nor is the end in sight. During the 1960s, about 26 million youth will seek entry into the labor market, a far greater number than the United States has ever had to educate, train, and absorb into employment in any previous decade. The number of children five to thirteen years of age will increase from 34.5 million in 1963 to 37 million in 1968; the number of youth fourteen to seventeen years of age will grow from 13.4 million in 1963 to 15.7 in 1970 and to 16.7 in 1975; and the college-age group (eighteen to twenty-one years old), which numbered 11.1 million in 1963 will increase to 14.3 million in 1970 and to 16.0 million in 1975.[15]

At the same time, schools have been encountering a financial rival in old age pensions and other necessary provisions for the security and welfare of the population sixty years and above. As the number in this age group has increased in proportion to that of the population as a whole, so the problem of equitable distribution of public funds in support of young and old has become more acute. Already, in a number of states, commitments to the aged have led to the curtailment of appropriations for education and other social services. To meet the legitimate needs of young and old alike, in addition to the requirements of defense for an indefinite future, calls for a quality of statesmanship and foresight only too infrequent in these days of comparative abundance.

A number of recent trends point toward a more economically favorable age distribution in the near future. Although projections indicate substantial increases in the population sixty-five years and over, the rate of growth of this age group is expected to decline. In various population projections, the median age, which was 28.5 in 1964, is expected to decline to 26.4–27.4 in 1970, and to 25.9–27.5 in 1975.[16] Moreover, as more young people enter the labor force, the dependency ratio is expected to be more favorable by the early 1970s.[17]

13. Erick L. Lindman, "Financial Status of the Public Schools, 1964," *NEA Journal*, November 1964, p. 39.

14. *Digest of Educational Statistics, op. cit.*, p. 131.

15. "Projections of the Population . . . ," *op. cit.*, pp. 5–6.

16. *Ibid.*, pp. 7–8.

17. "The U.S. Labor Force . . . ," *op. cit.*, p. 62.

Productivity and Education

Among other favorable considerations, possibly the most important are the rising productivity rate and the growing affluence of the American people. Productivity rose at an average rate of 2.4 per cent annually over the period 1909–1963. During the postwar period 1947–1963, the increase averaged 3.0 per cent, while the annual increase for 1960–1963 averaged 3.6 per cent.[18] Most projections anticipate a continued rise of the productivity rate during the coming decade.[19]

Moreover, the GNP *per capita* increased by 121.5 per cent by the early 1960s from the 1912–1916 average, at the same time as the population expanded enormously and the average hours worked per week in the manufacturing industry decreased about 20 per cent.[20] The national income per pupil in public elementary and secondary schools rose from $101 in 1919–1920 to $329 in 1949–1950, and to $518 in 1961–1962.[21] It is important to note that economists agree that the rising educational level of the population probably contributed more than any other factor to the rise in productivity during recent decades and that added education would now contribute much more than it has in the past.[22]

These data take on added significance when we recall that many countries—including Russia, Poland, Holland, Norway, Belgium, and Japan—have been spending a significantly higher proportion of their national income on education than has the United States.[23] There can be no doubt of our ability to provide adequate funds for education and for other social needs. As Professor Raymond E. Callahan has written:

18. U.S. Department of Labor, *Manpower Report of the President and A Report on Manpower Requirements, Resources, Utilization, and Training* (Washington, D.C.: U.S. Government Printing Office, 1964), p. 46.

19. See, for example, Warren L. Smith, "The Report of the Commission on Money and Credit," *American Economic Review*, May 1962, pp. 302–19.

20. U.S. Department of Labor, *Labor in America: 1913–1963* (Washington, D.C.: U.S. Government Printing Office, 1963). Pages in this pamphlet are not numbered.

21. *Digest of Educational Statistics, op. cit.*, p. 12. The data are in adjusted dollars, corresponding to 1961–1962 purchasing power.

22. See Moses Abramovitz, "Economic Growth in the United States," *American Economic Review*, September 1962, pp. 769–70; E. F. Denison, "How to Raise the High-Employment Growth Rate by One Percentage Point," *American Economic Review*, May 1962, pp. 71–72; T. W. Schultz, "Investment in Human Capital," *American Economic Review*, March 1961, pp. 10–13.

23. UNESCO, *Basic Facts and Figures: International Statistics Relating to Education, Culture, and Mass Communication* (Paris: UNESCO, 1962), pp. 72–78.

"Any nation that spends almost three times as much on the purchase and operation of automobiles as it does on education has a problem in values, not in economic capability." [24]

Until the twentieth century, no society could afford more than a small number of educated people. No progressive society today can afford *not* to provide open opportunities for all of its citizens to receive both a general and a specialized education.

The Shifting Occupational Patterns

The joint rise of productivity rates and educational levels is closely associated with a number of other factors which are vital in weighing the role of the school in preparing youth for the world of work. The following two tables provide an introduction to some of these essential

TABLE 3

OCCUPATIONAL GROUPS AS A PERCENTAGE OF THE TOTAL
LABOR FORCE IN REPRESENTATIVE YEARS

Occupational Group	1900	1947	1960	1975 (projected)
White-collar workers	17.6	34.9	43.1	47.8
Professional and technical	4.3	6.6	11.2	14.2
Managers and proprietors	5.8	10.0	10.6	10.7
Clerical workers	3.0	12.4	14.7	16.2
Sales personnel	4.5	5.9	6.6	6.7
Blue-collar workers	35.8	40.7	36.3	33.4
Craftsmen and foremen	10.5	13.4	12.8	12.8
Semiskilled operatives	12.8	21.2	18.0	16.3
Laborers (exclusive of farm and mine)	12.5	6.1	5.5	4.3
Service workers	9.0	10.4	12.5	14.3
Farm workers	37.6	14.0	8.1	4.5

SOURCE: Grant Venn, *Man, Education, and Work* (Washington, D.C.: American Council on Education, 1964), p. 8.

24. *Education and the Cult of Efficiency* (Chicago: University of Chicago Press, 1962), p. 261.

considerations. The first table shows the long-term shifts in the occupational distribution of the labor force.

Some additional figures may help to interpret the significance of these data for the employment opportunities, education, and training of youth.[25] Of the gainfully employed in 1870, over half were farmers. At present, less than one worker in every fifteen is a farmer, and by 1975 the proportion will be about one in twenty. Within the blue-collar occupations, only the skilled—craftsmen, foremen, and kindred workers—will grow at a rate equal to the projected increase in total employment between now and 1975. The estimated increase of over 2 million workers in this group will raise the number of skilled workers to more than 11 million. Semiskilled industrial workers—operatives and the like—the largest occupational group, will probably have a slower-

TABLE 4

MEDIAN YEARS OF SCHOOL COMPLETED (1962) BY
OCCUPATIONAL GROUPS AND PROJECTED PER-
CENTAGE CHANGE IN EMPLOYMENT IN
OCCUPATIONAL GROUPS (1960–1975)

Occupational Group	Median Years of School Completed (1962)	Projected Percentage Change in Employment (1960–1975)
Professional and technical	16.2	65
Managers and proprietors	12.5	32
Clerical workers	12.5	45
Service workers	10.8	51
Sales workers	12.5	34
Skilled workers	11.2	30
Semiskilled operatives	10.1	18
Laborers (except farm and mine)	8.9	0
Farm workers	8.6	−28

SOURCE: *Manpower Report of the President . . . , op. cit.,* pp. 13, 100.

25. The data in this paragraph are taken mainly from Ewan Clague, "The Occupational Outlook," *Bulletin of the National Association of Secondary-School Principals,* November 1964, pp. 37–44; Committee on Education and Labor, House of Representatives (Eighty-eighth Congress), *The Federal Government and Education* (Washington, D.C.: U.S. Government Printing Office, 1963), pp. 134–38; U.S. Department of Labor, *Mobility and Worker Adaptation to Economic Change in the United States,* revised (Washington, D.C.: U.S. Government Printing Office, 1963), pp. 14–15, 29, 34.

than-average growth, although their numbers may rise from 12.5 million in 1963 to about 14 million by 1975. The number of managers, officials, and proprietors (except farm owners), occupations that demand considerable educational preparation, has been growing rapidly. Although the growth rate of this group will be slower than that of any other white-collar group, it will number about 9.4 million by 1975, an increase of more than 20 per cent over the 1963 level. Finally, professional, technical, and kindred workers, the fastest-growing group during the past two decades, will probably grow almost twice as rapidly as employment as a whole between 1963 and 1975. Estimates of employment in this group by 1975 range from 12.3 to 12.7 workers.

Symbolizing the basic occupational-educational trend are two reversals, shown in Table 3, which have taken place in the twentieth century. About the middle of the 1950s, the United States and Canada became the first industrialized nations of the world in which white-collar employment exceeded blue-collar employment. Also, a country with a labor force in which one in ten is an unskilled laborer and one in twenty is a professional person will have different educational and training requirements than a country in which one in ten is a professional person and one in twenty is an unskilled laborer. Roughly speaking, this kind of reversal took place between 1900 and 1960.

Table 4 underlines the fact that, in general, those occupations which are expected to grow most rapidly are those which also require the longest educational preparation.

During the early part of the twentieth century, youth with relatively little schooling usually could find employment on farms, in local distribution trades, in factories or shops. But, as the data indicate, these conditions no longer prevail. "We face an unprecedented growth in the number of young people and a substantial reduction in the number of jobs traditionally open to youth." [26]

The Changing Nature of Work

In the lives of individuals the historically shifting occupational patterns take the form of increasing "occupational mobility," that is, individual occupational changes. For some, this may mean advancement; for

26. President's Committee on Youth Employment, *The Challenge of Jobless Youth* (Washington, D.C.: U.S. Government Printing Office, 1963), p. 2.

others, "displacement" or temporary unemployment; and for those whose life experiences and general education have left them unprepared for learning anew, it may mean more or less permanent unemployment.[27]

The occupational shifts are not merely movements from one position to a similar position with, say, a different firm. Automation and other changes which will probably eliminate about 2.5 million jobs annually during the 1960s [28] also produce millions of new jobs, and in recent years about one half of all job changes have been movements from one occupational category to another.[29] Moreover, the data on occupational mobility do not reveal the greatly increasing need for retraining and continuing learning within occupations because of developments in knowledge, instruments, machines, skills, and organizational patterns.[30] All signs point to the conclusion that occupational mobility and the need for continuing learning on the job will increase at an accelerated pace.[31] As we have already noted, for example, the typical subprofessional person entering the labor market today can expect five or six occupational shifts during his working years.

In this context of rapidly changing occupations and skills, it is not surprising that an increasing number of industrial, military, and governmental organizations, particularly those which employ large numbers of workers,[32] find it necessary or desirable to expand their prejob and on-the-job training programs in order to provide the specific skills and information which, for an increasing number of occupations, are unobtainable in schools. "Today's industrial workers are often hired without specific skills and are trained on the job to perform skilled industrial operations. As technology changes, those same workers are retrained for different operations." [33] The full extent of this occupational

27. See Walter Buckingham, "The Great Employment Controversy," *Annals of the American Academy of Political and Social Science,* March 1962, pp. 46–52.
28. Edward T. Chase, "Learning to Be Unemployable," *Harper's Magazine,* April 1963, p. 34.
29. See, for example, *Mobility and Worker Adaptation to Economic Change. . . , op. cit.,* p. 23.
30. See, for example, George E. Arnstein, "Vocational Education," *Bulletin of the National Association of Secondary-School Principals,* November 1964, pp. 56–58.
31. See "Lifetime Occupational Mobility of Adult Males," *Current Population Reports* (Technical Studies), May 12, 1964, pp. 1, 3, 10.
32. *Mobility and Worker Adaptation to Economic Change . . . , op. cit.,* p. 40.
33. Lawrence L. Bethel, and others, *Industrial Organization and Management,* 4th ed. (New York: McGraw-Hill Co., 1962), p. 425.

training by employing organizations is not known, but it seems likely that in recent years the funds spent on this training have amounted to at least half of the expenditures for public education.[34]

At the same time, schools often neglect basic training for fields whose opportunities for entry jobs are expanding. For example, less than 20 per cent of urban high school students receive any sort of specific preparation for work, and 95 per cent of high schools offer no training in merchandising or selling, although job opportunities in these fields now outnumber those in production.[35] On the other hand, restricted by archaic legislation and equipment and by rather inflexible teaching skills and aims, schools produce unneeded workers, such as woodworkers and weavers, while the demand is for business-machine repairmen, electrical servicemen, and so on.[36]

To be sure, the effects of technological changes on the nature of work are not uniform.[37] Many jobs involve the performance of apparently simple, repetitive operations. However, the ability to acquire these skills—not to mention the ability to learn new principles and techniques—usually requires a broadening and deepening of the general education foundation for modern occupational training. The same requirement is highlighted by the increasing demand for people in many occupations—from professional and managerial work to production, sales, clerical, and service work—who can receive, interpret and apply information of varied kinds and who can understand the relation of their task to associated tasks.[38]

It is true that many new jobs involve the performance of tasks in relative isolation and, thus, decreased contacts with other workers. Some of the demands for "lonesome pay" and some of the experiments with "job enlargement" stem from this situation.[39] However, it is clear that security and advancement for the individual in the vocational field,

34. T. W. Schultz, *op. cit.,* pp. 9–10.
35. Edward T. Chase, *op. cit.,* p. 33.
36. See, for example, Marshall L. Schmitt, "Trends and Developments in Industrial Arts," *American School Board Journal,* March 1963, pp. 32, 35–36, 38.
37. See Leon C. Megginson, "Automation: Our Greatest Asset—Our Greatest Problem?" *Academy of Management Journal,* September 1963, pp. 232–44.
38. Seymore L. Wolfbein, "Automation and Skill," *Annals of the American Academy of Political and Social Science,* March 1962, pp. 58–59; Howard M. Vollmer and Donald L. Mills, "Nuclear Technology and the Professionalization of Labor," *American Journal of Sociology,* May 1962, pp. 690–96.
39. Charles R. Walker, ed., *Modern Technology and Civilization* (New York: McGraw-Hill Book Co., 1962), pp. 129–36, 168–75.

broadly conceived, turn more and more upon qualities of personality and character, capacity for cooperative and creative relations with people, capacity for continuing learning, habits and values which promote responsible and efficient performance of tasks, and general intelligence and education. Less exclusively than was once the case does vocation depend upon training of a purely technical character.[40]

Obviously, this does not mean that technical skills are unimportant. Modern technological society would suffer acutely were it to fail to maintain an open road for highly specialized abilities. The moral is rather that (1) education on all levels should concern itself with social and emotional aspects of development as well as the "intellect," with conditions that make for health of personality rather than exclusive emphasis upon training of the "mind" (or the "hand") in lonely isolation, and (2) attention must be given to bridging the traditional gap between general and vocational education on secondary and post-secondary school levels.

Schooling Replaces Work

It is an anachronism that the Bureau of Labor Statistics still uses fourteen as the age of entry into the labor market, since the average age of entry is now nineteen and will continue to rise as more high school graduates go on to college and to graduate schools.[41] Accompanying the steady rise in wealth and in the standards of education and skills imposed by business and industry, there has been a steady decline in the percentage of youth who participate in the labor force. The percentage of boys fourteen to nineteen years of age who were working (full- or part-time) declined as follows: 45.3 per cent in 1949; 40.8 in 1954; 36.5 in 1959; and 31.7 in 1963.[42] The situation in 1963 stands in sharp contrast to that of the early years of the century when about 60 per cent of boys fourteen to nineteen years of age were working, and

40. See Henry Borow, ed., *Man in a World at Work* (Boston: Houghton Mifflin Co., 1964), pp. 198–212, 414–29; Sigmund Nosow and William H. Form, eds., *Man, Work, and Society* (New York: Basic Books, 1962), pp. 69–87, 126–35, 287–305.

41. Thomas B. Curtis, "Automation: Change and the Technological Process," *Bulletin of the National Association of Secondary-School Principals*, November 1964, p. 19.

42. *Manpower Report of the President* . . . , p. 210.

when one of every five boys ten to fifteen years old was already a worker.[43]

Such data provide a partial explanation for the rapid increase in school enrollments during recent decades. School enrollment of children five to thirteen years of age rose from 73.7 per cent of this age group in 1910 to 95.3 per cent in 1963.[44] Very significant, too, are the figures which indicate that the average number of school days attended by pupils five to seventeen years of age has more than doubled within a century, increasing from 78.4 days in 1869–1870 to 121.2 in 1919–1920 and to 162.3 in 1961–1962.[45]

The general exclusion of young people from economic life has been reflected dramatically in secondary school enrollments. Toward the end of the nineteenth century, a minority of youth fourteen to seventeen years of age was in school. By 1910 the percentage of this age group who were enrolled had risen to 58.9, and by 1963, it had risen to 92.9.[46] Public elementary and secondary school enrollments reached a record 41.4 million in 1964. But enrollments in secondary schools are increasing much more rapidly than those in elementary schools. In 1964, secondary school enrollments totaled 15.2 million, a gain of 5.4 per cent over 1963; the 26.2 million pupils in elementary schools in 1964 represented an increase of only 1.7 per cent.[47]

During 1963–1964 the number of public high school graduates jumped by 18.1 per cent to a record 2,021,000. This number represented 73 per cent of the students who had entered the ninth grade four years earlier.[48] Estimates for the coming ten to fifteen years indicate that for each three public high school graduates in 1960 there will be an average of four graduates annually after 1965.[49] Another indica-

---

43. Seymore L. Wolfbein, "Labor Trends, Manpower, and Automation," in *Man in a World at Work*, Henry Borow, ed. (Boston: Houghton Mifflin Co., 1964), p. 157. See also Samuel Saben, "Work Experience of the Population," *Monthly Labor Review*, January 1964, pp. 20–22.

44. The figures for 1910 and 1963 are taken, respectively, from Bureau of the Census, *Historical Statistics of the United States: Colonial Times to 1957* (Washington, D.C.: U.S. Government Printing Office, 1960), p. 214, and "Facts on Education: Pupils," *NEA Research Bulletin*, May 1964, p. 44.

45. *Digest of Educational Statistics*, p. 10.

46. See the same references, and same pages, mentioned in footnote 44.

47. *Kansas City Times*, January 7, 1965.

48. *Ibid.*

49. Donald J. Bogue, "Population Growth in the United States," in *The Population Dilemma*, Philip M. Hauser, ed. (Englewood Cliffs, N.J.: Prentice-Hall, Inc., 1963), p. 78.

tion of the extent to which schooling has replaced work within a single generation is a comparison, made in 1962, of the educational attainment of men twenty to sixty-four years of age with the educational attainment of their fathers. About 55 per cent of the men, compared with 24 per cent of their fathers, were high school graduates; and 26 per cent of the men, as against 10 per cent of their fathers, had completed one or more years of college.[50]

General, universal education has moved up the age scale from the elementary school (once characterized as the common school) into the upper years of the secondary school and the lower levels of college. Today educators are discussing the need for terminal education in the junior college in much the same terms that, about fifty years ago, they applied the concept to the junior high school. At this level, too, educators are raising the question of a general education appropriate to the needs of young people who seemingly are unable to pursue the type of curriculum traditionally designed for the few rather than the many.

Some data add flesh to the proposals of educators and of many public leaders. The percentage of youth eighteen to twenty-one years of age who were enrolled in college rose from 22.1 in 1946 to 40.4 in 1963.[51] In recent years, college enrollments have been increasing at a more rapid rate than enrollments at any other level. During the period 1958–1963, total school enrollment increased by 17.4 per cent; high school enrollment increased by 31.1 per cent and college enrollment went up by 33.7 per cent.[52] One typical estimate is that the present number of students in college will more than double by 1975.[53]

The truly amazing growth of junior colleges or, as many of these institutions are now called, "community colleges," is one of the most significant developments on the educational scene. The first two-year college was founded in 1902.[54] In 1925 there were 153 of these institu-

50. "Educational Change in a Generation," *Current Population Reports* (Population Characteristics), September 22, 1964, pp. 1, 9.
51. *Digest of Educational Statistics*, p. 75.
52. "School Enrollment: October, 1963," *Current Population Reports* (Population Characteristics), July 24, 1964, pp. 3–4.
53. Donald J. Bogue, *op. cit.*, p. 79.
54. Most of the data in this paragraph are taken from (1) *Digest of Educational Statistics*, p. 84; (2) *Saturday Review*, December 19, 1964, pp. 50–54, 64; and (3) "Schooling for All Through Grade 14?" *Phi Delta Kappan*, February 1964, p. 264.

tions, and two thirds of them were privately controlled. In 1963 there were about 700 junior colleges; two thirds of them were publicly controlled, and these public institutions enrolled almost 90 per cent of the one million students in junior colleges. It has been estimated that by the early 1970s most communities of 50,000 or more will have at least one junior college and that 80 per cent of all college-bound high school graduates will enroll in such institutions. Usually maintaining an open-door admission policy for all high school graduates, offering both terminal and college transfer credit programs, the public junior colleges enable large numbers of youth to extend their education at minimum cost and provide academic preparation for occupations which require education beyond the high school but not a baccalaureate degree.

The Challenge to Society and the School

Clearly, the past few decades have been of unusual significance in their influence upon the status of youth. All of the data point to the fact that schooling is replacing work as a formative influence on the lives of boys and girls; the school is now the major institution for preparing youth for the world of work.

Social and educational arrangements for guiding youth toward adulthood and occupational competence have not kept pace with the consequences of technological changes. The coexistence of shortages (totaling some four million jobs) of trained manpower, widespread pockets of poverty in the midst of affluence, a fairly constant group of four to five million unemployed potential workers, and sharply rising educational needs has generated an increasingly massive national attack on some of the intertwined roots of poverty, unemployment, and cultural and educational deprivation. Educational, philanthropic, and civic organizations, state and local governments, and, most of all, the federal government are pouring billions of dollars into programs which range from slum clearance to the extension and improvement of counseling services, from provisions for prekindergarten programs, subsidized work experiences, summer camps, cultural enrichment programs, and special services for culturally disadvantaged youth to measures for training and retraining of adults and out-of-school youth.

Some older federal legislation relating to the support of vocational education has been updated to permit the extension of aid to training in newer fields of work, and the Vocational Education Act (1963) provides for job training and the transfer of funds among the various categories in the older federal acts.[55] Among the proposals being considered for channeling youthful energies into constructive and ego-involving tasks are those calling for the establishment of a Youth Conservation Corps and a National Service Corps—programs which would provide for educational, often remunerative, and socially useful work experience on national, state, and local service projects. Employers and unions are being urged to reconsider their personnel policies in order to eliminate practices which discriminate against minority groups and which unduly restrict the entry of youth into beginning jobs. In order to promote vocational preparation and employment opportunities for youth, some states and cities are establishing various formal commissions and informal relations among organizations concerned with youth employment—employers and labor groups, schools, employment and welfare agencies, and others.

Thus, in this national attack on the problems of manpower shortages, poverty, and unemployment, the schools are slowly but increasingly becoming involved in cooperative relations with other social agencies. The problems faced by schools are enormous. The basic problem is that despite the extension of schooling over time and to larger numbers of young people, the level of education and skills required by modern life and work is rising more rapidly than the educational attainments of our people.

Various considerations, including some we have already mentioned, reveal that the educational situation is not a healthy one. During the movement of students from the fifth grade to the twelfth grade, the educational system loses about 33 per cent of its enrollees.[56] Then, roughly 45 per cent of the high school graduates fail to go on to college,[57] and the colleges (at least during the period 1959–1964) lose over 40 per cent of their entrants.[58] Roughly speaking, out of every 100 boys and girls in the fifth grade, about 67 complete high school,

55. George E. Arnstein, "Vocational Education," *Bulletin of the National Association of Secondary-School Principals,* November 1964, pp. 70–71.

56. *Digest of Educational Statistics,* p. 120.

57. *Digest of Educational Statistics,* p. 120; Grant Venn, *Man, Education and Work,* p. 2; John C. Flanagan, "Project Talent," *NEA Journal,* January 1964, p. 10.

58. *Digest of Educational Statistics,* p. 75 (table 53) and p. 94.

only about 37 of these high school graduates go on to college, and about 20 complete their college education.

A number of studies have shown that hundreds of thousands of young people who could benefit from a college education do not go on to college. One large-scale study revealed that 20 per cent of the top 25 per cent in academic aptitude did not enter college, at least within one year of graduation from high school.[59] Studies by the National Science Foundation indicated that, nationally, less than half of the youth in the top third of their high school graduating class went on to graduate from college. Again it is obvious that an adequate solution to the problem of vocational education cannot be reached without close attention to the general education of youth. Too, the failure of large numbers of able students to extend their education reduces the job opportunities open to less academically able youth, since the academically able but undereducated youth "take jobs at less than their potential capacity, thus overshadowing other young people with lower abilities who would be able, nevertheless, to handle the jobs adequately if they could get them." [60]

By and large, employment conditions for youth under twenty give little assurance of permanency or regularity. In 1963, when the general unemployment rate was 5.5, about 18 per cent of the high school graduates who were in the labor market were unemployed, and the unemployment rate for high school dropouts was 32 per cent.[61] These general figures do not reveal the heavy underemployment of young people with little schooling, nor the fact that in minority ghettos the unemployment rate for teenagers often exceeds 50 per cent. Moreover, since a person is counted as unemployed only if he has been actively seeking a job, the figures do not reveal the existence of at least 350,000 young people between fourteen and twenty-four years of age who have stopped looking for work because they have found no opportunities for undereducated people.[62]

As we have indicated, the school alone cannot solve these problems.

59. John C. Flanagan, and others, *Project Talent: The American High School Student* (Pittsburgh: University of Pittsburgh, 1964), pp. 11–12.
60. *The Challenge of Jobless Youth*, p. 3.
61. Vera C. Perrella, "Employment of High School Graduates and Dropouts in 1963," *Monthly Labor Review*, May 1964, pp. 523–24.
62. Robert Theobald, "Cybernation: Threat and Promise," *Bulletin of the National Association of Secondary-School Principals*, November 1964, pp. 24–25.

But again and again—whether we consider the increasing time a growing percentage of youth spend in schools during their formative years,
or the rising standards of education and skills, or the narrowed and
even dehumanized lives of undereducated people—we find that modern society has developed a challenging and central role for the school.

General Education as the Foundation for Vocational Education

In their report to the President of the United States, the Panel of
Consultants on Vocational Education wrote as follows:

> Skills in reading, mathematics, and other general education
> fields are essential for acquiring specific vocational competence
> and the higher levels of education needed for many occupations.
> . . . The early school leaver who has not acquired the basic skills
> is not only unable to find satisfactory permanent employment but
> is also greatly handicapped in acquiring specific vocational train-
> ing as an adult.[63]

Virgil M. Rogers, director of the Project on the Educational Implications of Automation, sponsored by the National Education Association,
elaborates on one of the points made by the President's Panel when he
writes: "To retrain quickly for specialized jobs, adults must have a
command of the fundamental tools of learning: reading, writing, arithmetic, oral communications, and human relations. With these skills
students will be equipped to take more training or retraining when job
changes become necessary." [64]

The data we have examined concerning the increasingly "cognitive"
nature of work, occupational mobility, and the qualities of personality
required by modern work, all point to the conclusion that a good general education is the foundation for vocational education.

Thus, educators and the public should be vitally concerned about
the many studies which show that students in vocational high schools
tend to have ability much below average in the "tool" subjects of general education.[65] At the same time, as Grant Venn reports, "in many

63. *Education for a Changing World of Work*, p. 5.
64. "What Kind of an Education in a World of Automation?" *Bulletin of the
National Association of Secondary-School Principals*, November 1964, p. 53.
65. See, for example, John C. Flanagan, "The Implications of Recent Research
for the Improvement of Secondary Education," *American Educational Research
Journal*, January 1964, p. 2.

technical curricula only 10 per cent of the school time is allotted to general education subjects." [66]

Despite such facts, proposals are being made which look toward converting skilled workers into teachers through a few college courses.[67] The problems of vocational education are difficult and numerous, and they are not likely to be solved by such proposals in the modern world of elevated educational standards and changing skill requirements in an increasing number of occupations. More than ever before the problems of general education—obtaining well-educated teachers, adapting curricula to individual differences, providing for interrelations between subjects and between students from varied backgrounds, and so on—should become basic concerns in plans for vocational education. It would be wise to make the general education of culturally disadvantaged children a major part of the educational program for these young people.

As we envision general education, it is not merely a program calling for the learning of verbal skills. For example, the field experiences and the social service and work projects discussed in Chapter 13 provide opportunities for acquiring not only academic skills and social and economic understandings, but also the basic habits of industry and the attitudes associated with efficient and cooperative work. In many ways, general education can contribute to the development of a sense of personal involvement which can heighten the satisfaction derived from work or, where work is routine, can provide interests leading to other ego-involving activities in civic, social, and family life.[68]

Hundreds of thousands of youth enter the labor market annually with little or no carefully supervised work experience which has contributed to growth in social maturity, general work habits and attitudes, and occupational skills. On the other hand, at the beginning of the 1960s, one (or one plus) out of every six youths between the ages of fourteen and seventeen in attendance at school was either employed or looking for work.[69] The increasing cost of education requires many young people to engage in part-time work while pursuing their studies, and part-time

66. *Man, Education, and Work*, p. 32.

67. For a criticism of one of these proposals, see George Arnstein, *"Quo Vadis* Vocational Education?" *Phi Delta Kappan*, April 1963, pp. 326–30.

68. Robert J. Havighurst, "Youth in Exploration and Man Emergent," in *Man in a World at Work*, pp. 226–35.

69. *Digest of Educational Statistics*, p. 148.

jobs may well attract an increasing number of students in high school and college.

These conditions suggest that the schools envisage a relatively new and promising function: cooperating with employment agencies of the community and with groups of employers to make part-time work experience educationally valuable not merely for students enrolled in vocational high school, but also for many of those engaged in general education.[70] Since the policies of private business and industry often restrict employment opportunities for youth, and since the private sector of the economy will absorb a decreasing percentage of the total work force in the foreseeable future, a growing number of schools are establishing cooperative arrangements with agencies which administer publicly subsidized programs involving urban renewal, conservation, and other service projects.[71]

Working as catalysts, some public agencies (such as state employment services) have brought together private industry and the school. A number of cities have already established junior placement bureaus which place high school graduates and dropouts. These bureaus should increasingly assist young people who wish to remain in school but must of necessity add to the family income or those who would profit in the maturing process from work experience.

Various agreements have been reached to provide for careful supervision of the young worker and to enhance the exploratory and educational values of his work experience. In many cases, the employment bureau, upon the basis of information supplied by the school, assists the youth to find a job appropriate to his abilities and needs, and either the school or the employment agency helps him to interpret and to use his work experiences most fruitfully. In any case, it is important to avoid (1) the immersion of students in work which will lead nowhere, (2) the isolation of work experience from an educational context, and (3) the kind of "made-work" which often is little more than a holding effort designed to get youth off the streets of the cities.

Cooperative work-study arrangements might very well strengthen the holding power of the school. We have noted that despite the steadily increasing proportion of young people who are attending school,

70. For descriptions of several kinds of work-study programs which, in general, are relevant to the orientation of this section, see George W. Burchill, *Work-Study Programs for Alienated Youth: A Casebook* (Chicago: Science Research Associates, Inc., 1962), pp. 1–15, 27–41, 123–65.

71. In this connection, see *The Challenge of Jobless Youth*, p. 7.

the percentage of nonattendance is still too high and suggests a waste of personnel that the country can ill afford, as well as a sad harvest of ultimate frustration and failure for those who, with appropriate schooling, might have lived contented and useful lives.

It is obvious that the holding power of the school has increased with the attractiveness of the curriculum, and that the attractiveness of the curriculum generally has increased with attempts to organize the work of the school so as to meet the growing needs of boys and girls. Units of work in the elementary school, for example, introduce children to economics by helping them to discover the ways in which people provide themselves with food, clothing, shelter, and other basic requirements for living. Moreover, in the upper years of the elementary school and in the junior high school, many field and service experiences and many projects which grow out of classroom work contribute to social insight and sympathy as well as to economic understanding. So, too, do work camps on the senior high school and college levels, when they are organized as self-governing communities and are devoted to the performance of tasks that are clearly as much social and civic as economic in character.

Nevertheless, as students move through the secondary school and the junior college, subjects of study should provide, for many students, an ever more specific orientation to economic life.

Although each subject in the curriculum (particularly the "general studies" or the "core curriculum") lends itself to the orientation of students to economic life, there is need for vocational information which is not covered by these fields. Modern life is sustained by thousands of specialized occupational pursuits. No school can hope to acquaint its students with them all. The complexities of the situation require guidance and information more specific than general education alone can provide. One means for providing such information is establishment of a working arrangement between guidance specialists and student advisors.[72]

Utilizing the Summer Vacation

Cooperative relations between school and community might also help to solve the problem of the summer vacation. This problem seems to

72. In this connection, see Henry Borow, ed., *Man in a World at Work*, chaps. 18, 21–22.

become increasingly acute for large numbers of young people. Rural life has long ceased to be the dominant pattern in this country, but it continues, nevertheless, to determine the character of the school year, with the result that large numbers of children and adolescents are confronted each summer with a long vacation which many find it difficult to use constructively. To be sure, for those who can afford it, the recreational camp helps to solve the problem, but a considerable proportion of young people are unable to take advantage of camps. Nor is it possible for the average community to provide temporary jobs of a worthwhile character either in private firms or in the various public, semipublic, and voluntary agencies for the large number of young people thus released from school.

These facts have led educators and laymen repeatedly to raise the question of an all-year school, with little tangible success. One difficulty is genuine doubt as to the wisdom of extending conventional schooling into the summer months, coupled with failure, as yet, to develop a convincing substitute for this schooling. Another difficulty is the added expense an all-year school would necessarily involve at a time when many communities are already restive under what they consider inflated school budgets.

On the other hand, public concern for what seems to be an increasing proportion of children and adolescents who become delinquents suggests that serious thought be given to the needs of children in their out-of-school hours. Nor are we without valuable experience upon which to draw. For many years and in various sections of the country, private agencies have developed programs which schools might well adopt and enlarge upon. For example, in New York City, the Play Schools Association, a private organization, has long conducted a summer play school program with the consent of and with some assistance from the Board of Education. These play schools provide experiences in art and shop and in dramatics and music, together with excursions and trips of an educational and recreational character, as well as games and other "play" activities. For older children, an extension of this basic plan would include special-interest projects in areas such as science, art, literature, dramatics, shop, and the like which might vitalize and enrich interests related to the work of the school year.

Here, as in other developments of the program of the school, experimentation on a voluntary basis wisely antedates efforts at universal application. Enough has been done, however, in developing summer programs with children and adolescents to establish the wisdom of their extension to larger numbers. Were schools open during the summer months for "special interest" groups and work projects of various types within the community, together with ample opportunities for play and recreation under supervision, the rewards would soon become evident to all.

Although many summer programs are devoted too exclusively to providing "make-up" or accelerated academic work, there has been a definite upswing of interest in summer programs in recent years.[73] Some communities, like Syracuse, New York, are establishing summer work and recreation camps in which children and youth, especially those from culturally disadvantaged homes, can have experiences in group living, the performance of useful work, recreation, and remedial work on school subjects. In 1964 the federal government allocated about fifteen million dollars to thirty-two states for the establishment of camps (which are not necessarily limited to the summer period) in which young men sixteen to twenty-one years of age will learn new skills, get remedial education, and contribute to the general welfare in conservation work.[74]

Vocational Education in a New Role

Vocational education has centered all too commonly upon training in specific skills and techniques, evidently on the assumptions that the responsibility of the school ended with the immediate preparation of the student for a job, and that once he possessed a skill, he could safely weather economic change. Neither assumption is valid today.

As we have noted, qualities of personality, broad intellectual and motivational characteristics, and competences associated with general education are increasingly important in determining vocational success. It is also true that rapid changes in methods, materials, and divisions of tasks in occupational fields lead to the scrapping of old processes and skills and the emergence of new ones.

Take, for example, the plumber who now works with metallic pipes

73. Gloria Cammarota, and others, *Extending the School Year* (Washington, D.C.: Association for Supervision and Curriculum Development, 1961), esp. pp. 1–10, 28–38, 58–60.
74. *Kansas City Star*, November 26, 1964.

amenable to treatment by blowtorch. Metallic pipes may soon be largely replaced by plastic pipes that come from a factory or are squirted to specification on the job.[75] Apparently, many plumbers may soon become victims of technological unemployment. If, as often happens, the plumber has had little general education, has had a vocational education limited largely to specific ways of processing certain specific materials, and has had little variety in work experience,[76] he may have great difficulty in finding new employment. However, an industrial arts education could—and sometimes does—include instruction in some basic and transferable technical principles: thermal principles, and their uses in activating, fusing, distilling, sterilizing, and fritting materials; chemical principles, and their uses in carbonizing, compounding, dissolving, analyzing, oxidizing, saturating, and slaking materials, and so on.[77] With some understanding of the broader technical principles of his trade and with some experience in their application to diverse materials and processes, the plumber might well find new employment—perhaps in something like the factory producing the plastic pipes.

In several documents, Earl J. McGrath has reported that this same general approach is increasingly being put into practice (despite some countertendencies) at the professional level. Many faculties in professional schools are replacing particularized courses with a core program dealing with principles and techniques of general applicability. Specialization and clinical, work-study experience (internship, practice teaching, and so on) come later. These professional faculties, Dr. McGrath states, believe that "a core of basic instruction provides the graduate with the adaptability required by the changing conditions of modern business and industry." [78] Indeed, in some of the most rapidly growing professional fields, no specific or highly specialized college programs are available or desirable. For example, the Manpower Systems Officer of the National Aeronautics and Space Administration writes about "the diversity of training and degrees possessed by aerospace technologists, who are doing the same kind of work." He goes on

75. George E. Arnstein, "Vocational Education," *op. cit.*, p. 56.
76. Delmar W. Olson, *Industrial Arts and Technology* (Englewood Cliffs, N.J.: Prentice-Hall, Inc., 1963), pp. 88–92.
77. *Ibid.*, pp. 104–15.
78. Earl J. McGrath, "The Ideal Education for the Professional Man," *Sixty-first Yearbook*, National Society for the Study of Education (Chicago: University of Chicago Press, 1962), part II, p. 285.

to state that "college training and academic degrees in any of the physical science or engineering disciplines appear to be a suitable foundation for most of the aerospace occupational specialties." [79]

In view of the pressing need for general education and for understanding of broad principles, many educators today are discussing the desirability of delaying specific occupational preparation until the junior college level. Obviously, however, no one rigid rule can govern the character of vocational education. This will vary with vocations, the capacity of individuals, and the circumstances operating upon young people. Two factors, however, would seem to be of importance. One is to encourage all who are competent to do so to continue their education. The second is to help each student to acquire a sense of progress toward a life goal, whether this be in a trade or a profession. For some, this will mean a continuation of general education, which would include a continuing economic orientation. For others, it will involve an earlier introduction to occupational skills with, if possible, some first-hand contacts with jobs.

The introduction of young people to economic life must include adequate guidance and provision for the placement of youth in jobs both while they are in school and after graduation. There are over 30,000 specialized and changing occupations in our society. The school is increasingly unable to provide the specific machines and skills found in the occupational world and must enter into cooperative arrangements with other community agencies concerning division of labor among the agencies, job placement of youth, supervisory activities, and relations of work and study appropriate to different individuals and circumstances. Moreover, since the qualities making for efficiency and happiness in work are not separable from general qualities of personality, and since many young people (particularly those from culturally disadvantaged backgrounds) have a heavy burden of personal and social problems, vocational guidance must be supplemented by personal and social counseling services.

These considerations and others call for the extension and improvement of guidance and counseling services. "The ratio of students to counselors needs to be cut down sharply from the present ratio of 700 students for every counselor. The ideal would be one for every 250 to

79. C. Guy Ferguson, "Manpower Futures in the NASA," *Higher Education,* May 1963, p. 4.

300 students." [80] The education of counselors needs to be broadened and elevated to a high professional level. Relations of guidance personnel with teachers, their general roles within schools, and their relations with out-of-school agencies need to be constantly reexamined and improved.

Because rapid change occurs in vocational as well as in professional practice, occupational education should enable the individual to meet the experiences of life with flexibility and to possess himself of a basic knowledge that has application to "families" of occupations. Since, moreover, the future of the individual as well as changes in occupations are unpredictable, vocational education should be like the hub of a wheel with many spokes: education building not only intellectual skills but also character; a set of diversified, exploratory, and educational work experiences; knowledge of general and transferable technical principles and occupational skills as well as appropriate specific skills; the extension of guidance services and of cooperative relations with other agencies concerned with the social development and employment of youth. All this means that vocational education is seen not as some separate "part" of an education but as "inextricably linked in myriad ways with the totality of common education." [81]

The Problem of Culturally Disadvantaged Youth

Alienated young people who are markedly unsuccessful in entering the normal patterns of the social-educational-occupational world may come from any kind of socioeconomic background. However, a large majority of them come from culturally disadvantaged homes.

As many middle-class families desert the central city areas for the suburbs, culturally disadvantaged youth become increasingly concentrated in the central city areas, and the education of these young people is developing into one of the major urban problems of our society. "In 1950, about one child out of ten attending public schools in the na-

80. Eli E. Cohen and Louise Kapp, "Youth and Work: The Second Challenge," *Children*, March–April 1962, p. 83.

81. Laurence D. Haskew and Inez W. Tumlin, "Vocational Education in the Curriculum of the Common School," in *Vocational Education*, Sixty-fourth Yearbook, National Society for the Study of Education (Chicago: University of Chicago Press, 1965), part I, p. 64.

tion's fourteen largest cities was culturally disadvantaged. In 1960, the proportion had risen to one of three. Some authorities believe that by 1970 it may be one out of two." [82]

These young people are the ones most shunted from the mainstreams of life, most limited in enriching contacts with adult members of the community. One study found that three fourths of the parents of these youth had never finished high school and that 52 per cent of the fathers were either unskilled workers or were unemployed.[83] A large majority of high school dropouts are lower-class youth. The dropout rates of these young people may be four or more times the rates found in substantial middle-class communities.[84] While the great majority of dropouts do not become juvenile delinquents, the rate of juvenile delinquency is much higher among dropouts than among high school graduates.

Even under their present developmental conditions, tens of thousands of dropouts have the general ability to finish high school, and many thousands have the scholastic potential to complete a college education. While about 30 per cent of the general population have I.Q. scores of 110 or higher, 11 per cent of the dropouts studied in three states were in this I.Q. range.[85] A national study found that entrance to college was closely related to family income level. For example, within the second highest quarter of the general aptitude scores (percentile ranks 50.0 to 74.9), it was found that "51.8 per cent of the boys and 74.8 per cent of the girls in families with annual income below $3,000 did *not* enter college, in families with annual incomes of $12,000 or more, only 20.3 per cent of the boys and 29.2 per cent of the girls did not do so." [86] It is significant, however, to note that, according to one rather typical study, many more high school students drop out because of lack of interest in education (35 per cent) and lack of scholas-

82. Frederick Shaw, "Educating Culturally Deprived Youth in Urban Centers," *Phi Delta Kappan*, November 1963, p. 91.

83. Daniel Schreiber, "Juvenile Delinquency and the School Dropout Problem," *Federal Probation*, September 1963, p. 17.

84. Leonard M. Miller, "The Dropout: Schools Search for Clues to His Problems," *The Dropout*, U.S. Department of Health, Education, and Welfare; Office of Education (Washington, D.C.: U.S. Government Printing Office, 1963), p. 4.

85. O. Ray Warner, "The Scholastic Ability of School Dropouts," in *Selected Reports and Statistics on School Dropouts*, U.S. Department of Health, Education, and Welfare; Office of Education (Washington, D.C.: U.S. Government Printing Office, 1964), pp. 11–12.

86. John C. Flanagan, and others, *Project Talent . . . ,* pp. 11–19.

tic success (18 per cent) than because of economic reasons (11 per cent).[87]

Clearly, schools have much room—and hope—for improvement in their work with culturally disadvantaged youth.

Programs and Proposals for Educating Disadvantaged Youth

A large share of the national attack on poverty, unemployment, and manpower shortages has been directed toward eliminating some of the social and educational causes of alienation and cultural impoverishment among youth. Many promising programs and proposals have been developed. Some, like work-study and summer camp arrangements, are elaborations of programs we have already discussed. Here we will consider briefly some plans which usually are aimed specifically at the problems of socially disadvantaged youth.[88]

Increased Subsidization of Education. Of course, the policy of easing the financial burden of education for worthy youth who would otherwise have to shorten their education is being increasingly effected in many ways, as in the establishment of community colleges. We suggest, as a more specific aid, extension of the principle implicit in the G.I. Bill of Rights and in the policy of subsidizing the education of potential scientists, medical specialists, and others needed for defense to all youth able and willing to continue their education. A step in this direction is the Higher Education Act of 1965 which, along with other authorizations, provides new scholarships, loans, and work opportunities for poor but able youth. Advisable as this policy is, it would leave unaffected a sizable proportion of young people who lack the background and motivation for higher education. Much more needs to be done.

87. Leonard M. Miller, "The Dropout . . . ," *op. cit.*, p. 3.
88. For discussions of some of these programs and proposals, see the following sources: (1) George W. Burchill, *Work-Study Programs . . .* ; (2) National Society for the Study of Education, *Vocational Education,* Sixty-fourth Yearbook (Chicago: University of Chicago Press, 1965), part I, chaps. 4–7; (3) A. Harry Pasow, ed., *Education in Depressed Areas* (New York: Bureau of Publications, Teachers College, Columbia University, 1963), part V; (4) U.S. Department of Health, Education, and Welfare; Office of Education, *Programs for the Educationally Disadvantaged* (Washington, D.C.: U.S. Government Printing Office, 1963). No single community is undertaking all of the measures we discuss, and thousands of communities are doing little or nothing about these problems. It will be evident that although the measures are discussed separately, many of them are not separable in practice.

The Economic Opportunity Act. The antipoverty program of the federal government was signed into law in 1964. Formally entitled the Economic Opportunity Act, this measure provides for the allocation of funds to a wide array of programs, including job-corps camps, possible birth control projects, and community rehabilitation projects. Youth opportunity centers are being established in a number of cities. These centers will test and counsel youth and direct them to manpower development and job training programs, to neighborhood youth corps projects where they can gain work experience and earn money to stay in school, or to remedial programs where they can receive both educational and medical attention.

One of the most promising features of this Act is the call for private and public groups at the local level to develop their own plans for a Community Action Program. Along with other agencies, a number of school systems are developing plans for combining work-study programs with the service and work projects envisioned in the Community Action Program. Some plans include the recruitment of volunteers to help in the remedial instruction of children or in field excursions and group activities; some include educational and recreational after-school activities for young people and adults.

The Elementary and Secondary Education Act of 1965. Under the provisions of Title I of this federal act, financial assistance (amounting to slightly over 1 billion dollars in the fiscal year beginning July 1, 1965) will be distributed to the states on the basis of the number of children aged five to seventeen who come from families with annual incomes below $2000 and the number from families receiving assistance under the aid-to-dependent-children program. As an expression of national concern for improving the quality of general education at the elementary and secondary school levels and for promoting equality of educational opportunity at these levels, this Act may well mark a revolutionary turn in the activities of the federal government in support of education.

Extending Relations with Parents. Recognizing that the home is one of the most powerful influences upon youth development, a number of schools are taking steps to improve parents' understanding of education, raise their educational levels and aspirations, and help them solve their family problems. At times, instruction is provided in reading, sewing, family relations, vocational skills, and other areas. Activities are being organized which bring family members together in common interests and tasks. "Visiting teachers" help to trace relationships between children's school and home problems. Since they have had special training in psychology and social work, these teachers may act as counselors for the family or may refer families to appropriate agencies and specialists for help.

Adaptations of the Curriculum and Instructional Procedures. There has been a growing realization that the content of the curriculum (its vocabulary; the events, things, and values which are considered or assumed; and so on) are taken largely from the middle-class way of life. In an effort to make education meaningful and interesting to lower-class children, some schools are developing their own curricular materials based on the experiences of lower-class children. In a few cases, the children themselves help to develop the materials by writing stories which are later incorporated into a reading series.

In some communities, the pupil-teacher ratio has been reduced to facilitate individualized instruction. Where the curriculum is generously conceived, arrangements have been made to promote the intermingling of young people from different backgrounds and to maintain an open road for the development of varied interests and abilities in both the regular and the extracurricular activities of the school.

Cultural Enrichment. Some programs emphasize the enrichment of culturally undernourished lives by bringing children into contact with social institutions and cultural activities which would otherwise often lie outside their experiences. A "school-community coordinator" may, among other things, arrange trips to museums, libraries, colleges, business establishments, concerts, governmental agencies, and plays. Use may be made of volunteers (who may be college and high school students or adults from the community) to provide not only excursion leadership, but also opportunity for the interaction of people from varied social class, racial, ethnic, and religious backgrounds.

Extension of Special Staff and Services. To help troubled and unhappy young people and to compensate for cultural deprivations, some schools are providing assistance to the central figure, the teacher, in the form of additional specialists—not only the visiting teacher and the school-community agent, but guidance personnel, teacher aides, coaching teachers in reading and other subjects, and special staff or consultants in the areas of sociology, social work, and psychology.

Preschool Programs. Writing about programs for socially disadvantaged children, Havighurst states that "There are strong indications, based on scientific data and experimental programs, that the earlier the child can be reached, the more effective the program will be." [89] After reviewing some of the relevant research studies, Benjamin S. Bloom concluded that "marked changes in the environment in the early years can produce greater changes in intelligence than will equally marked changes in the environment at later periods of development." [90] He believes that the preschool period and the early years of the elementary school are crucial in stimulating the development of the general learning which underlies later school achievement.

Lower-class children usually do not have what Bloom calls an "abundant" or stimulating environment. Compared with middle-class children, they generally have less interaction with adults and they receive less encouragement to ask questions and to solve problems logically. They are exposed to poor models of language usage and they have meager opportunities for direct and indirect (through books and pictures, for example) contact with a wide and variegated world.

It seems clear that organized kindergarten and nursery school programs could have far-reaching effects on the disadvantaged child's learning abilities and interests.[91] Thus, it is indeed unfortunate that relatively few school systems have established preschool programs for these children.

Improving the Preparation of Teachers of Disadvantaged Children. To guide youth so that they feel at home and secure in their school requires a professionally trained teacher. The difficulties increase enormously when the (usually) middle-class teacher has to guide and instruct lower-class children. The task demands of a teacher not only the usual professional competences, but also a thorough understanding of the social and psychological characteristics of children who, in terms of class, race, or ethnic origin, are "different" or "inferior." Given all this, the teacher must have an adaptability and maturity of personality capable of transcending the common barriers between social groups and of entering into the lives of disadvantaged children.

89. Robert J. Havighurst, *The Public Schools of Chicago,* p. 66.
90. *Stability and Change in Human Characteristics* (New York: John Wiley and Sons, Inc., 1964), p. 89.
91. See, in this connection, Martin Deutsch, "The Disadvantaged Child and the Learning Process," in *Education in Depressed Areas,* pp. 163–79.

Moreover, most teachers experience a "cultural shock" when they have their first intimate and prolonged encounter with lower-class patterns of behavior.[92] The teachers' reactions may range from patronizing sympathy to, more often, rejection of these children. Rarely do they respond with the liberality of spirit and the experience which can promote understanding and respect. Relatively few teacher-training institutions provide for special instruction and for guided, intensive, and relevant experiences for prospective teachers of disadvantaged children. The challenging and specialized professional task of teaching disadvantaged children must be recognized as such in terms of training, salary, and other signs of professional status.

The programs and proposals which we have mentioned are promising ones. However, we would not want to leave the impression that all goes well now in regard to the education of disadvantaged children. As a whole, the education of these children is alarmingly inadequate to their needs, the demands of a technological society, and the ideals of democracy. All too often, for example, even when a work-study program is available for disadvantaged youth, school and society provide these young people with narrow skills and an inferior general education. Instead of being one vital element within a program designed to attain the liberal objectives of the school, job-training becomes almost a substitute for these objectives. To be sure, it is difficult to reach children whose backgrounds have been limited, but this is a responsibility which must be met.

Suggested Reading

Borow, Henry, ed., *Man in a World at Work* (Boston: Houghton Mifflin Co., 1964), chaps. 2, 7, 10.

Burchill, George W., *Work-Study Programs for Alienated Youth: A Casebook* (Chicago: Science Research Associates, 1962), pp. 1–15, 27–41, 123–65.

"Educating the Culturally Deprived in the Great Cities," *Phi Delta Kappan,* November 1963, pp. 70–76, 82–97.

"Education and Automation," *Bulletin of the National Association of Secondary-School Principals,* November 1964, pp. 22–44, 56–82.

National Society for the Study of Education, *Vocational Education,* Sixty-

92. See Helen Storen and Robert Edgar, *Learning to Teach in Difficult Schools* (New York: Department of Education, Queens College, 1963), pp. 3–8.

fourth Yearbook (Chicago: University of Chicago Press, 1965), chaps. 2–6, 13.

Nosow, Sigmund and William H. Form, eds., *Man, Work, and Society* (New York: Basic Books, Inc., 1962), pp. 96–147, 408–48.

Passow, A. Harry, ed., *Education in Depressed Areas* (New York: Bureau of Publications, Teachers College, Columbia University, 1963), parts 3–4.

Venn, Grant, *Man, Education, and Work* (Washington, D.C.: American Council on Education, 1964), chaps. 1, 7–8.

U.S. Department of Health, Education, and Welfare; Office of Education, *Programs for the Educationally Disadvantaged* (Washington, D.C.: U.S. Government Printing Office, 1963).

Chapter 15

Some Aspects of the Intellectual Task of the School

What Constitutes Literacy?

The reader who has followed the discussion thus far has doubtless asked himself, "What of the distinctively intellectual task of the school? Surely, education has to do with the training of the mind. Do the authors suggest we by-pass this traditional function?"

Not at all. Changes in the social order carry with them an insistent moral for the "training of the mind."

Many of the items already discussed bear directly upon both the content and the method of education, suggesting at one time that the school put new wine into its old bottles, at another that it provide both new wine and new bottles. For example, the meager participation of young people in economic and social activities, to which we have repeatedly drawn attention, renders imperative new ways of introducing children to the three Rs and the abstract concepts of advanced subjects if their teaching is to be vital. In short, the moral of earlier chapters is that to equip young people to face the contemporary world resourcefully, we must train their minds in ways more relevant than those of the past. The times require a unique facility in the "arts of communication," superior to those developed in the traditional school; they also require a broader recognition of what is meant by the "arts of communication." No longer can we identify these arts solely with the verbal arts. They include, as well, the fine and practical arts, the use of radio and television, and cooperative relations with others in work and play. In fact, the arts of communication include any media which ease and free communication and deepen understanding among people.

This broader conception of the arts of communication in no way lessens the importance of verbal instruction, when it is conceived functionally. Take, for example, the concept of literacy as defined in the relatively simple agricultural and rural economy of yesterday and in the more complex society of today. A man was once considered literate if he could read sentences of a simple character and sign his own name to legal documents. Given the ability, in addition, to add and subtract, multiply and divide, or to perform the operations equivalent to those mastered easily by a child in primary school today, he was sufficiently schooled to meet the normal problems of living.

But if one is to be self-sustaining in an urban and industrial society a much higher order of ability to read and to write and "to figure" is required.

Take a member of a labor union, for example. To participate responsibly in the decisions of his union an individual must be able to read and evaluate the economic reports submitted to the membership by the trained economists the union has employed. Again, as an urban dweller, the individual of today depends upon his daily paper or trade journal for information regarding opportunities and responsibilities of which he would otherwise be ignorant. As a member of a committee to consider a problem of importance to his church or fraternal society or civic community, he must know how to search out, organize, and interpret information bearing upon a many-sided question. Unless he can find his way to a library and not become confused once he is inside, he is severely handicapped. Moreover, he needs to be able to protect himself against undue credulity with respect to what he reads. Reading cannot safely be identified with believing. Accordingly, our citizen has to learn how to weigh evidence, detect bias, identify prejudice, and resist the wiles of the propagandist.

Nor is literacy solely a matter of reading and reflecting upon what is read. The radio and television have accentuated the importance of the spoken word. This, too, calls for discipline and training in the art of listening: the ability to grasp an argument as a whole, not merely to hear one point or to become so preoccupied with one statement that the speaker's argument as a whole is misinterpreted. To the extent that radio and television are used in political campaigns and to sell ideas and programs in other areas of living, it becomes important for the citizen to develop immunity against abuses of those functions and the ability to listen critically and objectively to what he hears.

Again, as the influence of technology continues to permeate and transform our lives and to render men daily more dependent upon science and the applications of science, a rudimentary understanding of the biological and physical sciences, as well as the "mathematics" of everyday life (to say nothing of science as a method of thinking) becomes ever more important.

Finally, literacy, under conditions of the present, would seem to involve elementary acquaintance with media other than the verbal, whether written or spoken. Acquaintance with the graphic arts, too, ranging from the simplest illustrations in a daily newspaper to the most vivid methods of conveying statistical information, is essential in the equipment of a literate mind. In short, literacy involves a minimum degree of facility in finding one's way around in a world in which communication through plural media is a condition of intelligent living.

Uses of the Past

Some would insist that we have omitted a most important aspect of functional literacy, knowledge of the past, since few problems can be dealt with adequately without knowledge of the background out of which they emerge. Indeed, it might be argued that no present event can be fully understood apart from its known connections with the past. What is a present problem indeed, other than a unique combination of factors from the past, operating in the present and charged with tantalizing future implications?

Were the concept of functional teaching adhered to consistently in determining what of the past should find its way into the curriculum, there would be less sound and fury in educational circles regarding the place of history and the classics in general education. Unfortunately, neither the friends nor the foes of traditional materials are at all times loyal to the arguments they employ. Many, for example, ground their arguments on behalf of the inclusion of a generous background in his-

tory in the curriculum upon its functional value in the solution of contemporary problems. Upon winning their case, however, they proceed
to introduce not a functional history, but a special-privileged history,
that is, segments of historical experience of interest and concern to an
instructor or to a specialist, perhaps, but quite unrelated, so far as the
student can detect, to his interests and needs. On the other hand, the
ardent advocate of a plan in which contemporary materials in education take precedence over the classics and the "dead languages" is
equally prone to assume that the values he seeks reside in an arbitrary
subject matter rather than in the interplay between a student and subject studied. As one of the present writers has stated on another
occasion:

> There is a necessary content out of the past to which schools
> should introduce their students—a content not to be selected and
> listed arbitrarily in school and college catalogues as a uniform
> and required curriculum for all, but chosen lovingly and fearfully
> by teachers who seek to marry the peculiar promise of the stu-
> dent and the rich resources of our culture. Material that con-
> stitutes an open sesame to life's values for one student may defy
> the most skillful teacher's efforts with another. And for a very
> good reason. Values as such reside in Greek or Latin or mathe-
> matics in the same manner only that indigestion dwells within
> cold mince pies. The individual in each case is an important
> contributing agent. Values require for their emergence a living
> interplay between a unique personality and an appropriate sub-
> ject matter. Consequently there is no avoiding the necessity of
> selecting and adapting educative materials to groups and indi-
> viduals. Indeed, it is precisely this selection and adaption that
> defines the genius as well as the profession of teaching.[1]

Once it is realized that values are the resultants of several variables it
becomes clear that an "appropriate" subject matter will take character
from time, place, and circumstance. In one community, or with one
group of students, the struggle of the Romans to create and maintain a
government responsible to the people and mindful of their needs will
give perspective, depth, and meaning to present-day efforts at political

1. V. T. Thayer, *American Education Under Fire* (New York: Harper & Brothers,
1944), p. 178.

reform which contemporary material might lack. So, too, a comparative study of the relations between members of a Roman family and the family patterns of students in the class might help the latter to understand and appreciate the evolution of the family and to consider by comparison and contrast the role of child and parent which they would create for themselves. On the other hand, in a less historically minded community, with a class less gifted verbally, more reliance upon contemporary patterns might bring the desired results.

Not only do values change character from the interaction of subject matter and student, but they also vary with method employed. Take, for example, a freshman course in history as described by Elliott Dunlap Smith.

> Early in the course . . . the students are asked to study the essay on the Germans by Tacitus and to decide for themselves whether Tacitus had ever been in Germany, supporting their conclusions with evidence. Then they beat out in class, through the slow process of wrestling with their observations and their deductions, a judgment as to what validity the evidence of Tacitus has in giving them a picture of the Germans of that time, and what corrections and precautions they must take to bring their picture of the Germans into true focus. In the same way, the course proceeds, now exploring, for example, the bias of Gibbon, and now what is historical and what religious in the Acts of the Apostles.[2]

In the abstract, Tacitus is remote indeed from the immediate concerns of college freshmen. But when time is used as a conscious instrument for developing the ability to weigh and appraise the testimony of an observer and to exercise critical judgment, it ceases to operate as a dulling factor. With quite a different class group, however, these same characteristics of mind may require for their stimulation material of quite a different nature and on an altogether different level. Common to all situations, however, is the need to cultivate a habit of mind which confronts each problem with the queries: "How did you come to be what you are? What are your forebears? Your origins? Out of what background do you arise? What answers have men given to you in the

2. Elliott Dunlap Smith, "General Education in Practice," *Journal of Higher Education*, October 1951, p. 377.

past? With what results? How do the circumstances of successful solution in the past differ from the present? What data, then, are familiar, perhaps constant, and what novel, suggesting a new approach and perhaps a new solution?"

One function of the past then is to further perspective and to develop the habit of attacking a novel problem with an eye to its origins as well as its present context. Still another is to offset the limitations of provincialism and to accustom young people to the facts of diversity in life values. Nor need this realization lead, as some fear, to a serious undermining of purpose. Surely this is not the only alternative to a realization that what meets the deepest needs of one individual or one people may not do so for another. In *The Uses of the Past*, Herbert J. Muller asserts "that the admission of a principle of relativity and uncertainly should not simply be depressing."

> It enables a higher objectivity, a fuller understanding of present and past. It enables wiser choices among the possibilities open to us—among goods that are no less real because they are relative, and that are more relevant than arbitrary absolutes. Above all, this principle encourages a positive faith in positive values: of liberality, breadth of spirit, hospitality to new ideas, willingness to adventure, humility in admitting one's own fallibility and the limitations of the human mind—of the tolerance that is indispensable for the pursuit of truth, for social harmony, and for simple humanity. If these are not the highest values, none are more essential for world order and peace.[3]

The "Times" and Methods of Thinking

Intimately related to the use of the past is conscious emphasis upon methods of thinking which are keyed to a heterogeneous society and a period of history unique in rapidity of change, to a world in which values are plural and facts refuse to remain pinned down.

Serious consideration of these aspects of modern life suggests an appropriate emphasis on the intellectual task of the school. As the philoso-

3. Herbert J. Muller, *The Uses of the Past* (New York: Oxford University Press, 1952), p. 43. For an excellent discussion of the uses of the past in education, see Sidney Hook, *Education for Modern Man,* new ed. (New York: Knopf, 1963), pp. 119–37.

pher Alfred N. Whitehead has emphasized, the period in which we are living is unique in human history in that we can no longer assume, as men have safely assumed since Plato, that each generation will live amid conditions substantially the same as those which governed the "lives of its fathers and will transmit those conditions to mould with equal force the lives of its children." This follows from the fact, to continue with Whitehead, that in the past "the time-span of important change was considerably longer than that of a single life." Today, however, this time-span is "considerably shorter than that of human life, and, accordingly, our training must prepare individuals to face a novelty of conditions." [4]

The Changing Status of Facts

One moral to draw from Whitehead's analysis relates to the teaching of facts and principles. Too often these constitute the be all and end all of classroom instruction. Consequently, when classes increase in size, as they have on all levels of education in recent years, the temptation to evaluate the results of teaching in terms of facts memorized is difficult to resist. (Witness the widespread use of objective tests of a predominantly informational character on the college as well as the secondary and elementary school levels.)

Change both enhances and decreases the importance of facts. To acquire the habit of asking, "What are the facts of today as against those of yesterday?" is one way of avoiding error or of becoming quickly out of date. This puts a premium upon the techniques of searching out, organizing, and marshaling facts in every field of study. On the other hand, the ever present possibility that the validity of facts is of short duration requires constant checking and rechecking of their credentials. Nowhere is this more evident than in the field of science, where, presumably, the methods of procedure for identifying and validating facts and principles are most refined.

This suggests the importance of developing early the habit of regarding the facts of a situation with a healthy skepticism until they are rechecked, of accepting conclusions tentatively, of acting upon the basis of principles that one stands ready to revise in the light of new and more relevant data. Here, again, a word from Elliott Smith is pertinent.

4. Quoted in John L. Childs, *Education and Morals* (New York: Appleton-Century-Crofts, Inc., 1950), p. 113.

It is usually stated that general education is good in proportion as it serves to broaden or deepen a student's understanding of life as a whole. Our experience has taught us that this criterion is misleading. It is not that the concepts are wrong but that it is wrong in tense. After all, even in college, students are young and have a long life ahead of them. In this changing, perplexing, and indoctrination-ridden world, they must learn much more after graduation than they can possibly learn in school or college; and for the most part they must be their own teachers. What is important in any program of general education, therefore, is less what the students learn at the time than how well their education fits them to go on learning in the future.[5]

Few aims of education are mentioned more frequently than "teaching students to think." However, many teachers apparently equate sound reasoning with knowing a correct answer or understanding a statement. Yet, it is obvious that the ability to understand and recall a statement does not in itself provide the grounds for believing that statement. Moreover, correlations between knowledge and sound reasoning abilities are generally low to low-moderate.[6]

Even though the evidence is clear that there is no line where learning stops and thinking begins, and that children are developing reasoning abilities from the first years of their lives,[7] teachers not uncommonly believe that instruction in reasoning must necessarily be delayed until high school or college years. Many teachers hold the view that a child must first learn facts before he begins to think. Yet it is clear that experiences which focus almost entirely on developing the ability to reproduce the correct answer often weaken the abilities and attitudes associated with reflective thought.[8] Moreover, a number of studies have established the general facts that children in the early years of schooling can be taught to reason effectively and that such instruction

5. Smith, *op. cit.*, p. 374.
6. See, for example, David H. Russell and Henry R. Fea, "Research on Teaching Reading," *Handbook of Research on Teaching* (Chicago: Rand McNally and Co., 1963), p. 901.
7. Michael A. Wallach, "Research on Children's Thinking," in *Child Psychology*, Sixty-second Yearbook, National Society for the Study of Education (Chicago: University of Chicago Press, 1963), part I, pp. 237–40.
8. For a review of some relevant studies, see William H. Burton, Roland B. Kimball, and Richard L. Wing, *Education for Effective Thinking* (New York: Appleton-Century-Crofts, Inc., 1960), pp. 243–61.

does not lower but, on the contrary, usually raises significantly their level of knowledge of the facts they study while reflecting upon them.[9] Not children's abilities but teachers' beliefs and abilities are the primary obstacle in this matter.[10]

The largely undeveloped reflective capacities of children, the rapid advances in knowledge in many fields, and a world of changing individual and social situations calling for reflective ability, lend great weight to these words of Hullfish and Smith:

> Education, as opposed to deliberate indoctrination or normal cultural conditioning, is concerned with the process by which beliefs are formed and with the way in which they are held. Thus, *believing*, not a particular set of accepted beliefs, is the educational interest. This conclusion brings the reflective process to the fore in education. . . .[11]

The Traditional Emphasis of the School

An education that equips the individual to find his way in a precarious and uncertain world runs counter to the traditional emphasis and the original purposes of the school. In the colonial period, for example, the dominant purpose of the school was to transmit truths which could only be rejected on peril of eternal damnation. Religious orthodoxy was all-important, since the nonconformist was universally assumed to be a menace to himself and to his community. Sects differed in their conception of the truth but they were united in ascribing its source to an authority outside the experience of men. On this assumption John Cotton grounded his conviction that the desire for liberty is but the sinful prompting of the natural man. On this assumption, too, the early Puritans justified their conviction that the "elect" should govern in both church and state. Roger Williams, appealing to the same author-

9. See, for example, David H. Russell, "Higher Mental Processes," *Encyclopedia of Educational Research*, Chester W. Harris, ed. (New York: Macmillan Co., 1960), pp. 652–53, 657; N. E. Wallen, and others, "The Outcomes of Curriculum Modifications Designed to Foster Critical Thinking," *Journal of Educational Research*, July–August 1963, pp. 529–34.

10. In this connection, see Raymond B. Fox, "Difficulties in Developing Skill in Critical Thinking," *Journal of Educational Research*, April 1962, pp. 335–37.

11. H. Gordon Hullfish and Philip G. Smith, *Reflective Thinking: The Method of Education* (New York: Dodd, Mead and Co., 1961), p. 109.

ity, the Bible, argued on behalf of freedom of conscience and the separation of church and state. Neither questioned the assumption that truth is formulated *for* man rather than *by* man and is thus discovered rather than created.

This concept of truth as external long dictated the emphasis in schools. The methods of thinking employed and fostered bore little resemblance to those which spelled success on the farm, in trade and commerce, or in the budding new industries which quickly developed on American soil. Habits of mind symbolized by the term "Yankee ingenuity" seldom found their way into the classroom, even when teachers themselves engaged in original research. Thinking was restricted, rather, to deductions from a known principle or an axiom stated in the textbook, much as a minister of the gospel develops the moral of his sermon from a quotation taken from the Scriptures. First-hand experience, if recognized at all, was considered a poor second to the printed word, and children were taught that new truths are in reality old truths which have been lying dormant, much as the sleeping beauty of the fairy story awaited the reviving kiss of her lover.

Increasing Importance of Scientific Methods of Thinking

The gradual conquest of the frontier brought a change in methods of thinking which eventually penetrated the insulated walls of the school. In long-established and settled communities the practices which men follow successfully in agriculture, trade, and commerce, as well as in their associations with each other, assume the character of fixed principles or major premises in a syllogism from which the answers to individual problems can be deduced as they arise in the daily course of living. But when the farmer moves into new territory where new conditions of soil and climate confront him with novel problems and a contradiction of old precepts, the familiar axioms which have dictated when to plant, how to fertilize, and when to reap no longer hold good. New premises are called for and qualities of inventiveness assume an importance not previously accorded them.

It is precisely this necessity of coping with new conditions and discovering new processes and techniques, together with the readiness of a restless people, constantly on the move, to accept the new on the basis of equality with the old, that has transformed the American continent. Necessity has been the mother of invention, and the inventive spirit has furthered not only the development of modern science and technology but also a conscious formulation of methods of thinking better designed to control the novel.

To be sure, this change in attitude toward the natural environment is not exclusively American. Its origins antedate the discovery and settlement of the New World, and its revolutionary achievements in thought and action are written large in European history. In America, however, men were confronted with a unique situation, the repeated opportunity and necessity to create and re-create the physical and social conditions of a civilized existence. Successive generations cleared the forest, tamed the soil, and organized new communities, thus creating their own political, social, and civic institutions as well as their own customs and laws, manners and morals. Having done so, they moved on to a new location where their children proceeded to repeat the process.

The Influence of the Frontier upon Conceptions of Law and Morality

For one who establishes his residence on virgin soil and builds a community in cooperation with others of somewhat different background, it is indeed difficult to believe that institutions and ideas have a fixed, eternal character. Here the customs, laws, and morals originate largely with the people who make up the community, and the habit of evaluating institutions by their effects upon people comes naturally. Man, in the best sense, is thus the measure of all measures.

The American's notion that institutions are born of man and are designed to serve his needs led him also to change the age-old concept of the nature and purpose of law. Contrast, for example, the concept of law as expressed by the distinguished jurist, Chancellor Kent, in 1836, with that of Oliver Wendell Holmes some fifty years later. According to Chancellor Kent, "The law, as a science, is only a collection of general principles, founded on the moral law and in the common sense of mankind, and applied to particular cases as they arise, by the diligence of the bar and the erudition of the courts." [12]

12. From *An Address*, Boston, 1836, p. 6. Quoted in Richard D. Mosier's *Making the American Mind* (New York: Kings Crown Press, 1947), p. 63.

Here the law is viewed as an externally formulated body of general principles derived from moral laws that are likewise essentially foreign to the native spirit of mankind. Consequently, the correct application to specific cases is more likely to follow upon strict adherence to the rules of a syllogism than from a tender concern for what might be unique and individual in the case at issue. As the court sees it, justice is none too closely related to consequences. "Right for right's sake, though the heavens fall" marks the decisions of a just judge.

Doubtless it was reaction against a too rigid application of justice so conceived which prompted one jurist to remark that the wise decisions of Western courts followed more from an ignorance of precedents than from their knowledge of the law!

By 1881, the year in which Oliver Wendell Holmes published his lectures on *The Common Law,* the practical conditions under which Americans had created their institutions had prepared many to accept a more dynamic and experimental conception of law. As Holmes observed,

> The growth of the law is legislative. And this in a deeper sense than that what the courts declare to have always been the law is in fact new. It is legislative in its grounds. The very considerations which judges most rarely mention, and always with an apology, are the secret root from which the law draws all the juices of life. I mean, of course, considerations of what is expedient for the community concerned. Every important principle which is developed by litigation is in fact and at bottom the result of more or less definitely understood views of public policy; most generally, to be sure, under our practice and traditions, the unconscious result of instinctive preferences and inarticulate convictions, but none the less traceable to views of public policy in the last analysis. And as the law is administered by able and experienced men, who know too much to sacrifice good sense to a syllogism, it will be found that, when ancient rules maintain themselves . . . new reasons more fitted to the time have been found for them, and they gradually receive a new content, and at last a new form, from the grounds to which they have been transplanted.[13]

13. Quoted in Max Lerner, *The Mind and the Faith of Justice Holmes* (Boston: Little, Brown & Co., 1945), pp. 54–55.

As with law, so with certain aspects of morality. Diversity in background, characteristic of most American communities, has fostered competition for men's loyalties in matters spiritual as well as things material, and the principle that "by their works ye shall know them" has seemed to many as appropriate to apply in choosing between rival conceptions of the good life as in other areas.

At the same time, Americans have been and still are a religious people. Moreover, they are disposed to take their religion seriously. Despite the differences that separate Protestant from Catholic, or Catholic from Jew, and even Protestant from Protestant, one common assumption has run through the faith that each holds: the assumption that religion is both the source and the indispensable undergirding of morality. From which it follows that only a valid religion can yield a valid morality!

Here would seem to be the seeds of an inevitable conflict; and, indeed, rivalry and conflict there has been. On the whole, however, a spirit of tolerance and the disposition to live and let live in matters of religion characterizes the American today, in contrast with an earlier insistence upon orthodoxy and a none too gentle handling of the nonconformist. If we ask ourselves how this has come about, the answer is found in the use of two concepts of morality without overly conscious awareness of their contradiction. The one, sectarian and authoritarian in character, regulates relations within the family and parochial group, dictating how one should spend the Sabbath, whether he should smoke or drink, play cards or dance, practice birth control. The other, secular and more specifically public in its applications, is a morality of common agreements which the individual and his neighbors have worked out together and come to accept as standards with which to channel their common interests, resolve conflicts, and, in general, to ease and free relations with each other.

In this manner American communities have narrowed the range of sectarian morality and widened that of the secular.

Doubtless the emergence of the nonsectarian school aided this trend. Originating in the Middle Colonies, it quickly spread into the North and the South and the rapidly expanding West. Characteristic of its instruction was a centering upon elements of faith common to all religious groups within the community and the bypassing of tenets upon which its patrons disagreed. This formula was followed by

Americans in the development of public education in communities as multicolored as the traditional coat of many colors.

None the less, nonsectarian instruction perpetuated two assumptions in education which, relevant and appropriate as they might have been a century ago, many challenge today.

Contributions and Limitations of Nonsectarian Education

First, it assumed that pupils are to remain passive in the learning process and that teaching is a procedure in which the ideas of the instructor or the assertions of the textbook are to be conveyed to the mind of the student without change en route. Mansfield's *American Education,* published in 1851, put this neatly as follows: "What is the business of the teacher? . . . His position is strictly that of a conveyor of knowledge—moral and intellectual—to a yet unoccupied and growing mind. To do this successfully, requires that his instruction should carry to that waiting mind a conviction of its *truth,* and that he should also *connect* that truth with the *duties* of life."

Second, nonsectarian instruction assumed that items of controversy were to receive silent treatment in the school. In short, a device which originated in the effort to avoid the heat of controversy in a society religiously plural and highly sensitive to creedal differences was extended as well to other areas of significant difference. Were this principle adhered to logically, nothing but the commonly agreed upon would find a legitimate place in the curriculum of the school, and young people would emerge from the classroom, as, indeed, they have done all too frequently, wanting in the discipline of effective methods for coping with problems upon which men disagree and the final answers to which may be known only to the future.[14]

An Intellectual Discipline Relevant to a Pluralistic Society

As indicated earlier, the principles by which people direct their lives in a one-patterned society easily become identified with the inner struc·

14. See, in this connection, Peter A. Soderbergh, "Dogmatism and the Public School Teacher, *Journal of Teacher Education,* September 1964, pp. 245–51.

ture of the universe. Once these life patterns become plural, however, a stubborn insistence that my neighbor mold his life according to my sacred convictions may do violence to convictions equally sacred to him. It may even threaten the integrity of his personality. At the same time, there is no avoiding the fact that we live in an interrelated society, one in which interests overlap and the way in which each lives his life becomes of increasing moment to others. How then, can we manage not only to dwell together in comparative peace, but to transform our associations into mutual benefit?

Lawrence Frank provides one answer in an article entitled "Responsible Living." Having developed the thesis that contemporary changes in our political, economic, civic, and social life render less obvious a single path of duty or responsibility, he insists that this confusion is not altogether bad. Characteristic today is an increasing sensitiveness to the consequences of our actions upon the lives of those affected by them. Not only is the "right" less easily identified in specific situations than it once was, but each of us is less content to follow the maxim of "right for right's sake" regardless of the consequences to others. That is, the situation or context of a problem as well as a general principle looms large in arriving at a decision. As Frank puts it:

> What today seems significant is that we are increasingly evaluating what people do or refrain from doing, not as measured by impersonal rules and conformity to super-human standards, or obedience to legal and moral codes, but by its meaning and significance for others as personalities. We are realizing that, in whatever we do, we should have, to use an old Quaker word, a *concern* for others—a feeling of sensitive awareness of what we are doing to and for others, how others feel and what we may be evoking from them.[15]

Now, if we seek a formula with which to justify and explain this increasing tendency to resolve moral issues and conflicts of interest in terms of the effect of any decision upon the personalities involved rather than in the logical deductions from an abstract principle, we find it in the concept of a democracy of absolutes.

15. Lawrence Frank, "Responsible Living," *The Standard,* January–February 1951, p. 208.

Applying the Golden Rule to Absolutes

But this concept is double-edged in its application. It guarantees to each individual or group freedom to think and to act in accordance with its own absolutes in private life and many of the more personal relationships. But once men venture into the public market place, their absolutes are required to discard their royal and sovereign robes and to clothe themselves in a garb befitting a democracy in which loyalties are free to compete on an equal and fair basis. In other words, when absolutes overlap or conflict, they are to be evaluated in terms of their potential contribution to the general welfare rather than by their pedigrees.

Seeing the World Through the Eyes of Others [16]

The first step leading toward peace and understanding in a world of plural values is thus an application of the Golden Rule to absolutes. But this is only the first step. Second is the disposition and habit to enter sympathetically and appreciatively into the lives of our neighbors, with a view to seeing the world as nearly as possible through their eyes.

There was a time when traveling abroad was considered to be the last stage in the completion of a formal education. This was intended, at its best, to confront the student with the customs and manners and life values of a people different from his own. The hope was that the values he was ultimately to make his own would be ripened and seasoned from observing the customs and codes of others. Rich in possibilities as travel is, the experience of a critical comparison and contrast of values cannot be safely left to the last days of schooling. Rather should the discipline begin in the primary school, with the young child's friendly interest in people who differ from his own, and continue as an intercultural education through the elementary and secondary school and college. It is this that gives plausibility to recent emphasis upon a curriculum based upon the "great books" in school and college and the central place of the humanities in general education. But it is also this

16. For discussions of relevant points, see Warren G. Bennis, Kenneth D. Benne, and Robert Chin, eds., *The Planning of Change* (New York: Holt, Rinehart and Winston, 1961), pp. 141–48, 250–76, 408–20, 456–76, 503–58.

purpose which reveals the limitations in one arbitrary list of books for a student to read. Not only will a relevant selection of books vary with individuals and local circumstance, but the "great books" taken alone are insufficient. To them should be added opportunity for enrichment of experience in art and music, the science laboratory and industrial shop, and, above all, first-hand contact with people under conditions that further seeing life as others see it.

William James once remarked that no one has adequately refuted another's philosophy until he not only has laid bare the principles of the rival system, together with their limitations, but has also clarified what caused his opponent to see life as he does. So it is with all conceptions of life with which one must come to terms. As Lawrence Frank has said, wherever men live they encounter persistent problems of living. The different answers they devise for these problems constitute their assumptions about nature and the world. But since all experience is limited, no assumption does full justice to the needs or the potentialities of living of all people in all times and places. This should humble the claims of any system of values. To acquire the disposition and skill, as well as the courage, to sift and winnow from the past and the contemporary scene that which will mature and ripen and render ever more relevant one's own life assumptions is the never ending purpose of a liberal education. Perhaps it was this realization which led Pascal to remark, "Thought makes the whole dignity of man; therefore endeavor to think well—that is the only morality."

The application of the Golden Rule to all contenders for truth and an honest attempt to afford a fair field for all rivals for men's loyalties comprise two aspects of an intellectual discipline keyed to a pluralistic world. A third is what Max Otto termed creative bargaining.[17]

The Art of Creative Bargaining

The term "creative bargaining" is not altogether a happy one to apply to the process we have in mind, since there is a tendency to identify bargaining with the disposition to accept half a loaf today with the expectancy of further gains tomorrow. (Perhaps "creative consensus"

17. "Creative Bargaining," *The Standard*, March 1951, pp. 263–69. See also, Max Otto, *The Human Enterprise* (New York: F. S. Crofts and Co., Inc., 1940), chap. V.

would be a better term.) Bargaining, or compromise, so conceived testifies neither to growth in the understanding of the needs and interests of others nor to change in the evaluation of one's own position. It suggests merely a shrewd adaptation of means to inflexible ends. What Otto had in mind was the possibility of a wiser and more generous formulation of objectives resulting from conference, deliberation, investigation, and an earnest attempt on the part of the participants in a discussion to put themselves in the place of others.[18]

There are, to be sure, occasions when creative bargaining cannot run its full course, and education in the art of compromise requires full recognition of this fact. Disputes between sovereign national powers often are of this character. Frequently the possibilities of agreement hinge upon the ability of neutrals to persuade the disputants to bypass their absolutes and to give serious consideration to the consequences of indefinite deadlock or precipitous action not only upon themselves but upon the entire world. Thus, for example, one political scientist states that deliberations within the United Nations have "tended to induce the American government to accord respectful attention to the future in forming its own present policies. On the whole this incentive is a useful prod to farsightedness. . . ."[19]

Agreement in cases of this character involves an appeal to an overarching ideal more compelling than the principles in conflict or to an aroused sensitiveness to the context of the problem sufficient to bring about the weighing of principle against contingent circumstance.

The controversy over the teaching of religion in public schools illustrates further the difficulties which often beset creative bargaining. According to the principle of separation of church and state, as interpreted by the Supreme Court, public schools are forbidden to engage in religious instruction. This does not preclude, however, an objective and impartial study of religion. Nevertheless, few communities are willing to subject religious tenets to comparative study. They are satisfied only when school authorities indoctrinate their pupils in one or another religious faith or in a "common core" of religious doctrine. Lacking a willingness to subject religious tenets to scrutiny, most

18. For an analysis within this same general orientation, see the little volume by Kenneth D. Benne, *Education in the Quest for Identity and Community* (Columbus, Ohio: College of Education, Ohio State University, 1962).

19. H. B. Westerfield, *The Instruments of America's Foreign Policy* (New York: T. Y. Crowell Co., 1963), p. 508.

schools have found it expedient to exclude from the curriculum all study of issues in religion upon which men do not see eye to eye.

Nor is religion unique in this respect. In recent years numerous groups have come forward to censor textbooks and to control the manner in which teachers deal with controversial issues. They wish no unbiased or impartial weighing of evidence, since, as they see it, there is but one side to a question. Failing to appreciate that the issues upon which people are divided often constitute the growing points of society and thus, when properly handled, afford the young most fruitful opportunities from which to acquire methods of thinking and ways of living of inestimable value in the contemporary world, they seek to confine the classroom either to the innocuous or to questions of a hothouse variety.

Pressure groups within the community and well-meaning but overly ardent or intolerant advocates of special causes likewise present obstacles to the educational handling of controversial issues and moot questions, since they generate an emotional atmosphere that precludes suspending judgment pending a calm and dispassionate hearing of all points of view. Often, too, in the discussion of an issue the members of a class generate a heat that militates against light. Under these conditions the instructor performs a valuable service when he insists upon a "cooling off period," or discontinuing discussion until the group can demonstrate a proper degree of maturity.

The atmosphere which permits or forbids the handling of critical issues in the classroom pervades the community as well as the school. Fortunately, schools start with an initial advantage in that the average community gives lip service, at least, to the principle that it is the school's function to educate people to have an open mind. But, like a wayward pupil, it needs to be reminded of its convictions and the implications of these convictions.

The principal of one school reports a happy incident of this character. A teacher in social science succeeded in stimulating discussions of controversial issues to the point where they overflowed the classroom and extended into the homes of his students. A number of parents found their convictions challenged and protested to the principal that the classroom was being used to promote false and dangerous notions. They demanded either an end to discussion or an acceptable weighing of conclusions.

Instead of yielding to this pressure, or advising the teacher to "go slow," the principal invited the irate parents to spend an evening in his home and there to meet the offending teacher. This they agreed to do. In this informal atmosphere, the parents were led to state their objections to the procedures of the classroom. The instructor described the objectives he sought and reviewed some of the questions discussed. In the discussion which followed he inquired, innocently, of the group how they would have dealt with one of these questions. The suggestions that followed were in no way unanimous and before long an animated debate was in progress. So rewarding, indeed, was the evening that it concluded with the organization of the group into a discussion club!

Not all community objections have such happy outcomes. Few instructors are as successful in calming worried citizens or in helping them to see that in areas of controversy the function of the school, as the representative of the public at large, is to promote understanding rather than to grind the ax of any one segment of community opinion.

Collective bargaining between capital and labor constitutes one field of creative bargaining. Certainly, unions and managements often resort to force—disciplinary actions against workers, strikes, and so on. By and large, however, since the extension of collective bargaining in and after the 1930s, "resort to force seems to be a steadily declining practice." [20] Both unions and managements have moved in the direction of more responsible (that is, responsive to each other and to public interests) settlement of disputes through negotiation, arbitration, outside evaluation, and the like.[21] The "Quaker Way" of dealing with knotty problems [22] testifies to its extension in still other areas where the interests or the ideas of one impinge upon those of another. Morris Llewellyn Cooke has described the manner in which this method is gaining ground in the work of committees and commissions in government and "is being adopted by numerous directors of public and private organizations in various parts of the country."

In striking contrast with traditional methods of debate and reliance

20. Edwin F. Beal and Edward D. Wickersham, *The Practice of Collective Bargaining* (Homewood, Ill.: R. D. Irwin, Inc., 1959), p. 632.
21. Sumner H. Slichter, and others, *The Impact of Collective Bargaining on Management* (Washington, D.C.: The Brookings Institution, 1960), p. 958.
22. See Jessamyn West, ed., *The Quaker Reader* (New York: Viking Press, 1962), pp. 437–42, 463–72, 479–87.

on majority rule, which, according to Cooke, assume "there exists a
divergence of interests rather than a common purpose," the Quaker
Way concentrates upon the importance of a consensus.

The first step is to divorce the individual as nearly as possible from
emotional identification with one position as against another. For this
reason, in a Quaker meeting,

> . . . a subject is introduced not by presenting a resolution but
> by "reading a query." This is usually done by the chairman—or
> "Clerk of the meeting," as he is known in Quaker groups. Such a
> departure from parliamentary order is by no means a petty one,
> for by this simple device, the issue seems to come from the group
> as a whole instead of being sponsored by one faction within it.
>
> Various points of view on the subject are expressed by individ-
> ual members—whoever wishes to contribute. But strong words,
> provocative language and repetitive discourse are taboo: mem-
> bers are encouraged to speak just once on a given point, and only
> after careful thought. And, most significant of all, the individual
> speaks not simply as a man, expressing his own conscience but as
> the voice of the group addressing itself to the issue at hand. If a
> contrary viewpoint is raised, it is considered as if it were one's
> own for the purpose of treating it objectively. "Getting under the
> weight" of the other man's doubts is the term the Quakers some-
> times use to describe this attitude of respect for a minority view-
> point.
>
> If conflict at any point becomes so heated as to make an agree-
> ment doubtful, the Clerk may halt discussion and ask members to
> consider the subject for a while in thoughtful silence.[23]

These illustrations suggest that a new and more democratic method
of conference, deliberation, and decision are in process of evolution,
methods more sensitively attuned to a complex and interdependent society than are the older methods of debate in which protagonists for
one side strive to overwhelm those of another. They also render clear
that success in arriving at a consensus turns upon a discipline in cooperative thinking no less rigorous than the individualistic procedures
of the past. Just as the schools have sought to develop in their students

23. Morris Llewellyn Cooke, "The Quaker Way Wins New Adherents," *The New
York Times Magazine,* June 17, 1951, p. 21.

the skills and techniques requisite for the one, so it is now incumbent upon them to provide opportunities for the acquisition of the other —and to determine when the one is appropriate and when the other. For this reason, it may be helpful to identify the crucial factors that make for either a consensus or a generous understanding of problems upon which honest men disagree.

Crucial Factors in the Conference Method

First is the habit of insisting upon a knowledge of relevant facts.[24] To be sure, the method of debate is not unmindful of the importance of facts, but it stresses a selection and organization of data favorable to the winning of converts. The method of conference, in contrast, is less biased, since the question under consideration has been posed as a query, not as a bone of contention.

When facts seemingly conflict or differences in their implication become obvious, there is need for further data. A wise moderator, at such a time, will assign the task of further research to individuals who most need training in objectivity, with the injunction that they are now the servants of the group, not partisans!

It is one thing, of course, to sense the need for additional data with which to clarify a problem and another thing to gather, organize, and present them. What the latter involves will vary with the nature of the problem under study. It calls for the exercise of many skills, techniques, and methods. Intelligent participation in problem solving, be it individual research or group study, rests upon both prior and supplementary training in methods that are pedagogically different: the methods of the laboratory, of historical inquiry, of the social sciences, of weighing values. To acquaint students with these methods and to enable them to determine when one as against another is called for is one of the functions of general education.

Some years ago a class in elementary science undertook to dissect a chicken as a practical means of identifying the organs of the body and its bony structure. Not only was the flesh removed but the skeleton was taken apart as well. This being done, several pupils suggested that the

---

24. H. Shepard and R. R. Blake, "Changing Behavior through Cognitive Change," *Human Organization,* Summer 1962, pp. 88–96. This reference elaborates on some of the points discussed in this section of the text.

bones be restored to their original position. No sooner said than attempted, and with success—up to one final bone. This stubbornly refused to reveal its original position. Where did it belong? One theory after another was proposed, tested, and found wanting. As the end of the period approached closer and closer, tension and frustration mounted. Finally, one boy exclaimed, "Let's vote on where it belongs."

This experience afforded the teacher a rare opportunity to impress upon the children the difference between the type of situation in which voting may lead to a satisfactory solution and one in which it is valueless. When different methods are thus involved, the school can be helpful in leading pupils to appreciate the circumstances under which one method or the other is applicable.

But let us return to our unsolved problem. The need for additional facts temporarily halts discussion. Emotional squalls may also inhibit intelligent consideration of points at issue. When these occur, it is the responsibility of the moderator to order a cooling-off period.

Not all cooling-off periods succeed in a permanent reduction of temperature, but—in education, particularly—the values sought derive less from the ultimate solution of a problem than from the habits distilled in the process. The discipline of recognizing when emotion is blocking intelligence is one of the lessons a school can impart. For a class to observe that it lacks sufficient maturity with which to continue a discussion may constitute in itself a valuable educational experience.

Finally comes the stage of summing up or concluding a discussion and evaluating what has been done. Here again each situation is unique and the concluding session will take its character from this fact. The class may have discovered that the problem must continue as an open question, that circumstances do not permit a definitive conclusion, or that the best authorities on the subject are themselves divided. Other problems are equally inconclusive as regards evidence, but the circumstances may require action on the basis of a tentative judgment. Still other discussions may have ended in a consensus, but even in these instances the participants should have learned that time plays tricks upon certainty and that what seems altogether evident today may be under suspicion tomorrow.

Whatever the outcome of a specific discussion, the training it yields is not complete until its members have summarized and appraised what has happened. The urgency of this training is evident to anyone who observes the reaction of many who listen to a lecture or a discussion on the radio or television. How eagerly they seize upon one point with which they agree or disagree to the neglect of all others! They have lacked experience in considering an argument as a whole, or the relation of one item to its qualifying context. But, if we reflect upon the future use of the radio and television as media for the discussion of critical issues, the discipline of listening so that one acquires what John Locke termed "a round-about knowledge" of a topic assumes increasing importance. Consequently we must turn again to the school for the development of the art of listening, an art that comes only from the necessity of repeated listening and of reporting fairly and objectively upon what one has heard and summarizing for others as well as for oneself the "pros" and the "cons" of a discussion.

Cooperative thinking, as we have hurriedly described it, demands the exercise of a number of functions for which the school can train its students: (1) the functions of a moderator, whose duty it is to subordinate his own feelings and to insure a fair hearing for all points of view, to keep his finger upon the pulse of the group, and to identify occasions when additional facts are required, a cooling-off period is advisable, or the time is ripe for concluding the discussion; (2) the function of fact-gathering or resource leader; (3) the function of observer and critic of the discussion; and, (4) the function of a direct participant whose thinking has been refined and tempered by repeated practice in these other functions.

Opportunities to develop these habits, dispositions, and skills abound both in classrooms and the general life of the school—wherever, indeed, ideas and interests come into conflict. When so used, conflict and disagreement constitute happy occasions for developing the habits of mind and character upon which our contemporary world places a premium, for, to repeat, we live in a world of rapid change in which confirmed ways of thinking, feeling, and acting are constantly being challenged. It is a world of increasing interdependence, of chain reactions, in which no man and no people can safely live in isolation. It is a world of variegated communities and plural cultures with contrasting and contradictory life values, but a world, nevertheless, in which men of different codes and standards must traffic with each other in accordance with principles and procedures which promote a community of interests. Given this kind of a world, an important task of the school would seem to be to develop the logic and the ethics of thinking which might encourage even the lion and the lamb to deal with each other in peace and good will.

Finally, it should be carefully noted that we have not advocated the intellectually and morally calamitous position of equating the true and the good with the consensus in a society or group. A consensus is itself to be evaluated in terms of "the logic and ethics of thinking." Is it constructed in accordance with the principles of right reason? Does it develop, within a group and among groups, the enlargement of vision and of sharing upon which individuals can thrive? Does it leave room for differences, even fundamental disagreements, within a set of procedural rules which provide for continuing and generous inquiry? [25]

The Curriculum and Methods of Thinking

Little has been said about the content of the curriculum. This is indeed relevant to any consideration of the intellectual task of the school. It is unwise, however, to assume an arbitrary and dogmatic attitude with respect to the essential content of education above the level of "primary adjustments" or the minimum essentials of the elementary and early years of the secondary school. Most people would agree that every individual is handicapped severely in modern life if he lacks facility in elementary mathematics, is unable to read simple material in the vernacular, is unable to express himself clearly in oral and written language, is ignorant of the facts and principles of science which enter into everyday living. But precisely at what point requirements in these various fields should end for students on the secondary level is by no means conclusive. In a world of shifting emphasis in the demands of society and the needs of young people, it is likely that the answer to the question of when general education should end and special education begin will always vary with time and place and individual. Consider, for example, the suddenness with which educators, as well as the public at large, have awakened to the serious consequences which may ensue as a result of the neglect of science in the schools. Revolutionary

25. For an excellent analysis of the relations of consensus theory to democracy and the logic of social inquiry, see Irving L. Horowitz, "Consensus, Conflict and Cooperation: A Sociological Inventory," *Social Forces*, December 1962, pp. 177–88.

changes in technological development at home and abroad bear directly upon what constitutes an appropriate curriculum in school and college.

Nor is the problem clarified by insisting merely that the "permanent studies" should comprise the heart of the curriculum, since this in no way solves the problem of what specific content within these studies is appropriate today in contrast with yesterday. Probably the best we can do is to seek agreement on the broad fields which should be included in the program of each school, leaving more specific definition of content within each field or area to the results of a cooperative study by curriculum planning groups within each state and locality: teachers, administrators, students of adolescent development and of society, experts within the various fields. By and large, there is unanimity of belief that these fields should include language and literature, the social studies (history, sociology, geography, psychology, anthropology), mathematics, foreign languages, science, the fine and practical arts. To these conventional fields many would add, either as subjects for special courses or as inherent parts of the above, experience which looms large in importance from a functional analysis of significant "relationships of living": personal-social, social-civic, economic, personal development.

The past few decades have witnessed much discussion about "erasing subject matter lines" or developing "integrated," "problem-centered," or (at the college level) divisional courses. With the development of the generally subject-centered "new curricula" in recent years, interest in this movement has notably declined. However, much can be said on behalf of this approach as a corrective for the insulation of subjects which characterizes instruction in many schools—an insulation, incidentally, more or less inevitable when the preparation of teachers becomes overly specialized or, at the other extreme, when teachers are required to teach subjects for which their preparation is inadequate.

Nor are the conventional divisions within a given field, such as science or mathematics or the social sciences, pedagogically justified in all instances. Mathematics teaching, for example, might well improve were algebra, geometry, trigonometry, and calculus taught with less emphasis upon rigid sequence and greater attention to the evolving structure of mathematics and the lives of students. Just as, outside the school, the psychologist sometimes advances his work best when he draws upon biology or physiology, or the physiologist upon chemistry, so, within the curriculum of the school, learning is often enriched and vitalized by crossing over or "erasing" traditional subject-matter lines.

The theory of the "core curriculum" illustrates the point we are making. Where this has been most successful, attention has centered upon helping young people to understand and to cope with "growing pains" within relationships of living commonly omitted from or insufficiently emphasized by the traditional subjects. Consequently, by concentrating upon life problems without necessary reference to the lines which separate science from social science, literature from art, history and economics from psychology, students are helped to face their "developmental tasks" more effectively than in a school which adheres to traditional subject-matter divisions. Furthermore, within the subjects themselves, certain areas of investigation are dependent upon materials drawn from other subjects. For example, a problem in the social studies having to do with public health cannot be solved without drawing upon science, and many problems in science cannot be solved without the aid of mathematics. Good teaching, in other words, often requires ignoring rather than adhering to the dictum that each subject should stick to its last.

Granted this, it is nevertheless true that great emphasis should be given to the differences in the methods and procedures used in the various disciplines. To be sure, certain rules of right reason and good evidence are common to all disciplines. Nevertheless, each of the disciplines involves the use of a more or less unique and distinctive set of intellectual tools which the student must acquire. The procedures employed in solving a problem in a laboratory science differ in many respects from the procedures employed in resolving a historical question or in determining the relevance of one moral principle as against another in a conflict between individuals. Again, despite some basic structural similarities, language and mathematics represent quite distinctive methodologies in the analysis of experience. The art approach and the realm of values in literature yield still other disciplines. To help young people acquire the basic concepts and the methods of thinking appropriate to each is one of the most important contributions of education. Without this discipline and these methods, one's knowledge scarcely goes beyond the level of information about specific items of little permanent value.

The New Curricula and the Structure of a Discipline

Since the late 1950s, stimulated by the knowledge explosion, the educational demands of a technological society, and public anxiety concerning the Soviet Union's advances in science, subject specialists have been turning to a field they had long neglected—the school curriculum. A multiplying number of curriculum projects, supported by public and private funds, are under way. These projects have centered especially on the designing of new curricula in mathematics and the natural sciences. However, this dangerous imbalance is being somewhat corrected as the curriculum ferment expands into the social studies and the humanities.

The subject specialists have found that much of the traditional school curricula was obsolete. Schools were teaching (and, in general, still continue to teach) arithmetic, algebra, and geometry as separate subjects, not as aspects of evolving, unified mathematical structures. Elementary school children were spending much more time studying American Indian culture than, for example, Russian or French culture.

One of the potentially valuable characteristics associated with the curriculum-reform movement is the idea that students should be taught not an encyclopedic collection of facts, but the basic principles and concepts and methodology which impart meaning and organization to the details and data of a subject. Often the term "the structure of a discipline" is used to refer to the substantive concepts of a discipline; less often, the term includes the methodological rules and principles. Since these concepts and principles are basic and are involved in all the content of a discipline, they can be taught, as Professor Bruner has said, in some "honest" fashion at all levels.

Another characteristic of some of the new curricula is the emphasis on having pupils learn principles by the "discovery method," through dealing with situations from which the principles can be extracted by the pupils, rather than by having teachers tell the pupils about the principles.

Interest and reflection certainly can be stimulated by methods other than the discovery method. However, as Cronbach remarks, the value of discovery lies "in two transfer effects: in attitude toward a field of knowledge, and in improved ability to discover principles." A student who has discovered a generalization, Cronbach continues, "has become less dependent on authority. He has a new sense of his own intellectual power and a clearer view of the nature of knowledge. He expects other generalizations to make sense, and also begins to understand the limitations of knowledge derived from evidence of the sort he used." [26]

As we have indicated, the curriculum-reform movement has many promising aspects. Here, in the interest of realizing as much of this promise as possible, certain cautionary notes should be sounded.

Many teachers and some of the leaders in the movement (including Jerome Bruner, who was one of the earliest formulators of certain ideas which characterize the movement) [27] often speak as if a discipline has *a* single structure. Bruner writes, for example, that "every subject has a structure, a beauty, a rightness." [28] Yet it is clear that many sciences—and, even more, many social and humanities studies—have more than one structure, and that even in the advanced sciences, structures are not neat and complete. There is more than one economic theory. In the field of English there exist the conceptual systems of traditional grammar, several varieties of "structural grammar," and the new "transformational grammar." As Graham C. Wilson has remarked, there is good reason to doubt that "an over-all structure in the discipline called English can be satisfactorily demonstrated." [29] There are numerous conceptual problems within physical theory, including relativity theory.

Often the assumption is made that only a single theory or set of principles can explain and predict the phenomena studied by a discipline. This is an erroneous view of the complex process of verification. Were this view correct, numerous theories—which did explain and predict certain historically limited data—would not have been abandoned, as they have been. The teacher who can control a child and predict his behavior does not necessarily have an adequate understanding of the

26. Lee J. Cronbach, *Educational Psychology*, 2d ed. (New York: Harcourt, Brace and World, Inc., 1963), p. 380.
27. Jerome S. Bruner, *The Process of Education* (Cambridge: Harvard University Press, 1960).
28. Jerome S. Bruner, "Structures in Learning," *NEA Journal*, March 1963, p. 26. See also, Jerome S. Bruner, "Introduction: The New Educational Technology," *American Behavioral Scientist*, November 1962, pp. 5–8; Shirley H. Engle, "Thoughts in Regard to Revision," *Social Education*, April 1963, pp. 182–84, 196.
29. "The Structure of English," in *The Structure of Knowledge and the Curriculum*, G. W. Ford and L. Pugno, eds. (Chicago: Rand McNally and Co., 1964), p. 85.

child. His ideas about what motivates the child or about how the child will behave as an adult may be quite wrong.

The principles of verification involve not only the concepts and the methodological rules of a discipline, but also general principles of sound reason and good evidence. They also involve concepts studied in other disciplines—as when an economist uses an assumption about motivation, an assumption which he might "verify," to some degree, by looking at psychological, sociological, and anthropological data.

What we are cautioning against is not the search for structure, but the search for one rather fixed structure which can be grasped without a wide array of considerations that go far beyond intuitive guessing and picking up of hints that may be built into instructional procedures and the materials presented.[30] (Pupils can be led to "discover" *only* a principle toward which they have been carefully, if unobtrusively, guided.) What we are cautioning against is the definite trend toward insulated, even if improved, subjects.[31]

There is also some tendency to regard the structure of a discipline as the main, if not sole, guide for the selection and organization of materials in a subject. The term "logical" often is applied to an organization based on this criterion, the implication being that any other kind of organization is not logical. Clearly, however, not only psychological principles and the needs and abilities of particular students, but also the relations of one discipline to others and to vital social problems and values must also be considered in developing a curriculum. Moreover, as we have indicated already, to provide students with experience in defining problems and in using materials from a number of fields may be crucial in the effort to achieve some worthy intellectual aims.

The archaic conditions of large portions of the school curriculum which, in part, have led to the possible overemphasis on insulated subjects, demonstrate the need for a "continuing self-renewal of the current curriculum reform movements." [32] This effort should involve the

30. The writings of Joseph J. Schwab contain many illuminating discussions and illustrations of problems involved in formulating and teaching the structures of disciplines. See, for example, Joseph J. Schwab, "Structures of the Disciplines: Meanings and Significances," in *The Structure of Knowledge and the Curriculum*, pp. 6–30; Joseph J. Schwab, "The Teaching of Science as Enquiry," in *The Teaching of Science*, Joseph J. Schwab and Paul F. Brandwein (Cambridge: Harvard University Press, 1962), pp. 3–103.

31. John I. Goodlad, *School Curriculum Reform in the United States* (New York: Fund for the Advancement of Education, 1964), p. 78.

32. *Ibid.*, p. 85.

institution of cooperative relations among the various specialists concerned with education—subject specialists, research experts, administrators, students of society and philosophy, teachers, and teachers-in-training.

Again we note that the school's responsibility for fostering an intellectual discipline unique in the history of civilization is indeed complex and challenging. Subjects and their structures and relations, logic and values, concern for truth and for others, are all aspects of a larger discipline which the student, guided by the school, must make his own.

Suggested Reading

Bennis, Warren G., Kenneth D. Benne, and Robert Chin, eds., *The Planning of Change* (New York: Holt, Rinehart and Winston, 1961), chaps. 3, 6, 8–9.

Burton, William H., Roland B. Kimball, and Richard L. Wing, *Education for Effective Thinking* (New York: Appleton-Century-Crofts, Inc., 1960), chaps. 2–3, 12–15.

Elam, Stanley, ed., *Education and the Structure of Knowledge* (Chicago: Rand McNally and Co., 1964), chaps. 1–3, 5–6, 8.

Goodlad, John I., *School Curriculum Reform in the United States* (New York: Fund for the Advancement of Education, 1964).

Hook, Sidney, *Education for Modern Man,* new ed. (New York: Alfred A. Knopf, 1963), chaps. 2, 6–7.

Horowitz, Irving L., "Consensus, Conflict and Cooperation: A Sociological Inventory," *Social Forces*, December 1962, pp. 177–88.

Hullfish, H. Gordon and Philip G. Smith, *Reflective Thinking: The Method of Education* (New York: Dodd, Mead and Co., 1961), chaps. 4, 12–15.

Kaplan, Abraham, *The Conduct of Inquiry* (San Francisco: Chandler Publishing Co., 1964), chaps. 9–10.

Phenix, Philip H., *Realms of Meaning* (New York: McGraw-Hill Book Co., 1964), part 3.

PART IV

CRITICAL ISSUES IN CONTEMPORARY EDUCATION

Chapter 16

Public Education Under Fire

Early Criticisms of the Schools

It is commonly assumed that the strength and vitality of a democracy derive from the responsiveness of its institutions to the will of the people. In contrast with the conformity of mind and will upon which the survival of an autocracy depends, it is (at least, ideally) the governed who govern in a democracy. Criticism thus constitutes the life's blood of a free society.

If this be true, the American public school has received generous injections of good red blood in recent years. Nor is there evidence that the original springs of vitality are in process of drying up! The flood of articles and books devoted to the problems and failures of public education increases steadily in volume and threatens at times to become a torrent.

Prior to 1950, indictments of failure gave the appearance of local origin, or, as in the case of Robert M. Hutchins and other intellectuals in the 1930s and the early 1940s, testified to a widespread but healthy concern of the friends of public education that instruction in the schools be brought to higher levels of efficiency. The enforced resignation of Dr. Willard Goslin from his position as Superintendent of Schools in Pasadena, California, in the fall of 1950, however, indicated that criticism was neither exclusively local in origin nor designed merely to improve and strengthen the public schools.

One of the first to draw attention to a national pattern in these attacks and to identify individuals and organizations fostering them, together with their obvious motives, was Robert Skaife of the National Commission for the Defense of Democracy Through Education. In a series of articles written in *The Nation's Schools,* beginning in January 1951, Skaife undertook to expose the propaganda methods and procedures of these "critics" of public education.

Criticisms of Public Education in the 1950s and Early 1960s

What was the nature of these criticisms?

One was to identify progressive practices and curricular revisions in the schools with undisciplined instruction and the clever designs of educators to subvert American education in the interests of communism and collectivism. The fear of subversion was acute in the early 1950s, when United States Senator Joseph McCarthy was engaged in an investigation of communism in American life, particularly in the departments and agencies of government, industries related to national defense, and education.

For a time, a number of organizations thrived upon this indictment. Prominent among these was Allan Zoll's National Council for American Education. Zoll's pamphlets found their way into communities of virtually every state in the union. Their purpose may be inferred from the title of one pamphlet, "They Want Your Child." Our schools, it was stated, "were founded to preserve the American form of government and the American institutions of freedom and individual liberty. It can safely be asserted that ninety per cent of the texts and teachers in our schools today are in considerable measure subversive of these basic American principles." [1]

Lending support to charges of subversion were a number of prominent radio commentators and journalists. Consider, for example, the obvious inference that anxious parents might draw from these words addressed to them by George Sokolsky, whose syndicated column appeared in leading newspapers from coast to coast:

> You need to know what a teacher believes. The teacher says that it is none of your business. The teacher says that the Constitution, under the Fifth Amendment, protects a citizen in his beliefs. That is absolutely true. A citizen can believe anything he

1. Other pamphlets distributed by the National Council for American Education were "Progressive Education Increases Delinquency," "How Red Are the Schools?" "Private Schools: The Solution to America's Educational Problem."

likes: That the moon is made of green cheese, that Karl Marx is as great an historic figure as Moses, Jesus, Aristotle, and Plato; that John Dewey was the greatest philosopher of all time. That is a teacher's private business. . . . No child need be sent to a school whose teachers offend a parent's beliefs. The child must have a certain amount of "education," according to the law. That may require the parents to pay for the upkeep of two schools. Many do.[2]

Charges of subversion in education also received support from a number of educators who claimed first-hand acquaintance with the doctrines and influence of John Dewey, William Heard Kilpatrick, and their associates. One of these "experts," Dr. Felix Witmer, professed to speak out of seventeen years of teaching experience at the New Jersey State Teachers College in Montclair, New Jersey. Witmer resigned from this institution to devote himself to writing and lecturing. As one admiring editor put it, what he had to reveal "exploded over the national scene like well-placed time bombs."

One of his articles on "The Initiators of Operation Socialism," began with these words:

Have you ever read a book on "curriculum development"? No one should blame you if you haven't. If you have, you may understand a little better what has happened to the schools in your community, and how it has come about.

As the years went by and your children passed through the grades, you may have noticed that a change was going on. Subject matter, teaching methods, types of study, everything changed. If you put two and two together, you realize that the emphasis shifted from the individual to the group.

Your children learned that the Communist Manifesto ranked among the great works of world literature and that the Soviet Union was an "economic democracy." Competition, it seems, had become old hat. "Attitudes" and "group relationships" were the thing.

Just who was responsible for the changes you could not say. "Trends of the times" hardly seems to be a penetrating explana-

2. "Do You Know the Teachers? What Do Teachers Know?" *Rochester Times-Union,* December 28, 1951.

tion. Fact is that a relatively small group of educators, who have gravitated toward Columbia Teachers College, have in the course of 20 years turned thousands and thousands of teachers into missionaries of the collectivist, i.e., socialistic, creed. These thousands of converts have brought about the change.[3]

A second source of subversion, in the eyes of many in the 1950s (and today) were textbooks and the manner in which they were used to deal with controversial issues in the classroom. Textbooks and teachers alike, it was said, are indoctrinating for a new social order. Consequently, "patriotic citizens" were used to purge public education of both textbooks and teachers who were seemingly bent upon undermining American institutions. This followed, since the valid purpose of education, in the words of one enthusiastic partisan, should be that of "instilling traditions which are not subject to re-examination."

Efforts to control the selection and rejection of textbooks were extended as well to topics that schools are permitted to consider in the classroom.

Equally serious—perhaps even more serious—was the growing tendency of governing boards, on state as well as local levels, to limit the choice of textbooks, reference materials, and the content of teaching to that which promoted an uncritical acceptance of the status quo. Typical of these efforts were the criteria for the selection of textbooks as unanimously adopted by the Denver School Board in December 1952. No textbook or other instructional material, declared this Board, might be used unless it was first established that its "author supports the principles of American Constitutional government" and "the nature and content of the material are consistent with the principles of American Constitutional government."[4]

Of these trends, George F. Kennan, former ambassador of the United States to Russia, was moved to remark:

> I have lived more than ten years of my life in totalitarian countries. I know where this sort of thing leads. I know it to be the

3. See "The Initiators of Operation Socialism," *National Republic*, June 1953, p. 13.
4. The decision of school authorities, in a number of instances, to prohibit the study of the United Nations and its agencies serves as a further illustration of the attempts of partisan groups to use the schools to promote their ideologies. That this tendency is still with us is evidenced by the recent effort of certain religious groups to control the manner in which the concept of evolution is dealt with in public schools today.

most shocking and cynical disservice one can do to the credulity and to the spiritual equilibrium of one's fellow men. . . .

In this way, we begin to draw about ourselves a cultural curtain similar in some respects to the Iron Curtain of our adversaries. In doing so, we tend to inflict upon ourselves a species of cultural isolation and provincialism wholly out of accord with the traditions of our Nation and destined, if unchecked, to bring to our intellectual and artistic life the same sort of sterility from which the cultural world of our Communist adversaries is already suffering.[5]

Periods of hysteria come and go. Unfortunately, however, their after-effects are not always healthy. The number of teachers in American schools whom the patriotic groups succeeded in identifying not merely as communists but, as Senator McCarthy phrased it, those "who think as communists," has been small indeed; but the procedures employed in searching them out and depriving them of their positions have tended to weaken instruction and to deprive young people of the opportunity to develop that intellectual discipline which comes from wrestling with problems to which the immediate answers are unknown. Indeed, there is evidence of a cultural lag on the part of the schools. Outside educational institutions, the courts have rendered a number of significant decisions designed to reaffirm the constitutional guarantees of freedom of thought and expression. Consequently, there has come about an obvious relaxation in the public mind that permits freedom of thought and expression which once seemed on the point of eclipse. Within the field of education, however, this movement is less evident.

Writing in 1951, the Committee on Tenure and Academic Freedom of the National Education Association stated that the "Presence in the school curriculum of items to which a partisan group is sensitive is causing a greater degree of voluntary censorship than ever before." The committee asserted further "that voluntary censorship by administration and teachers—to avoid conflict with groups—is far more insidious than the overt acts of boards and legislatures."

These statements describe the situation of some years ago. Unfortunately, as we shall see in the chapters which deal with the questions

5. From an address delivered on May 15, 1953 at the University of Notre Dame, on the occasion of the dedication of the new I. A. O'Shaughnessy Hall of Liberal and Fine Arts.

"How Free is Freedom to Learn?" and "How Free is Freedom to Teach?" problems of integrity of instruction are still with us.[6]

Education Is Said to Cost Too Much

A second charge commonly made in the 1950s as well as today, is that the schools are guilty of waste and extravagance. Education, it has been said, costs too much.

This criticism coincided with the attempts of many communities to float bond issues and to levy special taxes with which to better teachers' salaries, erect new school buildings, and improve facilities—all of which were rendered imperative by rapid increases in the school population, so characteristic of the 1940s.

It is obvious, of course, that accusations of waste and extravagance are best checked when they are examined concretely and specifically. It is possible that individual communities here and there may have spent more for materials and supplies or for building construction than the circumstances warranted. If so, this might have been determined by careful and objective investigation. Surely the professional educator, as well as the taxpayer, should be concerned to see that a dollar's value is received for every dollar spent. Toward this end, laymen and professional men can be of help to each other, the educator interpreting to the layman the physical necessities of an effective education and the layman contributing his practical knowledge as businessman, architect, or contractor to insure most economically the translation of these needs into actual construction.

This practical method of cooperation, however, was not always followed. Thus the public was informed that modern education (or "progressive education") inevitably involves waste with its fads and frills and its "activity curriculum." That "public education costs more money every year" was asserted over and over again in the campaign waged against Superintendent Willard Goslin in Pasadena, but one specific objection to the Goslin budget, seldom mentioned openly, was his plan to improve the educational facilities available for the underprivileged children of the city, namely, the Mexican and Negro children.

6. See Jack Nelson, "What is the Problem?" *NEA Journal,* May 1963, pp. 19–21. See also Paul Goodman, "Don't Disturb the Children," *New Republic,* March 16, 1963, pp. 19–20.

Public Education as an Undesirable Monopoly

From the contention that public education costs too much to the argument that public schools enjoy an unfair advantage in competition with nonpublic schools is but a step. In support of the latter position we find a curious assortment of individuals and groups, ranging from those who would abolish public schools altogether to those who contend that, since both public and private schools "perform a public function" and are thus "integrally a part of what is basically a dual system," government support for the one and not the other is fostering an undesirable monopoly of education.

An ardent advocate of the abolition of public schools for a decade or more has been Robert Cyrus Hoiles, the owner of ten newspapers in Texas, California, Colorado, New Mexico, and Ohio. A formidable opponent of bond issues in support of public education, Hoiles utilizes news items and educational events to promote the thesis that the concept of public education is anti-American and that "Government schools are leading us to socialism and communism." "It is impossible," he contends, "for tax-supported education to teach American principles. They can only teach foreign principles, collectivism, fascism, might-makes-rightism and the end justifies the means." [7]

The charge that public education constitutes an undesirable monopoly has also been made by representatives of both Protestant and Catholic sects and is as commonly heard in the 1960s as it was in the 1950s. Partisans of this position point out that under the decision of the United States Supreme Court in *Pierce* v. *Society of Sisters* in 1925, parents are assured the constitutional right to satisfy the requirements of compulsory school attendance laws by sending their children to either a private or a public school. They further point out that since the private school provides instruction in secular subjects in a manner similar to that of the public school, it performs a public service and is entitled to public assistance in those areas of instruction precisely as is the public school. For government to deny the nonprofit private school this assistance is to fail to realize that the private school "has a higher

7. A description of the campaign waged by Hoiles and his newspapers may be found in an article by Lewis C. Fay, written for *The Nation's Schools,* August 1952, under the title "Abolish Public Schools." Statements ascribed to Hoiles are derived from this source. We include Hoiles in this discussion for the reason that his views are still more widely held than many realize and because his newspapers are as active in opposition to public education today as they were in 1952.

legal status than the mere non-profit voluntary organization because those who elect to use this institution *must* attend it for a designated period under penalty of violating the state's truancy laws," [8] and is to accord to public education an unfair monopoly in the use of public funds.

These groups also argue that sound public policy runs counter to the assumption by government of functions that constitute the "appropriate tasks" of other social institutions and agencies. This position was ably argued by Robert C. Hartnett, editor of *America*. In an article on "The School in the American Community," Hartnett stated that

> the state can fail to perform its proper functions in two ways: one, through lack of initiative, as when it allows the economically powerful to exploit the economically weak, or allows private interests to pillage the natural resources of society or in any one of a dozen ways permits the benefits and burdens of social life to be apportioned without regard to social justice . . . [and, two, through] excessive and too far-reaching interference in the free areas of social organization. In trying to redress the balance in favor of social justice, the state often extends its coercive arm much farther into such fields as education, health, and social welfare than is at all necessary or compatible with the nature of a free society. Ideally, the state should always aim to assist social institutions and agencies to perform their appointed tasks, rather than to *replace* them with public (i.e., political) agencies [italics in the original].[9]

A partial correction of this mistake, it is felt, would be made were the state to assist private as well as public schools. To adopt such a policy, however, would require a reinterpretation of the principle of separation of church and state in its application to education. To this problem we will devote Chapters 17 and 18.

The Schools Are Agents of Irreligious Influences

These charges have ranged from the thesis that moral education without positive religious instruction is futile to the charge that our schools "are dominated by a naturalistic religion" and the equally extreme in-

8. Robert F. Drinan, S.J., *Religion, the Courts, and Public Policy* (New York: McGraw-Hill Book Company, Inc., 1963), p. 126.
9. *America*, April 9, 1952, pp. 65–68.

dictment that they are turning out "millions of uncontrolled delinquents."

The object of these charges seems to be twofold: (1) to convince a
doubting public that it is in its interest to lend financial support to
church-related schools; (2) to replace the accepted policy of neutrality in public education in matters of religious conviction with one of
positive indoctrination.

The first of these objectives, as we indicated above, bears directly
upon the American principle of separation of church and state. The
second rests upon the assumption of an inseparable relationship between moral education and a religious faith (which one does not seem
to matter!). It is this assumption that has led many earnest people to
view with alarm the decision of the United States Supreme Court in
Abington School District v. *Schempp* (1963) in which the Court
banned Bible reading and the use of the Lord's Prayer as devotional exercises in public schools. Congressman Frank J. Becker was reported
to have said that the Court in this decision has aided and abetted "cyn-
ics, atheists, and unbelievers," in their efforts to "outlaw God, step on
God, ridicule God, and deny God in our public institutions." [10]

Thus convinced, Congressman Becker and others of like mind undertook to bring about a reversal of the Court's decision by constitutional
amendment. Altogether some 147 resolutions toward this end were
considered by the House Judiciary Committee. The testimony before
the Committee centered chiefly on the most prominent of these proposals, the so-called "Becker amendment." [11]

To the surprise of many, formidable opposition to the Becker
amendment came from representatives of organized religions—
Protestants, Catholics, Jews—as well as from distinguished members of
the legal profession. The latter stressed the point that once we start to
tinker with the Bill of Rights,

10. *The Catholic Chronicle,* Toledo, Ohio, May 1, 1964.
11. This amendment was intended to insure the following interpretation of the
First Amendment of the Bill of Rights:

Section 1. Nothing in this Constitution shall be deemed to prohibit the offering,
reading from, or listening to prayers or Biblical scriptures, if participation therein
is on a voluntary basis, in any governmental or public school, institution or place.
Section 2. Nothing in this Constitution shall be deemed to prohibit making reference to belief in, reliance upon, or invoking the aid of God or a Supreme Being in
any governmental or public document, proceeding, activity, ceremony, school, institution, or place, or upon any coinage, currency or obligation of the United States.
Section 3. Nothing in this article shall constitute an establishment of religion.

to amend them here, and to amend them there, we will soon find
good reasons for restricting this liberty, or narrowing that safeguard, and will eventually wake up to find that we have lost
essential safeguards which these Amendments can and should
protect.[12]

Typical of the arguments bearing upon the religious implications of
the Court's decision by those opposed to the Becker amendment was a
statement submitted to the Committee by William J. Kenealy, S.J., of
the Boston College Law School on May 8, 1964. In addressing himself
to the principles enunciated by the Court in *Engel* v. *Vitale* (in which
the Court outlawed the use of a prayer in the public schools of New
York as formulated by the Board of Regents of that state) and in
Abington School District v. *Schempp*, Father Kenealy stated in part,

> I do not subscribe to what seems to me the Court's uncritical
> invocation of the "wall of separation" metaphor, nor to its simplis-
> tic interpretation of the "establishment of religion" clause of the
> 1st Amendment, nor to its mechanistic incorporation of that
> clause into the "due process" clause of the 14th Amendment. But
> I do believe that the prayer and Bible readings condemned by
> *Engel* and *Schempp* were violative of the fundamental constitu-
> tional and personal right of the "free exercise" of religion, ex-
> pressly protected against federal action by the 1st Amendment,
> and properly protected against state action by the "due process"
> clause of the 14th Amendment.

Father Kenealy, in common with others who believe that religious
exercises should be excluded from public schools, insists that interests
other than the school—the church, the home, the religious school, "the
groups and associations which carry on study, discussion, teaching,
writing, and publishing on matters philosophical and theological"—are
the proper custodians of the religious heritage of America; that the
"public school, as an official agent of the religiously neutral *state,* cannot, without betraying the religious neutrality of its principal, provide
religious devotions or exercises of its pupils."

So much for the principle of religious liberty as viewed by those who

12. Erwin N. Griswold, Dean of the Law School, Harvard University, in a
letter addressed to Congressman Emanuel Celler, Chairman of the House Committee on the Judiciary, April 15, 1964.

oppose the use of religious services in the public school. But what of the assumption that without instruction in a religious faith moral education is without substance and force? To this question we will return in Chapter 19 on "Religion and Morality in Public Education."

The Schools of Today Are Inferior to Those of Yesterday

Early criticisms of the schools bore down most conspicuously upon their assumed failure to ground their pupils in the three Rs. This is a recurrent argument, repeated generation after generation. However, it is one that can easily be refuted, if statistical evidence of children's accomplishments are accepted in preference to the undocumented inferences of parents and teachers who seem forever disposed to prefer the past to the present.

For example, as early as the 1920s, Caldwell and Courtis, in a volume entitled *Then and Now in Education,* conclusively answered this argument for their generation. Having come into possession of examinations administered to school children in Boston in 1845, the authors arranged to subject children of the 1920s to the same tests. Despite the fact that in the 1840s only superior pupils were privileged to undertake these examinations, whereas the children examined by Caldwell and Courtis were from a cross section of the school population, the children of the 1920s demonstrated a superiority of performance over those of 1845.

As criticism in the 1950s continued to increase in volume, educators undertook to meet charges of inferiority with the results of research. For example, William H. Burton pointed out in 1952 that over 275 separate studies were then available in magazines and master's theses to establish the fact that the schools "are teaching the Three R's today far more efficiently than ever before in history. The children, generally, have far greater skill than their parents and forbears. Modern methods are measurably superior to those used formerly, or, in my day.' " [13]

In 1951 a thoroughgoing survey was conducted by a graduate seminar in education at Ohio State University under the direction of Professor Harold Alberty. From its review of the major experiments and research studies bearing upon the effectiveness of instruction in the

13. See "Get the Facts: Both Ours and the Other Fellow's," *Progressive Education,* January 1952, pp. 82–90.

basic skills "in the present-day curriculum as compared with the older and more traditional practices," the seminar concluded that "The evidence of growth in basic skills, both at the elementary and the secondary levels, reveals clearly that in the modern curriculum these skills are achieved as well or better than in the conventional curriculum. This is true for the basic skills discussed here, namely, skills in reading, arithmetic, and language." [14]

A comparison of high school and college education at mid-century with that at the turn of the century leads to a similar conclusion. Critics of modern education have either forgotten or are ignorant of the conditions which prompted the National Council of Education in 1892 to appoint a Committee of Ten, under the chairmanship of Charles W. Eliot, with instructions to bring order, if possible, out of a chaotic and confused situation. This committee was confronted with the absence of any consistent policy on the secondary level for preparing students either for college or "for life." Subjects taught varied from school to school. There was no uniformity as to time allotments, and grade placements of topics or subjects pursued in one institution did not have any obvious relationship to time allotments and grade placements in another. Writing in the *Arena*, for June 1890, on "The Gap Between Common Schools and Colleges," President Eliot stated,

> The elementary or common-school system, in both city and country, is tolerably organized in many States; but between the elementary schools and the colleges is a wide gap very imperfectly bridged by a few public high schools, which conform to no common standards and are under no unifying control. The masses of the rural population—that is to say, three quarters of the American people are unprovided with secondary schools.

Speaking of his own state, Massachusetts, one of the leading states of the period, Eliot continued,

> The plain fact in Massachusetts is that not one tenth of the schools called high habitually maintain a course of study which enables the pupil to prepare himself for admission to Harvard College, or to any other college in the State which enforces its requirements for admission as stated in its catalogue. If this is the

14. *Let's Look At Attacks on Our Schools* (Columbus, Ohio: College of Education, Ohio State University, 1951), pp. 21–29.

condition of things in what may be called an urban State, what must it be in a rural one? [15]

An examination of the nature of instruction afforded in college prior to the turn of the century is equally fatal to the argument that the salvation of American education depends upon restoring to the colleges "the kind of education in the liberal arts which American colleges had furnished well into the nineteenth century." [16] The plain fact is, as Professor Frank Freeman has demonstrated, "Comparisons of entrance requirements, college curricula, textbooks, and methods of instruction" support the conclusion that "until 1890–1900, the courses and the teaching in most colleges in this country did not make as great demands upon the mental abilities of their students as do the average academic high schools of today." [17] As to the "sound intellectual discipline" the liberal arts were supposed to convey, the record seems to indicate, continues Freeman, that

> College education, down through the 19th Century, was largely a matter of memorization and repetition of textbook lessons in the classical languages, grammar, rhetoric, some logic and philosophy, some mathematics; and, in some colleges, a bit of French, German, and elementary English. The sciences, and the arts, and the humanities properly understood, certainly were not dominant in secondary or in college education up to the decade 1890–1900.

In describing the intellectual discipline provided by colleges in this period, Henry James remarks, in his biography of Charles W. Eliot, that college teaching consisted in "drilling rudiments into boys, who, most of them, brought no enthusiasm for the particular subject in the classroom . . ." and from whom the college "exacted . . . as little as possible." [18]

Since the decade 1890–1900 our high schools and colleges have expanded phenomenally. Enrollments have increased, new curricula have been added, and the education afforded is far richer and more

15. Reprinted in *Educational Reform, Essays and Addresses* (New York: The Century Company, 1898), p. 199.
16. See Stringfellow Barr, "The Education of Freemen," *The New Republic,* August 13, 1942, pp. 248–50.
17. From a paper read before the Academy Conference of the American Association for the Advancement of Science in Philadelphia, December 1951.
18. Quoted by Freeman from Henry James, *Charles William Eliot* (Boston: Houghton Mifflin Co., 1930).

varied than ever before in the history of this nation—or, for that matter, of any other. To be sure, rapidity of growth is not always best for quality. That the standards of education in high school and college today are not what they should be the educator should be the first to concede. Moreover, in seeking to minister to the needs of individuals who no longer constitute a selected group, school and college alike have increased the complexity of their tasks immeasurably. It is one thing, however, to recognize that the schools have not been entirely successful in meeting the requirements of both quality and diversity in education, or that in their attempts to serve all types of minds (those whom Robert Ulich suggestively classifies as humanists, scientists, executives, artisans, workers),[19] equal and exact justice is not meted out to all, and quite another thing to attribute this failure to the "excesses of progressive education."

Despite the significant changes and problems mentioned in the preceding paragraphs, the results of research studies continue to refute charges concerning the declining quality of education. With respect to the elementary school, for example, comparative studies indicate that the children of today are mastering reading at an earlier chronological age than in previous years and on a level of proficiency superior to that of which their parents and grandparents sometimes boast.[20] The great majority of studies at high school and college levels add weight to this refutation.[21]

Today's Challenge to Education

It is reasonable to conclude that little evidence supports the statement that schools and colleges of today are inferior to those of yesterday. Important as it is to establish this fact in the interests of accuracy, it is not sufficient. The times require a clarification of the tasks confronting the schools in the light of conditions that obtain, if they would prepare the young to cope with the winds of change. Consequently, we

19. See Robert Ulich, *Crisis and Hope in American Education* (Boston: Beacon Press, Inc., 1953), chap. III.

20. Arthur I. Gates, "The Teaching of Reading—Objective Evidence Versus Opinion," *Phi Delta Kappan*, February 1962, pp. 197–205.

21. See, for example, Norman E. Wallen and Robert M. W. Travers, "Analysis and Investigation of Teaching Methods," in *Handbook of Research on Teaching*, N. L. Gage, ed. (Chicago: Rand McNally and Co., 1963), pp. 470–74; *Phi Delta Kappan*, March 1964, p. 319.

will conclude with a brief consideration of the major concerns of education in the 1960s.[22]

First are the implications that follow from the quickening pace with which a once predominantly rural and small-town civilization has become a metropolitan, industrial, scientific civilization. Today, for example, over 70 per cent of the people of the United States live in metropolitan areas. Between 1950 and 1960 the urban population of the United States increased by 6 per cent, but of this 28 million gain in the urban population some 97 per cent took place in metropolitan areas. Rural families now comprise less than 10 per cent of all families in the United States. And for this decreasing number the farm is no longer the attractive haven it once was for the illiterate and the unskilled.

Equally significant are the contrasts between conditions of living in urban communities of yesterday and of today. Cities were once aggregates of neighborhoods and the term "community" still referred to a geographical area in which one lived and worked more or less intimately with others as a citizen. Ease of transportation and communication have transformed all of this. Yesterday the individual exercised his responsibilities as an individual and in a specific location. Today he tends to do so more and more through membership in an organization —a labor union, an employers' association, a political party, a civic group—in which his voice is blended with those of others.

This new situation creates new problems for young and old. It renders imperative a type of education in childhood and adolescence that will enable the young person to bridge the gap between the complex and relatively impersonal world of adults and the more insulated and limited circle of relatives and friends (the "nuclear family") in which young people now live, move, and have their being. Particularly is this true of the period of adolescence which now constitutes a new and critical stage of development in American society. This suggests that the school, as a supplementary institution, organize its work—the curriculum, the life of the school, its administrative structure—in full awareness of the fact that it functions as a major "highway to adulthood." [23]

22. For a more detailed discussion of the factors discussed here, see V. T. Thayer, *Formative Ideas in American Education* (New York: Dodd, Mead and Company, 1965), Chapter 15, of which this section, in the main, is a summary.

23. For a comprehensive discussion of this concept, see "The High School's Role in Adolescent Status" in B. J. Chandler, Lindley J. Stiles, and John I. Kitsuse, eds., *Education in Urban Society* (New York: Dodd, Mead and Company, 1962). See also Chapters 13 and 14 in the present text.

A second factor of critical importance today is the fact that Americans are no longer a self-sufficient people. It is not long since the United States was a heavy exporter of raw materials. Today it is the world's biggest market for the exports of other countries, consuming about half of all the industrial raw material produced in the free world.

Admiral Rickover has drawn attention to the rapidity with which the energy resources of the United States and, indeed, the world are being depleted and the moral that follows with respect to improving the quality of education in school and college, if the American people are to retain their position of leadership in the free world.[24] It is not surprising that he, as scientist and engineer, should emphasize the importance of science and mathematics as a condition of our future material and cultural development. Relevant as this is, interdependence in the modern world involves much more than the economic and the scientific. It highlights the importance of foreign language, literature, and the arts as means of acquiring a sympathetic insight into the values, the habits, and the customs of other cultures. Indeed, interdependence renders imperative a new approach to virtually every subject in the school. What scientists and mathematicians are attempting in the way of introducing elementary and secondary school pupils to new concepts in the light of contemporary research, the social scientists (anthropologists, sociologists, historians, economists, psychologists, and psychiatrists) should undertake cooperatively in order to correct narrow and outdated conceptions of man and his institutions which now inhibit creative and constructive relations between people of different origins and cultural values.

Nor is this task exclusively one of new subject matter and new types of experiences. It also involves resolving problems and conflicts through cooperative thinking, feeling, and acting relevant to a world at once sensitively interrelated and varied in its patterns.[25]

This takes us to the ever increasing role that science has come to play in modern life. Ralph Tyler, Director of the Center for Advanced Study in the Behavioral Sciences at Palo Alto, California, has well illustrated the extent to which the applications of science have revolutionized economic life. It is estimated, he states, that more than 50 per cent of the occupations in which today's college graduates will find employ-

24. See his chapter on "Energy Resources and Our Future," in *Education and Freedom* (New York: E. P. Dutton & Co., 1959).

25. For an amplification of this point, see Chapter 15 on "The Intellectual Task of the School."

ment did not exist when these young people were born! [26] Still more startling is a statement by Lawrence Stessen to the effect that research in business and industry brings forth some 900 new products each day.[27]

In the light of these developments, it is understandable that Clark Kerr, President of the University of California, should compare the effects of the "knowledge industry" upon the second half of this century with that of the railroads upon the second half of the nineteenth century.

The applications of science and technology to all phases of American life are fast denying to the unskilled a significant role in economic life. Not only is it increasingly necessary to acquire an education prior to entering the labor market, but continuous education, even re-education and re-training, have become essential conditions for sharing in the advantages that flow from the "knowledge industry." To be sure, schooling has long been recognized in American society as a means for bettering one's station in life. In one sense, therefore, the importance accorded schooling today merely accentuates a traditional value. What is novel today is the fact that without formal education the individual is hopelessly lost!

It is unfortunate that in discussions of the place of science and mathematics in the schools too little mention is made of the potential contributions of science to an intellectual and moral discipline appropriate to the modern world. Not the least of the tasks of the school is to acquaint young people with the concepts of modern science that are forcing a revision of what Lawrence K. Frank terms the "many obsolete, archaic concepts and assumptions, the long accepted criteria of credibility, that are no longer valid." Frank believes we should

> earnestly endeavor to acquaint all students, beginning with their first years in school, with contemporary scientific ideas and assumptions, helping them to understand that to live in the contemporary world, they need this orientation because our social order, as well as our individual living, is being transformed by scientific thinking and its applications in technology.[28]

26. Quoted by Maurice B. Mitchell in a special supplement to *The New York Times* on "The Knowledge Explosion," May 26, 1963.

27. "Business Goes on a Manhunt," *The New York Times Magazine*, November 8, 1964.

28. *The School as an Agent for Cultural Renewal* (Cambridge, Mass.: Harvard University Press, 1960), pp. 17–18.

It is often said that a democratic society is an open society—that progress in all significant areas of living depends upon the right to freedom of thought and expression. Now, for both the formulation and the application of the principle of free inquiry we are heavily indebted to the example of the scientific community. In this community, dissent from established truth or the projection of a new idea is viewed, ideally, as a stimulus to progress, not as heresy to be suppressed or repelled. In the scientific community, also, the principle that conflicts are best resolved through the use of rational methods of discussion and investigation has long been an axiom. That is to say, for the scientist, it is not authority, tradition, or superior force that determines the truth or the validity of an idea but its relevance to the circumstances or the context in which it arises, its implications and consequences in the deepest and fullest sense of those words. In short, in science, there is no better test than "By their fruits, ye shall know them."

Similarly, other characteristics of science as a method of thinking have relevant implications for relations between people. Over and above its applications in a specific field (characteristics which John Dewey has described in his *How We Think*), science, as a method, has developed methods of procedure which go far to implement the democratic ideal.

Traditionally, both the subject matter and methods of instruction in our schools have been keyed to the imparting of facts and principles already salted down. More and more, however, we find ourselves today in the position of the college student serving as a guide to an "old grad" who, in a sentimental mood, had decided upon a visit to his alma mater. After visiting one after another of his favorite haunts, he thought to inquire after his former teachers, in particular, a professor of economics. "Oh," replied the student, "he is still teaching, and he continues to ask the same ten questions in his final examinations."

"That should make it easy for you," commented the old grad. "All you have to do is to remember the questions and 'bone up' on the answers."

"Well, it is not quite so simple as that," replied the student ruefully. "You see, the old boy studies the trends and changes the answers!"

To study the trends and to change the answers, including some of the major premises that have come down to us, is one of the imperatives of modern life. Moreover, for our schools to fail to impart this discipline to the young is more serious today than it was yesterday, in view of the trends in economic and social life to which we called attention in Chapter 14. There, it will be recalled, we pointed out that for a steadily increasing proportion of our youth, schooling has come to replace responsible participation in life outside the school.

A fourth factor to which educators are being asked to give increasing attention is the mobility of our population.

That large numbers of our people are continuously on the move is, to be sure, no novel characteristic of American life. Since the first attempts of Europeans to establish a foothold on the continent, Americans have used change of location as a means of solving their problems —economic, religious, social. What is more common, indeed, than the expression, "If you don't like it, why don't you get out?" This suggestion is so frequently followed with successful results that one explanation of the traditional American optimism is repeated confirmation of the assumption that opportunity waits just around the corner!

What is new in the contemporary situation is the close relationship that has developed between mobility of population and formal education. No community today lives sufficient unto itself. Consequently, when the impoverished Negro from the South or a displaced white farmer moves to a large metropolitan center in order to improve his economic and social status, the failure of the community of his origin to provide him with an essential education may cause him and his children to become both an economic and an educational burden upon the community of his adoption.

The movement of population from one geographical section to another is in no way restricted, however, to the underprivileged and the disadvantaged. Statistics from the Bureau of the Census indicate that the better educated in our population move most frequently, and the higher the educational level of people the more likely are they to move. For example, less than 40 per cent of the male population twenty-five years of age and over, with eight years or less of schooling, moved between 1950 and 1960, whereas over 50 per cent of those who had attended or graduated from college moved during the same period. "The man who leaves home," writes William H. Whyte, Jr., "is not the exception in American society but the key to it." Whyte goes on to show that the records of long-distance movers indicate that "The greatest single group of their clients—between 40 and 50 per cent—is com-

posed of corporation people. . . . If to this group are added government, Army and Navy people, and corporation people leaving one
company for another, roughly three quarters of all moves are ac-
counted for by members of large corporations." [29]

These facts, as we shall emphasize in Chapter 23, bear directly upon
the problem of federal aid to education in the states. It is not the children of the impoverished and the inarticulate alone who suffer from
inequality of educational opportunity; it is also the children of that rapidly growing professional, technical, and managerial middle class
whose members are increasingly on the move. For these people education is one of the most prized of life's advantages. Accordingly, we may
expect from this group mounting pressure in favor of educational
measures that eliminate differences between communities, thus providing a new setting for an ancient controversy over uniformity in education versus flexibility and adaptation to local conditions in the construction of curricula.[30]

A fifth characteristic of today is a renewed determination to close the
gap between ideal and reality with respect to equality of educational
opportunity. Some of the implications of this reaffirmation of faith in a
traditional American ideal were discussed in Chapter 5. It may be relevant, however, to mention several reasons for a revitalized concern by
thoughtful Americans for equality of educational opportunity.

One is the continuing competition between the free world and the
totalitarian powers, with its twofold emphasis upon our translating this
faith into works and offsetting the present serious waste of talent in
young Americans; (2) the Civil Rights Movement and its identification with attempts to eliminate segregation and discrimination in education. To this we devote Chapter 22. (3) The Antipoverty program
of the Johnson administration with its special provisions for the education of underprivileged children and assistance to disadvantaged communities.

Growing dissatisfaction with contemporary programs of teacher education constitutes a sixth factor of concern today.

With a renewed appreciation of the importance of education in

29. *The Organization Man* (New York: Simon & Schuster, 1956), pp. 297–98.
30. For an interesting forecast of the future influence of the rapidly expanding
professional, technical, and managerial middle class, not only upon education but
upon other aspects of American life, see Peter F. Drucker, "American Directions:
A Forecast," *Harper's Magazine*, February 1965, pp. 39–45.

today's world and the need to improve its quality, it was inevitable that attention should turn to the status of the teacher in American society and what is essential in his preparation. That salaries are inadequate and that teaching as a profession lacks general respect have long been recognized, but, as Mark Twain once remarked about the weather, everyone talks about it but no one seems to do anything about it. This has been true of the status of the profession of teaching. Today, however, there are indications of change.

If respect is to be lasting it must be merited. Critics have not been wanting in recent years to downgrade the quality of teacher education and the methods of teacher accreditation in the United States.[31] Prior to 1900 both the determination of the content of subjects taught in the secondary school and the preparation of teachers were largely in the hands of the faculties of liberal arts colleges. With the rapid expansion of the secondary school population in the first decades of the twentieth century and the plain necessity of adapting the school to the needs of "all American youth," in contrast to the much simpler task of serving the needs of a relatively homogeneous student body of an earlier period, considerations other than preparation for college began to control the selection and organization of subject matter. (Contrast, for example, the assumptions underlying the Report of the Committee of Ten in 1893 with the implications of the Seven Cardinal Principles of secondary education as put forth by the Commission on the Reorganization of Secondary Education in 1918, with respect to both the content of subjects to be taught and to the organization and conduct of the school.) Parallel with the introduction of new objectives in the education of the young came a withdrawal of interest and involvement of college teachers in problems of instruction in the lower schools, and, unfortunately, a corresponding lack of mutual confidence and respect on the part of the faculties of education and the faculties of the liberal arts.[32] James B. Conant gave voice to a dominant attitude on the part of professional educators when he stated, "College professors of the liberal

31. A conspicuous example is James D. Koerner, *The Miseducation of American Teachers* (Boston: Houghton Mifflin Company, 1963).

32. From lack of mutual respect to expression of suspicion and hostility is but a step. See in this connection Arthur Bestor's description "of the debasement which the teaching profession is undergoing at the hands of the interlocking directorate of professional educators" in his *Educational Wastelands: The Retreat from Learning in Our Public Schools* (Urbana, Ill.: University of Illinois Press, 1953), pp. 120–21.

arts often discuss school problems as though schools operate in the stratosphere—that is, in a social vacuum." [33] But he, like many others, is nevertheless convinced that educators, in their attempts to cope with change, have sadly neglected the gifted child and, in their teacher education programs, have expanded unnecessarily "educational courses" to the exclusion of potential contributions from scholars in the preparation of teachers. The immediate task of teacher education, as Conant sees it, is (1) to bring about a better understanding and to establish cooperative relationships between the faculties of the arts and sciences and the faculties of education in the training of teachers with a view to reducing the present number of required courses in education and increasing the contributions of scholars within the subject-matter fields; (2) to strengthen programs of practice teaching and probationary periods of employment under expert guidance. [34]

John Dewey once remarked, "If we once start thinking no one can guarantee where we shall come out, except that many objects, ends, and institutions are doomed. Every thinker puts some portion of an apparently stable world in peril and no one can wholly predict what will emerge in its place." This may well follow upon current criticisms of teacher education, the curriculum, and the administrative organization of schools. There is encouraging evidence today of serious thinking about American education, not only on the part of professional educators, but of many others, including the faculties of liberal arts colleges, social reformers, and statesmen. What will result from this thinking it is too early to forecast in detail, but there is every reason to believe that out of new cooperative relationships between interested groups much of value will emerge.

Criticism as a Questioning of Basic Assumptions

From this survey of public education under fire it would appear that a number of basic assumptions which have given character to American education in the past are undergoing reexamination by influential seg-

33. *The Child, the Parent, and the State* (Cambridge, Mass.: Harvard University Press, 1959), pp. 64–65.

34. Conant's analysis of teacher education in the United States, together with his recommendations for its improvement, are found in *The Education of American Teachers* (New York: McGraw-Hill Book Company, Inc., 1963). See also his *Shaping Educational Policy* (1964) by the same publisher.

ments in our population. As an introduction to the chapters that follow, it may be helpful to mention these assumptions briefly.

First is the assumption that both private and public education realize their unique functions best when private schools receive support solely from private sources and public funds are used exclusively for public education. This principle dates from the beginnings of public education in this country. Although it is true that in the eyes of many today this principle derives its strength from the interpretation which the United States Supreme Court has given to the First Amendment to the federal Constitution, its origin and general adoption resulted from painful experience of the states with public support of nonpublic schools. As Justice Frankfurter remarked in *McCollum* v. *Board of Education,* "Separation in the field of education . . . was not imposed upon unwilling states by superior law. In this respect the Fourteenth Amendment merely reflected a principle then dominant in our national life. To the extent that the Constitution thus made it binding upon the States, the basis of the restriction is the whole experience of our people."

Today, however, this basic assumption is questioned on the theory that insofar as Congress and state legislatures are enjoined to "pass no law respecting an establishment of religion," this prohibition was intended to do no more than to forbid government from assisting one religion to the exclusion of others and was in no sense designed to prohibit the extension of aid to all religions on an "equal and fair" basis. It is also questioned as sound public policy on the ground that there is no actual violation of the religious clause of the First Amendment when public assistance is limited to the support of instruction in secular subjects and the nonreligious activities of church-related institutions.

A second assumption defines the task of the school in areas of controversy and doubt and in matters on which a community is not of one mind. No one has formulated this principle of procedure more clearly than Charles W. Eliot in his inaugural address as President of Harvard College in 1869. In the course of a review of the educational values implicit within the main branches of learning, he came to the "philosophical subjects." These, he insisted, should never be taught with authority.

> They are not the established sciences; they are full of disputed matters, open questions, and bottomless speculations. It is not the

function of the teacher to settle philosophical and political controversies for the pupil, or even to recommend to him any one set of opinions as better than another. Exposition, not imposition of opinions is the professor's part. The student should be made acquainted with all sides of these controversies, with the salient points of each system. . . . The very word education is a standing protest against dogmatic teaching.[35]

Few would contend that this principle has found consistent application in problems upon which the public is as a house divided against itself, but despite distortion and open violation, it has nonetheless remained a fixed star by which good teachers have sought to direct their course. It is also an ideal that elicits the support of American communities once the issues become clear and they are asked to decide between education and indoctrination. But in times of crisis, when waves of fear and hysteria seep through the country, that principle easily becomes blurred.

Still a third principle of public education is designed to insure equality of educational opportunity to all children, despite differences in economic circumstance, race, nationality, creed, or, indeed, any characteristic other than those which call for general attention in order to insure an open door to talent and ability.

Realization of the implications for democracy of equality in education has led to the substitution of the multiple-track and enriched curriculum for the narrow, single-track curriculum of an earlier day. It has also led to efforts on both state and national levels to offset the disadvantages that weigh upon children in states of low income through the creation of equalization funds and grants of federal aid. Repudiation of the principle of equality, in turn, explains the contrast that may be found all too frequently between the educational opportunities available to residents in a wealthy neighborhood and those afforded poorer districts of the same community or state, or between white schools and Negro schools where segregation is a persistent pattern.

Attacks upon this principle are seldom made openly, a fact which testifies to its potential and inherent vitality. For example, it is easier for those who oppose increasing school budgets designed to provide for greater equality in education to contend that "progressive education

35. Charles W. Eliot, *Educational Reform: Essays and Addresses* (New York: The Century Co., 1898), pp. 7–8.

costs too much" than to face squarely the question, "Shall this community guarantee to its minorities educational facilities equal to those possessed by the majority?" It is easier to assert that the curriculum of the school is robbing the home of its legitimate functions than to discuss frankly and openly the wisdom of providing courses in home economics, child care, or ample facilities for creative opportunities in art, crafts, music, and recreational activities. Again, it is easier to proclaim that the schools of today are "keeping young people in school too long for their own good" than to face realistically what fruitful alternatives are open to young people other than prolonged schooling in view of the steady exclusion of these young people from economic and social responsibilities in home and community.

Here as elsewhere, however, the choice is not always one between white and black. Nor are the dictates of equality at all times easy to interpret. How, for example, in constructing the school budget, shall we balance the necessity for providing an open road for talent and ability through adequate provision for the gifted against the equally important objective of prolonging the education of all in order to close the gap between the age at which universal education commonly ends and employment opportunities of a promising character begin? Differences of judgment between people who are equally devoted to the principle of equality seem to be inevitable.

Conflicting interpretations of equality likewise emerge from differences of philosophy. Does equality in education imply an identical curriculum for all, as Mortimer Adler, Robert M. Hutchins, and others insist, or does it suggest adapting the curriculum to the child from the first to the last day of his schooling?

Questions of this character are involved in our last assumption. This relates to the supplementary function of the school, to which we gave attention in Chapter 3. Schools are the institutional expressions of co-operative attempts on the part of a community to provide for the young what parents and guardians cannot provide individually.

From this survey of public education under fire it would appear that a number of principles that have given character to American education in the past are undergoing reexamination in the minds of influential segments of our population. Should we continue, for example, to deny public support to nonpublic schools or do new times suggest a return to an earlier policy of "cooperation" between government and religious organizations? Shall we insist that public education remain true to the principles of freedom of inquiry in dealing with problems on the cutting edge of the future or shall the customer, as represented by community sentiment, determine what is to be taught? What does the increasing concern of today for equality of educational opportunity for all groups in our population and all sections of our country suggest with respect to the responsibility of the federal government for education in the states?

The chapters that follow will deal with these and related questions in more detail.

Suggested Reading

Bestor, Arthur E., *Educational Wastelands: The Retreat from Learning in Our Public Schools* (Urbana, Illinois: University of Illinois Press, 1953).

Chandler, B. J., Lindley J. Stiles, and John I. Kitsuse, *Education in Urban Society* (New York: Dodd, Mead and Company, 1962), chaps. 4, 8, 16.

Conant, James B., *The Education of American Teachers* (New York: McGraw-Hill Book Company, Inc., 1963).

Conant, James B., *Shaping Educational Policy* (New York: McGraw-Hill Book Company, Inc., 1964).

Drinan, Robert F., S.J., *Religion, the Courts, and Public Policy* (New York: McGraw-Hill Book Company, Inc., 1963), Chapter 4.

Educational Policies Commission, "The Contemporary Challenge to American Education," *N.E.A. Journal*, March 1958, pp. 188 ff.

Frank, Lawrence K., *The School as an Agent for Cultural Renewal* (Cambridge, Mass.: Harvard University Press, 1960).

Keats, John, *Schools Without Scholars* (Boston: Houghton Mifflin Company, 1958).

Melby, Ernest and Morton Pruner, *Freedom and Public Education* (New York: Frederick A. Praeger, Inc., 1953).

Rudy, Willis, *Schools in an Age of Mass Culture* (Englewood Cliffs, N.J.: Prentice-Hall, Inc., 1965), chaps. 5–7, 9.

Thayer, V. T., *Formative Ideas in American Education* (New York: Dodd, Mead and Company, 1965), chapter 15.

Chapter 17

Church, State, and Education

The United States represents a unique experiment in relationships between church, state, and education. Prior to the passage of the First Amendment to the Constitution of the United States, the historic tradition in most nations had been for these three functions to be intermeshed. The Founding Fathers of this country, however, in the interest of religious freedom, sought to establish and protect a new principle of separation of church from state and, consequently, from public education.

The idea that government and government-sponsored education should be absolutely free from religious domination and vice versa has been the center of continuous controversy. Differences of opinion are made more intense by the fact that both organized religion and government share many common interests, such as interest in morality of behavior, family stability, community health and welfare, as well as in education. What should be the roles of each, and how mutual concerns and responsibilities for similar functions may be discharged without undesirable, or even unconstitutional infringement of one on the other continue to be the center of heated debates, continuing theoretical inquiries, as well as legal tests. The ongoing search for lasting agreements on such questions centers in the quest for religious liberty. Government and education sponsored by government in this pursuit are often viewed as threats to man's right to freedom to worship, a privilege so dear that it has been protected by the Constitution itself.

Separation of Church and State as Official Doctrine

In a discourse on religious liberty delivered over a hundred years ago, the distinguished jurist Jeremiah S. Black stated:

> The manifest object of the men who framed the institutions of this country, was to have a state *without religion* and a *Church without politics*—that is to say, they meant that one should never be used as an engine for any purpose of the other. . . . Our fathers seemed to have been perfectly sincere in their belief that the members of the Church would be more patriotic, and the citizens of the state more religious by keeping their respective functions separate. For that reason they built up a wall of complete and perfect partition between the two.[1]

This interpretation of the American principle of separation of church and state as embodied in the First Amendment to the Constitution [2] was emphatically affirmed by the United States Supreme Court in 1947 and again in 1948. Speaking for the Court in each instance, Justice Hugo Black declared,

> Neither a state nor the Federal Government can set up a church. Neither can pass laws which aid one religion, aid all religions, or prefer one religion over another. Neither can force nor influence a person to go to or to remain away from church against his will or force him to profess a belief or disbelief in any religion. No person can be punished for entertaining or professing religious beliefs or disbeliefs, for church attendance or non-attendance. No tax in any amount, large or small, can be levied to support any

1. Quoted by Justice Frankfurter in his concurring opinion in *McCollum* v. *Board of Education*, 333 U.S. 203 (1948). Frankfurter describes Black as "one of the most distinguished of American judges."

2. This reads in part as follows: "Congress shall make no law respecting an establishment of religion, or prohibiting the free exercise thereof. . . ." These two injunctions are commonly spoken of as the "Establishment" and the "Free Exercise" clauses. Of them Justice Brennan states in *Abington School District* v. *Schempp*, 374 U.S. 203 (1963): "These two clauses, although distinct in their objectives and their applicability, emerged together from a common panorama of history. The inclusion of both restraints upon the power of Congress to legislate concerning religious matters shows unmistakably that the Framers of the First Amendment were not content to rest the protection of religious liberty exclusively upon either clause."

religious activities or institutions, whatever they may be called, or whatever form they may adopt to teach or practice religion. Neither a state nor the Federal Government can, openly or secretly, participate in the affairs of any religious organizations or groups and vice versa. In the words of Jefferson, the clause against establishment of religion by law was intended to erect "a wall of separation between Church and State." [3]

This concept of complete separation of church and state was rendered less vivid in its applications to released time programs for religious education in a subsequent decision of the Court in *Zorach* v. *Clauson.* In the latter decision the Court sanctioned "adjusting the schedule of public school events to sectarian needs" so as to permit religious organizations to conduct classes in religion on school time but off the school grounds. Contrast, for example, the words quoted above from Judge Jeremiah S. Black with this equally crucial statement by Justice William O. Douglas, who spoke for the Court in the *Zorach* v. *Clauson* case:

> When the state encourages religious instruction or cooperates with religious authorities by adjusting the schedule of public events to sectarian needs, it follows the best of our traditions. For it then respects the religious nature of our people and accommodates the public service to their spiritual needs. To hold that it may not would be to find in the Constitution a requirement that the government show a callous indifference to religious groups. That would be preferring those who believe in no religion over those who do believe. Government may not finance religious groups nor undertake religious instructions nor blend secular and sectarian education nor use secular institutions to force one or some religion on any person. But we find no constitutional requirement which makes it necessary for government to be hostile to religion and to throw its weight against efforts to widen the effective scope of religious influence. The government must be neutral when it comes to competition between sects. It may not thrust any sect on any person. It may not make a religious ob-

3. In *Everson* v. *Board of Education,* 330 U.S. 1 (1947) and the *McCollum* case. Attorneys for the state of Illinois in the latter case had requested the Court to declare the statement quoted an *obiter dicta.* It was to deny this request specifically that Justice Black repeated the words quoted.

servance compulsory. It may not coerce anyone to attend church, to observe a religious holiday, or to take religious instruction. But it can close its doors or suspend its operations as to those who want to repair to their religious sanctuary for worship or instruction. No more than that is undertaken here.[4]

The Elementary and Secondary Education Act of 1965 draws heavily on the philosophy of cooperation stated by Justice Douglas in providing for dual enrollment programs between public and nonpublic schools. The Act, which was passed by the 89th Congress, also provides certain kinds of indirect financial support for nonpublic schools. This legislation represents the first direct federal[4a] aid to elementary and secondary schools since the period of federal grants to the states in support of education in the nineteenth century to which reference is made in Chapter 4. It is categorical in nature, in contrast to unrestricted support, in that funds must go to strengthen educational services to children of low income families, to provide library resources, textbooks, and other instructional materials, to support supplementary educational centers and services, to finance educational research, and to strengthen state departments of public instruction. The indirect aid to nonpublic schools must be administered by a public agency and comes in the form of access to certain instructional resources, the benefits of research and development programs, and support of certain costs in public schools that cooperate in dual enrollment plans. The supporters of the legislation argued for the principle enunciated in the G.I. Bill of Rights that the aid is intended to assist pupils rather than schools. The concept of "friendly cooperation" between state and church was emphasized. The constitutionality of the legislation has yet to be established.

Evolution of the Principle of Separation of Church and State

Union of church and state characterized a majority of the colonies during the colonial period. Only in Rhode Island and the Middle Colonies (Pennsylvania, Delaware, New Jersey) was there anything analogous to toleration of religious differences. Each community was

4. 334 U.S. 306 (1952).
4a. See James E. Gibbs, Jr., Carl J. Sololowski, August W. Steinhilber and William C. Strasser, Jr., *Dual Enrollment in Public and Non-Public Schools*, U.S. Department of Health, Education and Welfare, Washington, D.C. 1965, 85 pp.

convinced that religious orthodoxy was essential not only for the salvation of the individual's soul but for the well-being of the community as well, and deviation from the narrow path of conformity brought severe penalties. When Nathaniel Ward declared in early Massachusetts that "All Familists, Antinomians, Anabaptists, and other Enthusiasts shall have free liberty to keep away from us," he voiced sentiments by no means peculiar to his own colony or his own day. As late as the Revolution, in one Massachusetts town alone "eighteen dissenters were in jail for refusing to pay ministerial rates in support of the established worship, and in all but one colony (Pennsylvania) it was illegal to celebrate the mass in public." [5]

The evolution of religious liberty in America has been one of gradual emancipation of the individual from the consequences of this union of church and state. In general, it has involved the following steps: (1) the right of dissenters in religion to reside in a colony without molestation; (2) the right of an individual to refrain from attending the established church and to maintain the church of his choice, while, of course, continuing to pay taxes in support of the established church; (3) the prohibition of one established church; and (4) legalizing the principle, as Jefferson phrased it, that it is "sinful and tyrannical" for the state to force contributions from an individual in support of *any religious belief,* be this his own or that of another.[6]

We should not assume that these developments, particularly points (3) and (4) in the paragraph above, reflected a weakening of religious conviction on the part of the people in the colonies. Rather, they were the result of a conviction which many had come to share (the conventionally minded as well as rationalists, Deists, Unitarians, and others of an unorthodox point of view) that religious organizations and the

5. Leo Pfeffer, "The Meaning of the Establishment Clause," *Buffalo Law Review,* Spring 1953, p. 225. Even in the Virginia of Madison and Jefferson, a Christian who ventured to deny the Trinity was subject to three years' imprisonment, and, if a parent, he might be denied the custody of his own children.

6. Jefferson's own words were: "Whereas Almighty God hath created the mind free . . . to compel a man to furnish contributions of money for the propagation of opinions which he disbelieves, is sinful and tyrannical; that even the forcing him to support this or that teacher of his own religious persuasion, is depriving him of the comfortable liberty of giving his contributions to the particular pastor, whose morals he would make his pattern, and whose powers he feels most persuasive to righteousness." Section II of his Bill for Establishing Religious Freedom reads in part, "Be It Enacted By the General Assembly, That no man shall be compelled to frequent or support any religious worship, place, or ministry whatsoever. . . ."

state would thrive best when the interests of the one were completely divorced from the interests of the other.

For example, in 1785, the Virginia Baptists opposed a "Bill Establishing a Provision for Teachers of the Christian Religion" on the grounds that

> no human laws ought to be established for this purpose; but that every person ought to be left entirely free in respect to matters of religion; that the holy Author of our religion needs no such compulsive measures for the promotion of his cause; that the Gospel wants not the feeble arm of man for its support; that it has made, and will again through divine power make its way against all opposition; and that should the Legislature assume the right of taxing the people for the support of the Gospel, it will be destructive to religious liberty.[7]

And John Leland, a Baptist leader in Virginia, wrote in 1791 that "government has no more to do with religious opinions of men than it has with the principles of mathematics." [8]

Other religious leaders assumed an identical position, but for different reasons. The exercise of religion, as they saw it, was a "natural right" and was thus excluded from the legitimate area of governmental concern. Religious organizations were viewed as private corporations, free to operate within the state but dependent for their support upon the voluntary contributions of their members and friends. To men of this mind, Thomas Paine's statement in *Common Sense* seemed most sensible. "As to religion, I hold it to be the indispensable duty of government to protect all conscientious professions thereof; and I know of no other business which government hath to do therewith."

The determination of religionists and nonreligionists alike to separate religion from government is evidenced by attempts to abolish both single and multiple establishment. The traditional requirement that all men, regardless of their religious affiliations, should be taxed in support of an established church led dissidents to identify religious liberty not only with the freedom to worship according to one's own conscience but also with exemption from taxation in support of another man's religion. The significance of this identification of religious freedom with

7. Conrad H. Moehlman, *The Wall of Separation Between Church and State* (Boston: Beacon Press, 1951), p. 80.
8. Pfeffer, *op. cit.*, p. 229.

freedom from taxation in support of an alien faith, it is argued, is overlooked today by the advocates of nonpreferential assistance to religion. That Madison and Jefferson so conceived religious liberty seems amply demonstrated by their writings, as well as by their actions when serving as presidents of the United States.[9]

In a letter to Edward Livingston, dated July 10, 1822, Madison wrote of the American experiment with religious liberty:

> Notwithstanding the general progress made within the last two centuries in favor of this branch of liberty, and the full establishment of it, in some parts of our country, there remains in others a strong bias toward the old error, that without some sort of alliance or coalition between Government and Religion neither can be duly supported. Such indeed is the tendency to such a coalition, and such its corrupting influence upon both parties, that the danger cannot be too carefully guarded against. . . . It was the belief of all sects at one time that the establishment of Religion by law, was right and necessary; that the true religion ought to be established in exclusion of every other; and that the only question to be decided was which was the true religion. The example of Holland proved that a toleration of sects, dissenting from the established sect, was safe and even useful. The example of the Colonies, now States, which rejected religious establishments altogether, proved that all Sects might be safely and advantageously put on a footing of equal and entire freedom. . . . We are teaching the world the great truth that Governments do better without Kings and Nobles than with them. The merit will be doubled by the other lesson that Religion flourishes in greater purity, without than with the aid of government.[10]

9. In 1783 Jefferson proposed the following article for incorporation in the Constitution of Virginia: "The General Assembly shall not have the power to infringe this constitution; to abridge the civil rights of any person on account of his religious beliefs; to restrain him from professing and supporting that belief, or to compel contributions, other than those he shall have personally stipulated for the support of that or any other. . . ." [Saul K. Padover, *The Complete Madison* (New York: Duell, Sloan & Pearce, Inc., 1943), p. 113].

Both Madison and Jefferson (and, for that matter, Jackson) considered even the issuing of a Thanksgiving proclamation unconstitutional. To ease his conscience, after yielding to political considerations in this matter, Madison was careful to employ nonsectarian terms. Madison likewise considered the payment of chaplains for Congress a violation of the Constitution and suggested that their salaries be paid out of the voluntary contributions of the members of Congress.

10. Saul K. Padover, *op. cit.*, p. 309.

To perpetuate the beneficial results of a strict neutrality on the part of government in matters relating to religion, the framers of the First Amendment sought to establish as a constitutional principle the proposition that all authority over religion is prohibited to government. Credence is given to this interpretation by the obvious failure of the friends of multiple establishment to phrase the Amendment specifically so as to permit nonpreferential assistance to religion.

Two efforts of this character were made in the Senate after the amendment had passed the House. One suggested wording ran as follows: "Congress shall make no law establishing one Religious Sect or Society in preference to others, or prohibiting the free exercise thereof, nor shall the rights of conscience be infringed." [11]

The second read: "Congress shall make no law establishing any particular denomination of religion in preference to another, or prohibiting the free exercise thereof, nor shall the rights of conscience be infringed." [12]

Both of these suggested revisions failed of passage. The wording as we have it today was arrived at in conference between the Senate and the House. In the light of abortive attempts to legalize nonpreferential assistance to religious sects, it would seem that the wording finally arrived at was intended to ban public aid to establishments in the plural as well as in the singular.

This conclusion is further confirmed by trends within the states in the period immediately preceding and following the approval of the First Amendment by the people of the states.

Following their break with England, the original thirteen states faced the necessity of adopting constitutions to replace their colonial charters. In this process their attitudes toward the establishment of religion and freedom of conscience became clear. Between the years 1776 and 1791, nine of the thirteen states (including Rhode Island, which retained its original charter) wrote into their constitutions unmistakable prohibitions against establishments of religion, plural as well as singular. Evidently experience with multiple support of religious establishments (or, to use the contemporary phrase, "cooperation between government and religious bodies") had been no more satisfactory than that with single establishment. Consequently they had come to agree

11. *Journal of the First Session of the Senate of the United States of America* (New York: John Greenleaf, 1789), p. 116.
12. *Ibid.*, p. 117.

upon one and only one method of safeguarding both the integrity of religious organizations and the religious conscience: to deprive government of all authority to promote or to regulate religion or to impose taxes in its support.

Subsequent developments within the four lagging states were in harmony with the trend in opposition to government support of any and all religions. Maryland in 1810, Connecticut in 1818, New Hampshire in 1819, and Massachusetts in 1833 joined with their sister states to prohibit public support for any and all religious establishments.[13]

As is well known, when the First Amendment to the federal Constitution was adopted it was in no way binding upon the states. Each member of the Union was left free to determine for itself what should be its relation to religious corporations and, since education was clearly recognized as a state and not a federal function, the definition of the relation of government to public education became a matter of state rather than federal determination.

One of the first states to blaze the trail in definition was Connecticut. In revising its constitution in 1818 Connecticut faced the problem of utilizing funds received from the sale of public lands. Should these be devoted exclusively to the development of public education or should they be used to promote the interests of both public and private schools? The answer given was in harmony with the conviction that both state and church would profit from an absence of dependence upon each other. Accordingly, the constitution provided, first, that the support and maintenance of church buildings and ministers should be "by a tax of the members of any such society only, to be laid by a major vote of the legal voters assembled at any society meeting," and, second, that "the fund, called the School Fund, shall remain a perpetual fund, the interest of which shall be *inviolably appropriated* to the support and encouragement of the public, or common schools, throughout the State . . . and no law shall be made, authorizing said fund to be diverted to any other use than the encouragement and support of public or common schools. . . ."

Connecticut's example was followed by states in the East as well as

13. For example, the Maryland constitution of 1776 stated that the Legislature is authorized "in their discretion . . . to lay a general and equal tax, for the support of any particular place of worship or minister. . . ." In 1810 this wording was changed to read, "That it shall not be lawful for the General Assembly to lay an equal and general tax on the people of this state for the support of any religion."

by western applicants for admission to the Union, with the result that by the end of the century, all but two states had prohibited by constitutional provision or through legislative act either the teaching of sectarian doctrines in the public schools or the use of public funds for religious schools, or both.[14]

Since these developments antedated the applications of the First Amendment to the states through the Fourteenth Amendment, Justice Frankfurter was moved to remark in *McCollum* v. *Board of Education* that "Separation in the field of education . . . was not imposed upon unwilling States by force of superior law. In this respect the Fourteenth Amendment merely reflected a principle then dominant in our national life. To the extent that the Constitution thus made it binding upon the States, the basis of the restriction is the whole experience of our people."

The First Amendment Is Made Applicable to the States

Although education under the Constitution still remains primarily a state rather than a federal responsibility, the Congress of the United States has on numerous occasions both assisted education in the states and provided for educational projects under the auspices of the federal government. General assistance to education began, in principle at least, under the Continental Congress with a provision in the Ordinance of 1785 that "there shall be reserved the Lot 16 of every township for the maintenance of public schools within said township." Federal assistance has, on the whole, been in accordance with the twofold principle that public funds made available to education shall be used exclusively for public education and that public education shall remain free of sectarian instruction. In line with this policy, Congress in 1896, when appropriating funds for education in the District of Columbia, specifically stated: "And it is hereby declared to be the policy of the Government of the United States to make no appropriation of money or property for the purpose of the founding, maintaining, or aiding by payment for services, expenses, or otherwise, any church or religious

14. James O'Neill, *Religion and Education Under the Constitution* (New York: Harper & Brothers, 1949), pp. 143–44.

denomination, or any institution of society which is under sectarian or ecclesiastical control. . . ." [15]

Inasmuch as both state and federal governments are directly responsible to the people, it is not surprising to find the two keeping step in matters of supreme concern to the people. Not until well into the present century, however, was it clearly established that essential agreement on policy in the relation of religion to education was rendered obligatory by the Fourteenth Amendment to the federal Constitution.[16] In 1922, Oregon undertook to require all children to attend public schools. The obvious intention of this legislation was to abolish private schools. The constitutionality of this act was challenged by the Society of the Sisters of the Holy Names of Jesus and Mary, and the case found its way, eventually, into the United States Supreme Court. In rendering its decision, the Court declared that the Oregon statute "unreasonably interferes with the liberty of parents and guardians to direct the upbringing and education of children under their control" and violates the provisions of the Fourteenth Amendment that no state shall "deprive any person of life, liberty, or property, without due process of law. . . ." [17]

After this decision a more specific application of the Bill of Rights to the states was inevitable, and in 1925, in the case of *Gitlow* v. *New York,* the Court ruled that the rights of freedom of speech and press "which are protected by the First Amendment from abridgement by Congress . . . are among the fundamental personal rights and liberties protected by the due process clause of the Fourteenth Amendment from impairment by the States." [18] Subsequent decisions of the Supreme Court have confirmed the principle that the restrictions placed upon Congress in the First Amendment are now "wholly applicable to the states."

15. U.S. Statutes at Large, 29:411 (June 11, 1896). Again, when passing the Smith-Hughes Act, Congress stipulated: "No portion of any monies appropriated under this act for the benefit of the States shall be applied, directly or indirectly . . . for the support of any religious or privately owned or conducted school or college" [*Ibid.,* 39:936 (February 23, 1917)].

16. For a helpful discussion of the applications of the Fourteenth Amendment to the states in matters of religion, see Alvin W. Johnson and Frank H. Yost, *Separation of Church and State in the United States* (Minneapolis, Minn.: University of Minnesota Press, 1948), chap. I.

17. *Pierce et al.* v. *Society of Sisters,* 268 U.S. 510 (1925).

18. 268 U.S. 652 (1925).

Public Schools and Sectarian Practices

Despite Justice Frankfurter's assertion that the application of the First Amendment to the states through the Fourteenth Amendment "merely reflected a principle then dominant in American life," we should not conclude that the concept of a "wall of separation between church and state" has been uniformly interpreted within states and localities. Nor is this surprising when we consider that neither in theory nor in practice has the meaning of "separation" as applied to education been crystal clear. Indeed, the twin facts of wide variation in the religious composition of school communities and the practice of local autonomy in education have insured contradictory interpretations of the concept of nonsectarian instruction. In a predominantly Protestant population, for example, as was that of Massachusetts in 1827 when that state enacted a law forbidding school boards to purchase or use textbooks calculated to favor any particular religious sect or tenet, few if any objected to the required reading of the Protestant Bible or to religious exercises in the form of prayers and hymns of Protestant origin. Even Horace Mann, in his efforts in the 1840s to exclude sectarian practices from the schools, sought to disarm his critics by pointing out that while under his administration "sectarian instruction has, to a great extent, ceased to be given," the Bible, "the acknowledged expositor of Christianity" . . . has been restored "to schools in which it had previously been excluded." [19]

On the other hand, in communities far more heterogeneous in religious composition than those of Massachusetts, the concept of nonsectarianism assumed quite a different meaning. As Catholic and other religious minorities increased in numbers and influence, liberal educators and religious leaders came to realize that what constitutes nonsectarian instruction under one set of conditions is sectarian under another. Consequently, reading from the Protestant Bible, singing Protestant hymns, engaging in Protestant prayers, and performing other rites and ceremonies which seemed normal and natural, or at least remained unchallenged in Protestant communities, eventually took on a

19. For Horace Mann's views on religious education, see his Twelfth Annual Report to the Massachusetts State Board of Education. This is reprinted in *The Republic and the Schools: Horace Mann on the Education of Free Men,* Lawrence A. Cremin, ed. (New York: Teachers College, Columbia University, 1960).

sectarian hue and were objected to as an infringement upon the freedom of the religious conscience.

There was stubborn opposition in many quarters, however. School authorities were inclined to fall back upon the assumption that these exercises were positive factors in promoting individual morality and civic health. Accordingly, the first reaction to the demand that Catholic children be exempted from participation in these Protestant exercises was to compel compliance, often on pain of expulsion. On occasion, when Catholics ventured to express publicly their opposition to these violations of freedom of conscience, mobs rose up to demonstrate in mob fashion the superiority of the Protestant faith. In Philadelphia in 1844, for example, Catholic schools were burned by an irate mob in answer to a Catholic bishop's suggestion that public schools exempt Catholic children from the necessity of reading from the Protestant version of the Bible.[20]

Fortunately, a more charitable spirit gradually asserted itself, and the principle of the Golden Rule was seen to apply to Catholics and Jews—and even to atheists—as well as to Protestants.

In the emergence of this spirit the courts were often helpful. In 1872, to take one conspicuous example, the Supreme Court of Ohio sustained the board of education of Cincinnati in prohibiting "religious instruction and the reading of religious books, including the Bible," in the common schools of the city. Speaking for the Court, Judge Welch pointed out that the petitioners, who were bent on requiring the teaching of religion in the schools, were actually seeking to impose their own concepts of religion and to establish Christianity as the law of the state.[21]

Although court decisions were by no means consistent (the highest court of one state interpreting the Bible as a sectarian document and that of another holding it to be above sectarianism), the general trend in the latter part of the nineteenth century was toward tolerance and a growing conception of the public school as a secular institution. The

20. Howard Beale, *A History of Freedom of Teaching in American Schools* (New York: Charles Scribner's Sons, 1941), p. 94. Edward J. Richter and Berton Dulce in their *Religion and the Presidency* (New York: The Macmillan Company, 1962) provide a vivid description of ways in which "native Americans" greeted Catholic immigration early in the nineteenth century. Attacks upon Catholic schools and churches were but one phase of an unlovely role that religious intolerance has played in American life since the days of the Founding Fathers.

21. *Board of Education v. Minor*, 23 Ohio 211 (1872).

school came to be thought of as an institution which strives to minister to needs common to all young people in communities that are heterogeneous in matters of religion, and which carefully avoids indoctrination in a realm where, as Justice Frankfurter once said, "conflicts are most easily and most bitterly engendered."

By 1900 Massachusetts was the only state in the Union in which morning prayers and Bible reading were required by statute, although, to be sure, in many schools throughout the nation these practices were engaged in without statutory sanction or prohibition.

Then came a change in the tide. In 1913, the legislature of Pennsylvania passed a law which made the reading of the Bible compulsory in all public schools. By 1946, thirteen states had taken similar action, and in June of 1963, the month in which the United States Supreme Court declared unconstitutional both Bible reading and the reciting of the Lord's Prayer at opening exercises in public schools, it was estimated that nearly 42 per cent of all school systems in the nation were observing a daily routine of Bible reading.[22]

Religious instruction on "released time" likewise dates from 1913. By 1948, the year of the *McCollum* decision, it was estimated that approximately 2500 communities were providing religious instruction in "cooperation" with public schools for nearly 2,000,000 pupils.[23] Moreover, by mid-century, there was evidence of a growing demand for the inclusion of some form of direct religious instruction in the curriculum of public schools as one means of combatting what many considered a dangerous trend toward "secularism in American education."

As might be expected, these trends encountered opposition from advocates of strict separation of church and state. And again, as in the nineteenth century, appeals to the courts brought contradictory results.

22. According to a survey conducted by the *New York Times*, 76 per cent of all school districts in the South, 67 per cent of all in the East, 18 per cent of all in the Midwest, and 11 per cent of all in the West were engaged in the practice of Bible reading. Since close to 42 per cent of all school systems in the nation were reported as observing a daily routine of Bible reading, and a high proportion of these were large school systems, the study concluded that a majority of American school children were affected by the ruling of the Supreme Court. (*The New York Times*, June 18, 1963, p. 27.) In *School Life* for July 1962, pp. 8–9, August W. Steinhilber summarizes briefly the legal status of Bible reading and daily recital of the Lord's Prayer in the states.

23. For information on the extent of various types of sectarian practices in public schools at the time of the *McCollum* decision, see the Research Bulletin of the National Education Association, entitled *The State and Sectarian Education*, Washington, D.C., 1946.

In 1904 a Kansas court approved the required presence of all children in the classroom during the recital of the Lord's Prayer and the Twenty-third Psalm. A second court, in South Dakota in 1929 ordered the reinstatement of Catholic children whom a teacher had expelled for refusal to attend opening exercises at which the King James version of the Bible was read and the Lord's Prayer recited, but granted the legality of the practice provided children were permitted to absent themselves during the exercises. Still other courts (Illinois in 1910 and Louisiana in 1915) ruled that Bible reading in public schools was unconstitutional. A similar state of confusion obtained with respect to the legality of programs of religious instruction on "released time." [24]

By and large, before 1947 proponents of some form of assistance to nonpublic schools and of the introduction of religion in public education had reason to believe they were riding on the wave of the future. As Justice Rutledge was moved to observe in *Everson* v. *Board of Education,*

> Neither so high nor so impregnable today as yesterday is the wall raised between Church and State by Virginia's great statute of religious freedom and the First Amendment, now made applicable to all States by the Fourteenth. New Jersey's statute sustained is the first, if indeed it is not the second breach to be made by the Court's action. That a third and fourth, and still others may be attempted we may be sure.[25]

Judge Rutledge had in mind, as the first breach of principle, a decision of the Supreme Court in 1930 which sanctioned the furnishing of free textbooks to children attending parochial schools, as well as those in public schools. Here, as later in the Everson case, the Court saw no direct aid as such to a church school, holding rather that the child and not the institution was being assisted, and "the taxing power of the

24. For a review of court decisions with respect to all types of religious practices prior to the *McCollum* decision in 1948, see Johnson and Yost, *Separation of Church and State in the United States* (Minneapolis: University of Minnesota Press, 1948).

25. In *Everson* v. *Board of Education* (1947), the Supreme Court had ruled favorably on the right of New Jersey to reimburse parents for the expense of transporting children to parochial school in public conveyances and on public routes. The Court interpreted this provision as a public health measure. At the same time it laid down the general principle that the state cannot "aid one religion, aid all religions, or prefer one religion over another."

State is exerted for a public purpose" when the books distributed are identical with those used in the public schools and are nonreligious and nonsectarian in character.[26]

The decisions of the Supreme Court in *Cochran* v. *Louisiana State Board of Education* and in *Everson* v. *Board of Education* seemed to foreshadow a lowering of the "wall of separation" between church and state. Indeed, the words of Justice Hugo L. Black on behalf of the Court in the latter instance prompted Justice Jackson in his dissenting opinion to observe that the majority opinion seemed "utterly discordant" with the grounds upon which it had based its conclusions and reminded him of "Julia who, according to Byron's reports, 'whispering "I will ne'er consent"—consented.'"

Encouraged by the Court's evident intention to find ways of affording aid to children attending church-related schools, if not to the institutions themselves, friends of the latter began to insist that all federal legislation designed to aid education within the states should include provision for "auxiliary services" to nonpublic schools.

The *McCollum* decision appeared as a roadblock to these efforts with its reaffirmation of the principle that neither a state nor the federal government "can pass laws which aid one religion, aid all religions, or prefer one religion over another," nor can a tax in any amount, large or small, "be levied to support any religious activities or institutions, whatever they may be called, or whatever form they may adopt to teach or practice religion."

The immediate effect of this decision was to launch a debate, historical and legal, respecting the origin and meaning of the Establishment Clause of the First Amendment. Among the first to envisage the implications of Justice Black's words for future relations of government and church-related schools, as well as for religious practices in public schools, were the Catholic Bishops of America. In a statement issued on November 20, 1948 the Bishops asserted:

> To one who knows something of history and law, the meaning of the First Amendment is clear from its own words: Congress shall make no law respecting an establishment of religion or forbidding the free exercise thereof. The meaning is even clearer in the records of Congress that enacted it. Then and throughout English and Colonial history "an establishment of religion" meant

26. *Cochran* v. *Louisiana State Board of Education,* 281 U.S. 370.

the setting up of an official church which would receive from the government favors not equally accorded to others in the cooperation between government and religion—which was simply taken for granted in our country at that time and has, in many ways, continued to this day. Under the First Amendment, the Federal Government could not extend this type of preferential treatment to one religion as against another, nor could it compel or forbid any state to do so. . . . Lawyers trained in the American tradition of law will be amazed to find in the McCollum case the majority opinions pay scant attention to logic, history, or accepted norms of legal interpretations.[27]

On the other hand, both historical and legal talent were not wanting to document the contention that Madison and his associates in the First Congress intended the Amendment "to create a complete and permanent separation of the spheres of religious activity and civil authority by comprehensively forbidding every form of public aid or support for religion." [28]

The discussion thus begun has continued without abatement. The partisans of rigid separation of church and state insist the Court is correct in its assumption that at the time of the adoption of the First Amendment

> . . . the word "establishment" had a broad meaning comprehending almost every tangible manifestation of religion or at least organized or institutional religion. An incorporated church was a "religious establishment" in Madison's veto message. A place where persons worshiped was a "religious establishment." Jefferson considered even a non-sectarian Presidential proclamation of religion interdicted by the First Amendment. Madison considered the institutions of Congressional chaplains as religious establishments.[29]

A second group quotes from the record to sustain the position that the Amendment was

27. "The Christian in Action," published in *The New York Times*, November 20, 1948.
28. Justice Rutledge's words in *Everson v. Board of Education.*
29. Leo Pfeffer in a debate with James O'Neill on "The Meaning of the Establishment Clause," *The Buffalo Law Review*, Spring 1953, pp. 225–78.

designed to meet the wishes of the people of the various states who had adopted resolutions, memorials, and petitions, recommending that the Federal Constitution should make clear that "no particular sect or society ought to be favored or established by law in preference to others. . . ." The words "an establishment of religion" interpreted in the light of their history cannot properly be held to mean "any, even non-preferential assistance to religion." [30]

The Supreme Court Reaffirms Its Interpretation of Separation of Church and State

We must resist the temptation to review in detail the arguments for and against these interpretations of the intentions of the Founding Fathers in view of the extensive discussions of the issues involved by the Justices of the Supreme Court in the "prayer decisions" of June 25, 1962 and June 17, 1963.[31]

Conscious of serious division in the public mind as to the meaning of the Establishment and Free Exercise clauses of the First Amendment, Justice Clark, speaking for the Court, was at great pains to document carefully the Court's considered judgment as to the original intent of the First Amendment.[32]

30. James O'Neill, *op. cit.*, pp. 243, 247.

31. In the first of these decisions, *Engel* v. *Vitale,* 370 U.S. 421 (1962), the Court declared unconstitutional the daily recitation in public schools of a prayer formulated by the New York State Board of Regents. In June of 1963 it took similar action with respect to an act of the legislature of Pennsylvania and a regulation of the Board of School Commissioners of the City of Baltimore requiring the daily recitation of the Lord's Prayer and readings from the Bible, without comment, at opening exercises in public schools. The Court's decision affecting these two cases is commonly spoken of as the "Schempp-Murray decision" but is officially designated *Abington School District* v. *Schempp,* 374 U.S. 203 (1963).

Justice Brennan's concurring opinion in Schempp-Murray covered some 77 pages in the Supreme Court Report (Nos. 142 and 119, October Term, 1962), and consists of an exhaustive review of both the Establishment and Free Exercise clauses in their historical and legal setting. Together with Justice Rutledge's dissent in *Everson* v. *Board of Education,* and Justice Frankfurter's concurring opinion in *McCollum* v. *Board of Education* it may well become a classic statement on church-state relations in education.

32. Justice Stewart was the sole dissenter in *Abington School District* v. *Schempp.* He based his dissent, however, more on his interpretation of the facts in the two cases before the Court than on his difference with the basic position of the majority.

In so doing, he emphasizes three points, documenting each with copious references to prior decisions of the Court.

(1) "First," states Justice Clark, "this Court has decisively settled that the First Amendment's mandate that 'Congress shall make no law respecting an establishment of religion, or prohibiting the free exercise thereof' has been made wholly applicable to the States by the Fourteenth Amendment."

(2) "Second, this Court has rejected unequivocally the contention that the Establishment Clause forbids only governmental preference of one religion over another."

After documenting this conclusion by reference to decisions of the Court since the *Everson* case, the Justice adds, with seeming impatience:

> While none of the parties to either of these cases has questioned these basic conclusions of the Court, both of which have been long established, recognized, and consistently reaffirmed, others continue to question their history, logic and efficacy. Such contentions, in the light of the consistent interpretations in cases of this Court, seem entirely untenable and of value only as academic exercises.

(3) Third, quoting in this instance from *Cantwell* v. *Connecticut*, 310 U.S. 303 (1940), Justice Clark draws attention to the interrelationship of the Establishment and Free Exercise clauses of the Amendment. Taken together they require, as Justice Frankfurter wrote in *McCollum* v. *Board of Education,* that government "abstain from fusing functions of government and of religious sects, not merely to treat them all equally." [33] Which is another way of saying that in matters of religion government must maintain a position of "wholesome neutrality." To quote once more from the majority of the Court:

> The wholesome neutrality of which this Court's cases speak thus stems from a recognition of the teachings of history that powerful sects or groups might bring about a fusion of governmental and religious functions or a concert or dependency of one

33. In his concurring opinion, Justice Brennan also writes in this connection: "In sum, the history which our prior decisions have summoned to aid interpretations of the Establishment Clause permits little doubt that its prohibition was designed comprehensively to prevent those official involvements of religion which would tend to foster or discourage religious worship or belief."

upon the other to the end that official support of the State or Federal Government would be placed behind the tenets of one or all orthodoxies. This the Establishment Clause prohibits. And a further reason for neutrality is found in the Free Exercise Clause, which recognizes the value of religious training, teaching and observance and, more particularly, the right of every person to freely choose his own course with reference thereto, free of any compulsion from the State. This the Free Exercise guarantees.

Many who are willing to accept the Court's interpretation of separation of church and state nevertheless question the validity of its application to devotional exercises in public schools. They point out that public education, as we know it today, was nonexistent at the time of the adoption of the Constitution. On what grounds, then, can we assume that the Founding Fathers would have prohibited what they were unable to envisage?

To this argument Justice Brennan replies that in interpreting the Constitution we are concerned less with specific practices than with a general principle. "An awareness of history and an appreciation of the aims of the Founding Fathers," he states, "do not always resolve concrete problems." That is to say, when we seek to apply the First Amendment to religious practices of today we should ask ourselves not how Madison and Jefferson would have viewed them under conditions peculiar to their day, but whether or not they "threaten those consequences which the Framers deeply feared; whether, in short, they tend to promote that type of interdependence between religion and state which the First Amendment was designed to prevent." [34]

Justice Brennan also insists that the very fact that eighteenth-century schools were private institutions renders their practices inapplicable to public schools of today. "The structure of American education has greatly changed since the First Amendment was adopted," he reminds us. The population served by the public school of today is highly diversified as to religion. Our forefathers "knew differences chiefly among Protestant sects. Today the Nation is far more heterogeneous reli-

34. While granting the possibility that Jefferson and Madison might have considered religious practices in public schools permissible, Justice Brennan holds that such a conclusion is at best uncertain. He quotes, for example, Jefferson's admonition against "putting the Bible and Testament into the hands of children at an age when their judgments are not sufficiently matured for religious inquiries," and his suggestion instead that "their memories may here be stored with the most useful facts of Grecian, Roman, European and American history."

giously, including as it does substantial minorities not only of Catholics and Jews but as well of those who worship according to no versions of the Bible and those who worship no God at all." Consequently, practices "which may have been objectionable to no one in the time of Jefferson and Madison may today be highly offensive to many persons, the deeply devout and the non-believers alike."

Again, continues the Justice, we must consider fully the implications of the fact that public schools are supplied by "funds exacted not alone from parents, not alone from those who hold particular religious views, nor indeed from those who subscribe to any creed at all." This gives to them a "uniquely *public* function" implicit in the history and character of American public education:

> . . . the training of American citizens in an atmosphere free of parochial, divisive, or separatist influences of any sort—an atmosphere in which children may assimilate a heritage common to all American groups and religions. . . . This is a heritage neither theistic nor atheistic, but simply civic and patriotic.[35]

By way of summary, then, we may say that the principle of separation of church and state in the United States has come to mean the following:

(1) Religious convictions and religious organizations are, as James Madison expressed it, "wholly exempt" from "the cognizance of civil society." By this is not meant that government is either indifferent to or hostile to religion, but, rather, that the maintenance and the promotion of religious institutions and the regulation and control over religious ideas are denied to all governmental authority. The religious conscience is thus protected from infringement upon its free exercise, and religious corporations as private organizations are assured complete freedom to further their doctrines. But the price of freedom is a constitutional ban upon public support of sectarian interests.

(2) As applied to education, the principle of separation of church and state requires (a) that all funds appropriated by state and federal governments alike are to be used exclusively for public education; (b) that no public funds may properly be granted to any institution

35. This "uniquely public function" is one with the "wholesome neutrality" emphasized in the majority opinion. Of this Justice Clark states: "While the Free Exercise Clause clearly prohibits the use of state action to deny the rights of free exercise to anyone, it has never meant that a majority could use the machinery of the State to practice its beliefs."

in which sectarian doctrines are taught; and (c) that government can neither "employ the organs of government for essentially religious purposes," nor "employ religious means to serve secular interests, however legitimate they may be, at least without the clearest demonstrations that non-religious means will not suffice." [36]

It was apparently the hope of the Supreme Court in its careful documentation of the two "prayer cases" to erase much of the confusion and ambiguity that had followed earlier pronouncements. If so, the Court was soon to be disappointed. Both in the area of public assistance to church-related schools and in applying the concept of "neutrality" with respect to religious instruction in public education serious differences continue to beset educators and to disturb the communities they serve.

We turn now to contemporary dissatisfaction with a policy that restricts public funds exclusively to the support of education under public auspices.

Suggested Reading

Boles, Donald Edwards, *The Bible, Religion, and the Public Schools* (Ames, Iowa: Iowa University Press, 1963).

Butts, R. Freeman, *The American Tradition in Religion and Education* (Boston: Beacon Press, Inc., 1950).

Corwin, Edward S., "The Supreme Court As National School Board," *Law and Contemporary Problems*, Winter 1949.

Duker, Sam, *The Public Schools and Religion: The Legal Context* (New York: Harper & Row, 1966), Chapters 2, 3, 5–8.

Healey, Robert M., *Jefferson on Religion in Public Education* (New Haven: Yale University Press, 1962).

Howe, Marke de Wolfe, "The Constitutional Question," in *Religion and the Free Society* (New York: The Fund for the Republic, 1958).

Kempner, Maximilian, "The Supreme Court and the Establishment and Free Exercise of Religion," in *Religion and the Free Society* (New York: The Fund for the Republic, 1958).

Lardner, L. A., "How Far Does the Constitution Separate Church and State?" *American Political Science Review*, March 1951, pp. 110–32.

Pfeffer, Leo, "Freedom and Separation: America's Contribution to Civilization," *A Journal of Church and State*, November 1960, pp. 100–11.

———, "The Schempp-Murray Decision on School Prayers and Bible Reading," *A Journal of Church and State*, November 1963, pp. 165–75.

United States Supreme Court, *Abington School District* v. *Schempp*, 374 U.S. 203 (1963).

36. Justice Brennan in *Abington School District* v. *Schempp*.

Chapter 18

Public Assistance to Nonpublic Schools

Factors Which Weaken the Policy of No Public Assistance to Nonpublic Schools

The prevailing attitude of the American people toward public education at the turn of the century was well expressed in these words of Theodore Roosevelt:

> We could suffer no national calamity more far reaching in its effects than would be implied in the abandonment of our system of non-sectarian schools; and it is a very unfortunate thing for any man, or any body of men, to be identified with opposition thereto—it is not really a question of sects at all; it is merely an illustration of survival or importation here of the utterly un-American and thoroughly Old World idea of the subordination of the layman to the priest; it is an issue between intelligent American laymen of every faith on the one hand, and ambitious, foolish or misguided supporters of a worn out system of clerical government on the other. Our public schools are here to stay.[1]

Nevertheless, as was suggested in Chapter 17, there were by 1913 clear indications of a drift away from the principle that public funds are to be used exclusively for public education and that sectarian in-

1. Quoted by Agnes Meyer in an address delivered before the National Education Association, July 3, 1952. *Addresses and Proceedings*, vol. 90, p. 70.

419

struction should find no place in the classrooms of the public school. Multiple factors doubtless contributed to this change of mind.

Not least in importance is the fact that with the common acceptance of separation of church and state, the principle received slight emphasis in the curriculum of school and college. What one generation of Americans had struggled to attain and succeeding generations took for granted, many who came after knew only vaguely.

Heavy immigration from countries in which separation of church and state is unknown constituted a second factor related to the first. Thus, there is little in the conscious tradition of large segments of the population today to create acute awareness of the significance of the principle of separation in American experience.

Still a third factor is the expanded influence of the Catholic Church. Protestant denominations have expanded as well, but none has developed as extensive a program of church-supported schools. The general policy of the Catholic Church, in other countries as well as the United States, is to maintain its own church-administered schools. The curriculums include both secular and sectarian subjects and with some variations may allow an intermeshing of the two. Because historical practice in other countries is to provide state support for church schools, the Catholic Church quite naturally has favored governmental support of its schools in this country.

Generalizations about the impact of the Catholic Church in promoting public assistance for nonpublic schools must be interpreted against a background of certain factors, each of which may vary to some extent from parish to parish, diocese to diocese, order to order, and of course among individuals. The Catholic Church in the United States, many religious leaders point out, functions in its own environment and, hence, does not always follow as rigidly the doctrine that may characterize church bodies in other countries. Differences prevail among Catholic educators as well as laymen just as they do in other groups. Spokesmen who apparently "speak for the church" do not necessarily reflect a united and unquestioned support from the church leaders and laymen. Mention should be made, additionally, of the fact that any objective account of the controversy about public assistance to nonpublic schools must rely heavily upon statements by Catholic leaders favoring government assistance to church-supported schools since no other denominational group has been so active in this area. Nor has any other church body assumed such a burden for support of its own schools.

Catholic representation in the population of the United States has grown from 1 per cent in 1800, to 16 per cent in 1900, and to over 24 per cent in 1966. The growth is further reflected by the fact that today Catholics comprise about 37 per cent of the entire church membership of the country. As Irwin Widen has pointed out, "Catholicism does not approach majority status; but because of the fragmentation of Protestantism the Catholic Church is by far the largest single denomination in this country, with more than three times the membership of the second-ranking Methodist Church." [2]

Not only has the Catholic Church increased in numbers, but as its members have come to participate in manifold activities of the American community their views have naturally received more visibility. Not all Catholics agree, however, as to the proper relationship between church and state. Nor do all feel that a closer merging of religion and education is constitutionally possible. President John F. Kennedy, a Catholic himself, argued that general support for church schools by the federal government was unconstitutional. Nor has the general discipline of the church been uniformly followed. The church's traditional position that children of Catholics should attend parochial schools and that church members should contribute to the support of such institutions has provoked recent debate among laymen and clergy about the value of parochial schools. The sheer economic burden of maintaining church-supported schools for increasing numbers of students has stimulated proposals for modifications in policy for parochial education. Some Catholic educational leaders have seen in the new dual enrollment programs the answer to the growing burden of educational costs; others still favor outright federal aid to both nonpublic and public schools; another proposal is for government reimbursement for tax funds paid by Catholics to support public schools. [3]

Fourth, Catholics are not alone in their desire to maintain church schools or in their determination to persuade the state to relieve their

2. Irwin Widen, "Public Support for Parochial Schools: Why the Issue Has Re-emerged," *History of Education Journal*, Winter 1953, p. 60.

3. A recent suggestion is that parents of children in attendance at nonpublic schools receive credit upon their income tax returns for tuition paid to nonpublic schools.

For a discussion of the problem of Catholic education as Catholics view it, see patrons of the financial burden of so doing. As indicated earlier, members of the Protestant clergy in recent years are insisting with increasing vigor that public schools must either find ways of including religion in the curriculum or, as Henry P. Van Dusen, President of Union Theological Seminary puts it, they "will be driven to the expedient of the church-sponsored school." The decision of the United States Supreme Court on June 17, 1963 to the effect that "requiring the selection and reading at the opening of the school day of verses from the Holy Bible and the recitation of the Lord's Prayer by students in unison" in public schools, constitutes a religious exercise and thus a "fusion of governmental and religious functions" and therefore a violation of the establishment clause of the First Amendment, may well encourage the further development of church-related schools.

The emphasis in recent years upon education as a vital factor in national defense and the importance, consequently, of all schools', private as well as public, improving the quality of their education has emboldened the friends of church-related schools to increase their demands for federal aid to private and parochial schools. At the same time it has weakened resistance to this assistance by many who have traditionally insisted upon a strict interpretation of the principle of separation of church and state.

Finally, the concern of the nation for children from low income families, whose cultural backgrounds give poor support for educational attainments, has contributed to a growing philosophy that the federal government should help improve education for all children. This principle of helping the individual child, whether in a public or nonpublic school, has found favor in certain legislatures as well as in congressional actions, such as the Elementary and Secondary Education Act of 1965.

The demand that church-supported schools share in proposed federal grants to education has, until recent years, been limited to "token assistance" in support of auxiliary activities—health, transportation, free textbooks, and instructional materials. A change in attitude became evident in 1961 when the Catholic Bishops of America publicly announced their opposition to legislation then pending in Congress on the ground that the proposed aid to education discriminated "against chil-

Urban H. Fleege, "Issues and Problems Facing Catholic Secondary Education," *Catholic Education Review,* November 1952, pp. 272–73; Neil G. McCluskey, S.J., "Public Funds for Parochial Schools? Yes!" *Teachers College Record,* October 1960, pp. 49–56.

dren attending nonpublic schools." Discrimination in this instance consisted in the failure of legislation to provide funds for nonpublic as well as public schools in support of "secular aspects of education," such as instruction in science, mathematics, and foreign language.

In the same year, the American Civil Liberties Union, long an ardent and consistent advocate of a strict interpretation of the principle of separation of church and state, submitted a statement to the Senate Committee on Labor and Education in which the Union attempted to draw a line of distinction between aid to church-related elementary and secondary schools and aid to church-related colleges and universities. The former, the Union argued, are created "for the precise purpose of communicating a body of religious doctrine" and are thus ineligible for aid, whereas the latter tend to "concentrate on higher education rather than upon the inculcation of religious doctrine." Consequently, the Union saw "no constitutional bar to the granting of building loans or grants to those church-related colleges and universities" that do not require indoctrination in the tenets of a specific faith as "a required part of the curriculum." [4]

Has Public Policy in the Past Weakened the Churches?

For a period in our history, states Charles Clayton Morrison, editor emeritus of *The Christian Century*, "Protestants welcomed with relief the shifting of the burden of general education from the church to the secular community or the state. They believed that they could supplement the work of the public school with effective religious instruction in the church and the home." This confidence they have now lost: "The modern home is notoriously incompetent in this field. The Sunday school with its one hour a week of religious instruction, by volunteer teachers, under conditions of slack discipline is barely a gesture toward education. It cannot command the respect of pupils accustomed to the

4. *Civil Liberties Bulletin*, September, 1961. See also an editorial on "Church-Related Schools" in *The New Republic* for March 2, 1963, in which the editors, in contrast with their position on public aid to church-related schools in the past, assert: "The state has an interest in ensuring that all pupils, whether publicly or privately educated, have a mastery of certain subjects, from the three R's to history and chemistry. The state can and should pursue this interest by subsidizing instruction in these subjects. So long as the student is mastering them it makes no difference to the state whether his instructors are Jesuits or agnostics, whether his classroom is owned by the Lutherans or the local school board."

vastly superior methods, discipline, and prestige of the public school."
Consequently, Morrison is forced to conclude, "Protestantism cannot
long maintain its position in American life while it allows its children to
grow up in religious illiteracy. Its devotion to the public gives it the
right to demand that the ban on religion in the curriculum be removed." [5]

Faced, as they fear they are, with the prospect of losing their dominant position in American religious life, many Protestants view with
increasing concern the evolution of the nonsectarian public school (often
of Protestant orientation) into a genuinely secular school. For this reason many of their leaders have joined with certain Catholic spokesmen
in charging public schools with promoting the "deadly menace of
secularism."

Yet this increased anxiety on the part of these Protestant and Catholic
leaders seems to have gone hand in hand with a steady increase in
church membership! For example, at the time of the adoption of the
Constitution, probably no more than one out of ten people [6] in the
population was affiliated with any church; today, church membership
includes some 63 per cent of the total population of the United States.

In the light of these data, it is difficult to conclude that the growth of
the secular public school has brought disastrous effects upon church
membership! On the contrary might we not infer, with some basis in
fact, that just as religious organizations in the United States, under
conditions of nongovernmental assistance, have manifested a vitality
superior to that evidenced in Europe under state support, so a system
of public education which refrains from indoctrinating in religion gives
evidence at least of no deleterious effects upon membership in religious
organizations?

Despite these facts, some church leaders have concluded that more
than an attitude of benevolent neutrality in religious matters is required
of public education.

Finally, some analysts see evidence of a distressed state of public
mind, widespread and varied in character, in the mounting demand for
religious instruction in public schools and the disposition to replace the

5. "Can Protestantism Win America?" *The Christian Century,* April 3, 1946,
pp. 425–27. It should be pointed out, however, that Morrison parts company with
all who would have the state subsidize nonpublic schools.

6. Richard Hofstadter, *Anti-Intellectualism in American Life* (New York: Alfred A. Knopf, 1963), p. 2.

secular school with private, religiously oriented schools. This unease, they hold, results from many causes: profound changes in ways of living, economic disturbances, the aftereffects of war, depression and dislocation of populations, together with the ever-present threat of atomic war. According to this interpretation, dissatisfaction with the work of the schools in the realm of values, as in other areas, is but one manifestation of a wider trend which finds expression in a "loss of nerve," a disposition to seek refuge in religion from the storms that beset the contemporary world.

Be this as it may, there is no doubt of the determination of numerous groups and individuals to discount the importance of protecting religious freedom and to ask for the allotment of public funds for education to private as well as public schools. This determination manifests itself on the federal level in attempts to incorporate assistance to nonpublic schools in practically all legislation designed to aid education in the states; on the state level sectarian groups have made an effort to obtain aid from the states through the merging of public and sectarian interests. What seems to the partisans of separation nothing less than an improper (and illegal) violation of public trust by boards of education looks quite different to laymen who are consistently exposed to the argument that right and justice require public support of both public and nonpublic schools.

We will turn now to a brief summary of the arguments employed to justify public support of nonpublic schools.

The Argument in Support of Public Assistance to Church-related Schools

A widespread argument for public support of nonpublic schools holds that since nonpublic schools render a public service, they are entitled to compensation or some form of assistance from government. For example, the Legal Department of the National Catholic Welfare Conference asserted in December of 1961 that Catholic schools, elementary and secondary, were providing education for four and one-half million children, around 13 per cent of the school population of the nation, at a saving to the American taxpayers in 1960 alone of 1.8 billion dollars.[7]

7. "The Constitutionality of the Inclusion of Church-Related Schools in Federal Aid to Education," later published in the *Georgetown Law Journal*, Winter 1961, pp. 399–455.

This contention has been made with considerable force in connection with proposed federal legislation on behalf of education. Since the financing of education through taxation is a responsibility of government, it is argued, government is obligated "to observe the norms of distributive justice" in the distribution of funds collected. "Since government has nothing to teach," Msgr. William E. McManus of the National Catholic Welfare Conference stated,

> and because government receives a full return from its educational investment when a school produces well-trained citizens, therefore every school to which parents may send their children in compliance with compulsory education laws of the State is entitled to a fair share of tax funds. Local and state governments which refuse to support schools not under the control of the local school board are guilty of an injustice against other qualified schools within the community.[8]

There can be no question that the existence of church-supported schools in a community reduces the costs of public schooling. Nevertheless, supporters of church-related schools recognize that the constitutions of both state and federal governments, as at present interpreted by the courts, prohibit the use of public funds in support of denominational schools. They contend, however, that (1) this prohibition is neither all-inclusive nor universal in its application; (2) it is not morally justifiable in the light of the composition of the present population of the United States.

Take first the point of universal application. This turns upon an interpretation of the Establishment Clause of the First Amendment to the federal Constitution, as embodied in two decisions of the United

8. Hearings on Federal Aid to Education before The Sub-Committee on Education and Labor of the House of Representatives, 1947, pp. 310–11. See also statement of the Catholic Bishops of America on *The Place of Private and Church-Related Schools in American Education* in which the Bishops stated: "The private and church-related schools are part of the American system. Manifestly, they exist; they exist by right; and they are unquestionably carrying a large share of the educational burden. Their teachers, religious and lay, have dedicated themselves to a high purpose, have labored hard to acquit themselves worthily, and the entire nation is their debtor. . . . The students of these schools have the right to benefit from those measures, grants, or aids, which are manifestly designed for the health, safety and welfare of American youth, irrespective of the school attended" (*The New York Times*, November 20, 1955).

States Supreme Court—*Cochran* v. *Louisiana State Board of Education*, 281 U.S. 370 (1930), and *Everson* v. *Board of Education*, 330 U.S. 1 (1947). In the first of these decisions the Court declared constitutional an act of the State of Louisiana which permitted the distribution of textbooks free to children in private as well as public schools. In so doing, the Court enunciated what is termed the "child-welfare theory." Stipulating that the books provided children in private schools must be identical with those used in public schools and must be nonreligious and nonsectarian in character, the Court emphasized that the interests thus served were primarily those of individuals and that the interests of an institution "were aided only as the common interest is served."

Again, in *Everson* v. *Board of Education,* the Supreme Court approved an act of New Jersey that sanctioned the refunding to parents of children attending parochial schools the cost of transporting their children in public vehicles to these schools. Here the Court emphasized once again the primacy of the public interest (in this instance safeguarding the health and safety of children) as against the benefits that might accrue "incidentally" to church-related schools. Said the Court:

> The State contributes no money to the schools. It does not support them. Its legislation, as applied, does no more than provide a general program to help parents get their children, regardless of their religion, safely and expeditiously to and from accredited schools.

The Court further added, "we must be careful, in protecting the citizens of New Jersey against state-established churches, to be sure that we do not inadvertently prohibit New Jersey from extending its general state law benefits to all citizens without regard to their religious belief."

Armed with these two principles, those of "child welfare" and of "incidental benefit," the advocates of public assistance to nonpublic schools concentrated for a time upon no more than public assistance for auxiliary services on both state and national levels. In an effort to dramatize the principle involved in these forms of assistance, representatives of the National Catholic Welfare Conference consistently opposed all legislation in Congress that excluded nonpublic schools from "fringe benefits" in the form of health services, transportation, textbooks, and instructional materials.[9] With the successful launching of Sputnik I by Russia in October of 1957, the hopes of advocates of public assistance expanded with the hopes of other Americans that competition with Russia in the exploration of space would induce Congress, at long last, to subsidize general education. Surely, it was felt, the obvious relationship between trained intelligence and national security in the emerging age—particularly in the fields of science and mathematics—would dissipate erroneous notions of constitutional restrictions upon public assistance to secular education in nonpublic schools.

To validate the principle of governmental assistance to secular instruction in nonpublic as well as public schools, the Legal Department of the National Catholic Welfare Conference issued its Study of "The Constitutionality of the Inclusion of Church-Related Schools in Federal Aid to Education." [10] In addition to arguments bearing upon the right of the parent to send his child to a nonpublic school and the danger that government might impose upon the people a single educational system, the Study draws attention to the full implications of Justice Black's frequently quoted statement in both the *Everson* and *McCollum* decisions to the effect that "no tax in any amount, large or small, can be levied to support any religious activities or institutions." Read in the light of what the Court actually decided in both *Cochran* v. *Louisiana State Board of Education* and *Everson* v. *Board of Education,* insists the Study, it does not follow that because government is forbidden to aid religion, it cannot assist nonreligious activities in church-related schools. On the contrary, it is both proper and essential, in the interest of the general welfare, to strengthen secular instruction in these schools.

So much for the constitutional argument. Equally important for

9. See, for example, William E. McManus, "Showdown on Federal Aid," *America,* June 20, 1949.

10. See footnote 7. This study was prompted in large measure by the refusal of the Kennedy Administration to recognize the constitutionality of grants to church-related elementary and secondary schools. It attempted to refute an opinion rendered by the Legal Department of the United States Department of Health, Education, and Welfare to the effect that the First Amendment renders unconstitutional "across the board" grants and loans to church schools and tuition payments for all church-related pupils. This opinion did grant, however, that the constitution might permit church-related schools to borrow funds with which to purchase equipment for the teaching of science, mathematics, and foreign languages when this instruction is clearly related to specific national purposes and its connection with religion is remote.

For a brief summary of both documents, see *NEA Journal,* May 1962, pp. 26–28.

an understanding of the issues involved is it to review the American doctrine of separation of church and state in the light of its origin and development in a society governed by what Robert F. Drinan, S.J., has characterized as "an informally established 'pan-Protestantism.'" [11] As we have seen, our early schools were denominational schools of Protestant vintage. When Connecticut, in 1818, resolved that its School Fund should be used exclusively for "the encouragement and support of public and common schools," a policy subsequently followed by other states, and when Horace Mann, Henry Barnard, and other nineteenth-century educators finally succeeded (in principle, at least) in eliminating sectarian instruction from schools supported by public funds, what they actually accomplished was to restrict religious instruction in public schools to common agreements between Protestants. Public schools "remained, in many places, generally Protestant in spirit, with Bible reading, the singing of hymns, prayers, and other activities mainly drawn from a Protestant way of life and Protestant sources." [12] This Protestant monopoly, fortified in numerous instances by court decisions approving Protestant religious exercises in public schools, forced Catholics, when possible, to establish parochial schools. Nor was the trend toward nonsectarian and secular instruction in public schools of assistance to a religious group that firmly believes religion should permeate all instruction. Since public policy renders some Catholics unable to use public schools, it would seem that concern for religious liberty and justice dictates a revision of the First Amendment as presently interpreted by the United States Supreme Court.

The transformation of a religiously oriented public school into a secular school has been accentuated in recent years by decisions of the United States Supreme Court which ban both prayers and readings from the Bible at opening exercises—a trend that is causing many Protestants to question the wisdom of their traditional attachment to

11. *Religion, the Courts, and Public Policy* (New York: McGraw-Hill Book Company, Inc., 1963), p. 4.

12. Bernard J. Kohlbrenner on "The Controversy Over Public Support to Parochial Schools," in *Religion, Government, and Education*, by William W. Brickman and Stanley Lehrer (New York: Society for the Advancement of Education, 1961), pp. 65–69. Kohlbrenner describes conditions in the United States in the mid-nineteenth century that promoted Catholics to develop parochial schools and explains why, today, they find themselves "in conscience unable to make use of public schools."

public education and clearly runs counter to the basic convictions of many Catholics. Furthermore, since Catholics today comprise over one fifth of the population of the United States, it is contended that justice and equity require a revision of a principle which received its formulation in a period when they constituted no more than 1 per cent of the population. The revision desired is replacement of the concept of a "wall of separation" between church and state with one of "friendly cooperation," one that assures to all young people, without discrimination, "the right to benefit from those measures, grants, or aids, which are manifestly designed for the health, safety, and welfare of American youth, irrespective of the school attended." [13] It should be noted that other religious groups and educational spokesmen favor "friendly cooperation" in place of complete separation.

A second argument in support of public assistance to nonpublic schools turns upon "implementing" the legal right of a child to attend a private school in lieu of a public school. As we have seen, this right was specifically affirmed by the United States Supreme Court in the case of *Pierce* v. *Society of Sisters,* in which the Court declared unconstitutional a statute of the state of Oregon designed to require all children to attend public schools. "The child is not the mere creature of the state," declared the Court; "those who nurture him and direct his destiny have the right, coupled with the high duty, to recognize and to prepare him for additional obligations." Among these rights and obligations is that of parental determination of the school, public or private, in which he shall receive his education.

But of what value is this right unless parents are genuinely free to exercise it? "If parents have the right to send their children to any adequate school, public or independent," one prominent member of the clergy has argued, "then obviously all these schools must be allowed to exist without unfair discrimination or undue favoritism." At present, however, the parent who chooses to send his child to a nonpublic school suffers from two handicaps: (1) he is disadvantaged when auxiliary services are provided for public school children and denied to children of nonpublic schools; (2) he is subjected to "double taxation" in that he pays a tax in support of public education as well as tuition to the nonpublic school in which he enrolls his child.

The second of these handicaps weighs heavily upon those church

13. Statement of the Catholic Bishops of America, *op. cit.*

bodies heavily committed to support their own schools, not merely as an additional financial burden in the education of their young, but because it seems to them an act of injustice on the part of the state. They consider it unjust for the reason that when a parent selects a nonpublic school for his child to attend, he selects an institution that has undertaken to implement the state's compulsory school attendance law in accordance with standards defined and enforced by the state. "A strong case can be made for the proposition that it is unfair and unwise," writes Robert F. Drinan, S.J., "to force *all* children to attend school and then require those parents who refuse to allow their children to go to a school 'wholly secular' to finance the education of their children entirely from their own resources." [14]

Closely allied to this second argument is the contention that to restrict public funds to the use of public schools is to create an undesirable monopoly of public education. This charge takes on special significance in a period of reaction to all measures suggestive of "creeping socialism" and constitutes an indictment that today is in no way limited to individuals and groups identified with religious schools. Private schools are now envisaged as exemplars of the spirit of free enterprise and public schools are condemned as representing a trend in the direction of totalitarianism.

Support is given to this position by the argument that the private school exemplifies at its best the American principle of private enterprise, and that the "state should always aim to assist social institutions to perform their appointed tasks, rather than to replace them with public (i.e., political) agencies." [15]

A note of urgency is given to the arguments reviewed above by the hard fact that nonpublic schools of all types are finding it increasingly difficult to maintain their existence in the face of rapidly rising costs of operation.

This burden falls especially heavily upon Catholics, since they face a religious injunction far more imperative than that imposed upon the members of other church groups. For example,

> Catholic children may not attend non-Catholic neutral or mixed schools, that is those which are open also to non-Catholics and it pertains exclusively to the Ordinary of the place to decide,

14. *Op. cit.*, p. 127.
15. Robert C. Hartnett, *America*, April 9, 1952, pp. 65–68.

in accordance with the instructions of the Holy See, under what
circumstances and with what precautions against the nature of
perversion, attendance at such schools may be tolerated. Neutral
schools are those which exclude religion by prescinding from it,
such as the public schools in the United States. Mixed schools are
those which admit pupils of any or no religion.[16]

It has never been possible, of course, for all children of Catholics
to be enrolled in church-supported schools. Despite heroic efforts by
educational leaders and devoted support by laymen to expand schools
to keep pace with enrollments, in many communities this mandate
cannot be enforced.

The financial strain upon Catholics has become heavier with the
years, not only as a result of increasing costs characteristic of the times,
but also because of increased efforts to expand the facilities of Catholic
secondary and higher education. If we bear in mind that secondary
education involves a higher per-pupil cost than does elementary education and that the shortage of nuns as teachers necessitates supplementing the teaching staff with more costly lay teachers, the financial
burden imposed becomes formidable indeed.[17]

Protestant church schools are unable to draw upon religious orders
for teachers to the same extent as Catholics; consequently, faculty costs
are higher for them. Neither do Protestant churches typically exercise a
discipline over their members sufficient to procure the funds essential
to establish and maintain schools that can compete with public schools.
It is not surprising, therefore, to find Protestant advocates of church
schools joining with Catholics in the demand that ways and means be
found for the state to subsidize private schools. This demand, too, can
be clothed in patriotic robes, as, for example, in the observation of
Professor Van Zyl of Calvin College that "if we want to have a healthy
social structure and preserve our democracy, and if private schools are

16. Canon Law 1347. T. Lincoln Boriscaren and Adam C. Ellis, *Canon Law;
Text and Commentary* (Milwaukee, Wisc.: Bruce Publishing Co., 1946), p. 704.
    17. For a vivid description of the problems confronting Catholic schools in the
United States today, see the report of a study made by Jack Star, Senior Editor of
Look, in the issue of October 22, 1963 of that magazine. Star draws attention to
the phenomenal increase in enrollments in Catholic elementary and secondary
schools in recent years (129 per cent since 1940, as against 53 per cent in public
schools); the shortage of religious teachers, which necessitates the use of lay
teachers at far greater expense; and the difficulty of financing building construction
and up-to-date methods and materials of instruction.

among the best guarantees of liberty and freedom, then we ought to give private initiative more support."

Finally comes the argument that to provide positive religious instruction to the children of our nation in itself constitutes a public service that the state cannot safely leave to the chance that private resources may be found to sustain it. Under interpretations of the First Amendment that exclude the reciting of prayers and readings from the Bible at opening exercises, public schools are circumscribed in their efforts to provide a genuine moral education. Public schools in the minds of some thus become "godless institutions." Not only is education in morality severely handicapped, continues the argument, but democracy is weakened since it, too, is dependent upon a religious underwriting of Judean-Christian origin. To perpetuate democracy we must make certain that religion be not excluded from education. Consequently, if the fact of religious diversity or rigid interpretation of the Constitution requires the omission of religion from public education, it is a matter of public moment that private schools assure its continuance. Certainly we cannot afford "to identify freedom of religion with freedom from religion."

Here, briefly summarized, are arguments which induce many to advocate an interpretation of the principle of separation of church and state which does no more than prohibit the state from favoring one religious orientation over others and which sanctions positive "cooperation" between the state and religious organizations.

The Argument in Support of a Policy of Nonassistance

We turn now to an examination of the position just reviewed and to the positive considerations favoring a strict interpretation of separation of church and state in education.

Let us examine first the argument that since nonpublic schools render a public service they are entitled to receive public support.

This argument overlooks the very important consideration that insofar as nonpublic schools do in fact relieve public schools of a pupil load, this follows not from common planning or mutual agreement, but from accident. Nor is there usually any effort to envisage the enrollment problem of the community as a whole as a preliminary to a decision as to how its pupil population can most effectively be housed and educated. Rather, the private school, on its own initiative, decides to serve its own clients. Not infrequently, as a result, the housing of the pupil population is far from economically determined, and it is an open question whether a community richly supplied with both private and public schools is not actually wasting the resources potentially available for the education of its young. And what shall we say of a public policy which requires the state to reward the competitors of an institution established to serve the public when these competitors weaken and circumscribe its activities?

The fallacy in the public-welfare argument also becomes evident when we inquire into the character of the education afforded by those nonpublic schools which are claimants for public assistance. Although leaders in religious education are not of one accord, the most often espoused purpose of the church-related school is not to provide young people with two types of education, the one secular and the other religious, each separately conceived and administered. Rather, is it to organize instruction so that all subjects are permeated with a sectarian interpretation. Consequently, in asking the public to finance such a school we are suggesting that the state support not only a concept of religion and of life that is peculiar to one segment of the public, but to promote as well general education of a sectarian character.

Indeed, it is the expressed purpose of insuring a sectarian interpretation of all subjects in the curriculum that justifies in the eyes of their patrons the maintenance of church-related schools. Science, literature, history—even mathematics—are not conceived solely as secular subjects to be taught in a manner more or less identical with that in a public school. On the contrary, they are designed to promote a uniquely religious interpretation of life.[18]

For individuals or groups to organize and conduct private schools with a view to furthering a sectarian conception of life is, of course, a right guaranteed under the Constitution. Are not the nonpublic schools precluded from a claim upon the public purse precisely because they are assured the right to utilize education for private rather than public ends? As Justice Jackson remarked in his dissenting opinion in the Everson case, "We cannot have it both ways. Religious teaching cannot

18. For a report on the content of textbooks used in Catholic parochial schools, see George R. La Noue, "The National Defense Act and Secular Subjects," *Phi Delta Kappan*, June 1962. Also, by the same writer, "Religious Schools and 'Secular' Subjects," in *Harvard Educational Review*, Summer 1962, pp. 255–91.

be a private affair when the state seeks to impose regulations which infringe upon it indirectly, and a public affair when it comes to taxing citizens of one faith to aid another, or those of no faith to aid all. If these principles seem harsh in prohibiting aid to Catholic education, it must not be forgotten that it is the same constitution that alone assures Catholics the right to maintain these schools at all when predominant local sentiment would forbid them." Obviously, what Justice Jackson writes with reference to Catholic schools applies to schools of all denominations.

The contention that parents of children in sectarian schools suffer from double taxation fails to distinguish between an assessment compelled by government in support of a public service (one from which society as a whole benefits and for want of which all are disadvantaged) and an assessment which one assumes voluntarily by virtue of his identification with a cause which he individually deems worthy and essential.

No one will deny that the development of a dual or multiple system of education in this country imposes a heavy burden upon the supporters of nonpublic schools, a burden which promises to become heavier rather than lighter. It is understandable, too, that individuals whose devotion to nonpublic schools is drawn upon to the point of exhaustion should seek ways of relief from taxation on behalf of a system of education in which they have little faith. Nor is the disposition to submit to public taxation in support of public schools, under these circumstances, strengthened by the charge, so frequently encountered today, that public education in being neutral towards religion is, in fact, hostile to it.

Even so, the remedy is not to exempt from taxation all who prefer to substitute private services for public. To adopt this as a principle would be to paralyze the most vital activities of government. What, for example, would be the consequences of its application in areas other than education? Should we exempt individuals and corporations from taxation for the support of a police department, for example, in the event that they prefer to substitute the protection of a private security guard? Or consider the example of the government's requiring each individual to be immunized in the face of a general epidemic of a contagious disease and providing vaccination free to all through the resources of a public health department to insure that this be done.

Would we sanction the state's assumption of medical fees paid to private physicians by those who preferred to substitute the services of their family doctor?

The obvious reply is "No," because the taxes so imposed have as their object the health, welfare, and safety of all, and it is to the interest of the public that no one be overlooked. Similarly, public schools are established because of general recognition of the fact that the community as a whole benefits from them and suffers from their neglect. Consequently, taxes in their support are imposed upon the childless as well as parents, upon nonpatrons as well as patrons.

A similar fallacy underlies the contention that the state must implement the legal right of a child to attend the school of the parents' choice. As we have seen, the United States Supreme Court, in *Pierce* v. *Society of Sisters*, clearly affirmed the parent's right to send his child either to a public or to a private school. From this, some infer that unless the parent is financially assisted in his decision to use the private school, and not disadvantaged by "double taxation," the right remains an empty right.[19]

The error here consists in the assumption that an obligation of government *to recognize* a right carries with it a corresponding obligation to underwrite *the conditions of its realization*. This, too, would be a hazardous principle for the state to adopt. Does the licensing of competent individuals or private corporations to perform valuable services in vital areas obligate the state to subsidize these activities and to insure for each that financial records be in the black? Does the fact, strongly emphasized by Catholic writers, that the state *forces* all children to attend school, while leaving them free to select a licensed private school in preference to a public school, obligate the state to finance this preference? Were this adopted as a principle, why should subsidies be limited to institutions? Why not subsidize as well the teaching activities of a competent private tutor, or remit to the parents of children so instructed the fees thus paid?

19. Another way of stating this argument is to say that parents who elect to send their children to a religiously oriented school merit special consideration if the guaranteed right to religious liberty is to become a reality. To this argument opponents of public assistance to church-related schools reply that what is termed a "parent's inalienable right" to send his child to a parochial school is, for many, more accurately described as conformity to an ecclesiastical injunction which the state is being asked to subsidize. Legitimate as it may be for a church to impose this discipline upon its members and for the latter to submit, it does not follow that failure of government to underwrite parental conformity constitutes a denial of an "inalienable right" or an infringement upon religious liberty.

But if we deny assistance in cases of this kind, upon what grounds do we insist the state should finance the right to attend any school of one's choice? Is not the freedom of a parent to send his child to a private school one thing and the obligation of the state to finance this right altogether another? Justice Rutledge, in *Everson* v. *Board of Education*, appropriately remarked in this connection:

> Of course discrimination in the legal sense does not exist. The child attending the religious school has the same right as any other to attend the public school. But he foregoes exercising it because the same guaranty which assures the freedom forbids the public school or any agency of the state to give or aid him in securing the religious instruction he seeks.
>
> Were he to accept the common school, he would be the first to protest the teaching of any creed or faith not his own. And it is precisely for this reason that their atmosphere is wholly secular that the children are not sent to public schools under the Pierce doctrine. But that is a constitutional necessity, because we have staked the very existence of our country on the faith that complete separation between the state and religion is best for the state and best for religion.

Confusion of thought, equally serious, applies to the charge that unless the public assists both nonpublic and public schools in the discharge of their "appointed tasks," it is guilty of fostering a monopoly in education.

In what sense is the term "monopoly" used here? Surely not in the sense that in controversial matters, such as in politics, economics, and religion, the public school is free to impress one and only one point of view upon the minds of the young. On the contrary, is it not a basic principle in public education (in contrast with a principle often sanctioned and sometimes lauded in private education) that in matters upon which the public mind is as a house divided, the school must carefully refrain from promoting only one point of view?

Nor is the "deadly monopoly" of public education in any way similar to state education in a totalitarian country, despite the overly zealous indictment of individuals to this effect.[20] One unique feature of public

20. See article by Lewis C. Fay, "'Abolish Public Schools,' Says Owner of Newspaper Chain," *The Nation's Schools*, August 1952.

education in the United States is its independence of the state, even of local governments, as Europeans understand state control of education. Indeed, there is no uniform pattern of American education—unless it be in the existence of a high degree of local autonomy exercised by boards of education. In the United States approximately 85 per cent of the school boards are elected by the people. This fact, together with the control such boards exercise over the curriculum of the school, hardly resembles the highly centralized control over education which emanates from ministries of education in European countries and this arrangement should insure the protection of the American people against the educational evils of the "slave state."

What, then, is meant when friends of church-related schools warn against the "monopoly" of public education? No more than the exclusive use of funds for public education and the obligations of self-financing that this imposes upon private education. Is it not misleading to characterize this as a monopoly when the field is left open to private intiative? And what is the alternative? For the state to finance free enterprise in education? Surely, this is a strange and novel conception of private initiative!

A strange interpretation, yes. But also a suggestion which, if followed, might prove equally disastrous to private and public education inasmuch as the hand that controls the purse is seldom satisfied until it also controls policy.

This takes us to the dangers of state interference in private and sectarian education implicit in governmental support. It is well to remind the advocates of state subsidies for nonpublic schools that this was once the practice in American education. Characteristic of this period also was government control of the education thus afforded. Americans are unaccustomed to the conception of relations between church and state in which the church functions as a self-determining agency in education and the state meekly assumes the burden of financing this education. Rather, it has been one in which state subsidies have led to a determining voice in matters of policy. Howard Beale, in his *History of Freedom of Teaching in American Schools*, recites instances in which the states presumed to dictate the internal structure of educational institutions to which articles of incorporation had been granted. Thus, in 1834, the legislature of Missouri, in approving a charter for an academy at Troy and Independence, stipulated that "no preference shall be given or any discrimination made (in the choice of trustees, professors, or teachers, or students) on account of religious sentiments; nor shall any trustees, professors or teachers at any time, make by-laws, ordinances or regulations that may, in any wise, interfere with or in any manner control the conscience, or the free exercise of religious worship." [21]

To be sure, the Missouri legislature, in this instance, was animated by what some would consider an excessive spirit of nonsectarianism. But this does not alter the fact that a government which pays the piper may decide at any time to call the tune. In fact there is some regulation of nonpublic schools even when there is no state support. And there seems to be ample evidence today of a growing disposition on the part of state legislatures, as well as the Congress of the United States, to dictate to educational institutions how they should order their houses. Should this not be sufficient to suggest to independent schools the folly of jeopardizing an autonomy that constitutes their *raison d'être?* They might well ponder Justice Jackson's words in *Everson* v. *Board of Education:*

> Nor should I think that those who have done so well without this aid would want to see separation between Church and State broken down. If the State may aid these religious schools, it may therefore regulate them. Many groups have sought aid from tax funds only to find it carries political control with it. Indeed this Court has declared, "It is hardly lack of due process for the Government to regulate that which it subsidizes." [22]

On the other hand, unless the state is privileged to regulate and supervise education within schools dependent upon it for support, it would be committed to an untenable principle.

There is no suggestion on the part of groups now seeking public aid that they accept public control or supervision over the education they

21. New York: Charles Scribner's Sons, 1941, p. 94.
22. The statement within the quotation is from *Wickard* v. *Filburn,* 317 U.S. 111 (1942). Of interest in this connection is the proposal of the American Civil Liberties Union to a committee of Congress in March of 1961. The Union would have Congress impose as a condition of granting aid to church-related colleges that each recipient of this aid (1) admit all students without respect to religion, (2) require no course in theology or attendance at religious exercises, and (3) place the control of the college in the hands of academic officials. (Hearings on March 21–29, 1961 before the Sub-Committee on Education and Labor, House of Representatives, 87th Congress, First Session, Part 2, pp. 1024–25.)

provide in return for assistance received. On the contrary, their basic position, sincerely and honestly stated, is that separation of church and state in education implies that the state shall finance, while the church defines and carries on, this education. Insofar as standards might be imposed by the state, they would be superficial and external, restricted to matters such as the physical conditions of buildings and, perhaps, the minimum and maximum salary to be paid to teachers, but unrelated in any vital sense to the content and quality of instruction. Certainly there would be no effective supervision of the nature, quality, and integrity of the thinking promoted by teachers, or a tender concern for methods of inquiry and reflective thinking which are indispensable in the education of free men.

If it is felt that these dangers to private education are largely theoretical, there is no denying the disastrous consequences that might follow for public education by the diversion of public funds to nonpublic schools. It is difficult to exaggerate the serious situation which already confronts public education for want of adequate support. School enrollments are mounting steadily. Additional school buildings are called for, and existing structures are sadly in need either of repair or replacement. Classrooms are overcrowded and large numbers of children are in schools which operate on a double (often a triple) session basis. A critical shortage of teachers exists, and there is no immediate prospect of remedying this situation substantially in the light of existing salary schedules. Surely, this is no time in which to weaken public education further by diverting into other channels funds so desperately needed.

While it is true that the existence of nonpublic schools reduces the cost of public education, apportioning of funds between different systems would not be a simple matter. There are at present some 256 religious sects in this country. Once the principle of state assistance to nonpublic schools begins to operate, many new systems would no doubt appear, each demanding its fair share (or, shall we say, a lion's share?) of the public purse. The inevitable result would be a steady expansion of appropriations on behalf of nonpublic schools and a contraction in those available to public schools.

Not only would subsidizing nonpublic schools sap the material resources of public education; it would also result in a lowering of educational standards in both types of institutions. What reason is there to believe that the character of nonpublic education would improve as each denominational school became the recipient of public aid? It is true that private schools have, on occasion, developed and tested new methods of teaching and new organizations of subject matter from which public schools, less free to use their pupils as guinea pigs, have profited. By and large, however, public education in this country has served as a stimulus for raising the standards and broadening the educational vision of nonpublic schools. If the bleeding process is inaugurated, however, and the vitality of the public schools lowered, we may expect the work of nonpublic schools to sag as well.[23]

Finally, a word is called for regarding the contention that the philosophy of church-state relations, as embodied in the establishment clause of the First Amendment and interpreted by the courts, requires revision.

Friends of the concept of separation of church and state have two answers to this argument. They point out, first, that it oversimplifies history. As a matter of fact, the "Protestant establishment" (if we may so describe those responsible for formulating the uniquely American concept from Roger Williams to James Madison, Thomas Jefferson, and others) in no way reflected the traditional conception as practiced in Europe and this country. In Protestant as well as Catholic countries, state support of religion was the accepted pattern. As was pointed out in the preceding chapter, painful experience with both single and multiple establishments prior to the Revolution led nine of the original thirteen states (including Rhode Island, which retained its original charter) between the years 1776 and 1791 to write into their constitutions prohibitions against any and all support of religion. Similar provisions were later adopted by other states and applied to church-related

23. Holland is frequently cited as a model for granting assistance to nonpublic schools, since in Holland all types of schools are assisted by government. It might be cited with equal force to demonstrate the disastrous effects upon public education of a policy of state support for both public and nonpublic schools. At the turn of the century, public schools in Holland enrolled 69 per cent of all children in school. Following the Primary Education Act of 1920, which established a formula for grants to nonpublic schools, enrollments in public schools began to decline. By 1959, approximately 28 per cent of elementary school children were attending public schools; 41 per cent attended Catholic schools, 27 per cent Protestant schools, and 1 per cent "other" schools. See Robert Gordis, in *Religion and the Public Schools* (New York: Fund for the Republic, Inc., 1959).

For evidence that Dutch schools, as at present supported, encourage a permanent division of the population into three worlds—Protestant, Catholic, and neutral— a segmentation that carries over into economic, social, and political life following school, see David O. Mobery, "Social Differentiation in the Netherlands," *Social Forces*, May 1961, pp. 333–37. See also Norman H. Wilson, "Dutch Schools and Religious Segmentation," *Comparative Educational Review*, 1959, pp. 19–24.

schools upon the emergence of publicly supported free schools. Far from reflecting an exclusively "pan-Protestant" influence in our history, constitutional denial of public support for all religious organizations represented an attempt on the part of far-seeing individuals and groups in this country to safeguard Americans from the internal troubles arising out of theological differences and the rival claims of church and state that had long vexed European states. As James Bryce stated in his monumental work, *The American Commonwealth,* "This whole vast chapter and debate and strife has remained virtually unopened in the United States. There is no Established Church. All religious bodies are absolutely equal before the law, and unrecognized by the law, except as voluntary associations of private citizens." [24]

In view of this happy experience, Americans should consider carefully before they revert to a policy that involves not only competition between public and private schools for public funds, but also rivalry between private schools for the favorite place at the public trough.

Second, in asserting the relevance of a principle to a present problem, it is important to distinguish between the origin of this principle and its applicability to contemporary conditions. It may be of interest to compare the religious affiliations of the American people in 1791 with their affiliations today. But the validity of the principle of separation of church and state turns less upon these data than upon whether or not its applicability to a religiously heterogeneous people that chanced to be largely Protestant still holds for a people of even greater diversity. Wisdom would seem to dictate that as differences multiply it becomes increasingly important for the state to hold fast to a principle that insures freedom of religion for all and entangling alliances with none.

Should Government Assist Auxiliary Activities in Private Schools?

As stated earlier, controversy in the 1940s and the 1950s centered chiefly upon the question of "fringe benefits" for nonpublic schools. Since 1958 (and the passage of the National Defense Education Act of that year), the issue has broadened to include the propriety of loans and grants in support of educational activities and facilities of a nonreligious character in religiously oriented schools and colleges. From

24. Second edition, revised. (New York: Commonwealth Publishing Company, 1908), Vol. II, p. 643.

this we should not conclude, however, that controversy over the use of public funds in support of auxiliary activities in private schools has in any way diminished.

Since both principle and practical considerations are involved, let us examine more closely this question of public support of auxiliary services in nonpublic schools.

In the first place, it is important to observe that they are not all of the same order. They differ significantly both in nature and importance. Since, however, the term is a blanket one it can be used to blur the line that legitimately separates aid to the individual (in this instance, the child) from aid to an institution with which he may be associated.

Take, for example, the public transportation of children to nonpublic schools. This has been sanctioned by the United States Supreme Court (*Everson* v. *Board of Education*) as a public health or safety measure. In dissenting from the majority decision, however, both Justice Jackson and Justice Rutledge pointed to inaccuracies of fact and interpretation in the majority opinion and the danger that the Court was engaged in broadening the concept of public welfare to such an extent that the purposes of the First Amendment might eventually be annulled. Justice Jackson emphasized that the New Jersey statute did not, in fact, provide for the free transportation of all children. Children attending private schools "operated for profit in whole or in part" were excluded under the terms of the act. The test of eligibility for assistance thus turned upon whether or not a child chanced to attend a school of a given type. Accordingly, the Justice concluded,

> It seems to me that the basic fallacy in the Court's reasoning which accounts for its failure to apply the principle it avows, is in ignoring the essentially religious test by which beneficiaries of this expenditure are selected. A policeman protects a Catholic, of course—but not because he is a Catholic; it is because he is a man and a member of our society. The fireman protects the Church school—but not because it is a Church school; it is because it is property, part of the assets of our society. Neither the fireman nor the policeman has to ask before he renders aid, "Is this man or building identified with the Catholic Church?" But before these school authorities draw a check to reimburse for a student's fare they must ask just that question, and if the school is a Catholic

one they may render aid because it is such, while if it is of any other faith or is run for profit, the help must be withheld.

Of the dangers involved in employing the concept of public welfare loosely, Justice Rutledge warned that it might well lead to an undermining of the First Amendment. This approach, he states,

> if valid, supplies a ready method for nullifying the Amendment's guarantee, not only in this case and others involving small grants in aid for religious education, but equally for larger ones. The only thing needed will be for the Court again to transplant the "public welfare–public function" view from its proper non-religious due process bearing to First Amendment application, holding that religious education is not "supported" though it may be aided by the appropriation, and that the cause of education generally is furthered by helping the pupil to secure that type of training.

That Justice Rutledge's reservations were not entirely imaginary seems obvious in the light of the actual operation of bus service for children in the two types of schools. Normally, transportation of public school children is furnished only within a defined area (that is, to children attending the school nearest their homes). This is not true in all cases of children in nonpublic schools. Court approval of the New Jersey statute has been used to sanction not merely free transportation on public highways, where traffic hazards are to be expected and the principle of public health and safety may be applicable, but to maintain bus routes without reference to place of residence and thus to render it convenient for children to attend the nonpublic school. Surely this goes beyond the necessities of public welfare and contributes directly to the advantage of the church school.[25]

25. That the *Everson* decision failed to establish clearly the principle of public financing of the transportation of parochial school pupils is evidenced by contradictory decisions of state courts since 1946. For example, the courts of Washington (1949), New Mexico (1951), Missouri (1953), Alaska (1955), and Wisconsin (1962) have ruled against the practice, while those of Maine (1959) and Connecticut (1960) have approved. Nor has clarity been added by the refusal of the United States Supreme Court to review cases from the states of Washington (1951), Connecticut (1960), and Alaska (1962). At present, some twenty-two states sanction public provision for the transportation of children by bus to private schools. With good will on all sides and an objective concern for the welfare of young people, it should be possible to provide essential transportation for all children without either discriminating against or favoring attendance upon nonpublic schools.

Free textbooks constitute a second category of auxiliary services and a unique problem. As indicated earlier, the furnishing of textbooks by the state to children in public and nonpublic schools was approved by the United States Supreme Court on the theory that the child, rather than the school, is aided thereby. In the words of the Louisiana court,

> One may scan in vain to ascertain where any money is appropriated for the purchase of school books for the use of any church, private, sectarian or even public schools. The appropriations were made for the specific purpose of purchasing school books for the use of the children of the state, free of cost to them. It was for their benefit and the resulting benefit to the State that appropriations were made. True, these children attend some school, public or private, the latter sectarian or non-sectarian, and that the books are to be furnished them for their use, free of cost, whichever they attend. The schools, however, are not the beneficiaries of these appropriations. They obtain nothing from them, nor are they relieved of a single obligation because of them.[26]

With this position Chief Justice Hughes was apparently in agreement. In upholding the decision of the lower court he also stated that the Fourteenth Amendment was not violated when the state supplies textbooks free to children in private as well as in public schools, provided, however, that the books thus distributed are identical with those used in public schools and are nonreligious and nonsectarian in character.

It should be noted that many teachers and officials in nonpublic, including church-supported, schools prefer textbooks used in public schools. It is true, nevertheless, that the proviso that the textbooks be nonsectarian runs counter to a widely accepted purpose of the religious schools, namely, to permeate all instruction with a religious point of view. Consequently there is a very real temptation for religious groups to exercise pressure upon those charged with responsibility for the selection of books to choose those which meet religious criteria. A conspicuous example of this pressure occurred in New Mexico a few years ago. Textbooks in the form of readers and books in the fields of history, geography, and the like, published specifically for the use of schools of one religious persuasion, were included in the official list of books

26. *Cochran v. Louisiana State Board of Education.*

adopted by the Department of Education and were used in public as well as nonpublic schools.

Needless to say, pressure upon public authorities to select textbooks favorable to a sectarian point of view might well endanger freedom of teaching. The determination of pressure groups to control teaching in controversial areas already constitutes a serious problem. If the number of states which provide textbooks free to children of all types of schools increases to fifty, the practice of impartial and objective teaching will encounter still graver obstacles. As one writer has pointed out:

> The privilege which parents enjoy of educating their children in private schools has a two-fold benefit. It insures freedom of private schools to deviate from what is generally accepted; even to experiment in methods and ideas, without severely injuring the public, and, on occasion, with benefit to the public. On the other hand, it leaves the public school relatively free to draw upon an objective and impartial scholarship in the selection of its teaching materials and in determining what it shall stress. True, a good school avoids indoctrination in controversial areas and is careful to call the attention of students to principles that are of doubtful validity or are in dispute. But it is one thing to be free to present all points of view and it is another thing to teach adequately when the weight and momentum of the institution is to prior commitment. Let the public adopt the practice of furnishing textbooks free to non-public as well as to public schools and education will cease to be free. Special interests and parochial conceptions under the guise of religious convictions or absolutes, which no one may question, will soon operate to destroy the integrity of textbook selection, corrupt the atmosphere in which textbooks are written, and render impossible the education of the free mind.
>
> These results will satisfy no one. To the extent that the state remains neutral and independent in its choice of the materials of education, it will be accused of unfair treatment of sectarian groups or of introducing "disturbing" materials of learning to the students. To the degree that parochial interests intervene and seek to control this selection they will exercise an unwarranted, even dangerous control over the education of children outside their legitimate spheres of influence. Inevitably, then, the furnish-

ing of free textbooks to children in parochial schools will result in that intermingling of secular and religious concerns which Madison, Jefferson, and others sought to prevent by the adoption of the First Amendment to the Constitution.[27]

Similar reservations found expression in the testimony of a number of witnesses before Congress with respect to Title II of the Elementary and Secondary Education Act which President Johnson signed on April 11, 1965. Interpreting generously the decision of the Supreme Court in *Cochran* v. *Louisiana State Board of Education,* to which we referred above, this bill allocates 100 million dollars to the states for the purchase of textbooks and library materials for use in church-related and other nonprofit schools, as well as public schools. Funds thus appropriated are to be distributed to the schools concerned by public educational authorities. The adoption of this legislation suggests a significant change is taking place in the public mind with respect to church–state relations in education. Indeed, many who vigorously opposed "fringe benefits" for private and parochial schools in the past now contend that the education of all American youth has become so important in today's world that they are willing to incur the "risks" thus involved.

The question of health services, in contrast to the problems of transportation and free textbooks, is relatively simple. In these days when the necessities of an adequate national defense and the draft confront the people of the United States, few would deny the public importance of insuring the minimum essentials of health care for every child. Nor is there objection to state intervention in order to protect a child from neglect or the mistaken notions of parents and guardians. With respect to health needs, the welfare of the child and the well-being of the community take precedence over all other interests.

These considerations should also control the organization and administration of health services. Several years ago the Federal Council of Churches of Christ in America made suggestions designed to meet the health needs of children and, at the same time, to prevent these suggestions being used for narrow interests. These suggestions involved the divorcing of welfare services from the question of aid to education. "By thus drawing a clear distinction between aid to schools and welfare services for children," stated the Council, "we believe that necessary

27. V. T. Thayer, *The Attack Upon the American Secular School* (Boston: Beacon Press, Inc., 1951), pp. 121–22.

assistance can be given to education without making it the object of sectarian controversy or compromising the principle of separation of Church and State for which the Council has always stood."

In line with this policy, the Council suggested that all health services which are publicly supported be placed under the supervision and administration of a public agency. By centralizing administration, it was hoped, overlapping and duplication of machinery would be avoided.

This may prove to be a happy solution with respect to health services and constitute a wise precedent to follow not only with health projects, but in the administration of other services of a public character to children. Certainly every effort should be made to prevent the duplication of facilities and personnel which would follow inevitably upon the division of administration of services between public and private agencies.[28]

The Problem of Desegregation Introduces a New Factor

Thus far we have discussed almost exclusively the efforts of religious groups to secure public assistance for nonpublic schools. Only incidentally have we referred to the attempts of individuals who, opposed to public education outright, seek to bring about a return to privately supported education.

Since the decision of the United States Supreme Court in 1954 which declared unlawful the exclusion of children from public schools on grounds of race, a new factor has been introduced into the situation and a new danger confronts public education. In a number of southern states, state constitutions have been revised and laws passed which permit the abolition of public schools and the subsidizing of private schools in the event that a federal court orders the admission of Negroes into a white school. Private schools, however, cannot spring into being fully equipped at a moment's notice. Furthermore, private schools now operating in the South are chiefly of sectarian affiliation and are thus not eligible to receive public assistance. Consequently, the

28. The National School Lunch Act of 1946 was written with this in mind. This act provides that in states where agencies of public education are forbidden to distribute federal-state funds to nonpublic schools, the latter may apply directly to the United States Department of Agriculture for their proportionate share of funds allocated by the federal government for free or reduced-cost lunches for school children. Surplus foods are distributed to private schools in a similar manner.

constitutional prohibition of public aid to nonpublic schools constitutes one of the most formidable obstacles to the southern program of "massive resistance" to desegregation. To meet this new situation, southern politicians, who, in the past, were vigorous supporters of public education, have switched their loyalty to private schools. Virginia, for example, was quick to repeal its compulsory school attendance laws following the outlawing of segregation by the United States Supreme Court. It also established the precedent of providing financial assistance to children in private nonsectarian schools. Subsequent federal legislation has served to reverse this trend by withholding federal funds from states and school districts that are not making acceptable progress toward desegregation. Nevertheless, the experience documents a danger to the principle of no public support for nonpublic schools.

Shared Time as a Novel Solution for an Old Problem

In recent years a group of educators representing the major religious denominations in the United States (Protestant, Catholic, and Jewish) have come forward with a novel solution for the problem of church-state relations in education. According to this plan, public schools would provide instruction in "neutral subjects" such as mathematics, science, foreign language, home economics, shop, art, and physical education, and sectarian schools would provide instruction in religion and those subjects in which religious orientation plays an important role— literature, history, social studies, and the like.

Proponents of shared time envisage a number of advantages in the plan, all of which should alleviate tension in religiously divided communities and ease financial strain upon both types of schools.

In one large city, for example, plans are under way for the construction of a Catholic high school near a new public high school. The 1600 students of the former are to receive instruction in religious courses, social studies, English, art, and music in the parochial school, and in science, foreign language, mathematics, commercial and technical subjects, and physical education in the public high school. By this arrangement Catholics hope to reduce tuition costs to parents and to double the capacity of their school. Public school officials, in turn, hope to receive increased sums from the state in the form of state aid, based upon pupil attendance, and united community support for future bond issues and increased taxes for the improvements of instruction in which all parents will now have an interest.

Educators favoring shared time also anticipate that it will relieve pressure upon public schools to incorporate religious instruction and religious practices in their program. Parents who are concerned that religious influences permeate instruction are assured cooperation from the public school, but this instruction will be given under church auspices. From this point of view shared time becomes an enlarged and generalized form of released time.

Not all communities are in a position to inaugurate shared-time programs *de novo,* as in the illustration above. Unless public and nonpublic schools are convenient of access to each other the shifting of pupils from school to school will create serious administrative problems of transportation and scheduling of classes. More serious, from an educational point of view, are the difficulties involved in realizing the potential values of a genuinely integrated school experience for students and thus to offset the divisiveness that frequently accompanies segregation on the basis of religion. As Phillip Jacobson has pointed out, "It would be self-defeating—and far worse—if there were a Lutheran or Jewish or Catholic school class in French or mathematics." [29] But to organize schedules so as to achieve genuine integration through mixed-class groups is obviously possible only in small schools or in schools where plural sections in the same subject are feasible.

In order for shared time to become an accepted pattern of relationships between public and church-related schools, serious compromises of principle are called for on the part of both public and church-school educators. For the first, it requires the virtual abandonment of an educational principle long accepted as basic in a pluralistic society that strives to become democratic—namely, that in areas where facts are in question and values in conflict sound teaching consists in developing an understanding and an appreciation of rival points of view as a necessary preliminary to well-grounded and uncoerced conclusions. For this principle, shared-time programs substitute the assumption that subjects which involve rival interpretations are best taught in a sectarian atmosphere and by sectarian instructors.

29. In "Shared Time, A Symposium," a reprint from *Religious Education,* January–February 1962, p. 26. This reprint consists of a 36-page symposium in which some 19 representatives of Catholic, Jewish, and Protestant faiths express their views on the advisability and feasibility of shared-time programs.

For the religious educator, on the other hand, shared time means an abandonment of the assumption that there are no "neutral subjects"; that aside from a very restricted area, such as typing or geometry or industrial arts, no subject can properly be divorced from religion; that even these subjects should be taught in a school where the religious atmosphere dominates.[30]

Shared time is still in its infancy. Credit for introducing the idea should doubtless go to Harry L. Stearns, Superintendent of Schools in Englewood, New Jersey. Stearns first proposed the plan in an article in *Christianity and Crisis*, September 18, 1961. The extent to which communities have embraced the plan varies widely. In some, nonpublic school children share only in physical education. In others, they attend public schools for a half day and their own schools for the other half. Nevertheless, the plan has spread widely since 1961, some 26 states using it in one form or another. In a number of states its use waits upon the removal of legal obstacles in the form of school attendance laws and the modification of school codes.

Congressional approval of the Elementary and Secondary Education Act of April 1965 may well result in the expansion of shared-time programs in the states and the modification of state laws that now inhibit their expansion. This legislation provides funds for the establishment of educational centers under public auspices in communities so electing. These centers will provide supplementary instruction for private and parochial as well as public school students in areas that require specialized teachers, such as the arts, sciences, foreign language, and technical training. It is also hoped that many of these centers will serve as model or demonstration schools with special provisions for teacher training.

That there is some doubt as to the constitutionality of these attempts to assist church-related schools was apparent in the debates within Congress that preceded the adoption of this legislation, as well as from

30. Arthur T. Geoghen, Superintendent of Catholic Schools, Diocese of Providence, deals with this problem in "Shared Time, A Symposium," *op. cit.*, p. 25. "It will take a great amount of persuasion to convince some religious leaders that science can be taught without reference to religion," he writes. But he adds, "For my part I think they [teachers] can." He suggests, however, "that the home-room teacher or a coordinator in the church school have a copy of the science text being used in the public school. In the course of the year there may be three or four instances which call for a religious, as well as a scientific examination. It would be incumbent upon the church school teacher to undertake the religious examination and to point out the harmony between science and religion."

the immediately announced intentions of a number of objecting groups outside Congress to appeal to the courts to determine whether "tax-raised funds can be spent constitutionally for the benefit of church-related schools." What the courts will decide ultimately rests with the future.

So much for the problem of public assistance, direct and indirect, to nonpublic schools. There remains the concern, to which we referred at the conclusion of the preceding chapter, that in adopting an attitude of neutrality toward religion public schools are neglecting an essential education in moral and spiritual values and are contributing to the weakening of the moral fibre of our democracy.

To this problem we now turn.

Suggested Reading

American Jewish Committee, *Religion in Public Education: A Statement of Views* (New York: American Jewish Committee, 1957).

————, *Summaries of Rulings of State Attorneys General with Respect to Church-State Questions as They Affect Public and Parochial Schools* (New York: American Jewish Committee, 1958).

Blum, Virgil C., S.J., *Freedom in Education: Federal Aid for All Children* (New York: Doubleday & Company, 1965).

Brickman, William, and Stanley Lehrer, *Religion, Government, and Education* (New York: Society for the Advancement of Education, 1961), chaps. 1, 2, 5, 6.

Catholic Bishops of America, *Statement on the Place of the Private and Church-Related Schools in American Education, The New York Times,* November 20, 1955.

Drinan, Robert F., S.J., *Religion, the Courts, and Public Policy* (New York: McGraw-Hill Book Company, Inc., 1963), chaps. One, Four, Five, Six.

Duker, Sam, "The Issue of Shared Time," *Educational Forum,* January 1965, pp. 235–41.

Freund, Paul A., and Robert Ulich, *Religion and the Public Schools* (Cambridge, Mass.: Harvard University Press, 1965).

Katz, Wilbur G., "The Case for Religious Liberty," in John Cogley, ed., *Religion in America* (Meridian Books, 1958), Part 2, chap. 2.

La Noue, George R., "Religious Schools and Secular Subjects," *Harvard Educational Review,* February 1961, pp. 91–95.

McCluskey, Neil G., S.J. "Public Funds for Parochial Schools? Yes!" *Teachers College Record,* October 1960, pp. 49–56.

Pfeffer, Leo, "An Analysis of Federal Aid to Parochial Schools," *Journal of Church and State,* November 1961, pp. 137–48.

Religion and the Schools (pamphlet) by Robert Gordis, William Gorman, F. Ernest Johnson, and Robert Lekachman (New York: Fund for the Republic, 1959).

"Shared Time: A Symposium," *Religious Education*, January–February 1962. Published also as a reprint by Religious Education Association, 545 West 111th St., New York 25, N.Y.

Chapter 19

Religion and Morality in Public Education

Religious Freedom as Originally Conceived

In his oration commemorating the two hundredth anniversary of the landing of the Pilgrims at Plymouth, Daniel Webster pictured these sturdy individuals as pledging, "If God prosper us, we shall here begin a work which shall last for ages; we shall plant here a new society, in the principles of the fullest liberty and the purest religion. . . ."

The debt which Americans owe to the founders of New England is in no way lessened by a more realistic appraisal of the motives which animated them. They were indeed determined, as were many others, to establish a new society in the New World, but they scarcely envisaged its realization through the application of the "principles of fullest liberty." On the contrary, to insure the practice of the "purest religion," as they conceived it, required the enforcement of the most rigid conformity of thought and conduct. The religious conscience which prompted them to establish communities in the New World, where they might worship without restraint, demanded that this worship not be defiled by the presence of individuals of a contrary conscience.

The original American settlements were thus religiously homogeneous and one major purpose of the schools was to transmit to the young the faith of the fathers without deviation. Nevertheless, the free air of America eventually fostered an identification of religious freedom with the freedom of individual conscience both in thought and in mode of worship. This carries with it the right to deviate as well as to conform, to travel at one's own risk as well as to follow the majority. Under the law, no American is now authorized to decide for another what is valid or invalid in religion. Truth and error in religious matters are exclusively determined by an authority higher than man.

One of the clearest statements of this principle is found in the decision of the United States Supreme Court in *West Virginia State Board of Education* v. *Barnette*, 319 U.S. 624 (1943). In conformity with an act of the state legislature, the West Virginia Board of Education in January 1943 adopted a regulation requiring the salute to the flag as "a regular part of the program of activities in the public schools." All teachers and pupils were required to participate in the ceremony. Failure of any pupil to do so was to be considered an act of insubordination to be dealt with by expulsion from school. Readmission to school was denied by statute until the student complied with the rule. In the meantime, the offending child might be proceeded against as a delinquent and his parents or guardians subjected to prosecution.

A number of children whose parents belonged to Jehovah's Witnesses, a religious sect that takes literally the Biblical injunction, "Thou shalt not make unto thee a graven image," and "thou shalt not bow down thyself to them nor serve them," refused to engage in the flag salute on the ground that the flag is an "image" in the sense forbidden. Eventually, the issue involved reached the United States Supreme Court, which sustained the refusal of Jehovah's Witnesses to salute the flag as a right guaranteed by the First Amendment. Speaking for a majority of the Court, Justice Jackson said in part,

> If there is any fixed star in our constitutional constellation it is that no official, high or petty, can prescribe what shall be orthodox in politics, nationalism, religion or other matters of opinion or force its citizens to confess by word or act of faith therein.

Contributions of the Nonsectarian School

As we saw in Chapter 17, acceptance of the principle that there shall be no indoctrination of religion in public education did not come suddenly (if, indeed, it is fully observed today). The establishment of the nonsectarian school marked the first step in its realization. Unlike New

England and the South, the Middle Colonies were heterogeneous in nationality and creed from the beginning. Here Quaker and Mennonite, Lutheran and Reformed German, Baptist and Methodist, Presbyterian and Anglican, even an occasional Catholic and Jew rubbed shoulders. Proximity and the financial difficulty each sect encountered in supporting its own school created conditions favorable to cooperation. Eventually the Quakers and, later, other denominations conceived the plan of enrolling in their schools the children of the unorthodox as well as the orthodox. The presence in the same school of pupils of varied religious origins under conditions favorable to mutual respect and understanding tended to shift the emphasis in religious instruction from points of sectarian difference to items upon which all denominations might agree. Thus nonsectarian instruction came into being.

Nonsectarian instruction was admirably adapted to the needs of education on the Western frontier where the population was varied in background, but it was also well received in the original colonies as these increased in numbers and diversity. During the nineteenth century it gave impetus to the states to extend the principle of separation of church and state to the field of education. Thus, as old and new states came to establish public school systems, they tended to erect a "wall of separation" between the public treasury and nonpublic schools through the adoption of constitutional provisions which restricted the use of public funds to public education and forbade the appropriation of any funds to any institution in which sectarian doctrines were taught.

In the beginning, however, nonsectarian instruction meant little more than the elimination of doctrines which divided Protestant from Protestant. Later, in a more complex situation, it became evident that the identical principle forbade instruction in matters that set Catholic apart from Protestant and both from Jew. Consequently, materials of instruction and practices that were once taken for granted came under review and were gradually eliminated from schools in communities of religiously heterogeneous populations. Most conspicuous of these practices was the reading from the King James version of the Bible, the reciting of Protestant prayers, and the singing of songs of an obviously sectarian tinge, to which Catholics, Jews, and other non-Protestants objected.

As indicated earlier, these developments did not occur without dissent, repeated appeals to the courts, and contradictory results. One state court, for example, would rule that the Bible is a sectarian document to be banned from the school, whereas another would hold that it is the "mother of sects" and thus overarches sectarian doctrines—that its use, accordingly, was not only appropriate but desirable.

Were we to generalize from practices actually followed in the schools through the country in the course of the nineteenth century, we should doubtless conclude that few institutions were genuinely non-sectarian. But this is to confuse the outward and visible expressions of principle with its inward and motivating spirit. What was progressively accepted by the public and the courts alike was the *principle* of the nonsectarian school, a principle that dictated, in substance, the exclusion from the public school of positive instruction, or indoctrination, in tenets of religion to which any group might object. In line with this policy, public schools in the states gradually abandoned compulsory reading of the Bible, singing of denominational songs, using parochial prayers, and other exercises of a sectarian character as objection to them became manifest.

Fifty Years of Reaction and the Situation Today

Then came a period of reversion to the required reading of the Bible and the recitation of prayers in public schools, in some states through local action under permissive legislation or the absence of prohibitive legislation; in others, in conformity with legislative mandate. Demands for compulsory Bible reading and a return to the daily use of the Lord's Prayer were followed by the introduction of programs of religious instruction on "released time," a device by which children are given instruction in religion on school time by teachers of the parents' choice. These programs were only partially checked by the *McCollum* decision in 1948, since, four years later, in *Zorach* v. *Clauson,* 343 U.S. 306 (1952), the Supreme Court ruled that public schools might adjust their schedules to permit pupils to attend classes in religion, provided those classes were conducted off the school grounds.

Despite this favorable ruling, released-time programs have not been altogether satisfactory, either from the standpoint of religious groups or from that of school administrators. The obvious disruption of the school schedule, the segregation of children into sectarian groups, the not infrequent isolation of the nonconformist child, and the frequent use of unskilled personnel for instruction trouble conscientious laymen as well as educators and have frequently induced boards of education to abolish programs once initiated. To this must be added, in all sincerity, the uneasiness with which many have viewed the willingness (if not insistence) of ardent advocates of released-time instruction to ignore both the spirit and the letter of the law, at the same time that they argue the indispensability of religious instruction as one means of fostering a healthy obedience to law in the hearts of the young! [1]

On the other hand, since these programs fall short of what many religious leaders would have the school assume as a sacred obligation —namely, to bridge the gulf between secular and religious education —demands mounted in the 1940s and the 1950s for the incorporation of religious instruction into the "heart of the curriculum." One suggestion was to introduce a "common core" of religious content into the curriculum, by which was meant religious beliefs accepted in common by the three major faiths—Protestants, Catholics, and Jews. This common core, according to one prominent advocate, was to involve "not merely the institution of courses in one department in the curriculum or required attendance in such courses," but, as well, "a fundamental re-orientation of every subject in the curriculum and its presence in every course." [2]

The demand that the public schools incorporate in the curriculum a common core of religious instruction enlisted, for a time, the active interest of a considerable group of Protestant leaders, some of whom, indeed, threatened to withdraw Protestant support from public education unless means were found to introduce religious instruction into the school. However, the net result of these efforts has been small, as

1. The willingness of school boards to comply with the decisions of the United States Supreme Court on matters of religion is not impressive. For example, from a study conducted by R. B. Dierenfeld in 1961, it was concluded that home-room devotional exercises were being conducted in 50.22 per cent of the schools of the nation; that released-time programs were operating in 29.66 per cent of the nation's schools, with every eighth school system permitting these programs to operate within school buildings in open violation of the Court's injunctions. *Religious Education,* May–June 1961, pp. 173 ff.

2. Henry P. Van Dusen, formerly President of Union Theological Seminary, New York City, in *God in Education* (New York: Charles Scribner's Sons, 1951), p. 78.

evidenced by a statement of the National Council of the Churches of Christ in the United States of America in 1963. The Council states:

> While both our tradition and the present temper of our nation reflect a preponderant belief in God as our Source and our Destiny, nevertheless attempts to establish a "common core" of religious beliefs to be taught in public schools have usually proven unrealistic and unwise. Major faith groups have not agreed on a formula of religious beliefs common to all. Even if they had done so, such a body of religious doctrine would tend to substitute for the more demanding commitments of historic faiths.[3]

In 1953, a committee on Religion and Education of the American Council on Education put forth a compromise proposal. This committee found that public schools are engaged at present in "three overlapping and confused policies and practices." These are avoidance of religion, planned religious activities, and a factual study of religion. Of the three, the committee preferred the third, the factual study of religion. "This approach," the committee stated, "has distinctive merits. It is thoroughly consistent with modern educational theory and practice. It is applicable to any school, college or university, in addition to, or in substitution for, other practices. Its justification lies principally in the requirements of a fundamental general education. Such a practice need not supplement planned religious activities, but it will tend to fill a vacuum caused by avoidance of religion." [4]

The committee recognized that genuine difficulties must be overcome if its recommendations are not to be used, on the one hand, as a Trojan horse for the introduction of sectarian teaching and, on the other hand, to sanction an objectivity which concentrates so exclusively upon bare facts that it fails to stimulate young people to come to terms with the issues of life. Consequently, it urged an experimental program "in a few carefully selected situations to discover what is involved, and, insofar as possible, to obtain answers to certain important questions" before communities generally attempt its adoption. The problem, as the com-

3. A Policy Statement of the National Council of the Churches of Christ in the United States of America on *The Churches and the Public Schools,* adopted by the General Board, June 7, 1963.

4. *The Function of the Public Schools in Dealing with Religion: A Report of the Exploratory Study Made by the Committee on Religion and Education* (Washington, D.C.: American Council on Education, 1953), p. 83.

mittee envisaged it, "is one which makes peculiarly imperative a scrupulous observance of the constitutional principle of religious liberty," and it is mindful that "one of the most important aims of such studies and experiments should be how this principle can be applied to all—minorities and majorities alike." [5]

Not all advocates of the study of religion and the "erasing of religious illiteracy" are as scrupulously concerned to respect the sensibilities of minorities or to realize the obligations of a teacher to his students in an area where honest men differ fundamentally. Indeed, they are convinced that "objectivity" is undermining both religion and the democracy which they believe derives its life blood from religion. The spirit of nonsectarianism, they contend, has overshot its mark and has led to a "religious vacuum" in public education which militates against religion. This vacuum they propose to fill by a "factual study of religion" which differs little, if at all, from that proposed by the advocates of a "common core" of religious instruction. Certainly, the "facts" presented constitute a none-too-critical description of the orthodox faiths and their organizational expressions in contemporary life and exclude an equally sympathetic presentation of the views of numerous groups which have abandoned orthodoxy, together with the grounds for this deviation. In short, the purpose is less the pursuit of truth in a highly confused and complex area of living and more the "saving of souls" as one segment of the community conceives salvation.

Finally, in this review of attempts to use the public schools in the interests of religion, mention should be made of courses in the teaching of moral and spiritual values. An assumption common to many of these courses is that belief in God undergirds both "loyalty to American ideals" and the principles of morality.[6]

In view of the widespread belief that moral character lacks substance in the absence of religious faith, it is not surprising that consternation in many quarters should follow upon decisions of the Supreme Court outlawing Bible readings and the use of officially approved

5. *Ibid.*, p. 86.
6. In a case involving the city of Miami similar to *School District of Abington* v. *Schempp*, 374 U.S. 203 (1963), the Supreme Court of Florida stated, "The concept of God has been and is so interwoven into every aspect of American institutions that to attack this concept is to threaten the very fibre of our existence as a nation." (*Chamberlin* v. *Board of Education*, 143 So. 2d 21, Florida, 1962.) On appeal to the United States Supreme Court, the latter directed Florida to reconsider its position in the light of the *Schempp* decision.

prayers in public education and, further, the Court's insistence that in dealing with religion, public schools must be "wholly neutral," neither "aiding nor opposing religion."

What Is Meant by "Religion and Morality"?

But how shall we interpret the injunctions of the Supreme Court? What does "wholesome neutrality" imply, positively and negatively, with respect to the responsibilities of the public school in relation to religion? To answer these questions we shall have to examine the nature of both religion and morality under the unique conditions of public education.

Let us begin with religion. In seeking a definition, we should bear in mind that definitions, in order to be helpful, must be relevant to a purpose. The purpose in the case under discussion is twofold: to achieve mutually supportive social contributions and mutually independent operations between the functions of religious organizations, on the one hand, and the functions of the school, on the other. Justice Frankfurter borrowed a phrase from Robert Frost to describe how to maintain this relationship in *McCollum* v. *Board of Education,* "good fences make good neighbors." Cooperating neighbors, each restricted from trespassing upon the other, is the goal sought.

A concept long employed by the courts, when considering relations between church and state, identifies religion with a theistic conception of the Deity and man's relation to Him. It was this definition that Justice Field propounded in *Reynolds* v. *United States,* 98 U.S. 145 (1878), when he stated, "The term religion has reference to one's views of his relation to his Creator, and to the obligations they impose of reverence for His being and character, and of obedience to His word."

This concept is also in harmony with the pronouncements of a representative group of educators and religious leaders in the 1947 Report of the Committee on Religion and Education of the American Council on Education. In stating what it meant by religion, the Committee wrote as follows:

> In simple terms religion implies an ultimate reality to which supreme allegiance must be given. To this ultimate reality men have from time immemorial given a name—God. The religious

man finds warrant for all his conceptions of worth, of right, of duty, and of human destiny in his relation to this ultimate reality. . . . Religion affirms overwhelmingly a reality that transcends the flux of events and constrains men toward the true and the good.[7]

Justice Field's definition of religion is also in agreement with that commonly held by advocates of positive religious instruction in public schools, as evidenced by the writings of responsible leaders such as Dr. Henry P. Van Dusen, Dr. Luther A. Weigle, and Bishop James A. Pike, as well as by earnest laymen who, as members of local school boards, have insisted upon daily readings from the Bible and prayers at opening exercises as one means of furthering moral education. The latter clearly conceives of God as both a Creator and a Lawgiver who has provided man with the Bible as a moral codebook from which all who read may derive His intentions. On this view, moral principles are formulated *for* man rather than *by* man, and learning from experience in moral matters is more a discovery of God's commandments than an original and creative act. As Dr. Luther A. Weigle, Dean Emeritus of the Yale Divinity School and one of the expert witnesses in *Engel* v. *Vitale* has stated, "The Bible is not a mere historical document to be preserved. And it is more than a classic of English literature to be cherished and admired. The Bible contains the Word of God to man. . . ."[8]

It was doubtless this conviction that prompted Dr. Weigle to assert of the decision of the Supreme Court in *McCollum* v. *Board of Education,* that it encourages an "uneasy working partnership between atheists and positivists on the one hand and religious individualists and ultra-fundamentalists on the other," who favor an interpretation of separation of church and state "which confines God to the church and

7. *Report of the Committee on Religion and Education,* American Council on Education Studies, Report of Committees, Vol. XI, No. 26, April 1947, p. 11. This report should not be confused with the 1953 report on *The Function of Public Schools in Dealing with Religion* to which reference was made above.

8. Quoted from *The English New Testament* at the hearings of *Schempp* v. *School District,* 177 F. Supp. 398 (E. D. Pa., 1959). Robert F. Drinan, S.J., remarks in this connection, "The profoundly religious and theistic presuppositions of the American state appear to be so deeply ingrained in American policy that it is doubtful if Congressional or Supreme Court endorsements of a neutral or secular state can, in the absence of a complete reversal of public opinion, change the fundamental direction of church-state attitudes in America." *Religion, the Courts, and Public Policy,* p. 7.

outlaws Him in the state." This neutrality, he further asserts, has the practical effect of foisting an atheism "or a non-theistic humanism" upon the schools which is inconceivable since "They may be neutral as to the strife of sects; but they cannot be neutral as to God." [9]

This concept of religion runs counter to the convictions not only of naturalists, but also of many religious liberals who hold to a concept of ultimate reality and of human nature significantly different from that of Weigle and his associates. Doubtless the same is true of many teachers who can hardly be characterized as religiously illiterate. Neutrality in religion would seemingly require these instructors to refrain from efforts to persuade their pupils to adopt the conception of an ultimate reality which appeals to them and the morality which derives from this partisan view. But if they suppress the evangelical impulse to promote the faith to which they are committed, are we to insist that they inculcate doctrines which they themselves cannot accept? In discussing this dilemma, some years ago, I. N. Thut remarked,

> The constitutional provisions for religious freedom clearly recognize the limitations in man's ability to know God fully and completely. . . . It is a deep-rooted American tradition that a man's God-theory is his own personal business and that he has a right to keep it as private as his breakfast or his bath. . . . In this atmosphere of freedom, it is small wonder that a multiplicity of God-theories has appeared. There is, for example, the Quaker theory, which looks upon God as a kind, loving father, who walks so closely with each of his children that no man or institution should be permitted to come between them. Then there are the well-known Congregationalist and Unitarian theories which disagree so sharply on the question of whether God has three forms or one. Similarly, the Mormon theory and the Shaker theory lead to decidedly opposite views on the matter of procreation. Some sects picture God as a fearful Being likely to punish violently anyone who dares approach Him without proper credentials. Others look upon Him as a somewhat vague, formless spirit that may be felt in one's heart but may not be known otherwise directly.[10]

9. These quotations are from an article entitled "Freedom of Religion and Education," *Christianity and Crisis,* July 24, 1950, pp. 97–103.

10. "Shall the Public Schools Teach Religion?" *Teacher Education Quarterly* (Connecticut State Department of Education), Winter 1951, pp. 75–79.

Recent decisions of the Supreme Court indicate that the "wholesome neutrality" it now enjoins upon public education involves more than neutrality with respect to what Thut terms "God-theories." In 1961 (*Torcaso* v. *Watkins*, 367 U.S. 488), the Court stated, "Neither [a State nor the Federal Government] can constitutionally pass laws nor impose requirements which aid all religions against non-believers, and neither can aid those religions based on a belief in the existence of God as against those religions founded on different beliefs." And, in a footnote, Justice Black, speaking for the Court, added, "Among religions in this country which do not teach what would generally be considered a belief in the existence of God are Buddhism, Taoism, Ethical Culture, Secular Humanism and others." [11]

It would seem, then, that the concept of wholesome neutrality in religion on the part of the public school precludes positive action in the form of instruction or practices, authorized and permitted by the school, which have in mind either promoting or undermining specific religious commitment.

Are we to conclude, then, that religious concepts are to go unmentioned in the school?

Religion as Structure Versus Religion as Function

Some have sought a middle ground by drawing a distinction between religion as a "structure" and religion as a "function." By religion as a structure is meant what Thut has characterized as a "God-theory." Essentially, it is a theology together with its implications for conduct (specific doctrines with their rituals and symbolism and approved practices, which distinguish one faith from another). Religion as a function refers to a "quality of behavior" or to the ideals and standards which, presumably, all religious structures in a given culture approve and which, it is believed, can be distilled and promoted independently of any one specific faith or creed.

As we shall see later, this distinction between common ideals and the

11. This, together with other decisions of the Court, particularly *McGowan* v. *Maryland*, 366 U.S. 420 (1961), and *Engel* v. *Vitale*, 370 U.S. 434 (1962), served as a basis for the following statement by Justice Clark in *Abington School District* v. *Schempp*, 374 U.S. 203 (1963): "While the Free Exercise Clause clearly prohibits the use of state action to deny the right of free exercise to anyone, it has never meant that a majority could use the machinery of the State to practice its beliefs."

sectarian systems of belief which are thought to underwrite them has some value. But we may question whether the use of the term "religion" to designate both content and function may not confuse rather than clarify when applied to the practical problem of whether or not public school classrooms should be used as a medium of instruction in religion.

One source of confusion derives from the fact that advocates of the distinction between structure and function are by no means in agreement as to where the one leaves off and the other begins. Some draw the line in such a manner as to differ little, if at all, from the advocates of a common core of religious content. Others, for example Ward Madden,[12] conceive of function as analogous to, if not identical with, the process of education. As such, it is none other than the weighing of one proposed line of conduct against another, the resolving of conflicts among ideals through the reconstruction of an old or the creation of a new ideal which will guide men as a cloud by day and a pillar of fire by night. Activities of this character are common to all men. They involve the thoughtful process of matching the assumptions or major premises common to one's family, local community, or national culture against the context of ever changing circumstance, with a resulting clarification or reinterpretation and, on occasion, even revision of these basic assumptions and principles. If this is what we are to mean by religion as a function, it embraces, as Ward Madden admits, atheists as well as religionists and, indeed, all men who live in the same culture. Moreover, if the term "religion" is to be applied to this process, religious education obviously becomes an essential ingredient of all good education.

The concept of religion as a function furthers a spirit more democratic than that which insists upon incorporating a specific content of religion in the curriculum of the school. It is more democratic in the sense that its advocates would not have the school display favoritism toward any particular religious faith. It also runs counter to the assumption which has so frequently pitted brother against brother, namely, that adherence to one arbitrary faith is an indispensable condition of morality. Rather, is it more in harmony with a favorite phrase of John Adams, "There was virtue in the world before there was orthodoxy in it."

12. *Religious Values in Education* (New York: Harper & Brothers, 1951).

This tolerance is a decided asset to education in a society in which the religious atmosphere resembles the tower of Babel. Nevertheless, many will prefer a more neutral term to designate the objectives of the functionalists. They see little value and potential danger in maintaining a distinction that is essentially fictitious: one of thought rather than actuality. They fear that when a teacher in a classroom attempts to develop the "religious attitude" he will be tempted to ground this attitude in a religious premise, one which he may believe inoffensive or nonsectarian but which others will immediately identify as sectarian.

As we shall see later, it is possible to avoid this difficulty by recognizing that the sources of morality are plural and more fundamental than any one religious faith, as conventionally understood.

What Place, if Any, Has Religion in Public Education?

We return, then, to our original query. Is there no place for religion in public education? Must we insist upon its total elimination from the school?

The answer is "No." Certainly there is a place for religion, so long as the school sincerely attempts to avoid indoctrination. Theoretically, at least, the educational task in matters relating to religion is no different from that confronting the classroom in other areas where the community (not merely the local community, but also the wider community) is heterogeneous. Under these circumstances, and insofar as it is possible to deal with the topic educationally (that is, in the absence of emotional tensions which render impossible a sympathetic and generous understanding of rival points of view), it is the obligation of the school to inform, enlighten, and further appreciation and understanding of religious institutions. Ideally, consideration in the school of religion and its expressions, institutional and personal, should result in the members of one denominational group viewing the adherents of another more sympathetically and generously than they did prior to study. This should hold true for the orthodox and the unorthodox, the believer and the nonbeliever. It would also be desirable for each individual to clarify his own position, which may or may not be that of the instructor or a fellow student.

What this implies specifically will vary with the age of young people and with circumstance, but the principle is identical on all levels. It draws a clean-cut distinction between the "factual study of religion," as occasion arises in history, literature, science, music and art, the social studies, and the like, and all efforts on the part of the school to determine for a student his religious faith. As different and contrasting points of view become evident, young people will doubtless appreciate and respect the position of a teacher who makes clear that religion is no exception to the general rule that in controversial matters the public school is the representative of society as a whole and the partisan of no one segment.

Theodore Brameld,[13] in a Letter to the Editor in *The New York Times* of June 24, 1963, stated this position effectively as follows: The decision, he wrote, referring to the Supreme Court's ruling on Bible reading and the use of the Lord's Prayer at opening exercises in public schools,

> invites long overdue reconsideration of how public education may provide effective study of the role of religion in the experience of mankind, and how it may do so without loading the dice through indoctrination. To be sure, this new opportunity will be far from easy to implement. It will require, for example, comparison of all the great religious movements—not merely the Judaic-Christian but the Buddhist, Hindu, Humanist and others. It will need carefully trained teachers. It will afford first-hand acquaintance with the practices of these religions. And it will offer completely free opportunity for any learner to reconsider his own religious preferences should he care to do so.

Educational Adventure

This kind of teaching and learning, which is antithetical to the kind of indoctrination finally outlawed by the Supreme Court, opens a new frontier for educational adventures. At first, to be sure, experimentation in religious study should be attempted only on the senior high school level and in carefully selected communities. As it proves workable, however, I am convinced that it will become acceptable to most communities. For it will demonstrate to the American people that the choice is not between teaching one religious doctrine and teaching none at all. Rather the choice

13. © 1963 by The New York Times Company. Reprinted by permission of The New York Times and Theodore Brameld.

is between bad education and good education—between the teaching that forces beliefs of any sort upon learners and teaching that enables them to grow into citizens capable of evaluating, comparing, examining, and finally choosing for themselves.

Were classroom instruction in religion to deal justly with all faiths, the "study of religion" would include not merely the views of the orthodox faiths but the religious convictions of minority groups, including the "liberals," the agnostics, the humanists, and others who may have abandoned orthodoxy. It would not emphasize exclusively factors which impel some men toward religion, but would investigate as well the grounds that have persuaded people equally sincere to seek the solutions to life's problems in nonconventional formulas.

It is obvious that few communities will venture to introduce religion into the curriculum of the public school under these broad and generous conditions, despite the fact that in a democracy which aspires to raise up free men, responsible and seasoned in their thinking, it is a goal toward which to strive. In the meantime, and until a community has reached the point where it will permit a genuinely objective consideration of religion rather than merely using a "factual study" as a device with which to promote the theological convictions of dominant groups, we must view "the study of religion" with extreme caution. Certainly, to authorize the use of school time for instruction in religion by its partisans is to sanction an educational procedure we should roundly condemn were it applied to other areas of disagreement and controversy.

Does Moral Education Require a Religious Underpinning?

Some will object to these conclusions on the ground that they represent a grudging concession to the claims of religion. "How," they may exclaim, "is it possible to educate in moral and spiritual values, if religion is permitted only when sicklied over with the pale cast of thought?"

This takes us to the heart of our problem. How can the school educate for character without positive instruction in religion? In dealing with this problem we must repeat that by "religion" is meant a specific content of belief, a "God-theory," as Thut has well described it, or a theological concept upon which men are by no means agreed. By "qualities of character" and "moral ideals" is meant those common and accepted ways of thinking and feeling and acting in our relations with others which all men recognize will raise the standard of our living together.

Despite its importance for public education, this distinction is none too clear in the popular mind. Many still cling to a oneness in thought between doctrine and conduct characteristic of an homogeneous rather than a heterogeneous culture.

In a discussion of the nature of religion in various societies, John Herman Randall, Jr., tells us that there are some societies in which the social materials of religion are "moral, or imaginative or artistic rather than intellectual." In these societies religion is as much a way of life to be pursued as it is a set of beliefs to be accepted as true. But, as he points out, these societies are characteristically homogeneous in their religion. In the Western world, which has lacked this homogeneity for centuries and in which Protestantism has long been an important influence, the theoretical aspects of religion have consistently loomed large.[14]

It was the theological aspect of religion which concerned our fathers when they instituted the policy of separation of church and state. They had come to realize from painful experience that the traditional assumption of a one-to-one relation between religious belief and individual and social morality was no longer sound and that, however essential it may have been in the past to insure social cohesion, in a land of many faiths it had become destructive of unity.

This was, of course, a revolutionary insight and led to an equally radical change in public policy. For ages men had assumed that conformity in thought was the *sine qua non* of social morality. It was this assumption which seemingly justified religious wars and pitted brother against brother and child against parent.

We cannot review here the many factors in American life which led our people to abandon the one-religion, one-society theory. Were we to do so, however, the nonsectarian school would loom large both as a cause and an effect, since one logical outcome of religious instruction in this institution was the obvious conclusion that the virtues common to

14. William Ernest Hocking, Brand Blanshard, Charles William Hendel, and John Herman Randall, Jr., *Preface to Philosophy* (New York: The Macmillan Co., 1946), p. 314.

the members of diverse religious denominations are rooted in something more basic that the creedal differences which divide them religiously.

This basic unity seemed, for a time, to reside in a common core of Protestant theology, but with further diversity and the sharing of common experiences by Catholic and Protestant, an extension of the theological basis of morality became necessary, and Christianity, as distinct from its denominational expressions, was accepted as a foundation of sound morality. Then came the Jew and other non-Christians to participate in American life, and the more liberal-minded individuals were impelled to modify still further their conceptions of an indispensable religious basis for morality. Thus what was once exclusively Christian has become the "Judeo-Christian metaphysics." It is this basic content of religious belief that we are now told must be imparted to all children in the public school if they are to acquire and practice virtue.[15]

But the end is not yet! Modern means of communication and the emergence of the United States as a world power, with interests and responsibilities penetrating into all corners of the earth, render imperative further insight into and further extension of the foundations of a morality common to all peoples, regardless of differences in religion. A condition of realizing "One World" is the emergence of a one-world morality, by which is meant ways of thinking, feeling, and acting common to all men which harmonize interests, channel differences, and foster rich and creative relations between individuals and groups.

One step in this direction is to recognize the limitations in the common view of a *necessary* relation between religion and morality.

John Stuart Mill was one of the first to question this necessary relationship when, in his *Three Essays on Religion,* he pointed out that the Greeks serve as an illustration of a people whose morals were independent of religious sanction. Indeed, for them, the problem was to instruct their gods, since the morality of mortals was obviously superior to that of the immortals! The religion of Buddha likewise refutes the common Western notion that morality is dependent exclusively upon a power outside ourselves that makes for righteousness. Buddhism is primarily a system of ethics, of conduct, without the inducements of reward and punishment characteristic of Western religions. A follower

15. American Council on Education Studies, *Reports of Committees and Conferences,* February 1945, p. 33.

of Buddha strives for self-control, wise moderation in the indulgence of passion, and brotherly love and living sympathy with others, but he denies a creation or a creator and spurns the notion of personal immortality.

It is important to observe what has been said up to this point and what has not been said. We have said that the building of a morality which overarches parochialism and renders possible mutually fruitful ways in which people can live together in a heterogeneous society and a world of plural cultures requires recognition of no *necessary* connection between religious dogma and moral conduct. But we have not said that this holds true of all men and in all places. A basic assumption of a democratic society is the right of each man to determine for himself the foundation of morality.

The Sanctions of Morality Are Plural

These facts define the responsibility of the public school in matters of religion and morality. They suggest that, psychologically, at least, both the sources and the sanctions of morality are sectarian and secular. From this it follows that the public school should avoid indoctrinating for the narrowly sectarian and encourage intelligent identification with ideals and standards general in the culture.

Religious denominations, for example, vary widely in what they reject or sanction as approved conduct for their members. One may oppose birth control; another may justify such practice. Some sects forbid the use of certain foods and beverages for reasons others do not understand. Some frown upon smoking, card playing, and dancing. Others provide social halls for such activities. Not only are differences found between approved behavior among religious groups, the mores approved for one generation may be changed by a denomination for the next.

Contradictory and conflicting as these standards are, they have in common the injunctions or the sanctions of religious authority as the faithful conceive and interpret that authority. But this authority is sectarian and the public school cannot with justice indoctrinate its pupils in either a sectarian religion or a sectarian morality. Insofar as it deals with the sectarian at all—and to avoid it completely is impossible—it should do so exclusively on an informational level and in a manner designed not to convert, but to further mutual understanding, appreciation, and toleration.

So much for one category of moral codes and principles. A second consists of standards and ideals, directions for living, common to a wider culture. For example, the constituents of the "American way of life" despite some local differences embrace southerner and northerner, New Yorker and Californian, in a community of ideals and attitudes and dispositions of sufficient potency to set them apart as a unified group (Americans) from the members of other national and cultural groups.

Broader still are the ideals of the "free peoples" as these find expression in the day-by-day relations within family and community life, in contrast with those of peoples long denied direct and effective participation in determining their own destinies. Although the average citizen in a democracy is often unable consciously to formulate these ideals, honoring them all too frequently in the breach, these ideals nevertheless give form and substance to his daily activities. High on the list of these ideals are an essential respect for the worth of the individual and the uniqueness of his personality; the concept of a reciprocal relation between society and the individual of such an order that, on the one hand, the validity of institutions and laws is measured by the degree to which they meet the needs and enrich the lives of people and, on the other hand, the appropriateness of individual action and expression is judged by their effects upon others; and, finally, the principle that conflicts between interests are best resolved through the mediating operations of intelligence, a process in which all contestants are accorded a fair hearing and the solution arrived at consists of the most reasonable adjustment and the most adequate and happy harmonizing of these interests.

Broad and general as these ideals, concepts, and principles are, they lead to a thousand and one practices and accepted ways of living which distinguish a democratic culture from an autocratic and totalitarian one.

Now, this democratic morality, if we may so characterize it, has evolved in the modern world out of diversity and the practical effort to encourage creative and mutually fruitful relations between individuals and whole peoples within a pluralistic culture. Although it is possible

—and, indeed, it has often happened—that the principles and precepts of various religious sects have contributed to the development of democratic morality, it is also true that they have functioned at times as obstructive agents, particularly when dogma dominated other considerations.

This suggests a difference in the methods of thinking characteristic of the two types of morality, a difference of significance for the school. Morality linked to a religious sect commonly starts with an accepted major premise in the form of a precept or principle derived from tradition and authority. Consequently, the solution of a moral problem consists, in the main, in identifying the appropriate moral injunction applicable to the situation in doubt. Once this is identified, the answer to the problem follows as the conclusion from the premises of a syllogism. A morality that is designed to ease and free and enrich relations among people who share some principles in common but differ fundamentally in others involves a procedure more flexible and more complicated.

Insofar as the problem at issue relates to premises upon which there is no agreement among the participants, there comes into operation what might be termed a Golden Rule as applied to absolutes. That is, the devotees of each sacred principle are expected to respect the convictions of their neighbors and to act on the assumption that what one man accepts as of ultimate validity for himself shall be of no more than relative or suggestive value in the thinking or the conduct of the other.

In many situations this will be as far as the participants can go, a willingness to abide by the principle of live and let live. But the process contains the seeds of a more embracing morality, one sensitive to considerations to which the prior absolutes were blind, i.e., the changing circumstances of life. A sensitive response to changing circumstance in moral matters leads to conclusions different from those characteristic of narrowly sectarian morality—the difference, shall we say, which marks off the Pharisee from the Good Samaritan. It recognizes an organic connection between the individual personality and his surroundings and, in consequence, a degree of relativity in moral matters to which dogmatism closes its eyes.

We may illustrate with family relationships. In the homogeneous community there grows up a generally accepted and rigidly enforced pattern of relationships between man and wife, child and parent. Woman in this type of society "knows her place" and tends to keep it!

So it is with other members of the family. As we move from one cultural group to another, however, the definition of what constitutes the right and proper behavior varies significantly. In one family the patriarchal relationship between father and child persists. In another, this has given way to a democratic familiarity between parents and children in which all are known by their first names and the family council includes the child as well as the adults. In other families still other patterns obtain. If representatives of these contrasting family groupings are brought together in the same community, under conditions in which the children play together, attend the same school, form friendships, and eventually intermarry, problems of differing values that are of unique importance for education emerge. The problems posed by contrasting values are particularly acute during adolescence when an individual begins to be concerned about the respective roles of boy and girl, young man and woman, husband and wife. Nor are these young people helped in their progress toward healthy, responsible, and mature personalities by the efforts of adults to impose upon them one arbitrary concept of a child's duty to his parents or the ideal marriage relationship. Rather, the most satisfying and creative patterns will vary from individual to individual, reflecting in each instance experiences peculiar to that person.

Narrowly sectarian morality and the morality of a wider culture in a dynamic and changing society thus differ significantly in their attitudes toward principles and their applications of those principles. The first commonly derives its directives from sources outside the lives of the individuals immediately employing them. These directives not only constitute the "eternal verities," but in their applications to practice they are detailed and specific. Since they fall within the category of "right for right's sake though the heavens fall," they allow for little adaptation to circumstance. Morality of the wider culture and interacting relationships, on the other hand, consists of principles which permit greater flexibility of application. Consequently, the goal of education with respect to them is less that consistency which Emerson considered the hobgoblin of small minds and more a moral thoughtfulness which weighs principle against principle and novel data against both principle and familiar circumstance. Toward this end all subjects of the curriculum, the daily life of the classroom, extracurricular activities, and school-community relations have contributions to make. Moral education in school, in other words, is not so much a special subject to be taught as it is a central concern permeating all school experience.

Finally, in our classification of moral values, are the universals of still wider application, universal in the sense that they overarch and penetrate all civilized communities. To these all good men are true, regardless of race, nationality, creed, or class. They constitute the social cement of all civilized societies and range from principles such as the Golden Rule to such common virtues as honesty, reliability, temperance, and self-control.

These values and virtues, like those in our second grouping, are formal and abstract in statement. Only when they are applied to specific situations by individuals under conditions that are at once novel and familiar do they come to life. This accounts in part for the ineffectiveness of purely verbal instruction in moral principles. Only in individual action, in day-by-day associations with people under circumstances that are never quite identical, can precept and practice give vitality and meaning to each other.

Their formal and abstract character in no way weakens their importance, however. They lack specificity merely because they are the essence of wisdom gleaned by generations of men under all manner of conditions. They are the tested and validated formulas for harmonizing and channeling relations between person and person, individual and group, group and group, and for carving out ever widening and more profitable spheres of community action in a world where basic differences and disagreements stubbornly persist. Moreover, the universals, in common with the second order of values, are more solidly grounded when they are recognized as independent of and superior to the claims of any one sectarian religion. Indeed, as the anthropologists have fairly well established, religion is less the source and validator of this morality than is moral experience the matrix and the ultimate testing ground of what is durable and valuable in religion.

Legitimate Areas of School Concern

We conclude, then, that for the practical purposes of public education moral and spiritual values may be grouped under three headings. First are the sectarian values, intimately associated with one religious sect. In American society these values are the cherished ways of living peculiar to one or more of the subgroups within a larger all-embracing culture. Occasionally they dominate one community or one region and give to the inhabitants of that area the false sense of a universally shared morality. Second are the nonsectarian and secular values common to the members of a diversified culture (as, for example, the people of the United States as a whole) despite differences in race, nationality, and creed. Last, but of supreme importance for the evolution of morality in the future, are the universal values which enlist the loyalties of all men in all cultures.

This classification should help us to determine what is legitimate and what is illegitimate with respect to religion and morals in the field of public education. Neither sectarian religion nor sectarian morality is properly to be "taught" in the public school, if by "taught" we mean manipulating the school situation with an eye to molding the lives of young people into conformity with them. Positive instruction here should be clearly and exclusively the responsibility of family and church. Values in the second and third categories, on the other hand, are of a different order. They are the values common to all members of a culture and are acknowledged by all to be the primary conditions for fruitful communication and mutually beneficial relationships. They are the tested general formulas for promoting the interpenetration of interests and resolving conflicts between people as these conflicts arise. Helping young people recognize, acquire, and wisely apply these values calls for more than indoctrination in specifics. In involves rather the acquisition through practice of disciplined but flexible ways of thinking, feeling, and acting that have as their objective "raising the standard of men's living together."

As we have seen, one significant contribution of the nonsectarian school was the discovery that common values are grounded in something more fundamental than the creeds which divide men into warring schools. Their primary source is the imperative need of people to communicate in mutually fruitful ways and to engage in transactions of mutual benefit and concern. The public school is uniquely qualified to promote these common values precisely because of its public and secular character. Consequently, were the American people to yield to the temptation to ground the common principles of morality exclusively in one or more religious orientation, be this narrowly denominational or as vague and general as "Judeo-Christian affirmation," they would succeed only in warping their character and limiting the range of their application. On the other hand, once the American public school interprets its function as the development of disciplined ways of thinking, feeling, and acting which ease and free communication and further profitable interrelationships among men of all faiths and many cultures, it will contribute to the eventual realization of an era of peace on earth and good will toward men.

Suggested Reading

AASA, *Religion in the Public Schools* (Washington, D.C., 1964).

Boles, Donald Edwards, *The Bible, Religion and The Public Schools* (Ames, Iowa: Iowa University Press, 1963).

Bower, W. C., *Moral and Spiritual Values in Education* (Lexington, Kentucky: University of Kentucky Press, 1952).

Center for the Study of Democratic Institutions, *Religion and American Society, A Statement of Principles* (New York: The Fund for the Republic, 1961).

Committee on Religion and Education, *The Function of the Public Schools in Dealing with Religion* (Washington, D.C.: American Council on Education, 1953).

Drinan, Robert F., S.J., *Religion, the Courts, and Public Policy* (New York: McGraw-Hill Book Company, Inc., 1963), chaps. 2–3.

Educational Policies Commission, *Moral and Spiritual Values in the Public School* (Washington, D.C.: National Education Association, 1952).

Ehlers, Henry J., and Gordon C. Lee, *Crucial Issues in Education*, 3rd ed. (New York: Holt, Rinehart and Winston, 1964), Part 2.

Johnson, F. Ernest, ed., *American Education and Religion* (New York: Harper & Brothers, 1952).

Madden, Ward, *Religious Values in Education* (New York: Harper & Brothers, 1951).

McCluskey, Neil Gerard, S.J. *Public Schools and Moral Education, The Influence of Horace Mann, William Torrey Harris, and John Dewey* (New York: Columbia University Press, 1958), chap. XI.

Miller, William Lee, "Religion and Americanism," *A Journal of Church and State*, May 1963, pp. 15–26.

"Religion in the Public Schools: A Symposium," *Religious Education*, July–August 1955, pp. 211–46.

Thayer, V. T., *The Attack upon the American Secular School* (Boston: Beacon Press, Inc., 1951), chaps. X, XI.

Chapter 20

How Free Is Freedom to Learn?

"Ye Shall Know the Truth, and the Truth Shall Make You Free"

In Chapter 16, we drew attention to a number of assumptions which have given form and character to American education. One of these, the assumption that in areas of controversy and doubt the function of the school is to develop in students an understanding and sympathetic insight into relevant points of view, but not to indoctrinate, served to guide the discussion of Chapter 19. Its application, however, is by no means restricted to the disputed role of religion in public education. It defines as well the function of instruction in other areas where ideas and suggested programs of action compete for the loyalties of men. Here, too, its validity has been openly challenged in recent years by individuals and groups determined to purge textbooks and libraries of subversive influences and to control education in harmony with narrow partisan interpretations of the orthodox.

To these developments we now turn.

It is sometimes said that once the public grasps the full implications of education in a free and changing society, problems of censorship will take care of themselves and pressure groups will find it difficult, if not impossible, to control teaching. There is much to be said in support of this view since, in the last analysis, public opinion both erects and sustains the bulwarks of a free education. But to win and to retain public support is no easy accomplishment.

One difficulty derives from the very nature of a free society, that is, a society in which the loyalty of its members is not constrained. Under

478

normal circumstances this gives both an inner stability and a durability lacking in an autocratic and totalitarian society. But it also fathers delay in organizing resistance to impending dangers and often enables the enemies of democracy to gain their ends through piecemeal tactics. Too frequently a school board or the governing body of an educational institution under attack delays forthright action on behalf of freedom to teach, on the theory that the storm may blow over, only to discover, too late, that issues which should have been clear are blurred. Or representatives of an institution free from assault hesitate to speak out in defense of a sister institution on the principle of "Why respond when our ox is not being gored?" Or "Why call 'Wolf! Wolf!' when there is no wolf at our door?" Or, still again, "These criticisms are not new. They have been made frequently before and the situation has righted itself. We may be certain that history will repeat itself." In the meantime, the public is ill prepared to cope understandingly with the issues involved.

As we shall see, attempts of individuals and organized groups to determine what the schools shall teach within sensitive areas (religious, political, economic, social) are not new. They have characterized American education from the colonial period to the present. What distinguishes the period since World War II (followed as it has been by a Cold War of apparently endless duration) has been the rise of numerous self-styled "patriotic" organizations, operating on a national scale and dedicated to the elimination of "atheistic, communistic, and collectivistic" influences in American life and education. The efforts of these groups are altogether legitimate in a democratic society—until they begin to identify as subversive all views which deviate from their own ideology and adopt pressure tactics in order to control the selection of textbooks and other classroom materials, the choice of library books and magazines, and the hiring and firing of teachers so as to insure the propagation of the one true gospel. During the 1950s attacks of this character upon the integrity of public education were sufficiently novel to receive the attention of press and magazine and, as a consequence, to generate counterefforts in support of academic freedom. Since the period commonly termed the "McCarthy period," [1] less attention has

1. A term used to describe the campaign waged by United States Senator Joseph McCarthy to weed out communists and "communist sympathizers" from government, industries related to national defense, and schools and colleges by the use of methods none too sensitive to the reputations or the rights of individuals investigated.

been given to attacks upon local school systems, although attempts to influence boards of education, state legislatures, and textbook publishers have continued unabated. Between 1958 and 1962, for example, textbooks "came under fire" in nearly a third of the state legislatures.[2] Indeed, the findings of the Committee on Tenure and Academic Freedom of the National Education Association, published in the *NEA Journal* of May 1951, are still relevant. Said the Committee:

> Presence in the school curriculum of items to which a particular group is sensitive is causing a greater degree of voluntary censorship today than ever before.
>
> The committee has evidence to indicate that voluntary censorship by administrators and teachers—to avoid conflicts with groups—is a far more insidious force than the overt acts of boards or legislatures.
>
> Organized minority groups representing fraternal, patriotic, religious, business, labor, and racial organizations often are unwilling to recognize that points of view other than their own have a right to be presented by teachers in any study of current controversial issues. Such groups need help in understanding that the schools must guarantee the right of the learner to have access to all relevant information in studying society's unsolved problems.
>
> These problems deal with management and labor; local, state, national and foreign governments; communism, fascism, isolationism, socialism; public housing; ownership of public utilities; socialized medicine; universal military training; federal aid to education; sex education; consumer education; race and religion.

On the other hand, instances are not wanting to demonstrate that once the issues of a free education are clearly envisaged by the public, many communities will give loyal support to the principle that "Ye shall know the truth, and the truth shall make you free."

Typical of this attitude was the manner in which citizen groups in Arlington, Virginia, faced an attack upon textbooks used in their schools. Immediately following a widely publicized charge that six

2. For a description of the organizations and the methods adopted by lay groups to screen textbooks and to remove "objectionable" books from school and public libraries and to control the manner in which controversial topics are to be dealt with in the classroom, see Jack Nelson and Gene Roberts, Jr., *The Censors and the Schools* (Boston: Little, Brown and Company, 1963). See also Mary Ann Raywid, *The Ax-Grinders* (New York: The Macmillan Company, 1962).

textbooks in history and economics were "slanted toward collectivism and socialism," a committee of citizens representing civic organizations subjected this indictment to detailed examination. One subcommittee reported as follows upon one book:

> Of the eighteen direct quotations offered . . . as "proof" of this alien slant, only five were found to be accurate in the sense that the actual words were actually found in the textbook, and that the meaning of the sentence was not changed by the surrounding material. In the opinion of the sub-committee, none of these five quotations prove much of anything unless it is that the world has changed in the past twenty-five years.
>
> The other quotations which we managed to locate were falsifications and distortions. Either qualifying material given with the sentence was omitted in order to present a false impression, or the sentence itself was perverted, twisted and mutilated to give a meaning never intended by the author.

Community action of this character constitutes a healthy contrast to the often hasty decision of boards of education to remove books from classroom and library with little or no investigation of the accuracy of charges leveled against them or summarily to dismiss teachers who have been indiscreet enough to bring controversial materials into the classroom and to encourage their students to think critically about them.[3]

Two Conflicting Traditions in American Education

We commonly speak of the "right" to free inquiry as an American tradition, and, in evidence, we are prone to point to the First Amendment of the federal Constitution with its guarantee of freedom of

---

3. Encouraging, also, was the action of the school board of Hanover, New Jersey, in the spring of 1958. An English teacher had asked her pupils to read John Hersey's *Hiroshima* and to write essays based upon the book. Several of the papers were published in the school paper, some of them critical of the use of the atomic bomb. Veteran groups in the community responded angrily and demanded that the teacher be dismissed. The teacher, in turn, submitted her resignation to the Board of Education, admitting to "an error of judgment." Whereupon, the Board refused to accept the resignation and emphasized the importance of teaching "students to think by presenting all the facets of a problem and challenging their minds into making free decisions . . ." (*The Washington Post and Times Herald*, June 20, 1958).

thought and expression. But is this strictly accurate? To understand better the problems of freedom in American education we should remind ourselves that, in strict accuracy, there are two traditions operating within our schools—one is a tradition of conformity and education for indoctrination and the second is education for the free mind. Nor is it established as yet which of these two trends is to prevail.

We will consider briefly these two traditions.

Education for conformity is consistent with the original purpose and character of our early schools. These, as we have observed, were established by religious communities for the purpose, among other things, of raising up the young in the one true faith and to fortify them against the wiles of that "Old Deluder Satan," who was known to use even the Scriptures for his ends. Under these conditions, it was highly important that methods and materials of instruction meet standards of orthodoxy. Accordingly, the Bible, together with approved commentaries, constituted the chief objects of study and the criteria with which to appraise other materials. Rigid censorship operated on all levels of education, from infant school through college. "Let the master take special Care," enjoined the Charter and the Statutes of the College of William and Mary, "that if the author is never so well approved on other accounts, he teach no such Part of him to his Scholars, as insinuates anything against Religion and Morals." [4]

A second factor leading to education for conformity has been the rapid development of our country with its spectacular increase in population, leading, in each generation, to a phenomenal growth in numbers of schools. At all times, as a people, we have been driven by an insatiable appetite for education. But at no time (and this is pathetically and critically true of the present) has the supply of adequately equipped teachers matched the needs of school and college. A considerable proportion of the instructors has consistently lacked preparation and training, and at no time have the rewards of teaching, either in salary or status, attracted permanent personnel of a quality equal to that drawn to the law, to medicine, or to the higher echelons of business and industry. Throughout our history teaching has suffered from the lure of rival occupations, with the result that it has been, to a considerable extent, an occupation of transients, individuals who use

4. Quoted in Elmer Ellsworth Brown, *The Making of Our Middle Schools* (New York: Longmans, Green & Co., 1914), p. 130.

teaching as a steppingstone to a more attractive career. This, too, has influenced the nature of teaching and the methods of thinking and learning common to our schools. The textbook, for the ill-prepared teacher as well as for the pupil, has been an authoritative source of information, a body of material to accept with little question rather than to weigh and ponder and appraise. What the Bible has been to the orthodox clergyman and the faithful layman, the textbook has been to large numbers of teachers and pupils. In each instance, reading is conceived of as a skill one acquires in order to identify what to believe and seldom, if at all, as an operation essential and preliminary to the sifting and winnowing process of critical thought.

To these considerations we should add the evangelical purpose with which Americans have commonly endowed their schools. Beginning with the extensions of manhood suffrage in the period following the Revolutionary War and continuing throughout the nineteenth century with each successive wave of new immigrants, the school has constituted a melting pot of conformity for new entrants into American life, political and civic as well as economic. For the children of the newly enfranchised as well as for the children of immigrants the school has exercised a molding influence essentially conservative in character. Its functions, as conceived by the dominant forces within the community, have been more to transmit a culture than to welcome new ingredients, to assimilate the children of immigrants (often creating out of them strangers to their parents) rather than to encourage the evolution of new patterns of living from the ever changing contributions of the newcomers to the American scene. Richard D. Mosier, in his suggestive study of the McGuffey readers,[5] reveals the motives which long gave character to the content of these books. Both manhood suffrage and immigration quite naturally disturbed the conservative mind, but this mind also recognized that if one generation were introduced to the solid middle-class virtues of American society, all might be well. Moreover, with an open frontier and a rapidly expanding economy, there seemed for a time to exist a pre-established harmony between the Puritan virtues and those which make for individual success. Accordingly, we find the authors of the readers accepting "the premise that the Christian virtues of thrift, labor, honesty, punctuality and good-will

5. *Making the American Mind* (New York: Kings Crown Press, 1947). See Chapter IV particularly on "The Morality of the Middle Classes."

carried men to the successes which daily would be witnessed by the humblest citizen." [6] At the same time the use of texts for this evangelical purpose tended to confirm a concept of teaching and learning friendly to conformity and relatively indifferent to the empirical use of first-hand experience in resolving the issues of life.

Finally, the psychology of learning should be mentioned, since for a long period in our educational history it conceived of the mind as a receptacle to be filled with the appropriate information, ideas, and principles. "What is the business of the teacher?" asked the author of *American Education,* a volume published in 1851. He replied, "His position is strictly that of a conveyor of knowledge—moral and intellectual—to a yet unoccupied and growing mind. To do this successfully, requires that his instruction should carry to that waiting mind a conviction of its *truth,* and that he should also connect that truth with the duties of life." [7]

This conception of the relation between teacher and pupil is in agreement with the popular notion, long dominant in American life and education, that schooling serves the practical purpose of disposing youth to accept a culture essentially foreign to native interest or to acquire a trade, a vocation, or a profession with which they can better their stations in life. One need not deprecate the phenomenal achievements of American education in technological advancement and in raising the cultural level of our people in order to realize its limitations in fostering a discipline keyed to novelty and the solution of problems whose answers are neither known in advance nor derived from the application of the rules of a syllogism.

Here, then, are a number of influences which have affected generation after generation of Americans in school and college, with the result that large numbers of students have left these institutions with the conviction that a major purpose of education is to mold men's minds rather than to impart a discipline which will enable young people to become in fact the architects of their own fortunes. Nor should we be surprised when earnest citizens and conscientious parents, concerned with the shape of things to come, consider it a sacred obligation to keep a

6. *Ibid.,* p. 122.

7. Quoted in William Heard Kilpatrick, *Source Book in the Philosophy of Education* (New York: The Macmillan Co., 1923), p. 270. See also, Alfred Auerback, "The Anti-Mental Health Movement," *American Journal of Psychiatry,* August 1963, pp. 105–11.

watchful eye upon the contents of the textbooks which properly are to constitute the warp and the woof of the growing mind. Again, when communities, once homogeneous in character, become heterogeneous and include individuals who advocate a variety of conflicting and "questionable" points of view, we should not be surprised to find that some individuals and groups turn to censorship. Are not, indeed, the waves of hysteria and conformity which so often threaten to submerge the spirit of free inquiry in the classroom the logical outcome of the school's own activity?

There is a tradition of conformity in American education. But there is a second tradition, one born of diversity, which thrives on differences, creating solid bonds of unity within these differences on both local and national levels. This tradition has profound implications for the emerging role of the United States in world affairs.

As indicated earlier, this tradition of freedom found expression first in sectarian and later in secular education, both logical developments of religious toleration and freedom of conscience. But the growth of religious liberty was no isolated phenomenon. It, in turn, was derived from multiple factors: the continuous immigration of people of diverse religious faiths and national backgrounds; the westward movement with its continuous creation of new communities of mixed origins and traditions; the leavening influence of wars which did much to wear down provincialism and to promote the idea of a common allegiance to common principles—political, economic, moral; and the intellectual contribution of European thinkers, particularly the English forerunners of freedom. Consequently, when the authors of the Declaration of Independence asserted on behalf of the American colonies, "We hold these truths to be self-evident, that all men are created free and equal, that they are endowed by their Creator with certain unalienable rights . . ." and "That to secure these rights governments are instituted among men, deriving their just powers from the consent of the governed," they were giving utterance to a way of thinking which had become firmly grounded in the daily experience of ordinary men and women, as well as in the philosophical speculations of the distinguished members of the Continental Congress. Indeed, it was doubtless first-hand contact with democratic communities in evolution on the frontier, direct observation of the actual creation and maintenance of law and order through the efforts of the people themselves, that enabled the intellectual leaders—Thomas Jefferson, John Adams, Benjamin Franklin, and others—to envisage an application of John Locke's words more radical by far than contemplated by that philosopher:

> Men being by nature all free, equal and independent, no one can be out of this estate and subjected to the political power of another without his own consent, which is done by agreeing with other men, to join and unite in a community for their comfortable, safe and peaceable living, one amongst another, in a secure enjoyment of their properties, and a greater security against any that are not of it. . . . When any number of men have so consented to make one community of government, they are thereby presently incorporated, and make one body politic, wherein they the majority have a right to act and include the rest.[8]

On the other hand, when Jefferson was moved to swear "upon the altar of God eternal hostility against every form of tyranny over the mind of man," he was but applying to his own day, and in a unique manner, a principle which John Milton a century and a half earlier had urged upon Oliver Cromwell in the latter's hour of victory: "Again, it is my earnest wish," wrote the blind poet to the Protector,

> that you would give permission to those who are inclined to freedom of inquiry, to publish what they have to communicate at their own peril, without the private inquisition of any magisterial censor: for nothing could contribute so much to the growth of truth; nor would all science be forever measured out to us in a bushel, and be bestowed at the pleasure of the half-learned. . . . Lastly, it is my fervent wish, that you should not be afraid to listen either to truth or falsehood, of whatever description that may be: but that you should listen the least of all to those, who never fancy that they themselves are free, unless they deprive others of their freedom; who labor at nothing with so much zeal and earnestness, as to enchain not the bodies only, but the consciences of their brethren; and to introduce into the church and state the worst of all tyrannies, the tyranny of their own misshapen customs and opinions. May you ever take part with those

8. John Locke, *Treatise on Civil Government,* chap. VIII.

who think it just that not their own sect or fashion alone, but all the citizens alike should have an equal right to be free.[9]

English political thought found in America fruitful soil for further growth and development. Under European conditions, and in the daily presence of ancient institutions and confirmed habits and customs of an authoritarian background, a concept of the relation of the individual to his government was necessarily of slow growth; but under American conditions it easily acquired the status of an axiom. Of these axioms, the principle of freedom of thought and expression loomed large as indispensable for the discovery of truth and the maintenance of a healthy society. But since the colonies had to fight a War of Independence to secure these blessings of liberty and freedom, our fathers deemed it wise to include a Bill of Rights in their new constitutions. That they were prudent in so doing is evidenced by the numerous occasions in which the courts have since found it necessary to reaffirm the sacred status of freedom of inquiry and expression in the face of repeated attempts to undermine them.

Implicit in the concepts of freedom of inquiry and expression is the ideal of an open society. An open society, writes Herbert J. Muller, in his *Uses of the Past,*

> is an adventurous society that has broken with universal prehistoric custom of regarding ancient customs as magical or sacred, that views its institutions as man-made for human purposes, that welcomes variety and change instead of enforcing rigid conformity, and that accordingly provides its members with personal opportunities beyond mere obedience. It is Athens as opposed to Sparta.[10]

An open society neither comes into being through spontaneous generation nor perpetuates itself without effort. It requires of its members a discipline of mind and spirit which its schools cannot safely neglect to develop in the young, disciplined ways of thinking and living that give reality to Abraham Lincoln's concept of a government of the people, by the people, and for the people.

This second tradition, the tradition of free inquiry, is now embodied

9. Quoted in Irwin Edman and Herbert W. Schneider, *Fountainheads of Freedom* (New York: Reynal and Hitchcock, 1941), p. 334. (This title is published by Harcourt, Brace & World, Inc.)

10. New York: Oxford University Press, 1952, p. 71.

in the constitutions of both state and national governments and finds classical expression in the Bill of Rights. Nevertheless, its applications in education are far from commonplace. All too few are the schools and colleges which appraise their work in terms of their success or failure in equipping students with the habits of mind and character requisite for effective living in an open society.

Implications for Subject Matter and Method

Obviously these two traditions dictate quite different procedures in school, from the standpoint of method and the choice of subject matter.

First, a word with respect to method.

It must be emphasized that education for the free intelligence as against education for conformity in no way precludes instruction in the specific and definite. There are bodies of knowledge, for example, as well as techniques and skills in human relations and in practical affairs that have met not only the tests of time but all known criteria of validation. These must be imparted to the young, if the latter are to carry on from where their elders left off. For example, no educator worth his salt would object to a mastery of the three Rs or to the conscious acquisition by his pupils of an abiding loyalty to the common virtues and the ethical principles of a democratic culture. On the contrary, these must be transmitted to our youth if modern civilization is to survive, let alone progress.

But the *methods* of imparting the definite and the specific need not be, nor can they safely be, distinguished sharply from instruction in the uncertain. They should be keyed to an open rather than a closed society. The student of an ancient civilization should be trained in the habit of forming tentative judgments on many items since further research may require their revision. In this respect he is not unlike his fellow student who specializes in constitutional law, which can be fully understood only when past decisions of the courts are weighed against both present and probable future trends, or the medical student who is planning to devote himself to medical research, or still another who is entering upon a trade or a vocation in which a skill of today may be replaced by a new process tomorrow. In short, there are few (if any) areas of learning today in which either facts or processes can wisely be taught as unchangeable. Even in the operations of simple arithmetic, the pupil who has learned to question the accuracy of his work until he has verified it has an advantage over his comrades who follow only a rule of thumb. And when we consider how persistently time undermines knowledge that had presumably been pegged down, education for conformity and passive acceptance in any area should be recognized as slender reeds upon which to lean.

Now, methods which perhaps are no more than questionable when one is dealing with the certain and the noncontroversial become handicaps in areas where uncertainty and doubt or irreconcilable differences in values are characteristic. But these are precisely the aspects of life with which the contemporary mind is increasingly called upon to deal. To employ methods of indoctrination in these areas or to fail to develop the discipline of mind essential to living resourcefully with tentative conclusions is to do a disservice both to the student and to the society in which he is preparing to play a responsible role.[11]

Viewed in this perspective, classroom consideration of questions for which there are no immediate or conclusive answers constitutes indispensable grist for the educational mill.

Not all problems of a controversial nature, however, lend themselves to classroom consideration, since what is desired is growth in the ability to enter with understanding into points of view which run counter to one's own convictions and habits. When community sentiment or divisions within a class group reach a degree of partisanship and emotional excitement which precludes objective discussion and investigation, the most valuable lesson the instructor can convey is to announce, "We shall have to postpone further deliberation on this problem until we are sufficiently mature to cope with it."

This necessity of reducing factional excitement and the goal of promoting insight into the world views of others render debate a questionable tool. In comparison with a sincere effort to gather and to examine critically *all* the data relating to an issue, debating encourages the highlighting of data favorable to but one point of view and the playing down or elimination of equally relevant facts which may be unfavorable to a partisan conclusion. To be sure there are occasions in

11. It seems clear that many courses or units constructed in the early 1960s to "teach children about Communism" would perform this disservice. See Melvin Rader, "Teaching About Communism," *Teachers College Record*, April 1963, pp. 577–83.

life when one is called upon to assume the position of a debater; but debate as an educational tool, designed to foster a genuine search for truth and nothing but the truth, is severely limited. Indeed, it is more appropriate in the professional training of an attorney, a salesman, or a lobbyist—one whose occupation requires the skills of an advocate and a special pleader—than in the education of a responsible citizen striving to find his way in a world in which objectivity and suspended judgment and an ever watchful eye for the neglected aspect are of critical importance.

Controversial problems thus constitute a valuable means for education in the democratic and cooperative methods of thinking discussed in Chapter 15. To exclude them from the curriculum or to educate for certainty where there is no certainty is to ask our schools to commit intellectual suicide.

Functions of the Textbook

The contrast between instruction in an authoritarian and totalitarian society, on the one hand, and a free society, on the other, applies as much to content as to method, a fact not fully realized by those earnest individuals who would safeguard our institutions from "subversion" by means of a rigid censorship of textbooks and other materials of instruction. Well might the latter ponder these words of David K. Berninghausen:

> The enemy of free public education can frequently be spotted by his attitude towards materials of instruction. He cannot escape the consciousness that if he were in complete control of education he would see to it that only *approved* literature could be found in classrooms and libraries. To his mind, a textbook is equated with the official, orthodox doctrines to be taught to the young people; a magazine by its very presence in the school library, must be considered approved, authoritative information. Therefore, any teaching material allowed in the school is "correct" and not to be questioned by pupil or teacher. Because teaching and indoctrination are one and the same, he distrusts free inquiry, he becomes a censor and demands the banning of any materials he finds objectionable.[12]

12. *Harvard Educational Review*, Summer 1951, pp. 138–54.

But what positively should we expect of a textbook, apart from the technical requirements of size of type, appropriateness to age level, ample illustrative material, appropriate level of vocabulary, and the like?

Certainly, in a text which purports to deal with contemporary society and its developments, including its "growing pains," we should expect a clear and unbiased account of the factors and conditions that have given rise to the present. This calls for an objective presentation that lays a solid foundation in fact sufficient for the student to appreciate "all points of view," as well as a fair and unbiased description of the schools of thought which divide men with respect to proposed lines of action.

By "objectivity" we have in mind something more than a coldly intellectual attitude or the mere listing of the pros and cons of a question at issue, analogous to a balancing of the credits and debits in an account book. What is required is a mature understanding of the problems of change at points where change has disturbed living relationships that have long been cemented. This can be conveyed at times by representative accounts in the text of an intimate and personal character, by supplementary reading, or by a moving picture, a novel, a play, or other dramatic material designed to convey to the student a full and rich understanding of why individuals think, feel, and act as they do with respect to the issues of life. To the extent a textbook or other classroom material imparts this "roundabout" knowledge of issues in dispute, it fulfills a major mission.

Finally, in a good text, we should look for suggestions and references which stimulate and assist an instructor and his students to engage in further investigation and inquiry.

Objectivity, then, looms large in the appraisal of any textbook which presumes to deal with areas of doubt in any field. Its major function, within this context, is to supplement the work of the teacher in helping the young to realize how few are the fields of knowledge in which the frontiers are closed and to acquire not so much the answers to life's problems as the courage and the will and, above all, the habits of creative inquiry with which "to follow knowledge like a sinking star, beyond the utmost bound of human thought."

Richard M. Pearson, at one time Director of the Educational Division of The Macmillan Company, described the purpose of the textbook in common-sense terms in answer to the question, "Can Textbooks Be Subversive?" "Textbooks," he suggests,

> are neither purveyors of opinion nor molders of young peoples' minds. They are instruments of learning, selected locally in most cases nowadays, to meet local needs and to suit local preferences. . . . The main job of education, in which textbooks assist, is not to fill children full of facts. It is rather to help them and keep them, as their mothers and fathers were before them, alert, self-reliant, intellectually inquisitive human beings, capable of thinking for themselves, making their own choices, forming their own opinions and responding to the challenges that life offers. Textbooks can help in that process, not only by telling young people what their fathers long since knew but by encouraging them to be on the lookout for things that their fathers have never known.[13]

Once a textbook meets the criteria of objectivity, there is no reason why its author should not share with his readers his conclusions on moot questions. Not to do so in areas in which he may have done original research or in which he has special competence might result only in depriving his readers of valuable raw material for their own thinking. In other words, the test of the value of a text is not whether the author expresses views in agreement with those of the instructor or confirms the opinions and prejudices of groups dominant in the community. Rather, is it a question of the degree to which a book (or other instructional material) functions as an adequate educational tool; whether, in short, it both introduces students to significant areas of the field under study and stimulates them to engage in original thought with respect to problems discussed, with the full knowledge that they are coming to grips with issues upon which honest men do not see eye to eye.

To appraise a textbook in these terms is a professional responsibility, a task for experts rather than for the man on the street or the layman with his own ax to grind. Nor is it altogether identical with a procedure keyed primarily to "good public relations," a procedure in which a committee of representative laymen is asked to pass judgment upon books under attack or to serve as an "advisory committee" in the

13. *Phi Delta Kappan,* January 1952, pp. 248–50. See also, Stanley E. Ballinger, "The Social Studies and Social Controversy," *School Review,* Spring 1963, pp. 97–111.

winnowing and sifting of books to be used in library and school. The solution of the textbook problem, in the present atmosphere, is less one of calming troubled waters or of freeing specific texts from criticism than it is that of educating the public to a full understanding of the educational functions classroom and library are to serve.

Some years ago the board of education of one of our large eastern cities established a committee on human relations, consisting of representatives from civic organizations, to suggest ways for using the schools as a means of improving intercultural relations within the city. The committee recognized the strategic importance of textbooks and classroom instruction in furthering mutual understanding of the many religious and racial groups represented in the schools. This moved one earnest member of the committee to suggest that the group undertake to read all textbooks in use in the schools for the purpose of identifying passages to which anyone might object! These passages were to be called to the attention of publishers and their elimination insisted upon as a condition of retention and use. It required long and strenuous argument to convince this individual and others that a procedure of this character might well result in texts barren of any point of view and with all the juices of life extracted from them, and that, in addition, it would deprive teachers and pupils of the educational opportunity of identifying these passages on their own initiative and weighing and appraising their worth from the standpoint of accuracy, objectivity, bias, and prejudice.

This is not to suggest that expressions of bias and prejudice are to be searched out for inclusion in the curriculum (although on occasion this might very well be a valuable exercise). Unfortunately, not all teachers are sufficiently competent to assist their students to cope constructively with open expressions of prejudice or gross inaccuracy, and fewer still are competent to detect more subtle deviations from truth. For this reason great care must be exercised in the choice of material used in the school. But this does not sanction substituting lay for professional judgment in the selection of educational materials or appraising these materials apart from the context in which they are to be used. There is a very real danger that lay committees, composed of representatives of special-interest groups—labor unions, chambers of commerce, racial and religious organizations, and the like—who lack expertness in the fields covered by the text, will arrive at conclusions regarding its use that will deprive the classroom of the opportunity and the responsibility for engaging pupils in critical thinking or will restrict attention to the least common denominator of common agreement on moot issues.

Conflicting Views As to the Role of the Public

Does this mean that we should exclude the public altogether from participation in the selection of educational materials?

Some educators answer in the affirmative. They believe with Professor Preston H. Epps of the University of North Carolina that "So far in our history, no group has been able to view our society and set-up as objectively and intelligently as a group of professional scholars. So far, we have wisely looked to such scholars to write the textbooks through which we want our youth to be introduced to the various fields of knowledge." [14] And they fear with Edward N. Saveth that to involve the public,

> is not without its own perils: by inviting the community to participate in the defense of textbooks, is there not some risk of further inflaming tempers and ideologies, of further widening the gap between objective criticism and partisan denunciation? Is there not real danger of further involving teachers and teaching materials with sections of the community that may be ignorant, irresponsible, and all too willing themselves to flex the muscle of censorship? Might it not end with an ugly spectacle of stereotype pitted against stereotype, smear against smear? [15]

Other educators go so far as to employ the analogy between physician or surgeon and teacher. What parent, it is asked, would presume to advise the medical expert on the comparative merits of different prescriptions for an illness or suggest to a surgeon the instruments he should use in performing an operation? Is it not equally rash for the layman to invade the territory of the expert in promoting the health of mind or warding off illness?

This analogy overlooks a significant difference between the status of the medical profession and that of teaching. In the eyes of the layman,

14. Quoted in an article on "What To Do About Dangerous Textbooks" by Edward N. Saveth. Reprinted from *Commentary*, February 1952, pp. 99–106, and distributed by the American Jewish Committee.
15. *Ibid.*, p. 10.

the licensed teacher and the licensed physician are by no means comparable. He knows full well that the average physician possesses a competency the layman cannot match, whereas all too frequently teachers are encountered who are sadly wanting in background and training. On both the elementary and secondary school levels the classroom teacher is called upon to deal with subject matter in areas where his knowledge is frequently less accurate or extensive than that of many parents of students in his class, and the occasions are all too common in which professional incompetence has been sufficiently obvious to lower the status of the profession in the eyes of the public. Add to this the common knowledge that low salaries together with an indifferent social status have attracted the mediocre and discouraged the able from entering the profession of teaching, and we can readily understand why the average citizen or parent accords less weight to the professional judgment of his child's teacher than to that of the family physician.

But even if the public were to accord respect where respect is due, there are other significant differences between the relations of the medical and the teaching professions to their clients. What surgeon, for example, would insist that the success of an operation turns upon the active participation of a child's parents? Many educators, on the other hand, argue with sound reason that the education of a child is incomplete without the active cooperation of his parents. With what consistency, then, can the school demand the exclusion of the latter from areas in which they are most vitally concerned?

It would seem that the solution of the problem of community participation in professional activity turns upon the avoidance of two extremes: a professional insulation which deprives the young person of significant interrelationships with his social as well as his natural environment, on the one hand, and the erasing of all distinctions between lay and professional responsibility in determining the content and method of instruction, on the other. It is one thing to recognize the need for functional participation of both layman and professional in the work of the school. It is another to assume that these functions are identical.

This suggests a concluding word with respect to ways and means of vitalizing instruction and generating confidence in the professional work of the school.

A Constructive Role for Parents

The advantages of utilizing the specialized knowledge and experience of lay experts in the community in the construction of courses of study and resource units, in the selection of equipment, and, occasionally, in the work of the classroom have long been recognized. Particularly is this applicable to vocational education where it is most essential that the skills and techniques imparted should keep in step with developments outside the school. But equally valuable results follow in general education when the work of the classroom is recognized by pupils as of living concern to men and women of talent and ability outside the school. In some institutions advisory committees of parents, whose special interests and abilities parallel the work of the school, have been organized to serve as resource groups to which departments, such as art, science, language, and literature, as well as vocational subjects, might turn for advice and counsel and, on occasion, for classroom participation. From these groups teacher and student may derive the stimulus that comes from direct contact with adult practitioners. On the other hand, in these instances of cooperation it remains the responsibility of the teacher, with his special knowledge of child development and psychology, to keep clear the distinction between adult standards and criteria, or the expectations of the specialist, and those relevant and appropriate to the age levels of the learners.

As the school receives from the adult community, so should it contribute. Parents are appreciative when the school shares with them and interprets for them modern methods of teaching and learning in the traditional subjects and the principles of healthy emotional and social development which give character to child rearing in home and school. As one of the present authors has elsewhere stated,

> There is an intimate connection between the psychology of child rearing we employ and the kind of society in which we hope our young people are to live, move, and have their being. To help children make their own the discipline that marks the difference between democratic and autocratic ways of living is no easy task. What it demands of parent and teacher varies with age level and stage of development of children. Theoretically, at least,

the school is the professional agent of the community in child rearing. To discharge its function wisely and effectively involves an understanding relationship with the parent community. Let this be achieved, and, again, ill-informed attacks upon the schools to the effect that "progressive education increases delinquency" will gain little headway.[16]

Relations of intimacy and mutual understanding between home and school which give substance and vitality to education under normal circumstances constitute a first line of defense when textbooks or instructional materials are subject to attack. Once mutual understanding between school and home has become a two-way street, charges of subversion are less easily generated than is possible where school and home and community lack intimacy of contact. But in either case, criticism should be met, if possible, in an *educational* manner. On the principle that "Ye shall know the truth and the truth shall make you free," the first step should be to welcome an investigation. Boards of education do well, under these circumstances, to appoint a committee of representative and competent citizens to examine the validity of criticisms made and to render a report to the board and the community. These reports should, if possible, do more than answer the specific question of whether or not criticisms are accurate or false. They should attempt as well to clarify for the public the basic principles that are to guide teacher and student and community in a democracy when dealing with problems upon which not even experts are agreed or the answers to which are of necessity in doubt.

Nor should the students—particularly on the secondary and college levels—be excluded from participation in determining the truth or falsity of charges made. What is more vital in arousing the interests of students, both in the topic under study and in the appropriateness of its treatment by the text or the instructor, than to set the young people themselves upon the task of determining the accuracy of indictments made? What better way, in fact, might students gain insight into methods of sound evaluation and techniques of valid criticism?

We conclude that there are very important respects in which laymen of specialized ability as well as the average citizen of intelligence and understanding, even the students themselves, may be involved in

16. V. T. Thayer, *Public Education and Its Critics* (New York: The Macmillan Co., 1954), p. 159.

evaluating materials of instruction without infringing upon the unique function—indeed, the obligation—of the teaching staff to exercise an essential freedom in the selection and use of the tools of its trade.[17]

Thus far our discussion has centered upon freedom to learn. What shall we say of the freedom of the instructor, his rights and his obligations as a citizen and a teacher?

The problem merits a special chapter.

Suggested Reading

Alberty, Harold B., and Elsie J. Alberty, *Reorganizing the High-School Curriculum*, 3d ed. (New York: The Macmillan Company 1962), pp. 362–77.

American Civil Liberties Union, *Combatting Undemocratic Pressures on Schools and Libraries* (New York: American Civil Liberties Union, 1964).

Hodgkinson, Harold L., *Education in Social and Cultural Perspective* (Englewood Cliffs, N.J.: Prentice-Hall Publishing Company, 1962).

King, Joseph A., "Books and Banners: A Case History," *Saturday Review*, November 9, 1963, pp. 28, 29, 66.

Krug, Mark M., " 'Safe' Textbooks and Citizenship Education," *School Review*, Winter 1960, pp. 463–80.

McKeon, Richard, Robert K. Martin, and Walter Gellhorn, *The Freedom to Read: Perspective and Program* (New York: The National Book Committee, 1957).

Miller, Richard I., "An Approach to Teaching About Communism in Public Secondary Schools," *Phi Delta Kappan*, February 1962, pp. 189–192.

Nelson, Jack, and Gene Roberts, Jr., *The Censors and the Schools* (Boston: Little, Brown and Company, 1963).

Phi Delta Kappan, issue devoted to the topic "Textbooks and the Schools," January 1953.

Raywid, Mary Ann, *The Ax-Grinders* (New York: The Macmillan Company, 1962).

Robinson, Donald W., "The Teachers Take a Birching," *Phi Delta Kappan*, February 1962, pp. 182–88.

Shaw, Archibald B., "What Can the Superintendent Do?" *NEA Journal*, May 1963, pp. 22–23.

17. For a suggestive analysis of the "extreme variability in initiative and compliance" that schools may display in response to social pressures, see Ronald G. Corwin, *A Sociology of Education* (New York: Appleton-Century-Crofts, 1965), chap. 12.

Chapter 21

How Free Is Freedom to Teach?

The Rights of a Teacher and His Rights as a Citizen

"The kind of virtue that can be produced by guarded ignorance," writes Bertrand Russell in his *Unpopular Essays,* "is frail and fails at the first touch of reality."

If this observation be valid, it would seem that a school or a college, dedicated to the interests of the public as a whole, should assure its teachers every freedom to teach without the limitations of outside dictation. Nevertheless, freedom to teach, like freedom in other areas, must be responsible and in no way implies the freedom of an adult to decide at will the pattern he would give to a growing mind.

What does responsible freedom to teach imply in a world of conflicting and confused ideologies?

As a general proposition, it implies the right of a teacher to function as a citizen, to speak his mind on public issues without losing his professional status thereby; to read without fear that other citizens are looking over his shoulder to determine the fitness of what he reads or scrutinizing his mail with a view to ascertaining what magazines and books come into his home; to attend meetings addressed by all manner of speakers without being judged guilty of subversive leanings. Indeed, freedom to read and freedom to hear should be recognized as professional obligations in areas of controversy as well as privileges of citizenship, since they constitute one means of enriching class instruction.

All of this needs to be recognized more clearly in view of the danger that governing boards of schools and colleges, influenced by the loyalty and security programs of state and federal governments (especially colleges and universities engaged in research associated with national defense) will adopt similar criteria of reliability and thus reinforce the traditional ivory tower existence of the teaching profession.

This is not to say that the line of distinction between the rights and obligations of the teacher as citizen and those of teacher as teacher is clearly marked at all points. An instructor's tender concern for the quality of his influence upon the young (particularly in the elementary and secondary school) often renders impossible a consistent and clean-cut distinction between his functions as citizen and his functions as teacher. It is one thing, for example, for a teacher, imbued with the spirit of reform, to participate actively in political and civic movements in a large metropolitan area, where he often lives in one place and practices his profession in another, and quite a different matter to undertake to remake the out-of-school environment of his pupils in a small and intimate community. In the latter instance the effects of his actions upon relations with his pupils as well as his "rights" as a citizen will have to determine both the extent and the manner of his participation in out-of-school activities. Again, it is impossible for the teacher of small children, let us say of kindergarten and primary age (where the teacher functions as a parent substitute, and success depends upon the teacher's ability to share his professional knowledge with parents, helping them to guide constructively the emotional and social as well as the intellectual development of their young), to live two lives—one, the confidant of old and young alike, the other, an active reconstructionist of the social order. Nor is the role of an instructor of boys and girls at the hero-worship stage identical with that of a college professor. In the first instance, the teacher must be mindful of the tendency of young people to idealize his behavior and to use what they believe they see in the structure of his personality (qualities often read into his person by the admiring pupil rather than actually present) in the building of their own personalities. This suggests circumspection with respect to ideas expressed, a deliberate effort to highlight the details of democratic methods of thinking and of living, and perhaps a more conscious practicing of what one preaches than is demanded of a teacher on the college and graduate levels. In the latter case, the views of the instructor can be viewed objectively, somewhat on a par with those of a reference book in the library, whereas with the teacher of the young, views easily become living ingredients in the pupils' personalities. For these reasons, the activities and behavior of the teacher outside as well as within the classroom and school carry a different moral at different age levels and cannot be a matter of indifference either to the instructor or to those responsible for his selection and retention.

It would seem, then, that although the rights of a teacher as a citizen are to be respected and, certainly, teachers as a class are not to be disfranchised, the two are not as east and west which never meet. It is also clear that teaching involves a unique relationship between teacher and taught, a relationship which at some points and at some age levels involves the home and the community within the professional concerns of the teacher more intimately than at other points and other age levels. But at no time do the rights of the teacher as citizen sanction the corruption of his activities and responsibilities as a teacher. When these two areas overlap to the point of conflict, then the instructor must decide upon which to concentrate exclusively. "Teachers," to quote Bertrand Russell once again, "are more than any other class the guardians of civilization." This implies a respect for the personality of the growing individual and, on the teacher's part, the exercise as well as the transmission of discipline keyed to a future essentially unknown. This discipline precludes molding others either in the image of a teacher's own ideas or his own personality. In this sense (not in the sense of caprice or lack of direction) the classroom should be child-centered, and neither the privileges of citizenship nor the obligations of teaching sanction the affiliation of a teacher with any organization or pressure group, be this religious, political, economic, or social, which presumes to dictate to him what and how he should teach. The moment an instructor subordinates himself to an external discipline of this character and attempts to mold the minds of his students according to predetermined patterns or seeks to transform them into passive instruments for the ends of others, he is guilty of conduct unbecoming a teacher and should be dealt with accordingly.

A classic statement of policy emphasizing a respect for the integrity of the student as well as the obligation of a free society to keep open the channels of knowledge is found in the declaration of the First Committee on Academic Freedom of the American Association of University Professors in 1915. This runs, in part, as follows:

Members of the academic calling have as their function . . . to deal at first hand, after prolonged and specialized technical training, with the sources of knowledge; and, to impart the results of their own and of their fellow specialists' investigation and reflection, both to students and to the general public, without fear or favor. . . . To the degree that professional scholars, in the formation and promulgation of their opinions, are, or by the character of their tenure appear to be, subject to any motive other than their own scientific conscience and a desire for the respect of their fellow experts, to that degree the university teaching profession is corrupted; a society at large fails to get from its scholars in an unadulterated form, the peculiar and necessary service which it is the office of the professional scholar to furnish. . . .

An inviolable refuge from tyranny should be found in the university. It should be an *intellectual experiment station,* where new ideas may germinate and where their fruit, though still distasteful to the community as a whole may be allowed to ripen until finally, perchance, it may become a part of the accepted international food of the nation or of the world.

Underlying this concept of academic freedom is the assumption stressed above, namely, that the right to inquire, to learn, and to teach is more than a personal privilege or an individual right. It is one of the conditions of a free society's remaining free. As Justice Frankfurter remarked at the Anniversary Dinner in honor of John Dewey's ninetieth birthday, "Without open minds there can be no open society, and if there be no open society the spirit of man is mutilated and enslaved."

Has Academic Freedom Gone Too Far?

Convincing as this may be in the abstract, it is obviously unsatisfactory as a universal principle to many people who are fearful that alien and un-American ideas are undermining American institutions. They believe large numbers of teachers are utilizing academic freedom not to sustain and enrich democracy, but with the deliberate purpose of destroying it. Consequently, they are convinced that the procedures that have become established in law and practice in order to assure the right of students to learn and of teachers to teach require review and modification. As Sidney Hook insists, it is one thing to father heresy and quite another to engage in a conspiracy against society.

Be this as it may, there is no question but that the existence in America of a Communist conspiracy and the methods of infiltration employed by Communists in the 1940s and 1950s, and the methods employed by extreme "right-wing" groups to combat "subversion," together with the measures adopted by state legislatures, boards of education, and trustees of institutions of higher education to deal with faculty members under suspicion, have forced a review not only of the principles of academic freedom but also of the relation of political authority to education.

In an essay entitled, "Academic Freedom Revisited," [1] T. V. Smith states that encroachments upon academic freedom have commonly had three sources: (1) First, "sacerdotalism," or the "bellicose orthodoxy of those who hold that in matters religious and spiritual all that is essential has already been discovered and is in fact owned by him and his group." Individuals and groups of this persuasion set themselves up as watchdogs to determine the limits and conditions of instruction in matters of religion. (2) Second, "big business," which has often exercised pressure upon faculty selection and retention, with an eye to safeguarding economic interests from heretical concepts or from criticisms hostile to the status quo. (3) A third source of criticism and attempts at coercion of academic freedom, according to Smith, is political and comes from the politicians. In each case, observes Smith, the attacks have come from outside the institution concerned and have been directed against specific individuals. Their object has been conservative, that is, to shield parochial and partisan groups from the dangers sensed by these interests as implicit in untrammeled inquiry. Moreover, their antagonists, or victims, have been individuals rash or bold enough to challenge conventional notions or the prevailing practices of firmly entrenched groups. On these occasions, friends of academic freedom have appealed to the principle of free enterprise in ideas so admirably expressed in the familiar words of Justice Holmes:

> But when men have realized that time has upset many fighting faiths, they may come to believe even more than they believe the very foundations of their own conduct that the ultimate good de-

1. T. V. Smith in *Essays in Honor of Horace Kallen: Vision and Action* (New Brunswick, N.J.: Rutgers University Press, 1953), chap. I.

sired is better reached by free trade in ideas—that the best test
of truth is the power of the thought to get itself accepted in the
competition of the market, and that truth is the only ground upon
which their wishes safely can be carried out. That, at any rate, is
the theory of our Constitution. It is an experiment as all life is an
experiment. . . . While that experiment is part of our system I
think we should be eternally vigilant against attempts to check
the expression of opinions that we loath and believe to be fraught
with death, unless they so imminently threaten immediate interference with the lawful and pressing purposes of the law that an
immediate check is required to save the country.[2]

The necessity to defend innovation in ideas against attack from those
congenitally committed to the principle that

> Come weal, come woe,
> My status is quo,

has generated certain habits of mind which characterize the liberal in
education as elsewhere. One is the habit of looking for the truths of
tomorrow within the nonconformities of today. This has given to non-
conformity as such not only a respectability but an aspect of urgency.
He who would be wise must be a nonconformist. Would you elicit the
respect of future generations? Then honor the ideas of the minority
rather than of the majority, of the radical, not the conservative of today!

Second, past attacks upon academic freedom have been commonly
identified with onslaughts upon individuals who are sufficiently able
and courageous to think creatively and with an originality denied the
common run of men. Accordingly, those who anticipate a tomorrow
different from today easily assume that the interests of the future require giving sympathy and support to educators under attack.

For these reasons, liberals, lay and professional, were ill-prepared in
the 1940s and 1950s to cope with the invasion of American educational
institutions by well-organized, disciplined disciples of the left. The in-
vaders themselves were the pliant tools of outside groups who deliberately used academic freedom as a screen to conceal the indoctrination
of the young in a dogmatic philosophy—one that required of its fol-

2. *Abrams* v. *U.S.*, 250 U.S. 616, 624 (1919).

lowers not the encouragement but the extinction of originality and independence in thought and behavior.

This novel situation, the presence in public education (in institutions of higher learning particularly, but in elementary and secondary schools as well) of teachers devoted not to freedom of inquiry and unbiased instruction, but to its ultimate extinction, confused and divided liberals. This situation has undoubtedly weakened efforts in the 1960s to safeguard school systems and teaching staffs from the onslaughts of the "radical right," groups equally determined to transform public schools into instruments of indoctrination. Some educators continue to insist, with Thomas Jefferson, that there is no ultimate danger so long as reason is left free to cope with error, and, therefore, they insist that the traditional methods of procedure which the lovers of freedom have sought to incorporate into administrative procedure are equally applicable to the Communist and the non-Communist. Others insist upon distinguishing between the "heretic" and the "conspirator" and would modify the principles determining selection and retention of faculty members in the light of this distinction. This difference in fundamental point of view among the friends of academic freedom is serious and is reflected in the pronouncements of members of the profession, both as individuals and as professional organizations, and in attitudes assumed with respect to the activities of investigating committees of Congress and state legislatures with respect to "subversion" in American education.

The Problem of Membership in Organizations Outside the School

In March 1952, the Committee on Academic Freedom and Tenure of the American Association of University Professors submitted to the annual meeting of the Association its conclusions regarding university policy bearing upon faculty membership in the Communist Party and Communist front organizations. Declared the committee, with the approval of the delegates,

> The tests of the fitness of a member of the academic profession should be his professional competence, his integrity and character, and his ability and willingness to engage in vigorous, objective instruction and research; these to be measured by the accepted principles and standards of the profession. A teacher

who is guilty of misusing his classes or his other relationships with his students for biased partisan propaganda, or is guilty of a legally defined subversive act, is responsible as an individual for the violation of professional principles or the law of the land, as the case may be, and should be dismissed, provided his guilt is established by evidence adduced in a proceeding in which he is given a full measure of due process. . . .

In discussing the intent of this resolution, Ralph Himstead, formerly General Secretary of the Association, added,

It is clear from this excerpt that the American Association of University Professors does not accept the formula of guilt by association. The views it has stated on this subject are, we believe, realistic, and what is more important, consonant with the principles of the Academic Profession, of Anglo-American Law and of our Constitutional System. We believe that our colleges and universities can be protected, and are being protected against subversive individuals without doing violence to these basic principles. Pursuant to the affirmative tests of professional fitness, set forth in the resolution cited, higher education is protected not only against subversive acts of teachers who may be members of the Communist Party, but also against subversive acts of teachers who are "fellow travelers" or crypto Communists.[3]

Himstead and the American Association of University Professors evidently grounded their position on the theory that the principles of both academic and constitutional freedom are designed to protect the individual as teacher and as citizen. Basic to these guarantees is the fact that *actual conduct* rather than mere association constitutes guilt or innocence. Consequently, he insisted that membership in an organization outside an educational institution, in and by itself, should not imply conduct "unbecoming a teacher"; that the test of a teacher's fitness turns rather upon his activities within the classroom and/or actual behavior outside the classroom.

If this be granted, it follows that the responsibility of a board of education, when a competent teacher comes under attack for present

3. *Academic Freedom in the United States.* Papers contributed to the Fifteenth Annual Spring Conference of the Division of the Social Sciences of Howard University (Washington, D.C.: The Howard University Press, 1953), p. 13.

or past membership in an outside organization (as long as this organization is or was legal at the time of membership), becomes one of educating the community in the principles of academic freedom rather than yielding to pressure and dismissing a teacher who comes under fire. All too frequently, however, school authorities have been tempted to follow the example of Arlington, Virginia. When one of its public school teachers was found in 1958 to have joined the Communist Party in the mid-1930s, she was "persuaded" to resign from her position in the course of the school year, despite the fact that she had become disillusioned and had resigned from the party in the 1940s, that in all known respects her work was above reproach, and that it was clear her original motives for joining the party had been idealistic rather than subversive.

An example quite different was set by the school board of Fullerton, California, in its refusal to discharge a school counselor who was being subjected to an abusive campaign of letters, telephone calls, and demands for dismissal from a right-wing group. His offense consisted of, (1) membership in the American Civil Liberties Union; (2) former membership in American Youth for Democracy; and (3) permitting a controversial figure to address a meeting in his home. According to Donald W. Robinson, a school official had been assured by a member of the organization seeking the counselor's dismissal that if the board would discharge the offender he would "call off about fifty people who are going to the newspapers" about the case.[4]

It should be added that dismissal of teachers under the conditions described is of doubtful legal validity. Thus, in passing upon the constitutionality of an Oklahoma statute which required a loyalty oath of all state and local employees, the United States Supreme Court, Justice Clark speaking for the Court, stated:

> Due process does not permit the dismissal of folks solely on the basis of organizational membership regardless of their knowledge concerning the organization to which they may belong. A state servant may have joined a proscribed organization unaware of its proclivities and purposes. In recent years many completely loyal persons have severed organizational ties after learning for the first time the character of the groups with which they have

4. "The Teachers Take a Birching," *Phi Delta Kappan*, February 1962, p. 185.

belonged. At the time of affiliation the group itself may not be known to be subversive. Under the Oklahoma Act the fact of association alone determines disloyalty and disqualification. It matters not whether the association existed innocently or knowingly.

To thus inhibit individual freedom of movement is to stifle the flow of democratic expression and controversy at one of its chief sources.

We hold that the distinction observed here is a basic distinction. Indiscriminate classification of the innocent with knowing activities must fall as an assertion of arbitrary power. This oath offends due process.[5]

When Is Membership in an Out-of-School Organization "Conduct Unbecoming of a Teacher"?

The assured right of a teacher to associate himself with an organization outside the school, be it religious, political, civic, or social, without jeopardizing his position as a teacher is by no means a one-sided privilege. As I. B. Berkson has well stated, "academic freedom is an obligation rather than a right." It is a professional discipline. "It is a corollary of the belief in the value of scholarship and scientific inquiry for the extension of knowledge and the service of human welfare. In substance, it makes the ethics of the profession of scholars and scientists supreme over the arbitrary control of outside forces—of the state, the church, the political party, and, not least, of public opinion." [6] Consequently, in guaranteeing the right of free association it must be assumed that the organization does not presume to control the activities of the teacher as teacher.

The 1950s, however, brought exhaustive investigations and reports of commissions (such as that appointed by President Truman to determine whether the American Communist Party should register as an agent of a foreign power), the publicizing of testimony on communism gathered in judicial proceedings, and the sad experiences of numerous educational institutions with communist activity on campus and in the classroom. During this period, many liberals became convinced that

5. *Wieman* v. *Updegraff*, 344 U.S. 183 (1952).
6. *The Ideal and the Community* (New York: Harper & Brothers, 1958), p. 258.

membership in the Party did in fact carry with it submission to an external discipline. They were also willing to concede that in itself Party membership constituted conduct unbecoming a teacher. As they saw it, nevertheless, the difference is clear between protecting a teacher in the exercise of his privileges and obligations as a citizen and the corruption of the teaching function that follows when an instructor, with a "captive audience," identifies his functions as a teacher with those of a citizen engaged in propaganda.

The 1950s constituted a period of soul-searching with respect to the rights and obligations of the teacher. We should not assume, however, that violations of academic freedom came from left-wing sources only. Had this been the case, both the issues involved and their resolution might have been simpler. Instances were common then, as they are today, in which an individual's interest in nonconventional ideas, and his sense of obligation to give these a fair hearing in the classroom, were equated with communism, or "thinking like a communist." Moreover, the names of individuals so branded have a way of finding a place in the unevaluated files of legislative committees investigating un-American activities and of being used uncritically by "patriotic" organizations to harry and embarrass, even to blacklist, otherwise innocent individuals.[7]

Under these circumstances every effort should be made to enable educational institutions under public control (and private institutions as a condition of professional self-respect) freely to exercise the right and the obligation to judge a teacher on the basis of professional conduct, rather than intellectual orthodoxy as defined by the self-appointed guardians of orthodoxy.

Who will contend, for example, that the colleges of California would long retain their professional integrity if the testimony of Richard M. Combs, Chief Counsel of the California State Senate Committee on Un-American Activities, before the "Jenner Committee" of the United States Senate, became a permanent policy? Mr. Combs outlined an arrangement which he stated existed between the State Senate Committee and the college presidents of the major California colleges. According to this arrangement, the colleges undertook to employ, as full-time members of the staff, ex-F.B.I. agents and ex-navy and military intelligence people. These people, to quote a U.S. Senate report,

7. See, for example, Ralph S. O'Leary, "Minute Women, Daughters of Vigilantism," *The Nation*, January 5, 1954, pp. 26–28.

. . . maintain a liaison with our committee. We in turn make available to them the accumulated documentation, the material that we have accumulated during the 14 years. But we soon found that it was even more necessary to prevent people from getting on faculties and obtaining positions in the educational institutions than it was to get rid of them once their positions became solidified.

So the committee developed a procedure whereby applicants for positions are referred to us, their names are, and if we do have any documentation concerning their Communist activity over a long period of time we make that available to the university as a guide to indicate whether or not the individual should be employed.[8]

According to the testimony of Mr. Combs, some one hundred faculty members were severed from their positions during the period June 4, 1952 and the date of his testimony on March 24, 1953.

Observe that nothing was said by Mr. Combs or in the report of the Jenner Committee to indicate the manner in which "people who are either Communists or about whom there is evidence of Communist activity" were so identified. Since, however, the California Senate Committee was one and the same as that which recommended the banning of textbooks from public schools which offended by listing in their bibliographies the writings of Charles A. Beard, Stuart Chase, Dorothy Canfield Fisher, Lewis Mumford, and others similarly distinguished, we may question the scrupulous care with which this committee determined the fitness or unfitness of the one hundred undesirable faculty members!

To draw a clear line between conduct unbecoming a teacher and the appropriate area of private conviction is not always easy. Nevertheless, the attempt of governing boards to hew to this line is practical insurance against situations that are all too common, if subversion is identified with what officials consider anathema in ideas.

Some, however, reject the attempt to maintain this distinction as the equivalent of appeasement. To appease the enemies of freedom in the

8. *Report of the Subcommittee to Investigate the Administration of the Internal Security Act and Other Internal Security Laws to the Committee on the Judiciary,* United States Senate, July 17, 1953, p. 12.

academic world, they contend, is as fatal as it is to appease the enemies
of democracy in the political arena. Nor will they agree that we have
drawn the line accurately between conduct and freedom of thought.
"Surely," they argue, "membership in a lawful organization should not,
in and by itself, disqualify a person from functioning within the academic community."

To this we reply that the distinction between membership in a lawful as against an unlawful organization is not of necessity relevant to
the point we are making. Today, the Communist Party is an outlawed
party. Consequently, membership in it may properly disqualify an individual from employment in a school or a college which is conducted
under public auspices and supported by public funds.[9] But this does
not render moot the question of membership in *any* organization outside an educational institution which presumes to dictate the functions
and responsibilities of a teacher as teacher. No one will contend, for
example, that membership in a religious organization, such as a church,
should disqualify an individual from teaching in a school or college.
Far from it! Indeed, in a church-related school and in many public
schools church membership is considered an asset to be added to a
teacher's professional qualifications. But in a number of states the question of whether members of a religious order that requires submission
to a discipline superior to all other disciplines, as well as a commitment
to spread the doctrines of the parent church, shall be privileged to
teach in public schools has become an acute issue. Nor is this issue disposed of by the suggestion that conventional clothes be substituted for
distinctive religious garb when members are engaged in the act of
teaching. It is not the outward and visible insignia that is in question
but the inner commitment which lends itself to the possibility of partisan and narrowly sectarian instruction.

The same may be said of membership in any organization, be it religious, political, economic, or social. The moral is clear, although, ad-
mittedly, its administration is difficult: The obligation of governing
boards and teachers alike is to serve the public by insuring the rights of
students in a public institution to receive a broad public education
rather than a narrow partisan one.

9. For discussions of the legal and ethical questions involved in this position, see
Milton R. Konvitz, *First Amendment Freedoms: Selected Cases on Freedom of
Religion, Speech, Press, Assembly* (Ithaca, New York: Cornell University Press,
1963), pp. 550–84.

Criteria for Determining the Retention or Dismissal of Teachers

The position outlined above differs little from that suggested by one of the authors as early as 1943, when the friends of academic freedom were more divided than they are today on the problem of Communists as teachers or of membership in well-disciplined organizations outside educational institutions which presumed to control the performance of teachers. It was necessary then as it is imperative now to stress safeguards for teachers whose academic fitness has been challenged.[10]

1. Both the criteria and the procedures to be followed in the selection of a staff member are different from those which might be used appropriately when considering his dismissal. Too often this difference is ignored. On the elementary and secondary levels particularly, and to a lesser degree in colleges and universities, factors other than competence in classroom instruction enter prominently. Since the concerns of the school have been enlarged to include objectives other than exclusive emphasis upon intellectual development—guidance in emotional and social growth, education for character as well as of the "mind"— the qualifications for teaching have likewise increased in number and quality. The selection of a prospective teacher is thus influenced of necessity by factors such as the complexion of the community, the character of the parent as well as the student body, and the kinds of relationships which obtain or are desired between school and society. These more varied and intimate concerns are receiving ever greater attention in the selection of members of the staff of the modern school and college and are relevant factors as well in determining retention. Nevertheless, the two—factors of selection and retention—are not identical. Nor need the evidence required to refuse employment in the first place be as conclusive as that justifying dismissal.

2. Again, every precaution should be taken to insure competent and professional judgment on the conduct of any teacher who may be charged with the abuse of his functions. The American conception of justice has been sorely tried, if not corrupted, in recent years. As

10. We can do little more at this point than to state the general principles of procedure. For a more detailed consideration of methods to follow in determining fitness to teach, see *A.A.U.P. Bulletin* on *Academic Freedom and Tenure*, March 1958. American Association of University Professors, 1785 Massachusetts Avenue, N.W., Washington 6, D.C. See also, "Academic Freedom and Tenure: 1940 Statement of Principles," *A.A.U.P. Bulletin*, June 1963, pp. 192–93.

against the traditional axiom that a man is innocent until proven guilty, the reverse has too often been the case. How many people today hold to the principle that it is better for ten guilty men to go free than for one innocent man to be declared guilty? Surely an educational institution should set an example of equal and exact justice. Specifically, this entails judgment by one's peers and meticulous reliance upon due process. In deciding the fate of a teacher as a teacher there is no place for the use of anonymous witnesses, the refusal of the right to confront and to cross examine one's accusers, or the practice of keeping secret from the accused the nature of the charges against him. Unless our educational institutions observe scrupulously procedures designed to protect the innocent as well as to identify the guilty, we shall move rapidly into a situation in which the American people will have transformed their way of life in the image of the totalitarians. Repeated experience should have taught us that the most effective way to deal with heretical ideas is to subject them to open criticism, not to suppress them, to refute heresy and dangerous ideas with intelligence, not to do violence to their advocates. As Henry Steele Commager has wisely observed,

> There is no real choice between freedom and security. Only those societies that actively encourage freedom—that encourage, for example, scientific and scholarly research, the questioning of scientific and social orthodoxies and the discovery of new truths— only such societies can hope to solve the problems that assail them and preserve their security. . . . A nation that silences or intimidates original minds is left only with unoriginal minds and cannot hope to hold its own in the competition of peace or of war. As John Stuart Mill said in that essay on Liberty to which we cannot too often repair, "A state which dwarfs its men in order that they may be more docile instruments in its hands . . . will find that with small men no great thing can really be accomplished." [11]

The nature of academic freedom is clearer in the minds of laymen as well as members of the profession than before the "Communist conspiracy" threatened the integrity of academic performance. But we should recognize also that the manner in which governing boards have

11. "Is Freedom Really Necessary?" *The Saturday Review,* February 21, 1953, pp. 11 ff. See also, Paul G. Kauper, *Civil Liberties and the Constitution* (Ann Arbor: University of Michigan Press, 1962), pp. 108–13.

dealt with teachers under suspicion has probably injured the cause of free inquiry as much if not more than have offending members of the profession, for the latter have been relatively few in numbers. Seldom have the protections which institutions of higher learning extend to members of their faculties been afforded to teachers of elementary and secondary schools who were under attack from without. Here summary dismissal without appeal has all too often been the rule. Indeed, one may question whether the principles of academic freedom as defined by the American Association of University Professors have any genuine application to public education below the college level. On these lower levels both the definition and the applications of the principles of freedom are as virgin soil awaiting cultivation. How open, for example, is the opportunity for unbiased consideration of the problem of desegregation in education in a southern classroom today? How genuine are the rights of the teacher either as teacher or as citizen in a southern state which writes into law the provision that any institution which employs a teacher who is known to have contributed to the National Association for the Advancement of Colored People thereby sacrifices its right to receive public funds? Nor is the South alone in this frame of mind. Let an issue equally acute arise in a northern community and similar pressures will play upon the schools.

Despite these discouraging facts, it is doubtless true, speaking generally, that both the lay public and members of the teaching profession are more keenly aware of the nature and the value of academic freedom today than they were a decade ago. If the attempt to resolve the problem of communism in American education has in fact contributed to this end, perhaps the sacrifice of many an innocent victim will not have been altogether in vain.

Suggested Reading

Academic Freedom Committee of the American Civil Liberties Union, *On the 1953 Statement of the Association of American Universities, "The Rights and Responsibilities of Universities and Their Faculties"* (New York: American Civil Liberties Union, 1958).

American Association of University Professors, *Academic Freedom and Tenure, A.A.U.P. Bulletin,* March 1958.

American Civil Liberties Union, *Combatting Undemocratic Pressures on Schools and Libraries,* A Guide for Local Communities (New York: American Civil Liberties Union, 1964).

Berkson, I. B., *The Ideal and the Community* (New York: Harper & Brothers, 1958), chap. XV.

Chandler, B. J., "Freedom of Inquiry Is in Jeopardy," *Phi Delta Kappan*, May 1960, pp. 356–58.

Commager, Henry Steele, "Is Freedom an Academic Question?" *Saturday Review*, June 20, 1964, pp. 54–56.

Goodman, Paul, "Don't Disturb the Children," *The New Republic*, March 1963, pp. 19–20.

Hook, Sidney, *Heresy, Yes. Conspiracy, No.* (New York: John Day Company, 1953), chaps. VI, VIII, IX, XII.

Hutchins, Robert M., *Freedom, Education and the Fund: Essays and Addresses, 1946–1956* (New York: Meridian Books, 1956), pp. 152–56.

Murphy, William P., "Educational Freedom in the Courts," *A.A.U.P. Bulletin*, December 1963, pp. 309–27.

Taylor, Harold, *On Education and Freedom* (New York: Abelard-Schuman, 1954), chap. VII.

Woodward, C. Vann, "The Unreported Crisis in the Southern Colleges," *Harper's Magazine*, October 1962, pp. 83–89.

Chapter 22

Segregation in American Education

Class and Caste in American Society

Distinctions of class are present in all communities, although the degree of their visibility varies widely. Of the visibility of caste, however, there is no question. Nor is there reason to doubt that caste distinctions foster inequalities in education.

Even so, the implications of caste are by no means everywhere the same. They differ as between groups affected, a fact which renders it easier for the members of some groups than for members of others to emancipate themselves, as witness the comparative ease with which an educated Mexican or an Oriental—even an Indian—can break through caste barriers, in contrast with the difficulties confronting a Negro. These implications likewise differ with geographical location. In Hawaii, for example, caste distinctions based on race and nationality are of low visibility, despite the fact that some thirteen or more ethnic and racial groups live side by side in a relatively small area.

In contrast with the hospitable attitude in Hawaii, we find states of the Union, primarily in the North and the West, in which discrimination exists but is publicly frowned upon and people are highly sensitive to the rights of minorities, but for reasons quite different from those in Hawaii. The population is heterogeneous in composition and most, if not all, races and creeds represented have suffered at one time or another a minority status. In seeking equality for its members each group realizes that consistency and expediency dictate that what one claims for himself should be accorded to another. Consequently, organized

516

efforts are made to insure this general equality through law and education. In New York, for example, both "fair employment" and "fair educational" practices have the sanction of law, but the machinery of enforcement relies as much upon the use of persuasion as upon penalties
for violation. It seeks to erase false apprehensions from the minds of
employers and employees regarding the consequences of non-segre-
gated working conditions or from the minds of parents who fear violence if their children attend mixed schools; it furnishes expert advice
on ways and means of introducing new practices and of avoiding, if
not eliminating, difficulties that have their roots in racial and religious
prejudice.

Despite these attempts to insure equality of treatment for all races,
evidences of the reverse are obvious outside as well as within the
South. What William R. Mong wrote in 1952, the recent agitation for
"first-class citizenship" for Negroes has demonstrated to be true still.
He said,

> There are public schools and local school systems with racial
> patterns and practices hardly distinguishable from the segregated
> school patterns of the Deep South. Among these states are New
> York, Pennsylvania, Illinois, Ohio, Arizona and New Mexico.[1]

These pockets of resistance result often from restrictions of residence,
either accidental or by design. Again, they follow upon the invasion of
a community, long homogeneous in its racial complexion, by groups
different both in race and cultural level. This holds true of the immigration of Mexican laborers into the West and Southwest and of the
heavy migration of Negroes from the Deep South into northern and
western communities. Even in communities where concepts of equality
were thought to have been firmly rooted in tradition and law, devices
of one sort or another have been resorted to in order to bring about
segregation in schools, residential districts, housing developments, and
employment.

In some instances, as in the states of New Mexico, Arizona, Kansas,
and Wyoming, this sentiment found expression, prior to the Supreme
Court decision of 1954, in the passage of laws which rendered segregation optional in education.

1. "The Elimination of Segregation in the Public Schools of the North and
West," *Journal of Negro Education*, Summer 1952, p. 265.

Finally, there is the South in which distinctions of caste have become deeply rooted in both custom and law, and segregation accurately expresses long-accepted ways of feeling, acting, and thinking. People have passed from childhood into adolescence and on into adulthood without either experiencing or contemplating a relationship other than one of segregation between the races. What seems axiomatic to the liberal in the North is viewed by the southerner as a threat to the foundations of his society, and the attempts of the former to change the ways of the latter seem an unwarranted invasion by an outside meddler.

Rigid as caste distinctions are, there is little consistency in either definition or practice when it comes to identifying the status of individuals of mixed blood. Lord Bryce, in his *American Commonwealth,* observed that "In Latin America whoever is not black is white." [2] This is not so in the United States. Interestingly enough (but tragic in its implications), the decision of the United States Supreme Court in the case of *Plessy* v. *Ferguson,* 163 U.S. 537 (1896), which gave legal sanction to the "separate but equal" doctrine, grew out of an incident in Louisiana in which the plaintiff, whose great-grandparent was a Negro, had ventured into a passenger car reserved for whites. M. R. Konvitz states that the definitions of a Negro "are all made from the standpoint of the white person who seeks to avoid contact with a person who *he* considers to be a Negro, without regard to what the latter may have to say about the matter." [3] In some states "everybody having a known trace of Negro blood in his veins, no matter how far back it was acquired—is classified as a Negro." [4]

Enforced segregation of the races likewise varies among the states. Prior to the 1954 decision of the United States Supreme Court on segregation in education, twenty-nine states forbade the marriage of a white person and a Negro, five the marriage of a white and an Indian, and fourteen marriage of a white and a "Mongolian" or an Oriental. In 1951 segregation on buses and on street cars was mandatory in eleven states. Similarly, the states of Arkansas, Georgia, Louisiana, Missouri, Oklahoma, South Carolina, Tennessee, and Virginia had enacted statutes requiring segregation in the use of parks, playgrounds, bathing and

2. 1910, vol. II, p. 555.
3. M. R. Konvitz, "The Extent and Character of Legally Enforced Segregation," *Journal of Negro Education,* Summer 1951, p. 526.
4. Gunner Myrdal, *An American Dilemma* (New York: Harper & Brothers, 1944), p. 113.

fishing facilities, boating facilities, amusement parks, race tracks, billiard and pool rooms, circuses, theaters, and public halls.[5] Segregation in hospitals and penal institutions was likewise common. Oklahoma required that separate telephone booths be installed when "there is a demand for such separate booths." Separate washrooms are, of course, common in factories, in business houses, and in public and semipublic institutions. South Carolina forbade Negroes and whites in the cotton textile factories to work in the same room, to use the entrances and exits at the same time, or to "use the same stairway and windows at the same time." [6]

Mandatory segregation has assumed many forms. Most frequent is that forbidding the marriage of whites with individuals of another color. Mandatory segregation in education ranks second. In 1950, sixteen states insisted upon segregation in their colleges and universities and twenty states either required or rendered permissive segregation in public schools.[7]

It should be observed that in most instances the seventeen states which, prior to 1954, had rendered mandatory a dual system of education (Alabama, Arkansas, Delaware, Florida, Georgia, South Carolina, Louisiana, North Carolina, Tennessee, Kentucky, Texas, West Virginia, Missouri, Maryland, Oklahoma, Mississippi, and Virginia) fall within the low per capita income belt. That is to say, those states which have found it most difficult to provide adequate educational facilities for their children, irrespective of color, have been most insistent upon maintaining dual systems of education. The inevitable result is to lower the level of education for both white and Negro children and to render deplorable, in many instances, the educational status of the latter.

Efforts to Realize Separate But Equal Education in the South

Immediately prior to the decision of the Supreme Court in 1954, prompted in no small measure by the fear that the courts would even-

5. Konvitz, *op. cit.*, p. 431.
6. *Ibid.*, p. 432.
7. *Ibid.*, pp. 427–28. Since the decision of the United States Supreme Court on segregation in education the United States courts have rendered a series of decisions declaring laws of the character described above unconstitutional and, of course, the passage of the Civil Rights Act by Congress in 1964 renders illegal discrimination on the basis of race in employment, voting rights, and the use of public accommodations and facilities, as well as in education.

tually declare segregation in education unconstitutional, southern states undertook to bring about a greater semblance of equality between Negro and white schools. Heavy bond issues were launched for this purpose, and ambitious building programs were undertaken. In some instances this resulted in larger per capita expenditures for the Negro than for the white pupil and, temporarily at least, superior physical facilities. Thus it was possible for the Virginia court to state, in *Dorothy E. Davis et al.* v. *County School Board of Prince Edward Co.*, that "in 29 of the even hundred counties in Virginia, the school facilities for the colored are equal to the white schools, in 17 more they are now superior, and upon completion of work authorized or in progress, another 5 will be superior. Of the twenty-seven cities, 5 have Negro schools and facilities equal to the white and 8 more have better schools than the white."

In Missouri the per capita expenditures for the education of colored pupils in 1948–1949 was $175.32 as against $166.31 for white pupils.[8]

Both Virginia and Missouri are richer in financial resources than most southern states. When we consider the problem which confronted the South as a whole of equalizing building facilities, teachers' salaries, pupil-teacher ratio, instructional materials, and other essentials, the task would have been Herculean. For example, in 1946, states with a dual system spent on the average $104.66 per white pupil and $57.57 per Negro pupil. To equalize expenditures would have required either doubling the cost per pupil for Negro children or reducing severely the amounts then available for white pupils. In view of the fact that twelve of the sixteen southern states were already taxing themselves more heavily than the national average of effort,[9] it is questionable whether equalization would have been brought about without lowering the standards below an acceptable level.

It is too late to do more than speculate on what might have evolved

8. Federal Security Agency, Office of Education, Statistical Circular, No. 286, January 1951.

9. *Facts on Federal Aid* (Washington, D.C.: National Education Association, September 1950). One study of the educational situation in the South estimated that in 1954 it would have taken $350,000,000 to equalize the physical facilities of Negro schools with those provided for whites in 13 southern states. Harry S. Ashmore, *The Negro and the Schools* (Chapel Hill: University of North Carolina Press, 1954), pp. 119, 156.

For a detailed comparison of all types of expenditures for the education of white and Negro schools in the South, see *Southern Schools: Progress and Problems* (Southern Education Reporting Service, Nashville, Tennessee, 1959).

out of a sincere effort to apply the doctrine of "separate but equal facilities" in education in the South. Many who cannot justify segregation on principle nevertheless believe that equal though separate schools for the two races would have prepared the ground for a more peaceful transition from segregation to integration than now seems possible.

There is much to be said for this assumption. But it is also pertinent to ask whether emphasis upon equal but separate facilities might not have resulted in confirming or perpetuating the custom of separate schools, unless they had been used deliberately as a transition program (which, of course, was quite the opposite of the intentions of southern leaders). In each instance, much would have depended upon the nature of the education provided. How realistic is it to suppose that those who are opposed to integration would administer a separate education so as to lead to its eventual elimination?

Moreover, can equality in education be in fact realized in an atmosphere of compulsory segregation in other areas of living? Are not conditions outside the school as well as inside essential in order to insure equality of instruction in any genuine sense? Surely it is futile to suppose that schools will provide differentiated opportunities for children in education on a segregated basis unless, upon the conclusion of that education, there exists something akin to an open door to business, the professions, and other positions of dignity and respect in the community.

Steps Leading to the Decision of the Supreme Court of May 1954

Before considering the implications of the momentous decision of the United States Supreme Court in May 1954, on the question of segregation in education, it might be well for us to review briefly the steps which led more or less inevitably to the ultimate rejection of the "separate but equal" doctrine.

The history of the doctrine reveals a steady transformation in its meaning, beginning with the period in which the eyes of the courts were exclusively upon separation, with little concern for the facts of equality or inequality, to the final period in which it was recognized that genuine equality and separation are irreconcilable.

Prior to the Civil War, civil rights and the conduct of education were the exclusive prerogatives of the states. Upon the defeat of the seceding states and as a condition of their readmission to the Union, Congress undertook to insure the equality of the Negro with the white. These efforts assumed the form of specific acts of Congress relating to civil rights, the adoption of the Thirteenth, Fourteenth, and Fifteenth Amendments to the federal Constitution, and a requirement that all applicants for statehood would have to include in their constitutions provision for the establishment and the maintenance of free public schools. The most notable of these acts of Congress was that of 1875, which stated as its purpose "to Protect all Citizens in Their Civil and Legal Rights." This act provided that

> All persons within the jurisdiction of the United States shall be entitled to the full and equal enjoyment of the accommodations, advantages, facilities and privileges of inns, public conveyances on land and water, theaters, and other places of public amusement; subject only to the conditions and limitations established by law, and applicable to citizens of every race and color, regardless of any previous condition of servitude.[10]

By 1883, when the Supreme Court of the United States declared the Civil Rights Act unconstitutional, the people of the North had become sufficiently weary or disgusted and ashamed of the excesses of the Reconstruction period to leave the fate of the Negro in the hands of the South, and white supremacy under state autonomy was quickly reestablished. Disfranchisement under one guise or another and segregation in education as in other areas followed.

It was during this period that state courts developed the doctrine of "separate but equal" facilities as applied to education, which later received approval on a national basis at the hands of the United States Supreme Court. The occasion for this was a statute enacted by the state of Louisiana which required segregation on railroad trains. With Justice Harlan dissenting, the Supreme Court in *Plessy* v. *Ferguson* confirmed prior decisions of state courts to the effect that segregation is not discrimination when equal but separate facilities are provided.[11]

10. This act was declared unconstitutional on the ground that the restrictions of the Fourteenth Amendment applied to state action and not to individuals. It is for this reason that Congress, in passing the Civil Rights Act of 1964, based this legislation upon the Commerce Clause of the Constitution as well as upon the Fourteenth Amendment.

11. For an excellent review of these decisions, see Harry E. Groves, "A Reexamination of the 'Separate but Equal Doctrine,'" *Journal of Negro Education*, Fall 1951, pp. 520–34.

In arriving at this decision the Court, as we have said, drew upon prior rulings of state courts, which, in turn, oddly enough, derived from a decision of a Massachusetts court in 1849.[12]

The Massachusetts constitution contained a clause to the effect that all persons are equal before the law "without distinction of age or sex, birth or color, origin or condition." A Negro child claimed the right under this clause to attend the school nearest her home rather than the one to which she was assigned because of her race. In denying this right, the Court stated in part:

> But when the great principle (of equality) comes to be applied to the actual and various conditions of persons in society, it will not warrant the assertion, that men are legally clothed with the same civil and political powers, and that children and adults are legally to have the same functions and be subject to the same treatment; but only that the rights of all, as they are settled and regulated by law, are equally entitled to the paternal consideration and protection of the law, for their maintenance.

Thus, according to the Court, equality is a philosophical rather than a practical principle!

The decision of the Court in *Plessy* v. *Ferguson* was quickly extended to education. In *Gong Lum* v. *Rice*, 277 U.S. 78 (1927), the principle received explicit recognition by the United States Supreme Court. A Chinese girl in Mississippi had objected to compulsory attendance at a Negro school and sought to compel her admission to a white school. Speaking for the majority of the Court, Chief Justice Taft stated that "it is the same question which has been many times decided to be within the constitutional power of the state legislature to settle without intervention of the Federal courts under the Federal Constitution."

The decision in *Gong Lum* v. *Rice* gave little consideration to the actual facts of "equality" of facilities. Nor did earlier decisions. So intent had the courts been upon approving the provision for *separate* facilities that they overlooked the other side of the equation; not until late in the 1930s did the term "equal" receive critical appraisal.

In 1938, the United States Supreme Court refused to sanction the mere existence of separated facilities in education, and, in the absence of equal facilities for Negroes, the Court ordered the University of

12. *Roberts* v. *The City of Boston*, 5 Cush. 198, 206, Mass. (1849).

Missouri to admit a qualified Negro applicant to its law school. This decision seemed to establish the principle that where equal facilities were not provided, Negroes were entitled to be admitted to the corresponding white institutions. It was this more detailed attention to the fact of equality which led the Supreme Court in *Sweatt* v. *Painter*, 339 U.S. 629 (1950), to insist upon the admission of Herman Sweatt to the University of Texas Law School, despite the existence of a law school established exclusively for Negroes, which was, however, inferior to the white school. In making its ruling the court called attention to the fact that the Negro law school could not possibly provide equal preparation for legal practice because of differences in student body, faculty, library, and other intangibles "incapable of objective measurement." It also pointed out that the prospective lawyer would be at a disadvantage to prepare for practice in an academic vacuum, apart from association with the body of classmates with whom he must deal when admitted to the Texas Bar.

Keener appreciation of what constitutes genuine equality in education received further emphasis in *McLaurin* v. *Oklahoma State Regents*, 339 U.S. 636 (1950), with Chief Justice Vinson again speaking for the Court. In response to a decision of the District Court to the effect that the state of Oklahoma was obligated under its constitution to afford McLaurin "the education he sought as soon as it provided that education for applicants of any other group" and that the Oklahoma statutes under which McLaurin had been denied admission to the university were unconstitutional, the Oklahoma legislature amended its statutes so as to permit the admission of Negroes to institutions of higher learning along with white students when identical courses were not available in Negro schools. But the legislature also stipulated that instruction under these circumstances "shall be given at such colleges or institutions of higher education upon a segregated basis." In conformity with this legislation, McLaurin was admitted to the graduate school of the University of Oklahoma, but under regulations which required him, as the Court emphasized, "to sit apart at a designated desk in an anteroom adjoining the classroom, to sit at a designated desk in the mezzanine floor of the library, but not to use the desks in the regular reading room; and to sit at a designated table and to eat at a different time from the other students in the school cafeteria."

Justice Vinson pointed out that these regulations set "McLaurin apart from the other students. The result is that the appellant is handicapped in his pursuit of effective instruction. Such restrictions impair and inhibit his ability to study, to engage in discussions, and exchange views with other students, and, in general to learn his profession."

The Sweatt and McLaurin cases bore upon the admission and the treatment accorded Negro students in higher education. It was inevitable that cases involving the "separate but equal facilities" for education on the elementary and secondary levels should eventually find their way to the Supreme Court. Kansas, South Carolina, Virginia, and Delaware, together with the District of Columbia, soon fulfilled this expectation.

In the Kansas case the state court had ruled that under the *Plessy* doctrine segregation constitutes no violation of the Fourteenth Amendment, but it had also held that education under segregation is not and cannot be equal. On the other hand, the courts of South Carolina and Virginia had refused to grant that segregation of necessity spells inequality. On the contrary, the Virginia court boldly proclaimed that "Maintenance of the separate school system has not been social despotism" but has even "begotten greater opportunities for the Negro." In each instance, however, the courts recognized existing inequalities in facilities and ordered the school board concerned, in the words of the Virginia court, "to proceed with all reasonable diligence and dispatch to remove the inequality existing."

It is obvious that in order to remedy conditions of inequality even "with all reasonable diligence and dispatch" takes time. In the Sweatt and McLaurin cases the Court took this fact into account and ordered immediate relief for the victims of injustice. Similarly, a Delaware court drew attention to the fact that to grant an extension of time in which to remedy general conditions of inequality is, in effect, to ignore the rights of the individuals who are presently appealing for a redress of grievances.

In the Delaware case, Negroes resident in one school district were denied admission to the elementary and secondary schools reserved exclusively for whites and were required to attend schools for Negroes which were both remote from their homes and inferior in quality. The defendants denied that segregation in education violates the federal Constitution and produced evidence to demonstrate that building programs were, in part, on their way and, in part, in a planning stage to offset whatever inequalities might exist.

Chancellor Seitz, who rendered the opinion for the Court, concluded "that the separate facilities and opportunities offered these plaintiffs, and those similarly situated, are not equal to those afforded white children . . . and that, in consequence, the State by refusing these plaintiffs admission to Claymont solely because of their color, is violating the plaintiffs' rights protected by the Equal Protection Clause of the Fourteenth Amendment."

These cases, together with one from the District of Columbia, quickly found their way to the United States Supreme Court. Since the cases from Kansas, South Carolina, Delaware, and Virginia, although premised on somewhat different facts and different locations, nevertheless involved a common legal question, they were considered together and were consolidated in one opinion. The Court's decision, delivered by Chief Justice Warren, was rendered on May 17, 1954. With it, compulsory segregation in education in the United States ceased to be legal. In the language of the Court:

> We conclude that in the field of public education the doctrine of "separate but equal" has no place. Separate educational facilities are inherently unequal. Therefore, we hold that the plaintiffs and others similarly situated for whom the actions have been brought are, by reason of the segregation complained of, deprived of the equal protection of the laws guaranteed by the Fourteenth Amendment.

At the same time, "because of the great variety of local conditions," continued the Court, "the formulation of decrees in these cases presents problems of considerable complexity," and it requested the parties involved to present further argument on questions propounded by the Court. These questions were discussed before the Court in the fall of 1954 by representatives of the states involved, the District of Columbia, and the Attorney General of the United States. On May 31, 1955, the Court rendered a final decree regarding methods of implementing its original decision. This decree left the way open for the localities affected to bring about a gradual transition from segregated to nonsegregated schools. Under the supervision of the district courts, consideration was to be given to problems peculiar to each locality, provided "the defendants make a prompt and reasonable start toward full compliance with our May 17, 1954 ruling." The Court made it clear, however, that flexibility is not to be confused with any retreat from its original decision that segregation is unconstitutional. It goes without saying, emphasized the Court, "that the vitality of these constitutional principles cannot be allowed to yield simply because of disagreement with them."

It is obvious that although the rate at which communities would be expected to conform to the Court's decision might vary, the direction in which all must move was clear. Compulsory segregation in education as an established institution belongs to the past.

Recent Changes in the Status of the Negro

It is sometimes said that the Supreme Court is not insensitive to public opinion and that it, no less than Congress—although less rapidly to be sure—follows "election returns." This may or may not be true. It is nevertheless relevant to observe significant changes that have taken place in the status of the Negro in American life since the *Plessy* v. *Ferguson* and the *Gong Lum* v. *Rice* decisions, changes of which the Court must have been aware in outlawing compulsory segregation.

First has been the emergence of what Harry S. Ashmore terms an indigenous leadership. This leadership, unlike the earlier leadership of Booker T. Washington, demands more than the opportunity to secure an economic toehold in American society. It demands full recognition of the Negro's right to the privileges of first-class citizenship in voting, in employment opportunities, in housing and residence, in the use of public facilities, and in public education as an indispensable condition for their adequate realization.[13]

Although Negroes are still far from attaining the goals their leaders have set for them, significant progress has nonetheless been made. Slowly, they have gained entrance into a number of the professions— law, medicine, education, and the like—and have succeeded in secur-

13. The Report of the United States Commission on Civil Rights to the President, entitled *Freedom to the Free: Century of Emancipation, 1863–1963* (Washington, D.C.: U.S. Government Printing Office, 1963) contains an excellent summary of the progress and the present status of the Negro in voting rights and political participation, in employment, in housing, in desegregation in education and religion, and in other significant areas.

ing membership in a considerable number of professional organizations in the South as well as in the North. For example, as early as 1948, the Missouri State Teachers Association admitted Negroes to its fold, and by 1950, twenty-seven state and county medical societies, including the southern states, had either admitted Negro physicians or amended their rules so as to make this possible. In 1950, eight states had enforceable fair employment acts upon their statute books. By 1963, the number had increased to twenty-one.[14]

Despite improvement in employment opportunities for Negroes in recent years, a comparison of their general position—economic, cultural, educational—with that of whites of comparable education and training reveals striking inequalities. For example, in a nationwide broadcast on June 11, 1963, President Kennedy stated that the Negro has about one half as much chance of completing college as a white student, one third as much chance of becoming a professional man, twice as much chance of becoming unemployed, about one seventh as much chance of earning $10,000 a year, and "a life expectancy seven years shorter."[15]

A comparison of the median income of the heads of white and nonwhite families in 1961 yields the following information:[16]

Years of school completed	Total	White	Nonwhite	Nonwhite per cent of white
8 years elementary	$4872	$4911	$3338	68.0
4 years high school	6302	6390	4559	71.3
4 or more of college	9264	9315	7875	84.5

It remains true, of course, of Negroes as of young people in the labor market, that they are the last to be hired and the first to be discharged.[17]

14. *Ibid.*, p. 132.

15. *The New York Times*, June 16, 1963.

16. *Economic Status of Non-white Workers, 1955–62*, Special Labor Force Report, No. 33. Bureau of Labor Statistics, United States Department of Labor, p. 8.

According to the Census of 1960, the median annual earnings of white professional workers was $8536 as compared with $6552 for nonwhite; for white farmers, $3252 as against $1168 for nonwhite; for white managers, officials, and proprietors, $8451 and for nonwhite $5319; for white craftsmen and foremen, $6570 and for nonwhite, $4654; and for white nonfarm laborers, $4845 and for nonwhite, $3450. U.S. Department of Commerce, Bureau of the Census of Population, 1960: *United States Summary: Detailed Characteristics*, Table 230, pp. 1, 610–11.

17. In July of 1963, when the unemployment rate for whites was 5.1 per cent,

Even so, the status of the Negro in American society has improved remarkably in recent years. Particularly is this true in the South, despite resistance of certain groups to Negro voting rights, to their economic progress, and to desegregation in education. Speaking of the great mass of southerners in the early 1940s, Professor Howard W. Odum stated they identified the Negro "as a Negro and nothing more." They "did not appraise the Negro as the same sort of human being as they themselves." [18] Once this attitude is changed, however, and the Negro is recognized as a *person*, the groundwork is laid for a new attitude toward the restrictions that have kept him as a thing apart. This change, in turn, follows upon the improved educational, economic, and cultural status of an increasing number of Negroes characteristic of recent years. Deplorable as conditions of Negro education still are in several of the southern states, the progress of recent decades has bordered upon the miraculous. For example, in 1916 there were 69 Negro high schools in the South with less than 20,000 pupils in attendance.[19] By 1960, the median years of schooling completed by Negroes between the ages of twenty and twenty-four was 10.1 years, and for the population as a whole 10.8 years. In the South alone, Negro school attendance in the period 1940–1950 increased twice as fast as that of the total population. Moreover, on the higher levels of education in the South, as well as in other sections of the country, a steadily increasing number of white people, through their association with Negroes in institutions of higher learning, have come to appreciate qualities of intellect and character strikingly different from the conventional stereotype. Indeed, there are communities in the South as well as in the North in which there is no longer a wide gap separating the cultural status of the Negro from that of the white.

Nevertheless, as we have seen, opportunities for education and cultural progress, in the sense of an open road for Negroes to positions of responsibility and trust in the higher echelons of business and industry, lag far behind those for whites. In the South, particularly, supervisory

---

that for nonwhites was 11.2 per cent. The situation for nonwhite boys and girls between the ages of 14 and 19 was considerably worse—25 per cent as against 12 per cent for white youth of the same age range. (*The New York Times*, August 28, 1963.) For the unemployment rates of experienced workers by color and major economic groups between 1955 and 1962, see *Economic Status of Non-white Workers, 1955–62*, p. 4.

18. Ashmore, *op. cit.*, p. 130.
19. *Ibid.*, p. 19.

and white-collar positions in business and industry are difficult to secure. However, the situation is not altogether static. The Negro is finding a place in the professions. Here and there the policy of total exclusion from labor unions or recognition only on condition of lower status
and pay is being modified. Furthermore, the exodus of Negroes from
agriculture and the increasing proportion who have become white-
collar workers foreshadow change in both economic and social status.
Thus the proportion of Negroes employed in agriculture, in the country
as a whole, declined from 21 per cent in 1948 to 11 per cent in 1962.[20]

The improved economic status of the Negro is related to the shift in
the center of Negro population from the rural areas in the South to

TABLE 5

MEDIAN SCHOOL YEARS COMPLETED BY PERSONS
25 YEARS OLD AND OVER BY REGIONS AND COLOR,
ACCORDING TO THE 1960 CENSUS

Regions	White	Nonwhite
North East	10.8	9.2
North Central	10.8	9.0
South	10.4	7.1
West	12.1	10.0
U.S.	10.9	8.2

SOURCE: *Digest of Educational Statistics,* U.S. Department of Health, Education,
and Welfare, Office of Education (OE 10024–62), p. 14.

urban localities and from the South as a whole to the North. The consequences of this migration are revolutionary in their possibilities and
may well transform the problem of segregation and integration in education.

For example, one area of intense resistance to integration in education is the rural community, with its fixed prejudices and its caste prescriptions firmly rooted in custom and tradition. But it is precisely from
the rural South that the Negroes are migrating in the largest numbers.
One consequence of the transfer of Negroes from agriculture to industry is to leave some counties in the South without any Negroes in the
population "and others where Negroes have become so few that segre-

20. *Economic Status of Non-white Workers, 1955–62,* p. 2.

gation in the schools is already coming to be looked upon as a nuisance." [21]

Most significant is the migration of the Negro from the South in recent decades. In 1900, about 90 per cent of the Negro population was found in the South. By 1950, this had declined to 68 per cent and, by 1960, to 60 per cent. During the decade 1950 to 1960 alone, approximately 1,500,000 Negroes migrated from the South, chiefly to the cities of the North and West.[22] As compared with the South's 16 per cent loss in its nonwhite population in the decade 1940-1950, and 14.1 per cent in 1950–1960, all other sections of the country experienced a sizeable increase. Table 6 provides a state-by-state comparison of the percentage of gain or loss in the population of eleven southern states resulting from white and nonwhite migration in the period 1940–1960.

TABLE 6

State	White Gain or Loss		Nonwhite Gain or Loss	
	1940–1950	*1950–1960*	*1940–1950*	*1950–1960*
Alabama	− 7.6	− 6.9	−20.5	−22.8
Arkansas	−17.6	−19.1	−32.4	−35.0
Florida	+40.8	+70.0	+ 2.7	+16.6
Georgia	− 2.4	− 0.4	−22.2	−19.2
Kentucky	−13.3	−13.7	− 7.9	− 7.6
Louisiana	− 0.2	+ 2.4	−17.0	−10.4
Mississippi	− 9.7	− 9.3	−30.2	−32.7
No. Carolina	− 3.7	− 4.0	−16.2	−19.2
Oklahoma	−17.1	− 9.5	−31.5	−13.0
So. Carolina	− 2.2	− 0.3	−25.3	−26.5
Virginia	+ 9.6	+ 3.3	− 3.9	− 9.5

SOURCE: *Statistical Abstract of the United States, 1963,* U.S. Department of Commerce, Bureau of the Census (Washington, D.C.: U.S. Government Printing Office, 1963), p. 39.

21. Ashmore, *op. cit.,* p. 128. Taking the country as a whole, the white population in urban areas for the decade 1950–1960 increased by 29.3 per cent and decreased by 0.8 per cent in rural areas, in contrast with an increase of 48.7 per cent in urban areas for Negroes and a decrease of 8.8 per cent in rural areas. Bureau of the Census, *op. cit.,* Table 42, pp. 1–143.

22. The per cent of increase in the nonwhite population resulting from migration from the South to the Northeast in the decade 1940–1950, was 34.3 and for 1950–1960, 26 per cent; to the North Central region for these two decades it was 42 and 23.8 per cent respectively; to the West 60.5 per cent and 23.6 per cent. *Statistical Abstract of the United States, 1963,* Bureau of the Census, p. 39.

The term "nonwhite," as used by the Census, is broader than that of "Negro," but as applied to the South in this discussion it is practically identical with "Negro."

From these data it is clear that the proportion of Negroes to whites in the South is rapidly shrinking. In the North, it is rapidly gaining. Of importance for education is the fact that migration in all regions is predominantly from rural areas to cities. The basic causes of migration on the part of both whites and nonwhites are to better economic status and to profit from superior educational and cultural opportunities. The following table provides interesting data with respect to leading cities of both North and South.

TABLE 7

GROWTH OF POPULATION, NEGRO–WHITE, FOR
SELECTED CITIES, 1950–1960

City	1960			1950		
	Total	White	Negro	Total	White	Negro
Atlanta	487,455	300,991	186,464	331,314	209,898	121,416
Baltimore	939,024	612,435	326,589	949,708	723,655	226,053
Chicago	3,550,404	2,712,748	837,656	3,620,962	3,111,525	509,437
Dallas	685,814	562,367	123,447	434,462	377,199	57,263
Detroit	1,670,144	1,182,970	487,174	1,849,568	1,545,847	303,721
Houston	938,219	720,547	217,672	596,163	470,503	125,660
Los Angeles	2,479,010	2,061,808	334,916	1,970,358	1,758,773	211,585
Philadelphia	2,002,512	1,467,479	529,240	2,071,605	1,692,637	378,968
New York	7,781,984	6,640,662	1,087,931	7,891,957	7,116,428	775,529
San Francisco	742,855	644,755	98,100	775,357	693,888	62,635
Washington	763,956	345,263	418,693	802,178	518,147	284,031

SOURCE: *Southern School News,* July 1962, p. 15.

It is interesting to observe from this table that while the cities of Baltimore, Chicago, Detroit, Philadelphia, New York, San Francisco, and Washington added significantly to their Negro population in the decade 1950–1960, all registered a decline both in their total and their white populations. "As dramatic as has been the increase in the urban Negro population during the past two decades," writes the *Southern School News,* "the increase in enrollment of Negro children in public schools doubled while that of white children for the same period either declined or increased only slightly." [23] To the problems thus engendered, we shall turn shortly.

Finally, the integration of the armed forces should be mentioned in this enumeration of factors leading to a new status for the Negro. This

23. *Southern School News,* July 1962, p. 15.

policy is both cause and effect in that it could not have been brought about without a change in public mind, and it is operating to undermine traditional attitudes. Intimate associations on the battlefield as well as in training camps, together with the demonstrated efficiency of integrated units in the Korean conflict, have transformed the sentiments of many in the armed forces with respect to the Negro and challenge the validity of discriminatory practices in civilian life. Taken together with the pressing need to counteract Communist propaganda abroad, which pictures the Negroes as submerged and oppressed and uses this picture as evidence of the American's attitude toward all colored peoples, integration within the services clearly foreshadows desegregation in other areas of living.

Desegregation in the North and the Border States

An early reaction to the concentration of a Negro population in northern communities was educational segregation. In some instances this resulted more or less naturally from residential patterns, but it was not uncommon for school administrators and boards of education through gerrymandering of school districts and other administrative devices to bring about a segregation neither authorized nor required by law. Today, paralleling the more recent invasion of the non-South by the Negro, a dominant sentiment in opposition to segregation has developed. Prior to the Supreme Court decision in May of 1954, only four states outside the South—Arizona, Kansas, New Mexico, and Wyoming —had authorized local communities to segregate children in school on the basis of race. Eleven states lacked legal provision regarding segregation, and sixteen had adopted laws expressly prohibiting it.[24] In large measure the trend away from segregation testifies to the influence of a

> . . . general redefinition of minority rights which has occupied the nation since it took up arms against a racist enemy in World War II. This has been reflected in persistent pressure from Negroes now organized as never before, and from human relations agencies, church and civic groups, and school administrators themselves. The threat of legal action has played a part, too, as has the economic fact that it is often cheaper to integrate than to

24. Ashmore, *op. cit.*, pp. 67–68.

provide new or improved facilities for a small group of Negro pupils. The press of the non-South has been a positive force in the process, for even the most conservative newspapers are now generally sympathetic to the Negro's demand for equal treatment.[25]

The change in public attitude in the non-South with reference to segregation, plus differences in state law and means of enforcement have contributed to considerable variation in methods employed in the transition from segregated to integrated pattern in education. For example, in 1949, Indiana adopted an act forbidding segregation in the schools of the state but incorporated in the law no provision for its enforcement.[26] In Illinois, legislation in opposition to segregation dating from 1874 was strengthened in 1945 to assure desegregation, but the means of enforcement were largely financial; that is to say, an amendment to an appropriation bill in the 1949 Legislature provided that "No part of the money appropriated by this act shall be distributed to any school district in which any student is excluded from or segregated in any public school, within the meaning of 'The School Code,' because of race, color, ancestry or national origin." [27] On the other hand, New Jersey, in revising its constitution in 1947, incorporated a clause which expressly forbids segregation in the public schools "because of religious scruples, race, color, ancestry or national origin." [28] Not content with this, the state set up an agency which has endeavored to prepare communities for the transition from segregation to integration by means of expert guidance.[29] In New York both fair employment and fair educational practices acts have been on the statute books for some years, with the result that there is no legal basis for segregation in either the faculties or the student bodies of public schools. Consequently, the segregation that exists results primarily from gerrymandering of school districts or from residential patterns. Spurred on by energetic cam-

25. *Ibid.*, p. 68. See also, "De Facto Segregation," *NEA Research Bulletin*, May 1965, pp. 35–37.
26. For the text of this law, see Robin M. Williams and Margaret W. Ryan, *Schools in Transition* (Chapel Hill, N.C.: University of North Carolina Press, 1954), p. 10.
27. Illinois Statutes, 1949, H.B. 1066, p. 53.
28. Article I, Section 5.
29. See Joseph L. Bustard, "The New Jersey Story: The Development of Racially Integrated Public Schools," *Journal of Negro Education*, Summer 1952, pp. 275–85.

paigns of recent years on behalf of civil rights for Negroes, both the courts and state educational authorities in the North are committed to the elimination of "racial imbalance" in public schools to every extent possible.

Ironically, these efforts have encountered legal difficulties when race is used as a factor in correcting *de facto* segregation. Nor have the courts succeeded in clarifying the powers of boards of education in meeting the problem. For example, the attempt of school officials in New York City, in September of 1963, to correct racial imbalance by redrawing the demarcation lines of school districts was declared to be in violation of the State Education Law which provides, "no person shall be refused admission into or excluded from any public school in the State of New York on account of race, creed, or national origin." This decision, however, the New York Court of Appeals reversed by a vote of six to one. On the other hand, a United States Court of Appeals, in upholding the neighborhood school policy of Gary, Indiana, in November 1963, ruled that the Fourteenth Amendment would be violated if some students were required "to leave their neighborhood and friends and be transferred to another school, simply for the purpose of balancing races in the various schools."

Contradictory as these decisions seem to be, the United States Supreme Court has refused to accept them for review, a fact which seems to imply that local school boards have broad constitutional discretion to deal with racial patterns, provided such action is not designed deliberately to maintain segregation.[30] This conclusion seems to follow from a decision of the United States Supreme Court on June 3, 1963 (No. 217, October Term, 1962). Said the Court, in reversing a prior decision of the United States Court of Appeals of the Sixth Circuit which had approved a pupil transfer plan of the Board of Education of Knoxville, Tennessee, and in remanding the case to the lower courts for appropriate action, "Not only is race the factor upon which the transfer plans operate, but also the plans lack a provision whereby a student might with equal facility transfer from a segregated to a desegregated school." And, again, "no official transfer plan or provision of which ra-

30. In the New York case, for example, the State Court of Appeals noted that the children concerned were entering a new junior high school and hence no one was being transferred against his will nor would he have to travel farther in order to attend one school as against another. The Court did not indicate whether its decision would have been different had the facts been different.

cial segregation is the inevitable consequence may stand under the Fourteenth Amendment."

If this recital leaves the reader in a haze of uncertainty, he may be assured that our highest court will eventually find it necessary to provide further clarification!

The Problem of the Deep South

As we move from north to south through the border states, we observe a progressively hardening resistance to desegregation. In May 1958, four years after the decision of the United States Supreme Court outlawing segregation, a survey conducted by the *Southern School News* revealed that 764 school districts had begun or completed desegregation and 2125 biracial districts still remained segregated. Six years later, in September 1964, the same source reported that 2255 school districts out of a total of 2993 in the eleven southern states had desegregated in one form or another; of these, 127 had desegregated in the fall of 1964 (102 voluntarily). Furthermore, with the beginning of desegregation in Mississippi (four districts), every southern state had established biracial classes in both public graded schools and public colleges and universities.

These facts reflect gradual abandonment of a policy of "massive resistance" to desegregation and willingness in an increasing number of instances to move toward integration without waiting upon court action. On the other hand, what is officially termed "desegregation" in no way implies the total elimination of racial discrimination in education in the "hard core" states. In many instances nothing more than "token integration" has occurred, by which is meant the admission of a few Negro pupils into a predominantly all-white school. For example, according to the September 1964 issue of the *Southern School News,* the number of Negroes enrolled in the public schools of eleven southern states was less than 2 per cent of some 2.9 million Negro students in this region. In some instances, laws designed to retard integration continue to operate. These states have established pupil-placement boards armed with multiple criteria, "other than race," with which to keep to a minimum the number of Negroes who may transfer from one school to another. This tactic has slowed down integration considerably. In still other instances, once legal attempts to block desegregation have failed, southern states have adopted tuition-payment plans designed to assist parents who wish to transfer their children from public to private schools. The establishment of state pupil-placement boards and the adoption of tuition-payment plans, together with other measures designed to transfer control of education from local school districts to the state, have placed the future of public education in the South in jeopardy. To what extent the "carrot and the stick" provisions of the Civil Rights Act of 1964 (one, the provision in Title IV that the Office of Education provide technical and financial assistance, if requested, to local school systems undertaking to desegregate their schools; two, the requirement in Title VI that the Office of Education withhold federal funds from school districts otherwise entitled to receive such funds but which engage in discrimination in education) will speed desegregation remains to be seen.[31]

Suggestions for Effecting a Transition from Segregation to Desegregation

What suggestions emerge from events in the states which have undertaken seriously to comply with the rulings of the United States Supreme Court?

Apart from specific suggestions that follow, it is important to realize that desegregation is still in its early and experimental stages. This implies that just as communities differ (some rural, some urban, some liberal, some conservative, and all stages in between) within the same geographical region as strikingly as do different sections of the country, so do methods that bring success in one school district encounter difficulty in another.

With these qualifications in mind, it may be said: (1) In the vast majority of instances desegregation has proceeded with less stress and strain than anticipated. This is true despite occasional violence in the South and the equally stubborn, if less conspicuous opposition to integration on the part of middle- and upper-class communities outside the

31. On December 2, 1964 the United States Court of Appeals for the Fourth Circuit struck down the Virginia plan of paying the tuition of students who wished to transfer from a public to a private, nonsectarian school. The decision forbids two districts to continue payments to students attending all-white "private academies" on the ground that this constitutes "a transparent evasion of the 14th Amendment." This decision may be said to have signaled the death knell of similar devices in the southern states to thwart desegregation.

South. Indeed, the dramatic failure of Governor Barnett of Mississippi in 1962 and of Governor Wallace of Alabama in 1963 to nullify court decrees ordering the admission of Negroes to previously all-white institutions has demonstrated the inevitability of desegregation in the "hard core" states as well as in states less resistant to desegregation.

(2) A direct relationship has been found to exist between advanced planning on the part of boards of education, the administrative staff of the schools, and teachers, and success with integration. Louisville, Kentucky, is a striking illustration of a city in which foresight and careful preparation designed to bring about cooperation between school and community organizations rendered possible rapid transition from segregation to integration. On the other hand, a do-nothing policy or evidence of irresolution, uncertainty, and confusion of purpose (particularly indifference on the part of the police) serves to encourage resistance and to provide a fertile opportunity for the invasion of forces bent upon maintaining segregation.

(3) Closely related to the above is the importance of channels of communication between racial and cultural groups within the community. Where committees or organizations concerned with bettering human relations are active, the transition proceeds with relative ease. If difficulty threatens, resources are at hand with which to meet it. In a number of instances, these groups have conducted forums and discussion meetings designed to prepare parents of the schools, as well as citizens at large, for impending change, to clarify problems, and to anticipate their constructive solution. Similarly, within the school system, prior preparation on the part of the administration, including the careful selection of principals and faculty for areas in which difficulties are expected, has marked the difference between success and failure.

(4) Both on the higher and the lower levels of education, surprisingly little resistance has been found in student bodies. Moreover, where tension and outright disorder have occurred, the sources of difficulty have frequently been from outside rather than inside the institution. A remark frequently made by students is, "We would get along all right if our parents and outsiders would only leave us alone."

This should not blur the fact that to bring Negro and white children together in a public school in a southern community, in which members of each race have long viewed those of the opposite race as another order of being, involves a strain upon both groups. As Robert

Coles points out in his suggestive study of the effects of intermingling in southern schools, effects vary with individuals, their home and community backgrounds, and with what *"actually happens* in the room between the Negro child and his classmates and teachers." [32]

(5) There is evidence to suggest that a policy of gradual integration is less successful than more ambitious attempts to bring about transition. Gradual integration, often, not only prolongs the agony of change but inhibits organized efforts to effect desegregation. When but one grade in an elementary school, for example, undertakes integration, the parents of the school as a whole are less concerned about cooperating actively with the administration. Divisions and contrasts within the school itself are easily used to keep the pots of opposition boiling. On the other hand, advocates of a gradual approach contend that piecemeal integration provides an opportunity to prepare Negroes more effectively to hold their own educationally in mixed schools and eases the difficulties involved in merging Negro and white personnel on the teaching staff. Robert Coles discusses this problem in the concluding chapter of his study. Most educators and doctors, he states, would agree that, from the standpoint of teaching and the emotional effects upon the child (the comparative absence of racial bias in the very young child), much is to be said in favor of starting integration in the early grades.[33]

(6) Finally, despite the conviction of middle- and upper-class parents that integration will lower educational standards, this is by no means inevitable. Indeed, the evidence from a number of communities and school situations has shown the opposite to be true. For example, tests of academic achievement administered to pupils in Louisville, Austin, Baltimore, and Washington, D.C. several years after integration have indicated in each instance substantial gains in scholastic achievement. Pertinent in this connection is the statement of Frank H. Stallings, following a survey of the Louisville schools:

> Perhaps the safest generalization that can be drawn from the study is that for the period of time considered, integration need

32. *The Desegregation of Southern Schools: A Psychiatric Study* (Atlanta: Southern Regional Council, July 1963), pp. 9–10. This study in depth gives one an excellent picture of the effects of desegregation upon both Negro and white children and upon teachers and the classroom.
33. *Ibid.*, pp. 20–25.

not adversely affect the scholastic achievements of white pupils and it can favorably affect that of the Negro. The study, therefore, offers reassurance to those who fear that the immediate effect of integration must automatically lower the level of achievement.[34]

One obvious benefit that seems to have resulted from desegregation has been the highlighting in the minds of the public, as well as of the educational staff, of the inferior education previously afforded Negro children. For example, Walter N. Tobiner, President of the Board of Education in Washington, D.C., states that one of the major problems revealed by desegregation has been "a very disheartening and almost appalling disparity between Negro achievement level and white achievement level." He adds, however, that this follows more from the previous opportunities afforded in each instance than from known facts of potentiality. Indeed, under integration, he adds, "a greater number of children are getting a better education than before." [35]

These conclusions are reassuring, but it should be borne in mind that they apply to school systems as a whole and not to individual schools nor to individual children. Nowhere are valid conclusions regarding the relative merits of administrative programs or methods of sectioning children more contingent upon community sentiment, parents' attitudes, and quality of the teaching staff than in dealing with problems of transition from segregated to integrated schools.

Some Significant Aspects of the Problem

One difficulty in dealing with a problem as complex as desegregation in education is the temptation to oversimplify. This tendency is accentuated in this instance because the problem is, in fact, both simple and complex. As a legal problem, it is relatively simple insofar as the law insists that all people be viewed as individuals and not as members of a

34. "Changes in the Academic Achievement Since Integration in the Louisville Public Schools, in *Second Annual Conference on Education*, Gatlinburg, Tennessee, March 1960, by the United States Commission on Civil Rights (Washington, D.C.: U.S. Government Printing Office, 1960), p. 149.

This report of the United States Commission on Civil Rights provides a helpful survey of the effects of desegregation upon academic standards and social adjustment of both white and Negro students in a number of school systems.

35. *Washington Post and Times Herald*, April 7, 1958.

group, be it racial, religious, economic, or social. Accordingly, in its decision of May 17, 1954, the Supreme Court said no more than that Negroes are persons and that no person can be denied the services of an institution established and maintained by the public by virtue of his racial background. The Court did not say that all schools must be integrated or that some schools may not be segregated. This will depend upon circumstances. It did say, however, that no qualified pupil may be denied admission to a school because he is black rather than white, yellow rather than brown, etc. Indeed, as mentioned earlier, the 1954 decision of the Supreme Court has been used to inhibit the efforts of civil rights groups and school officials to offset racial imbalance in schools by means of the compulsory transfer of children from their neighborhood schools to more distant schools.

Both as an educational and as a social problem the transition from a segregated school and community to one more in harmony with democratic ideals is extremely complicated. Nor is it rendered simpler by the disposition of both those who would continue segregation and those who would eliminate it to center upon one or two factors in the situation and to ignore others. For example, the segregationalist tends to ignore the effects of segregation upon the personalities of white and Negro children alike, but particularly the Negro. Moreover, he insists upon grouping all Negroes under one stereotype and refuses to consider the scientific conclusions of anthropologists with respect to race. Indeed, he frequently goes farther and excludes from libraries and classrooms materials bearing upon racial distinctions, lest they influence the minds of the young in ways opposed to his own convictions. On the other hand, the northern opponent of segregation is equally prone to ground his position on an abstract principle, one that ignores the stubborn influence of long-established folkways and patterns of living upon the mind and disposition of the southerner. For this reason, the northerner needs to be reminded that not all opposition to integration in the South is racial or solely racial. Many a southerner—mistakenly or not—objects to the education of his child with Negroes on cultural grounds. Faced with the necessity of sending his children to school with children of an obviously lower cultural level, a school in which the majority of the children may possess habits of speech and conduct altogether different from those he wishes his children to acquire, he vigorously opposes this intermingling. If he is unsuccessful, he is disposed to follow the example of many a northerner and, if he can, send his child to a private school.

This is understandable. It is less understandable, however, that he fails to recognize similar feelings on the part of the educated and cultured Negro, whom he would force to keep his children in a segregated school of deplorable status. The latter, too, may wish his child to receive the best possible education and can view only with frustration and indignation a situation in which the principle of nondiscrimination permits white children of cultural backgrounds high and low to intermingle in the same school from which his children are excluded solely on the basis of race.[36]

Two basic principles are operating in the South with respect to segregation. One is the traditional assumption of the equality of all individuals before the law. As applied to public institutions and their services, this means that each person, irrespective of birth, has an equal claim upon these institutions and services. It also means that each individual is to be judged in terms of what he is and can demonstrate himself to be, not in terms of the accidents of race, creed, or economic circumstance. Each child is thus assured an inherent right to reach for the stars. Nor is it for the state to cripple his arms!

The second principle is one of practical procedure, born of repeated experience in creating and maintaining ever widening opportunities for individuals with the help of government. It holds that the opening of new roads to opportunity, as reform through governmental action, is better achieved through education than compulsion. Not until a goodly proportion of our people came to realize the importance of school attendance was it possible for the state to enforce compliance with laws which made mandatory the attendance at school of all children within a given age range. However, once compulsion reflected public senti-

36. It may be appropriate to point out in this connection that what constitutes race in the segregation picture is also sadly oversimplified. Writing in this connection, Max Lerner states, "But, even when you single out pigmentation from all other genetic traits, there are still a bewilderingly large number of color gradations and combinations in America that would defy a corps of skilled ethnologists: the varieties of black, white, yellow, red, mulatto, quadroon, octaroon, almost white, 'passing,' Creole, Indian-white, Indian-Negro, Caribbean-Latin, Hawaiian-Filipino-Chinese mixtures. Where the culture is, like the American, made up of human material from many ethnic groups that were crossbred to start with, and where it has carried the biological and cultural cross-breeding so far, the stalking of ethnic purity has an ironic irrelevance, and to base caste on it becomes a cruel fantasy." [*America As a Civilization* (New York: Simon and Schuster, 1957), p. 515.]

ment, the enforcement of compulsory attendance laws was not difficult. It remains to be seen whether the decision of the United States Supreme Court with reference to segregation is at all analogous to the passage of compulsory school attendance laws.

The danger of oversimplification is also apparent in well-meaning attempts of reformers in the North to bring about immediate integration where segregation and racially imbalanced schools have come into being. In many instances, this has led to serious differences between educators, sociologists, and others intimately concerned with the needs of children in underprivileged areas, on the one hand, and ardent advocates of civil rights on the other. The first group views the problem of segregation in the North as one quite different from segregation in the South. In the North both official policy and public sentiment, in large measure, oppose segregation on principle. With few exceptions, it is the direct result of housing and residential factors slow of remedy and over which school officials have no control. Consequently, the status of the underprivileged Negro child is not unlike that of the underprivileged white child. For both the educational problem is essentially to find ways and means of offsetting the injurious effects of cultural deprivation in home and community—and, all too often, inferior schools as well. As educators see it, the demand of lay advocates of equality that these children be merged suddenly with children who have long enjoyed more favorable economic and cultural advantages may well result in no more than surface integration.[37]

Writing of protests and pressures in northern states to correct *de facto* segregation, Fred M. Hechinger, of *The New York Times*, remarks,

> The "racial imbalance" theory may hold some danger of creating an educational racism all its own; for it implies that a white

37. Inge Lederer Gibel, an active worker on behalf of civil rights, the white wife of a Negro, and the mother of a child in a newly integrated school, draws attention to a lack of communication between some civil rights leaders and parents of underprivileged children. The latter, Mrs. Gibel contends, are more concerned with the improvement of the neighborhood school than with integration. She also points out that the common practice in northern cities of sectioning children in schools on the basis of ability, a device that enables teachers to adapt their instruction to children with relatively similar academic needs, results in identifying the culturally deprived child as inferior, in his own mind as well as in the minds of his schoolmates, thus defeating one major purpose of integration. See, "How Not to Integrate the Schools," *Harper's Magazine*, November 1963, pp. 57–66.

majority is necessary for good schooling. This assumption may be true as long as the white pupils are middle-class and the minority pupils are from the lower socio-economic strata. But the same assumption would be an insult to Negro or Puerto Rican pupils if they were (as it is assumed they will be) on an equal socio-economic level.[38]

Surveys of parent sentiment in segregated communities within large cities also reveal objections to the elimination of segregation by means of the mass transfer of children.[39] These objections are based upon a number of factors: the desire of parents to keep their children near home; a conviction that the time consumed in transportation and the necessity of adhering to bus schedules would deprive children of an opportunity to participate in extracurricular activities at school as well as in the local community (activities often sponsored by the city and settlement houses); and a conviction, shared by the more sophisticated residents, that the transfer of children out of the local school district would deprive the latter of able leaders within school and community and thus inhibit fruitful school and community relationships.

Since northern communities are experiencing the growing pains of desegregation with which southerners will also have to contend, once token integration gives way to genuine efforts at desegregation, a brief summary of methods commonly employed in the non-South may be relevant.

(1) In relatively small and medium-sized communities, the merging of white and nonwhite children has been accomplished with little difficulty, as the experience of Clinton, Tennessee, demonstrates, despite an initial period of violence. Indeed, in many instances, the elimination

38. Hechinger also points out that the transporting of children in and out of segregated districts in order to correct racial imbalance in "some suburbs or smaller cities . . . would call for transfer from outside the deeper ghettos; in New York, it would call for shipments from other boroughs. This opens the question whether the parents' right to select the area of residence, with a special view to their children's schooling, can be abridged." "Segregation Protest in the North Obscures Educational Problems," *The New York Times,* September 8, 1963, Section 4, p. E9.

39. See, for example, Joseph P. Lyford in *The Negro as an American, An Occasional Paper on the Free Society,* published in 1963 by The Center for the Study of Democratic Institutions, Fund for the Republic, Inc., 133 East 54 Street, New York City. Lyford conducted an intensive study of some sixty square blocks in New York City inhabited by both Negroes and Puerto Ricans. Similar conclusions are reported by Mrs. Gibel in the *Harper's* article to which reference was made above.

of segregation has resulted in both financial economies and increased educational effectiveness.

A method commonly adopted in these communities, as well as in large cities where schools are not far from each other, has been termed the "Princeton Plan." Under this plan, all children of certain grades (let us say, from kindergarten through third or from fourth through sixth) are assigned to one school. This plan retains the advantages and potentialities of the neighborhood school.

(2) "Voluntary transfer" is another method used in some communities. By this term is meant granting the requests of parents to withdraw their children from a school considered inferior and to send them to another in order to insure advantages that would otherwise be denied.

This plan, as well as an "open enrollment plan," serves somewhat as a safety valve for ambitious parents who see little prospect of reforming a backward school in time to benefit their own children.

(3) Of far more importance, in the long run, than the above method is concentration upon meeting the unique problems of slum schools by means of educational measures keyed to the special needs of disadvantaged children and their parents. The major purpose in these cases is to provide educational facilities and conditions that will insure an open road to opportunity for the individual child and the contributions to society potentially present in underprivileged children.

This is a formidable task that can receive little more than brief reference here. It means transforming the slum school for both whites and nonwhites into a combination settlement house and conventional school, staffed with teachers trained specifically to cope with the complex problems of the slum school and neighborhood; teachers who are also social workers and who receive salaries commensurate with their special competence and unique responsibilities.

In conclusion, it should be said that educators who look forward to the eventual elimination of segregation in education should give serious attention to the problems which arise outside the classroom as well as within. Here the experience of integrated systems has provided a fuller understanding than in the past of the cultural handicaps which afflict Negro children under segregation. We have in mind items such as the essentials of health education, standards of social behavior, and identification with moral and ethical values which free one from the limitations and the handicaps of a parochial grouping and insure for him the opportunity of wholesome participation in American society.

One of the valid arguments in opposition to segregation has to do with the effects of enforced separation upon a child's personality. A dual system of education, under the most favorable conditions, cannot prevent serious injury to the personalities of many who are thus set apart as inferior. Numerous investigations have established this fact. Convincing evidence of the judgment of experts in this field comes from an investigation conducted by Max Deutscher and Isador Chein and published under the title, "The Psychological Effects of Segregation." [40] These writers undertook to determine the judgments of anthropologists, psychologists, and sociologists concerning the effects of segregation when equal provision of physical facilities exist. Out of 517 replies to the questionnaires sent to 849 social scientists, 90 per cent indicated their conviction that enforced segregation yields detrimental effects on the segregated groups, 2 per cent that it has no harmful effects, and 4 per cent refrained from expressing an opinion. Among the injuries reported were: the stresses created in the minds of children by the conflict between democratic schooling and its implications of equality and the practices of segregation with its implications of inferiority; the development of submissiveness, martyrdom, feelings of persecution, withdrawal tendencies, self-ambivalence in the personality of the "inferior group"; distortions in the sense of reality as a consequence of enforced segregation; the higher price paid for adjustment by members of the segregated groups who are necessarily maladjusted.

Impressive as this list is of the effects upon personality which result from segregation, we must not conclude that all evils will end with its abolition. The experience of a colored child in an integrated school in which his white brother enjoys the advantages of superior class status can be as harmful as segregation. Indeed, when a colored child is in the minority and can find no healthy outlet for his ability or is banned from equal participation in the normal activities of the school because of the mere fact of his color, it is questionable whether the effects are not as serious, if not more so, than normal relations with his fellows in a segregated school. This poses a problem which must be faced in the nonsegregated school if all children are to be permitted to enter into their birthright.

40. *Journal of Psychology,* October 1948, pp. 259–67. See also, Ralph M. Dreger and Kent S. Miller, "Comparative Psychological Studies of Negroes and Whites in the United States," *Psychological Bulletin,* September 1960, pp. 361–402.

Thus the problem continues. Once segregation ends, problems of integration begin!

Suggested Reading

Brink, William, and Lois Harris, *The Negro Revolution* (New York: Simon and Schuster, Inc., 1964).

Clift, Virgil A., Archibald Anderson, and H. Gordon Hullfish, *Negro Education in America* (New York: Harper & Row, 1962), Parts, I, III, IV.

Coles, Robert, *The Desegregation of Southern Schools: A Psychiatric Study* (Atlanta: Southern Regional Council, 1963).

Committee on Social Issues, *Psychiatric Aspects of School Desegregation* (New York: Group for the Advancement of Psychiatry, 1790 Broadway, May 1957), Report No. 37.

Gibel, Inge Lederer, "How *Not* to Integrate the Schools," *Harper's Magazine*, November 1963, pp. 57–66.

Ginzberg, Eli, and Alfred S. Eichner, *The Troublesome Presence: American Democracy and the Negro* (New York: The Free Press of Glencoe, 1964).

Handlin, Oscar, "Is Integration the Answer?" *Atlantic Monthly*, March 1964, pp. 49–64.

Humphrey, Hubert H., ed., *Integration vs. Segregation* (New York: Thomas Y. Crowell Company, 1964).

Lerner, Max, *America As a Civilization* (New York: Simon and Schuster, Inc., 1957), pp. 501–25.

Morland, J. Kenneth, *Token Desegregation and Beyond* (Atlanta: Southern Regional Council, 1963).

Peters, William, *The Southern Temper* (Garden City, New York: Doubleday and Company, Inc., 1959).

Silberman, Charles E., *Crisis in Black and White* (New York: Random House, 1964), chapter IX.

Southern School News, Nashville, Tenn. (An invaluable monthly publication for anyone seeking information on progress in desegregation. It was established by southern editors and educators in order to provide information on developments in education with respect to desegregation.)

Chapter 23

Federal Aid to Education in the States

Traditional Federal–State Relations in Education

In Chapter 4 we observed that the ideal of local autonomy in education has given character to the organization and conduct of our schools since early in the seventeenth century. Only after local communities had first set the example did state authorities undertake to require of all communities a responsibility which the pioneering few had already assumed. We also saw that education, in the course of time, has become a state function, and insofar as the subdivisions of the state do, in fact, exercise local control and self-determination, it is by virtue of authority delegated to them by the Constitution and the legislature of the states. An illustration of the manner in which the right of local autonomy once granted may be rescinded is found in the pupil placements acts of a number of southern states, acts which remove from local boards of education all authority to determine what schools individual pupils may attend.

Earlier chapters have also described the relation of the federal government to education. Immediately following independence from England, Benjamin Rush and his associates in the American Philosophical Society undertook to devise plans for a national system of education. As late as 1795, indeed, the Society offered an award for the most effective plan of this character. With the adoption of the Constitution, however, together with the Tenth Amendment, it became increasingly clear that responsibility for education was to become primarily a state, rather than a federal, responsibility.

The decision to lodge primary responsibility for education in the states did not, however, preclude all federal participation. Precedents set by the Continental Congress in 1785 and 1787 in connection with the sale of public lands in the Northwest Territory inaugurated a policy which the federal government has followed throughout the years. Beginning with the admission of Ohio to the Union in 1803, the central government adopted the practice of stipulating that the sixteenth section of public lands granted to the states be devoted to the support of public schools and two townships to the establishment of a university. To these provisions have been added, from time to time, grants of land and generous sums of money from government surplus funds.[1] Contributions from the federal government in support of special types of education—some permanent, some temporary—began with the passage of the Morrill Act in 1862 and have continued with little interruption since.

With few exceptions (such as aid to vocational education, the establishment of the National Youth Administration, and the Civilian Conservation Corps) federal grants have been free of attempts to exercise federal control and supervision over the educational activities thus fostered. That is to say, the principle that education, even when assisted by the federal government, is a state and local function has been carefully observed.

Most educators and laymen who favor federal aid to education are agreed that this is as it should be. It was this conviction which prompted the Educational Policies Commission in 1941 to oppose the continuance of the National Youth Administration and the Civilian Conservation Corps as federal agencies, despite the invaluable services they had rendered American youth in the 1930s, and to urge the trans-

1. For example, a significant portion of the surplus revenue was allocated to the states by the federal government in 1837 for purposes of public education. Other grants included the Direct War Tax Refund to three states in 1891; the Forest Reserve Income Act of 1908 (which assigned 25 per cent of the funds received from each forest reserve to schools or roads in states containing these reserves); and the Mineral Royalty Act of 1920. For a summary of federal grants to education, see Charles A. Quattlebaum, "Federal Policies and Practices in Higher Education," in Douglas M. Knight, *The Federal Government and Higher Education* (Englewood Cliffs, New Jersey: Prentice-Hall, Inc., 1960).

fer of their functions to the states, but with continued financial assistance from federal appropriations.[2] Similarly, in all legislation suggested or supported by organizations such as the National Education Association, the Council of Chief State School Officers, and the like, it has been carefully provided that funds so appropriated are to be turned over to the educational officials of the states for administration and distribution.

Within recent years the federal government has been asked for more than just grants-in-aid for specific activities such as vocational education, adult education, school lunch programs, nursery education, and so on. Many have felt that both the national welfare and the ideal of equality of educational opportunity require that the federal government supplement state efforts in the support of general education.

What has led to these new demands upon the central government and what are the arguments employed both in support and in opposition to programs of federal aid?

Factors Which Suggest Increased Federal Participation in Financing Education

Educators are fond of quoting the Founding Fathers on the close correlation between education and free government. It was this early recognition which prompted Washington to stress in his Farewell Address that "it is essential that public opinion should be enlightened" and to urge his successors to "Promote, then, as an object of primary importance, institutions for the general diffusion of knowledge." Nor were those who followed him in the presidency indifferent to this injunction. From Jefferson to John Quincy Adams, presidents continued to recommend to Congress that it devote the proceeds from the sale of public lands to the advancement of education as well as to roads, rivers, and other "objects of public improvement." "The great object of the institutions of civil government," wrote John Quincy Adams,

> is the improvement of the conditions of those who are parties to
> the social compact, and no government, in whatever form constituted, can accomplish the lawful ends of its institutions but in

2. See the report of the Educational Policies Commission, *The Civilian Conservation Corps, the National Youth Administration and the Public Schools* (Washington, D.C.: National Education Association, 1941).

proportion as it improves the condition of those over whom it is established. . . . Among the first, perhaps the very first, instrument for the improvement of men is knowledge, and to the acquisition of much of the knowledge adapted to the wants, the comforts, and enjoyments of human life public institutions and seminaries of learning are essential.

Unfortunately, these convictions were those of the enlightened few rather than of the majority. The economy of the period was predominantly rural and the population thinly scattered over wide areas. Means of communication and transportation were also limited. Only the rare person was competent to envisage injury to the nation as a whole from the neglect of education in any one segment of the population.

No Community Lives Unto Itself Alone

But this situation does not prevail in America today. Increasing mobility of population has become dramatically evident. The steady trend toward industrialization, together with improved means of transportation and communication, has fostered movement from place to place at an ever accelerating pace. As W. H. Whyte, Jr., has shown in *The Organization Man,* corporate development has multiplied middle-class occupations many times. With this has come a phenomenal increase in the number of individuals who, with their families, periodically change their place of residence. To be sure, Americans have always been a mobile people, but the extent to which this has become a normal characteristic on all levels of society is peculiar to contemporary life. According to the Census of 1960, some 33 million Americans move each year, of which 10 million make long distance moves. To be sure there are significant differences among communities and sections of the country. Of moment to educational policy, however, is the movement of large numbers of young people from states in which economic conditions and educational facilities are most inadequate into states more favored. Conspicuous in this category are both Negro and white migrants from the rural South to northern metropolitan areas. The city of Chicago, for example, receives some 20,000 "functional illiterates" each year. Similar problems of immigration confront other northern cities.

Writing in 1958, Arthur F. Cory, of the California State Teachers Association, stated that the population of that state was increasing at the rate of more than 500,000 a year, thus confronting California with the task of staffing new schools "at the rate of one eighteen-classroom building per day, 365 days a year." [3] New York State has likewise served as a mecca for the underprivileged, as evidenced by an appeal of the Board of Education of the City of New York to the federal government on October 22, 1964, for assistance in the construction of 300 new schools to eliminate overcrowding, short-time classes, and obsolete facilities. In supporting this appeal, James B. Donovan, President of the Board, stated that over 800,000 Puerto Ricans and Negroes from the rural South had migrated to New York City since World War II.[4]

A shift of population of this magnitude from underprivileged areas into areas of better economic status creates a severe strain upon the educational systems of the latter, rendering it difficult to maintain former standards and often necessitating significant changes in curriculum and teaching procedures.

Intimately related to facts of mobility are the consequences which follow upon the steady elimination of unskilled labor from the American economy. The localities which today attract the ill-educated are not the meccas for the unskilled they once were; rather is the reverse true. Take, for example, the phenomenal exodus of population from rural communities to urban centers, an exodus that decreased the total number of farm workers by 1,100,000 between 1950 and 1960. For those young people who remain on the soil (approximately one out of ten, according to present trends) the applications of science and technology to farming assume ever increasing importance. For those who move to urban areas an education that insures an introduction to occupations requiring both a general and a technical education is most essential. Unfortunately, however, the rural schools which serve both groups seldom provide either the training or the guidance relevant to their futures. If, however, this is not done the social, correctional, and educational agencies to which many of these young people move must assume added responsibilities.

3. "California Schools Do Educate," *Atlantic Monthly,* December 1958, pp. 63–66.
4. *The New York Times,* October 23, 1964.

Closely related to the above are the changes in the employment picture resulting from automation. Taken together, these developments render ever more critical the need for improving the quality of vocational education and salvaging the future of dropouts from both elementary and secondary schools (estimated at some 700,000 to 1,000,-000 each year). In recent years educators have come to realize that problems of education and re-education, of training and re-training thus accentuated are inseparably associated with programs of slum clearance, urban renewal, and "antipoverty" measures to which the federal government is giving increasing attention. Certainly, both the problems and their solutions call for research, experimentation, pilot projects in curriculum reorganization (a domestic Marshall Plan as some suggest) from which local school systems can profit, but which few are either competent or able to provide.

Inability to Finance Education

Failure on the part of a number of states to educate their youth is not entirely the result of ignorance or indifference, although, as opponents of federal aid are quick to point out, these factors are not altogether absent. As we saw in Chapter 5, it is often the lack of financial resources in many communities which explains inequality of educational opportunity. For example, an unfortunate correlation obtains at present between states of low personal income per pupil enrolled in public schools and high percentage of school-age population on the one hand, and high personal income per pupil enrolled and low percentage of school-age population on the other.[5]

In his testimony before the Subcommittee of the Committee on Labor and Education of the House of Representatives, on April 30, 1958, Dr. Edgar Fuller, Executive Secretary of the Council of Chief State School Officers, pointed out that the real-property tax, upon which local public services commonly depend, "is so unevenly distributed in every State that thousands of school districts find adequate local public school financing impossible." To offset this lack, the states supply nearly 5 billion dollars annually to school districts from state re-

5. For a comparison of the fifty states in this respect, see *NEA Research Bulletin,* Vol. 39, No. I (February 1961), pp. 11–15.

sources. In 1958, according to Fuller, approximately 50 per cent of these state funds were distributed to local school districts, the amount varying in accordance with the need. Even so, this was not sufficient to finance adequate programs of education in all districts. To secure additional funds has become increasingly difficult "because the financial incentives offered by the Federal Government to State legislatures through matching grants for welfare, health, highways and other services give these services priorities over education in the competition for State appropriations." [6]

Studies conducted by the National Education Association likewise indicate the necessity in the future of federal support of education. These studies reveal that the school population is growing more rapidly than the total population. Between 1950 and 1960, for example, the school-age population increased by 47 per cent in contrast with an increase of 18.5 per cent in the total population of the United States.[7] Nor is there any present indication that this trend will not continue for some time. On the other hand, the National Education Association studies point to a continuing inability on the part of the states to cope adequately with needs still unmet (classroom shortages, inadequate salaries for teachers, limited instructional equipment, and so on) solely out of state and local resources.

Wide differences in the ability of the states to finance education result in corresponding differences in per capita expenditures for education. Thus, in 1961–1962, the average expenditure per pupil in the states varied from less than $200 in districts of lowest expenditure to over $700 in those of highest expenditure.[8] These glaring contrasts among the states give the phrase "equality of educational opportunity" a hollow sound. Since, however, the federal government has access to resources far in excess of those of the poorer states, it seems both logi-

6. Committee on Education and Labor, House of Representatives, *Hearings on Federal Grants to States for Education,* Eighty-fifth Congress, Second Session (Washington, D.C.: U.S. Government Printing Office, 1958), p. 172.

7. *NEA Research Bulletin,* Vol. 39, No. 1 (February 1961), p. 1.

8. According to the National Education Association, more than 65 per cent of all school districts spent from $300 to $499 per pupil in 1960–1961. The highest expenditures per pupil are in the large cities,where the median expenditure ranges from $400 per pupil in districts of 75,000 to 99,999 average daily attendance to $424 per pupil in districts of more than 100,000 average daily attendance. Eleven districts in California, New Jersey, New York, and Ohio reported an expenditure of over $600 per pupil and one district in New York, $948. *NEA Research Bulletin,* Vol. 40, No. 1 (February 1962), pp. 29–30.

cal and necessary that it employ them to offset the handicaps described.

National Defense Requires a High Level of Education

In addition to economic and cultural considerations which seem to point to the necessity of federal aid to education, there are the imperatives of national defense. Startling advances in Russian scientific achievements have drawn attention to Russian emphasis upon science and mathematics and their application to areas in which Russia and the United States are in keen competition. In this competition, however, the United States is sadly deficient in numbers upon which to draw, both in the way of students to teach and in competent instructors. Consequently, for the United States to perpetuate conditions which involve waste of personnel and inferior instruction becomes a matter of national concern, and the institution of a program to offset educational deficiencies is therefore an important aspect of national defense.

Statistics of rejection from the armed forces for reasons of "educational deficiency" reveal not only a serious waste of personnel, but also the extent to which lack of education in one state or one section of the country imposes burdens upon another. In the Southeast, for example, 202 out of each 1000 Negroes examined in World War II were rejected on grounds of "educational deficiency" in contrast with 50 rejections in the Far West out of each 1000 Negroes examined. A similar comparison of the rejection rate for whites, although less striking, is nevertheless significant: 52 persons per 1000 examined in the Southeast were rejected, as compared with 9 rejections per 1000 in the Far West.

The consequences of differences in educational opportunities afforded Negroes and whites become evident when we compare Negro and white rejections. In the Southeast, where, as we saw, rejections of Negroes numbered 202 per 1000 examined, rejections for whites stood at 52 per 1000; and in South Carolina, every county, without exception, had a Negro rejection rate of 175 or more per 1000 examined in comparison with a white rejection rate of 47 per 1000.

Nor have these differences between the states changed significantly since World War II, as evidenced by preinduction and induction examinations for military service. These examinations are based on mental tests composed largely of educational materials. In 1960, rejections in the different states ranged from 4.7 per cent to 56.5 per cent.[9]

From these data it is evident that what one community within a state or one state sows in the way of educational neglect, another community or state often reaps. It is also evident that failure to educate all young people up to the level of their ability bears directly upon the reservoir of talent available for the varied purposes of national defense, as well as for continued advancement in a technological civilization. For this reason, as many now see it, to oppose federal aid to education testifies to a narrow-mindedness that may result in tragic consequences for the nation as a whole.

The Case for the Opposition

A policy which seems imperative to one group appears in quite a different light to another. Opponents of federal aid to education insist that it would result inevitably in an extension of federal control over matters that should remain exclusively within the authority of the states and would impose an unfair burden upon one section of the country in order to offset neglect and indifference in other sections.

Fear of Federal Control

Fear of federal control is based upon the common experience of identifying sources of financial support with centers of control. This fear need not always be realized. As we have seen, within the states the enlargement of units of finance has not resulted necessarily in centralizing school administration. Moreover, the vast majority of educators as well as laymen who are desirous of increasing the contributions of the federal government to education are determined to disassociate aid from control. "Nothing contained in this act shall be construed to authorize any department, agency, officer or employee to exercise any direction, supervision or control over . . . any state educational insti-

9. National Education Association, Research Division, *Rankings of the States, 1962* (Washington, D.C.: National Education Association, 1962), p. 32. For a discussion of the loss to the nation from our unused talent in the uneducated, see Eli Ginzberg and Douglas W. Bray, *The Uneducated* (New York: Columbia University Press, 1953).

tution or agency" is a common insertion in all proposed federal aid legislation.

In spite of these precautions the fear of ultimate federal control persists. Nor have the decisions of the United States Supreme Court on religion and segregation in education helped to dispel this fear. In *School District of Abington* v. *Schempp* the Court has outlawed Bible reading and the use of the Lord's Prayer at opening exercises in all public schools. Similarly, in its decisions of 1954 and 1955 on segregation in education, the Court forbade the barring of any child from admission to any public school solely on grounds of race. Still again, in the Civil Rights Act of 1964, with its provisions for the denial of federal money to schools that persist in defying the Court and of affording both advice and financial assistance to schools that request assistance in desegregating, we have, it is said, federal control both direct and detailed. If the federal government can substitute its authority for that of the state and locality in these areas today, who will say it will not preempt authority in other areas in return for federal aid tomorrow?

Prominent among the opponents of federal aid to education is the Chamber of Commerce of the United States. This organization bases its opposition on these grounds: (1) Federal control over education is certain to follow federal appropriations and will thus discourage state and local initiative, self-determination, and experimentation. (2) Unless control does in fact accompany federal grants, there is little assurance that backward states and communities will better present conditions. On the contrary, they will be tempted to use federal funds in order to lessen the present tax burden. (3) The assumed inability of the states to finance education out of their own resources is not well grounded. It is want of will rather than the absence of resources that accounts for the sad state of education. Once these states are persuaded to reform their tax structures, ample support for education will be forthcoming. Let us examine these arguments in more detail.

State and Local Initiative Will Be Undermined

In support of the proposition that state and local initiative will be weakened if communities are permitted to receive federal funds for education without federal guidance and supervision, the Chamber of Commerce points to states in which increasing dependence upon state as against local revenues for education has already had this result. According to John R. Miles, Manager of the Education Department of the Chamber of Commerce, if heavy support from the state treasury brings these results, may we not expect communities to go even further "in such local irresponsibility by resorting to the Federal Treasury"? Miles points out that in many states, "where local taxes provide only 10 to 30 per cent of school expenditures, the misuse or underuse of the property tax is quite evident. In such states, both the rates and the ratio of assessments of property to true value are quite low." [10]

If these are the consequences of the assumption by state governments of major responsibility for the support of local schools under state control, what may we expect from federal appropriations carefully divorced from control? What inducements would local school systems have to review present practices and standards critically?

Not only would federal appropriations in support of general education in the states, unaccompanied by federal guidance and supervision, be unwise, continues Miles, they would be without precedent. All grants to the states in the past have been instituted under the "defense and welfare" clause of the federal Constitution and none have sought "to modify the organization of the systems of general education then existing or otherwise to intrude upon the prerogatives of the states, or communities, or private agencies to maintain the educational institutions they had developed." That is to say, in the interests of national defense and/or to promote the general welfare, these grants have had in mind encouraging the states to undertake new responsibilities. Thus the Morrill Acts were intended "to press the states to establish agricultural and mechanics arts institutes to train manpower for the industrial revolution during the transition of this country from an agrarian to an industrial economy." The Smith-Hughes Act of 1917 was in recognition of our increasing competition with the nations of Western Europe and our need of skilled craftsmen. "To guarantee against the exploitation of child labor while training our own craftsmen, the responsibility for the program was handed over to the public schools. . . . This new function of secondary education was again a Federal decision to use Federal money to implement a Federal purpose through state plans that were federally approved and supervised." [11]

10. *Government and Education: The Responsibility of State and Local Government* (Washington, D.C.: Chamber of Commerce of the United States, 1963), p. 11.
11. *Ibid.*, p. 3.

A final illustration of federal assistance to education of a specific rather than general character is the National Defense Education Act which was passed in order to meet "a presumed national emergency in scientific manpower."

The major purpose of each of these programs, continues Miles, has been to induce state and local boards of education to assume new educational functions and only superficially have they "disclaimed Federal power to supervise the changes that were intended." But equally important, they have not intruded upon the "right or the ability of the people to develop general educational programs appropriate to their cultural background under state, local, and private auspices." The responsibility for general education remains as it has been from the beginning, a state and local right and duty.[12]

It was stated above that a majority of educators who favor federal aid to education wish this granted in such a way as to eliminate all possibility of federal control. Not all educators, however, grant the wisdom of this insistence upon state and local autonomy in the use of federal funds. Indeed, a number of factors in contemporary American life are causing many educators and laymen to question the validity of earlier assumptions of local autonomy in education. These present factors include the increasing proportion of middle- and upper-class families that move each year from state to state (members of the military establishment, corporation executives, scientists and technicians engaged in new occupations resulting from the "knowledge explosion," and others) and many conditions mentioned earlier in this book which render imperative raising the level of general education. Prominent among educators who question the efficacy of local autonomy in contemporary American education is Theodore Brameld. According to Brameld, the validity of an appeal to the federal government in support of education rests upon three important premises: (1) the desirability of providing equal opportunity in education for all citizens "regardless of race, creed or economic status"; (2) "the necessity of an educated citizenry for the nation as a whole"; and, (3) "the increasingly collective" and interrelated structure of modern society.

It is clear, states Brameld, that educational equality cannot be provided in a number of states without outside assistance. Nor is there any assurance that the process of simply handing over federal funds will

12. *Ibid.*, p. 4.

bring about equality. "Vast amounts of money can be spent by ingenious but irresponsible public officials without any certainty whatever that the children and adults for whose benefit it is intended will enjoy plentiful and excellent textbooks, well-trained and well-paid teachers, or up-to-date equipment." Consequently, it is time for the American people to face reality and to provide federal aid to the states with an essential degree of federal supervision.[13]

What Brameld terms "facing reality," opponents of federal aid to general education interpret as a deliberate attempt on the part of "educationists" to wrest control of the schools from local school boards and "to decide for the people what schools should be and how the people should pay for them." These educationists

> recognize that such professional domination is impossible as long as the people, by direct vote at state and local levels, control the purse strings to their schools. With fiscal control, the people will continue to have substantive control through authorized state and local school boards of education. Federal assistance is the means of by-passing such popular control.[14]

In order to check these trends toward centralization, the Chamber of Commerce appeals to businessmen to exercise leadership in the maintenance and the improvement of state and local school systems.

> Our public school system is traditionally and distinctively a community responsibility. The states and their school districts should accept full responsibility for the financing of public education.
> Broad based tax programs at state and local levels should provide the revenues needed to maintain high-quality educational opportunity for all.[15]

Obviously, if the ideal of educational equality is to be realized, a serious dilemma confronts the advocates of federal aid. Brameld and

13. "The Bugaboo of Federal Control," in *Education for the Emerging Age* (New York: Harper & Brothers, 1961), pp. 145–51.
14. John R. Miles, *op. cit.*, p. 5.
15. *Education Policies and Projects of the Chamber of Commerce of the United States* (Washington, D.C.: Chamber of Commerce of the United States, 1964), p. 3. This pamphlet enumerates ways in which the Chamber believes the business community may discharge its responsibilities to education in the light of its "vital stake in our schools, our junior and senior colleges, our institutes and our universities." See also, *Education—An Investment in People* (Washington, D.C.: The Chamber of Commerce of the United States, 1964).

other advocates of federal aid, with associated federal guidance, are undoubtedly correct in their insistence that the sums of money required in order to raise the level of education in the poorer states to that in the more fortunate states are far larger than any amounts thus far proposed in Congress. The best that can be said of past proposals is that they have sought to establish the principle of federal obligation to assist in bringing about a semblance of equality of education among the states. Is it reasonable to assume that the huge sums required to give substance to this objective should be appropriated without assurance that they will be wisely spent? Can we assume that states and communities long underprivileged and backward (often, politically as well as culturally) can transform their educational systems without guidance? Have we a right to require the wealthy states to tax themselves for the improvement of others without guarantees respecting the use to which these taxes will be put?

On the other hand, is it not too much to expect that a centralized authority in Washington will supervise expenditures with an eye sufficiently sensitive to differences in needs among communities and in a manner best calculated to stimulate local pride and initiative and self-determination?

Is there no alternative, on the one hand, to federal grants without federal control and, on the other, to overly centralized control in Washington?

Some years ago one of the writers suggested a plan for the administration of federal aid to general education which was designed to avoid both the dangers of centralized control and the limitations of an exclusively state and local self-determination in the use of federal grants.[16] He still believes it merits consideration. It involves the creation of regional boards which, acting under general directives, would undertake to establish regional standards and criteria to be met by the states and communities of each region. These regional boards should be composed of representatives from state departments of education, laymen of public vision from each region, and representatives of the federal government. From regional boards thus composed, a unique combination of federal and regional direction of education might emerge, involving control over expenditures of federal funds but equally, if not

16. V. T. Thayer, *American Education Under Fire* (New York: Harper & Brothers, 1944), pp. 133–36.

more important, the cooperative definition and realization of standards and criteria appropriate and relevant to the needs of the states and localities affected.

Federal Assistance to Localities Is Not Needed

We come now to the contention that there is in fact no necessity for the federal government to supplement state and local resources in support of education. To tax the more progressive states to assist the less progressive, it is argued, not only imposes an unfair burden upon the former but assumes that the backward states are in fact in genuine need of this assistance.

The Chamber of Commerce contradicts the assertion that states and localities have reached the limits of their taxing ability in support of education. Rather, it insists that inertia and antiquated state tax structures explain the seeming lack of financial resources. Take, for example, West Virginia. Harry A. Stansbury, Managing Director of the West Virginia Chamber of Commerce, testified before the Subcommittee on Education and Labor of the House of Representatives, that in twenty of the fifty-five counties of West Virginia, not one dollar of school-building bonds had been issued for more than twenty-five years, despite the fact that these counties were possessed of "aggregate assessments of $1,243,567,000 and school-bonding authority of $37,306,000 under the 3 per cent constitutional provisions." In one county, according to Mr. Stansbury, the state provides 55 per cent of all money spent on public schools. Even though this county has an idle bond capacity of $4,180,000 without a dollar standing against it, it spent in 1957 only $16,239, or half of 1 per cent, for school construction. In still another county, fully able to tax itself generously, the state furnishes 85 per cent of all money spent on public schools. Were the federal government to provide additional funds, it is argued, a sense of responsibility to promote good schools would shrink still further.[17]

Unfortunately, West Virginia is not the only state in which communities have permitted their schools to deteriorate rather than imposing local taxes.

17. *Hearings on Federal Grants to States for Education, op. cit.,* June 3, 1958, p. 403.

Again, opponents of federal aid draw attention to recent improvements in the educational picture that suggest a "go-slow" policy with respect to federal aid to general education. There is evidence, for example, that the educational crisis of the 1950s is in process of correction.

A number of factors have contributed to this improvement. Of prime importance is the decrease in the rate at which school enrollments have expanded in relation to the increase in the rate of growth of the gross national product. According to the Census Bureau, all educational enrollments between 1950 and 1962 grew 66 per cent, but are expected to expand no more than 14 to 21 per cent (an average of 17 per cent) between 1962 and 1970. At the same time the GNP, which grew at a slower rate than school enrollments in the 1950s, is now growing faster and is expected to advance between 27 and 37 per cent (an average of 32 per cent) between 1962 and 1970.[18]

These facts indicate increasing ability on the part of states and localities to finance education on all levels. This increasing ability is already reflected in significant developments in school construction, teacher supply, and teacher salaries. Thus, it is pointed out, a shortage of 600,000 classrooms which President Kennedy stated in his message to Congress in February 1961, would have to be corrected in the 1960s was reduced by 210,000 in the first three years, a decrease that corresponds to a decennial construction rate of 700,000.

More than normal progress in meeting the shortage of teachers characteristic of the 1950s and in bettering salary schedules also marks the decade of the 1960s. Thus Paul Woodring, Education Editor of the *Saturday Review,* could write in the January 18, 1964 issue of that magazine:

> For a decade we have been reading annual reports of a national teacher shortage of 120,000 to 140,000. Those who read only the headlines have been led to believe that many classrooms are without teachers and many children are going untaught. These figures are misleading and require interpretation.

18. Data quoted from the Census report of January 10, 1962, by Roger A. Freeman before the Senate Committee on Labor and Public Welfare of the 88th Congress, First Session. Reprinted in House Document No. 164 under the title, *Guaranteeing an Opportunity for Higher Education to all Qualified High School Graduates: Should the Federal Government Participate?* (Washington, D.C.: U.S. Government Printing Office, 1963), p. 81.

Woodring proceeds to show that the 120,000 figure represents merely the number of teachers required when the number of new teachers available is subtracted from the number required annually in order to replace those leaving the classroom, plus the number needed in order to meet increased enrollments, to provide additional services, to reduce class size, and to replace those now teaching on temporary certificates. He adds, however, that "Today the number of teachers who hold some kind of legal certificate and are willing to teach approximately equals the total number of actual jobs available in the nation."

It remains true, of course, that there still exists a serious imbalance between the types of teaching positions available and the number of teachers who are properly prepared for these jobs, but the data on the number of students who are preparing for teaching positions is reassuring as to the future. In the fall of 1963, for example, "the field of education led all others in enrollments for advanced degrees." [19]

This marked increase in the number of young people who are preparing to teach doubtless results, in part, from significant improvements in teachers' salaries. Although the average salary for teachers is still considerably lower than that of other professional workers, an increase of 67.3 per cent in the past ten years (from an average of $3428 to $5735 annually) [20] promises well for the future.

Opponents of federal aid conclude from these data that the states are well on their way toward meeting their educational problems without incurring the dangers of federal control that are certain to follow upon federal financing of general education. Far better, they insist, would it be for states to reform their tax structures and, if necessary, for the federal government to return to the states for their unrestricted use a portion of the revenue it now collects from them.

Educators do not deny these improvements in the educational picture nor the wisdom—indeed, the necessity—of fundamental changes in the manner in which education is financed by the states. They point out, however, that the improvements mentioned above are not uniform throughout the nation nor have they erased the serious differences in the ability of the states to finance education. For example, the percentage gain in teacher salaries over the past ten years varies from

19. *NEA Journal,* November 1964, p. 3.
20. From "1963–64 Salary Schedules," in *NEA Research Bulletin,* Vol. 41, No. 4 (December 1963).

state to state, from 17.8 per cent in South Dakota to 87.1 per cent in Mississippi; but the average salary in South Dakota still exceeds that in Mississippi by $340 per year. Or take Alabama, with its 39.8 per cent gain in the past ten years and a projected future gain of the same percentage in the next ten years. If this is realized, the average salary in that state will still be $160 below today's average for all states.[21]

Nor will this inequality in the ability of states to finance education, with its accompanying inequality of educational opportunity, be corrected by having the federal government return to the states funds it now collects from them. Were this policy adopted, present inequalities would be accented rather than lessened, since the rich states would have returned from the federal government sums that might otherwise be used to raise the level of education in the poorer states.

Federal Scholarships Are Likewise Uncalled For

The Chamber of Commerce of the United States, in conjunction with other groups, questions not only the need of federal aid to general education, but also recent proposals for a program of federally supported scholarships. John M. Stalnaker, president of the National Merit Scholarship Corporation, is quoted as telling a House Committee that of the top 7500 students drawn from each state in proportion to population, 97 per cent are in college and of the next 7500 about 95 per cent are already in college.[22] He concludes that well over 90 per cent of the young people who might be eligible for federal scholarships are already encountering no difficulty in attending college. It is argued further that lack of motivation rather than want of financial resources keeps many young people from continuing with their education beyond high school graduation. Therefore, he concludes that federal grants would have little effect other than to establish an unfortunate precedent.

Needless to say, educational groups challenge the representative character of these statistics as well as the validity of the conclusions drawn from them. Granted that lack of motivation operates to keep too many able young people from attending college, it still remains true

21. *Ibid.*, p. 99. See also, *NEA Research Bulletin*, May 1965, pp. 48–55.
22. Quoted in *Sizing Up Federal Scholarships* (Washington, D.C.: Education Department, Chamber of Commerce of the United States, 1958).

that a sizable number fail to go on for want of financial resources. Nor are educators in agreement with Stalnaker's data. Indeed, it would appear that Stalnaker himself has modified his views since 1958 with respect to the availability of scholarships for worthy young people. In an address delivered at a conference on the topic "Equal Opportunity for Higher Education," sponsored by the American Federation of Labor in cooperation with the Association of State Universities and Land-Grant Colleges in January 1962, Stalnaker is quoted as saying,

> You may have seen the statement that scholarships are plentiful, that scholarships go begging, that any ambitious student can get help to get a college education. We have studied this issue and find such statements false and misleading. There is a relatively small amount of scholarship money and the applicants for each scholarship of any value are numerous and growing. The competition is fierce.[23]

Stalnaker also states in the same address that "Most of the college-controlled scholarship money is held by a small group of private colleges. Three per cent of the colleges control over one third of the scholarship funds." [24] That financial inability to meet the costs of attendance at college keeps large numbers of able students from receiving a higher education is confirmed by the testimony of Dr. Rexford G. Moon, Jr., Director of the College Scholarship Service of the College Entrance Examination Board, before the House Committee on Education and Labor in 1963. Moon calls attention to the results of Project Talent which, in that year,

> indicate that at least 120,000 youngsters whose high school performance indicated the ability to achieve success in needed professional areas—doctors, teachers, engineers—did not enter college last fall. The number of students who started college but were unable to meet their expenses and did not return is not know at this date, but the loss over a 4-year period probably will exceed 40 per cent of the total. Obviously, family finances have much to do with this problem.[25]

23. Quoted in *Guaranteeing an Opportunity for Higher Education to all Qualified High School Graduates: Should the Federal Government Participate?*, p. 35.
24. *Ibid.*, p. 35.
25. *Ibid.*, pp. 23–24.

A New Approach to Federal Aid

As we saw in the chapter on "Public Assistance to Nonpublic Schools," opposition to federal legislation in support of general education in the states is not limited to those who fear federal control or who question its need. Opposition has also come from religious groups that object to all legislation of this character unless it includes assistance for non-public as well as public schools. So determined has been this opposition that no legislation in unqualified support of general education in all elementary and secondary schools has thus far succeeded in passing both houses of Congress. To this opposition has been added in recent years that of segregationists who fear that federal appropriations will be used to enforce desegregation in education.

This record of failure to secure legislation in support of general education for all public elementary and secondary schools led the United States Commissioner of Education, in cooperation with educational organizations, to abandon the battle for general aid in the 88th Congress and to concentrate first, upon securing support for "special projects" as a supplement to the original provisions of the National Defense Education Act of 1958, and, second, upon provisions for meeting other pressing needs of a wide-spread character. The success of this procedure was evidenced in the passage of a surprising number of significant acts by Congress in 1964 and 1965, such as amendments (in 1964) to the National Defense Education Act of 1958, the Economic Opportunity Act of 1964, and the Elementary and Secondary Education Act of 1965.

The National Defense Education Act of 1958 had represented a crisis approach to education and was designed to improve instruction in areas obviously related to national defense—science, mathematics, and foreign language. The amendments of 1964, under the "special projects" approach, resulted in the appropriation of 76.6 million dollars for the improvement of instruction in elementary and secondary schools in the fields of history, civics, geography, English, and reading, as well as in science, mathematics, and foreign language. The money thus made available may be used for a variety of purposes: to remodel classrooms and laboratories, to purchase equipment, such as remedial reading devices, laboratory apparatus, reference books, maps, films, teaching machines, and electronic equipment, and to improve programs of teacher training, state supervision, and administration. In addition, 1 million dollars were appropriated for use as direct loans at low interest to non-public elementary and high schools.

The Economic Opportunity Act and the Elementary and Secondary Education Act represent still further extensions of the principle of federal assistance in support of state and local efforts to meet specific educational needs; to improve, for example, the status of school drop-outs, to establish preschool nurseries for slum children, special services for teachers in distressed neighborhoods, after-school classes for parents, music and art classes for underprivileged children, and to establish and operate special educational centers in cooperation with agencies in the community, private as well as public. These centers are to offer educational enrichment opportunities to elementary and secondary school students in the project area.

The "special project" approach to federal aid should be credited also for expanded assistance to institutions of higher learning. The Higher Education Act of 1965 is unique, for example, in its major emphasis upon undergraduate education, its encouragement of universities and colleges to assist in the solution of community problems in areas such as housing, poverty, recreation, youth opportunities, transportation, health, and land use, and in its provisions for teachers and other experienced personnel who wish to enter or re-enter elementary or secondary school work. Likewise, in the face of the opposition to outright grants to students in college, this act provides several types of assistance to academically qualified students in the form of outright grants to those of exceptional ability but in financial need, the expansion of programs of low-interest insured loans for students, and assistance to colleges in the expansion of programs for the part-time employment of students.

One distinctive feature of the "special projects" approach to federal aid is its attempt to provide assistance to nonpublic schools and colleges as well as to public, on the assumption, of course, that only nonsectarian and secular activities are to be assisted, and on condition, as President Johnson has emphasized, that the federal government refrains from exercising either the "wish" or the "power to dictate education."

It is doubtless too early to foresee all that the "special project" approach holds for the future as a means of securing federal aid for education in the states. However, if we may judge from the legislation briefly reviewed and the overwhelming vote in Congress in April, 1965 in favor of President Johnson's request for an appropriation of slightly more than 1 billion dollars with which to upgrade education in needy school districts in direct proportion to the number of children in these districts of families with less than $2000 of annual income, the use of this method is still in its infancy.

Suggested Reading

Benson, Charles S., *The Cheerful Prospect* (Boston: Houghton Mifflin Company, 1965).

Brameld, Theodore, *Education for the Emerging Age* (New York: Harper & Brothers, 1961), Chapter 14.

Chamber of Commerce of the United States, *Education—An Investment in People* (Washington, D.C.: Chamber of Commerce of the United States, 1964).

Committee on Education and Labor, House of Representatives, 88th Congress, First Session, *The Federal Government and Education* (Washington, D.C.: U.S. Government Printing Office, 1963).

Educational Policies Commission, National Education Association, *Educational Responsibilities of the Federal Government* (Washington, D.C.: National Education Association, 1964).

Hazelton, Paul, "Education and Politics," *Saturday Review*, June 15, 1963, pp. 62 ff.

Lieberman, Myron, *The Future of Public Education* (Chicago: University of Chicago Press, 1960), Chapters 2, 3.

Miles, John R., *Government and Education; The Responsibility of State and Local Government* (Washington, D.C.: Chamber of Commerce of the United States, 1963).

Miner, Jerry, *Social and Economic Factors in Spending for Education* (Syracuse, N.Y.: Syracuse University Press, 1963).

National Committee for Support of the Public Schools, *Changing Demands on Education and their Fiscal Implications* (Washington, D.C.: National Committee for Support of the Public Schools, 1963).

Shermis, Sherwin, "The Semantics of Federal Aid and Federal Control," *Phi Delta Kappan*, October 1961, pp. 35–37.

Index